THE MEANINGS OF DRESS

THE MEANINGS OF DRESS

FOURTH EDITION

KIMBERLY A. MILLER-SPILLMAN
University of Kentucky

ANDREW REILLY
University of Hawai'i, Mānoa

FAIRCHILD BOOKS
NEW YORK · LONDON · OXFORD · NEW DELHI · SYDNEY

FAIRCHILD BOOKS
Bloomsbury Publishing Inc
1385 Broadway, New York, NY 10018, USA
50 Bedford Square, London, WC1B 3DP, UK

BLOOMSBURY, FAIRCHILD BOOKS and the Fairchild Books logo are
trademarks of Bloomsbury Publishing Plc

Second edition published 2004
Third edition published in 2012
Fourth edition first published in the United States of America 2019

Reprinted 2019 (twice), 2020

Cover design by Anna Perotti/ByTheSky Design | Cover image: Dancers perform during a dress
rehearsal of "Ahnsim Dance" by South Korean choreographer Eun-Me Ahn, at Maison de la
Culture, Clermont-Ferrand, on October 3, 2017. © THIERRY ZOCCOLAN/AFP/Getty Images

Library of Congress Cataloging-in-Publication Data
Names: Miller-Spillman, Kimberly A., author. | Reilly, Andrew Hinchcliffe, author. | Damhorst,
Mary Lynn. Meanings of dress.
Title: The meanings of dress / Kimberly A. Miller-Spillman, University of Kentucky, Andrew
Reilly, University of Hawai'i, Manoa.
Description: Fourth Edition. | New York : Fairchild Books, 2019. | "Third edition published
2012"—T.p. verso. | Includes index.
Identifiers: LCCN 2018026615 | ISBN 9781501323874 paper | ISBN 9781501323881 ePDF
Subjects: LCSH: Clothing and dress—Psychological aspects. | Clothing and dress—Symbolic
aspects. | Fashion.
Classification: LCC GT524 .D36 2019 | DDC 391—dc23 LC record available at https://lccn.loc.
gov/2018026615

ISBN: PB: 978-1-5013-2387-4
ePDF: 978-1-5013-2388-1

Typeset by Lachina Creative, Inc.
Printed and bound in the United States of America

To find out more about our authors and books visit
www.fairchildbooks.com and sign up for our newsletter.

CONTENTS

PREFACE

Since 2012 we have made several changes for the fourth edition of *The Meanings of Dress*. Kimberly Miller-Spillman and Andrew Reilly both return as co-editors. In an effort to streamline the fourth edition there is one less chapter and fewer readings compared to previous editions. (The third edition had 92 readings whereas the fourth edition has 42.) There are two new chapters, one on gender and one on sexuality; all other chapters have been revised and updated. Thirteen chapters are in the fourth edition, along with the addition of 28 new readings (and 14 readings retained from the third edition). In addition to dress and culture, we have increased information on theory, choosing readings that make the link between theory and practice.

EMPHASIS ON CULTURE AND THEORY

Cultural perspectives are key to the fourth edition. We worked to include as many perspectives as possible. For example, there are readings on the hijab, kente cloth from Ghana, American hip-hop style, African body image, Afghani gender politics, unisex fashion and politics in Sweden circa 1960s, Indian Hijaras, Bolovian Cholas, and Sikhs. The authors of these readings vary in gender, ethnicity, cultural background, age, and work roles. We hear from academics, journalists, business professionals, novelists, and students. They demonstrate how dress is a central factor in most areas of everyday life, such as work, school, sports, rituals and celebrations, fantasy, and play.

The Meanings of Dress also takes an interdisciplinary approach. Articles relate to psychology, sociology, anthropology, material culture, history, communications, semiotics, aesthetics, consumer behavior, marketing, business management, consumer economics, popular culture, gender studies, feminist scholarship, minority studies, and more. Dress is a multifaceted phenomenon; therefore, one viewpoint is just not enough.

PLAN OF THE BOOK

We reorganized the text for easy flow of concepts and topics. Chapter 1 introduces the book while Chapter 2 discusses the theoretical underpinnings of fashion. Chapter 3 discusses the nonverbal aspects of fashion and dress, and Chapter 4 discusses the body in different cultures. Chapters 5 and 6 examine gender and sexuality, while Chapter 7 focuses on race and ethnicity. Chapter 8 examines religious dress and Chapter 9 focuses on dress in the workplace. Chapter 10 looks at media-related issues connected to dress, Chapter 11 at the role of fantasy in dress, Chapter 12 at the role of technology in dress, and we conclude with Chapter 13, which examines ethical issues in dress.

Chapter 1: Introduction to Dress, Culture, and Theory provides definitions of terms and explanations of theories that are fundamental to the text. Connecting theory to dress is another goal of this chapter, allowing the reader to make these connections throughout the text. One objective of this chapter is to challenge students to think about their own culture from another's cultural perspective and we introduce readings on the hijab, clothing etiquette when traveling, the meaning and interpretation of sagging pants, and the history of cargo pants.

Chapter 2: Fashion as a Dynamic Process illustrates how fashion can be explained through theory. It includes a new concept—microtrends—and how they reflect current dress phenomena, how one designer—Heide Slimane—changed the silhouette of menswear in early 20th century, and the role of fashion bloggers in fashion change.

Chapter 3: Dress as Nonverbal Communication considers how messages are conveyed through dress. The first reading looks at the meaning of Kente cloth, while the second reading tackles the issue of clothing theft in 18th-century England and why clothing was important to status. The third reading explores the social strata of expensive "worn" jeans.

Chapter 4: The Body includes a classic reading on the meaning of beauty in different cultures but added to this chapter are readings on the increase in plastic surgery butt lifts in Africa and why popular tattoo locations on the body change.

Chapter 5: Gender now is its own chapter. We retain Patrik Steorn's article on unisex clothing in Sweden, and Katalin Medvedev and Lioba Moshi's analysis of politics and gender in a socialist society. A new article compares and contrasts the India Hijaras and American drag queens.

Chapter 6: Sexuality also now has its own chapter. A returning reading includes the often-discussed topic of tween fashion and modesty. New articles to this chapter include one on dress and lesbians, followed by one on gay men and dress.

Chapter 7: Race and Ethnicity examines how racial and ethnic identity are manifested in dress and then—controversially—adopted into fashion. The first article examines the lack of appropriate shades of makeup for women of color. We follow this with two returning articles—Puerto Rican traditional clothing and ethnic semiotics in college dress. The last article is new and examines the traditional and modern take on the Chola in Bolivia.

Chapter 8: Dress and Religion has been overhauled and considers the ideology of several religions and how ideology affects religious dress. New readings include Amish and Mormon dress, dress in the Middle East, and why Sikhs are mistakenly targeted for hate crimes.

Chapter 9: Dress in the Workplace is updated with all new readings. This chapter examines some of the ways that dressing for work has changed and how it has remained the same. It also looks at some recent controversies related to dress in the workplace and how specific dress in the workplace may identify a person's status or rank. And a reading about the reasons why so many bloggers.

Chapter 10: Dress and Media returns to this edition. This chapter focuses on some of the controversies related to appearance and clothing as discussed in articles from popular magazines, research journals, and newspapers. One new article is included, about the re-occurrence of ads and editorials that mix violence to women with fashion. Two favorites return about the media pressure to sustain a youthful look and how that expectation can affect young girls' body image.

Chapter 11: Fashion and Fantasy returns to this edition. This chapter focuses on the many ways that fashion and fantasy are intertwined through the lens of the public, private, and secret self model. Readings cover Disney princess costumes, costuming the imagination, and a new reading about the difficulty of making historic dress fit contemporary bodies for reenactments.

Chapter 12: Dress and Technology focuses on the relationship between technology, fashion, and culture. New technology trends and how they will transform the fashion industry are included as is the push to interest girls in STEM careers through their interest in fashion. Also included is the irony of efforts to send secondhand clothing to poorer countries while, unintentionally, ruining that country's efforts to create a textile industry of their own. Lastly, the apparel industry in the United States is considered in this chapter, especially regarding how slow the industry has been in adopting methods that promote sustainability.

Chapter 13: Ethics. This chapter proved popular in the prior edition and returns with readings on the ethics of eco-fashion, sweatshops, and "ethical fur."

The Meanings of Dress STUDiO

Fairchild Books has a long history of excellence in textbook publishing for fashion education. Our new online STUDIOS are specially developed to complement this book with rich ancillaries that students can adapt to their learning styles. *The Meanings of Dress Studio* features online self-quizzes with scored results, personalized study tips and flashcards with terms/definitions.

STUDIO access cards are offered free with new book purchases and also sold separately through www.fairchildbooks.com.

Instructor's Resources

Instructor's Resources offered online for teachers are: Instructor's Guide, which provides suggestions for planning the course and using the text in the classroom, supplemental assignments, and lecture notes; Test Bank, which includes sample test questions for each chapter; PowerPoint™ presentations that include images from the book and provide a framework for lecture and discussion.

ACKNOWLEDGMENTS

The fourth edition of readings and activities is the result of the combined efforts of many individuals. We thank all who helped for their time, effort, and support.

We thank the writers who eagerly allowed us to include their work. They have added critical perspectives to the book. We especially thank the contributors of original manuscripts for their interest in the book and their willingness to comply with our editorial suggestions.

We commend our editorial team, including Joseph Miranda, Edie Weinberg, and Bridget MacAvoy for their patience and understanding in dealing with our already full schedules.

Kimberly Miller-Spillman would like to acknowledge Andy and her co-editors on this and all editions of *The Meanings of Dress*. A special thanks to Fairchild for their willingness to update and renew editions based on instructor feedback.

Andrew Reilly expresses gratitude to his co-editor, Kimberly Miller-Spillman, as well as prior editors of *The Meanings of Dress* for creating an important work that is now in its fourth edition. He also thanks the authors who have written new articles. He also acknowledges his family and friends for their support.

We wish to acknowledge and thank Mary Lynn Damhorst and Susan O. Michelman for their work on the first and second editions of *The Meanings of Dress* and Patti Hunt-Hurst for her work on the third edition of *The Meanings of Dress*. Without their contributions to the framework of the text, the current edition would not be possible.

January 2018
Kimberly A. Miller-Spillman
Andrew Reilly

The publisher wishes to gratefully acknowledge and thank the editorial team involved in the publication of this book:

Acquisitions Editor: Wendy Fuller
Development Manager: Joseph Miranda
Editorial Assistant: Bridget MacAvoy
Art Development Editor: Edie Weinberg
Production Manager: Claire Cooper
Project Manager: Courtney Coffman, Lachina Creative, Inc.

CHAPTER 1
INTRODUCTION TO DRESS, CULTURE, AND THEORY
Kimberly A. Miller-Spillman

After reading this chapter you will understand:

- The definition of basic terms used in the scholarly study of dress
- The importance of cultural diversity to our world
- How scientific theories can be used to study dress
- How global awareness is created through a study of dress

Dress is often considered simultaneously important and unimportant, resulting in a complex field of study. Dress is a tool that tells individuals how to behave in social situations; it helps us to define gender, age, profession, and interests. All people wear clothes or adorn their bodies and learn from an early age how to "read" the dress of others. From this perspective dressing is unique to humans. However, some people take dress for granted and believe it is not a valid field of scientific inquiry. The goal of this book is to illuminate the vast amount of cultural information communicated through dress every day. For instance, we will examine the daily assumptions and stereotypes that people subconsciously make within seconds of encountering another individual based on his or her appearance.

Another goal of this book is to foster the reader's global awareness through a study of dress and appearance. We will study **culture**: what it means, how it works, and what we can learn about our own culture while studying the culture of others. Our hope is that this book will develop readers' critical thinking skills related to culture instead of teaching the specific dress details of any one particular culture.

Theory is another topic that is central to this text. We have purposefully chosen readings that illustrate the connection between theory and dress. Each chapter includes examples of readings from experts in the field of dress and culture.

DEFINING BASIC CONCEPTS

Dress

Dress is defined as any intentional modifications of the body and/or supplements added to the body (Roach-Higgins & Eicher, 1992). This includes garments worn on the body but also includes spray-on suntans, color contact lenses, makeup, earrings, shoes, tattoos, and diet and exercise that change one's body shape. Other terms used to refer to dress are "fashion," "costume," "clothing," "apparel," and "adornment." For the purposes of this book, we will use the term "dress" to encompass each of these terms and more.

There is evidence that dress has powerful effects in situations of human interaction such as job interviews (Damhorst & Fiore, 1990), first impressions (Rucker, Taber & Harrison, 1981), and experiments (Haney, Banks, & Zimbardo, 1973). Research confirms that initial impressions are made within the first five seconds of encountering a stranger; we also know that first impressions affect the outcome of job interviews. First impressions have also been studied when asking a stranger for change or to complete a survey. A few studies have also demonstrated the power of clothing on perceptions, such as in legal cases when the clothing of a rape victim is introduced as evidence in court (Lennon, Lennon, & Johnson, 1992–1993). Dress is powerful because it communicates who one is and who one is not.

A dress experiment carried out by a college student illustrates the power of dress. You can refer to this reading at the end of this chapter. In 2010, Cassidy Herrington decided to conduct a post-9/11 experiment that resulted in unanticipated reactions from those around her. In the reading "'Undercover' in Hijab: Unveiling One Month

Later," Herrington, a reporter for her college newspaper, wore a hijab (head scarf) for one month while continuing her normal routine as a student. She wore the hijab to use her "affiliation with 'white,' non-Muslims to build rapport with the Islamic community." One month after completing the experiment, Herrington spoke to a general education diversity class and reported that her newspaper column resulted in 30,000 emails from 122 nations representing the largest number of responses to any article in the paper's history (Herrington, personal communication, November 17, 2010). Herrington's experiment required personal courage and fortitude.

A similar experiment in 2017 was conducted by high school students (http://peoriapublicradio.org/post/hijab-day-sparks-conversations-richwoods-high-school#stream/0). Given the tension between Muslims and Americans, these experiments illustrate how much dress—such as a simple square of fabric—can affect interactions in daily life (see Figure 1.1).

Given the preceding examples, it is clear that dress is far from inconsequential.

Culture

Another concept that is instrumental to this book is that of culture. **Culture** is studied by many disciplines, including anthropology, psychology, business, and family and consumer sciences. There is no one universally agreed-upon definition of culture. We will use the following definition:

> Culture is defined as a set of human-made objective and subjective elements that in the past have increased the probability of survival and resulted in satisfaction of the participants in an ecological niche, and thus became shared among those who could communicate with each other because they had a common language and lived in the same time and place (Triandis, 1994, p. 22).

This definition distinguishes objective elements of culture (which include tools, buildings, dress, media outlets, etc.) from subjective aspects of culture (which include categorization, associations, norms, roles, and values). The objective elements refer to a culture's artifacts or objects made by humans. Dress is an artifact that throughout history reveals (among other things) different levels of technology used to make fabric and garments. For example, a simple back-strap loom compared to a computerized loom illustrates the range of technology used to make clothing (see Figure 1.2a and b).

The subjective elements of each culture are organized into unique patterns of beliefs, attitudes, norms (shared expectations of behavior), and values. Social stratification is an example of a subjective element of culture in which

Figure 1.1 Diverse Americans interact on a college campus.

Figure 1.2 Cultural tools to create fabric for dress can range from a simple back-strap loom (a) to a computerized loom (b).

humans create categories for people according to age, race, and income level. This also includes social norms, stereotypes, and prejudices.

In addition to defining culture, Triandis identifies four cultural syndromes that apply to all cultures: cultural complexity, cultural tightness, individualism, and collectivism.

Cultural complexity In complex cultures, people make large numbers of distinctions among objects and events in their environment. This means that generally societies that subsist on hunting and gathering tend to be simple; agricultural societies tend to be somewhat complex; industrial societies are more complex; and information societies are the most complex. The contrast between simple and complex cultures is considered the most important factor of cultural variations in social behavior (Chanchani & Theivanathampillai, 2002). In an information society such as the United States, dress is varied. For example, Silicon Valley employees may dress in casual T-shirts, jeans, and tennis shoes because they work on computers and seldom interact face-to-face with customers. Another example would be CEOs of large corporations, who may choose to dress in expensive business suits. Generally speaking, dress choices of complex cultures are far greater than those of simple cultures.

Tight and loose cultures Cultural tightness has clear norms, and deviations within tight cultures are met with sanctions. In tight cultures, if a person does what everyone else is doing, he or she is protected from criticism. Tightness is more likely when norms are clear; this requires a relatively homogenous culture. Loose cultures have unclear norms and tolerate deviance from norms. Cultural heterogeneity, strong influences from other cultures, and crowded conditions can lead to looseness. Urban environments are usually looser than rural ones. Tight cultures would likely frown upon those who do not strictly adhere to dress norms. If you grew up in a small town in the United States, you can probably relate to the tighter constraints on rural dress compared to urban dress.

Individualism and collectivism Individualists place high value on self-reliance, independence, pleasure, affluence, and the pursuit of happiness. The behavior of individualists tends to be friendly but non-intimate (i.e., emotionally detached) toward a wide range of people outside the family. Individualists thrive on individual expression through dress and can be found among those wearing subcultural styles such as piercings, tattoos, Goth, punk, and so on. Adolescent dress in the United States is a good example of individualist dress. Generally, adolescents are permitted to experiment with dress and "try on" different identities without penalty.

Characteristics of collectivists often (but not always) include organization in a hierarchical manner with a tendency to be concerned about the results of their actions on members within their close-knit groups, sharing of resources with group members, feeling interdependent with group members, and feeling involved in the lives of group members (Hui & Triandis, 1986). Collectivists also feel strongly about the integrity of their groups. Amish dress is a good example of a collectivist culture in the United States where all members are supported by the group and held to certain standards of behavior, including dress (Boynton-Arthur, 1993).

In addition to the preceding information about culture, there are two theoretical concepts that directly connect dress and culture and were developed or adapted by dress scholars. First, dress is a part of the material culture of the society in which it is worn. A **material culture analysis** consists of procedures to examine the artifacts created or utilized in a society or community. Through the material culture of a society, it is possible to explore the nonmaterial aspects of the culture: the values, ideas, attitudes, and assumptions present in that society. A material culture process has been developed by dress scholars specifically to study clothing as material culture (Severa & Horswill, 1989). Within this method are three stages. These stages are (1) determining modal type; (2) analyzing material, design and construction, and workmanship; and (3) examining identification, evaluation, cultural analysis, and interpretation.

Elements of the material culture, such as dress, are often related to the nonmaterial culture of a society in complex ways (Tortora, 2010). For example, in some cultures wedding dresses are preserved and worn only once (i.e., sentiment is valued over recycling a dress or conserving space), but other cultures may wear a wedding dress many times after the wedding.

When conducting a material culture analysis on a wedding gown, one must critically examine the styling details of a wedding dress to determine whether or not they match the fashion of the period. If the styling details do not match the fashions for the date of the wedding, it is possible that the dress was repurposed for a later occasion. For instance, a wedding gown bodice from 1892 was embellished with silver-lined beads. The beading was found to be quite elaborate compared to other wedding gowns of that period. Also, the sleeves were short and puffed compared to the more conservative long, fitted

sleeves on wedding dresses of the period. The bodice embellishment and the sleeve style indicate that the wearer repurposed the gown at a later date—perhaps for a ball gown (Blackwell, 2012). Even though the owner of the dress married into a wealthy family, she chose to repurpose her dress for another occasion several years after her wedding. The results of this material culture analysis include that this wealthy family valued conservation despite their ability to buy a new gown.

Second, **cultural authentication** is a process of assimilation through which a garment or an accessory external to a culture is adopted and changed. With this change, over time, the artifact becomes a vital, valued part of the adopting culture's dress (Vollmer, 2010). The steps of cultural authentication are (1) selection, (2) characterization, (3) incorporation, and (4) transformation. Cases of cultural authentication have been documented. One study connects Indian madras plaid to the Kalabari in Nigeria (Eicher & Erekosima, 1995). The Kalabari use a cut-thread method to create another design on traditional madras fabric. Another example of cultural authentication is the Hawaiian holoku (Arthur, 1997). The holoku is a loose-fitting dress with no defined waistline. It was fashioned after a muumuu-style dress worn by Western missionaries to Hawaii in 1820. The indigenous Hawaiians adapted the muumuu-style dress into what they now refer to as the holoku. Look for other examples of material culture and cultural authentication throughout this text.

Why Does Culture Matter?

Many universities have created diversity requirements for their students. Although the effort is not always perfect (Miller-Spillman, Michelman, & Huffman, 2012), the general consensus is that American college students will need cultural competencies (see Figure 1.3) in order to navigate a world that is increasingly diverse. Unless you plan to inherit a family-owned business that operates among a narrow, select clientele, chances are you will need interpersonal skills while working with a range of diverse individuals (i.e., cultural competencies). In addition, many people would likely argue that being a global citizen is part of being an educated person.

Travel to other parts of the world can increase one's cultural competencies. Davis (2008) offers this advice:

It may sound naïve, but when you enter a cross-cultural situation, you are by definition an ambassador

Cultural Competence Model ™

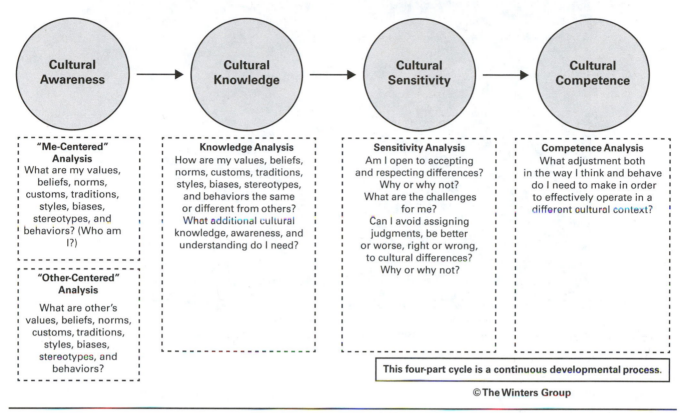

Figure 1.3 Consult the Cultural Competence Model at the beginning and the end of your course to track your progress toward pluralism.

for your culture. Decency and pride dictate that we present ourselves well, with respect and integrity. . . . Whether we travel as tourists, journalists, or academic anthropologists, it is our comparative wealth that allows us to be in these places, to have these life-affirming interactions. . . . The goal of travel is to return transformed. (pg 21 in MOD 3rd edition)

Cultural insensitivity while traveling can be seen when an American tourist demands American food while refusing to try the local fare. One cannot expect a burger and fries everywhere they travel. Culture is important to everyone and Americans who have chosen to arrive in another country uninformed about the culture they are visiting shouldn't be surprised to be dismissed or ignored by the locals. It is a matter of mutual respect of each other's culture.

Obviously, being culturally sensitive when you travel will be appreciated by the people with whom you interact. Learning a few basic words in their language will be appreciated by the locals even if you don't get the pronunciation exactly correct. Having the ability to converse with locals about their country's history and the current political issues will also be appreciated. Knowledge of their cultural dress is also valuable. One way to blend in is to understand the culture and dress accordingly. For instance, is this a modest culture in which women should cover their hair? Or is this a culture which accepts immodesty in women's dress?

See the reading "Etiquette 101: Dress Codes" (at the end of this chapter) for examples of what type of dress is worn at a meeting, on the street, and at a party in several different countries. Review and consider the dress advice for different countries. Some may surprise you.

THEORY

Theories are helpful to scholars and individuals who wish to explain a particular phenomenon. Dress scholars, for example, may wish to formally explain the emphasis on individual expression through dress in Western cultures versus the emphasis on traditional dress in some non-Western cultures. In addition, an individual encountering

Figure 1.4 Multiple face piercings may cause an observer to theorize about why a person would do that.

a barista at a coffee bar may speculate (or theorize) why a person would want several face and ear piercings (see Figure 1.4).

A variety of scientific theories helps us understand the effect of dress on interpersonal relationships. **Symbolic interaction theory** explains how an individual defines herself or himself through interactions and relationships with others (Mead, 1934). Symbolic interaction theorists contend that to develop a sense of self as a human being, one must interact with other people. Other people respond to an individual (both verbally and nonverbally) about how he or she is doing, what he or she is supposed to be doing, what the value or worth of that individual is, and how the individual is identified (Stone, 1965). Continuous presentation of **programs** of dress (programs could include other types of behavior) and reflection upon others' **reviews** or reactions to dress allow an individual to gain a sense of how others see and assign meaning to him or her (Stone, 1965).

Because dress is a part of our interactions with others, we learn some things about ourselves through the responses others give to our appearance. This is the process of discourse involving the presentation of appearance programs and receiving reviews. In addition, we interact with others on the basis of what their appearance means to us (Shilling, 1993; Stone, 1965). For example, consider

this in light of your own behavior with classmates versus authority figures.

Cooley (1902) compared the process of development of self to looking in a mirror. He outlined the general process as follows:

1. Individuals attempt to perceive themselves by imagining how others perceive them or by reflecting on reviews by others.
2. Individuals may reject or accept other people's reflections of the self, but these reflections nevertheless have an impact.

This process of using other people as mirrors to tell us who we are is the **looking glass self** process. So, who we are depends very much on the people with whom we interact, their reactions to us and evaluations of us, and our reflections on these reactions as guides to future behavior, including how to dress. We continually try out new presentations of self through dress or stick to old ways of dressing that we feel are successful or safe. A process of learning who we are through continued reflection and action with others and constant experimentation and exploration is the **self-indication process** (Blumer, 1969). Our reflections on others' responses or how we interpret what other people mean is as crucial to self as is our own behavior and the responses of others. Our interpretations may not always be accurate; we develop skills throughout life at placing the self in another person's position in order to understand the other or to understand the self from the other's point of view (Mead, 1934). Taking other people's perspectives to understand their responses is called **taking on the role of the other**. Herrington's experiment wearing the hijab is an excellent example of taking on the role of the other, in this case a Muslim woman. (See "'Undercover' in Hijab" at the end of this chapter.) Therefore, seeing the self and the world from another person's perspective is crucial to the looking glass self. An integral part of the self are the roles we take on. **Role theory** helps us to understand the roles we play and how dress is a part of those roles. **Roles are positions that people occupy in a group or society** (Biddle & Thomas, 1966). These positions are defined by social relationships; people take on roles in relation to other persons. Performance of a role is guided by social expectations for the role-player's behavior (including dress), knowledge, and attitudes.

Adults tend to have multiple roles that define different parts of the self. At any one time, a man may be 42 years old (age role); male (gender role); Puerto Rican (ethnic role); a chef and a boss to junior chefs (employment roles); a father, a husband, a brother, a son (family roles); a best friend of another man (social role); and a coach for a girls' soccer team (community leadership role). He may express some of these roles through dress but not all of these roles in any one appearance. These roles are parts of the puzzle that make up the man's **identity**. Other aspects of identity include unique personal traits and interests that are not necessarily role related. The Puerto Rican man might run five miles alone every morning and think of himself as defined in part by running. He, in a sense, has many identities that make up his total self. We would need to examine his total wardrobe to begin to grasp the multiple identities of this man, but some of his identity might never be expressed through dress.

Lastly, one sociologist used a **dramaturgical approach** to study dress and appearances. Goffman (1959) introduced the idea that life is played out on a stage and is similar to the theater in that actors can appear on the front or back stage. Goffman pointed out that individuals behave differently depending on the audience. Front stage behavior includes dress that is planned and controlled, whereas backstage dress is casual and impulsive. An example in retail would be the dress and behavior that sales associates display while on the sales floor with customers. Sales floor decorum may include professional dress or dress items from the retail store along with friendly, helpful behavior such as helping the customer pick out clothes for an upcoming event. Once the sales associate steps backstage into an area labeled "Employees Only," where she is no longer seen by the customer, she may grab a bite to eat, smoke a cigarette, chew gum, complain about customers' demands, and take off a jacket or untuck a shirttail. The dramaturgical approach also has common features to dress and the public, private, and secret self, as described in Chapter 11.

How Theories Help Us to Study and Understand Dress Meanings

Meanings of dress are central to this area of study. Symbolic interactionist Gregory Stone (1965) proposed that meaning can vary from boring (so mundane that no one even notices it) to nonsense (mixing many styles together, making their meaning unintelligible). Typically, individuals use those around them at home and work to gain ideas about dress. More formal avenues are fashion magazines, newspapers, television shows, and movies. More recently, social media (e.g., Facebook and YouTube) are adding to the influences on how we interpret dress (La Ferla, 2011).

Dress scholar Marcia Morgado provides readers with a process for discovering the meanings of dress in the reading "Uncovered Butts & Recovered Rules: Sagging Pants and the Logic of Abductive Inference" at the end of this chapter. Morgado uses the field of **semiotics**, the study of signs, to describe how dress items carry meanings. Morgado frames her work on sagging pants using a theoretical construct known as **abductive inference**. Follow her process of extracting meanings of sagging pants to understand how abductive inference works.

Collective Selection Theory

Often the terms "fashion" and "dress" are used interchangeably but they are two different concepts. Many products, if not all, are affected by fashion, from vehicles to home decor to "fashionable" places to eat and drink. Fashion has a specific meaning and is related to time. If a significant number of consumers decide to adopt the style, it actually becomes a fashion, though only certain segments of consumers may wear the style. The style may take on the added meaning of representing the lifestyles of people who adopt the new look (see Chapter 2 for more information on the fashion cycle).

Collective selection theory is a theory related to fashion (Blumer, 1969). Americans often believe they are individuals acting upon impulses that are uniquely their own; to some extent that is true. Americans are less likely to acknowledge the collective forces that shape their impulses, such as our clothing choices. Blumer called this collective selection because many individuals' choices are needed to make a dress item a fashion. And our choices are created by similar forces (e.g., what we see in the media and in conversation with others). See more on collective selection in Chapter 11.

Cargo pants were recently featured on *CBS Good Morning* (2016) and other media outlets because of the cargo pants wars that often divide husband and wife (see Figure 1.5). Cargo pants are a good example of **world dress** (Eicher, Evenson & Lutz, 2008) because of their

global reach. Similar to blue jeans, you can see cargo pants anywhere in the world. **Transnational style** is another term used to describe the cargo pant style that occurs simultaneously in several worldwide locations (Eicher & Evenson, 2015). See the reading by Joseph Hancock titled "Cargo Pants: The Transnational Rise of the Garment That Started a Fashion War" (at the end of this chapter) as he tracks the interesting historical growth of cargo pants.

What's the Benefit of Being a Global Citizen?

In this book, the authors combine dress and culture while discussing ideas beyond simply what is fashionable. However, people use dress as a vehicle to learn more about our culture as well as other cultures. Fashion is certainly a global phenomenon thanks to the Internet (see "Cargo Pants" section in this chapter). Knowing how to comfortably interact with those from other cultures is a life skill worth cultivating. In this section we consider why it is important to become a **global citizen**.

What's so great about being a global citizen? Does being a global citizen mean that you can no longer appreciate where you grew up? Davis (2008) provides examples of why being an American is not necessarily better than being from another country. He also points out that languages are dying out at an alarming rate because they are no longer being taught to children. Even though we may not feel the impact of a language dying out, eventually if we all speak the same language we will have lost a great amount of richness in diversity.

Americans are often accused of believing that they are the center of the universe and everyone else is looking at Americans for ideas on how to dress, live, and enjoy life—a very ethnocentric view. But how does the rest of the world view the United States? "Etiquette 101: What the World Thinks about Us" by Kachka (2008) features a list of ten common misperceptions about American culture. Compare these stereotypes of Americans to stereotypes that Americans have of people from other cultures.

Ethnocentrism is judging people from other cultures and backgrounds by one's own cultural standards and beliefs. **Pluralism** is the acceptance of differences in others while not necessarily wanting to adopt those differences for the self. In other words, you do not have to turn your back on your upbringing and cultural roots in order to become more pluralistic. However, becoming more pluralistic may help you to succeed in business or any public arena

Figure 1.5 Transnational style: cargo pants.

(such as local government). Moving from an ethnocentric view to a pluralistic one is a goal of this course. Since we see another's dress before we speak, assumptions are made based on dress and appearance alone. We see skin color, hair texture, and items of clothing and—without talking to this person—make assumptions based on stereotypes. In a fast-paced world, we cannot speak to everyone; our judgments of others are made quickly.

Summary

Dress is a complex topic because meanings are based on personal experience as well as cultural rules. This chapter serves as an introduction to basic concepts needed to study dress and culture. In this text we explore the intersections of dress and culture; theory is used to explain dress meanings. Dress, culture, and theory are recurring themes throughout the text that enable the reader to expand his or her knowledge of dress meanings and interpretations. Global awareness and critical thinking about dress and culture are skills necessary to be successful in a world of increasing complexity. Learning how to become a global citizen and following the steps to increase your cultural competencies are skills that will serve you well for the rest of your life.

Key Terms

Abductive inference	Ethnocentrism	Programs	Symbolic interaction theory
Collective selection theory	Global citizen	Reviews	Taking on the role of the other
Cultural authentication	Identity	Roles	Theory
Culture	Looking glass self	Role theory	Transnational style
Dramaturgical approach	Material culture analysis	Self-indication process	World dress
Dress	Pluralism	Semiotics	

Learning Activity 1.1

BODY SPACE DIFFERENCE BETWEEN CULTURES

Pair off in the classroom with the person sitting either directly in front or in back of you. While standing, face the other person with your toes touching and talk to each other for 60 seconds. After you are seated, share with the class how it felt to participate in this exercise. Most comments will relate how uncomfortable it was to be that close while talking. This can lead to a discussion about body space across cultures. Americans tend to stand an arm's length apart when speaking and have issues with closeness such as bad breath, food in teeth, and body odor. Some cultures have a closer body space. Conversations between two people from different cultures can sometimes result in a humorous "dance" in which one partner is advancing and the other partner is backing up.

Learning Activity 1.2

RESOLVING A CROSS-CULTURAL MISUNDERSTANDING—JOGGING ALONE

Objectives

- To understand that cross-cultural misunderstandings are common occurrences.
- To identify a solution to a cross-cultural misunderstanding.

Procedures

1. Read about the way in which individuals in the Dominican Republic misunderstood an American Peace Corps volunteer who was doing something that in the United States is perfectly normal.

2. Read the Peace Corps volunteer's account titled "Jogging Alone." Think about how you might solve the dilemma as you read. Work in pairs with your classmates to respond to the questions that follow.

3. Offer responses to each question during a class discussion. Allow for differing responses to be considered. DISCUSSION 1

Jogging Alone: An Account of a Peace Corps Volunteer Serving in the Dominican Republic

When I first arrived in my village in the Dominican Republic, I began to have a problem with my morning jogging routine. I used to jog every day when I was at home in the United States, so when I arrived in my village in the Dominican Republic, I set myself a goal to continue jogging two miles every morning. I really liked the peaceful feeling of jogging alone as the sun came up. But this did not last for long. The people in my village simply couldn't understand why someone would want to run alone. Soon people began to appear at their doorways offering me a cup of coffee; others would invite me to stop in for a visit. Sometimes this would happen four or five times as I tried to continue jogging. They even began sending their children to run behind me so I wouldn't be lonely. They were unable to understand the American custom of exercising alone. I was faced with a dilemma. I really enjoyed my early morning runs. However, I soon realized that it's considered impolite in Dominican villages not to accept a cup of coffee or stop and chat when you pass people who are sitting on their front steps. I didn't want to give up jogging. But, at the same time, I wanted to show respect for the customs of the Dominican Republic—and not be viewed as odd or strange.[1]

Endnote

1. This and other classroom activities can be accessed from Building Bridges: A Peace Corps Classroom Guide to Cross-Cultural Understanding Coverdell World Wise Schools, https://files.peacecorps.gov/wws/pdf/BuildingBridges.pdf Peace Corps. (2002). *Building bridges: A Peace Corps classroom guide to cross-cultural understanding*. Washington, DC: Peace Corps Paul D. Coverdell World Wise Schools.

Discussion Questions

1. What was the American's point of view here?
2. What American cultural norm, or custom, did the American think would be viewed as perfectly normal in the Dominican Republic?
3. Describe a way you think that the American could respect the Dominican need to show hospitality to a stranger and, at the same time, not have to give up jogging.
4. What was the Dominicans' point of view here?
5. What was the reason for the Dominicans' point of view? What cultural norm did the Dominicans have that made them view the American's behavior as strange?
6. How might the Dominicans begin to understand and respect American cultural norms and, at the same time, satisfy their own need to show hospitality to strangers?

_____

1. An extended version of this article appears in *Critical Studies in Men's Fashion* 2 (2 & 3), 107–126.

References

Arthur, L. (1997), "Cultural Authentication Refined: The Case of the Hawaiian Holoku," *Clothing and Textiles Research Journal*, 15(3): 125–39.

Biddle, B. J. and E. J. Thomas (1966), *Role Theory: Concepts and Research*, New York: Wiley.

Boynton-Arthur, L. (1993), "Clothing, Control, and Women's Agency: The Mitigation of Patriarchal Power," in S. Fisher & K. Davis (eds.), *Negotiating at the Margins*, 66–84, New Brunswick, NJ: Rutgers University Press.

Blackwell, C. R. (2012), "A Family Affair: An Analysis of the Means-Seaton Family Wedding Gowns from 1885–1892." Unpublished master's thesis, University of Kentucky.

Blumer, H. (1969), *Symbolic Interactionism: Perspective and Method*, Englewood Cliffs, NJ: Prentice Hall.

Chanchani, S. and P. Theivanathampillai (2002), "Typologies of Culture," University of Otago, Department of Accountancy and Business Law Working Papers Series, 04: 10/02. Dunedin: University of Otago.

Cooley, C. H. (1902), *Human Nature and the Social Order*, New York: Charles Scribner's Sons.

"Cross-Cultural/International Communication" (2012), *Encyclopedia of Business* (2nd ed.). Available online: http://www.referenceforbusiness.com/encyclopedia/Cos-Des/Cross-Cultural-International-Communication.html

Damhorst, M. L. and A. M. Fiore (1990), "Women's Job Interview Dress: How Personnel Interviewers See It," in M. L. Damhorst, K. A. Miller, and S. O. Michelman (eds.), *The Meanings of Dress*, 92–97, New York: Fairchild Publications.

Davis, W. (2008), "On Native Ground," *Conde Nast Traveler*, November 11. Available online: https://www.cntraveler.com/stories/2008-11-11/on-native-ground.

Eicher, J. B. and T. V. Erekosima (1995), "Why Do They Call It Kalabari?: Cultural Authentication and the Demarcation of Ethnic Identity," in J. B. Eicher (ed.), *Dress and Ethnicity*, 139–64, Oxford: Berg.

Eicher, J. B. and S. L. Evenson (2015), *The Visible Self: Global Perspectives on Dress, Culture, and Society*, New York: Fairchild Books.

Eicher, J. B., S. L. Evenson, and H. A. Lutz (2008), *The Visible Self: Global Perspectives on Dress, Culture, and Society*, New York: Fairchild Books.

Goffman, E. (1959), *The Presentation of Self in Everyday Life*, New York: Doubleday.

Haney, C., C. Banks, and P. G. Zimbardo (1973), "A Study of Prisoners and Guards in a Simulated Prison," *Naval Research Reviews*, Office of Naval Research, Washington, DC, 1–17.

Hui, C. H. and H. C. Triandis (1986), "Individualism and Collectivism: A Study of Cross-Cultural Researchers," *Journal of Cross-Cultural Psychology*, 17: 225–48.

Kachka, B. (2008), "Etiquette 101: What the World Thinks of Us," *Conde Nast Traveler*, October 14. Available online: https://www.cntraveler.com/stories/2008-10-14/etiquette-101-what-the-world-thinks-about-us.

La Ferla, R. (2011), "The Campus as Runway," *The New York Times*, October 13. Available online: https://www.nytimes.com/2011/10/13/fashion/on-campus-taking-fashion-seriously.html.

Lennon, T. L., S. J. Lennon and K. K. P. Johnson (1992–1993), "Is Clothing Probative of Attitude or Intent? Implication for Rape and Sexual Harassment Cases," *Law & Inequality: A Journal of Theory and Practice*, 11(2): 391–415.

Mead, G. H. (1934), *Mind, Self, and Society* (Charles W. Morris, Ed.), Chicago: University of Chicago Press.

Miller-Spillman, K. A., S. O. Michelman and N. Huffman (2012), "Are Required Cross-Cultural Courses Producing Pluralistic students?" in K. Miller-Spillman, S. Michelman and N. Huffman (eds.), *The Meanings of Dress*, 599–611.

Roach-Higgins, M. E. and J. B. Eicher (1992), "Dress and Identity," *Clothing and Textiles Research Journal*, 10(4): 1–8.

Rucker, M., D. Taber and A. Harrison (1981), The Effect of Clothing Variation on First Impressions of Female Job Applicants: What to Wear When," *Social Behavior and Personality*, 9: 53–64.

Severa, J. and M. Horswill (1989), "Costume as Material Culture," *Dress*, 15: 51–64.

Shilling, C. (1993), *The Body and Social Theory*, Newbury Park, CA: Sage.

Stone, G. P. (1965), "Appearance and the Self," in M. E. Roach and J. B. Eicher (eds.), *Dress, Adornment and the Social Order*, 216–45, New York: John Wiley.

Tortora, P. (2010), "Introduction to Cultural Groups," in *Berg Encyclopedia of World Dress and Fashion: Volume 3—The United States and Canada*. Available online: www.bergfashionlibrary.com/view/bewdf/BEWDF-v3/EDch3062a.xml.

Triandis, H. C. (1994), *Culture and Social Behavior*, New York: McGraw-Hill.

Vollmer, J. (2010), "Cultural Authentication in Dress," in *Berg Encyclopedia of World Dress and Fashion: Volume 10—Global Perspectives*. Available online: www.bergfashionlibrary.com/view/bewdf/BEWDF-v10/EDch10009.xml.

1.1
'Undercover' in Hijab: Unveiling One Month Later
Cassidy Herrington

Hilton Als, an African American writer, says our worldview and sense of "otherness" is created in our mother's lap.

Mother's lap is protective and familiar. Leaving this worldview can be uncomfortable, but I can assure you, the rewards are much greater.

Hijab

Last month, I climbed out of my "lap" and wore a hijab, the Muslim headscarf (Figure 1.6). I thought this temporary modification of my appearance would bring me closer to an understanding of the Muslim community, but in retrospect, I learned more about my place in the world.

Simplified, one piece of fabric is all it takes to turn perspectives upside-down.

The hijab is a contested, sacred, and sometimes controversial symbol, but it is just a symbol. It is a symbol of Islam, a misconstrued, misunderstood religion that represents the most diverse population of people in the world—a population of more than one billion people.

I realized the best way to identify with Muslims was to take a walk in their shoes. On Oct. 1, I covered my head with a gauze scarf and grappled with the perceptions of strangers, peers, and even my own family.

Because of perceptions, I even struggled to write this column. My experience with the hijab was personal, but I hope sharing what I saw will open a critical conversation.

My hijab silenced, but simultaneously, my hijab brought unforgettable words.

Idea

In the first column I wrote this semester, I compared college to an alarm clock saying, "we see the face of a clock, but rarely do we see what operates behind it." At the time, I did not realize how seriously I needed to act on my own words—as a journalist, a woman and a human.

A few weeks after I wrote that piece, a guest columnist addressed Islamophobic sentiments regarding the proposed "ground zero" mosque. The writer was Muslim, and she received a flurry of feedback.

The comments online accumulated like a swarm of mindless pests. The collective opinion equated Islam to violence and terrorism.

In response to her column, one comment said, "[The writer] asks us to trust Islam. Given our collective experience, and given Islam's history I have to wonder what planet she thinks we are on."

Although I did not know the voices behind these anonymous posts, I felt involuntarily linked to them—because I am not Muslim. I wanted to connect people, and almost instinctively, I decided that a hijab was necessary. A hijab could help me use my affiliation with "white," non-Muslims to build rapport with the Islamic community and at the same time, show non-Muslims the truth from an unheard voice. Above all, I wanted to see and feel the standard lifestyle for so many women around the world—because I'm curious, and that's why I'm a journalist.

Before I took this step, I decided to propose my idea to the women who wear headscarves every day. Little did I know, a room full of strangers would quickly become my

Figure 1.6 Student journalist Cassidy Herrington (a) wore a hijab (b) for one month to better understand the Muslim-American community.

This article originally appeared in *The Kentucky Kernel*, student newspaper of the University of Kentucky. Reprinted with permission.

greatest source of encouragement and would make this project more attainable.

The Handshake

Initially, I worried about how the Muslim community would perceive a non-Muslim in a hijab, so I needed its approval before I would start trying on scarves. On Sept. 16, I went to a Muslim Student Association meeting to introduce myself.

When I opened the door to the meeting room, I was incredibly nervous. To erase any sign of uncertainty, I interjected to a girl seated across the room, "meeting starts at 7, right?" The girl, it turns out, was Heba Suleiman, the MSA president. After I explained my plan, her face lit up.

"That is an amazing idea," she said.

I felt my tension and built-up anxiety melt away. In the minutes following, I introduced myself to the whole group with an "asalaam alaykum," and although I was half-prepared for it, I was alarmed to hear dozens of "wa aylaykum asalam" in response.

Before I left, several girls approached me. I will not forget what one girl said, "this gives me hope." Another girl said, "I'm Muslim, and I couldn't even do that." It did not hit me until then, that this project would be more than covering my hair. I would be representing a community and a faith, and consequentially, I needed to be fully conscious of my actions while in hijab.

First Steps "Undercover"

Two weeks later, I met Heba and her friend Leanna for coffee, and they showed me how to wrap a hijab. The girls were incredibly helpful, more than they probably realized. Although this project was my personal undertaking, I knew I wouldn't be alone—this thought helped me later when I felt like ripping off the hijab and quitting.

Responses to my hijab were subtle or nonexistent. I noticed passing glances diverted to the ground, but overall, everything felt the same. Near the end of the month, a classmate pointed out that a boy had been staring at me, much to my oblivion. The hijab became a part of me, and until I turned my head and felt a gentle tug, I forgot it was there.

For the most part, I carried out life as usual while in hijab. I rode my bike and felt the sensation of wind whipping under my headscarf. I walked past storefront windows, caught a glimpse of a foreign reflection and had to frequently remind myself that the girl was me. Hijab became part of my morning routine, and on one morning

I biked to class and turned around because I realized I left without it. At the end of the day, I laughed at my "hijab hair" pressed flat against my scalp.

The hijab sometimes made me uneasy. I went to the grocery store and felt people dodge me in the aisles—or was that just my imagination?

I recognize every exchange I had and every occurrence I report may be an assumption or over analysis because few of my encounters were transparent. The truth is, however, very few of my peers said anything about the hijab. My classmates I've sat next to for more than a year, my professors, and my friends from high school—no one addressed the obvious, and it hurt. I felt separated from the people who know me best—or so I thought.

A gap in the conversation exists, and it's not just surrounding my situation.

Just over a week ago, I turned on the news to see Juan Williams, a former NPR news analyst fired for commentary about Islam. Williams said, "If I see people who are in Muslim garb and I think, you know, they are identifying themselves first and foremost as Muslims, I get worried. I get nervous."

His statement revealed an internalized fear. And I saw this fear when my colleagues dodged the topic. When I went back to ask "why?," several said it was too "touchy" or insensitive to bring up.

A hijab [is] a symbol, like a cross, a star or an American flag. I am still the same Cassidy Herrington—I didn't change my identity, but I was treated like a separate entity.

Talk Is Not Cheap

When someone mentioned my hijab without my provocation, I immediately felt at ease. A barista at my usual coffee stop politely asked, "Are you veiling?" A friend in the newsroom asked, "Are your ears cold?"

My favorite account involves a back-story.

I love Mediterranean and Middle Eastern cuisine, and I garnered an appetite when I was young. My childhood home neighbored my "third grandmother," the most loving second-generation Lebanese woman and exceptional cook (not an exaggeration, she could get me to eat leafy vegetables when I was a child zealot of noodles and cheese). I remember knocking on her back door when I was five, asking for Tupperware brimming with tabouleh.

When King Tut's opened on Limestone, my school year swiftly improved to a fabulously garlicky degree. At least once a week, I stopped by to pick up the tabouleh, hummus or falafel to medicate my case of the newsroom munchies.

On Oct. 21, the owner, Ashraf Yousef, stopped me before I went inside.

"I heard about your project, and I like it," he said. "And you look beautiful in your hijab." This encounter was by far the best. And it made my shawarma sandwich taste particularly delicious. I went back on my last day to thank him, and Yousef said, "I'm just giving my honest opinion, with the hijab, you look beautiful. It makes your face look better."

Yousef asked if I would wear the hijab to his restaurant when the project was over. I nodded, smiled and took a crunchy mouthful of fattoush.

False Patriotism

I did not receive intentional, flagrant anti-Muslim responses. I did, however, receive an e-mail allegedly "intended" for another reader. The e-mail was titled "My new ringtone." When I opened the audio file, the Muslim prayer to Mecca was abruptly silenced by three gunshots and the U.S. national anthem.

I spoke to the sender of the e-mail, and he said, "It was just a joke." Here lies a problem with phobias and intolerance—joking about it doesn't make it less of an issue. When was it ever okay to joke about hatred and persecution? Was it acceptable when Jews were grotesquely drawn in Nazi cartoons? Or when Emmet Till was brutally murdered?

The e-mail is unfortunate evidence that many people inaccurately perceive Islam as violent or as "the other." A Gallup poll taken last November found 43 percent of Americans feel at least a "little" prejudice against Muslims. And if you need further confirmation that Islamophobia exists, consult Ann Coulter or Newt Gingrich.

Hijab-less

I've been asked, "Will you wear the hijab when it's over?" and initially, I didn't think I would—because I'm not Muslim, I don't personally believe in hijab. Now that I see it hanging on my wall and I am able to reflect on the strength it gave me, I think, yes, when I need the headscarf, I might wear it.

Ashraf said, "A non-Muslim woman who wears a hijab is just wearing a headscarf" (and apparently, my face "looks better"). Appearances aside, when I wore the hijab, I felt confident and focused. I wore the hijab to a news conference for Rand Paul, and although an event coordinator stopped me (just me, except for one elusive blogger) to check my credentials, I felt I accurately represented myself as an intelligent, determined journalist—I was not concerned with how I looked, but rather, I was focused on gathering the story.

So now, I return to my first column of the year. I've asked the questions, and I've reached across the circles. Now, it's your turn. You don't have to wear a hijab for a month to change someone's life or yours. The Masjid Bilial Islamic Center will host a "get to know your neighbors" on November 7, and UK's Muslim Student Association is having "The Hajj" on November 8. These are opportunities for non-Muslims to be better informed and make meaningful connections.

I want to thank Heba for being a friend and a resource for help. Thank you to Ashraf Yousef and King Tut for the delicious food and the inspiration. Finally, I apologize to the individuals who feel I have "lied" to them about my identity or who do not agree with this project. I hope this page clears things up—you have the truth now, and I hope you find use for it.

Why are we so afraid to talk about this? We are not at war with Islam. In fact, Muslim soldiers are defending this country. Making jokes about terrorism is not going to make the situation less serious. Simply "tolerating" someone's presence is not enough.

If you turn on the news, you will inevitably hear the prefix, "extremist," when describing Islam. What you see and hear from the media is fallible—if you want the truth, talk to a Muslim.

Discussion Questions

1. What do you think caused Herrington to make the decision to wear a hijab for a month, and why do you think she stuck to it?

2. Would you take on a Muslim dress code for a month? Why or why not?

3. How instructive do you think this exercise was on a personal level for Herrington, on a university level, and internationally?

DISCUSSION 1 -

Rule 1: Leave the Fanny Pack

What makes an Ugly American ugly? Is it the timbre of our voices? Or the way we travel in herds? Or is it (as we suspect) our love of sweatpants, baseball caps, and yes, fanny packs, no matter the occasion or place? While it can sometimes seem that the world has fallen victim to a sort of sartorial globalization, where jeans are welcome anytime, anywhere, the truth is—of course—more nuanced. What works in surprisingly laid-back Singapore will be greeted with looks of horror on the streets (or in the boardrooms) of Paris. And ladies, while you can (and should) pile on the gold and jewels in Greece, quirky and stripped-down is the way to go in Germany. So here are the rules on looking not just appropriate but actually stylish around the globe, whether you're in a meeting, at a party, or just walking outdoors. Plus: Tips on how to wear a head scarf, what to pack for safari, and how to play European for a day. Ugly American? Fuhgeddaboudit.

Africa/The Middle East

In general, coverage is key. But while merely clothing your collarbone is enough in Jordan, just an inch of shoulder skin could get you arrested in Iran; over in Dubai, you'll need a brand or two to make it big. Men are usually fine in long pants, and women carry shawls for a quick conservative fix, but consider yourself forewarned: Style is a sensitive subject here.

Dubai

At a meeting: Women's pantsuits should be sheeny and glam; men's duds are buffed, black, and paired with slim ties.

On the street: The mall, not the street, is the social arena. Here, girls in T-shirts (their shoulders covered out of respect and as a remedy against the freezing AC blasts) tote the latest Louis Vuittons. Carry a pashmina to cover up in case you find yourself in a traditional souk—although you'll see miniskirts and shorts, they're for people who know the city

well enough to avoid ultra-conservative quarters. On men, reflective aviators abound, as do Gucci sandals.

At a party: Go glam to the gills: No Swarovski is too shiny and no Giuseppe Zanotti is too high. Men wear Y3 trainers and tailored blazers over graphic tees.

P.S. Put on clean socks if you're going to a local's house—you'll leave your shoes at the door.

Iran

At a meeting: Men wear crisp Italian suits and shined shoes. A chador (hooded floor-length cloak) is needed for a woman meeting a clerical group, but for most gatherings, she should slip on a black manteau (a loose coatlike garment), low closed-toe pumps, and an Iranian hijab. Locally bought products drape best and look contextually refined.

On the street: Special police enforce the Islamic dress code, which requires women (non-Muslims included) to be covered from head to toe. The working classes wear full-length black chadors, but a manteau over jeans is an acceptable alternative. Hijabs are often patterned or pinned with pretty brooches. Makeup should be minimal, and while bright lipstick isn't allowed, flawless eyebrows are an absolute must.

At a party: Wear whatever you want under your outer cloak; the young remove their voluminous robes to show off tight jeans and strappy stilettos at friends' informal gatherings. Older intellectuals conceal elegant suits under their cloaks.

P.S. They're credited with creating the first perfume, so it's no surprise that the Iranians are scent savvy: Although women might be cloaked, they're often doused in glam, sexy fragrances like Azzaro's vetiver and pimento tonics.

Jordan

At a meeting: Suits and shoes should be simple, and dresses work for women provided they're shin-length and sleeved. Big hair is not for the Jordanian boardroom: Tie

Eimear Lynch/Conde Nast Traveler © Conde Nast

long locks into chignons and keep short dos neat. The "Hillary Clinton look" is a woman's best bet, according to John Shoup, author of *Culture and Customs of Jordan*.

On the street: Rich red embroidery is popular, so Western women can don detailed tunics over loose trousers (many local women wear pants) or black cotton dresses embellished with traditional needlework. Men wear khakis and collared shirts.

At a party: King Abdullah II is a sartorial guide; he's almost always dressed in navy suits for nighttime (gray for daytime) and a light-colored silk tie. Queen Rania set a haute new tone by sporting Lanvin, Dior, and Elie Saab to evening affairs, but the first lady covers her shoulders and legs (with couture) when she's out in Amman.

P.S. The veil's a release of sorts for trendy young women, who can show a little more skin as long as the head is covered.

What to Wear on Safari

Conjure "safari style" and you'll likely envision a smart pocketed Proenza Schouler ensemble or Cavalli's sheeniest leopard-print dress—but show up wearing either in an actual African wildlife reserve and you'll spend the week banished to the back of your camp's SUV. The safari-bound have plenty of things to avoid: The color red spells danger to lions; military fatigues look fraudulent; perfumes, hair gels, and aftershaves bother the animals; and shiny baubles might catch a leopard's roving eye. In the bush, form usually takes a backseat to function.

These issues notwithstanding, weight is your biggest concern. Hippo Creek Safaris, for example, limits baggage to 35 pounds, and Premier Tours' camping safaris allow you only 26. For successful stalking style, pack a Kelty duffle (which measures 30 inches but weighs only one pound) with basic pieces that are both snappy and sound: a Polartec fleece and long pants for chilly morning game drives, a pair of khaki pants or shorts (or pants that zip into shorts—though these we won't sartorially condone), and for women, a tank top to layer under a muted Ralph Lauren linen button-down. "I roll it to the elbow in the morning, unbutton it all the way if I'm really hot, and wear it at night with a nice piece of jewelry," says Nina Wennersten, a travel specialist with Hippo Creek Safaris. Teva sandals will work for every stroll through the African bush, so leave the heavy hiking boots at home.

Come evening, "nobody wants to sit down to dinner and feel schleppy next to the perfect Italian tourists at camp," Wennersten says. Channel Romans on holiday in black slacks (no skirts, since malaria-ridden mosquitoes come out after dark), driving shoes, your trusty linen button-down, and a silver necklace or silk scarf. Don't worry about re-wearing: Laundry's taken away in the morning and returned by sundown every day.

How to Wear a Hijab

A head scarf is a head scarf is a head scarf—right? Not really. You can actually tell a lot about a woman by the way she wears her scarf. Here, we show you how to wear your hijab no matter the occasion—and, of course, what not to do as well.

Start by pinning your hair back securely, then tie it in a bun at the nape of your neck. A high bun whose outline can be clearly seen through the hijab is viewed as provocative.

At a Gathering

Although women are traditionally expected to wear a black scarf tightly secured so as to show only the oval of the face, today's young Iranian women push the envelope by pulling a printed colored scarf loosely around the head and leaving an inch or two of the hairline daringly exposed.

At a Bazaar

In the throng of a crowded market, a loosely tossed scarf isn't fashionable; it's troubleome. Women tired of worrying about crooked head coverings instead float a large scarf over the crown and clip it below the chin (special clasps are made for this particular purpose, but safety pins work too), then throw each of the long ends over the opposite shoulder.

At an Informal Meeting

Large kerchiefs worn babushka-style work for informal meetings with nonsecular colleagues. To get the look, fold a square scarf into a triangle and rest the base of the triangle at the top of the forehead, then tie the ends below the chin. Make sure the back tip of the triangle covers the nape of your neck.

At Official Places

The most classic hijab, and the most universally acceptable, is the Al-Amira style—essentially a hood that reaches past the bust, with a hole for the oval of the face. It comes in cotton, silk, rayon, and a myriad of prints, from florals to fleur-de-lis.

At Religious Places

Forget the hijab; it's time to break out the big guns: the chador. A mark of piety and the easiest way to go unnoticed in the most religious areas of Kuwait and Iran, the full-length, cloaklike chador is thrown over the hair and held closed in the front.

At a Young, Liberal Party

Flashing a hint of hair in Iran is like showing a little leg in the United States, so girls keep their bangs pinned back and their scarves opaque unless they're headed somewhere young and free. At such parties and private gatherings, it's coquettish to have bangs peeking out from under a sheer scarf.

Headbands = Nerdy

Layering a stretchy headband under a tight-fitting hijab screams "dork" to trendy young Iranians. The same hijab sans headband is socially acceptable.

Asia

You'll need a myriad of outfit options for a transcontinental Asian trek. Miniskirts and monochrome black are safe bets from Jakarta to Japan, but women in India and Pakistan cover their legs and sport vibrant, rich hues. In fact, very few styles would work in every country: Flip-flops, for instance, are trendy in Singapore, verboten in China, and, in Indonesia, acceptable only for shower wear. Here's how to prep before you pack.

Japan

At a meeting: "The Japanese word for dress shirt, wai shatsu, comes from the English for 'white shirt,' which gives you an idea of the range of colors worn at work," says Dan Rosen, professor at Tokyo's Chuo Law School, who recommends basic black suits. In 2005, the government launched a Cool Biz initiative meant to lower AC costs by encouraging lighter work attire; it's been met with fierce resistance by the jacket-and-tie-loving Japanese working class.

On the street: For Tokyo youth, nothing's too studied or over-the-top, so the laissez-faire American norm is seen as slovenly. Women should wear heels, makeup, and a dose of frills, and men must be clean shaven and must spend time on their hair.

At a party: Agnès B. and Louis Vuitton are the easiest icebreakers, since the Japanese love labels—along with the stylish shapes by local designers like Yohji Yamamoto. No sweat suits, please!

P.S. Planning to shop here? Note that Japanese sizes run significantly smaller than those in the States. If you wear a medium in the United States, a Japanese XL might be a squeeze.

Singapore

At a meeting: You wouldn't think so, given Singapore's rules-happy reputation, but business meetings are actually super casual here (well, dresswise at least). Jackets aren't required, ties are rare, and both sexes wear oxfords and slacks. For women, trendy peg-leg pants are often permissible.

On the street: Those in their 20s and 30s strut in tank tops, hot pants (board shorts for boys), and flip-flops. A polo shirt by Fred Perry or Ralph Lauren is a popular option, as well as anything from casual mass-market stores.

At a party: "A Marni dress with Giuseppe Zanotti sandals for house parties," says Aun Koh, director of Singapore-based Ate Consulting. Brands are important to upper-class dames, who competitively collect Hermès bags. Men wear designer jeans from the likes of G–Star Raw and Dr. Denim.

P.S. Hems are worn high at every age—get your gams ready.

Europe

If there's one hard and fast sartorial rule in Europe, it's this: Shabby is never chic. And no one, whether in London or Leipzig, likes the American travel-comfort gear of clunky sneakers and shapeless skirts. That having been said, style varies wildly from country to country. The mullets that will make you a star in Moscow won't fly in peg-leg-trousers-crazed London or sleek Paris. So how should you dress? Just stay simple, look to the locals, and follow a few basic rules.

France

At a meeting: Dark, tailored, unflashy suits by Dior Homme or Jil Sander for both women and men (who need not wear ties).

On the street: Avoid bright colors—even kids' clothes come mainly in cream, navy, gray, and brown—and take care to shun the plethora of other offenses: pleated chinos, walking shorts, sport sandals, baseball caps, golf attire, loud logos, sneakers, T-shirts, and sexy clothes. "In France, it's always best to keep things simple, neutral, and classic rather than too trendy," says Miles Socha, European editor for *Women's Wear Daily*.

At a party: On a normal night out, overdressing's okay, but if it's black-tie, underdress: Men should wear business suits sans ties, women should slip on cocktail dresses, and for a normal night out, femmes should keep it simple, silky, and black.

P.S. "One's shoes and belt should always match," advises François Delahaye, former general manager at Paris's legendary Plaza Athénée. But, he adds, a man's tie should never mirror his silk pocket square.

Turkey

At a meeting: Neither men nor women should go without manicures, since Turks are known for being perfectly groomed. Hair should be trimmed, suits fitted (jackets and pants need not match), button-downs left open and worn without undershirts peeking through. Tailoring is a primary indicator of class, so no matter how cheap the suit, it should fit well.

On the street: "I once heard that a woman had trouble getting a tea-man to serve her because she dressed like a frumpy housewife," says White. So dressing down is not an option. Men and women cultivate a studied casual look in designer jeans, Tod's loafers, and ironed high-end T-shirts (like James Perse)—never shorts.

At a party: Visible brand names are seen as cheap and low-class. Truly chic women wear Matthew Williamson florals rather than triangle-stamped Prada, and accessorize with one large statement bauble, like a giant cocktail ring by Turkish born Sevan Biçakçi. Hair is tightly pulled back. Men wear open shirts under light jackets with dark pants (or vice versa).

P.S. "Never wear a long raincoat," White says. "Even when it's pouring, a secular Turk will wear a short coat so as not to be mistaken for a conservative Islamist."

United Kingdom

At a meeting: The downtown banking-and-newspaper bustle calls for a suit and tie (no tie on Fridays), but you'll be laughed out of Soho or Kensington ad agencies in the same getup: There, cool execs don a uniform of the newest Nikes and skinny jeans.

On the street: Quirky Kate Moss inspired London girls throw on a high-low mix of Top Shop and Temperley; they're freer and less polished than other city style–setters. Men wear peg-leg trousers in primary colors with plaid shirts or tees. Don't opt for chinos and polos—the preppy look won't fly in London.

At a party: Skinny jeans take a girl or boy from meetings to a cutesy mews (switch from heels to Chuck Taylors) to a Shoreditch pub crawl (back to heels).

P.S. Wellies might be as British as it gets, but they're really country wear. Do take them off if you're lounging indoors.

A Tale of Two Cities

Can anyone really not call Paris and Milan the fashion capitals of the world? After all, one is home to Chanel and Dior, the other to Prada and Armani. But how can you tell your Milanese hipster from your Parisian sylph? We asked Scott Schuman, the mastermind behind the popular fashion blog The Sartorialist, for some clues (his book, *The Sartorialist*, was released in August).

Milan

Hair should be up.

"The Milanese girl wears whatever's on trend in a sexy, overt way. She doesn't do anything vintage or sporty."

Must be a colorful print.

"The overall effect is resilient and formal. She's not one to mess around."

"Milanese girls' style is set: all Italian, all big brands, all off the runway. She loves D&G. Prada's too intellectual, Marni's too quirky."

Skin should be tanned.

"Shoes must be high to show off her legs."

Paris

Hair must be mussed.

"Unlike the Milanese girl, she's not brand obsessed: The Parisian will mix vintage with French brands like Isabel Marant and Vanessa Bruno, and throw in some cheap stuff from A.P.C."

Oversized white tee falling off her shoulder.

"There's a come-hither kind of sexiness to a Parisian girl: She's covered up but seems somehow barer, more fragile. She's more precious than your Milanese young thing: The Parisian girl is like a gift, with a sultry quality that's underlying but never plain."

These are her boyfriend's.

Her shoes are Balmain.

Discussion Questions

1. Which countries' dress code surprised you the most? Why?
2. Where do your assumptions about dress come from?
3. Were you aware how most non-Americans view the American habit of wearing a fanny pack?

1.3
Uncovered Butts & Recovered Rules: Sagging Pants and the Logic of Abductive Inference

Marcia A. Morgado

Sagging is the contemporary label for a subculture dress form typically associated with black boys, young black men and hip-hop culture (Figure 1.7). It is characterized by trousers worn low or below the hips with underwear, covered butt cheeks, and sometimes butt cracks conspicuously exposed. Although the name is new, early versions of sagging have been evident for nearly 30 years. Throughout this time the style has variously, and often simultaneously, functioned as an identity marker in youth subcultures; a contemporary mode of urban street dress; a designer runway fashion, the trappings of hip-hop celebrities; and a global youth style. The origins of sagging, popularly attributed to the ill-fitting, beltless garb of prison inmates and as a sign devised by prisoners to signal sexual availability, likely contribute to both the appeal and the offensiveness of the style. But issues of race and racism, public decency, and ethnic pride contribute, as well. Since inception, the dress form has ignited controversy, outrage, and fear.

Like other subculture appearance forms, characteristics associated with sagging evolved over time. In its original form, salient elements included oversized jeans turned back to front, with hemlines that dragged the ground, crotches extended to the knees, and dramatically lowered waistlines. Peculiar accessories, such as athletic shoes with unusual or untied lacings were common. A swaggering or penguin-like gait and the wearer's ethnicity—assumed to be African American—were also salient signs of the appearance form. White youngsters and young white men who identified with and adopted the style self-identified and were referred to as *wiggers*. Wiggers were typically accused of co-opting a black, inner-city dress form, and the wigger appellation served as a direct reference to the epithet *nigger*. Over time, the baggy trousers slimmed down, the dropped waistlines were further lowered—often below the butt cheeks—and the visibility of the underwear (necessarily boxers) and underwear label (necessarily 'designer')

increased in importance. Meanwhile, the significance of the swaggering gait and assumptions about the ethnicity of wearers remained intact, with the term '*saggin*' understood as a reverse spelling of the *niggas* epithet.

Sagging is a peculiar dress form. It is peculiar in terms of its obvious rupture with conventional dress, although much contemporary fashion is predicated on challenges to convention. Sagging, however, is peculiar in terms of the public reaction it ignites. Concerns are raised over physical health issues such as hip, joint and nerve damage

Figure 1.7 Sagging is a controversial dress form that serves as an identity marker in youth subcultures; a contemporary mode of urban street dress; a designer runway fashion, the trappings of hip-hop celebrities; and a global youth style.

Adapted from an article that originally appeared in *Critical Studies in Men's Fashion*.

that are proposed to result from the requisite swaggering gait; crusades are initiated to encourage young men to 'Pull Your Pants Up', ... public figures wage campaigns against sagging as an 'insidious spectacle of imposed ridicule,' and ordinances designed to criminalize sagging are not uncommon.

In this paper I suggest that the controversy surrounding sagging enhances opportunities to examine the structure of meanings that are attributed to, interpreted as, or otherwise presumed to inhere in contentious dress forms. My work is framed on *abductive inference*, a theoretical construct proposed in the work of the American logician, mathematician, philosopher, and semiotician Charles S. Peirce (1931/1958). Peirce postulates abduction as a natural, instinctive mode of reasoning that is hard wired into human cognition and expressed though 'spontaneous conjectures' that provisionally explain unusual observations. It is the process that results in what we sometimes describe as having an "ah ha!" experience or an act of insight. As an example, Peirce invites us to imagine the following situation:

Suppose I enter a room and there find a number of bags containing different kinds of beans. On the table there is a handful of white beans; and, after some searching I find one of the bags contains white beans only. I at once infer as a probability, or as a fair guess, that this handful was taken out of that bag (2:623).

This inference is an abduction. Abductive arguments are diagramed in a format similar to that used in presenting formal deductive and inductive logic arguments: The observation is positioned as a *Result*. The rule connecting the result to a conclusion is recorded as a *Rule*. The inference or conclusion derived from the *Rule* is identified as a probable or likely *Case*. Peirce's abduction regarding the source of the white beans is diagrammed like this:

Result: These beans are white. *Rule*: All the beans from this bag are white. *Case*: These beans are from this bag (probably).

Peirce describes abduction as the means through which we interpret peculiar circumstances. But contemporary scholars describe it as the primary mechanism through which we comprehend much of the phenomena of everyday life, and as the principle method of reasoning in interpretations of virtually all visual and verbal phenomena. The implication is that interpretations of dress-related phenomena likely occur through abductive inference. Most contemporary dress, however, is interpreted in terms of rules or codes that are relatively stable and somewhat commonly acknowledged. For example, there is a good deal of agreement as to the features that constitute appropriate dress for business professionals; we generally understand and similarly interpret business dress codes. But new and/or unfamiliar dress forms are often more difficult to interpret, as the rules or codes governing these may be unclear or yet-to-be established.

The highly transgressive nature of sagging and the extraordinary level of controversy it aroused led me to wonder at the nature of rules that might be engaged to infer meaning to the dress form at its inception as a youth subculture style. In the absence of pre-established codes for interpreting the style, what rules were engaged against which to assess its meaning? Peirce's description of the inferential process suggests the possibility that one's abductive inferences can be consciously reconstructed, and this implication is evident in the works of others who write on abductive inference, as well (e.g., Mick, 1986). To explore this possibility I examined my own inferences in response to arguments that occurred in the context of natural discourse during the early rise stage of the sagging pants phenomena. The arguments were captured in the live airing and written transcript of a televised *Oprah Winfrey Show* titled *What is a Wigger?* (Harpo, 1993). My examination was based on the following assumptions: (a) that contentious dress exemplifies what semiotician Umberto Eco (1968) calls an "open message" or "under-coded condition" (p. 165, cited in Noth, 1995, p. 427): a situation wherein pre-established rules for assessing meaning are largely absent; (b) that, in the absence of convention, we generate our own rules in order to link dress with meaning; in other words, we generate fresh abductions; (c) that arguments surrounding contentious dress enhance opportunities to examine the structure of abductive inferences; and that (d) abductive inferences can be consciously reconstructed.

I watched and took notes on the original airing of the televised show, and subsequently studied the official transcript which I obtained from Burrelles Information Services. The examination was conducted as follows: Where an argument led me to interpret statements as inferring meaning to the style, I recorded the statements as the "Result." I recorded the inference I drew from the statement as the probable "Case." In each instance, I then asked how I derived the inference: what rule might have led me to connect a result with a case? And I reflected on how my personal circumstances might account for the inferences and rules I generated.

At the outset, I anticipated that the transgressive nature of the style, its empty, open, or otherwise under coded condition, and the unique interpretive frame I brought to the study would lead to peculiar and highly idiosyncratic rules. The results were surprising. Here are examples of the abductive inferences I generated:

Example #1

Winfrey says: *Ok, you obviously white guys sitting here. So you wear these saggy clothes because what?* Teenager #4 responds: *We wear the clothes because this is what we want to wear* (Harpo, 1993, p. 3). My abduction is as follows:

Result: They wear baggy clothes because they want to. *Rule*: It's a free country.

Case: The clothes are a sign of freedom of expression (probably).

Discussion. My mother, a Latvian immigrant who typically espoused American values with considerably more energy and enthusiasm than did her American-born friends, often justified her unconventional behaviors with the dictum 'Vell, it's a frree cuntree. I can do anysing I vant' (*sic*). It is likely I interpreted the youngster's statement in terms of free expression because my family history is rich in the 'free country' platitude.

Example #2

A white youth is drawn into a discussion of the intended message conveyed by the peculiar lacing of his athletic shoes. It has been suggested that the youngster is aping a black appearance style and that the behavior is offensive. Winfrey says: *So—what do you want this to say about you?* Teenager #6 responds: *When I went to buy these shoes, they didn't tell me that I had to be black to buy these shoes. They just told me how much they were. You know, and I bought the shoes. You know?* And Winfrey responds: *Good point. Good point* (pp. 3–4).

Result: Some people believe only black people buy this type of shoe. The white youngster bought the shoes. *Rule*: People can buy what they can pay for.

Case: The shoes signify as an ordinary commodity (probably).

Discussion. The youngster elides Winfrey's question. Rather than address what the laces says about him, he identifies a false rule: only blacks buy this type of shoe. He then offers an ostensibly objective assessment of the conditions under which the shoes were purchased, providing the shoes with meaning anchored in conventions governing ordinary marketplace exchange.

Example #3

Winfrey engages the mother of a white, baggy-clad youngster in a discussion of parental concern over the dress form. She says: *What is a parent to do when a child starts wearing clothes 12 sizes too big? First up is Peggy Harman and her nine-year-old son Tim. . . . So this looks pretty, OK, though? This isn't too big.* Ms. Harman replies: *I think it's nice.* Winfrey: *You think it's ok.* Ms. Harman: *I think it's big. I think it's wonderful. I'm into hip-hop.* Winfrey: *You're into hip – who would have thought it?* (p. 4).

Result: Ms. Harman thinks baggy clothes on youngsters are wonderful. *Rule*: Fashion is fun.

Case: Baggy clothes signify as a cute youth fashion (probably).

Discussion. The saggy style that originated in an urban subculture was quickly appropriated by mainstream designers and marketed as Big! Fun! Fashion! I read Ms. Harman from the perspective of a fashion marketer, and interpreted her comments on the garb as the response of a particular market segment: white, suburban, mass-fashion-conscious mom.

Example #4

Black woman #3 shifts the focus of discussion to significant issues of racism and stereotyping: *I just think it's one more way that—that whites are capitalizing on this. I mean, if I were, you know, a young person and I'm walking down the street with your large clothes on and everything else, I'm considered to be a hoodlum, I'm considered to be a gun-toting, rap singing, whatever, grabbing my crotch and everything else. But if you wear it, you end up on the cover of Vogue magazine. I mean, look at Marky Mark, look at Kate Moss and all these people walking around and they're swinging and everything else. And they're embraced by the rest of the white society because you're white. But you can take off your clothes and you can still be white and walk into any situation. Where, I speak well, I'm a normal person, I'm from the suburbs and . . .* (pp. 8–9).

Result: Ethnicity governs perceptions of social role and character traits. *Rule*: The ethnicity of the wearer contributes to the meanings of dress.

Case: Baggy clothes on white people signify trendsetter; on black people the saggy clothes signify hoodlum (probably).

Discussion. Here, the result and case appeared connected through a rule that represents common knowledge among apparel scholars: visible indicators of social status and ethnicity are elements of the contexts in which the meanings of dress are interpreted.

Example #5

Black woman #5 expresses frustration over the direction of the dialogue: *There's not a point of – problem with them dressing like that, but they come into our neighborhoods and they see how we're dressing. And then they take it to the stores and overprice it. Then when we try to go in, we can't even get what we already started* (p. 12).

Result: The fashion industry draws on black dress forms for inspiration, but markets the styles at prices beyond the reach of the black community. *Rule*: Mainstream (white) commerce rips off black culture.

Case: The baggy style signifies fashion industry appropriation of black culture (probably).

Discussion. Initially, I was inclined to read woman #5's comments as I suspect she intended: commentary on the high prices attached to fashion-forward clothes. However, my readings in Marxist critique subsequently led me to feel more satisfied with an interpretation based on capitalist culture's appropriation of the creative products of marginalized subcultures.

In initiating this study I assumed that the rules I inferred would be highly idiosyncratic; that they'd reflect the exaggerated features of the dress form, its transgressive nature, and my unique interpretive frame. But this was not the case. None of my hypothesized rules were peculiar or even marginally original. Rather, the rules represented a common cliché: it's a free country. They reiterated principles identified in scholarly works on the social psychology of dress: the ethnicity of the wearer contributes to the meanings of dress; designers draw inspiration from street fashion and subculture styles. And they spoke to common marketplace wisdom: people can buy what they can pay for; fashion is fun. Berger writes that 'culture must cover as much of a given person's world of experience as it can' (1984, p. 168), and my study supported this, in that the abductions I generated drew on ready-made cultural rules that enabled me to correlate comments about a highly unconventional dress form with very conventional meanings. Thus, the assumption that my abductions would reveal idiosyncratic rules was not supported. However, the results of the study did support the assumption that I could consciously reconstruct my inferences, in that I was able to identify rules that appear to link my observations with likely, or possible, conclusions.

References

Berger, A. A. (1984). Signs in contemporary culture. An introduction to semiotics. Salem, WI: Sheffield Publishing Co.

Eco, Umberto (1976), *A theory of semiotics*, Bloomington, IN: Indiana University Press.

Harpo Productions, Inc. (1993, September 9), 'What is a wigger?' [Transcript of television series episode], *The Oprah Winfrey Show*, Available from Burrelles Information Services, Box 78, Livingston, NJ 07039.

Mick, David Glen (1986), 'Consumer research and semiotics: Exploring the morphology of signs, symbols, and significance', *Journal of Consumer Research, 13*, pp. 196–213.

Noth, Winfried (1995), *Handbook of Semiotics*, Bloomington, IN: Indiana University Press.

Peirce, Charles. S. (1931/1958), *Collected papers of Charles Sanders Peirce* (Charles Hartshorne, Paul Weiss and Arthur W. Burks, Eds.), MA: Harvard University Press.

Discussion Questions

1. How do you view 'sagging'? What is your opinion of sagging? Describe the possible origin(s) of your opinion (influenced by authority figures or a previous personal experience, etc.).
2. Have you ever adopted the fashion of sagging? Or know someone who did? If so, what were the reactions from friends, family members, teachers, etc.?
3. Since sagging has been around for nearly 30 years, what reasons can you give for the persistence of sagging?

An extended version of this article appears in *Critical Studies in Men's Fashions* 2 (2 & 3), 107-126.

1.4
Cargo Pants: The Transnational Rise of the Garment That Started a Fashion War

Joseph H. Hancock, II

The Summer War of 2016

On 1 August 2016, the Wall Street Journal printed a story discussing how Ashleigh Hanson, the wife of Dane Hanson, had been systematically throwing out her husband's collection of cargo shorts (Hong 2016). The article went on to discuss that relationships (mostly of a heterosexual nature) across the United States were being threatened by the inability of men to stop wearing these shorts. Transversely, many upscale golf courses have banned cargo shorts and do not allow them on their greens. In 2012, Michael Jordan was refused entry onto a course in Miami while wearing the said shorts (Hong 2012).

However, despite being bullied by women for men to stop wearing these garments, the cargo industry (pants and shorts) still accounts for over USD700 million worth of revenue for retailers in the United States, according to market research firm NPD Group (CBS This Morning 2016). Also, the industry database, Worth Global Style Network (WGSN), in 2015 reported that cargo shorts made up over 15 percent of new short styles sold, up from 11 percent in 2014 (Bhasin 2016). Additionally, there is an assumption that this garment has a much higher market share globally—being continually worn in countries such as Australia where they have over twenty-four different types of shorts (Lonnborn 9 October 2016 Interview).

Because of this controversy, and as the scholar who wrote his dissertation on cargo pants (Hancock 2007), I recently became the center of the cargo shorts debate and was featured on many radio and talk shows discussing the rise of cargo pants as a garment of twentieth century fashion that has now become somewhat despised by some women. But the media hype, or what I am calling *cargo-mania*, has risen without much discussion of the actual evolution of the actual garment and its origins.

I was elated when *CBS This Morning* was actually interested in an interview for their story. Off-camera, we discussed how after the barrage of media was over perhaps I needed to reiterate the cargo pants/shorts story for the academy in a new publication. Also, I agreed after being bullied myself by many female scholars from around the globe who found the fact I did my dissertation on cargo pants completely idiotic. One such email was from a professor of criminal justice who found the topic ridiculous, to which I simply replied, "Have you noticed what some police officers wear for pants?" She did not reply.

I have not written about cargo pants since 2010 in the *Australasian Journal of Popular Culture* (Hancock & Augustyn) but I feel it is time to tell the story again. Furthermore with the new propaganda hype concerning this transglobal garment it was important that the misnomer be replaced with facts and that the actual fashion story of the pants be told. During the late 1930s or early 1940s, cargo pants were designed, manufactured and developed as a utility garment for use in the military. During the last century, these pants have gone from being a traditional military uniform to a popular casual pant worn by almost every segment in the global consumer market. Despite their fashionable rising popularity and a large market share of retail dollars, little has been written about these pants. While they are visually prevalent in popular culture, and at times, dominate fashion trends (especially menswear), much about cargo pants still remains a mystery.

Since the 1970s, when hippies wore army surplus vintage styles as a sign of protesting against the Vietnam War until today, cargo pants have undergone a considerable transformation, changing both in fabrications and form. They are a part of the basic core of casual garments that has grown and developed over the last forty years. With casual dress having secured its place in the workplace today, in

Original for this text

addition to changes in consumers' active lifestyles, and a growing awareness and development of global brands and mass fashions, cargo pants no longer relate to their original use as just a functional utility work garment.

These pants have become part of styles that Eicher, Evenson and Lutz refer to as **world dress** (2008: 52). Like jeans, cargo pants have become a **transnational style** worn in both Western and Eastern cultures as everyday fashion and defined as a "quickly shifting style of dress worn simultaneously in many worldwide locations" (Eicher, Evenson and Lutz: 54). From retailers such as Abercrombie & Fitch in the United States, to similar styles found at Uniqlo in Japan, they are sold globally. This chapter will present the origins, histories and myths surrounding the development of cargo pants as a military garment. It will also highlight the induction of cargo pants into mass culture through various popular culture intermediaries such as the military, subcultural style, film, media, retail and merchandising; demonstrating how this garment has become part of world dress and **transnational mass fashion**, as well as an icon found in many global popular culture narratives.

The History, Origins and Myths of Cargo Pants

Where did cargo pants come from? Was there a design genius that suddenly created the pants? Or did they evolve over time developing from other military garments? This investigation began with the intention of discovering where cargo pants originated and what division of the military developed these pants. However, cargo pants do not have a single history, but multiple histories, among various regimes of global military divisions that have incorporated various styles of these types of pants into their regimes. This creates a conflicting dialogue as to the exact originator of this particular garment and to whom the credit should be given. History and research reveals that cargo pants were inspired by other garments already in existence in the military and were most probably developed because of utilitarian necessity.

Cargo pants do not seem to have come from one specific country, although evidence does suggest that they evolved across the military regimes of Great Britain, Spain, and the United States almost simultaneously. More than likely, various countries influenced each other's uniforms and dress in a similar fashion that today's designers are influenced by one another (Hanson 5 October 2006 Interview). Since the design process of military uniforms during this time required a lead time of about a year, it is quite possible that various armed services discussed future designs with each other, or that the manufacturers of these uniforms were the same across these regimes, much like fashion companies today produce divisions of garments under one roof. This is the case with the American designer Ralph Lauren, who manufactures most of the garments for his men's divisions such as Polo Ralph Lauren, Ralph Lauren Black Label, Ralph Lauren Double RL, Rugby, Ralph Lauren Home, Ralph Lauren Outlet, and the new Ralph Lauren Denim & Supply under the same manufacturers (Crawford 7 July 2010 interview).

With one leader, Ralph Lauren, the structural format of information dissemination and design ideas, across various boundaries and divisions, is somewhat inevitable and signifies the global branding process. Although each division services a specific male consumer lifestyle market, and they represent a specific division of the company, it is most likely, that each of these divisions influence one another. This may explain why the various divisional lines may look similar or appear to mimic each other because Ralph Lauren apparel is developed under the same guise of fashion trends, styles and aesthetics. For example, during the Spring 2011 season, Ralph Lauren Double RL featured a Grand Canyon Ripstop Cargo Pant for USD225.00, Polo Ralph Lauren featured a similar pant Authentic Army Parachute Pant for USD145.00, while Rugby their Patrol Cargo Pant for USD118.00. This divisional aesthetic of functional fashion is quite similar to the divisions of the Army, Navy, Air Force and Marines that are all housed under the purview of the United States Government, each operating under different leadership, but having one Presidential Commander-in-Chief.

Military Beginnings and Original Cargo Pant Identities

In the United States, the word "cargo pants" originated from the military battle dress pant known as *fatigues*. Sometimes they are referred to as Two-pocket, Six-pocket, Seven-pocket, Eight-pocket etc. . .depending on the number of pockets on the garment. Like most military garments, each pant was assigned a numerical identity for instant recognition and for the assemblage of entire uniforms for soldiers. Ralph Lauren, Levis Dockers, Abercrombie & Fitch, as well as other designers, have adopted these same numeric identifiers in order to give the garment a sense of authenticity for consumers. For example the contemporary D-2 cargo pant is what most

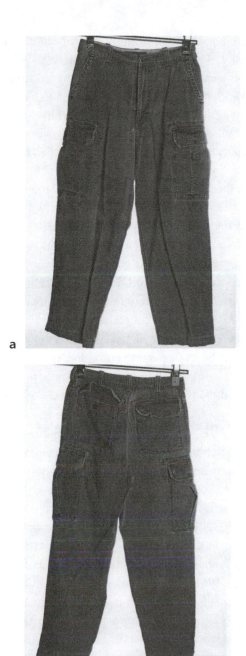

a

b

Figure 1.8a and b Abercrombie & Fitch-2003 D-2 Cargo Pants. The viewer will notice the two-side "cargo" pockets, two front pockets off the waistband, and the two back pockets off the waistband. This pant is sometimes referred to as a Six-Pocket Cargo Pant (a: front view; b: back view). © Joseph Hancock, All Rights Reserved.

people associate as the standard cargo pant (Figures 8a and b). D-2 cargo pants can also be referred to as an 8-pocket because it has 2-cargo pockets on the side legs, 2-front pockets off the waistband, and 2-back pockets off the waistband. This type of pant is called a field pant because of its use primarily as battle dress and not for

formal and ceremonial military regime. Cargo pants are usually produced from fabric such as wool, cotton, polyester, silk, and nylon and in fabrications and weaves such as plain, twill, herringbone and brushed flannel.

Chris McNab writes in *Modern Military Uniforms*, that the leg pocket on military uniforms was not present prior to the late 1930s and seems to have been designed during World War II (2000: 6–13). McNab credits the Air Force for developing leg pockets on the front of flight pants as the first sign of cargo-like styles. Since the cockpit of many fighter planes are so narrow, Air Force pilots required pockets on the front of their flight uniforms, allowing them access to supplies during flights. This allowed the pilots to feel more comfortable while being cramped in the plane's cockpit. McNab's theory is reinforced through such military uniforms as the Airman Bomber Command Royal Air Force England 1939 uniform (2000: 221), the US Marine Corps Bougainville 1943 uniform (McNab 2000: 263), and the Bomber Crewman 8th Army Air Force England 1945 uniform (McNabe 2000: 275).

Luther Hanson, curator of the military museum in Fort Lee Virginia for the past twenty-five years and a national military uniforms expert, claims that global retailers and designers visit the large collection of military uniforms for inspiration in creating the latest military looks. According to Hanson, versions of American field cargo pants did not appear until 1942. The concept for fatigues came from the Paratrooper Jump Coat Model #1 during World War II. He suggests that the design for cargo pants would have come from a Quarter Master Sergeant. Also during World War II, the Quarter Master regime designed uniforms at a rapid pace sending orders to various manufacturers who worked as a team specifically tailoring uniforms to each of the battle units. During these world wars, military uniforms became a method for identifying specific units. There was a functional design and the mass production of uniforms for both world wars and many specifications required rapid production alterations when the original planned design did not work.

Specifically with regards to cargo pants, it was Major William P. Yarborough who helped design the pant for field soldiers in 1942 (Amazing Stories: 2010: 72). Yarborough, also known as the "Father of the Modern Green Berets," was given the military assignment to design paratrooper's boots, uniforms and qualification badges (Bernstein 2005). At Fort Benning in Georgia, with the help of the quartermaster regime, Yarborough probably developed what would eventually be called the four-pocket cargo, which contained two deep side pockets that hung below the thigh and two back pockets.

Terry Sullivan credits the British for inventing cargo style pants (2003: 44). He suggests that British soldiers and paratroopers used these pants prior to the Americans. His article identifies that the major reason for cargo pockets was for soldiers to carry ammunition when they were climbing or hiding in high places. He believes the pockets cushioned and reduced noise where utility belts did not. Sullivan's theory reflects the uniforms worn by British Soldiers during this time such as the uniforms worn during World War II by the No. 1 Commando Unit at St. Nazaire (McNab 2002: 232).

Ironically, during this time, many of the United States' military webbing for uniforms was being produced in the United Kingdom, while many of the British uniform garments were produced in American manufacturing facilities. This was due to the United States having more space and not being considered a major battle zone. Since the manufacturing of British battle dress began in January 1943 from specifications drawn up in autumn 1942, it would have been quite simple for the United States to borrow design elements from the British and vice versa suggesting that each country was influenced by the others military uniforms and therefore design of cargo pants (in conversation with Hanson).

The Spanish Generalissimo Francisco Franco has also been credited for the design and manufacturing of cargo pants, or what he called 'Franco Pants' (Ziegler 1986: 92–93). During the Spanish Civil War from 1930–39, Franco would become enraged when he viewed his soldiers placing their hands in their front pant-pockets. To remedy this problem, the Fascist general had the pockets of the pants moved to below the upper thigh. His new pants were very similar to the 2-pocket fatigue pants (Figure 1.8), with back pockets as well. Franco was also recognized for developing the reinforced bulls-eye patterned patch that appears on the seat between and surrounding the buttocks that you see, even today, on contemporary styles of cargo pants. Whether the invention of the Generalissimo Francisco Franco, Great Britain, Major William Yarborough, the Air Force, the Army, the Navy or even Marines, there is a general consensus that cargo pants did not appear in military uniforms until the late 1930s. It can be safe to assume that the origins of cargo pants definitely relate to military uniform traditions and their original use was based upon function and not fashion.

With the military continuing to reinvent cargo styles during the 1940s and into the 1950s, unique styles of cargo pants that were designed and manufactured include the wool khaki battledress pants of 1951, the F-1 sage nylon air force pants of 1955, and a green polyamide hot weather fire resistant cargo pant in 1979 (Hanson). Each of these styles represents the evolution of cargo pants during the early to mid-twentieth century.

While there were many styles of cargo pants developed by the military, as previously stated, most individuals associate the D-2 style as the true cargo style (Figure 1.8). This pant seems to have become the iconic style most commonly replicated not only by the military, but designers and retailers too (Hanson). Even today, cargo style pants have been, and continue to be, worn by military troops across almost all countries. The traditional forms of 2-pocket, 6-pocket, and fatigue styles of cargo pants continue to be copied and reinvented in almost every country making cargo pants a true transnational garment and world dress (Eicher, Evenson, & Lutz 2008: 52).

Cargo Pants in Popular Culture

The connotation of cargo pants changes with each decade and is influenced by mainstream popular culture. During the 1950s and 1960s, cargo styles are still mainly associated with military themes. But, they were soon adopted by Hollywood, not only for movies related to war, but for movie themes exploring exotic travel and safari. Who can forget Red Buttons (1919–2006) as Pockets in the *Hitari!* (1961). In this film, John Wayne leads a group of highly qualified professional game hunters in the wilds of Africa. His group sets out to capture animals for zoos and circus attractions. Red Buttons plays his assistant Pockets, usually seen wearing green herringbone 2-pocket cargo pants similar to those in Figure 1.8. Throughout the entire film, Pockets keeps valuable items needed for the safari in his cargo pockets. In the movie, Wayne and other characters refer to the distinction of cargo pant pockets differentiating them from regular, traditional pants pockets. This movie marks a direct reference to cargo pockets that still remains unique in film history.

Another major popular cultural event occurred in 1958 when Che Guevera (1928–1967) was photographed wearing cargo pants while playing baseball (Amazing Stories 2010: 70). During the 1960s and early 1970s, cargo pants took on a new connation while becoming incorporated into protests and the Hippie movement. In protests against Western consumer culture and the

Vietnam War, much of the Hippie style clothing was self-made. Personalized and embroidered garments such as old military fatigues become part of anti-fashion outfits worn during this time. By re-stylizing traditional military dress, the hippie movement illustrated its counterculture attitudes toward the assimilation and strict codes of soldier dress (Baldwin et al: 1999: 340–341).

In his book, *Don We Now Our Gay Apparel*, Shaun Cole identifies garments such as military fatigues and cargo pants as part of sub-cultural dress in the mid-to-late 1970s. Gay men who wanted to identify as extremely masculine and butch became obsessed with clothing that symbolized ruggedness (Cole 2000: 93–106). Cargo pants were one of these items since they had originally been associated with signifying the military and the combat soldier. Music bands such as the Village People reinforced these style notions. The group referenced hyper-masculine stereotypes such as Alex Briley, the army soldier, (in addition to other looks such as the construction worker, the cowboy, the Indian, and the leather daddy), giving him a "homo-stylized" look for singing such songs as *In the Navy* and of course, *Macho Man*.

Since cargo pants are a part of military dress and represent an aspect of traditional American culture, it was not surprising that during the 1980s these pants became associated with the high social status of the *preppy look*. With designers such as Ralph Lauren, Izod, Liz Claiborne, and Calvin Klein, and retailers such as L.L. Bean, Eddie Bauer, Lands' End, The Gap, and Banana Republic leading the *preppy fashions* of the 1980s, cargo pants became a part of the conservative style (Birnach: 1980).

With the media exposure of movies such as, *Sixteen Candles* (1984), cargo pants were visually represented to both the teen and *preppy* markets. As a preppy teenager in high school, heartthrob Jake drives a Porsche, has very successful parents, lives in a mansion, has lots of money, is the most popular senior, and dresses in conservative, yet hip fashions. Jake appears on the cover of the current DVD and in the motion pictures main poster wearing a plaid woven shirt, cargo pants, and deck shoes.

During the 1980s, and into the early 1990s, cargo pants were adopted by the new countercultures such as mainstream punk, new wavers, rappers, grunge and various other Music Television (MTV) generation icons. Inexpensive military surplus stores became the major suppliers of garments for music groups such as, The Clash, Bananarama, The Belle Stars, Thompson Twins, Sex Pistols, Nirvana, Beastie Boys, Run DMC, and The Fat Boys who influenced mass fashion by wearing garments such as cargo pants on stage in their music video clips (Amazing Stories 2010:70). In response, teenagers flocked to similar military surplus stores hoping to find garments and styles worn by their favourite music videos performers.

In the United States, retailers such as The Gap, County Seat and manufacturers such as Bugle Boy gained popularity by copying MTV looks and selling their products in the teen market. During the 1991 Super Bowl, Bugle Boy debuted their television ad that featured the 1980s iconic band, The Go-Go's, to sell their cargo pants (Bugle Boy 1991). In the middle of *We Got the Beat* Belinda Carlisle of the band stops the music to ask a male audience member 'Excuse me. . .are those Bugle Boys you are wearing?' While Internet searches and bloggers suggest this ad is for jeans, it is actually for the line of cargo utility pants that the company was producing at the time as the company expanded into this apparel. By producing trendy fashionable styles of cargo pants, retailers such as The Limited and Express gained popularity with their cargo pant brands such as *Outback Red* and *Forenza* for women.

During 1998–99, Limited Brand's Structure (now Express) decided to investigate how many companies actually carried cargo pants in their assortment. The company wanted to decide if producing mass quantities of the pants would prove profitable. The American retailer discovered that cargo pants were being sold at almost every specialty store retailer in the nation. Specialty retailers, from high-end to low-end, had the pants well represented on their sales floors. The company also discovered that, not only did these retailers carry the pant, most had as many as five or six styles on their selling floors. Cargo pants had become a basic part of every mass fashion retailers' basic assortment. According to Leslie Wexner, C.E.O. of Limited Brands, the retailer Abercrombie & Fitch was leading the resurgence of cargo pants (Structure).

Abercrombie & Fitch had gained the attention of the public with their controversial advertising campaign that featured half-naked American college graduates (coeds), with photographer Bruce Weber as the creative genius behind the company's advertising campaign. Consequently, sales at Abercrombie & Fitch soared.

Twenty-First Century "Fashionable" Cargo Pants

Target, the U.S.'s second top retailing big box retailing giant, featured cargo pants during their 'Get A Jump on

School. . .Go Cargo,' 17 August, 2003 weekly newspaper circular demonstrating the significant monetary market share that these pants have when it comes to consumer spending in their stores. At the same time, this advertisement reveals how cargo pants have reached market saturation in their popularity, or lack of it. The advertisement below not only features cargo styles for men and women, but also gives evidence of how cargo pants have influenced contemporary fashion styles such as shorts and skirts in various consumer markets.

Target continued to merchandise and brand cargo pant styles through its new designer line by former British singer and songwriter Keanan Duffty. Graduating from St. Martin's College, University of the Arts, London he has displayed his designs on runways in Italy, London, and the United States, becoming one of Britain's high-end designers specializing in clothing that resembles garments from other fashion designers such as Vivienne Westwood. Duffty not only designs high-end runway garments, he also produces and directs music videos and his aim is to build a brand that is heavily influenced by both music and fashion.

Gentlemen's Quarterly recognized cargo pants as a successful and "wonderful addition to the mass fashion business" (Sullivan 2003: 44). Even the Cotton Incorporated's Lifestyle Monitor (2003: 2) section of the fashion wear industry's leading newspaper *Women's Wear Daily*, noted what they called 'The New Cargo Pants' coming from such fashion houses as Prada and Jil Sander in luxury fabrics. Similarly, the British men's magazine *Fantastic Man* published the article 'The Fashion Test Cargo Pants' that conducted an experiment to see which style of premium priced cargo pants were the best and incorporated garments from Thom Browne, G-Star, Dolce & Gabbana, and Ralph Lauren Black Label (Jonkers 2010: 33–34).

The proliferation of cargo pants continues with fashion styles from retailers such as Uniqlo's (RE)cargo for USD39.90, J.Crew's Stanton urban slim fit cargo for USD79.50, Country Road Australia's Engineered cargo pant for AUD119.00, all the way up to Ralph Lauren's Double RL rugged versions ranging from USD225 to USD328.00 make it clear that these pants are a fashion icon in popular culture. In addition, the recent rise and focus of most retailers in the area of men's fashion have some male consumers infatuated with finding the perfect pair of cargo pants.

Style editor of the *New York Times Magazine*, Carrie Donavon (1928–2001), was featured in an advertisement for American fashion label Old Navy stating, "I love these pants, they're so fab, and they have pockets!" Old Navy gained an increase in market share in this pant Old Navy's 2010 Back-to-School in-store presentation of cargo pants reveals that even in the twenty-first century, it considers it to be a basic style at USD29.50. The retailer merchandises and dedicates an entire wall to cargo pants housing it among other styles such as pleated and plain-front pants. This large item-impact display signifies the importance of cargo pants in merchandise assortments (especially at a large volume, mass discount retailer like Old Navy) during this time period (Hancock and Augustyn 2011).

The mass merchandising and rebranding of cargo pant has shifted people's perception of this garment. Their high price points and fashionable silhouettes have changed the perception of some consumers who now see these pants as quite stylish even when offered at expensive price points (Figure 1.9). In her *New York Times* column, Lily Burana (2006) suggests that consumers love the appeal and style of military fatigues and find them sexy. They have a quality that makes women (and men) feel like they are wearing a part of cultural heritage and style. There is something special about them that will never go away. And commentators who have issue with this garment need to reassess its cultural significance because they no longer represent the same thing as they did in past. Having been significantly reinvented, re-appropriated and restyled their transglobal heritage will endure.

References

Baldwin, Elaine; Longhurst, Brian; McCracken, Scott; Ogborn, Miles; and Smith, Greg (1999), *Introducing Cultural Studies*, New York, HarperCollins Publishers, Inc.

Bhasin, Kim (2016), 'They may be ugly, but cargo shorts are still king', *Bloomberg.com*, 16 September, http://www.bloomberg.com/news/articles/2016-09-16/they-may-be-ugly. . .ce=twitter&utm_medium=social&cmpid%3D=socialflow-twitter-business, Accessed 16 November 2016.

Bernstein, Adam (Thursday 8 December 2005), Lt. Gen. William Yarborough Dies. *The Washington Post*, [Online], Available from: http://www.washingtonpost.com/wp-dyn/content/article/2005/12/07/AR2005120702473.html, Accessed 9 July 2011.

Figure 1.9 The author wearing Fall 2016 Ralph Lauren Double RRL priced at USD390.00. Photo Courtesy of Dan McQuade.

Birnach, Lisa (1980), *The Official Preppy Handbook,* New York, Workman Publishing Company, Inc.

Bugle Boy (1991), '*We got the beat- Bugle Boy*', [Online], Available from: http://adland.tv/commercials/bugle -boys-go-gos-1991-030-usa, Accessed 7 November 2016.

Burana, Lily (2006), 'Army's fashion Fatigue', *New York Times*, 5 October, p. A29.

CBS This Morning (2016), 'Cargo shorts debate: To wear or not to wear?', *CBS This Morning*, 25 August, http://www.cbsnews.com/news/cargo-short-debate-to -wear-or-not-to-wear-fashion-faux-pas/, Accessed 7 November 2016.

Cole, Shaun (2000), *Don We Now Our Gay Apparel*, Oxford: Berg Publishers.

Cotton Incorporated (2003), Lifestyle Monitor: The new cargo pants. *Women's Wear Daily*, 27 February, p. 2.

Crawford, Corey (2010), Personal communication, New York interview, 7 July.

Eicher, Joanne; Evenson, Sandra Lee; and Lutz, Hazel A. (2008), *The Visibile Self*, New York, Fairchild Books.

Esquire (2010), 'Amazing stories: The intrepid history of three style icons', *Esquire The Big Black Book*, Spring/Summer, pp. 69–72.

Hancock, Joseph (2007), *These Aren't the Same Pants Your Grandfather Wore!: The Evolution of Branding Cargo Pants in 21st Century Mass Fashion*, https://etd .ohiolink.edu/ap/10?0::NO:10:P10_ACCESSION _NUM:osu1174323221, Ohio Link: Columbus, OH.

Hancock, Joseph and Edward Augustyn (2010), '"Fashionable Pockets": The transnational rise of cargo pants into popular culture', *Australasian Journal of Popular Culture* 2:2, pp. 183–195.

Hancock, Joseph and Augustyn, Edward (2011), Pants, trousers. Updates. [e-book] In: Eicher, Joanne. (ed.) *The Berg Encyclopedia of World Dress and Fashion*. Available from http://www.bergfashionlibrary.com/.

Hanson, Luther (2006), Personal communication interview phone call, 5 October.

Hawks, Howard (1961), *Hitari*, USA: Paramount Studios.

Hong, Nicole (2016), 'Nice cargo shorts! You're sleeping on the sofa', *The Wall Street Journal*, 1 August, http://www.wsj.com/articles/nice-cargo-shorts-youre -sleeping-on-the-sofa-1470082856. Accessed 7 November 2016.

Hughes, John (1984), *Sixteen Candles*, USA: Universal Studios.

Jonkers, Gert (2010), The Fashion test: Cargo pants. *Fantastic Man*, Spring/Summer, pp. 32–33.

Lonnborn, Harriet (2016), Personal communication interview phone call, 9 August.

McNab, Chris (2000), *Modern Military Uniforms*, New
Jersey, Chartwell Books, Inc.

McNab, Chris (2002), *20th Century Military Uniforms*,
New York: Barnes & Noble.

Structure. (2000), *Back-To-School Actual Report*,
Columbus: The Limited Corporation Publication.

Sullivan, Terry (2003), Cargo Pants. *Gentlemen's
Quarterly*, January, p. 44.

Ziegler, Mel and Ziegler, Patricia (1986), *Banana
Republic Guide to Travel and Safari Clothing*, New
York, Ballantine Books.

Discussion Questions

1. Do you currently, or have you in the past, owned
cargo pants? For what occasion did you buy them? To
go camping? Hiking? As a fashion statement or to fit
in?

2. Explain to someone the concept of World Dress using
cargo pants as an example. Do you believe that cargo
pants have surpassed blue jeans as a transnational
fashion?

3. What new information about cargo pants did you
learn from this reading? Its nebulous origin? Its
decade by decade dissemination? Its availability at
many price points? Google cargo pants to see how
many hits you get in return.

CHAPTER 2
FASHION AS A DYNAMIC PROCESS

Andrew Reilly

After you have read this chapter, you will understand:

- **Why fashion is a social process that continually changes and evolves**
- **The complex interaction of cultural, industrial, group, and individual factors that fuels fashion change**
- **That many theories are useful for explaining the fashion change process**

FASHION LIFE CYCLE

Fashion is a social process that encompasses many different groups of people who meet at different junctures, each with their own particular function. Fashion is created and influenced by one's culture, one's social organization, and one's psyche. Though each is necessary for the dissemination of fashion, they are not mutually exclusive for they support and interact with each other. And interlaced through culture, society, and one's psyche is the fashion system, which strives to serve the needs of each.

It is virtually impossible to trace the origin of a fashion trend. Fashion, by definition, is what is popular, and popularity is required for something to be observed and documented as a trend. Who was the first to wear or invent a style before it became a trend is often unknown, though fashion designers are often cited as contributing to the consumption of a style. For example, although Chanel did not invent the little black dress and Mary Quant did not invent the miniskirt they were influential in popularizing them.

What can be traced and understood with more certainty is the life cycle of a fashion trend, which mimics a bell curve (see Figure 2.1). A life cycle can last for a few months or even years. The process of fashion diffusion begins when fashion innovators wear a new article of clothing or devise a new way of wearing an existing piece. **Fashion innovators** are people who create a new style; they can be fashion designers or individuals with an artistic, unique sense of style. Some innovators, like designers, have changed the way people dress with a drastic change to the status quo. Christian Dior revolutionized women's wear with his *New Look* (more below) and Gianni Versace completely changed the fashion landscape by offering in-you-face-sexuality for men and women. In his article "Hedi Slimane and the reinvention of menswear", Jay McCauley Bowstead recounts the dramatic change in men's clothing and style in the early 21st century. Whereas men's clothing was once cut for the muscular physique, Slimane's designs were made for a slim physique and cut appropriately so. This was so unique and so different that is revolutionized the menswear industry and altered the way fashionable men have dressed for the past 20 years.

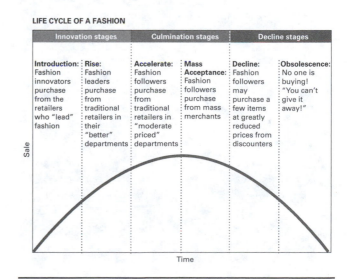

Figure 2.1 The fashion curve illustrates the life cycle of a fashion, from inception to obsolescence.

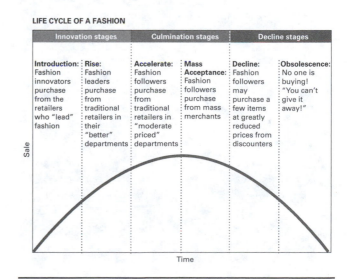

LIFE CYCLE OF A FASHION

Innovation stages		Culmination stages		Decline stages	
Introduction: Fashion innovators purchase from the retailers who "lead" fashion	**Rise:** Fashion leaders purchase from traditional retailers in their "better" departments	**Accelerate:** Fashion followers purchase from traditional retailers in "moderate priced" departments	**Mass Acceptance:** Fashion followers purchase from mass merchants	**Decline:** Fashion followers may purchase a few items at greatly reduced prices from discounters	**Obsolescence:** No one is buying! "You can't give it away!"

Sale / Time

Fashion leaders are people who are seen as authorities on clothing matters and are sought out for their opinions. Fashion leaders pick up on the new style and adopt it, increasing the number of people who see the trend. Examples of fashion leaders include celebrities such as A$AP Rocky and Kylie Jenner or business professionals such as Anna Wintour.

Some of the most influential fashion leaders today are bloggers who discuss, feature, and disseminate styles and trends through social media platforms like Instagram and personal websites. For example, fashion bloggers like Chiara Ferragni (The Blonde Salad), Leandra Medine (Man Repeller), Gabi Fresh, and Lisa Burg (Lala Faux Bois; see Figure 2.2) spend countless hours researching, creating, and contemplating posts and images to reach millions of followers with their thoughts on fashion and style.

In the article "Style and Substance: The Information Seeking Behavior of Fashion Bloggers," Kimberly Detterbeck, Nicole LaMoreaux, and Marie Sciangula look at what resources bloggers need in order to produce quality content. They also raise important issues like image citations and the need for authenticity.

By virtue of fashion leaders wearing a new style it is exposed to **early adopters** who increase the visibility of the style. By this point the trend has reached maximum exposure and starts to decline. **Late adopters** are the next category of consumers to adopt the style. They are people who do not feel comfortable wearing a new style until it has been established as a trend. Finally, **fashion followers** adopt the trend during the tail end when the style is nearing obsolescence. Some people argue that late adopters and fashion followers are people who cannot afford to wear the latest styles; this position may be accurate in some cases, but with the proliferation of fashion styles reaching all price points and markets nearly simultaneously, it is not an absolute.

The life of a fashion trend, however, is different from a fashion classic or fashion fad. A **classic** rarely changes drastically (a few stylish details might be altered); the overall concept remains recognizable from season to season. Blue blazers and white cotton shirts are often considered fashion classics. Their lives are long and strong, remaining fairly constant over time. The flipside of a classic is a **fad**, which has a short, energetic life. It appears on the fashion scene quickly, is adopted by many, and then dies soon after. Fads are easily forgotten and are remembered with horror (and laughter) when reviewing old photographs or yearbooks. Slatted sunglasses were a fashion fad in the 1980s and have made sporadic faddish returns for short periods since then.

A fashion classic can sometimes have trendy or faddish styling. For example, Converse shoes are considered a classic—their shape does not change from season to season, but their color can change to match the latest trend. The little black dress is considered a classic, but its particular rendering—the length of the hemline, the silhouette, the neckline, the fabric—can change (see Figure 2.3).

Figure 2.2 Fashion blogger Lisa Burg is an example of a fashion leader via her blog Lala Faux Bois.

Figure 2.3 The little black dress is a classic that can be styled to be fashionable.

Fashion is a complex process that cannot be explained by a single theory. Different theories examine different phases and sections of the fashion process. In order to understand the process, we use a continuum developed by Jean Hamilton (1997), who organizes fashion from the macro (or group) level to the micro (or individual) level. Hamilton's continuum argues that the cultural system influences the fashion system, which influences social groups, which influences individual choices. Further, these four levels of the continuum are interconnected and work together simultaneously.

Cultural System

The culture of a society determines whether a fashion system exists. Style change is found most frequently in cultures that value technological progress, individual expression, and capitalistic free-market exchange (Sproles & Burns, 1994; Kaiser, Nagasawa, & Hutton, 1995). Cultures that allow youthful experimentation and search for identity are also conducive to rapid changes in styles. An economic situation in which a significant portion of the population has discretionary income to spend on nonessentials is also necessary, as fashion change requires expenditure on new styles before clothing is completely worn out. Fashion has a difficult time existing—or must exist underground—in cultures where there is reverence for tradition or there is little freedom of individual expression. Native American and Japanese cultures value tradition and their traditional styles of clothing have remained relatively unchanged for generations. Cultures such as Communist China value the state over the individual, and fashion shows or fashion expression are often risky undertakings that could be met with punishment.

A new style is likely to be adopted when it fits with the **zeitgeist** (Blumer, 1969). *Zeitgeist* is a German word meaning "time" (*zeit*) and "ghost" (*geist*), translated as "spirit of the times," and fashion is a material reflection of the times. Nystrom (1928) identified five areas that comprise the zeitgeist: dominating events, dominating ideals, dominating social groups, dominating attitudes, and dominating technology. By examining these areas, one can see how they influence and affect fashion choices. The New Look exemplifies the relationship between fashion and the zeitgeist.

The New Look. When World War II ended, a young man named Christian Dior wanted to open his own fashion house. He had worked for other designers and had the knowledge and talent to design, but he did not have the financial capital. He asked a man named Marcel Boussac to fund his business. Boussac was an entrepreneur who owned many textile companies and agreed to finance Christian Dior's business, providing he used lots of fabric and purchased the fabric from Boussac's companies. Dior agreed. He then had to figure out how to design beautiful clothes using lots of fabric. Fortunately, an exhibition of the Belle Epoch was held in Paris at the time; Dior used this era of excess in fashion as his inspiration. And although Dior could design beautiful clothing, he could not be certain that women would wear his clothes. By the time World War II ended women had been dressing in masculine, tubular, close-fitting dresses for nearly a decade due to shortages of fabric, and they were ready for a change. When Dior unveiled his first collection for the House of Dior in 1947—full of voluminous skirts, wide collars, pleats, and a definite feminine flair—women were excited. Carmel Snow, then editor in chief of *Harper's Bazaar*, called it a "new look" for women. The New Look is an example of the zeitgeist because it combines economics, business, history, aesthetics, and the general attitudes of the day (see Figure 2.4).

Figure 2.4 Dior's New Look revolutionized women's fashion in 1947 and embodied the zeitgeist of the era.

Today's zeitgeist is the combination of social media, desire for instant gratification, and the fashion industry's desire to meet that demand. The result is a fashion system in hyperdrive, continually churning out new styles that are soon replaced by even newer styles and consumed promptly. Andrew Reilly and Jana Hawley term this "Attention Deficit Fashion" and provide a framework to understand current practices in the industry.

Fashion System

The fashion system works simultaneously with the cultural system. It is a globally based set of business establishments, small entrepreneurs, industry and government institutions, trade unions, and other agencies that have an impact on what products the consumer has to choose from in the marketplace. Economic interests drive most fashion system decisions, though government interests such as a trade agreement with, or boycott of, a nation, can also affect choices. George Sproles (1985) refers to this as the **market infrastructure theory**. Not everything is available at any given time; rather, the fashion system has pared down from the untold thousands of options and variations that its leaders believe the consumer wants. While some researchers have argued that is the consumer who has the power in the industry (Kaiser, Nagasawa, & Hutton, 1995), others, like Kean (1997), argue that consumer choice is dramatically limited by the industry because the industry makes many fashion and style decisions based on such matters as cost, production feasibility, government import quotas, and gut-level guesses about what will sell to the mass market, market segments, and niche markets.

Gatekeepers are people who make choices for consumers. In the late 19th and early 20th centuries, at the height of couture, fashion was a top-down business, meaning decisions made by designers such as Charles Worth and Cristobal Balenciaga were deemed infallible; they set the trends in fashion. However, fashion is a different sort of business today, with trends coming from a number of other sources such as cultural niches, political movements, or celebrities. These numerous, varied potential fashion influences make it difficult for one person to predict the next big trend. Fashion forecasters are a type of gatekeeper who help designers, marketers, and buyers make decisions about what will sell in the future. Fashion forecasting services help other fashion businesses by researching the current influences on fashion and organizing the material in books that provide guidance. The books offer "styles" and "looks" that are predicted to become popular. Fashion forecasting services can be very lucrative—providing, of course, that their predictions are accurate.

Designers, marketers, and buyers use the style guides offered by forecasters when making their decisions. This creates an interesting theoretical conundrum: those who use forecasting services know their competition does too and know their competition is looking at the same or similar guides. Therefore, they have a good idea of what their competition will offer and know they need to offer similar products so they do not lose their own consumers. This is one reason why a trend, such as the military trend in the early 2000s, appears simultaneously in many designers' collections and retail stores—everyone is looking at the same sources of information. Of course, not all businesses can afford forecasting services, and some must rely on their own instinct, observation, and skill at assessing society's current and future climate.

Social System

Regardless of how much power gatekeepers have and what they decide to offer consumers, it is ultimately the consumers who make a style fashionable. A number of theories have been proposed and studied in an attempt to understand why styles are adopted and discarded. These theories come from disciplines such as psychology, economics, sociology, marketing, politics, and art.

One of the earliest theories of fashion change is known as the **trickle-down theory** (Simmel, 1904; Veblen, 1912). This theory is based on the idea of social class emulation. High society introduces new styles, which are seen and copied by the middle class. Once the middle class has adopted the style, the lower class adopts it. When the upper class sees their style adopted by the lower classes, they discard that particular style in favor of a new one, and the cycle begins again. This theory is relevant in cultures that have distinct social strata, such as Edwardian England, but today it is difficult to find styles that begin in the upper class. Each social class in the United States may have its own aesthetic and may not necessarily want to look like their social "superiors." A variation of this theory is known as the **trickle-across theory** (King, 1963). King argues that a style can appear simultaneously in all class strata, just at different price points. This is due to designers and merchandisers with a keen understanding of fashion forecasting and with multiple lines for different markets (e.g., Giorgio Armani Privé, Giorgio Armani, Armani Collezioni, Emporio Armani, EA7, Armani Exchange, Armani Jeans, and Armani Junior; or Polo Ralph Lauren, Double RL, Ralph Lauren Collection, Ralph Lauren Purple Label, Ralph Lauren Black Label, Ralph Lauren Blue Label, Ralph by Ralph Lauren, Chaps, Polo Sport, RLX, Pink Pony, Polo Lauren Children, Denim & Supply Ralph Lauren, and Lauren) and retail giants offering similar trends at different price points in order to capture a larger market share. Another social-class theory is the **trickle-up theory** (Hebdige, 1979; Sproles, 1985), where fashion begins in the lower classes and is copied by a society's higher classes. An example of this theory is denim jeans. Originally intended as work wear for miners during the California gold rush of 1849, denim jeans were eventually worn by artists, rebellious teenagers, and the mass population (see Figure 2.5).

Sociologist and researcher Herbert Blumer (1969), however, had other ideas about fashion change. He argued that it was not class imitation and differentiation that drove fashion but rather any group that captures the zeitgeist. As long as their dress reflected the attitudes and desires of the time, they were likely to inspire fashion

Figure 2.5 Jeans are an example of the trickle-up theory because they originally were worn by working class miners but eventually adopted by the middle and upper classes.

trends, as people outside the group found those attitudes and desires relatable. In the 1970s, hippies had an impact on driving fashion, in the 1980s, yuppies (Figure 2.4) and punks, and in the 1990s, grunge and rap musicians all influenced the fashion scene to some degree. Blumer called his theory **collective selection** and sometimes it is referred to as the **subcultural leadership model** (Sproles, 1985).

Closely related to this is **social identity theory** (Tajfel & Turner, 1986). According to this theory, people strive to either align with or distance themselves from specific categories of people. One way to achieve this is through clothing. As people dress to align themselves with their race or sexual orientation or political views or economic aspirations, and so on, the group's style might become noticed by fashion innovators as something unique. Goths, punks, gamers, gay men, and lesbians are just some examples of groups whose distinct style illustrates these concepts.

THE INDIVIDUAL

The theories discussed so far examined fashion at the macro (group) level. Now we will examine fashion at the micro level. Whereas the macro level is about negotiations with culture or society or the fashion system, the micro level is about negotiations with the self. The macro level will offer and guide fashion selections, but the individual's unique tastes will also shape the adoption of new styles. Economic, political, sexual, and psychological circumstances can largely determine what consumers can afford and are willing to use. Each individual has his or her own speed at becoming accustomed to and accepting (or rejecting) new aesthetic combinations and forms (Sproles, 1985).

Symbolic interaction theory (Kaiser, Nagasawa, & Hutton, 1995) strives to explain the relationship between the macro level and the micro level. Contrary to other theories that argue that fashion starts at the social or cultural level, this theory argues that fashion starts at the individual level. In short, the theory proposes the idea that people experience ambivalence when they feel conflicted or pulled in different directions. The marketplace is simultaneously offering new, appearance-modifying commodities to express such ambivalence; appearances created using these products also convey ambivalence. The meaning of these ambivalent creations is negotiated in social settings; styles that prove meaningful are adopted.

If the style does not resolve ambivalence then it will be continually modified until it does. For example, a new shirt can be worn different ways—tucked in, untucked, partially tucked, collar up, collar down, sleeves cuffed, and so on—until it is deemed "right" or "appropriate" or "cool."

One could also argue that fashion at the macro level is about conformity and the desire to look like others. Fashion at the micro level can support this desire by adopting what is currently in fashion or it can disrupt the progress by not conforming. The desire to be different is addressed by the **uniqueness theory**, which argues that fashion trends begin when people adopt a style that is exclusive or distinctive to current modes.

Interestingly—and ironically—is that once the unique style is adopted by enough people to be considered "fashion," it loses its impact as something innovative, and people striving to be different must find something new to wear that expresses their individuality. At this point we can see the relationship between uniqueness and fashion innovators, for fashion innovators are usually people willing to take a risk to look unique or different from others. Thus, the fashion cycle begins anew.

Summary

Macro-level and micro-level factors and influences help shape individual choices about dress. We look to others, to industry offerings, and to cultural themes and trends to help in deciding what to wear. Fashion systems require social interaction. Individuals who are innovative, as well as consumers who are conforming, are both necessary for the process of fashion diffusion. Industry marketers or famous designers alone cannot make fashion trends happen without consumer acceptance and adoption of styles.

The process of fashion change and individual adoption or rejection is complex and involves all levels of society. Characteristics of culture are reflected in the fashion trends of a society. Trends in the arts, technology, and popular culture shape style trends. Large population groups sometimes shape fashion trends because of their vast market potential. Smaller groups—such as segments of the upper class, punk rockers, or rappers—may inspire fashion trends if they capture the zeitgeist. But rejection of the status quo can also inspire fashion change.

Key Terms

Classic	Fashion innovators	Subcultural leadership model	Uniqueness theory
Collective selection	Fashion leaders	Symbolic interaction theory	Zeitgeist
Early adopters	Late adopters	Trickle-across theory	
Fad	Market infrastructure theory	Trickle-down theory	
Fashion followers	Social identity theory	Trickle-up theory	

Learning Activity 2.1

THE LITTLE BLACK DRESS

Find images of the little black dress throughout the 20th century. What elements of this garment make it a classic? What were some trend influences of the time that were incorporated into it? Illustrate or draw how you would reinterpret the little black dress for the next fashion season. What classic elements would you keep? What trendy elements would you incorporate?

BRAND MARKETS

Find images of a trend that appear in all lines of a brand (e.g., Giorgio Armani, Armani Collezioni, Emporio Armani, Armani Exchange; or Polo, Polo Purple Label, Polo Black Label, Polo Blue Label, Chaps, Polo Sport, RLX, and Lauren). List how the trend is reinterpreted for the different markets and discuss your list with your classmates.

References

Blumer, H. (1969), "Fashion: From Class Differentiation to Collective Selection," *Sociology Quarterly*, 10: 275–91.

Hamilton, J. A. (1997), "The Macro-Micro Interface in the Construction of Individual Fashion Forms and Meanings," *Clothing and Textiles Research Journal* 15(3): 164–71.

Hebdige, D. (1979), *Subculture: The Meaning of Style*, London: Methuen.

Kaiser, S. B., R. Nagasawa and S. Hutton (1995), "Construction of an SI Theory of Fashion Part 1: Ambivalence and Change," *Clothing and Textiles Research Journal* 13(3): 172–83.

Kean, R. (1997), "The Role of the Fashion System in Fashion Change: A Response to the Kaiser, Nagasawa and Hutton Model," *Clothing and Textiles Research Journal*, 15(3): 172–77.

King, C. W. (1963), "Fashion Adoption: A Rebuttal to the 'Trickle-Down' Theory," in S. A. Greyser (ed.), *Toward Scientific Marketing*, 108–25, Chicago: American Marketing Association.

Nystrom, P. H. (1928), *Economics of Fashion*. New York: The Ronald Press Co.

Simmel, G. (1904), "Fashion," *International Quarterly*, 10: 130–55.

Sproles, G. B. (1985), "Behavioral Science Theories of Fashion," in M. R. Solomon (ed.), *The Psychology of Fashion*, 55–70, Lexington, MA: Lexington Books.

Sproles, G. B. and L. D. Burns (1994), *Changing Appearances*, New York: Fairchild Publications.

Tajfel, H. and J. C. Turner (1986), "The Social Identity Theory of Inter-Group Behavior," in S. Worchel and L. W. Austin (eds.), *Psychology of Intergroup Relations*, 33–47, Chicago: Nelson-Hall.

Veblen, T. (1912), *The Theory of the Leisure Class*, New York: Macmillan.

This introduction is based on a version originally written by Mary Lynn Damhorst and appeared in *Meanings of Dress* editions 1, 2, and 3.

2.1
Hedi Slimane and the Reinvention of Menswear

Jay McCauley Bowstead

Foreword

In 2001 I spent six months in Paris working in a health-food shop and living in a small, un-plumbed bedsit in the eaves of a nineteenth-century apartment block. I was ecstatically happy: Paris seemed to be a city alive with possibility, and I spent hours wandering the Marais, Saint-Germain-des-Prés, around the Beaubourg and the – then slightly edgy – area of Oberkampf and Canal St Martin where many French designers had their studios. The nascent changes to menswear of the late 1990s and early 2000s had not entirely eluded me, an avid consumer of *Dazed and Confused* and *Sleaze Nation*. But it was in that year that I noticed that people's responses to me changed: my stringy form and androgynous appearance had suddenly come into fashion. A photographer at the École des Beaux Arts asked to take some pictures of me, I now think, trying to capture some of my youthful uncertainty; it was the look at the time.

In this context, the changes to fashion and to representations of masculinity that Hedi Slimane introduced in the early 2000s, had a particularly strong and positive impact on me. The dominant models of masculinity of the 1990s had seemed unobtainable – I was never going to ripple with muscles or achieve a deep tan – nor did the mainstream gay scene of the late 1990s contest this model, as much in thrall to hegemonic masculinity as the straight world. Rather, the smallish indie scene represented by club nights like Trash at The End – with more than its fair share of queer youth – offered a true alternative in which more diverse modes of masculinity could be explored. As I will go on to suggest, in some ways indie subculture in the 1990s acted as the progenitor or at least as the guardian of the elements of Slimane's style, for which the 1970s 'underground' remained a particularly important reference.

At art school between 2002 and 2006, I saw myself as part of the vanguard of this new menswear, to which

many of our lecturers were highly ambivalent. This was the period in which Shoreditch and Brick Lane were becoming increasingly well known, as a new scene of dressed-up dandyism emerged amongst an arty crowd of clubbers, musicians, interns and struggling designers. Nights like Anti-Social and Boombox in Shoreditch as well as music venues including the George Tavern and the Rhythm Factory in Whitechapel became important places to dance, dress-up and be seen. This fashionable East London style was characterized by many of the features, including the very slim silhouette, that Slimane was pioneering at the time.

In 2005 I undertook work-experience for a large casual-wear firm based in Northern Italy, who remained singularly unconvinced that skinny jeans were a trend likely to take off in any big way. I and my student colleagues, immersed to various extents in an arty milieu, saw the company's less than rapturous response to our designs as both provincial, and lacking in foresight: but it was indicative both of the pace and the uncertainty of shifts in menswear at that point. It is important to remember that the fashionable scenes of cities including London, Paris and Berlin – while influential – were at some remove from the broader culture and even the mainstream fashion industry (see Figures 2.6 and 2.7).

Introduction

In the following I hope to locate Slimane's intervention in men's fashion and masculinity within a specific historical and disciplinary framework; to establish how and why Slimane's work enjoyed critical and commercial success; and to suggest how this success related to changing models of gender in the early to mid-2000s. My intention is to produce an account bringing together an analysis of fashion both as a creative discipline and as a producer of multiple masculinities. To this end, I have engaged closely with a range of materials, particularly documentation of

Figures 2.6 and 2.7 Design by Jay McCauley Bowstead (2005), drawings showing the clear influence of Slimane.

Hedi Slimane's collections for Dior Homme from 2001 to 2007 and, as far as possible, with his preceding collections for Yves Saint Laurent Rive Gauche.

In the past three decades a rich body of literature has emerged to reveal the links between fashion and broader social and cultural processes (Hebdige 1979; Wilson 1985; Barnard 1996; McRobbie 1998; Kaiser 2012). Drawing on sociology, psychology, semiotics, structuralist and post-structuralist thought, authors have sought to describe the manner in which fashion reflects the preoccupations of a particular society while acting variously to reproduce or challenge dominant cultural and economic relationships. But though these analyses have done much to provoke more serious and engaged discourses surrounding fashion, they have tended to underplay the significance of fashion as an *authored text* in which the designer – in particular – may consciously employ dress not only to reflect upon but to actively intervene in culture. In the following, I hope to demonstrate how Hedi Slimane's innovations in men's fashion during the 2000s were designed to disrupt dominant representations of fashionable masculinity while assessing the reach, success and potential limitations of his approach.

As I have described, my own experience of this new model of masculinity pioneered by Hedi Slimane – was one of some emotional and creative investment. And while I am no longer so directly engaged in fashion design practice, nor to the same extent in the 'construction' of my identity, it would clearly be disingenuous to attempt

to absent myself and my subjectivity from this analysis. I hope that my experiences of men's fashion, subculture and design inform my account, at the same time as maintaining an awareness of the specificity of my subject position, and the possibility of other interpretations. As writers and thinkers from both feminist and queer theory perspectives have described, personal experience is often a useful point of departure from which to consider broader questions of culture, society and politics, not as an avoidance of a rigorous or theoretically informed analysis, but rather as a way of accounting for the complexity and specificity of experiences that may not fit into existing accounts and orthodox models (Hanisch 1970).

Hedi Slimane and the Reinvention of Menswear

Seductive style to take your breath away, the like of which the world of menswear has rarely dared to imagine. (Cabasset 2001: 70)

From the middle of the 1990s to the end of that decade, scholarship focused upon masculinity and fashion enjoyed a sudden, and ostensibly unexpected, flowering. A range of new texts from a variety of perspectives explored the ways in which men constructed their identities through an interaction with fashion and consumer culture, for example: *The Hidden Consumer*, Christopher Breward (1999); *Men in The Mirror*, Tim Edwards (1997); *Hard looks*, Sean Nixon (1996); and *Cultures of Consumption*, Frank Mort (1996). These studies broke new ground in the analysis of an area that had been historically marginalized, and indeed, the foundational work of these authors has been crucial references in establishing the parameters of this article. While this is not the forum to rehearse this set of discourses in detail it would be fair to characterize Nixon, Edwards and Mort as suggesting that the emergence of a more sophisticated market in men's fashion – along with the lifestyle journalism, advertising and photography which surrounded it – had opened up sites for a newly commodified performance of masculinity. Indeed, in a chapter entitled 'New men and new markets' Frank Mort (1996: 15–27) explicitly links economic change in the 1980s, new models of masculinity associated more with consumption than production, and the development of a new menswear market. Somewhat divergently, Christopher Breward's *The Hidden Consumer* (1999) with its focus on men's fashion of the late nineteenth and early twentieth centuries, sought to locate menswear consumption in these periods as a locus of spectacular display linked to an emergent consumer culture. But despite the apparent divergent nature of Breward's writing in terms of its historical scope, all of these studies seem to point towards a scholarly engagement in men's fashion reaching a point of amplification in the final years of the twentieth-century.

It is intriguing and paradoxical, nevertheless, that this wealth of academic work engaging in men's fashion took place at a time when menswear as a design practice was anything but fecund. The late 1990s was a period in which arid and lifeless ideas were recycled on a seemingly endless loop: unstructured tailoring, workwear, sportswear, with the occasional bare muscled torso to add some semblance of vivacity. While, of course, some original and creative practitioners did prevail in this singularly inhospitable environment – Raf Simons, Helmut Lang and Tom Ford at Gucci spring to mind – there was a strong feeling amongst those engaged in men's fashion, strangely anticipated by the scholarly works to which I have alluded, that change in menswear had to come. To this end Adrian Clark of *The Guardian* asked: 'Does menswear really have to be so boring? What it has lacked for over a decade, is some drive, some guts and a wider choice' (1999a).

At the turn of the millennium a feeling pervaded the press, industry and academy that the representation of a greater diversity of masculinities had to be possible through the medium of menswear. Hedi Slimane, designer for Yves Saint Laurent Rive Gauche from 1997 to 2000, was cited as an increasingly important influence by those in the know during the late 1990s, combining a new radically slim silhouette with precise tailoring and 'edgy' play with form and fabrication (Clark 1999a). But it was Slimane's 2001 launch of a new label Dior Homme that acted as his decisive critical intervention in menswear, pointing towards the formal and aesthetic approaches that would go on to characterize the practice of men's fashion in the coming decade. The claims made for Slimane at the time evoked messianic imagery: 'It was on the last day of the presentations, however, that Paris was saved, by Hedi Slimane' (Clark 1999b). With the eyes of the world upon him, Slimane proposed a vision of menswear that seemed, at that moment, entirely new, fresh and exhilarating. In the words of Charlie Porter in *The Guardian*:

Nothing exciting is meant to happen in men's fashion. Yet in Paris right now, the talk is all of Hedi Slimane, the designer whose work at the newly established

Dior Homme is provoking a radical rethink in the stagnating ateliers of menswear. (2001)

In Slimane's inaugural collection for Dior, and in his final collection for Yves Saint Laurent, some of the core semantic and formal elements that went on to define his practice in the 2000s are already observable. First, there is a renewed emphasis on tailoring, as evidenced in Richard Avedon's iconic campaign photograph of Eric Van Nostrand for Autumn/Winter 2001/2002, in which the jacket has simultaneously regained its structured form – darted through the waist and padded and rolled at the shoulder – while losing the carapace-like excess of canvas that frequently characterizes traditional tailoring (Avedon 2001). The prioritization of elements of formal and evening wear, though the pieces were rarely worn as conventional suits, reflects a dandyish, nostalgic aspect to many of Slimane's collections. This should be read as a reaction to the dominance of sportswear in the 1990s, and to the oversized structureless silhouette introduced by Armani – both of which, ironically, rendered the hyper-traditionalist elegance of men's evening wear a subversive pose. Lest the implicit subversiveness of these two collections be too weakly felt, Slimane introduced an abstracting approach, shearing away at garments to reveal their pure forms. For Yves Saint Laurent Autumn/Winter 2000/2001 shirts were finished without buttons or, more dramatically, reinterpreted as a bolt of silk suspended from the neck, animated as the model progressed along the catwalk (Slimane 2000). In this outfit, in particular, a knowledge and respect for the core sartorial forms of menswear is joined by a willingness to challenge and radically subvert them. Moreover, the bared skin and more especially the sensuousness of the drape introduced an eroticism to the catwalk that would have been much less strongly felt had the model simply been shirtless. This sense of ambiguous eroticism was also seen in Slimane's contrast of monochrome against deep necklines and sheer fabrics, creating a graphic juxtaposition between the white of the models' chests and the black of their garments. Nods to Young Americans era Bowie and Roxy Music – in the form of tipped fedoras, leather and gold lamé trousers – appeared throughout the collection, but the exuberance of these gestures was always balanced against the coolness and minimalism of the styling. Similarly, in Solitaire for Dior Homme Autumn/Winter 2001/2002, the cleanness of the stripped back tailoring was complimented by subtle elements of decoration. The fabric corsage attached to the lapel of the tailored jacket in the celebrated Richard Avedon photograph was made using haute couture womenswear techniques for which Dior are well known, but these potentially conflicting elements of precision and decoration were balanced with a measured restraint (Avedon 2001). The impression we are left with, reflected in the fashion journalism of the time, is both of the audacity of the work, and simultaneously its strong and determined sense of purpose.

Return to the Demi-monde

In his desire to reconfigure and reform menswear Slimane turned to the past, to a period preceding the baggy sportswear inspired styles and glistening musculatures that had dominated the 1990s catwalk. In the advertising campaign for Autumn/Winter 2005, a model lounges in a moodily lit but chic 1970s interior. His black fedora, glossy black-leather trench-coat, drain-pipe trousers and gold Cuban heels evoke a set of overlapping 1970s underground scenes: pre-Berlin Bowie, the New York Dolls, The Factory, and early Robert Mapplethorpe. The period in which proto-punk and glam interacted was also the point at which a flirtation with queer signifiers was at its apogee. Drag queens interacted with beat poets; boys and girls wore gold trousers, black leather jackets and bore their chests (O'Brien et al. 2005). The iconography of a queer coolness, of aw 'mash-up' collaged approach to butch and femme, soft and hard becomes the visual language of rebellion in the 1970s. It is not by mistake, therefore, that Slimane returns again and again to this milieu paying homage to its images and icons.

In Slimane's Spring 2002 campaign for Dior Homme, again photographed by Richard Avedon the fine, sensuous features of model Tiago Gass are picked out by stark directional lighting: hair brushed dramatically over his face he looks directly into the camera, at once challenging and seductive. The model's shirt – shorn of its sleeves in a quiet nod to punk – is preternaturally crisp, its narrow collar finished with the closest of edge-stiches (Avedon 2002). A slim black tie bifurcates Gass' torso. But the controlled minimalism of the scene is interrupted by a dramatic stain to the left side of the model's chest, a splotch complete with dark droplets which on closer inspection reveals itself to be a motif of hand-embroidered sequins. The image certainly possesses a cool beauty, but suddenly, looking through Roberta Bayley's photographs of punk pioneers I realize that the advertisement is a direct quote. It references a series of pictures of former New York Doll

Johnny Thunders and his band The Heartbreakers whose blood-stained shirts evidence a (clearly staged) shot to the heart (Bayley [1976] 2005: 96–97). The figure on the centre right of Bayley's image, the obvious prototype for Avedon's 2002 photograph, is the seminal proto-punk Richard Hell whose carefully calculated style went on to be highly influential, providing a bridge between the glamour of the early 1970s and the nihilism that characterized the later part of the decade. The seductive, if not quite effortless cool of New York's 1970s demi-monde is certainly a rich source of inspiration for Slimane, we can see its influence particularly strongly felt in his Autumn–Winter 2005/2006 collection at Dior Homme, and already in his Autumn–Winter 2000/2001 collection for Yves Saint Laurent with its early Robert Maplethorpe styling, in Spring–Summer 2007 in a more punkish incarnation, and inflecting various of Slimane's collections with their emphasis on metallics, high sheen leathers and the eroticization of the chest.

A New Man?

For Slimane, the 1970s underground exercised a fascination linked to the ambiguous and provocative model of masculinity embodied by figures like Richard Hell (Name & O'Brien 2005). However, the power of these subversive references can be more strongly felt when contrasted against the fashionable masculinities that preceded Slimane's intervention in fashion. Dominant media representations of masculinity, from the mid-1980s and throughout the 1990s, privileged archetypes typified by a muscular eroticism inspired by neo-classicism and World War II propaganda of various hues. Workwear and military garments were particularly important references, while a highly muscular gym-honed body was reflected in menswear shoots that nodded to Greco-Roman statuary, socialist–realist imagery and images of early twentieth century industrial workers. Models were often shot shirtless, or in underwear, in a manner that combined a frank eroticization of the male form with the suggestion of a powerful, highly physical and active masculinity. Photographer Bruce Weber's iconic images for Calvin Klein, including his 1982 campaign featuring pole-vaulter Tom Hintnaus, anticipated the tone of the decade, by 1987 his Obsession For Men campaign, seemingly channelling Leni Riefenstahl, reflected a recognizable archetype of fashionable masculinity (Weber 1982). Accompanying this prioritization of a muscular physique, sportswear, casual wear and elements of workwear increasingly dominated popular men's fashions of the late 1980s, nor was this a passing trend (Anon 1988; Anon 1994a).

Indeed, the continued traction of über-masculine modes of self-presentation is still apparent in the Spring/Summer 1994 edition of *Arena Homme+*. A story entitled 'Military precision' features models in a variety of rumpled pseudo-utility garments, the editorial adding:

This year's action man is primarily a creature of the desert, with shades of sand, gunmetal and stone [. . .] Combat trousers are a particular favourite, with chunky thigh pockets [. . .] in which to stash those all-important maps, secret codes and poison pellets. (Anon. 1994b: 64)

This reliance upon a highly conservative notion of maleness, celebrating explicitly military imagery perhaps reflects a retrenchment in cultures of masculinity. In a US context, the Culture Wars of the 1980s had seen gender become a highly fraught and polarizing issue. In Western Europe the 1980s and 1990s saw many of the certainties of the progressive post-war consensus challenged, along with economic uncertainty gender and sexuality were also increasingly contested. But whether primarily as a response to gender-politics, or to economic uncertainty, masculinity of the early late 1980s and 1990s was located as a crisis-ridden space, a notion reflected in the discourses around the new-man, yuppie and new-lad by writers including Sean Nixon, Tim Edwards and Frank Mort.

Tim Edwards in his text of 1997 *Men in the Mirror* eloquently evokes the ambivalence and contradiction that underpinned the figure of the new-man, whom he describes as having emerged from 'the crystallization of consequences in economics, marketing, political ideology, demography and, most widely consumer society in the 1980s (1997: 39–40). As Edwards recounts, the new-man occupied an ambiguous position: located in media discourses both in relation to second-wave feminism and to an increasingly acquisitive model of capitalism: overtly commercialized and sexualized, while simultaneously reliant upon a curiously conventional image of masculinity. Despite the associations of the new-man with contestation and change, Edwards suggests, the explosion of new-man imagery in the 1980s was strangely safe and repetitive:

Yet despite this apparent plethora, the content of these representations remains quite extraordinarily fixed. The men in question are always young, usually white,

particularly muscular, critically strong jawed, clean shaven (often all over), healthy, sporty, successful, virile and ultimately sexy. (Edwards 1997: 41)

He goes on to characterize fashionable masculinity of the period as centred around the dominant archetypes of the expensively suited businessman and of the sporty, often scantily clad 'outdoor casual'. So while the imagery of the new-man of the 1980s emphasized fashionable consumption, grooming and desirability, it did so in a manner, as we have seen, that reinforced existing dominant modes masculinity privileging the physical strength of the athlete and the economic prowess of the businessman.

In this sense, fashions of this period reflect anxieties pervading the performance of masculinity within a still strongly heterosexist society experiencing rapid social change. The eroticization of the male body – which took place to an increasing extent in the late 1980s and 1990s – used hyper-masculinity as a way of displacing the unease which went along with the objectification of the male body. In this way, advertisers, designers and image-makers had their cake and ate it: giving themselves the permission to commodify male bodies, while employing the symbols of male power to neutralize the subversiveness of the act:

In effect the bodybuilder was the fleshy representation of the New Right's regressive revolution: in tune with developments of popular culture but deploying them for a right wing agenda. (Simpson 1994a: 24)

For Nixon, Edwards and Mort the increased commodification of the male body and incitement to the homospectatorial gaze (Fuss 1992) are linked to the figure of the new-man, as male consumers are exposed to increasingly diverse ways of 'consuming their masculinities'.[1] However, the notion of the new-man, with its progressive connotations, sits uneasily with images which, as I have described, present a somewhat antediluvian model of masculinity. Indeed, writers such as Mark Simpson and Niall Richardson (2010: 37–38) draw attention to the relationship between bodybuilding and the rightward shift in American politics of the 1980s and early 1990s, particularly as manifested in homophobia and in the fear of effeminacy. In this way, the aesthetic nature and semantic content of these commodified and eroticized images are not coincidental, but point to the ambivalence and anxieties that surrounded the commodification of

---

1. A similar association is heard in Mark Simpson's coinage of the term 'metrosexual' (1994).

masculinity in the 1980s and 1990s and which, in the context of resurgent right-wing economic and social politics, relied on distinctly conservative masculine iconographies.

Beyond the Homospectorial Gaze

The centrality of gay identities to the recent history of men's fashion is one that until very recently was elided and ignored. Shaun Cole has undertaken valuable work in revealing the significance of gay men as innovators of twentieth-century menswear introducing styles that came to be associated with Teddy Boys and Mods. As he explains, the first menswear shop on Carnaby Street in the early 1960s, catered at first to a predominantly gay clientele:

> [It is] clear that the dress choices of gay men were influential on mainstream men's fashion: 'Vince sold clothes that once would have been worn by no one but queers and extremely blatant ones at that'. (Cohn 1971 cited in Cole 2000: 74)

Similarly, Frank Mort (1996: 16) makes a case for early gay lifestyle magazines in the late 1960s, post decriminalization, as having acted as precursors for later mainstream men's publishing. But I would argue that the figure of the gay man has occupied a more central role at the level of symbol in men's fashion, style and in fashionable images of men than is widely acknowledged.

Central to the subversiveness of Mod, Carnaby Street, and later Glam and New Romantic/Blitz Kid styles, for both gay and straight participants, was their flirtation with queer signifiers. Something we see reflected explicitly in Slimane's preoccupation with historical and contemporary subculture. The symbolic power of transgressing acceptable heterosexual dress remained both a site of anxiety for purveyors of 'mainstream' men's fashion and a source of fascination and excitement for subcultures. In this sense, fashionable images of men from the 1960s onwards have often operated as the site of negotiated, complex and contested masculinities in which the spectre and augur of homosexuality have been an important part of the mix.

In *Hard looks* Sean Nixon (1996: 180–85) explores how influential style-magazine *The Face* explored a range of what he terms 'hard' and 'soft' signifiers in shoots styled by Ray Petri. My own research has brought me to similar conclusions. For example, in the October 1985 edition of *The Face* (Petri and Morgan 1985: 66–71)

Petri's styling features a range of disparate but iconic masculine signifiers: military and naval accessories, workwear, sportswear, flags and the hard musculature of the models. Against these masculine cues, elements of eclectic 'ethnic' and specifically Native American decorative elements serve to add a complexity to the images that elevates them from mere Tom of Finland camp. As Nixon puts it: 'the choice of model and some of the elements of clothing . . . have a strong intertextuality with certain traditions of representation of masculinity aimed at and taken up by gay men' (1996: 185). But to what end are these references to gay strategies of self-presentation employed? I would argue that the implicit aim of Petri's quotation of gay masculinities is more significant than a semi-coded nod to knowing viewers. Crucially, the creative intention of Petri and *The Face* was to produce innovative images imbued with an exotic, ambiguous and subversive energy.

For fashion designer Jean Paul Gaultier, the 'queering' of hegemonic models of masculinity through the application of camp was a key aspect of his aesthetic. His 1984 collection L'Homme Objet applied irony to normative masculinity through the application of gay clichés with muscle-bound models in cropped and backless T-shirts and miscellaneous naval accessories. In a more sophisticated mode, a famous publicity image from his Autumn/Winter 1985 collection shows a muscular black model, coded masculine by his developed physique, beard and shaven-head, wearing a full quilted satin skirt which he ruches in a clenched fist (Roversi 1985). Gaultier, like Petri, adopts elements of camp to expose the inherent performance of gender. But while his designs problematize hegemonic masculinity, they also reinforce the dominance of the 'virile' muscular, male figure as a locus of desire and identification. For both Petri and Gaultier, masculine, clone-like modes of self-presentation originating in the 1970s were still strongly felt. And while this look is ironized and aestheticized – in the mid-1980s at a time of homophobic media hysteria in the United Kingdom and a worsening AIDS crisis – the representation of a queer identity embodied through physical strength and resilience had particular resonance.

In contrast, Hedi Slimane's designs for Yves Saint Laurent and from 2001 for Dior Homme are neither ironic in intention, nor do they celebrate masculinity as conventionally conceived. Moreover, while Slimane frequently quotes from subcultural scenes that feature elements of camp, his own designs maintain a certain restraint and seriousness, that resist the label camp. This seriousness can be heard in Slimane's interview with Patrick Cabasset for L'Officiel:

A men's collection can be creative, desirable, enlivened [. . .] Menswear can become fashion too. I don't think this should be forbidden for men. I'm looking for a way through. I want to create something with a closeness, a sense of intimacy, a directness. (2001: 70)

Mark Simpson in his book *Male Impersonators* explains the issue of homophobia by evoking the fundamental fragility of masculinity: 'the problem of de-segregating homosexuality from a private ghetto into a heterosexual world that depends on homosexuality remaining invisible, encapsulates the problem faced everywhere in popular culture today by this frail phenomenon we call masculinity' (1994a: 6). Yet more strongly, from a psycho-social perspective, David Plummer makes the case for homophobia operating as a structuring agent in masculinity: 'In men's spheres, the yardstick for what is acceptable is hegemonic masculinity and what is unacceptable is marked by homophobia and enforced by homophobia' (1999: 289). The 'queering' strategies of Jean Paul Gaultier find their echoes in Simpson's writing that seeks to expose the performed or 'impersonated' nature of masculinity. However, by the approach of the millennium, there was a sense in which strategies of this sort were beginning to exhaust their usefulness. Homophobia that had acted as a structuring agent for hegemonic masculinity, while providing much of the sense of transgression and taboo for subcultural masculinities, had by the late 1990s ceased to be such a dominant force. In this context, Hedi Slimane made his intervention not only in men's fashion, but also in the symbolic language of masculinity.

There is a psychology to the masculine: we're told don't touch it; it's ritual, sacred, taboo. It's difficult but I'm making headway, I'm trying to find a new approach. (Slimane 2001 cited by Cabasset 2001: 70)

Slimane's collections for Dior Homme, as we have seen, acted as an explicit challenge to dominant representations of masculinity. But it was an intervention not content to sit at the peripheries of visual culture. Hedi Slimane may have drawn his inspiration, substantially, from niche and subcultural art and music scenes, but Maison Christian Dior, a multi-million euro company and one of the world's most famous fashion brands, was certainly not subcultural. To send explicitly androgynous figures down a menswear catwalk was not in 2001 totally without precedent[2], but to do so with the backing of a goliath company, with the eyes of the world upon him, and with an equally unequivocal advertising campaign was indeed radical.

A Transformation of Menswear

A comparison of two collection reviews from the menswear industry journal *Collezioni Uomo* prove instructive in assessing Slimane's impact on Maison Christian Dior. Separated by just ten years, the autumn/winter 1997 collection for 'Dior Monsieur' and the spring/summer 2007 collection for its successor label Dior Homme embody starkly divergent aesthetics: here, the changes wrought by Hedi Slimane on Christian Dior's menswear offering are overtly apparent. The boxy plaid jacket of autumn 1997 – three buttoned, broad lapelled, with a high break-point – has been replaced in spring 2007 by a draped, tropical-weight wool jacket, narrow peaked lapel, low break-point, tying – peignoir like – just below the waist. The model's vivid orange shirt of 1997, has been reworked in fine white poplin, and elsewhere replaced by translucent gossamer-like T-shirts with asymmetric draped appendages and geometric cut-outs. Sage-green corduroy trousers are superseded by fitted leather jeans, while a cool palette of reflective greys, tints of sand and glossy black takeover from a rural theme of terracotta, sage, textured browns, charcoal and blues. While Dior Monsieur imagines his man wandering through the countryside, Dior Homme evokes an urban milieu with eveningwear references – sequins, bare chests and shoulders and plays on 'le smoking' – contrasted against military styling in cotton twill and black nappa.

It is hard to understand at whom exactly the 1997 offering of Christian Dior Monsieur is aimed. In a collection undistinguished by any original design features, one wonders why a customer would not prefer to patronize a traditional men's outfitters. But in Slimane's own words 'At the end of the day, the men running the companies wanted the clothes to look like the kind of clothes they would wear, and they didn't really see a world beyond that' (Slimane 2001 cited in Porter 2001). As for Dior, so for

---

2. Raf Simons had presented androgynous menswear collections in the 1990s including A/W 1996 We Only Come Out at Night and S/S 1997 How to Talk to Your Teen but this influence was predominantly felt within a niche, experimental, fashion literate crowd. Tom Ford also pioneered a closer fit in his Gucci menswear collections during the 1990s. Though both designers were significant, they do not attract the claims of paradigm shift made by various journalists about Slimane.

much of the men's market whose CEOs, removed from their target audience by age, class and social aspiration, frequently projected their own conservatism onto menswear as a whole. Slimane's creation of Dior Homme was of considerable commercial significance to Christian Dior, as chairman Bernard Arnault pointed out in 2007: 'Dior Homme experienced sustained growth across its entire product line (city, sportswear, and accessories)'. But a much broader significance of Slimane's success was in innovating menswear more generally, as fashion companies saw a market ripe for capitalization.

In the early 2000s Slimane's influence began to exert itself strongly amongst designer and middle-market brands who adopted much slimmer silhouettes and focused increasingly on tailoring. In spring 2003 *Arena Homme+* featured slim tailoring from Italian label Iceberg: a brand previously strongly associated with oversized casual-wear and knit (Anon 2003). By spring 2005, an advertisement for Calvin Klein unexpectedly presented a model in a fitted two-tone suit, replacing the muscular topless men the brand had focused upon in preceding years (Meisel 2005). Slimane's former protégé Lucas Ossendrijver was appointed head of Lanvin's men's line in 2006 to revitalize their faded menswear offering. While high street companies especially Topman, but also brands including H&M, River Island and Zara, begin to feature styles heavily influenced by Slimane. Between 2007 and 2010 dandyish tailoring, scoop-necked fine gauge T-shirts, and very slim trousers became almost ubiquitous on the high street (Topman 2009). Style-blogs attest to the enthusiastic take-up of this style particularly among a demographic in their late teens and early twenties (Verhagen 2009). It is arguable that Slimane's strongest influence was felt after he had left Dior Homme in 2007 as his silhouette, punkish influences, androgyny and emphasis on tailoring began to infuse popular culture.

Integral to the new slim silhouette that Slimane pioneered were the models he cast for his catwalk shows and advertising campaigns. In the Autumn/Winter 2001 edition of *Arena Homme+* an article entitled 'Adam's ribs' asked:

> Who puts the slim into Slimane's shows? It's a transformation to confound Darwin [. . .] the male model has transformed into a much sleeker animal. Gone are the grinning, pumped-up, all-American-types that dominated the Eighties [. . .] In their place we have the less burly, more surly European skinny-boy. (Healy 2001: 163)

Slimane understood this new physique as representing a more authentic and less overtly constructed masculinity (Richardson 2010: 25–39): 'do real exercise, such as swimming or martial arts. Stay and be as natural as possible. Lean doesn't mean vulnerability but strength' (Slimane 2001 cited by Healy 2001: 163). It is equally clear that he saw his choice of model as a deliberate intervention in the language of gender: here cited by Charlie Porter (2001) in an article entitled 'Body politic' for *The Guardian* 'Muscles don't mean masculinity to me [. . .] and long hair does not define your sexuality'.

Raf Simons and Hedi Slimane rejected the 'built' body, a staple of the catwalks throughout the 1990s, in favour of slim, youthful-looking models. It was a strategy that attracted considerable press attention, particularly for Slimane, but that also signified a different set of aspirations for fashionable masculinity in the new millennium. Tellingly, both Simons and Slimane, made explicit borrowings from the Indie music scene and their choices of model – sometimes scouted from clubs and music venues – can be read as an extension of this aesthetic with its connotations of creative integrity and youthful rebellion.

The notion that a slender silhouette represents authenticity is clearly a highly problematic one, failing to account for the bodily regimes required to retain an appearance of perpetual adolescence and at risk of fetishizing youth and vulnerability. The symbolic power of Slimane's choice of models was in repudiating the normative model of masculinity of mainstream fashion imagery, but in doing so he arguably risked replacing one form of body-despotism with another.

Slimane's aesthetic owed much to the influence of mid-1990s Indie subculture typified by the groups of vintage clad teenagers who congregated around Camden-Market and frequented clubs like the Camden Palace, The Scala in Kings Cross and Trash – off Tottenham Court Road. Integral to the sensibility of the scene was the rejection of the commercial values of mainstream fashion and music expressing itself in an adoption of miscellaneous 1970s alternative references, and a tendency towards androgyny. Musicians such as Jarvis Cocker of Pulp and more particularly Brett Anderson of Suede were exemplars of a punk and glam inflected Ziggy-Stardust-manqué aesthetic, which processed through the filter of the 1990s, gained an additional patina of tatty nihilism. The rake-thin silhouette of these frontmen was part of their appeal: dramatically at odds with the pumped-up look of male musicians in commercial pop and mainstream male models.

Echoing a 1970s New York 'vibe' in a CBGBs mode, The Strokes emerged in 2000 their Ramones-like look and guitar-oriented sound becoming immensely influential. As Alex Needham, culture editor of *The Guardian* formerly of *The Face* and *NME* described to me:

The Strokes were immediately embraced by the fashion world. When you think what The Strokes were wearing at the time – jeans with suit jackets – that pretty much lasted the whole decade, and Converse as well. It was an updated version of a New York punk-band look which goes right back to the Velvet Underground, and that was what the music was like too. (1 February 2013)

By 2004 Hedi Slimane's engagement with indie music had become explicit as he dressed bands including Franz Ferdinand and the White Stripes. Already a keen photographer of emerging bands and youth tribes, who in turn influenced his collections, he embarked on an ambitious project with *V* magazine documenting up-and-coming bands in collaboration with journalist Alex Needham (then of *NME*) resulting in the book *Rock Diary* (2008).

As I have described, a set of 1970s subcultural milieux formed an important source of inspiration for Slimane directly reflected in his design. But while Slimane's interpretation was often imaginative, it was through contemporary youth culture and particularly musical culture that these references had retained their currency.

Conclusion: Beyond the Glass of Fashion

Each season brings . . . various secret signals of things to come. Whoever understands how to read these semaphores would know in advance not only about new currents in the arts but also about new legal codes, wars and revolutions. – Here, surely, lies the greatest charm of fashion. (Benjamin 1999: 64)

During his time at Dior Homme and Yves Saint Laurent, Hedi Slimane developed an aesthetic characterized by a focus on clarity and elegance. Clarity expressed through neat tailoring and an attenuated silhouette, and elegance communicated via drape, fine fabrics and a new dandyism nodding both to traditional eveningwear and to women's haute couture. As I have described, Hedi Slimane saw himself as intervening not only in the field of menswear, but in masculinity itself.

Slimane is heralding a more sensitive interpretation of male self-image, at odds with the pumped-up gym stereotype that has dominated menswear for the past two decades [. . .] It's almost a pain to have to insist that those elements do not say anything today. They are archaic, and for me they have nothing to do with the projections men have of themselves, or that their lovers or girlfriends have of them. [. . .] I don't know when it's going to happen, but it absolutely has to change'. (Slimane 2001, cited in Porter 2001)

By rejecting an exaggerated performance of masculinity in favour of a more ambiguous model Slimane's collections schematized the precarious nature of male identity in the opening decade of the twenty-first century. While the figure of rarefied ethereal beauty that he proposed was in some ways a problematic one – fetishizing youth, slimness and vulnerability – his intervention did act materially to open up discourses around the representation of masculinity. Slimane's ability to catalyze discourses and create new possibilities is evidenced both in media responses to his work and in his influence on popular and high-street fashions that I describe in the section 'A transformation of menswear'.

If fashion heralds social and political change, as Walter Benjamin suspects, it is intriguing to consider the place of Slimane's millennial man in a new ideology of gender. As I have described, Slimane's contribution to men's fashion was significant not only at the level of form and aesthetic but, through a deft manipulation of visual semantics, as an intervention in the language of masculinity. That this intervention was experienced as meaningful and significant, is evident both in the journalistic accounts of the early 2000s, and indeed, in my own more personal observations.

The notion that fashion acts as a *reflection* of society's values and mores is found in both Baudelaire (1864: 12) and Benjamin, and is an assumption implicit to much scholarly writing in the field. In this article, I have attempted to move beyond the model of fashion as a mirror by explicitly locating Hedi Slimane as a cultural actor. This approach is founded in my belief that fashion can be 'read' as an authored text as much as analysed as subtext, and can act as an intervention in culture as much as a reflection.

While it is difficult to anticipate the extent to which Slimane's design will continue to resonate in the future, his significance in the development of men's fashion in the first decade of this century is difficult to overstate.

The attention Slimane bought to Dior Homme instigated a renewed interest in menswear reflected in today's proliferation of menswear magazines, dedicated fashion weeks and new labels. By demonstrating that men's fashion could experiment with silhouette and fabrication, and with the language of masculinity, Slimane effectively expanded the parameters of what was deemed possible in his field, his influence is clearly evident in the work of contemporary designers including Kris Van Assche, Lucas Ossendrijver and Damir Doma who share many of his concerns for silhouette and fabrication. Beyond these direct influences, Slimane's formation of Dior Homme has gone on to embolden and enliven a new generation of designers by proving that creative menswear could be commercially viable. In this way, the formal and aesthetic diversity of contemporary men's fashion, and the new possibilities for the expression of gender it offers are the legacies of Slimane's pioneering approach.

Acknowledgements

I am indebted to Shaun Cole, Director of History and Culture of Fashion at the London College of Fashion for his insights into the theorization of menswear – and particularly gay men's dress, and to Professor Christopher Breward for his thoughts on the shifting critical discourses surrounding men's fashion. Alex Needham, Culture Editor of *The Guardian* was hugely generous in providing contextual knowledge of Slimane's inspiration and design methodologies during the early 2000s, for which I remain very grateful.

References

Anon. (1988), 'Mab Review: So Subtle', in Cliff Waller (ed), *Men's Wear*, 15th September, 35.

Anon. (1994a), 'Trends, military precision', in Kathryn Flett (ed), *Arena Homme +, 1, Spring/Summer 1994*, London: Wagadon, pp. 64–73.

Anon. (1994b), 'Chevignon' [advertisement], *Arena Homme+*, 1, Spring/Summer.

Anon. (2003), 'Iceberg, Homme+ SS03 Fashion: Second Skin', *Arena Homme+*, 19, Spring/Summer. p. 98.

Arnault, Bernard (2007), *2006 Annual Report: Combined Ordinary and Extraordinary Shareholders' Meeting*, Paris: Christian Dior.

Avedon, Richard (2001), 'Solitaire, Hedi Slimane for Dior Homme' [advertisement], *Arena Homme+*, 16, Autumn/Winter.

Avedon, Richard (2002), 'Dior Homme' [advertisement], *i-D*, no. 218, Spring/Summer.

Barnard, Malcolm (1996), *Fashion as Communication*, London [u.a.]: Routledge.

Baudelaire, C. (1864), *The Painter of Modern Life and Other Essays* (trans. J. Mayne), London: Phaidon Press.

Benjamin, W., & Tiedemann, R. (1999). *The Arcades Project*. Cambridge, Mass.: Belknap Press.

Breward, Christopher (1999), *The Hidden Consumer*, Manchester: Manchester University Press.

Cabasset, Patrick (2001), 'Portrait: Hedi Slimane: Le petit prince new-look de Dior Homme', 'Portrait: hedi slimane: the new-look little prince of dior homme', in Frédéric Beigbede *L'Officiel de la Couture et de la Mode de Paris*, No. 854, Paris: Les Éditions Jalou, pp. 66–71.

Clark, Adrian (1999a), 'All About Yves; As the new looks for the new millennium hit the catwalk last week, one label stood head and shoulders above the rest', *The Guardian*, 3rd of February 1999, Accessed 1 January 2012. Retrieved from http://www.theguardian.com/theguardian/1999/feb/03/features11.g2.

Clark, Adrian (1999b), '21st century boys', *The Guardian*, 9th of July 1999, Accessed 1 January 2012. Retrieved from http://www.theguardian.com/lifeandstyle/1999/jul/09/fashion4.

Cole, Shaun (2000), *Don We Now Our Gay Apparel: Gay Men's Dress in the 20th Century*, Oxford: Berg.

Edwards, Tim (1997), *Men in the Mirror: Men's Fashion, Masculinity and Consumer Society*, London: Cassell.

_____ (2006), *Cultures of Masculinity*, Oxford: Routledge.

Fuss, Diana (1992), 'Fashion and the homospectorial look', *Critical Inquiry*, 18:4, Accessed 10 April 2013. Retrieved from http://www.jstor.org/discover/10.2307/1343827?sid=21105561392353&uid=2&uid=4

Hanisch, Carol (1970), 'The personal is political', in S. Firestone and A. Koedt (eds), *Notes from the Second Year*, New York: Women's Liberation, pp. 76–78.

Healy, Murray (2001), 'Adam's ribs', in Fabien Baron, *Arena Homme+ Autumn/Winter 2001*, London: Wagadon, pp. 163–64.

Hebdige, Dick (1979), *Subculture: The Meaning of Style*, Abingdon, Oxfordshire: Taylor & Francis.

Kaiser, Susan B (2012), *Fashion and Cultural Studies*, London: Berg Publishers.

McRobbie, Angela (1998), *British Fashion Design: Rag Trade or Image Industry?*, London: Routledge.

Meisel, Steven (2005), 'Calvin Klein collection' [advertisement], *Arena Homme+*, 23, Spring/Summer.

Mort, Frank (1996), *Cultures of Consumption: Masculinities and Social Space in 20th Century Britain*, Oxford: Routledge.

Needham, Alex (2013), personal interview (Royal College of Art), 1 February.

Nixon, Sean (1996), *Hard Looks: Masculinities Spectatorship & Contemporary Consumption*, London: UCL Press.

Name, B., & O'Brien, G. (eds.), (2005), *Bande à part*, Paris: Éditions du Collectionneur.

Petri, Ray and Morgan, Jamie (1985), 'Pure Prairie: London cowboys lay down the law', *The Face*, October. pp. 68–71.

Plummer, David (1999), *One of the Boys: Masculinity Homophobia and Modern Manhood*, Binghampton, NY: Harrington Press.

Polhemus, Ted (1994), *Streetstyle: From Sidewalk to Catwalk*, New York: Thames and Hudson.

Porter, Charlie (2001), 'Body politic: In menswear it counts as a thrilling revolution: Hedi Slimane tells Charlie Porter why he's not interested in the musclebound look', 30th June 2001, *The Guardian*, Accessed 1 January 2012. Retrieved from http://www.theguardian.com/lifeandstyle/2001/jun/30/fashion1

Richardson, Niall (2010), *Transgressive Bodies: Representations in Film and Popular Culture*, London: Ashgate.

Roversi, Paolo (1985), 'Le Charme coincé de la Bourgeoisie', *Jean Paul Gaultier*, Autumn/Winter 1985/86, Accessed 30 March 2013. Retrieved from http://fashstash.net/post/8086980992/re-defining-the-gender-boundaries-in-fashion

Simpson, Mark (1994a), *Male Impersonators: Men Performing Masculinity*, London: Cassell.

____ (1994b), 'Here come the mirror men', *The Independent*, 15 November, Accessed 3 April 2013. Retrieved from http://www.marksimpson.com/here-come-the-mirror-men/.

Slimane, Hedi (2000), 'Yves Saint Laurent: Paris Ysl Fittings Winter 2001 January 2000', Autumn/Winter 2000/2001, Accessed 2 April 2013, Retrieved from http://www.hedislimane.com/fashiondiary/index.php?id=35.

____ (2005), 'Dior Homme, Autumn/Winter 2005/2006' [advertisement], *Another Man*, no. 1.

Sontag, Susan (1966), 'Notes On "Camp"', *Against Interpretation*, New York: Farah Straus and Giroux, pp. 275–92.

Topman (2009), 'Antony Price for Topman: In the trench', Spring/Summer, Accessed 9 April 2013. Retrieved from http://www.dazeddigital.com/fashion/article/6917/1/in-the-trench.

Verhagen, Damien (2009), 'Un été désastreux. Une journée formidable' lookbook.nu blog, Accessed 11 April 2013. Retrieved from http://lookbook.nu/look/213166-Louis-Vuitton-Evidence-Sunglasses-Jeanpaul-Gaultier

Walter, B. (1982), *The Arcades Project* (trans. H. Eiland and K. McLaughlin), Cambridge, MA: Harvard.

Weber, Bruce (1982), 'Tom Hintnaus models *Calvin Klein Underwear*', Accessed 2 April 2013. Retrieved from http://swanngalleriesinc.blogspot.co.uk/2011/04/calvin-kleins-controversial-ads-then.html

Wilson, Elizabeth (1985), *Adorned in Dreams*, London: Virago.

Discussion Questions

1. Why were Slimane's designs so well received? What qualities did they possess that made men want to consume the clothes?

2. What do you foresee as the next big revolution in menswear and what fashion innovators or fashion leaders do you feel will initiate the change?

2.2
Style and Substance: The Information Seeking Behavior of Fashion Bloggers

Kimberly Detterbeck, Nicole LaMoreaux, and Marie Sciangula

Introduction

Investigating the information seeking behaviors and research methods of particular populations is a well-established practice in librarianship. For example, one can easily find studies on how chemists look for information, how art historians do (or do not) use librarians, or how lawyers engage with research and resources. Building off of this theoretical model, we, the myMETRO Fashion Blogging Team, chose to investigate the research behaviors and methods of fashion bloggers. As per the description of the pilot project, we chose to study fashion bloggers because it is a population not traditionally associated with libraries nor traditional research methods. We saw this as an opportunity to reach out to individuals who don't necessarily view themselves as researchers or have any relationship with librarians or information professionals. Most library literature on blogs is concerned with two things: "how libraries can use them as communication or marketing tools for their library, and how librarians are using them as information resources for their own professional knowledge" (Eades, 2011, p. 12).

In contrast, our report focuses on the creation of blog posts and the information needs and gathering methods required for said creation. The premise of our study was to find out how bloggers function as researchers and knowledge creators. The research we conducted, via surveys and email interviews, aims to shed light on this process, albeit on a small scale, and helps to assist other librarians who may work with and/or serve this particular user group. The intended audience of this report will likely be librarians, information specialists, archivists and other researchers serving and working with the fashion industry.

For the sake of this report, we recognized the accepted definition of a blog as "a contraction of the words 'web' and 'log.' Blogs are internet sites on which individuals regularly publish their thoughts on a particular subject." Blogs are comprised of individual posts, often displayed in reverse chronological order, and often contain text, images, video, and music (Rocamora, 2011, p. 408). Fashion blogs are one subset of blogs that focus on fashion and style. Fashion blogs generally encompass three sub-genres (or types): street style ("blogs that highlight the 'best' of street fashion by capturing and posting photographs online"), personal style ("bloggers post pictures of themselves documenting their style"), and commentary and coverage of the industry's events, news, and shows (Leung, 2011, para 3 & Rocamora, 2011, p. 407).

Literature Review

For the purposes of this report and research study, we limited the scope of literature consulted and included in our literature review. We honed in on literature from library and fashion publications that specifically discuss how fashion bloggers find and use information. We purposely avoided literature on blogging and bloggers in general as to stay within the limited scope of our investigation. We also steered clear of literature on the broader fashion industry as fashion bloggers are a unique subgroup. We gathered background information from journal articles, interviews, conference keynote speakers, and books published by some of the more prominent fashion bloggers of the world.

Much of the literature, both scholarly and popular, about fashion blogging has focused on consumption (how the reader interacts with blogs, finds blogs, etc.); how fashion blogging relates to traditional fashion journalism; and the growing incorporation of bloggers into various sectors of the fashion industry.[1] Very little scholarship focuses on the creation of fashion blogs from the bloggers' point

---

Please see Alobaidat (2009), Claire (2009), Corcoran (2006), Dodes (2006), Grauel (2009), La Ferla (2008), Pham (2011).

of view—what goes into making a post or an entire blog; what type of research, if any, fashion bloggers conduct; and how fashion bloggers obtain and use information for the creation of their blogs. Even less literature exists on fashion blogs in library literature. What does exist focuses on how blogs serve as information sources for library patrons not on the blog creators themselves and on library resources for fashion students and faculty. The oft-cited article "Inspiration and Information: Sources for the Fashion Designer and Historian" by Gaye Smith (1989) comes closest to what we hope to achieve. Smith outlines where fashion designers and historians look for information and inspiration, emphasizing the importance of serials and magazines for following fashion trends and seeking visual information. Fashion bloggers seek some of the same information. Smith alludes to predictions of style, market trends, and visual sources of creative inspiration in her study. Vivienne Eades' article "Fashion blogs: too trendy for libraries or useful resources?" offers a justification for fashion blogs as a legitimate source of information for fashion students. While Ms. Eades does not look at fashion bloggers as a user group, the information seeking behaviors she describes for fashion students might be just as relevant for fashion bloggers as they can be, in some cases, one in the same.

In conducting our literature review, we found three notable researchers investigating fashion blogs and bloggers: Alice Marwick, Agnès Rocamora, and Eleanor Snare. Alice Marwick, a postdoctoral social software researcher in the Social Media Collective at Microsoft Research New England, studies online identity and consumer culture. Specifically Ms. Marwick investigates social status and conspicuous consumption online as demonstrated by fashion bloggers. In her presentation "Conspicuous and Authentic: Fashion Blogs, Style, and Consumption" Ms. Marwick provides a succinct summary of the fashion blogging universe which provides macro level context to our study. Although the bulk of her presentation focuses on how fashion bloggers exemplifies conspicuous consumption in the 21st century (a topic not immediately relevant to our investigation), her research does expound upon topics that inform the analysis of our survey results such as the importance of authenticity or perceived authenticity to the success of blogs and recognition of style curation as a valued and legitimate skill.

Also studying the practices and social impact of fashion bloggers is Eleanor Snare, who completed a dissertation on the relationships between fashion bloggers, the fashion industry, and contemporary social structures at the University of Leeds in 2011. Ms. Snare's research focuses on fashion blogs as "an important element of the contemporary fashion commodity chain" (p. 2). Her paper explicates the many tasks fashion bloggers undertake in order to run a successful blog, which serves to inform their information needs and practices. It should also be noted that Ms. Snare also uses empirical knowledge as gleaned via an online questionnaire, i.e. survey. Like us, Ms. Snare polled fashion bloggers on what they do although she did not explicitly ask them about how they conduct research or look for information.

Most notable and relevant to our study is the work of Agnès Rocamora, Senior Research Fellow and Senior Lecturer in Cultural and Historical Studies at University of the Arts London. Ms. Rocamora has written extensively on fashion blogs as a new media and interplay between fashion blogs and tradition fashion journalism as evidenced in magazines and newspapers. Ms. Rocamora's 2012 article "Hypertextuality and Remediation in the Fashion Media" was especially enlightening since it discusses some of the practices that go into creating blog posts. Ms. Rocamora explains that posts, fashion blogposts in particular, are often comprised of a series of links to other web material. This linking not only makes up the content of the blog but also serves as the most basic and most accepted form of citation in the blogosphere. The author also explains the transient nature of blog post creation and the post themselves; like much of the Internet's content, blog posts are expected to be created and consumed quickly. Fashion bloggers are expected by their readers to create hyper-up-to-date content, increasingly involving "live blogging" e.g. writing about an event in real-time. Rocamora also develops the idea of "expert paradigm" or the shifting notion of expertise in light of user-generated content. The expert paradigm plays into how fashion bloggers develop content for their posts and informs their information seeking methods.

Methodology

Fashion blogging, like all blogging, has grown exponentially. According to Blogger.com, slightly more than 2 million bloggers, as of July 2010, were classified as being "with an industry of fashion" (as cited in Rocamora, 2011, p. 409). While we would have loved to survey all 2 million of those fashion bloggers, we realized that we needed to identify a more manageable research population with which to work. A fashion blogger colleague, Pamala Gomes, directed us towards the professional fashion blogging network Independent Fashion Bloggers (IFB). IFB, founded in 2007, has a community of about 3,000 registered users, all of whom must have an independent fashion website in order to participate as a member. With both well established and emerging bloggers represented in IFB's membership, along with (what we perceived as) easy avenues to member communication, we determined that IFB provided an ideal research population.

We took a two-fold approach to gathering information about fashion bloggers' research methods. First we distributed a public survey using a Google form: http://goo.gl/x4Ji8. The survey questions explicitly asked bloggers what information they need to write posts, where they find that information, and how they would utilize the expertise of an information professional. Also included were demographic questions and details about their specific blog. We constructed the questions as simply as possible, avoiding words like "research," "methodology," "library," and "citation" as these terms do not resonate with fashion bloggers and would probably discourage participation in the survey. Pointed and directed questions allowed us to extract the information seeking methodologies of fashion bloggers without using explicit "library" jargon. We also included a question asking participants if they would be willing to be contacted for follow-up questioning.

The largest challenge we faced by far was distributing the survey and soliciting responses. Our initial method was to approach Jennine Jacob (née Tamm), IFB's founder and site administrator, in hopes of having the survey mentioned and/or linked to from IFB's homepage. What we realized and what we continued to experience, was that fashion bloggers, especially those at the level of Ms. Jacob, are saturated with a variety digital communications (emails, texts, Tweets, Facebook messages, etc). In this message rich environment, it was impossible to stand out among the crowd of emails Ms. Jacob receives daily and thus we never received a response.

Realizing that we would not enjoy the wide exposure that having a presence on IFB's homepage would grant, we explored other avenues of disseminating the survey. A large channel of distribution was through social networking sites such as Facebook, Twitter, Pinterest, Tumblr, LinkedIn, and the IFB member discussion board. The aforementioned fashion blogger colleague, Pamala Gomes, is a member of the IFB community and offered to post a link to the survey on IFB's many discussion forums on our behalf. Her insight was invaluable when communicating with fashion bloggers because of her direct involvement with and membership in IFB. In order to make the survey attractive to fashion bloggers, Ms. Gomes advised us to make our marketing of the survey look like a typical fashion blog post, i.e. more images, less text! To that end, Ms. Gomes created an infographic for the survey using Polyvore, a social fashion and style community website.

The image evolved to become the logo of our project and the main mechanism for marketing, especially on social media sites. Finally, we sent targeted emails to fashion bloggers featured in the publication, Style Diaries: World Fashion from Berlin to Tokyo by Simone Werle, an international fashion blog directory. In all of our marketing communication, The Fashion Blogging Team struggled with finding a balance between coming across as professional yet approachable; we discovered that the world of fashion blogging is an informal and collegial one. In an effort to be taken seriously and to not be perceived as "spam" or "pitches," the tone of our communication with fashion bloggers was initially perceived as too formal and thus blatantly interpreted as outside their community. The image created in Polyvore certainly helped mitigate the disparity and bridge a gap between academic librarianship and fashion blogging but ultimately our survey suffered from a lack of exposure. As we are not part of this community, we did not have a direct nor far reaching pipeline to the fashion blogger membership.

Figure 2.8 myMETRO Fashion Blogging Team Survey Logo

In light of our shift in perception, we adjusted the tone of our direct communication to bloggers; we took a more informal and relaxed tone when using social networking tools and sending emails. The survey went live March 2012 and stayed active until the end of April. During that time, we received 31 responses, 19 of whom indicated that we could contact them for a follow-up interview.

Recognizing that the information needs and seeking behavior of fashion bloggers is probably too nuanced to be completely described a 20-question survey, we included the question about follow-up contact. We hoped to conduct in-depth interviews with the individual fashion bloggers who showed interest in being contacted further. We composed eight additional questions, two of which were individualized to the blogger's survey responses. Through these questions, we hoped to gain detailed insight into how the information gathered was used and how fashion blog posts are created. The initial survey sought to have respondents identify information needs and information acquisition. The follow-up questions aimed to address the use of information to create new knowledge, i.e. blog posts. After repeated emails, we have only received one answer to our follow-up interview request.

Results

Qualitative data is an important part of this study; therefore the majority of the survey questions were in-depth, open-ended questions about process and methods. The entire text of the survey can be found in Appendix I. Given the small sample size – only 31 fashion bloggers took our survey within a two month period – we understand that the conclusions drawn may not be representative of all fashion bloggers. As explained in the

Methodology section, we attribute the low response rate to difficulties connecting with fashion bloggers amid the sea of correspondence they receive.

Demographics of the Bloggers and Their Blogs

The fashion bloggers who responded to our survey represent a variety of ages and geographies. The vast majority (70.9%) fall within the 19–29 age group. 9.6% of respondents are 13–19 years of age, 12.9% are 30–39, and 6.4% are 40–49.

Our survey received responses from around the world. The largest percentage of bloggers said they are based in New York City (32.2%) with Los Angeles, Italy and Manila, Philippines (6.4%) tied for second place. Others locations represented are Alabama, Toronto, Miami, New Jersey, Australia, Florida, Edmonton, Scotland, Latvia, Milan, Glasgow, Barcelona, San Francisco, Chicago, and Germany. The 31 bloggers who participated in our survey represent 10 different countries; the fashion industry is no longer exclusively tied to major cosmopolitan cities like New York, Paris, and Milan.

In terms of gender, our survey participants are reflective of fashion bloggers as a whole. The majority (87%) of our respondents identify as female. According to Alice Marwick (2011), fashion bloggers are overwhelmingly female, especially high-profile bloggers who have received the attention of the fashion industry (p. 1). We did have a few male bloggers (9.6%) and one respondent did not answer.

Inspiration and information needed to create individual blog posts

Inspiration for the surveyed bloggers varied. The most common sources of inspiration come from fashion news

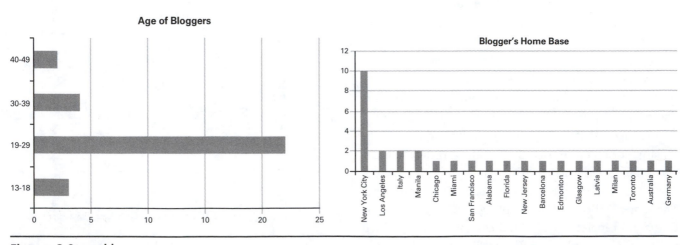

Figures 2.9a and b

and trends (18) and bloggers' personal experiences (12). Other sources of inspiration include:

- personal style (5),
- street style (4),
- entertainment and pop culture (4),
- budget and finance (3),
- websites and blogs (3),
- magazines, nature, music (2),
- content post to social networking sites such as Pinterest and Polyvore (1),
- travel (1),
- dreams (1)

In terms of information needs, almost half of all respondents (14) agreed that high-resolution images are key component to their fashion blogs. Other sources of information are press releases (2), historical trend data (4), statistics (1), prices and other cost considerations (2) and brand information (2). Some respondents said that magazines (3) and newspapers (2), model/styling information (1) were helpful elements in creating their own blog posts. Other needs included access to the Internet (4), laws regarding transgendered people (1), other blogs (2), background information on trends (1), personal accounts (4), and interviews with industry professionals (1).

Conducting research and gathering resources for individual blog posts

The survey revealed that most bloggers conduct their research using the Internet (90.3%). Other research methods include photographing street style (48.3%) and interviews with industry professionals (25.8%). Others said they use personal experience, magazines, and/or books to conduct their research (6.4%). Some use Fashion Weeks to help them conduct their research (9.6%). Other places included libraries, stores, conferences/expos, movies, and nature (3.2%). Most of the bloggers tend to use magazines and journals (26). Some respondents chose to use other blogs (24) and websites (23) to gather information regarding individual blog posts. Newspapers were also a big resource for our bloggers to use for their posts (12). One blogger each responded saying that they used events that they attended, books, and original interviews.

Collaborating with Others

All respondents reported that they do not collaborate with other bloggers to produce posts. However, three respondents (9.6%) indicated that they would collaborate with other fashion bloggers given the opportunity.

When asked which circumstances would inspire collaboration, the most common response emphasized the idea of a mutual partnership; whomever they work with would need to have the same aesthetic and/or beliefs as they do. Others were interested in cross-promotion for both their own blogs and the blog of the person with whom they collaborated (2). One person said that if they couldn't attend an event they would ask another blogger or a friend who was a good writer to attend and post on their blog on

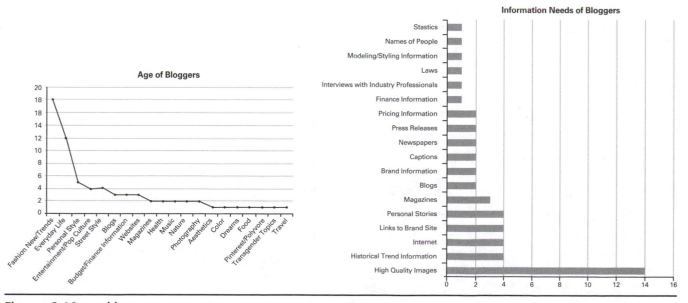

Figures 2.10a and b

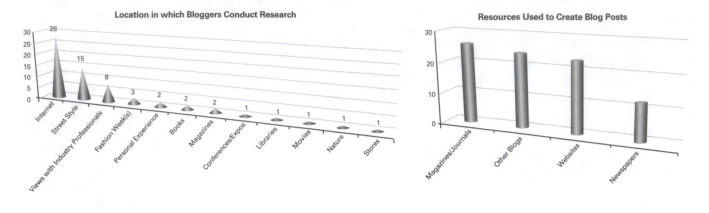

Figures 2.11a and b

their behalf. One respondent said they were interested in sponsorship (partnering with a brand). Others said travel inspires collaboration as well as the idea of working with someone who is expressive and inspiring (2).

Consistent Difficulty Finding Information Needed for Fashion Blogging

When we asked the surveyed fashion bloggers about what information is consistently difficult to obtain but is required to create their posts, most survey respondents left the question blank. One blogger stated that "nothing" is difficult to find when it comes to locating and obtaining information for their posts. Three other respondents stated that they know where to find the information they need. Among the challenges indicated were finding high-resolution images (3), and photographers (2). Unique and original content was also mentioned as a challenge. One blogger noted that that they had trouble finding information about Search Engine Optimization (SEO), in that they wanted to know more about what it is and how it can benefit their blog. Two respondents noted that they had trouble obtaining media passes required to gain entry into events and fashion shows. Other respondents indicated that they needed help finding unbiased information and information on products and advice for transgendered people.

The Role of Image Searching and Acquisition

We asked respondents to describe the role that searching for and acquiring images plays in the creation of their blogs posts. Sixteen commented that that they utilize their personal images and therefore do not have to worry about copyright issues. Others noted that they use other websites (13) and blogs (5) as a major source for images used on

their own blog. Some respondents said that they credit the sites from which they take these images and photos and use hyperlinks to link back to the original image. Several respondents noted that other image resources that they consult are websites like Tumblr, Polyvore, and Stock Photos. One respondent said that the companies would send products to photograph.

Image subscription services

Given the importance of images to fashion blogs, we were interested in whether or not bloggers use images services such as Getty Images, iStock Photo, or stock.xchng. Only two (6.4%) out of a total of 31 respondents subscribe to an image service, which often has copyright clearance included in the cost of the photo. Services specifically mentioned include Fashion Gone Rogue, Weheartit, and stock.xchng.

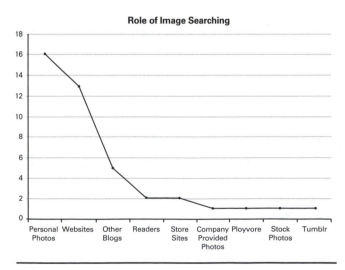

Figure 2.12

Information Subscription Services

Beyond images, we asked the fashion bloggers which information subscription services they use. Most bloggers reported that they use magazines to assist them with their blog posts such as Vogue, GQ, V Magazine, Glamour, Elle, InStyle, and Details (9). Others use various websites such as Refinery 29, Chictopia, and Style.com to assist them with the composition of their blog posts (7). The New York Times (NYT) and Women's Wear Daily (WWD) were popular answers as well (5). Two responded that they consult other bloggers for information. One respondent mentioned Flipboard (a social reader application) and another said when they have time they go to press sites to locate information for their posts.

Employing the services of professional researchers

We were interested in surveying fashion bloggers to find out what kinds of tasks they would want a professional researcher (librarian or other information professional) to perform or assist them with if they were able to employ such services. Most bloggers (10) responded that they either would not use a professional researcher or gave no answer to this question. If they were to utilize the skills of a professional researcher, they would have the researcher investigate:

- fashion forecasting (5),
- blog optimization (3),
- employing photographers,
- proper photo editing and acquisition,

- avenues for inspiration,
- celebrity culture and images (2)

Others would like help with pricing, reader needs, photo organization, unique content creation, Fashion Week scheduling, fit for various body styles and gender identities, effective social networking, and interview question construction.

Follow-up questions and visibility of the survey

The majority of bloggers indicated that they would be willing to be contacted for a follow-up interview about their blogging process (61.2%). Only one respondent stated that they would not be willing to be contacted for follow-up. However, after repeatedly reaching out to these bloggers, only one submitted responses to our follow-up questions. Many respondents discovered the survey via a direct email from the Researchers (35.4%). The second largest respondent group found out about the survey through a friend (12.9%). However, we did not ask this question on the original survey and therefore unintentionally missed 12.9% of our respondents. 9.6% of respondents did not answer the question.

Analysis & Conclusion

Although our sample size is small compared to the ever-growing number of fashion bloggers, there are general conclusions we can make about how this user group approaches research and information-seeking. Based on our research, we posit three observations about the information seeking behavior of fashion bloggers:

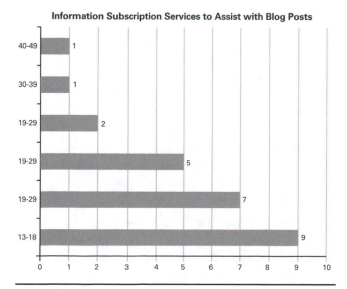

Figure 2.13

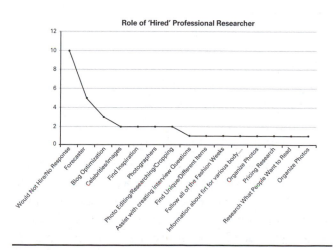

Figure 2.14

1. the importance of appearing authentic and knowledgeable discourages bloggers from consulting information professionals for research assistance;
2. the majority of fashion bloggers tend to access and use information in a manner characteristic of millennials. This along with blogging's inherently fast-paced nature stymies in-depth research;
3. fashion blogging hinges on information sharing among bloggers and other online sources but a fair and consistent standard of citation has not been established.

Authenticity

As evidenced by the literature on fashion bloggers and their qualitative comments, a bloggers' success is most often evaluated on the notion of authenticity or having a unique voice. Bloggers must demonstrate that their opinions have value and credibility; otherwise they will not obtain and retain readership and advertisers. "The indication of individual identity through the curation and display of clothing and accessories is in keeping with the ethos of social media, which emphasizes authenticity above all" Marwick 2010). To achieve this legitimacy, a blogger's opinions have to be rooted in a vast knowledge of fashion and style. Doing outside research and consulting an information professional for help would give the appearance that the blogger didn't have the sufficient knowledge base to run an impactful blog. When asked "If you could employ the services of a professional researcher, what would you have them do?" one respondent stated, "I wouldn't. That would take a large part of my work away that I truly enjoy doing." Another responder from Spain stated, "I prefer to be my own researcher." It is clear that the surveyed fashion bloggers hold authenticity in high regards and are reluctant to transfer responsibility of knowledge curation and acquisition to a professional (read: non-fashion blogger) researcher.

Most bloggers who responded to our survey did not answer our query about employing the services of a professional or stated that they do not need the help of the researcher. Those who did provide an answer to this question described tasks normally associated with the work of a personal assistant—keeping track of fashion industry events, taking photographs, and staying informed on fashion trends. In response to "What information do you need for fashion blogging that is consistently difficult to find or obtain?" a blogger stated "I have the opposite problem; I have too much content, too many products

to review (to the point that I now very rarely accept a product by mail), and an average of 8+ events/week to attend with generally very generous gift bags of products to try. Staying organized and on top of my calendar is the difficult part." Another blogger responded that they need help "organizing . . . my own images." A third stated, "I'd love my personal photographer for taking pictures when at fashion weeks and other go outs. But otherwise I like to do everything myself. I'm not very trustful when it comes to these kinds of things." These quotes indicate that fashion bloggers' immediate needs are not research assistance but instead personal and organizational assistance.

As reported in the literature and as demonstrated by our respondents, personal fashion blogs are primarily based on personal experiences and style and made up of self-generated content. Often the information needed for a new post literally resides in the fashion bloggers' closet and thus few secondary sources are needed to create a personal fashion blog post. As one blogger stated, "for me it's not difficult to find the information for my fashion blog because all the texts are made by me." Since much of fashion blog content is opinion based, it is not obvious or appropriate to conduct research in the traditional sense. A blogger from Alabama stated, "I am not sure that [hiring an information professional] would be useful for my blog, since I use mine mostly . . . [to] express personal opinions." These bloggers view themselves as individualists in both their style and opinions and therefore are hesitant to consult sources outside of themselves and their experiences.

Since fashion bloggers operate in an environment where authenticity (or perceived authenticity) is the defining factor of success, librarians need to present themselves not as information providers but as a "toolkit" for better information acquisition. Information professionals seeking to serve fashion bloggers would be advised to focus on marketing access to diverse and rich fashion-related materials, especially periodicals like Women's Wear Daily, Vogue, Harper's Bazaar and trend forecasting periodicals such as CAUSeffect, Close-Up, and Collezioni. Most bloggers are independent and not in the financial position to subscribe to these often costly resources. Although bloggers may not have institutional affiliations, most librarians, are willing and delighted to answer questions from the public.

Survey results also indicated that fashion bloggers tend to be confident searchers. In step with most millennials (and it should be noted that most, 70.9%, of our respondents are in the 19–29 age group) fashion bloggers believe that they already know how to find all the information they need. As one blogger stated, "It's not difficult to find if you know where to look. For me it's been this way." Another indicated, "Nothing is hard to obtain in this day and age if you know where to look" and a third stated, "I tend to find all that I need." While the millennial bloggers tend to believe that they know how and where to look for everything that they would need, we are sure that librarians would be able to assist in their search by offering their skills and knowledge of subject keywords and the workings of individual databases.

Prêt-à-porter le Blog

Blogging, fashion and otherwise, is a fast-paced endeavor. In order to attract and maintain readership and attention in the internet's crowded information sphere, a blog must provide frequent and timely updates. As Lovink (2008) puts it, "Technology such as the Internet lives on the principle of permanent change . . . The 'tyranny of the new' rule" (p. xi). "Witness the live streaming of fashion shows, events once the preserve of an elite given the privilege to see the collections months ahead of their appearance in print media and in shops" (Rocamora, 2012, p. 97). This need and want for instant gratification is demonstrated below.

Rocamora continues, "in their constant, often daily, updating of sites with new posts, fashion blogs feed into this tyranny of the new, constructing, more than any other media, fashion as transient, passing, already gone (p. 97). Not only must bloggers create content at a rate that keeps up with the industry and the expectations of its readers but also to remain competitive with other blogs. As on blogger stated, "It's very difficult to not write about the same news and write fashion news before other bloggers!" The pressure fashion bloggers experience to constantly update their blogs with new and unique postings causes them to prioritize quantity over well-researched, quality posts.

Fashion blogging's rapid pace does not lend itself to in-depth and complex research that is often the purview of librarians and libraries. The over 90% of fashion bloggers that reported they find the majority of their information on the Internet supports this information seeking practice; for information to be useful to a fashion blogger it must be easily and quickly accessible, without the need for complex searches or time-consuming investigations.

Fast-paced, easily accessible information seeking is also in line with that of millennials. As supported by the 2011 report "'If It Is Too Inconvenient, I'm Not Going After It:' Convenience as a Critical Factor in Information-seeking Behaviors," the "centrality of convenience is especially prevalent among . . .millennial[s] (Connaway, Dickey, & Radford, p. 22), citing the importance of complete and easy access to resources when appealing to this age group. As stated above, most bloggers who responded to our survey fall within this demographic. An excellent summary of the characteristics of the millennial generation is provided by Mark McMahon and Romana Pospisil (2005) in their article "Laptops for a Digital Lifestyle: Millennial Students and Wireless Mobile Technologies." They state:

The world in which millennial students have grown up is typically rich with technology, information and digital media and they have been exposed to IT from a very young age. The millennial generation stay connected by using SMS, mobile phones, chatrooms and email while they simultaneously play computer games, listen to music and watch TV (Frand, 2000, p. 18; Oblinger, 2003; Rickard & Oblinger, 2003). They have adapted to continuous multitasking and switch from one activity to another quickly and with minimal readjustment time (Brown, 2000, p. 13). These students are accustomed to fast food, fast everything and have zero tolerance for delays (Frand, 2000).

Librarians catering to fashion bloggers could consider the advice of Connaway, Dickey, and Radford:

In the current environment, most people do not have time to spend searching for information or learning how to use a new information source or access method. In order to be one of the first choices for information, library systems and interfaces need to look familiar to people by resembling popular Web interfaces, and library services need to be easily accessible and require little or no training to use (p. 28).

Librarians might not be able to assist with the immediacy of individual posts. However, we could aid fashion bloggers by providing access to information that would allow their posts to have original content as well as help to better equip bloggers with the skills and strategies necessary to quickly find quality information. As we stated above, if we present ourselves as 'toolkits' that provide access to information, we could potentially assist them in making their immediate postings unique. While there might be more than one blogger attending an event and uploading posts on the spot, with unique knowledge of said event or designer, the blogger who employs an information specialist or librarian could provide a unique spin on the posts.

Linking = Citing?

In both the survey and the personalized follow-up interview, bloggers stated that most of their images and blog posts come from personal photography and experiences. However, blogging also depends heavily upon borrowed text and images from other online sources. Rocamora (2012) refers to this concept as hypertextuality. "With the World Wide Web, however, and the blogosphere in particular, hypertextuality has proliferated. It is the very structure blogs rest on. When the reader clicks on a link, images (both still and moving), words and sounds can come at once on the screen, quickly succeeding and completing each other" (p. 95). She continues, "fashion blogs constantly relate to other blogs, be it through directly linking to them in a post or by including them in their blogroll, the list of blogs and the related links bloggers favour" (p. 96). As is clear, blogs refer to each other or "cite" not using an official citation standard like Chicago or MLA, like what is customary in traditional scholarship, but simply via the practice of "linking" or creating a hyperlink that refers back to the original source.

Since there are no clearly defined standards, the question then becomes one concerned with best practices for citing information sources. When asked during the follow-up interview, one blogger said "If there are any phrases or images I would like to borrow, I always make sure to cite all my sources by posting the links on where the reader may find them." When asked to describe the role of image searching and acquisition, many respondents said that they freely use images from other sites and expressed that they did not worry too much with regards to copyright. In order to feel as though they were citing the website or blogger of the photo(s) that they had used they either listed the site/blogger's name or linked back to their site. One stated, "In my full knowledge and opinion, it is very much acceptable for anyone and everyone to reuse all images off the World Wide Web PROVIDED they clearly and VISIBLY cite their references and all links to where they originally "borrowed" the images from." So much of fashion blogging is linking to other posts. It was a general consensus among the respondents that this is considered the accepted citation style of the fashion world.

The flipside of linking to a website or blog with regard to copyright and citation is whether or not bloggers are concerned with others linking to their own blogs, which can sometimes include their own original content. Do they use Creative Commons to protect their posts or do they use watermarks on their images? We had one respondent answer our individualized follow-up interview and stated that they did not believe that they were a well-known blogger so that this was not a current issue. She was:

> genuinely concerned about other bloggers or anybody who do not ask permission to use my original images. There is no current policy that protects all users on the internet for the images that they upload to be used without their consent. Right now, the internet can access anybody's images and anybody really can own any image found on the internet unless specified. Sad to say that not even watermarks on the images can deter people from editing them to claim it as their own.

What is most interesting about this sentiment is bloggers' desire for protection over their own images and texts while simultaneously assuming the right, entitlement, and flexibility to freely use third-party content without going through official clearance channels. This behavior is symptomatic of information sharing and exchange on the Internet, especially in the blogosphere which encourages and is built upon easy and seamless knowledge exchange.

IFB does offer some guidance for its bloggers. Taylor Davies, author of the post "Legally Blog: Know Your Rights," provides basic explanations of key copyright concepts such as fair use, plagiarism, and the Digital Millennium Copyright Act (DMCA). While this document is certainly a step in the right direction in standardizing sharing among blogs, the counsel offered is often vague and cursory. For example, Creative Commons Licenses, which in many respects are tailor-made for blog content, are not mentioned at all. Additionally when discussing fair use, the document states "Generally, say you republish a photo from another source to comment on it, or someone takes a paragraph from and then comments on it, that's okay. If you're not adding anything, – taking a photo from somewhere else and commenting on it it's usually okay." Unfortunately, the oversimplified language of this seemingly authoritative document does not arm bloggers with the tools needed to navigate complex and serious copyright concerns.

In another post, "Should Start-ups Get Permission to Use Blogger Images?," Davies (2012) questions the practice of aggregator sites drawing content from fashion and style blogs and instructs bloggers on how to protect themselves from sites borrowing their content. While the intended audience of this post is probably style bloggers (those bloggers who post images of themselves and do not rely on images from the open web or image services), the focus of IFB's input on copyright (and judging by the comments left by our respondents, bloggers themselves) concerns the protection of content creators, not proper and ethical information use.

If our respondents' comments and documents such as those produced by IFB are any indication, fashion bloggers are certainly in need of guidance and instruction on intellectual property and copyright. Librarians and information professionals trained in these areas are the ideal partners in this endeavor and opens up the possibility for enhanced collaboration between fashion blogosphere and the library world.

Future Considerations

As this project came to a close, we realized that there were several unanticipated avenues for further research. In the literature, especially trade periodicals and newspapers, fashion bloggers are often contrasted with traditional journalists. The next step in examining how fashion bloggers use and find information would likely be to find comparable studies of journalists within librarianship's literature and examine any parallels and/or deviations between the two populations.

Additionally, when constructing the literature review for this report, we came across several books authored by more prominent fashion bloggers. While many bloggers said that they felt like they did not need professional assistance in regards to daily posts, we had to wonder, would they need research assistance with a more substantial publication such as a book? More research could be conducted with regards to the publication process of putting together a book versus a fashion blog.

Finally, as fashion bloggers appear to share many of the habits of millennials, a more comprehensive examination of fashion bloggers as millennial information users is warranted. Are fashion bloggers truly unique in their information seeking methods or do they simply behave like millennials operating within a niche context? The more we analyzed the survey results and delved into the literature on millennials, the more this parallel resonated with us. Given the scope of this report, we were only able to touch upon this intriguing dynamic, but there is certainly much more to be explored and examined. It is also pertinent to examine the methods and behaviors of fashion bloggers not within the millennial age group. For example, our survey respondents included bloggers aged 30–39 (12.9%) and 40–49 (6.4%). We felt that it would be interesting to see how those populations seek for, interact with, and utilize information within the context of fashion blogging.

References

Alobaidat, W. (Ed). (2009). The Fashion Blogger Issue – Part I [Special Issue]. Sketchbook Magazine, 1. Retrieved from http://sketchbookmagazine.com/archive .php

Brown, J. (2002, Feb.). Growing up digital: How the web changes work, education, and the ways people learn. USDLA Journal 16 (2): 1–18.

Claire. (2009. Dec. 27). The New York Times catches on to the impact of fashion bloggers [Web log post]. Retrieved from http://fashionbombdaily.com/2009/12/27 /the-new-york-times-catches-onto-the-impact-of -fashion-bloggers/

Connaway, L. S., Dickey, T.J, & Radford, M.L. (2011). 'If it is too inconvenient, I'm not going after it.:' Convenience as a critical factor in information-seeking behaviors." Library and Information Science Research, 33: 179–190.

Corcoran, C. T. (2006). The blogs that took over the tents. Women's Wear Daily, 191.

Davies, T. (2012, April 30). Legally blog: Know your rights and protect your content [Web log post]. Retrieved from http://heartifb.com/2012/04/30/legally-blog -know-your-rights-and-protect-your-content/

Davies, T. (2012, April 20). Should start-ups get permission to use blogger Images? [Web log post]. Retrieved from http://heartifb.com/2012/04/20 /should-start-ups-get-permission-to-use-blogger -images/

Dodes. R. (2006, Sept. 16). Bloggers get under the tent. The Wall Street Journal. Retrieved from http://online .wsj.com

Frand, J. (2000, September/October). The information age mindset: Changes in students and implications for higher education. EDUCAUSE Review, 35(5), 15–24.

Grauel, J. (2009, Dec. 29). The growing Influence of fashion blogs: How fashion blogs are taking over the world [Web log post]. Retrieve from http://www .hercampus.com/style/growing-influence-fashion -blogs-how-fashion-blogs-are-taking-over-world

La Ferla, R. (2005, Sept. 8). Online, feisty critics. The New York Times. Retrieved from http://www.nytimes.com

Leung, B. (2011, March 8). The rise of the fashion blogger: Actual democratization of the fashion industry? Phreshly Squeezed. Retrieved from http://www.phreshly-squeezed.net/2011/05/rise-fashion-blogger-actual-democratization-fashion-industry/

Lovink, G. (2008). Zero comments: Blogging and critical internet culture. London: Routledge.

Marwick, A. (2011). Conspicuous and authentic: Fashion blogs, style, and consumption. Presented at the International Communication Association, Boston, MA. Retrieved from http://www.tiara.org/papers/marwick_conspicuousauthentic.pdf

McMahon, M. and Pospisil, R. (2005). Proceedings from Australasian Society for Computers in Tertiary Education. Brisbane, Australia. Laptops for a digital lifestyle: Millennial students and wireless mobile technologies. Retrieved from http://www.ascilite.org.au/conferences/brisbane05/blogs/proceedings/49_McMahon%20&%20Pospisil.pdf

Oblinger, D. (2003, July/August). Boomers & gen-xers, millennials: Understanding the new students. EDUCAUSE Review 38 (4): 37–47.

Pham, M.-H. T. (2011). Blog ambition: Fashion, feelings, and the political economy of the digital raced body. Camera Obscura, 26 (176), 1–37.

Rickard, W., & Oblinger, D. (2003, June 17–18). Higher education leaders symposium: The next-generation student, Redmond, Washington. Retrieved from http://www.educause.edu/ir/library/pdf/NLI0425a.pdf

Rocamora, A. (2012). Hypertextuality and remediation in the fashion media. Journalism Practice, 6(1), 92–106.

Rocamora, A. (2011). Personal fashion blogs: Screens and mirrors in digital self-portraits. Fashion Theory, 15 (4), 407–424.

Smith, G. (1989). Inspiration and information: sources for the fashion designer and historian. Art Libraries Journal, 14 (4): 11–16.

Snare, E. (2011). Work hard, consume hard: Fashion blogging as a site of labour and production on the fashion commodity chain (Dissertation). University of Leeds.

Werle, S. (2010). Style diaries: World fashion from Berlin to Tokyo. Munich: Prestel Verlag.

Discussion Questions

1. What steps would you take to establish authenticity in a blog and how would you communicate this to your readers?

2. What is your opinion of "borrowing" content from other bloggers without citing them? Is this an issue in the blogs you read? Do you think the originator of information or images should be cited?

2.3
Attention Deficit Fashion
Andrew Reilly and Jana Hawley

Introduction

This article offers a conceptual framework for understanding the current social and industrial structure that has resulted in what we term 'Attention Deficit Fashion (ADF). ADF is the result of the current condition of Internet fame, social media, fast fashion, the constant need for newness that is commonplace among the generations who are considered natives in a digital world (Prensky, 2001), the consumer power of this group, and the market's desire to meet this consumer demand. The result of these conditions are what we term mirco-trends.

Limited scholarship exists that examines fashion or the fashion industry under the rubric of post-postmodernism. Scholars have noted that the postmodern age appears to

Originally published in *Fashion, Style, & Popular Culture*

be waning and what is emerging is an era highlighted by (among other things) excessive consumption, waste, technology, and social media. The purpose of this article is to add to the literature on this subject. The framework that we offer can help guide researchers as they study current conditions and how they relate to fashion and appearance phenomena.

The Current Condition: Post-postmodernism

The fashion industry, as it was traditionally understood, was a product of the modern age. Although scholars argue over the historic dates of modernity (anywhere from mid-15th century to late 20th century), modernism is typically characterized by rejection of tradition and embrace of capitalism and industrialization (Osborne 1992; Toulmin 1990). During this time, fashion was seen as a social phenomenon influenced by economic development and corollary social changes. Fashion change was largely explained by the concept of the Trickle Down Theory (Simmel 1904) where class imitation was responsible for the dissemination of trends through society.

In the latter half of the 20th century, scholars noted social, cultural, and aesthetic changes, which became labeled as postmodernism.[1] Postmodernism is seen as a rejection of modernism and is characterized by rejecting objectivity and questioning authority, truth, and convention (e.g., Foucault 1973). These changes were attributed to new technologies, a new social order, and globalization (Best & Kellner 1991). Postmodernism is seen in fashion as a reaction to the rules and regulations of modernism and the upending of traditional models of fashion change, which were replaced by explanations such as style tribes, street style (Polhemus 1994) and branding.

Scholars in various fields from philosophy to sociology to literature to writing to art have argued that a new phase of existence is emerging, although they call the new era by many different appellations. Bourriard (1998/2002, 2009) dubbed the era altermodernism and noted features of it include collaborations between artists and consumers. Lipovetsky (2005) termed it hypermodern and identified its primary feature as excessive commercialization and consumption mixed with anxiety. Samuels (2008) labeled it automodernity and identified it as the combination of digital technology with human autonomy and theorizes that technology provides the youth with feelings of empowerment and independence. Kirby (2009) called the new era digimodernism and argued that it includes characteristics of fluidity, boundlessness, and multiple authorship.

Jameson argued that postmodernism was a result of a capitalist system in overdrive, in the sense of overconsumption of goods and services. However, today, the system appears to be on steroids, as witnessed by the *hyper*-consumption of goods and services. In *The Challenge of Global Capitalism*, Gilpin (2002) argued that by the end of the 20th century the open global economy could no longer be maintained due to political and national interests based on self-preservation. Polychroniou (2014) posited how global capitalism has changed in recent years, arguing, 'Today's brand of capitalism is particularly anti-democratic and simply incapable of functioning in a way conducive to maintaining sustainable and balanced growth' (n.p.). Using the term *predatory capitalism*, Polychroniou noted the three elements contributing to today's environment—financialization, neoliberalism, and globalization—constitute a return to the capitalist environment of the early 20th century when the majority of the world's wealth was controlled by a few individuals. In addition Nealon (2012) argued that capitalism in the post-postmodern age is an intensification of capitalism in the postmodern age.

Morgado (2014), using an umbrella term of post-postmodernism, conceptualized how these patterns are related to the fashion industry. Morgado acknowledged that some of her extrapolations based on post-postmodern scholars' propositions are not new but rather aspects of postmodern practices already in existence in the fashion industry; for example, heightened consumption and the advent of fast fashion. However, Morgado does postulate other examples that are novel to the fashion industry: 'The retail practice of intentionally destroying surplus inventories in order to eliminate the possibility that stale-dated garments will reach secondary markets is relatively consistent with Lipovetsky's thesis' (p. 334), and 'It is certainly the case that bloggers, their impact on fashion trends, their elevation to celebrity status, their influence on mainstream fashion media, and the integration of blogs with mainstream fashion enterprise offer fashion-related support for Kirby's proposition' (p. 335).

---

1. However, there exists in the academic literature ample critique of "postmodernism." For example: Dawkins (2003) argued that the postmodern theory explains everything and nothing and is therefore nonsense; Davis (2010) noted that the term "postmodern" is overused and inappropriately applied; and Jameson (1991), while not outright dismissing postmodernism, has argued its similarity to modernism in specific cases.

Changes in the Fashion Industry

In the western world, the concept of fashion began in West Europe in the mid-fourteenth century and spread throughout other parts of the world. During the industrial revolution of the late 18th century, fashionable dress moved from hand-made or custom sewn garments to manufactured goods produced at a speed and cost that allowed fashion to trickle down to the masses. When the department store concept emerged in the mid-19th century, fashion goods became widely available under one roof where merchandise was displayed by department. It was the department store that reshaped shopping habits that formed a culture of consumption that prevails today. Throughout the 20th century, the department store reigned as a preferred retail phenomenon that showcased haute couture, designer labels, and choices preferred by fashion leaders. Yet, according to government figures, while department store sales have been on the decline since the early 21st century, retail sales continue to realize steady, although slow, growth (US Department of Commerce, Census Bureau 2014), indicating consumers are using alternative venues for their purchases.

Whereas trends and styles were once determined by designers and manufacturers and showcased in the department store, today they are set by the consumers. Agins (2000) noted this change and wrote 'the power belongs to us, the consumers, who decide what we want to wear, when we buy it, and how much we pay for it' (p.8) In addition, fashion forecaster Lidewij Edelkoort declared that the fashion system is obsolete and fashion has been replaced by *clothes* ('It's the end of fashion. . .' 2015). While we do not disagree with Edelkoort entirely, we argue that the traditional fashion system has been replaced by fast fashion and what we identify as micro-trends.

Fast fashion has the objective of getting clothing to customers within the shortest time possible (Bruce & Daly 2006), but it is ultimately the consumer who will determine if the clothing is purchased. The result is a continual outpouring of new designs that are less than infrequently worn, if ever. Frustrated with the new system, designer John Paul Gaultier announced in 2014 his intent to leave the ready-to-wear market and focus only on haute couture because he was tired of design clothes that would never be worn. In fact, substantial evidence exists that clothes often are discarded with the original tags still intact (Hawley 2006).

The industry has also seen a rapid turnover of head designers at leading fashion houses. Typically, head designers remained with a brand for a decade or longer but a recent trend seems to have challenged this conception. Hedi Slimane headed Yves Saint Laurent for four years, Raf Simons headed Dior for three years, and Alexander Wang headed Balenciaga for less than three years. While in prior years the designer was the brand (e.g., Christian Dior, Valentino, Yves Saint Laurent), this revolving door of designers seems to indicate frustration with the changes in the fashion industry, either on the part of the head designers or on the part of CEOs and investors.

Digital Natives

Situated within the changes of the fashion industry are digital natives. Digital natives, also known as Millennials and Generation Y, include those born since the late 1980s. The central theme to support the concept of digital natives is that this group has been surrounded by, and interacted with, new technologies since they were toddlers. According to Prensky, 'Digital natives are used to receiving information really fast. They like to parallel process and multi-task. They prefer their graphics *before* their text. . .and thrive on instant gratification and frequent rewards' (2001, p. 1). Digital natives are often characterized as entitled, narcissistic, anxious, concerned for the environment and social justice, and constantly connected to social media.

It is estimated the Millennial generation represents 'about a fourth of the entire [US] population, control $200 billion in annual buying power. . .and are trendsetters. . .[in] fashion' (Schawbel, 2015, n.p.). Millennials buy more clothes than any other generation, with millennial women spending a third more on clothes than prior generations and millennial men spending twice as much on clothes that prior generations; in addition, millennial women shop nearly twice as often as other generations (Millennials Love Retail Spending, n.d.). Researchers have also noted that 52% of millennials are more likely to engage in impulse buying than any other generation (Tuttle, 2012) implying a need or instant gratification and got-to-have-it-now mentality.

Sago (2010) reported that 71% of digital natives use social media regularly with digital word-of-mouth communication serving as a primary driver of consumption. Within the context of the digital world, millennials create consumption opportunities through the electronic word-of-mouth concept which emerged when consumers could quickly and easily create and disseminate information through social media (Williams, Crittenden, Keo and

McCary 2012). Wasserman (2006) reminded us that the persuasive power behind electronic word-of-mouth is not the business itself, but the reference giver, the person who likes and shares information within his or her social network. In other words, more credibility is given to word-of-mouth endorsements because they are seen as independent sources of information. This consumer-generated media includes a variety of new sources of online information that is created, initiated, circulated, and used by consumers as a way to promote brands, services, issues, and products. Some have referred to this group as Consumers 2.0, a consumer who interacts with information in the context of purchase decisions (Rewardstream 2011). These consumers are described as more likely to access digital information, more comfortable buying online, and less reliant on their own physical experience in making a purchase decision. In other words, they have grown up with redefined notions of communications, interactions, relationships, brands, media, and technology.

As technology evolves, so does the connected consumer. According to Deloitte's 2016 study on digital democracy, consumer attention has increasingly spread across more devices, and the opportunity to capture their attention has decreased. Social media is also influencing buying decisions with online reviews now having more influence on buying decisions than television ads. Sixty-one percent of millennials reported that they learn about products from social media rather than a company's website. A significant issue comes from the increasing prevalence of ad-blocking software, with nearly 200 million millennials who indicate they have installed ad-blockers (Deloitte 2016). It becomes imperative, then, for successful brands to give attention to social media as a way of capturing the attention of millennials.

The term Web 1.0 generally refers to the first generation of web-based information that was unidirectional and the consumers simply consumed the information. Web 2.0 refers to the highly interactive platforms such as Facebook, YouTube, Twitter, or Instagram where users are not only consumers but also content-creators thus forming a social media ecosystem. Hanna et. al (2011) described the transformation of consumers from *bystanders* (where information is controlled by the advertiser) to *hunters* (where consumers control the interactivity) and finally to *participants* (where consumers create, consume, and share messages). According to recent Facebook Statistics, there are over 1.71 billion active Facebook users, and on a daily basis, there are 4.5 billion likes, 300 million photos uploaded, and 4.75 billion pieces of content shared. The largest demographic of users for Facebook are females (76%) between the ages of 25–35 (Zephoria, July 2016). This represents significant market space for social media efforts.

Important to note is that consumer attention is scarce—or as we argue 'deficit'. As consumer attention spans become shorter and shorter, brands must capture new and creative forms of micro-content to convince consumers to purchase. Berg and Gornitzka (2011) coined the term Consumer Attention Deficit Syndrome (CADS) defined as those consumers who develop competencies in specialized areas, but lack attention given to other consumer areas. They argue that in complex societies, consumers have attention capabilities for only some, but not all, of the market segments. As they point out, 'the complex attention mosaics that ordinary consumers are placed within is not only a problem at the level of the individual consumer; the market, too, will suffer from badly informed. . .consumers' (p. 173).

Commitment is now for shorter periods of time than before. Researchers have suggested a negative relationship between media usage and attention span (Ophir, Nass, & Wagner 2009; Wintour 2009) and a study by Microsoft found the average attention span of a person is now eight seconds (Gallagher 2015). Popular apps favored by digital natives exemplify this need for instant and short-lived gratification: SnapChat images last for no more than 10 seconds and Twitter limits texts to 140 characters. Hence, information and images need to be carefully curated and edited to have impact on consumers.

Selfies

Selfies, or a self-portrait, have become ubiquitous in the digital age. Some of the motives for posting selfies include to share an identity and attain affirmation from social media (Soerjoatmodjo 2016), to create an alternative version of oneself (Franco 2013), and to boost self-esteem (Alblooshi 2016). Not only are women are more likely to post selfies than men (Selfiecity 2014) but research finds young females are addicted to the 'likes' they get from posting selfies (Mascheroni, Vincent, and Jimenez 2015). Selfies are posted with the hopes of attaining '*instafame*, the condition of having a relatively great number of followers' (Marwick, 2015, p. 137). Hu, Manikoda, and Kambhampti (2014) noted that fashion and selfies are two of the eight most common Instagram posts and common fashion-related selfies include an image of the self with luxury purchases or bargain purchases (Marciniak & Budnarowska 2016).

The phenomenon of fashion selfies has not gone unnoticed by fashion brands, which have forged alliances between consumers and brands who hire them to wear their clothes and post pictures (e.g., fashion bloggers Danielle Bernstein, Georgia Bayliss, and Lexie Harvey). However, one does not need to be a brand ambassador to partake in the digital world of fashion selfies. Companies encourage consumers to post pictures of themselves in their brand outfits onto their social media venues; examples include Zara, H&M, Topshop, Adidas, and Nike. According to Peterson (2015), fast fashion companies have 'tapped the rise of street style and selfies, encourage their customers to become advertisers by posting pictures of themselves wearing the retailers' designs. Their followers are constantly bombarded by new products, beautiful images, and calls to action by brands in a strategic method to get them to buy more' (p. 80).

Whether one is hired by companies or one posts fashion selfies on their own time, one does not repeat the fashion faux pas of wearing the same outfit, leading to the popular hashtag #OOTD (outfit of the day). Carie Barkhuizen, of fashion brand Simply Be, noted 'pre-Facebook, women wouldn't think twice about wearing the same outfit to three or four events, especially if they were with different groups of friends' (quoted in Hendrlksz 2015). A research survey of 1500 women over the age of 16 found that 33% consider an item 'old' after no more than three wearings and 14% noted that they fear being 'tagged' on social media in same outfit on different occasions (Barnado's 2015). This fear is appropriately called tagophobia. No doubt, this leads to a rapid consumer turnover of different outfit combinations and the need to purchase new outfits frequently as consumers post images of their new outfit on a daily for numerous 'likes.'

Micro-trends

The fashion industry finds itself in a precarious situation. Youth have the consumer power; youth are digital natives and are conditioned to short time commitments. Youth use selfies to show their outfit of the day. Outfits cannot be seen more than once and are replaced quickly. Fast fashion brands market to the youth and encourage selfies which perpetrate the cycle. The result is an industry now predicated on micro-trends.

We define micro-trends as subtle and sometimes unnoticed changes in the fashion marketplace that involve only a small percentage of the total industry's activity. In fact, it is difficult to discern when a trend starts and when it ends, thus making it difficult for fashion companies to produce fashion that is sustainable—both economically and environmentally. A micro-trend is disseminated through one's digital network and adopted by followers but does not reach the wider, global population; therefore, a micro-trend could be limited to geography or demographics. In recent observations of college aged students in the southwest United States, fashion micro-trends for 2016 included open toed booties, oversized eyeglass frames, leather shorts, and Americana symbols that reflected support for Americans in the Rio Olympics. Whereas these trends may not necessarily grow to the wider marketplace, certain characteristics of the trend might be adopted in other locales or by other demographic groups. *leather pants*

Historically, fashion forecasters would release an abundance of information each season that ostensibly predicted the styles and fabrics that will be 'in'. But in today's world fashion is no longer predicted or forecasted. Instead, trend agencies provide inspirations to create trends and 'social media dictates trends' because the trends emerge overnight and disappear almost as fast (Abnett 2015). Today's fashion industry is driven by social media which has dramatically changed the way fashion companies do business, almost on a daily basis. As Abnett noted:

> Today, trends are born and die within an infinitely faster and more turbulent environment, in which brands, celebrities, magazines, bloggers and end consumers on social media all jostle for influence over what's 'in' and 'out' of fashion.

Conclusion

This manuscript utilized tenants of post-postmodernism to examine the current nature of Digital Natives' relationship with fast fashion, or what we term Attention Deficit Fashion (ADF). We argue that micro-trends are the result of a hyper-accelerated fashion cycle that rely on youthful consumers who are ravenous in their clothing consumption for social media purposes. Micro-trends are limited in geographic or demographic adoption. Fashion companies have had to become savvier in how they process information about trends in the marketplace. They must analyze which are the micro-trends that are or are not worth acting upon and which are the macro-trends that are worthy of significant investment. Often it comes down to analyzing whether the micro-trend fits the brand's image and the lifestyle of their customer. If it does not, it probably should be passed on in lieu of the next trend that better fits the brand's lifestyle. Retailers need to realize people may return clothes worn only once and expect to get their money back.

This manuscript also offers an addition to the literature on post-postmodernism and fashion or appearance styles. There is limited scholarship on this subject and similar to Morgado (2014) we found fashion-related examples that tie to scholars' conception of the new, dawning age. Bourrriard's (2009) argued that important feature of the age are collaborations between brands and consumers [and later supported by Morgado (2014) as a feature of post-postmodernism] and we argue that the platforms offered by brands to share their purchases and outfits (e.g., Facebook, Twitter, Instagram) illustrate this. Kirby (2009) tied the advent of Web2.0 technologies with superficiality and instantaneousness and we argue that #OOTD and tagophobia, fueled by the desire to receive adulation from social media followers, and combined with the immediate nature of social media, illustrate these points. Likewise, Samuels argued that a new psychology has developed from the constant engagement of humans with technology (e.g., cell phones, social media, iPads, etc.) that provides people with feelings of empowerment and (ironically) independence. Samuels illustrated this with educational practices, but we believe that the constant reliance of Digital Natives on technology when considering, selecting, or wearing their outfits illustrates the same mechanisms. Although the Attention Deficit Fashion framework does incorporate aspects of postmodern fashion, it also incorporates aspects of post-postmodernism, indicating a change in fashion as we know it.

Scholars and researchers of fashion and appearance can build on this article a number of ways. While this manuscript did not specifically examine gender, we did notice that many of our sources were related to women's experiences. Future research can use the Attention Deficit Fashion framework to examine differences in selfie posts, frequency of clothing purchases, and the micro-trends they generate or follow. Additionally, many of the selfies we observed focused on clothing styles not readily available in the market, such as plus-size clothing for young people, clothes for well-chested women, and clothes that showcase African roots. These subsets of Digital Natives maybe be looking for or inspiring micro-trends within their social circles.

References

Abnett, Kate (2015), 'Do fashion trends still exist?' *Business of Fashion*. https://www.businessoffashion.com/articles/intelligence/fashion-trends-still-exist. Accessed 19 September 2016.

Agins, Teri (2000), *The End of Fashion: How Marketing Changed the Clothing Business Forever*, New York City: William Morrow Paperbacks.

Alblooshi, Abdullah (2015), 'Self-esteem levels and selfies: The relationship between self-esteem levels and the number of selfies people take and post, and uses and gratifications of takin and posting selfies,' Masters thesis, Middle Tennessee University. http://jewlscholar.mtsu.edu/handle/mtsu/4760. Accessed 1 July 2016.

Barnado's (2015), 'Once worn, thrice shy—British women's wardrobe habits exposed!' http://www.barnardos.org.uk/news/media_centre/Once-worn-thrice-shy-8211-British-women8217s-wardrobe-habits-exposed/press_releases.htm?ref=105244 Accessed 1 July 2016.

Berg, Lisbet and Gornitzka, Åse. (2011). The consumer attention deficit syndrome: Consumer choices in complex markets. *Acta Sociologica*. 55(2), p. 159–178. Sage.

Best, Steven and Kellner, Douglas (1991), *Postmodern Theory. Critical Interrogations*, New York: The Guilford Press.

Bourriaud, Nicolas (1998/2002), *Relational Aesthetics* (trans. Simon Pleasance and Fronza Woods), Dijon, France: Le Presseus Dureel.

Bourriaud, Nicolas. (2009). *The Radicant* (trans. J. Gussen and L. Porten), chapter 1, Berlin/New York: Sternberg, mission17.org/documents/Nicolas Bourriaud_Ch1altermodernity_pp25-77.pdf. Accessed 10 February 2013.

Blackshaw Pete and Nazzaro Mike (2004), 'Consumer-generated media (CGM) 101: Word-of-mouth in the age of the web-fortified consumer,' http://www.brandchannel.com/images/Papers/222_CGM.pdf. Accessed 29 January 2011.

Bruce, Margaret, and Daly, Lucy (2006). Buyer behavior for fast fashion. *Journal of Fashion Marketing and Management,* 10(3), pp. 329–344.

Davis, B. (2010), 'The age of semi-post-postmodernism,' *Artnet*, 5 May, http://www.artnet.com/magazineus / reviews/davis/semi-post-postmodernism5-15-10 .asp. Accessed 1 February 2017.

Dawkins, R. (2003), 'Postmodernism disrobed,' in R. Dawkins (ed.), *A Devil's Chaplain*, Boston, Massachusetts: Houghton Mifflin, pp. 47–53.

Deloitte. (2016), *Digital Democracy Survey: Tenth Edition*. www.deloitte.com/us/tmttrends. Accessed 10 September 2016.

Eshelman, R. (2000/2001), 'Performatism, or the end of postmodernism,' *Anthropoetics*, 11:2, http://anthropoetics.ucla.edu/ap0602/perform.htm. Accessed 31 January 2017.

Foucoult, M. (1973), *The Order of Things*, New York: Vintage Books.

Gallagher, Danny (2015), 'Goldfish have a better attention span than you, smartphone user,' http://www.cnet.com/news/goldfish-the-actual-fish-not-the-crackers-may-have-a-better-attention-span-than-humans/. Accessed 2 February 2015

Gilpin, R. (2002), *The Challenge of Global Capitalism: The World Economy in the 21st Century*, Princeton, NJ: Princeton University Press.

Hanna Richard, Rohm, Andrew J., and Crittenden, Victoria L. (2011), 'We're all connected: The power of the social media ecosystem,' *Business Horizons*, 54, pp. 265–273.

Hawley, Jana. M. (2006), 'Digging for diamonds: A conceptual framework for understanding reclaimed textile products,' *Clothing and Textiles Research Journal*, 24(3), pp. 262–275.

Hendrlksz, Vivian (2015), 'How the selfie effect is disrupting the industry,' https://fashionunited.uk/news/fashion/how-the-selfie-effect-is-disrupting-the-industry/2015081317334. Accessed 12 April 2016.

Hu, Yugeng, Manikonda, Lydia, and Kambhampati, Subbarao (2014), 'What we Instagram: A first analysis of Instagram photo contest and user types,' *International Conference on Web and Social Media*, http://149.169.27.83/instagram-icwsm.pdf. Accessed 12 April 2016.

'"It's the end of fashion as we know it" (2015) says Li Edelkoort.' *DeZeen Magazine*, http://www.dezeen.com/2015/03/01/li-edelkoort-end-of-fashion-as-we-know-it-design-indaba-2015/ Accessed 1 February 2016.

Jameson, F. (1991), *Postmodernism, or, The Cultural Logic of Late Capitalism*, Durham, North Carolina: Duke University Press.

Kirby, Alan (2009), *Digimodernism: How New Technologies Dismantle the Postmodern and Reconfigure Our Culture*, New York: Continuum International Publishing Group.

Lipovestky, Gilles (2005), *Hypermodern Times*, Cambridge, MA: Polity Press.

Marciniak, Ruth and Budnarowska, Corinna (2016), 'Selfies: An exploration into the brand effects of visual imagery with earned media, http://eprints.bournemouth.ac.uk/22584/2/Nottingham%2520presentation%2520Ruth%2520final.pptx.pdf Accessed 1 August 2016

Mascheroni, Giovanna, Vincent, Jane and Jimenez, Estefanía (2015), *'Girls are addicted to likes so they post semi-naked selfies: peer mediation, normativity and the construction of identity online,'* *Cyberpsychology* 9(1). p. 5. ISSN 1802–7962

Millennials Love Retail Spending (n.d.). http://www.baynote.com/infographic/millennials-love-retail-spending/. Accessed: 9 March 2017.

Morgado, Marcia A. (2014), 'Fashion phenomena and the post-postmodern condition: Enquiry and speculation,' *Fashion, Style, & Popular Culture*, 1(3), pp. 313–339.

Nealon, J. T. (2012), *Post-Postmodernism, or, The Cultural Logic of Just-in-Time Capitalism*, Stanford, CA: Stanford University Press.

Ophir, Eyal, Nass, Clifford, and Wagner, Anthony D. (2009), 'Cognitive control in media multitaskers,' *Proceedings of the National Academy of Sciences*, 106(37)

Osborne, P. (1992), 'Modernity is a qualitative, not a chronological category: Notes on the dialetics of differential historic time," in Barker, P. Hulme, & M. Iversen (eds.), *Postmodernism and the Re-reading of Modernity*, Manchester, UK: Manchester University Press.

Peterson, Domenica (2015), 'Social media as a tool for social change,' in Janet Hethorn and Connie Ulasewicz (eds.) *Sustainable Fashion: What's Next? A Conversation About Issues, Practices and Possibilities*, 2nd edition, (pp. 76–99), New York: Fairchild.

Phelps, Nicole (2016), 'In-and-out creative directorships can't be good for fashion business,' http://vogue.com/contributor/nicole-phelps. Accessed 29 August 2016.

Polhemus, Ted (1994), *Streetstyle: From Sidewalk to Catwalk,* London: Thames & Hudson.

Polychroniou, C. J ., (2014), Predatory capitalism: Old trends and new realities, *Truthout*, http://www.truth-out.org/news/item/24732-predatory-capitalism-old-trends-and-new-realities, accessed March 30, 2017.

Prensky, Marc (2001), 'Digital natives, digital immigrants,' *On the Horizon*, 9(5), pp. 1–6.

RewardStream (2011), 'Do you know who Consumer 2.0 is?' Retrieved September 19, 2016 from http://rewardstream.com/do-you-know-who-consumer-2-0-is/. Accessed 10 September 2016.

Sago, Brad (2010), 'The influence of social media message sources on millennial generation consumers,' *International Journal of Integrated Marketing Communications*, 2(2), pp. 7–18.

Samuels, Robert (2008), 'Auto-modernity after postmodernism: Autonomy and automation in culture, technology and education,' In Tara McPherson (ed.), *Digital Youth, Innovation, and the Unexpected* (pp. 219–240), Cambridge, MA: The MIT Press.

Schawbel, Dan (2015), '10 New Findings about the Millennial Consumer,' *Forbes*. http://www.forbes.com/sites/danschawbel/2015/01/20/ 10-new-findings-about-the-millennial-consumer/#3d9ee60828a8. Accessed 1 February 1, 2016.

Selfiecity (2014), 'Selfiecity: Investigating the style of self-portraits (selfies) in five cities across the world, http://selfiecity.net/. Accessed 10 September 2016.

Shunatona, Brooke (2016), '7 fall clothes you're obsessed with but can literally only wear for 2 weeks,' *Cosmopolitan*. http://www.cosmopolitan.com/style-beauty/fashion/a63565/clothes-you-can-only-wear-during-fall/ Accessed 19 September 2016.

Simmel, George (1904), 'Fashion,' *International Quarterly*, 10, pp. 130–150.

Soerjoatmodjo, Gita Widya Laksmini, (2016), 'I *selfie* therefore I exist: A preliminary qualitative research on selfie as part of identity formation in adolescents, *Humaniora*, 7: 2, pp. 139–148.

Toulmin, S. E., (1990), *Cosmopolis: The Hidden Agenda of Modernity*, Chicago: University of Chicago Press.

Tuttle, Brad (2012), 'Millennials are biggest suckers for selfish impulse buys,' Time, http://business.time.com/2012/04/27/millennials-are-biggest-suckers-for-selfish-impulse-buys/. Accessed 9 March 2017.

US Department of Commerce: Census Bureau. (2014), 'Retail Trade,' https://www.census.gov/retail/index.html. Accessed 7 September 2016

Wasserman, Todd (2006), 'Word games, *Brandweek*, 47(17), pp. 24–28.

Williams, David L., Crittenden, Victoria L., Keo, Teeda. and McCarty, Paulette (2012), 'The use of social media: An exploratory study of usage among digital natives,' *Journal of Public Affairs*, 12: 127–136. DOI: 10.1002/pa 1414.

Wintour, Patrick (2009), 'Facebook and Bebo risk of "infantilising" the human mind,' *Guardina*. http://www.guardian.co.uk/uk/2009/feb/24/ social-networking-site-changing-childrens-brain. Accessed 5 September 2016.

Zephoria Digital Marketing (2016), 'The top 20 valuable Facebook statistics,' https://zephoria.com/top-15-valuable-facebook-statistics/. Accessed 19 September 2016.

Discussion Questions

1. What cultural, social, and technological conditions and changes lead to the current state of "attention deficit fashion"?

2. What are some "micro-trends" that you know of?

3. Is this system sustainable?

CHAPTER 3
DRESS AS NONVERBAL COMMUNICATION

Kimberly A. Miller-Spillman

After you have read this chapter, you will understand:

- **The substantial complexity underlying communication through dress**
- **The basic components of the structure of dress communication systems**
- **How people put together appearance according to "rules" or guidelines for dress shaped by cultural, historical, and group factors as well as personal tastes and preferences**
- **The characteristics of the present era that influence the way consumers "produce" appearances**

We express much through dress, including our personal identities, our relationships with others, and the types of situations in which we are involved. A phenomenal amount of information is transmitted in one's appearance, and human beings have an amazing capacity to make sense of a substantial amount of detail in a very short time. In this chapter we consider both the complexity of communicating through appearance and factors that influence messages sent through appearance. We look closely at the process of creating meanings about the self and society through dress.

WHAT IS NONVERBAL COMMUNICATION?

Dress is one of several modes of **nonverbal communication** that does not necessarily involve verbal expression through speaking or writing.[1] Other types of nonverbal communication include facial expressions, physical movement and actions (**kinetics**), the physical distances people maintain from one another (**proxemics**), touch (**haptics**), the sound of the voice while delivering verbal communications (**paralinguistics**), and hand gestures. All of these types of nonverbal communication involve behaviors that are informative and meaningful.

Dress serves as a backdrop while other forms of communication—verbal and nonverbal—occur. Unlike many other modes of communication, dress often tends to be stable or unchanging for many hours of the day. Dress, then, is usually **nondiscursive**—or fixed—behavior (McCracken, 1988). (See Chapter 12 for an update on how technology can change some clothing while it is being worn.) Two different definitions of communication are useful in understanding dress. One definition, mapped out by Burgoon and Ruffner (1974), contains a number of premises about sending and receiving messages:

1. **Communication** is an interactive process between two or more people. Millions of people can be involved when television and other media send messages to a vast audience. The performer may never interact directly with most viewers, but an interaction nonetheless occurs. For example, when presidential candidates run for office their dress is often scrutinized and critiqued as an indicator of what type of leader that person will be. People discuss with friends, on blogs, and in newspaper pieces the color, size, fabrications, and styles each candidate was wearing. In response, friends reply, people respond on blogs, and newspapers have letters to the editors for a continued discourse.

2. Communication involves the sending of messages to at least one receiver who, for a complete act of communication, sends a feedback message to the original sender. Feedback messages sent about dress are not always obvious and overt. Occasionally, one may receive a direct compliment or insult about dress. A long stare or whistle might constitute the feedback. In many instances, lack of comments serves

as feedback that nothing was terribly wrong with one's appearance. Getting a job or a date may indicate that one's dress was appropriate or approved.

3. Communication is a process that is ongoing and dynamic. Meanings are negotiated and created to reach common understanding. According to the three-part definition of communication, sender and receiver must come to a minimal level of agreement about the meanings of dress for a complete communication interaction to occur. This may happen to some extent in purposeful efforts at impression management, such as a suit worn to a job interview, a wedding dress, or a uniform for a job role. But for most, dress wearer and observer never converse specifically about dress and often do not completely agree on what each other's dress means (Tseèlon, 1992). Since dress is very **polysemic** (i.e., it sends a great amount of messages all at one time), it is difficult to find agreement on all of the meanings packed into one appearance.

A second, broader definition of communication emphasizes that dress is "the production and exchange of meanings" (Fiske, 1990, p. 2). A wearer puts clothing, hairdo, accessories, and grooming together to produce an appearance and may assign meanings to that assembled appearance. Each observer of that appearance may agree on some meanings but may also have a unique interpretation of the appearance. According to the second definition, disagreement does not mean that communication stops or fails. It is the sum of how the wearer and observers interact (or not) on the basis of appearance that produces meanings for the wearer and the observers.

Throughout much of the world during the early 21st century, dress meanings tend to be vague and hard to verbalize. A picture, such as an appearance, tells a thousand words, but those thousand words are difficult to pin down precisely. In addition, changing fashion trends continually modify meanings of dress, adding further to the lack of clarity of meanings. Umberto Eco (1976) refers to this vagueness of meanings as **undercoding**. Meanings of dress in U.S. society today are coded only generally and imprecisely, leaving much to the imagination of the perceiver.

In contrast to "modern" attire worn throughout the world today, dress in traditional cultures tends to change slowly over time and may incorporate long-used symbols that are steeped with meanings. One example of cultural meanings can be seen in Kente cloth worn by college graduates. As

Denise Oliver Velez writes in the reading "Power, Pride and Kente Cloth" (at the end of this chapter), the cloth that has been in production in Ghana since the 17th century has been banned during some graduation ceremonies. Kente cloth sends a strong cultural message and it is unmistakably African. Kente also has an established system of color meanings (e.g., blue portrays love) and status meanings (e.g., originally meant for royalty and wealthy). See images of Kente cloth in Figure 3.1.

THE STRUCTURE OF DRESS COMMUNICATION SYSTEMS

Channels of Transmission

Dress as a communication system is extremely complex. In any one appearance, messages may be sent simultaneously through a variety of channels. Berlo (1960) defined **channels of communication** as the five physiological senses. We often study how dress is used to communicate via the visual channel. However, we might also send messages via the hearing channel (e.g., the clanging of bangle bracelets, the clickety-clack of high heels on an uncarpeted hallway, the rustle of taffeta) or via the sense of smell (e.g., perfumes, deodorants to mask body odor, new leather). The sense of touch is inherent in perceiving clothing, as textiles have a tactile component. However, we can also look at a fabric sometimes and guess that it is soft (e.g., velvet) or slick (e.g., vinyl). These sensory transmissions may have meanings

Figure 3.1 Kente cloth is worn at graduation ceremonies in the United States. Kente cloth is the opposite of undercoding because it has precise meanings that have been around since the 17th century.

for observers. For example, many business dress advisors suggest that clanging jewelry and obvious perfumes convey an image that is less than professional in the office environment (Fashion Workshop, 1989; Fiore and Kimle, 1997; Roscho, 1988). The sense of taste is not strongly related to appearance. There are flavored lipsticks, balms, mouthwashes, toothpastes, and other grooming products, but because they are not easily seen their relationship to fashion is rarely used, other than a few amusing and/or erotic novelty dress products that are flavored. (For more information on dress and the senses, see Breu, 2007.)

An array of elements may be compiled on the body to complete a dressed appearance. When hairdo, facial grooming or makeup, clothing, scent, jewelry, shoes, and accessories are all combined, a tremendous amount of organization has taken place. The rules we use to put all of these components together on the body are loosely held guidelines for what is appropriate, fashionable, and attractive. The rules are a sort of grammar of dress. We learn the grammar of dress through the media and through groups and families to which we belong.

Any dress **grammar rule** can be broken; however, some rules are held seriously in some societies. For instance, in most communities in the United States today, it is illegal for women to go topless and for men to display their genitals in public. These laws stem from moral taboos related to a sense of modesty and sexual behavior.

In 18th century England, fabric and clothing thefts were associated with the desire to keep up with one's peers' fashionable dress (see the reading "The First Crime of Fashion: Eighteenth-Century English Clothing Theft and Emergence of Fashionability"). Scholar Lidia Plaza describes how items were stolen, for example, between servant and master, stealing clothing to sell to the secondhand market, or shoplifting once boutiques became all the rage (see Figure 3.2). Plaza's insightful statement that a stolen garment was not always taken because of its economic value but because the thief wanted to participate in clothing culture is an interesting idea. What do you think about applying this idea to today's shoplifting?

Elements of Dress Signs

According to the **model of clothing in context** created by Mary Lynn Damhorst, elementary components of clothing that may convey messages are listed in Figure 3.3 within the inner oval of the diagram. These are "perceptual elements" that are the integral units of fabric and apparel that can be

Figure 3.2 Because "keeping up appearances" was so important to 18th-century English society, fabric and clothing were often stolen.

perceived by humans. Many of these elements are the basic elements of design (Davis, 1980; Fiore & Kimle, 1997). Some of the elements have multiple subcomponents that influence meaning; for example, color has hue (the color family), value (lightness versus darkness), and intensity (brightness versus dullness). Fiber names can be meaningful (e.g., silk is a luxury fiber) as are fabrics such as denim (i.e., the fabric denotes America's casual lifestyle; Berger, 1984). These elementary units are relevant for clothing, but other aspects of dress such as hair, tattoos, and shoes have different sets of elementary perceptual units.

During the 20th century in North America, rounded design lines and flowing and delicate, translucent fabrics (such as voile) could be worn by women but were not traditionally seen in men's dress. Men tended to wear angular lines and sturdy, smooth, "hard" woven fabrics (McCracken, 1985). These differences in lines and fabrics reflected differences in traditional concepts of what is male (e.g., active, sturdy, strong) and female (e.g., soft, fragile). Today, women borrow masculine fabrics and design lines freely, as they take on roles and behaviors traditionally reserved for men. The increasing incorporation of

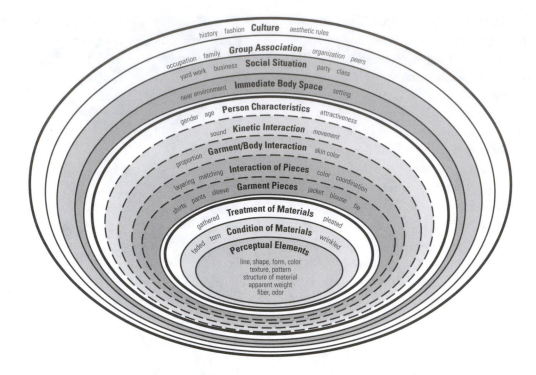

Figure 3.3 Model of clothing in context created by Mary Lynn Damhorst.

menswear symbols into women's wear is helping (along with other societal changes) to obscure the traditional gender meanings of design lines and fabrics.

Context of Use

In any appearance, a great number of **perceptual elements** are combined according to or in violation of some rules of grammar. How elements are combined and placed on the body, who wears them, and in what situation they are worn shapes meanings of perceptual elements. Combinations of elements and surrounding situations make up **context** (cf. Bateson, 1979). Figure 3.3 maps components of context that may shape meanings of clothing (Damhorst, 1984–1985).

The inner ovals of Figure 3.3 that surround the core perceptual elements pertain to "clothing materials" and how they influence meanings. For example, observers do not only see the clothing of another but they also take notice of the condition of the clothing such as how new/fresh it looks or how old/worn it looks. The condition of materials, such as stains or tears, could lower the impression given by a job applicant.

The meaning of fading and tears can vary with the whims of fashion, as noted by Troy Patterson's reading "Who Gets to Wear Shredded Jeans?" Distressed and stonewashed jeans have been popular for casual clothing for some time, but the cultural elite may have more societal permission to wear ripped jeans to a formal occasion than those with less social power. Patterson's acerbic article compares two schools of denim enthusiasts: (1) the over-dyed indigo jean

Figure 3.4 Axl Rose in shredded denim.

wearer with knife sharp pleats and (2) the music festival–going wearer of distressed denim. Patterson states that the over-dyed jean wearers are within good taste whereas the distressed denim wearer sends a message of disruption and masculine aesthetics (see Figure 3.4).

"Treatment of materials," another oval surrounding the core perceptual elements, includes gathers that may add fullness and softness to clothing, whereas pressed pleats may appear precise and sharp.

The next several layers of the clothing context model relate clothing to the body of the wearer. Garment pieces become familiar objects in a culture and are usually associated with coverage of one area of the body. Certain arrangements of elements (i.e., lines, shapes, fabrics, patterns) within a garment piece may then add meanings. For instance, denim jeans are a highly familiar garment symbol worldwide expressing the casual lifestyle of Americans.

The wearer's shape fills out a garment, and skin and hair coloring interact with garment elements. Body size also influences meanings of clothing. Clayton, Lennon, and Larkin (1987) found that garments worn by larger-size female models tended to be evaluated as less fashionable. This could pose a problem in marketing to larger-size women via catalogs and magazine ads. Do larger-size women see plus-size garments as less fashionable than garments worn by slim models? To approach the size issue cautiously, many mail-order firms feature plus-size models who are actually only a size 12 or 14, larger than average fashion models (size 0 to 4) but not in the size ranges offered in women's larger sizes (16W and up). Numerous characteristics of the wearer can also influence interpretation of clothing meanings. For example, an ice-cream stain on the shirt of a toddler may be perceived as cute or amusing, but might not be so cute on a 42-year-old.

The "interaction of pieces" section of Figure 3.3 refers to matching, color, and coordination. Within a particular occupation, some individuals adopt dress that becomes their signature style. Dolly Parton (Figure 3.5), the famous country music singer and songwriter, multi-instrumentalist, record producer, actress, author, businesswoman, and owner of Dollywood has a signature look. Dolly's large breasts and hairdo are a part of her public image. Dolly says that it takes a lot of money to look this cheap. Dolly's signature look contradicts her business acumen.

The outer layers of the model in Figure 3.3 relate to the situation surrounding the wearer. Let's leap to the outer rim and examine the all-encompassing context of culture (Firth, 1957). Elements and grammar of clothing take on meaning in cultural context. Consider the color red, for example. Red is an appropriate color for traditional Chinese bridal dresses, but what would the meaning of red convey in an American bride's dress? Similarly, bright red is the traditional color for funerals in Ghana, Africa, but is not usually an appropriate color to wear to funerals in the United States. In Chapter

Figure 3.5 Dolly Parton is known for her exaggerated figure and hairstyle, which fools some into believing she is an "air head."

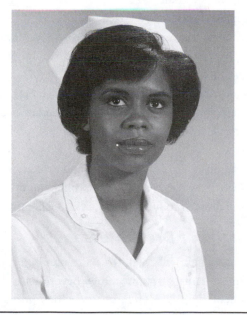

Figure 3.6 Nurses at one time wore a white starched cap, a white dress with hose and white shoes. Their position in the hospital hierarchy was easier to recognize then than it is today when many hospital personnel don scrubs.

5, the reading "Female Tradition in a New Context: The Case of the *Khanga*" discusses the varied meanings of the Tanzanian *khanga*, including politics, economic status, gender equality, and sexual intimacy.

Moving to the "group association" level of the clothing in context model, groups and organizations vary with each culture and over time, and the role of dress varies across groups. In North America prior to the 1980s, a hospital nurses' white cap, dress, hose and shoes were once associated with cleanliness, purity, and authority to carry out doctors' orders (see Figure 3.6). However, beginning in the 1990s, nurses adopted the scrub as uniform because it was easier to wash and work in than the traditional nurse's uniform. One complaint about nurses wearing scrubs is that patients cannot distinguish the nurse from physicians and other hospital personnel who also wear scrubs.

Dress helps us define social situations. Some social critics fear that the invasion of casual dress into business organizations diminishes the seriousness and professionalism of business interactions, while many workers enjoy the relaxed tone set on "casual days." Similarly, a party to which everyone wears tuxedos and formal gowns might have a different atmosphere or definition than a party to which everyone wears T-shirts and jeans.

Immediate surroundings of space and people can also influence interpretations of dress. The interaction between people and the immediate surroundings gives meaning and substance to dress. One particular item can be interpreted differently based on altering the "stage." For example a man in a multicolored wig at Mardi Gras in New Orleans provides a different interpretation than a man wearing a wig in a circus, an office, or an art gallery.

To summarize the model of clothing in context, it is not individual colors or garment pieces that dominate an appearance to create meanings. How all elements are combined on the body within cultural context is crucial for meanings. As Roach-Higgins and Eicher (1992) emphasized, dress is an assemblage. How the wearer uses clothing and other components of dress in context makes dress meaningful.

Meanings of Dress Messages

Semiotics, as you will recall from Chapter 1, is a field in which dress items carry meanings beyond the clothing objects themselves. Dress refers to meanings more abstract than the actual physical objects of dress. For example, dress makes visual proclamations such as "this person is male," "the wearer is competent at her job," "this person is fashionable," "this person is Nigerian," "I'm attending a black-tie affair," "I completed the Bluegrass 10,000," or "I wanna be like Lady Gaga." Many dress messages are such that we might feel a bit silly having to verbally announce them during first meetings with others.

McCracken (1988) contended that, because dress remains fixed or unchanged during most interactions, it tends to communicate stable characteristics of the wearer. Keep in mind, however, that many of us change our clothing and sometimes other aspects of grooming every day or more than once a day. The "stable" characteristics we communicate may be stable only for a few hours. One morning, a student might throw on a sloppy sweat suit to go to class because he's having a bad day and doesn't want to pay much attention to dress. Usually, however, that same student rarely wears sweats to class, preferring jeans and sweaters. Another student might dress in sweats every day; his attire might indicate personal attitudes about school, self, and dress. The meanings of his dress may be far more complex than not caring about his appearance, however. In the student's mind, and to the group he belongs to on campus, sloppy may be "cool." Surface-level interpretations do not always accurately reveal the meanings of dress.

The fact that dress can be misinterpreted was acutely demonstrated in rape and sexual assault trials at the end of the 20th century. Many men accused of rape claimed that the survivor's attire was a sign of consent. Many trials admitted as evidence the clothing the survivor was wearing, such as leopard-print underwear, a blouse with a plunging neckline that revealed a bra, or short and tight skirts. Lennon, Johnson, and Schulz's (1999) research found that a woman's motive for wearing "sexy" clothing was different from how it was perceived by men; women viewed their clothing as stylish or fashionable, while men viewed it as a sign the woman was interested in a sexual encounter. Today, in the United States, many states ban the admission of clothing into evidence as a sign of sexual consent, though it may be admitted as evidence of attack (e.g., torn fabric, blood stains). However, there are still disturbing cases where clothing is said to be a sign of consent.

Former South Africa President Jacob Zuma was accused of rape and during his trial he said the fact that his victim was wearing a skirt signaled to him that she was interested in sex. In Canada, the chief constable of police told women that they could avoid rape and assault if they didn't dress like a slut. One response to the social culture in which rape is blamed on clothing are demonstrations called "**Slut Walks**" as noted by Gillian Schutte (2011) in "South Africa: Semantics of the Slut Walk." After a young girl was brutally assaulted by taxi drivers for wearing a short denim skirt, women in many countries donned their skimpy dress to participate in organized events carrying slogans such as "Don't tell us what to wear—Tell men not to rape." Women, by way of these demonstrations, are reclaiming the right to wear sexy dress without fear of being raped. For another clothing example of fighting violence against women, see Hipple (2000).

THE PRESENT-DAY CULTURAL "MOMENT"

The present situation in U.S. culture very much shapes how consumers assemble appearances and send messages through dress. The characteristics of U.S. culture, as well as many cultures around the world, at the end of the 20th century and the beginning of the 21st century were sometimes referred to as **postmodern** (Gitlin, 1989). This term is useful in summarizing some present-day trends in consumer life. For a thorough analysis on postmodern influences on dress see Morgado (1996). We focus on four characteristics of consumer culture—eclecticism, nostalgia, questioning of rules, and simulation—that are reflected in how we currently purchase and present our appearances.

Postmodern appearances are **eclectic** in that consumers often mix and match a diverse array of styles and influences in any one appearance or throughout a wardrobe. For example, African-inspired fabrics (e.g., Kente cloth) are sewn into American styles; a Peruvian-knitted alpaca sweater might be worn with jeans. Consumers and designers borrow fabrics, hairstyles, jewelry, and diverse symbols across cultures, making the market for clothing very globally inspired (even though many consumers do not know the origin or meaning of what they borrow). Postmodern consumers are prone to mix diverse brands and designers in one appearance and buy parts and pieces of an ensemble at an array of price levels. Mixing Target and Gucci can be cool (Agins, 1999). Buying separates and mixing them with diverse accessories is quite common. Consumers mix and match not just to save money, but also to have more freedom in putting together unique combinations.

Nostalgia is another component of postmodernism. Nostalgia is yearning for another time that is viewed with reverence and longing. Nostalgia may explain the recurrence of past period styles in contemporary fashions. For example, flared pant legs popular in the 1960s and 1970s were common in the early and mid-2000s; likewise, aesthetics of the 1980s (big shoulders, neon colors, and pegged pants) are popular again in the 2010s.

Questioning traditions and rules seems to be a given during the postmodern era (Featherstone, 1991). We see fashionable combinations of masculine and feminine symbols, casual combined with formal, and interesting mixes of fabrics that challenge old rules about not mixing patterns in one look (see Figure 3.7). During a time when many traditional aspects of culture, such as gender roles, sexuality, bases of economic power distribution, and ethnic hegemony, are questioned, it is no wonder that questioning of traditional rules for dress should also occur. By the early 1990s, rap artists (certainly not mainstream power leaders) became a major source of fashion inspiration for young men in the United States (Spiegler, 1996). And tattoos and piercings became both fashionable and a statement of defiance against mainstream norms of body modification (Peace, 2001). Rap artists and piercings and tattoos questioned established traditions by challenging commonly accepted standards, values, and aesthetics. People began to accept different viewpoints and in doing so changed fashion.

Figure 3.7 This ensemble includes combinations of patterns not usually seen together. Would you say this outfit is postmodern chic or "fashion don't"?

Finally, Baudrillard (1983) suggested that during the postmodern era, **simulations** are becoming as valuable as what is real and rare. For example, since the late 1980s, animal prints and fake furs have been featured in top designer lines, perhaps to save endangered species while affording enjoyment of natural forms, even if they look fake. We also live in an era when cosmetic surgery is more accepted, when one can modify the natural body and acquire a "simulated" perfect figure or face. Simulations in general probably are increasing because of technological innovations that allow us to simulate materials (and bodies) effectively. Refer to Chapter 4 for more on this topic.

The issues surrounding postmodernism are numerous and complex; the issues they subsequently raise are not easy to solve. What is interesting is that some scholars are arguing that postmodernism is dead and a new era is upon us, though what that new era is—or even what to name it—is still up for debate.

Summary

The vast complexity of communicating through dress has become heightened during the postmodern era. Old rules of dress are questioned, symbols are borrowed and used out of historical and cultural context, and what is real can be simulated. Communicating through dress may less often involve clearly shared meanings.

The perceiver may have to work hard at making sense of a postmodern appearance. Nevertheless, dress is still significant human behavior that takes on a rich array of meanings within the surrounding context of individual wearer, social interactions, family, organizations, and culture.

Endnote

1. Verbal communications may be transmitted via dress, as when a brand logo is emblazoned on a garment or a saying or message is printed on a T-shirt.

Key Terms

Channels of communication	Kinetics	Perceptual elements	Simulations
Communication	Model of clothing in context	Polysemic	Slut walks
Context	Nondiscursive	Postmodern	Undercoding
Eclectic	Nonverbal communication	Proxemics	
Grammar rule	Nostalgia	Questioning traditions	
Haptics	Paralinguistics	Semiotics	

Learning Activity 3.1

DRESSING OUT OF CONTEXT

Objective

The experience of how others respond when your dress does not match with the social context in which you appear demonstrates how context affects meanings of dress. Using systematic observation techniques, record others' reactions to your dress and your own reactions to their feedback.

Procedures

Select one of the levels of context from the model in Figure 3.3. Plan to wear dress that is incongruent with that component of context during one day of the week when you will interact with others for several hours. For example:

Wear your out-of-context dress for at least six hours in one day. Try to wear it on a day when you will be seen by and interact with a variety of people you know, as well as people you know slightly or not at all. Pretend you think nothing is odd about your appearance. Let others react to you before explaining that you are doing an experiment.

EXPERIMENT PROCEDURES

Level of Context	Incongruent Dress Possibility
Culture	Wear dress that is normative to a culture other than the one in which you live or are from (e.g., wear a sari or a Scottish kilt to classes in the United States).
Social Situation	Wear a formal gown or a tuxedo to classes.
Person Characteristics	Wear an outfit that is appropriate for a person much younger or older than yourself.
Garment/Body Interaction	Wear an outfit that is too small for you or extremely large.
Interaction of Pieces	Wear unmatched plaids and prints together in one ensemble.
Garment Pieces	Wear a pair of jeans on your head all day.
Condition of Materials	Wear to class a garment that is notably stained or ripped.

Recording Your Experience

Carry a notebook to record your reactions and the reactions of others as the experiment progresses. Record:

- Positive and negative responses
- Responses from males and females
- Verbal and nonverbal responses
- Responses from acquaintances, friends, and strangers
- Your feelings and thoughts about yourself before you venture out wearing the costume and as the experiment progresses
- Comparisons of yourself with others' appearances

Also describe the places you went, situations you were involved in, types of people with whom you interacted, types of people you were seen by but with whom you did not specifically interact, date and times of day for each entry in your recordings, and weather conditions you experienced.

Questions to Ponder

1. Did you learn anything about how people respond to others on the basis of appearance? What types of meanings did various others seem to assign to your dress?
2. Was there more than one aspect of context affecting how your dress was interpreted?
3. What factors may have affected your accuracy in interpreting responses from others?
4. Will you ever dress this way again? Why or why not?

References

Agins, T. (1999), "Fashion: Cheapskate Chic," *Wall Street Journal,* June 11: W1.

Bateson, G. (1979), *Mind and Nature,* New York: E. P. Dutton.

Baudrillard, J. (1983), *Simulations* (P. Foss, P. Patton and P. Beitchman, trans.), New York: Semiotext(e), Inc.

Berger, A. A. (1984), *Signs in Contemporary Culture,* New York: Longman.

Berlo, D. K. (1960), *The Process of Communication,* New York: Holt, Rinehart and Winston.

Breu, M. R. (2007), "The Role of Scents and the Body in Turkey," in D. C. Johnson and H. B. Foster (eds.), *Dress and Sense: Emotional and Sensory Experiences of the Body and Clothes,* 25–38. Oxford: Berg.

Burgoon, M. and M. Ruffner (1974), *Human Communication,* New York: Holt, Rinehart and Winston.

Clayton, R., S. J. Lennon and J. Larkin (1987), "Perceived Fashionability of a Garment as Inferred from the Age and Body Type of the Wearer," *Home Economics Research Journal,* 15: 237–46.

Damhorst, M. L. (1984–1985), "Meanings of Clothing Cues in Social Context," *Clothing and Textiles Research Journal*, 3(2): 39–48.

Davis, M. L. (1980), *Visual Design in Dress*, Englewood Cliffs, NJ: Prentice Hall.

Eco, U. (1976), *A Theory of Semiotics*, Bloomington: Indiana University Press.

"Fashion Workshop: Real Life Cues to Clothes for Your Job," (1989), *Glamour*, October, 203–6.

Featherstone, M. (1991), *Consumer Culture and Postmodernism*, London: Sage.

Fiore, A. M. and P. A. Kimle (1997), *Understanding Aesthetics: For Merchandising and Design Professionals*, New York: Fairchild Publications.

Firth, J. R. (1957), *Papers in Linguistics, 1934–1951*, London: Oxford University Press.

Fiske, J. (1990), *Introduction to Communication Studies*, London: Routledge.

Gitlin, T. (1989), "Postmodernism Defined, At Last!" *Utne Reader*, July/August, 52–61.

Hipple, P. C. (2000), "Clothing Their Resistance in Hegemonic Dress: The Clothesline Project's Response to Violence Against Women," *Clothing and Textiles Research Journal*, 18(3): 163–77.

Lennon, S. J., K. K. P. Johnson and T. L. Schulz (1999), "Forging Linkages between Dress and Law in the U.S., Part II: Rape and Sexual Harassment," *Clothing and Textiles Research Journal*, 17: 144–56.

McCracken, G. (1985), "The Trickle-Down Theory Rehabilitated," in M. R. Solomon (ed.), *The Psychology of Fashion*, 39–54, Lexington, MA: Lexington Books.

McCracken, G. (1988), *Culture and Consumption*, Bloomington: Indiana University Press.

Morgado, M. A. (1996), "Coming to Terms with Postmodern: Theories and Concepts of Contemporary Culture and Their Implications for Apparel Scholars," *Clothing and Textiles Research Journal*, 14(1): 41–53.

Peace, W. J. (2001, Summer), "The Artful Stigma," *Disability Studies Quarterly*, 21(3): 125–37.

Roach-Higgins, M. E. and J. B. Eicher (1992), "Dress and Identity," *Clothing and Textiles Research Journal*, 10(4): 1–8.

Roscho, L. (1988), "The Professional Image Report," *Working Woman*, October, 109–13, 148.

Spiegler, M. (1996, November), "Marketing Street Culture: Bringing Hip-Hop Style to the Mainstream," *American Demographics*, 18(11): 29–34.

Tseèlon, E. (1992), "Self Presentation through Appearance: A Manipulative vs. a Dramaturgical Approach," *Symbolic Interaction*, 15(4): 501–13.

3.1
Power, Pride and Kente Cloth

Denise Oliver Velez

Across the nation, students graduating from historically black colleges and universities (HBCUs) like those in Howard University (Figure 3.1), don a cap and gown—and often accessorize them with stoles made of kente cloth.

Since at least the 1980s, many African American graduates—particularly university graduates—wear a kente cloth stole over their graduation robes. The kente cloth stole represents the graduates' pride in their African heritage, and their pride in their accomplishment of graduating. If they are members of a historically Black Greek lettered fraternity or sorority, the stole will be in the two colors of their organization.

The ceremonial use of kente cloth is familiar to many of us in the black community—not just for graduations, but also in other settings like churches and social events.

As such, I was surprised to see this story, and I posted it to twitter:

Black teen 'escorted out of high school graduation' for wearing African cloth

The student, Nyree Holmes, told the Black Star he wore the decorative cloth atop his graduation robes in order to wear something that represented his culture during the ceremony.

"I wanted to wear my kente cloth as a representation of my pride in my ancestors, to display my cultural and religious heritage," he said. "My particular cloth was made by Christians in Ghana, where the kente cloth has been worn by royalty and during important ceremonies for hundreds, if not thousands, of years."

Holmes, 18, who described the incident on Twitter, said the school's student activities director told him he was violating graduation dress requirements.

Holmes said he tried to talk to the director, but he would not engage and instead tried to prevent him from walking onstage and called authorities. When Holmes got off stage, he said, three sheriff's deputies were waiting to escort him out.

The school district statement said: "The student was allowed to walk across the stage to be recognized and

took a formal picture with the principal wearing the kente cloth. Later, the student was allowed to return to the area where students received their diplomas. The student was given his diploma."

Holmes said the school principal met his parents and apologized for the incident.

The school district statement added: "The district's approved graduation uniform is a cap and gown . . . Unfortunately, prior to the COHS graduation ceremony, school officials were not given the opportunity to discuss with the family the student's desire to wear the cloth."

It was gratifying to see that an apology was issued to Nyree Holmes and his family. However, after reading comments (both supportive and negative) on various articles about the incident, it became apparent that there are quite a few people who don't know much about kente, its history, and why it has a symbolic meaning for many African Americans.

This recent incident is not the first time that the wearing of kente cloth has been in the news. It goes back to a story that attracted quite a bit of attention in 1992. Black attorney John T. Harvey III was removed from a case by a white judge in Washington because he wore a kente cloth stole into the courtroom.

An objection from a judge about a lawyer's choice of attire has become the talk of legal circles in Washington, raising questions about where a lawyer's personal freedom collides with court procedures and whether clothing can influence a jury.

The questions arose after a lawyer, John T. Harvey III, was removed from a case last week by a judge after a dispute over Mr. Harvey's wearing of a striped stole made out of a colorful African fabric known as kente cloth. The judge, Robert M. Scott of the District of Columbia Superior Court, had said that the stole might unduly influence jurors' cultural sensitivities. Neither the prosecutor nor Mr. Harvey's client raised objections about the cloth.

Mr. Harvey has asked the District of Columbia Court of Appeals to reverse the order and to remove the judge from the case, and he vowed to appeal to Federal court if

As appeared on *The Daily Kos*

the ruling is not reversed. He cited not only his right to wear what he pleased, but also his right to wear a garment that holds religious significance for him. "An Orthodox Jew wears a yarmulke, an Indian wears a turban, and according to the case law they can appear before this judge," Mr. Harvey said in a recent interview. "What is the difference between a yarmulke or a turban and my stole?"

So just what is kente cloth, and what is its meaning?

Kente cloth is deeply intertwined with the history of the Ashanti nation. The Ashanti Empire or Confederacy, which was located in what is today Ghana, first emerged in West Africa during the seventeenth century. The Ashanti are members of the Akan people who speak the Akan or Ashanti dialect. The word "Kente" which means basket comes from the Akan or Ashanti dialect. Akans also refer to Kente as nwentoma, which means woven cloth. Kente cloth designs vary, with the different designs, colors, and patterns each having their own special meanings and stories. But Kente cloth also reflects the history of the Ashanti people, from the emergence of the various Ashanti kingdoms to the development of the slave trade up to and including contemporary life in Ghana.

According to Ashanti legend, two farmers, Krugu Amoaya and Watah Kraban, from the village of Bonwire, came across a spider, Ananse, spinning a web. Amazed by the web's beauty, the farmers returned to their homes eager to try and recreate the web. They wove a cloth first from white, and then black and white, fibers from a raffia tree. They then presented their cloth to the Ashanti Asantehene, or king, Nana Osei Tutu (who reigned from 1701 to 1717).

Here are the meanings of the colors in Ashanti kente cloth:

- black—maturation, intensified spiritual energy
- blue—peacefulness, harmony and love
- green—vegetation, planting, harvesting, growth, spiritual renewal
- gold—royalty, wealth, high status, glory, spiritual purity
- grey—healing and cleansing rituals; associated with ash
- maroon—the color of mother earth; associated with healing
- pink—assoc. with the female essence of life; a mild, gentle aspect of red
- purple—assoc. with feminine aspects of life; usually worn by women
- red—political and spiritual moods; bloodshed; sacrificial rites and death.
- silver—serenity, purity, joy; assoc. with the moon

- white—purification, sanctification rites and festive occasions
- yellow—preciousness, royalty, wealth, fertility, beauty

World leaders like President Bill Clinton and Nelson Mandela as well as celebrities like Michael Jackson and Muhammad Ali donned kente on visits to Ghana.

Wrapped in Pride: Ghanaian Kente and African American Identity, by Doran H. Ross, explores the history of kente in Ghana and its place in African-American culture.

Kente is not only the best known of all African textiles, it is also one of the most admired of all fabrics worldwide. Originating among the Asante peoples of Ghana and the Ewe peoples of Ghana and Togo, this brilliantly colored and intricately patterned strip-woven cloth was traditionally associated with royalty. Over time, however, it has come to be worn and used in many different contexts. In *Wrapped in Pride*, seven distinguished scholars present an exhaustive examination of the history of kente from its earliest use in Ghana to its present-day impact in the African Diaspora. Doran H. Ross is the former director of the UCLA Fowler Museum of Cultural History.

The *Wrapped in Pride exhibit* traveled from the Fowler to many museums across the U.S.

Kente reminds us that the world is larger than where you are. The world is larger than what you have suffered, what you have experienced. The world is large enough to step across the Atlantic, the Pacific, and to join people as people. So the significance to me is that it's a bridge joining worlds together. Kente cloth means dignity, freedom, liberation, joining hands, love.

—Reverend Cecil L. Murray, First A.M.E. Church, Los Angeles, 1997

Discussion Questions

1. The last statement in this reading is: "Kente cloth means dignity, freedom, liberation, joining hands, love". As a part of non-verbal communication, what are other ways that Kente cloth could be interpreted? Brainstorm in a group of classmates to come up with diverse terms that might be used to interpret Kente cloth.

2. Why do you think a lawyer wearing Kente to a court case provoked such a strong reaction from the judge?

3. Where have you seen people wear Kente cloth? Have you ever worn Kente cloth? If so, what was the occasion and what reactions did you receive from others?

3.2
The First Crime of Fashion: Eighteenth-Century English Clothing Theft and Emergence of Fashionability

Lidia Plaza

Introduction: An Eighteenth-Century Petticoat

Clothes are language. Even the simplest garment speaks volumes about its wearer–their gender identity, their socio-economic status, their beliefs, etc. Just like any language, clothes change over time; a quilted petticoat has no more a place in the modern closet than the use of "thou" in everyday conversation. A story like "Indusiata: or The Adventures of a Silk Petticoat," published by the *Westminster Magazine* in 1773, demonstrates just how different an eighteenth-century petticoat is from any twenty-first century garment.[1] This ten-part fictional serial story imagines the life of a petticoat from the petticoat's point of view, beginning with the petticoat's creation as an undergarment for the queen. Transition and transformation are the core themes of this story; the petticoat changes hands in almost every episode by being gifted, pawned, or, on one occasion, *stolen*. The petticoat is remade, altered, and repaired by its owners, and in turn the petticoat transforms its owners into participants of an increasingly industrious textile market. At the beginning of the eighteenth century, the English textile industry was still relatively unchanged from the homespun model that had existed for centuries. By the end of the century, however, textile manufacturing was becoming increasingly industrial. As the means of producing, selling, and buying textiles changed, the experience of owning clothes changed as well, transforming clothes into a much more expressive means of communication.

Soft Numbers and Hardened Criminals

One way to study the purchase of textile goods is to look at textile prices using a source like James E. Thorold Rogers' *A History of Agriculture and Prices in England: From the Year after the Oxford Parliament to the Commencement of the Continental War* (Vol. VII 1703–1793: Part I).[2] Using his data, one can calculate the average weighted price of textiles for each year and get a good sense of how textile prices fluctuated throughout the century. Based on Rogers' figures, it appears that textile prices gently fell by the end of the century (Figure 3.8).[3] In addition, it seems that this trend was unique in the eighteenth-century English economy, as wheat prices rose during that time (Figure 3.9). Furthermore, Figure 3.10 shows that consumers were buying more fabric around the same time that the price of fabric dropped.

Another way to look at changes in eighteenth-century textile consumption is to look at theft rates. As bizarre as it seems today, cloth and clothing theft is estimated to have accounted for 20–30% of all stolen items reported in early modern England, and it's easy to see why.[4] Clothes were easy to carry, easy to hide, and, thanks to a robust secondhand market, easy to resell.[5] Most importantly, in a time when everything had to be made by hand, a simple set of clothes could easily be worth the equivalent of a year's salary for the average laborer.[6] A well-made dress made of fine fabrics could be worth much more.

Figures 3.11 and 3.12 chart the rates of five categories of textile theft over the course of the eighteenth century in London using The Old Bailey Proceedings Online, a

---

Original for this text

1. (1773) "Indusiata: Or the Adventures of a Silk Petticoat." *The Westminster Magazine*, (Jun.) 365–368.

2. James E. Thorold Rogers. (1963). *A History of Agriculture and Prices in England, from the Year After the Oxford Parliament (1259) to the Commencement of the Continental War (1793)*. (Vaduz: Kraus).

3. The average weighted price is equal to the sum of each individual textile price multiplied by percentage of the overall market held by that specific item.

4. J. M Beattie. (1986). *Crime and the Courts in England, 1660–1800*. Princeton, N.J: Princeton University Press, 187.

5. For more, see Beverly Lemire. (1997). *Dress, Culture and Commerce: The English Clothing Trade Before the Factory, 1660–1800*. Houndsmill, Basingstoke, Hampshire, [England]: New York: Macmilan Press; St. Martin's Press, 127.

6. For more on the price of clothes see, and Carole Shammas. (1990) *The Pre-industrial Consumer in England and America*. Oxford, England: Clarendon Press, 212.

Figure 3.8 Average Weighted Price of Textiles in Rogers' *A History of Agriculture and Prices in England* from 1703–1793 measured in pence per yard.

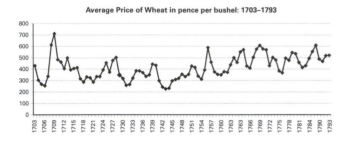

Figure 3.9 Average Price of Wheat in Rogers' *A History of Agriculture and Prices in England* from 1703–1793 measured in pence per bushel.

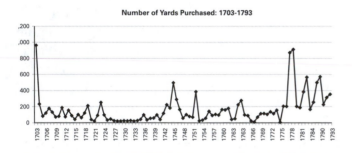

Figure 3.10 Number of Yards of Textiles Purchased 1703–1793 in Rogers' *A History of Agriculture and Prices in England*.

database of records from London's central criminal court.[7] Clearly, textile thefts increased generally as the century progressed, but raw textile theft far exceeded that of all other categories. However, these numbers were inflated by a few atypical cases in which thousands of yards of cloth were stolen at a time, and, if removed, the rate of raw textile theft would likely resemble that of clothing theft. More interestingly, clothing theft rates increased while the

<hr>

7. Data collection for this project used *The Old Bailey Proceedings Online*'s API, rather than the built-in search engine.

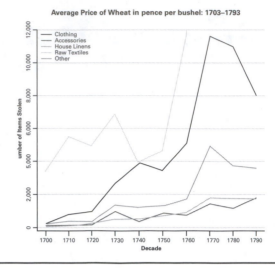

Figure 3.11 Eighteenth-century theft rates in *The Old Bailey Proceedings Online*, 1674–1913, for five categories of textile and apparel theft in eighteenth-century London: clothing, accessories, household linens, raw textiles, and other. Cases included in this graph are a representative sample of about 10% of all recorded eighteenth-century theft cases in Old Bailey.

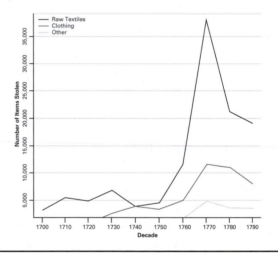

Figure 3.12 Eighteenth-century theft rates in *The Old Bailey Proceedings Online*, 1674–1913, for five categories of textile and apparel theft in eighteenth-century London: clothing, accessories, household linens, raw textiles, and other. Showing rate of raw textile theft.

theft of other kinds of textile goods became less common. This suggests that thieves were adjusting their tactics in response to an increase in clothing demand. Yet Rogers' data shows that the price of raw textiles had been dropping, making it more affordable to legally buy cloth and have clothes made, so why did theft increase? To resolve this paradox, we must take a closer look at these cases. The most common types of textile theft cases were instances of servants accused of stealing clothes from their masters, secondhand clothing merchants accused of selling stolen goods, and, a relatively new crime, shoplifting.

A Closer Look at Textile Theft

Masters, Servants, and the Problem of Ownership in the Household

The household was the most basic economic unit of early modern Europe, in which servants provided a large portion of the labor, and property dictated their relationship to the unit. Servants maintained and even helped produce the master's property, and in exchange they would receive some combination of wages, room, board, and/or clothes. A lucky servant might also receive property, including clothes, as a gift or as an endowment in their master's will. Livery—sometimes a generic term for clothes provided by a master, but more often used to describe the servant's uniform—was another way servants acquired clothes.[8] Yet the customs of the master/servant relationship were changing in the eighteenth century. The Industrial Revolution was taking shape, and it brought new ideas about how employers and employees should interact. Once thought of as members of the household, servants were becoming independent entities with their own economic agendas. As masters and servants redefined their relationships, clarifying ownership, especially of clothes, would become an increasingly important issue.

Theft was, of course, another way property moved between masters and servants, and this reality caused a great deal of social anxiety. Contemporary estimates claimed, "near one-third of the prisoners tried [in the year 1790] at the Old Bailey, were servants tried for robbing their master."[9] Yet the real terror of a servant's theft was that it undermined the core of eighteenth-century social structures, and, as one judge put it, "entirely destroy[ed] all the comfort and security of private families."[10] However, servants' intimate position in the household made it difficult to determine if there had been a theft at all. Servants often pleaded that they had simply taken the clothes for laundering or claimed that they had understood the clothes to be part of their payment. In addition, the parental nature of many master/servant relationships complicated matters. When accused of stealing from her mistress, Elizabeth Freeman pleaded, "I took the prosecutrix to be a mother to me, and she said to me I might make use of the goods when I wanted them."[11]

Disputes of ownership in the household were not limited to masters and servants. Consider the trial of William Badcock, accused of stealing his brother-in-law's clothes while living in his house. Upon hearing this case, the court was baffled and asked the brother-in-law, Mr. Story, "was it not customary for you to wear one another's Things?" Mr. Story answered, "Never but such Thing as a Coat."[12] To the court, Mr. Story's decision to prosecute his brother-in-law for theft was overdramatic, but it makes more sense when viewed from the perspective of a man using clothes as a form of self-expression. His garments were part of *his* construction of identity; they could not simultaneously be part of someone else's. Masters and servants may have come to similar conclusions. An eighteenth-century critic, Samuel Simon Witte, wrote, "[livery] concerns only the master and indicates only the master's taste," and servants were becoming eager to express their own tastes.[13] Servants may have been introduced to the culture of fashion while wearing their master's clothes, but to participate in that culture they would need to become their own masters in the clothing market. The first market they might have turned to was the secondhand one.

Secondhand Clothes, Firsthand Fashion

While today used clothing is a *secondary* market, it was a primary component of the early modern clothing economy, as many people could only afford to purchase clothing secondhand. Yet, just as ownership issues plagued the household, it was also a common dispute in this secondhand market. Secondhand dealers were constantly suspected of colluding with thieves to resell stolen goods,

---

8. See Anne Buck. (1979). *Dress in Eighteenth-century England*. New York: Homes & Meier, 108.

9. For more on servants see Bridget Hill. (1996) *Servants: English Domestics in the Eighteenth Century*. Oxford, UK: New York: Clarendon Press; Oxford University Press, 73.

10. Tim Hitchcock, Robert Shoemaker, Clive Emsley, Sharon Howard and Jamie McLaughlin, *et al.* (17 April 2011). The case of Mary Lawrence and John Lawrence (t17840526-75). *The Old Bailey Proceedings Online, 1674–1913*. (www.oldbaileyonline.org, version 6.0, 17 April 2011)

11. *Old Bailey Proceedings Online* (www.oldbaileyonline.org, version 6.0, 17 April 2011), April 1755, trial of Elizabeth Freeman (t17550409-11).

12. *Old Bailey Proceedings Online* (www.oldbaileyonline.org, version 6.0, 17 April 2011), April 1743, trial of William Badcock (t17430413-48).

13. Samuel Simon Witte, "An Answer to the Question: Would it be Harmful or Beneficial to Establish a National Uniform?" in Daniel Leonhard Purdy. (2004). *Rise Of Fashion: A Reader*. Minneapolis, Minnesota: University of Minnesota Press, 77.

but the only legal action that could be used against them was the charge of "receiving stolen goods knowing them to be stolen," as an accessory crime to a felony offence.[14] The problem was how to distinguish an honest dealer from a thief's accomplice. Rightful ownership of an item could be determined by the owner's "mark" on the item, a stamped symbol or embroidered initials. However, it was common practice for secondhand dealers to remove such marks upon accepting merchandise, and so this act alone could not implicate the dealer.[15] Not surprisingly, the crime of "receiving" accounts for only 4.3% of all theft cases brought to Old Bailey in the eighteenth century, and, of those accused, 70% were found not guilty.[16]

Ultimately, the secondhand market did become a secondary market. Secondhand dealers had been the primary means through which everyday people obtained ready-made clothes, but it was also the method through which the working and middle classes were exposed to the latest fashions and learned to be astute textile consumers.[17] Yet particularly discerning consumers would not be content in the secondhand market forever. Just as sharing ownership of a garment had become unacceptable to men like Mr. Story, buying clothes with previous ownership was becoming increasingly déclassé.[18] Secondhand dealers had thrived by providing whatever the market needed, but they unwittingly created a market that did not need them in return. Instead, middle-class Londoners became captivated by the new way to buy textiles: the modern shop.

Shopping and Shoplifting in the New Shopping Culture

"Shops" in the Middle Ages had been informal stalls or kiosks, but by the late eighteenth century shops had become specialized, fixed spaces more akin to a modern boutique. These new shops took London by storm, and the availability of cheaper textiles allowed textile shopkeepers to market to middle-class Londoners. They invested in elaborate window displays and made their shops exciting, enjoyable places to be, practices still used today.[19] Thus, they created a new kind of public space, and, with it, a new culture of shopping. This culture was particularly captivating to women, who did not otherwise have many socially acceptable spaces in the public sphere, and it transformed its disciples into a new kind of cultural and economic participant.[20] However, these new shops also created a new space for crime.

Though shoplifting was a relatively new crime, it was nevertheless considered a very serious thing; the Shoplifting Act of 1699 made the theft of goods worth over only five shillings a felony. Shoplifting accounted for only 4.3% of all eighteenth-century theft cases, but nervous shopkeepers felt that, if nothing else, the harsh measures helped discourage would-be thieves.[21] Shopkeepers felt prevention was key, for, even when a thief was caught, they could not always afford the expense and hassle of prosecution. In the few cases that did make it to Old Bailey, the prisoner was perceived as being obviously guilty and/or a professional shoplifter, sometimes described in terms of having "long had the Character of a Shoplifting."[22]

The real trouble was that thieves were supposed to be haggard vagrants, but many shoplifters looked just like the respectable, middle-class customers shopkeepers worked hard to attract. Even more troubling, an increasing number of shoplifters actually were respectable, middle-class customers, and, most upsetting of all, many of them

14. See Hitchcock, Shoemaker, Emsley, Howard, and McLaughlin et al. (2012). "Crimes Tried at the Old Bailey," *Old Bailey Proceedings*. Retrieved from https://www.oldbaileyonline. org/static/Crimes.jsp#theft.

15. One dealer admitted, "that he measur'd [the stolen goods] and cut off the Marks," but was still acquitted. *Old Bailey Proceedings* (www.oldbaileyonline.org, version 6.0, 17 April 2011), April 1719, William Cooling, (t17190408-42). See also Beverly Lemire. (1988). "Peddling Fashion: Salesmen, Pawnbrokers, Taylors, Thieves and the Second-hand Clothes Trade in England, C. 1700–1800." *Textile History*. (no. 1), 78

16. 1,807 cases of receiving out of 41,214 total theft cases. Old Bailey Proceedings Online (www.oldbaileyonline.org, version 6.0, 17 April 2011), Tabulating year where offence category is receiving between January of 1700 and December of 1799. Counting by offence. Also Old Bailey Proceedings Online (www.oldbaileyonline. org, version 6.0, 17 April 2011), Tabulating year against verdict category where offence category is receiving, between January 1700 and December 1799. Counting by offence.

17. See also Jan De Vries. (2008). *The Industrious Revolution: Consumer Behavior and the Household Economy, 1650 to the Present*. Cambridge; New York: Cambridge University Press, 145.

18. For more, see Beverly Lemire. (1 January 1998) "Consumerism in Preindustrial and Early Industrial England: The Trade in Secondhand Clothes." *Journal of British Studies*. (27, no. 1), 21.

19. For more, see Claire Walsh. (1 January 1995). "Shop Design and the Display of Goods in Eighteenth-Century London." *Journal of Design History*. (8. no. 3).

20. See Maxine Berg. (2005). *Luxury and Pleasure in Eighteenth-century Britain*. Oxford: Oxford University Press, 36-257.

21. Old Bailey Proceedings Online (www.oldbaileyonline.org, version 6.0, 17 April 2011), Tabulating year where offence category is shoplifting, between 1700 and December 1799. Counting by offence.

22. Old Bailey Proceedings Online (www.oldbaileyonline. org, version 6.0, 17 April 2011), February 1719, the case of Jane Scott, Ann Pierce and Sarah Scott (t17190225-7). Also, Old Bailey Proceedings Online (www.oldbaileyonline.org, version 6.0, 17 April 2011), August 1726, the case of Sarah Turner, and Katherine Fitzpatrick (t17260831-23).

were *women*.[23] Considering that respectable, middle-class women were the target market for the new shops, perhaps it isn't surprising that the same demographic composed its villains. Nevertheless, this phenomenon horrified eighteenth-century English society, which generally believed women to be incapable of committing such crimes, at least women of means and reputation. In addition, shoplifting violated a kind of social contract; it broke the rules of engagement in this new culture of shopping. However, it was precisely this culture that provided the motivation for this new type of thief. In essence, shoplifting was the price to pay for modern shopping.

Clothing to Fashion: A Revolution of Taste

Through the lens of cloth and clothing theft, we've examined several key cultural and economic shifts that drove the demand for textiles even as textile prices fell. Cases involving servants show how the ownership of clothing was becoming individualized, especially as the working class became more active participants of the clothing market. In cases concerning secondhand dealers and the reselling of clothes, we see how dealers took part in the negotiation of personal ownership, and how they helped refine the fashion pallets of eighteenth-century Londoners. Finally, shoplifting cases show how the eighteenth-century textile market created a new, modern public space and, in doing so, created a new drive for both consuming fashion and committing crimes. Yet, a major driving force of these developments rested neither the home nor the marketplace, but rather in the literal engines of the textile industry.

Innovations such as John Kay's flying shuttle, James Hargreaves's Spinning Jenny, and Richard Arkwright's water frame reinvented the entire textile industry in a process that is now considered beginnings of the Industrial Revolution. Nowhere was industry more revolutionary than in England. Early English textile manufacturing was dominated by the age-old industry of wool, but wool had lost favor among the fashionable people of eighteenth-century London who preferred French silks and Indian Chintz.[24] Some local textile producers pushed for legislation against these foreign imports, but more enterprising manufacturers responded by learning how to produce these fabrics at home. By the dawn of the nineteenth century, Great Britain had surpassed France and Italy as the powerhouse of textile production.[25] Yet cloth and clothes were not just cheaper and more abundant; they were becoming entirely different kinds of things.

Historian Daniel Roche once compared eighteenth-century clothing theft to modern-day car theft, and it's a useful metaphor.[26] A fancy car might express a person's socio-economic status, and a bumper sticker might express their political leanings. In early modern England, expensive clothes showed off the wearer's wealth and colored sashes or badges might indicate their political associations. However, modern-day clothes function as a means of expression and self-representation in ways that cars cannot. We change our clothes according to our mood, adjusting our wardrobes to fit ever-changing lifestyles, constantly recreating ourselves in textile form. This function of dress only became possible when everyday people could afford a variety of clothes, and, once they could, clothes became tools for expressing an individual's fashionability. Fashion is a quality of the garment, but fashionability is a quality of the person. Fashionability is the ability to create an expression of one's inner self and, in doing so, display a mastery of fashion culture through clothes. Today, to be fashionable isn't necessarily about wearing expensive clothes, or even nice clothes; it's about displaying one's prowess as a shopper and a consumer of fashion while also constructing a visual persona. As Samuel Simon Witte put it, "Costume thus does not dress the body, but rather the person."[27]

23. For more on women and shoplifting see Tammy C. Whitlock. (2005) *Crime, Gender, and Consumer Culture in Nineteenth-Century England*. Aldershot, Hampshire, England; Burlington, VT: Ashgate, especially 139 and 142. Also, Beattie, *Crime and the Courts in England, 1660–1800*, 179 and 237–243. Also Deirdre Palk and Royal Historical Society (Great Britain). (2006). *Gender, Crime and Judicial Discretion, 1780–1830*. Woodbridge: Royal Historical Society/Boydell Press, 39.

24. For more on English wool and textile production, see Maxine Berg. (1994). *The Age of Manufactures, 1700–1820: Industry, Innovation, and Work in Britain*. 2nd ed. London; New York: Routledge, 40. The ancient wool industry paved the way for England's textile industrial success; see Roze Hentschell. (2008). *The Culture of Cloth in Early Modern England: Textual Construction of a National Identity*. Aldershot, England; Burlington, VT: Ashgate, 3.

25. For more on English textile production and legislation see Buck, *Dress in Eighteenth-century England*, 189, 191. Also, De Vries, *The Industrious Revolution*, 137.

26. See Daniel Roche. (1994). *The Culture of Clothing: Dress and Fashion in the Ancien Regime*. Past and Present Publications. Cambridge : New York: Cambridge University Press.

27. Samuel Simon Witte, "An Answer to the Question: Would it be Harmful or Beneficial to Establish a National Uniform?" in Purdy, *Rise Of Fashion*, 77.

Conclusion

Today it would be downright comical for burglars to break into homes and steal nothing but the sheets. Craft stores are probably not overly concerned about customers shoplifting a yard of printed cotton. Yet the lack of cloth and clothing theft today, at least by eighteenth-century standards, is a direct result of the processes that once motivated that theft. In the two centuries to come, technological innovations continued to bring the cost of clothing down, and the textile industry was forced to re-conceptualize itself; the ancient industry of clothes became the modern industry of fashion. While eighteenth-century Londoners did not experience the fully-fledged fashion industry of today, they were already appreciating their clothes in deeper, more complicated ways. At some point, someone stole a garment—a dress, a shirt, or perhaps only a handkerchief—not for the monetary value of the object, but because they wanted to create a sartorial representation of themselves and participate in this new clothing culture. That was the first crime of fashion.

Reference List for First Crime of Fashion — Plaza

(1773) "Indusiata: Or the Adventures of a Silk Petticoat." *The Westminster Magazine*, (Jun.) 365–368.

Beattie, J. M. (1986). *Crime and the Courts in England, 1660–1800*. Princeton, N.J: Princeton University Press.

Berg, Maxine. (2005). *Luxury and Pleasure in Eighteenth-century Britain*. Oxford: Oxford University Press.

Berg, Maxine. (1994). *The Age of Manufactures, 1700–1820: Industry, Innovation, and Work in Britain*. 2nd ed. London; New York: Routledge.

Buck, Anne. (1979). *Dress in Eighteenth-century England*. New York: Homes & Meier.

Hentschell, Roze. (2008). *The Culture of Cloth in Early Modern England: Textual Construction of a National Identity*. Aldershot, England; Burlington, VT: Ashgate.

Hill, Bridget. (1996) *Servants: English Domestics in the Eighteenth Century*. Oxford, UK: New York: Clarendon Press; Oxford University Press.

Hitchcock, Tim; Shoemaker, Robert; Emsley, Clive; Howard, Sharon; and McLaughlin, Jamie, *et al.* (17 April 2011). *The Old Bailey Proceedings Online, 1674–1913*. (www.oldbaileyonline.org, version 6.0).

Lemire, Beverly. (1997). *Dress, Culture and Commerce: The English Clothing Trade Before the Factory, 1660–1800*. Houndsmill, Basingstoke, Hampshire, [England]: New York: Macmillan Press; St. Martin's Press.

Lemire, Beverly. (1988). "Peddling Fashion: Salesmen, Pawnbrokers, Taylors, Thieves and the Second-hand Clothes Trade in England, C. 1700–1800." *Textile History*. (no. 1).

Lemire, Beverly. (1 January 1998) "Consumerism in Preindustrial and Early Industrial England: The Trade in Secondhand Clothes." *Journal of British Studies*. (27, no. 1).

Palk, Deirdre and Royal Historical Society (Great Britain). (2006). *Gender, Crime and Judicial Discretion, 1780–1830*. Woodbridge: Royal Historical Society/ Boydell Press.

Roche, Daniel. (1994). *The Culture of Clothing: Dress and Fashion in the Ancien Regime*. Past and Present Publications. Cambridge: New York: Cambridge University Press.

Rogers, James E. Thorold. (1963). *A History of Agriculture and Prices in England, from the Year After the Oxford Parliament (1259) to the Commencement of the Continental War (1793)*. (Vaduz: Kraus).

Shammas, Carole. (1990) *The Pre-industrial Consumer in England and America*. Oxford, England: Clarendon Press.

De Vries, Jan. (2008). *The Industrious Revolution: Consumer Behavior and the Household Economy, 1650 to the Present*. Cambridge; New York: Cambridge University Press.

Walsh, Claire. (1 January 1995). "Shop Design and the Display of Goods in Eighteenth-Century London." *Journal of Design History*. (8. no. 3).

Whitlock, Tammy C.. (2005) *Crime, Gender, and Consumer Culture in Nineteenth-Century England*. Aldershot, Hampshire, England; Burlington, VT: Ashgate.

Witte, Samuel Simon. "An Answer to the Question: Would it be Harmful or Beneficial to Establish a National Uniform?" in Daniel Leonhard Purdy. (2004). *Rise Of Fashion: A Reader*. Minneapolis, Minnesota: University of Minnesota Press.

Discussion Questions

1. Do you think the author makes a credible case for clothing theft in 18th century England? Why or why not?

2. If you do believe the author's case to be credible, which part of her argument convinced you? For example, the graphs with clothing sales and clothing

thefts, her explanation that the Industrial Revolution created opportunities for easy shopping and easy thefts, or the description of the new retail shops and their social impact.

3. Explain how this reading serves as an example of the chapter title: dress as non-verbal communication.

4. Were you surprised to read that the patrons (middle-class women) of the new shops were not only the target consumer but they were also the thieves?

3.3
Who Gets to Wear Shredded Jeans?

Troy Patterson

Recently I scanned the statement of authenticity on a brand-new pair of good old bluejeans. Printed on the inside of the left pocket, beneath an equine insignia, an 1873 patent date and a boast of its status as "an American tradition, symbolizing the vitality of the West," Levi Strauss & Company reissued its ancient invitation to inspect the dry goods: "We shall thank you to carefully examine the sewing, finish and fit." The fit was slim, the sewing sound, the finish glamorously traumatized, as if intending homage to clothes Steve McQueen might have worn home from a bike crash.

A ragged extravagance of fraying squiggled from each knee, where an irregular network of holes was patched from behind by a white-cotton rectangle stretchier than sterile gauze. Knotted to a belt loop was a paper tag headed "Destruction," explaining that these Levi's, shredded to resemble "the piece you just can't part with," merited gentle treatment: "Be sure to take extra care when wearing and washing." The process of proving the denim tough had endowed it with the value of lace.

These jeans sent a dual message—of armor, of swaddling—in the accepted doublespeak of distressed denim. Pre-washed bluejeans are now sold already on their last legs: ripped, blasted, trashed, wrecked, abused, destroyed, sabotaged, devastated and, in what may be a borrowing of aerospace jargon for drones obliterated by remote control, destructed. Below this disaster-headline language, the fine print babbles smoothly about the soft comfort of deep familiarity, as the textile historian Beverly

Gordon observed in a paper titled "American Denim." These are clothes that suit the Friday-evening needs of Forever 21-year-olds buttressing their unformed selves with ceremonial battle scars, and they also meet the Saturday-morning wants of grown-ups who, arrayed as if to hint at having been out all night, enliven the running of errands by wearing trousers that look and feel like an opiated hangover.

The mass clique of distressed denim exists in polar opposition to another school of bluejean enthusiasm: the dye-stained cult of raw denim. The denim purists—looking professional in unsullied indigo fresh off the shuttle loom, in their natural habitat of bare brick walls and old gnarled wood and other textures invested with magical thinking—are likely to meet the approval of strict good taste. As opposed to people who buy their jeans prefaded and abraded, with a thumb-wide key punch in the watch pocket and the sham phantom of a wallet's edge in back. But sometimes good taste goes on holiday, to a music festival, for example, turned out in acid-streaked, bleach-stained, chaotically nasty cutoffs. This is the order of things. One point of beat-up bluejeans is to bother good taste, which is a muscular aesthetic stance, a canny market footing and an ambiguous moral position.

Some distressed denim is beauty-marked with subtle scuffs amounting to off-duty signs. Some is lavishly slashed into canvases for abstract craft work, with a fleeciness of bare threads asymmetrically outlined by stubby blue tufts, a kind of plumage for people treating a humble fiber as a vehicle for expressing splendor. There are bluejeans serially slit up the front, space striped as if by the shadows of window blinds in a film noir, and sometimes they are sold by shop assistants wearing jeans sliced to bare hamstrings, as if everyone's bored of the old ways of constraining the sight and shape of the body. There is a place in Paris that gathers old bluejeans as raw material for reassembled jeans that will cost $1,450 a pair. Which would be a bargain if you believed the piece worthy of framing as a collage deconstructing aperture and entropy and the tensions of a labor-class fabric reworked as universal playwear.

In 1973, writing a centennial lament for bluejeans in *The New Yorker*, the critic Kennedy Fraser discussed "one of the most bizarre twists of the whole extraordinary saga of innocent little denim and the giant, Commerce." The tastemakers of the rag trade had convinced the middle-aged establishment that denim was appropriate street wear, and these people, good bourgeois that they were, exchanged their money for putative luxury items. Meanwhile, everyone else kept buying durable old jeans as usual, including people who had no use for "fashion" but were nonetheless stylish and settled on jeans as an antifashion staple. Fraser wrote in "Denim and the New Conservatives" that "the fashion industry, spared the painful decision between catering to fickle trendsetters and to sheeplike followers, was able to trundle after both with piles of denim."

Bedraggled Denim

At the moment Fraser was writing, certain bands were tuning up (or not) to play anti-authoritarian costuming to the center of the popular stage. Bluejeans are sensually central to youth music—check out Elvis or Rihanna, query W. Axl Rose—and punk rock wrought its distraught energy on the uniform in a theatrically degenerate way. Boy-waifs in shrunken denim and shopgirls in shreds preened in the impropriety. The two most important influences on torn jeans are the kneecaps of Joey Ramone, bursting into view like the surly flesh of a malnourished Hulk. The third is the curt career of the Sex Pistols, a band that existed to promote a London boutique run by their manager, Malcolm McLaren, and his partner, Vivienne Westwood. McLaren's guiding ideology was Situationism, the post-Marxist movement remembered for its weary diagnosis of mass culture. The movement's texts were to him a playbook for turning battered bad attitude into a commodified style. "There is a certain aggression and arrogance in there that's exciting," McLaren once said of a Situationist anthology titled "Leaving the 20th Century." We might say the same of the 21st century's distressed denim, which struts its hostility to order by celebrating decomposition as a design element.

"Everything that was directly lived has receded into a representation," the Situationist theorist Guy Debord wrote in "Society of the Spectacle." He was describing a phenomenom now exemplified by new denim marketed as having been "aged to mimic look and feel of 11-year-old denim." The product lets its buyers slip into the approximation of a lived-in skin and by proximity, to enhance their own personal histories.

The insolence of indecent denim has evolved into a prefab mannerism, a marker of "punk chic" or "grunge cool." The holes can still reify a generation gap, I think, having heard a 35-year-old banker say that she cannot put on such jeans without imagining her parents' disapproval: "You should have worn those dungarees all day long until you wore them out yourself." But that purist's objection misses the point. The patent insincerity of distressed denim is integral to its appeal. What to make, glancing around the waiting room, of the precision-shredded knees of a pair of plainly expensive maternity jeans promoted for their "rock 'n' roll appeal"? No one supposes that a woman wearing an elasticized waistband to accommodate the fullness of her third trimester wiped out on her skateboard. The lie is not a lie but a statement of participation in a widespread fantasy. Contentedly pretending to be a dangerous bohemian, she is simply exercising the right to be her own Joey Ramone. We put on jeans with ruined threading in a self-adoring performance of annihilation.

This is a last frontier of conspicuous waste. Beyond the premise of a product enriched by terminal damage, there is the fact that making "trashed jeans" makes trash. Industrial laundries gobble water and spew poison. Garment workers choke on chemicals and dust. This is another of these limitless denim paradoxes: The threadbare surface of distressed denim implies to the eye that resources have been conserved and expenses reduced, but it is unsustainably costly. With a drought parching California, some distressers are now cutting back on prewashing in favor of ozone gassing, and some are scanning blueprints for lasers. Such innovations will lend a fitting postapocalyptic flavor to the future of the garment, matching the convoys of combat boots and motorcycle jackets essential to the everyday playacting of our era.

A few weeks ago, below the Tropic of Cancer, beneath the canopy shielding the glass face of a hotel lobby from the Caribbean sky, four tourists strategically picked through their suitcases while brass-buttoned bellhops stood by. The tourists were women who, early for check-in, chose to retrieve swimsuits and cover-ups for the sake of lazing poolside while their rooms were readied. One woman, completing this task, dropped upon her shoulder a silver satin sash, and her friends smoothed it to a photogenic drape. This was the aftermath of a pageant or something? Oh, no, obviously, right: This was a bachelorette weekend.

The bride wore white jeans stripped bare at the knees. Her friends wore jeans in mutually complementary pastels—pale blue and green and Nantucket-ruddy pink—all ripped at the knee line, with the remaining shreds of threads dynamic in perpendicular tension with patellar ligaments, denim blinking. This quartet of jeans was ideally socially suited to its moment, and the people wearing them sociologically coherent: a clique in sync, the details of ornament marking solidarity and order.

Denim is democratic. But though a great many of us are free to experiment with bedraggled chic, doing so requires a certain reserve of social capital. It is easy to imagine a worker showing up in distressed denim—showing up to do the kind of work likely to harm clothes—and being sent home to change. Claiming tatters as finery is a game not everyone can play.

Discussion Questions

1. Are pre-distressed jeans an homage to comfortable clothing or a streetwise trend?
2. Does Patterson approve or disapprove of pre-shredded jeans?
3. Are pre-shredded jeans the same as shredded jeans?

A version of this article appears in print on May 3, 2015, on Page MM24 of the Sunday Magazine with the headline: Who Gets to Wear Shredded Jeans?

CHAPTER 4
THE BODY

Andrew Reilly

After you have read this chapter, you will understand:

- Frameworks for viewing the body and dress
- Cultural expressions of beauty
- Potentially negative consequences of appearance-management behaviors

The human body has many possibilities for adornment; it can be considered a canvas for self-expression. Not only is it the foundation for the garments people wear, but it is also manipulated and decorated. For example, the body can be pierced, tattooed, injected with chemicals to remove wrinkles, have the fat sucked out, have its shape changed with undergarments, and have its texture altered with moisturizers or depilatories, among other possibilities. It changes with food intake, exercise, and age, and varies by gender and ethnicity. In this chapter you will read about different attitudes toward the body and how the body has been altered and changed to create different forms of beauty.

FRAMEWORKS FOR VIEWING THE BODY

Several scholars have devised ways to view the clothed body, and their work provides a basis not only for viewing the body but also for performing research studies on dress. Eicher and Roach-Higgins (1992) created a classification system for types and properties of dress. Body modifications and supplements can be sorted according to their respective properties. For example, skin can be transformed by tattooing (modification), which alters its color (property) and surface design (property). Body piercing not only modifies the body's skin, but allows for a ring to be attached to the body (supplement). See Table 4.1.

The taxonomy, created by Eicher and Roach-Higgins (1992), is a useful method to categorize and analyze body modifications and body supplements (see Table 4.1).

Susan Kaiser (1997) proposed a contextual perspective when viewing the body and dress. Awareness of the social, cultural, and historical influences at any given time is essential to understanding dress and its meaning, according to Kaiser. The contextual perspective draws from the fields of sociology, psychology, and anthropology, allowing researchers to understand meanings below the surface. See Figure 4.1.

Mary Lynn Damhorst created a model that considers the context of a person's dress and appearance (see Figure 3.3 on page 72). Underlying the contextual model are two premises: (1) in real life, we seldom see clothes divorced from social context, and (2) it has been demonstrated that interpretations of clothing vary along contextual lines (Damhorst, 1985).

Whether we approach the study of the body from a social, psychological, cultural, historical, or symbolic-interactionists or aesthetic perspective (or a combination of perspectives), one overarching concept remains clear: the body and all its modifications and attachments communicate volumes about an individual, a society, a culture, and a time.

CULTURAL STANDARDS OF BEAUTY

One connecting factor among all cultures is that we are all human beings, and many of us simply are not satisfied with what nature has given us. It seems to be human nature to want to "improve" upon the characteristics with which we were born. Because all cultures define ideals for their members, most individuals will spend time and energy

TABLE 4.1

CLASSIFICATION SYSTEM FOR TYPES OF DRESS AND THEIR PROPERTIES

Types of Dress**	Properties							
	Color	Volume & Proportion	Shape & Structure	Surface Design	Texture	Odor	Taste	Sound
Body Modifications								
Transformations of a. Hair b. Skin c. Nails d. Muscular/ skeletal system e. Teeth f. Breath								
Body Supplements								
Enclosures a. Wrapped b. Suspended c. Pre-shaped d. Combinations of ab,ac,bc,abc								
Attachments to Body a. Inserted b. Clipped c. Adhered								
Attachments to Body Enclosures a. Inserted b. Clipped c. Adhered								
Hand-Held Objects a. By self b. By other								

© Mary Ellen Roach-Higgins and Joanne B. Eicher

trying to attain that ideal. As social beings, we also want acceptance from others. One way to demonstrate that need for acceptance is the effort put into some approximation of one's cultural ideal. Consider these examples of beauty found around the world:

- In Africa, a large lip is considered beautiful among the Suri and Mursi women. Their teeth are removed and their lips pierced and stretched with a circular labret or disk made of clay or wood (see Figure 4.2).

- The Zöe men and women of Brazil use a m'berpót, a cylindrical plug made from the bone of a spider monkey or wood that in inserted through their chin as youth.

- Among indigenous people of North and South America, such as the Maya, Inca, Kwakiutl, Chinookan,

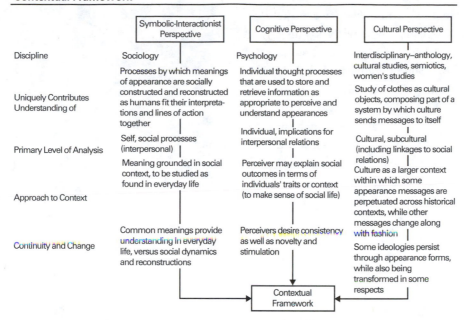

	Symbolic-Interactionist Perspective	Cognitive Perspective	Cultural Perspective
Discipline	Sociology	Psychology	Interdisciplinary–anthology, cultural studies, semiotics, women's studies
Uniquely Contributes Understanding of	Processes by which meanings of appearance are socially constructed and reconstructed as humans fit their interpretations and lines of action together	Individual thought processes that are used to store and retrieve information as appropriate to perceive and understand appearances	Study of clothes as cultural objects, composing part of a system by which culture sends messages to itself
Primary Level of Analysis	Self, social processes (interpersonal)	Individual, implications for interpersonal relations	Cultural, subcultural (including linkages to social relations)
Approach to Context	Meaning grounded in social context, to be studied as found in everyday life	Perceiver may explain social outcomes in terms of individuals' traits or context (to make sense of social life)	Culture as a larger context within which some appearance messages are perpetuated across historical contexts, while other messages change along with fashion
Continuity and Change	Common meanings provide understanding in everyday life, versus social dynamics and reconstructions	Perceivers desire consistency as well as novelty and stimulation	Some ideologies persist through appearance forms, while also being transformed in some respects

Contextual Framework

Figure 4.1 Susan Kaiser (1997) offers an approach to analyzing appearances that include symbolic-interaction, cognitive perspectives, and cultural perspectives.

and Choctaw, an elongated head was desirable. Modification began in infancy, when a child was bound to a cradleboard and pressure applied over time to change the shape.

- In China, circa 10th century to the mid-20th century, women with small feet were considered beautiful. A lotus foot measured three to four inches and was achieved through a process begun when a girl was approximately five years of age. The toes were folded under and pressed against the sole of the foot, broken, and wrapped with fabric bandages. The foot would then be adorned with silk embroidered shoes known as lotus slippers.
- The Kayan tribe of Thailand believe a long neck on a woman is beautiful. They use brass coils wound around the neck to push the shoulders down, giving the illusion of an elongated neck.
- The Moor Arabs of Mauritania view obese women as beautiful (and a sign of wealth). Beginning around age seven, girls are force-fed food in order to gain as much weight as possible and may even be sent to "wife-fattening" farms (Hartner, 2004).
- During a ceremony known as the Gerewol, where Wodaabe women of Niger can select new husbands, the Wodaabe men partake in a beauty contest and showcase bright eyes, white teeth, and faces painted yellow or red.

Figure 4.2 The women of the Mursi alter the size and shape of their lips using a disk.

- In the late 19th century, a beautiful ear was an important physical asset for European and American women, and was described as "neither too large nor too small, too fleshy nor too thin, too broad nor too narrow, too red nor too pale; it must be set neither too high nor too low on the head, and must neither stand out unduly from it or lie too close against it" ("Beauty and Hygiene, XV—Concerning the Ear," p. 152).

Ethnocentrism is the belief that one's own culture has the "right" way to do things. But when we make comparisons cross-culturally, can one honestly say that there is a difference between wearing high-heeled shoes and the bound lotus foot (bound Chinese foot)? Is scarification (cutting or branding the body) different from having a facelift or a nose job? Are lip plugs any different from ear, nose, and brow piercing? Cathy Newman, in "The Enigma of Beauty," points out just how elusive a definition of beauty can be. How do you describe beauty? How do you know it when you see it? Is beauty found only in physical characteristics? Or does "personality" factor into the equation? One way scientists have tried to quantify beauty is through symmetrical facial features. Newman's article includes an array of cultural and historical examples of beauty.

WESTERNIZED BEAUTY IDEALS: THIN AND MUSCULAR

The current Western ideal of thin and toned/muscular has not always been desired. In the Middle Ages, being overweight or obese was desirable because it indicated wealth (e.g., food during a time when food was limited). During the French Empire, women desired wide hips (a sign of fecundity) and could modify their silhouette with panniers. Beginning in the 16th century and moving into the 20th century slimness began to become more idealized as excess weight was synonymous with laziness or lack of self-control (Vigarello, 2013), although different silhouettes were fashionable during different times (e.g., hourglass, columnar). However, it was not until 1965 that a significant change took place in the fashion industry: Lesley Lawson was became a hugely popular model even though she deviated from the 1950s hourglass silhouette. Leslie was thin and became known as "Twiggy." From then on, thin was in, especially for models (see Figure 4.3).

However, the drive for thinness can be exacerbated and lead to negative consequences and the fashion industry bears part of the responsibility for this obsession. These expectations are placed on fashion models, and not meeting them results in models not being hired. Unfortunately, a number of models have died as a result of eating disorders in an effort to be or remain thin, including American model Margaux Hemingway in 1996, Brazilian model Ana Carolina Reston in 2006, Uruguayan sisters and models Luisel Ramos in 2006, Eliana Ramos

Figure 4.3 "Twiggy" epitomized a new look in fashion in the 1960s—that of a thin body.

in 2007, and French model Isabel Caro in 2010. Their deaths highlighted a growing concern about body image and led to some changes, such as Madrid Fashion Week instituting a minimum body mass index (weight to height ratio) and Italian fashion designers banning size 0 models, both in 2006. Dove, the soap company, instituted the "Dove Campaign for Real Beauty" in 2004 in hopes of changing perceptions of what is a "beautiful" body by using marketing with normal-size women in ad campaigns and videos.

Being thin is not idealized everywhere. Peck (2005) found that in Africa thinness is stigmatized. Those afraid of contracting HIV avoid thin individuals. This was also common among gay communities in the 1980s when thinness was equated with AIDS, regardless of one's HIV status. Among the Kalabari, also in Africa, fatness for women indicates a woman's fertility and therefore her value. In Jamaica, a thin person is viewed as someone who has low status and is not loved or cared for by others (Sobo, 1994). In Africa, a beauty pageant is held to celebrate a woman's plumpness (Knickmeyer, 2001). Knickmeyer (2001) noted the interesting cross-cultural observation that Americans focus on the size of a woman's bust line (as illustrated by Barbie, originally a German invention), while Africans focus on the size of a woman's derrière.

Westernized men, however, had more leeway with their body shape due to a patriarchal system where women were desired for their beauty and men for their financial economy (more on this in Chapter 5). Therefore, men's physiques were not necessary for attracting a desirable mate. But, as women entered the workforce in droves in the 1980s and became more financially independent, men realized they needed to attain a pleasing body. In addition, marketing changed and muscular models were now hired to sell everything from underwear to suits to cars to toothpaste. Of course, these are not the only reasons, as elements of class, race, and sexual orientation play a role in the development of the ideal body, too.

Body Image and Appearance Management

Body image is the mental construct people have about their bodies and includes "a person's perceptions, thoughts, and feelings about his or her body" (Grogan, 2008, p. 3). How a person views their body (body perception) affects not only how they present their physical selves to the public but also what they are willing to do in order to attain their ideal body. Several researchers have looked for a connection between body perception and self-esteem. Self-esteem involves individual feelings of self-worth (Rosenberg, 1985). Not surprisingly, when we feel better about our bodies, we feel better about ourselves. However, many people feel poorly about their bodies or experience body dissatisfaction.

Body dissatisfaction is common among the U.S. population and it is believed that very few people are perfectly satisfied with their bodies. Body dissatisfaction can lead to excessive exercise and dieting, self-induced vomiting, and plastic surgery. The extent of body dissatisfaction is not surprising, especially when one considers that comparing one's body to others and striving for a "better" body begins before becoming a teenager (Pope, Phillips, & Olivardia, 2000).

Body dissatisfaction was long thought to be only a woman's problem, but within the last few decades there has been an increase in men's concerns about the body. Men have likely been concerned about their bodies for longer than the last few decades, but two explanations can offer reasons why this focus has recently come to light. First, as women became more independent during the last several decades and did not need a man to support them, men had to compete with each other for female attention in ways other than economically; a desirable male body therefore became a commodity. Second, concerns about appearance had long been viewed as vain and feminine, and men likely thought it was unmanly to talk about their issues concerning weight, body shape, and muscle tone. Whereas women always have had a venue to discuss their anxieties, men have had to suffer in silence, until recently when diagnoses for body disorders became more frequent and support groups for men with body issues became more prevalent.

All people participate in **appearance management behaviors (AMBs)**: activities that create a desired aesthetic and generally relate to one or more of the five senses. For example, combing hair relates to the visual appearance, ironing clothing relates to the sense of touch, perfume to the sense of smell, the jingle of dangling bracelets or the sounds of taffeta to the sense of hearing, and flavored lip gloss to the sense of taste. More often, one AMB can overlap into multiple senses, such as mouthwash helping with both taste and smell or fabric selection addressing sight, sound, and touch.

AMBs can be divided into two categories, routine and non-routine. Routine AMBs are commonplace and tend to be non-painful, such as brushing teeth, shaving, moisturizing, trimming nails, painting nails, applying makeup, and so on. Non-routine AMBs are engaged in less frequently and tend to carry a degree of pain, discomfort, or health risk because of their invasive nature, such as liposuction, tattooing, branding (burning the skin with hot metal), and using anabolic steroids. Reilly and Rudd (2009) found the use of non-routine AMBs to be related to social anxiety, such that the more concerned or stressed someone is about being viewed in public situations, the more likely that person will consider a non-routine AMB activity. It appears that the non-routine AMBs offer some people a quick solution to their appearance worries.

Cosmetic surgery has become big business, and many people are turning to surgeons to change their appearance. According to the American Society of Plastic Surgeons, all cosmetic procedures have increased by 115 percent since 2000, with breast lifts and buttock lifts as the first and second, respectively, most popular invasive procedures and botulinum toxin (i.e., Botox) injections and soft-tissue fillers as the most popular minimally invasive procedures. Interestingly, men now account for more than 40 percent of cosmetic breast reduction surgeries. Buttock cosmetic surgeries had become the fastest growing type of procedure in 2015, with buttock augmentation, buttock lift, and buttock implants as the most popular (American Society of Plastic Surgeons, n.d.). Katie Pisa reports on this phenomena further in "Bottoms Up: Why Butt Lifts Are Big Business in Parts of Africa."

Altering skin tone is another common AMB related to body image. People believe a tanned person to be more attractive than an untanned person (Keesling and Friedman, 1987; Broadstock, Borland, & Gason, 1992; Garvin & Wilson, 1999); however, this was not always the case. Pale skin was once fashionable because it signified social and economic status. When European and American societies were based on agrarian manual labor, a tan indicated that one was a field worker, whereas pale skin indicated a life of leisure and indoor activities. In pre-Revolutionary France, members of the aristocracy would even paint blue veins on their skin to emphasize their paleness. However, with the increased rate of indoor work due to the Industrial Revolution, the perceptions of a tan changed. A pale pallor now meant that one worked indoors, while a tan indicated leisure activities outside.

Many people believe tanning can reduce or clear up acne (e.g., dry the oil glands), accelerate dieting (e.g., sweat out water retention), or aid in musculature (e.g., a tan helps define muscular curvature). However, tanning has its risks, including premature aging (ironic, considering the obsession with youthful beauty) and cancer. In one of the largest studies of its type, Geller et al. (2002) surveyed 10,000 children and adolescents on their tanning and sunscreen use and found they do not use recommended sun protection, found a notable difference between boys and girls, and found an increase in tanning bed use as age increases. At the opposite end of the spectrum are people who desire to lighten their skin tones and engage in skin-bleaching processes. Reasons appear to be similar to tanning (e.g., self-esteem, peer pressure, aesthetics), and Christopher Charles (2012) argues that a perception of beauty—not race—is a key factor due to **colorism**, or the privileging of lighter skin tones.

In addition to tanning and bleaching of the skin, a more permanent change to the body's color and texture is tattooing. Tattoos were once the domain of specific non-Western tribes and peoples (such as Pacific and African cultures), outlaws, sailors, and artists, but in recent decades they have become not only acceptable but fashionable. The desire to permanently mark the body can be attributed to personal identity, group affiliation, or aesthetic expression. The type or style of tattoo has been the effect of fashion forces (Negrin, 2007) and ranged from anchors and pinup girls to tribal to Japanese-style. However, Andrew Reilly argues that not only are types of tattoos symptomatic of fashion but their locations are as well in "Extending the Theory of Shifting Erogenous Zones to Men's Tattoos."

Summary

This chapter reviewed different ways that the body is considered beautiful and how people have altered the body—both good and bad—to achieve a cultural ideal. Some people focus on changing the entire body (e.g., silhouette), while others focus on smaller details (e.g., the ear). Beauty is not something that is easily attained—perhaps that is why everyone wants it so desperately—and the examples of what is beautiful change from age to age and culture to culture.

Key Terms

Appearance-management behaviors (AMBs)

Body image

Colorism

Ethnocentrism

FRAMEWORKS FOR CONTEXTUALIZING DRESS

Select either the model by Damhorst (on page 72 in Chapter 3) or the model by Eicher and Roach-Higgins (on page 92 in this chapter). Next, find a photograph of yourself, family member, or friend. Analyze the image using either one of the frameworks. When you are finished, consider how this helped you understand all the properties that work together to create a "look."

EXPOSED BODY PARTS

Review current and historic magazines to identify exposed body parts (e.g., shoulders, arms, chest, thighs, calves, etc.). For each category, note the year. Keep a list for women's images and a list for men's images. Do you notice any trends or eras when a specific body part was more prominent than others? Why do you think this was the case? Were there any gender differences?

test question

SELECTED IMAGES OF PREGNANCY THROUGH TIME

Pregnancy is an interesting stage of a woman's body that is associated with cultural expectations. For example, in the *Arnolfini Wedding Portrait* from 1434 (see Figure 4.4), the bride appears to be pregnant when in reality she is not. Her appearance is fulfilling a social expectation. In Europe at that time, great emphasis was placed on replenishing society because of losses from wars and plagues.

Most Americans reacted similarly after World War II by replenishing society, resulting in the baby boom generation. Postwar fashions for women are often noted for emphasizing a woman's reproductive capacities (Storm, 1987). A common example of this is Dior's New Look in 1947.

Moving ahead to the early 1970s, we see women exposing their pregnant bellies unapologetically (see Figure 4.5). One might assume that these women are hippies or those who adopted the philosophy of "let it all hang out" quite literally. No bashful pretenses here!

In the 1980s, Princess Diana (see Figure 4.6) took a very conservative approach to her dress for impending motherhood. Note the details of Princess Diana's dress: ruffles around the neck and wrists, white hose, and black

Figure 4.4 In Jan van Eyck's *Arnolfini Wedding Portrait* (1434), the bride is conforming to the 15th-century body ideal for European women.

Figure 4.5 Exposing abdomens in the 1970s was a way of visually challenging cultural expectations of pregnant women.

Figure 4.6 Princess Diana conservatively dressed in maternity attire.

patent leather shoes with bows. It appears as if she is dressed as the child she is about to give birth to! Certainly, cultural expectations of Diana greatly affected her choice of dress while pregnant with the future king of England. This is quite a shift from the previous 1970s illustration.

Also during the 1980s, there was a need for more professional dress than what Princess Diana was wearing (Miller, 1985). Many women in the 1980s were working to establish a career before having a family. You can imagine how difficult it might be for an attorney or physician to instill confidence in her professional abilities while wearing ruffles and bows to her law or medical office (see Belleau, Miller, & Church, 1988). Several companies during the 1980s developed a line of maternity clothing especially for professional women.

Now let's turn our attention to the 1990s. Actress Demi Moore was pictured on the cover of *Vanity Fair*, pregnant and nude, in 1991—quite a bold step that resulted in an interesting reaction to this issue. Some cities in the United States required that the magazine be wrapped in brown paper (much like pornographic magazines); other cities banned the sale of that issue completely. These reactions raise questions. Why was the cover of *Vanity Fair* so disturbing to some people that it had to be covered or banned? Why are Americans so uncomfortable with the sight of a pregnant woman (a natural state of the body)?

It would appear as though Demi Moore was making a brave and somewhat risky career move by posing nude for the magazine cover. It would also seem likely that she was interested in challenging cultural norms about the expectations of pregnant women. During the Victorian era in America, women were expected to stay at home and out of view when they were "in the family way." Demi very visibly challenged that old notion. Demi seems to have started a trend. After her daring cover other celebrity moms-to-be took similar turns posing nude on magazine covers: Britney Spears on *Harper's Bazaar* (2006), Cindy Crawford on *W* (2010), and Jessica Simpson on *Elle* (2012).

Today, showing off one's expanding body is a source of pride and seems to have returned to the sentiment of the 1970s. Not only is casual attire made for pregnant women, but so too are formal clothes. Heidi Klum's numerous walks down red carpets have represented another shift in attitudes toward pregnancy. Her sleek gowns are fitted, tailored, and revealing. With dresses exposing the leg through a high slit or strapless tops baring the décolleté, and feet in high heels, Heidi seems to be saying, "Yes I'm pregnant and I'm beautiful" (see Figure 4.7).

Writing Activity

Write a paragraph or two expressing your thoughts on why the Demi Moore photograph was covered in brown

Figure 4.7 Supermodel Heidi Klum proudly displays her pregnant figure on the red carpet.

paper or banned. Also include any ideas that came to mind while you looked at the images of pregnant women (real or imagined). How have ideas about pregnancy changed over time? How have those changes been reflected in dress? In the 1990s, concern for body weight affected some women's decisions regarding childbirth. More women were deciding not to have children because of the potential weight gain and difficulty in losing pregnancy weight (Garner, 1997). What implications does the decision not to have children have for American society? Also, consider the social class and status of the women illustrated. How might Princess Diana's status affect her dress as compared with the women from the early 1970s? How does today's emphasis on extreme thinness compare to Heidi's glamorous, figure-fitting gowns? How will this change perceptions about the pregnant body?

Group Activity

After writing down your thoughts, divide into small groups and share your ideas with your classmates.

References

American Society of Plastic Surgeons (February 25, 2016), "New Statistics Reflect the Changing Face of Plastic Surgery." Available online: https://www .plasticsurgery.org/news/press-releases/new-statistics -reflect-the-changing-face-of-plastic-surgery.

"Beauty and Hygiene, VI—Concerning the Ear," *Harper's Bazaar.* Reprinted in K. Miller-Spillman, A. Reilly and P. Hunt-Hurst (eds.), *Meanings of Dress* (3rd ed.), 152, New York: Fairchild.

Belleau, B. D., K. A. Miller, and G. E. Church (1988), "Maternity Career Apparel and Perceived Job Effectiveness," *Clothing and Textiles Research Journal*, 6(2): 30–36.

Broadstock, M., R. Borland and R. Gason (1992), "Effects of Suntan on Judgments of Healthiness and Attractiveness by Adolescents," *Journal of Applied Social Psychology*, 22: 157–72.

Charles, C. (2012), "Skin Bleaching: The Complexion of Identity, Beauty, and Fashion," in K. A. Miller-Spillman, A. Reilly, and P. Hunt-Hurst (eds.), *The Meanings of Dress* (3rd ed.), 154–60, New York: Fairchild.

Damhorst, M. L. (1985), "Meanings of Clothing Cues in Social Context," *Clothing and Textiles Research Journal*, 3: 39–48.

Eicher, J. B. and M. E. Roach-Higgins (1992), Definition and Classification of Dress, in R. Barnes and J. B. Eicher (eds.), *Dress and Gender: Making and Meaning*, 8–28, Oxford: Berg Press.

Garner, D. M. (1997, January/February), "The 1997 Body Image Survey Results," *Psychology Today*, 30(1): 30–44, 75–76, 78, 80, 84.

Garvin, T. and K. Wilson (1999), "The Use of Storytelling for Understanding Women's Desire to Tan: Lessons from the Field," *Professional Geographer*, 51(2): 269–306.

Geller, A. C., G. Colditz, S. Oliveria, K. Emmons, C. Jorgensen, G. N. Aweh, and A. L. Frazier (2002), "Use of Sunscreen, Sunburning Rates, and Tanning Bed Use among More Than 10,000 U.S. Children and Adolescents," *Pediatrics*, 109(6): 1009–14.

Grogan, S. (2008), *Body Image: Understanding Body Dissatisfaction in Men, Women and Children* (2nd ed.), London: Routledge.

Hartner, P. (2004), "Mauritania's 'Wife-Fattening' Farm," *BBC*. Available online: http://news.bbc.co.uk/2/hi/3429903.stm.

Kaiser, S. B. (1997), *The Social Psychology of Clothing* (2nd ed. rev.), New York: Fairchild Publications.

Keesling, B. and H. S. Friedman (1987), "Psychosocial Factors in Sunbathing and Sunscreen Use," *Health Psychology*, 6: 477–93.

Knickmeyer, E. (2001), "African Pageant Gives Weight to the Notion of Beauty," Associated Press, August 6. Available online: https://www.seattlepi.com/national/article/African-pageant-gives-weight-to-the-notion-of-1061896.php.

Miller, K. A. (1985), "Clothing Preferences for Maternity Career Apparel and Its Relationship to Perceived Job Effectiveness." Unpublished master's thesis, Louisiana State University, Baton Rouge.

Negrin, L. (2007), "Body Art and Men's Fashion," in A. Reilly and S. Cosbey (eds.), *The Men's Fashion Reader*, 323–36, New York: Fairchild.

Peck, D. (2005), "The Weight of the World," in M. L. Damhorst, K. A. Miller-Spillman, S. O. Michelman (eds.), *The Meanings of Dress* (2nd ed.), 42–43, New York: Fairchild.

Pope, Jr., H. G., K. A. Phillips and R. Olivardia (2000), *The Adonis Complex: The Secret Crisis of Male Body Obsession*, New York: Free Press.

Reilly, A. and N. A. Rudd (2009), "Social Anxiety as Predictor of Personal Aesthetic for Women," *Clothing and Textiles Research Journal*, 27(3): 227–39.

Rosenberg, M. (1985), "Self-Concept and Psychological Well-Being," in R. L. Leahy (ed.), *The Development of the Self*, 205–246, Orlando, FL: Academic Press.

Sobo, E. J. (1994), "The Sweetness of Fat: Health, Procreation, and Sociability in Rural Jamaica," in N. Sault (ed.), *Many Mirrors: Body Image and Social Relations*, 132–154, New Brunswick, NJ: Rutgers University Press.

Storm, P. (1987), *Functions of Dress*, Englewood Cliffs, NJ: Prentice Hall.

Vigarello, G. (2013), *The Metamorphoses of Fat: A History of Obesity*, New York: Columbia University Press.

This introduction is based on a version originally written by Kimberly Miller-Spillman and appeared in *Meanings of Dress* editions 1, 2, and 3.

4.1
The Enigma of Beauty
Cathy Newman

Sheli Jeffry is searching for beauty. As a scout for Ford, one of the world's top model agencies, Jeffry scans up to 200 young women every Thursday afternoon. Inside agency headquarters in New York, exquisite faces stare down from the covers of *Vogue, Glamour,* and *Harper's Bazaar.* Outside, young hopefuls wait for their big chance.

Jeffry is looking for height: at least five feet nine. She's looking for youth: 13 to 19 years old. She's looking for the right body type.

What is the right body type?

"Thin," she says. "You know, the skinny girls in school who ate all the cheeseburgers and milkshakes they wanted and didn't gain an ounce. Basically, they're hangers for clothes."

In a year, Jeffry will evaluate several thousand faces. Of those, five or six will be tested. Beauty pays well. A beginning model makes $1,500 a day; those in the top tier, $25,000; stratospheric supermodels, such as Naomi Campbell, four times that.

Jeffry invites the first candidate in.

"Do you like the camera?" she asks Jessica from New Jersey.

"I love it. I've always wanted to be a model," Jessica says, beaming like a klieg light.

Others seem less certain. Marsha from California wants to check out the East Coast vibes, while Andrea from Manhattan works on Wall Street and wants to know if she has what it takes to be a runway star. (Don't give up a sure thing like a well-paying Wall Street job for this roll of the dice, Jeffry advises.)

The line diminishes. Faces fall and tears well as the refrain "You're not what we're looking for right now" extinguishes the conversation—and hope.

You're not what we're looking for. . . .

Confronted with this, Rebecca from Providence tosses her dark hair and asks: "What are you looking for? Can you tell me exactly?"

Jeffry meets the edgy, almost belligerent, tone with a composed murmur. "It's hard to say. I know it when I see it."

What is beauty? We grope around the edges of the question as if trying to get a toehold on a cloud.

"I'm doing a story on beauty," I tell a prospective interview. "By whose definition?" he snaps.

Define beauty? One may as well dissect a soap bubble. We know it when we see it—or so we think. Philosophers frame it as a moral equation. What is beautiful is good, said Plato. Poets reach for the lofty. "Beauty is truth, truth beauty," wrote John Keats, although Anatole France thought beauty "more profound than truth itself."

Others are more concrete. "People come to me and say: 'Doctor, make me beautiful,'" a plastic surgeon reveals. "What they are asking for is high cheekbones and a stronger jaw."

Science examines beauty and pronounces it a strategy. "Beauty is health," a psychologist tells me. "It's a billboard saying 'I'm healthy and fertile. I can pass on your genes.'"

At its best, beauty celebrates. From the Txikão warrior in Brazil painted in jaguar-like spots to Madonna in her metal bra, humanity revels in the chance to shed its everyday skin and masquerade as a more powerful, romantic, or sexy being.

At its worst, beauty discriminates. Studies suggest attractive people make more money, get called on more often in class, receive lighter court sentences, and are perceived as friendlier. We do judge a book by its cover.

We soothe ourselves with clichés. It's only skin-deep, we cluck. It's only in the eye of the beholder. Pretty is as pretty does.

In an era of feminist and politically correct values, not to mention the closely held belief that all men and women are created equal, the fact that all men and women are not—and that some are more beautiful than others—disturbs, confuses, even angers.

Cathy Newman/NG Creative from January 2000 issue of *National Geographic.* Reprinted by permission of The National Geographic Society.

For better or worse, beauty matters. How much it matters can test our values. With luck, the more we live and embrace the wide sweep of the world, the more generous our definition becomes.

Henry James met the English novelist George Eliot when she was 49 years old. *Silas Marner, Adam Bede,* and *The Mill on the Floss* were behind her. *Middlemarch* was yet to come.

"She is magnificently ugly," he wrote his father. "She has a low forehead, a dull grey eye, a vast pendulous nose, a huge mouth, full of uneven teeth. . . . Now in this vast ugliness resides a most powerful beauty which, in a very few minutes, steals forth and charms the mind, so that you end as I ended, in falling in love with her."

In fairy tales, only the pure of heart could discern the handsome prince in the ugly frog. Perhaps we are truly human when we come to believe that beauty is not so much in the eye, as in the heart, of the beholder.

The search for beauty spans centuries and continents. A relief in the tomb of the Egyptian nobleman Ptahhotep, who lived around 2400 B.C., shows him getting a pedicure. Cleopatra wore kohl, an eyeliner made from ground-up minerals.

Love of appearance was preeminent among the aristocracy of the 18th century. Montesquieu, the French essayist, wrote: "There is nothing more serious than the goings-on in the morning when Madam is about her toilet." But monsieur, in his wig of cascading curls, scented gloves, and rouge, was equally narcissistic. "They have their color, toilet, powder puffs, pomades, perfumes," noted one lady socialite, "and it occupies them just as much as or even more than us."

The search for beauty could be macabre. To emphasize their noble blood, women of the court of Louis XVI drew blue veins on their necks and shoulders.

The search for beauty could be deadly. Vermilion rouge used in the 18th century was made of a sulfur and mercury compound. Men and women used it at the peril of lost teeth and inflamed gums. They sickened, sometimes died, from lead in the white powder they dusted on their faces. In the 19th century women wore whalebone and steel corsets that made it difficult to breathe, a precursor of the stomach-smooshing Playtex Living Girdle.

The search for beauty is costly. In the United States last year people spent six billion dollars on fragrance and another six billion on makeup. Hair- and skin-care products drew eight billion dollars each, while fingernail items alone accounted for a billion. In the mania to lose weight 20 billion was spent on diet products and services—in addition to the billions that were paid out for health club memberships and cosmetic surgery.

Despite the costs, the quest for beauty prevails, an obsession once exemplified by the taste of Copper Eskimo women for a style of boot that let in snow but was attractive to men because of the waddle it inflicted on the wearer—a fashion statement not unlike the ancient Chinese custom of foot binding (see Figure 4.8) or the 20th-century high heel shoe.

I am standing behind a one-way mirror watching a six-month-old baby make a choice. The baby is shown a series of photographs of faces that have been rated for attractiveness by a panel of college students. A slide is flashed; a clock ticks as the baby stares at the picture. The baby looks away; the clock stops. Then it's on to the next slide.

After more than a decade of studies like these, Judith Langlois, professor of psychology at the University of Texas in Austin, is convinced that this baby, like others she has tested, will spend more time looking at the attractive faces than the unattractive ones.

What's an attractive face? It's a symmetrical face. Most important, it's an averaged face, says Langlois. Averaged, that is, in terms of position and size of all the facial features. As the slides flash in front of the baby, I see what she means. Some faces are more pleasing to look at than others. It's a question of harmony and the placement of features. The picture of the young girl with wide-set eyes and a small nose is easier on the eye than the one of the

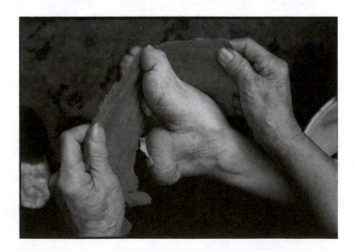

Figure 4.8 The tiny, narrow feet that resulted from the practice of foot binding were once considered beautiful by the Chinese.

young girl with close-set eyes and a broad nose. Extremes are off-putting and generally not attractive, Langlois says.

The idea that even babies can judge appearance makes perfect sense to Don Symons, an anthropologist at the University of California at Santa Barbara.

"Beauty is not whimsical. Beauty has meaning. Beauty is functional," he says. Beauty, his argument goes, is not so much in the eye as in the brain circuitry of the beholder.

In studies by psychologists such as Victor Johnston at New Mexico State University and David Perrett at St. Andrews University in Scotland, men consistently showed a preference for women with larger eyes, fuller lips, and a smaller nose and chin. Studies by psychologist Devendra Singh at the University of Texas show a preference for the classic hourglass-shaped body with a waist-hip ratio of seven to ten.

"That men prefer women with smooth skin, big eyes, curvaceous bodies, and full lips is anything but random," Symons insists. All these traits are reliable cues to youth, good health, and fertility. Take lips, which, plumped up by estrogen, reach their fullness at 14 to 16 when women enter the fertile stage of their life. With menopause and the loss of fertility, lips lose their fullness. Likewise lesions or sores on the skin signal the presence of infectious disease or parasites. Clear, smooth skin speaks of youth and good health.

In the scenario envisioned by Symons and other evolutionary scientists, the mind unconsciously tells men that full lips and clear skin equal health, fertility, and genetic soundness. It's an instinct honed over a hundred thousand years of selection, Symons believes. Because we are mortgaged to our evolutionary history, the instinct persists.

Not everyone agrees. "Our hardwiredness can be altered by all sorts of expectations—predominantly cultural," says C. Loring Brace, an anthropologist at the University of Michigan. "The idea that there is a standard desirable female type tells you more about the libidinous fantasies of aging male anthropologists than anything else."

Douglas Yu, a biologist from Great Britain, and Glenn Shepard, an anthropologist at the University of California at Berkeley, found that indigenous peoples in southeast Peru preferred shapes regarded as overweight in Western cultures: "A fuller evolutionary theory of human beauty must embrace variation," Yu says.

To think you've found a cultural universal is thrilling, says Elaine Hatfield, professor of psychology at the University of Hawaii, "but you don't want to deceive yourself into thinking that biology accounts for everything. The sociobiologists say we're trapped in our Pleistocene brains. The idea can be slightly bullying, as well as chauvinistic."

What about those who are not so symmetrical or well formed? Is anyone immune to feelings of inadequacy? Eleanor Roosevelt was once asked if she had any regrets. Only one, she said. She wished she had been prettier.

I knew I was an ugly baby when my parents gave me an electric toaster as a bathtub toy. . . . The joke is told by Joan Rivers, so I call her up—she lives in New York these days—to ask if the humor isn't just a little too dark.

"I always wonder what my life would have been if I had had that wonderful ingredient called beauty," the unmistakable raspy voice responds.

"Marilyn Monroe said to a friend of mine, 'I knew I had power when I was eight. I climbed a tree and four boys helped me down.'

"On the other hand, not being pretty gave me my life. You find other ways. It made me funny. It made me smarter. I wasn't going to get into college as Miss Cheerleader."

There's a hint of wistful in the voice. "Beauty is based on youth and on a certain look. When you're old, you're invisible. No matter how they lie to us and tell us Barbra Streisand is beautiful, if you woke up without her enormous talent would you rather look like her or Michelle Pfeiffer?"

In the world of beauty there are many variations on a theme, but one thing seems clear. Every culture has its bad hair day. In central Australia balding Aranda Aborigines once wore wigs made of emu feathers. Likewise, the Azande in Sudan wore wigs made of sponge. To grow long hair among the Ashanti in Nigeria made one suspect of contemplating murder, while in Brazil the Bororo cut hair as a sign of mourning.

Hair has other shades of meaning. Although the archetypal male hero in Western civilization is tall, dark, and handsome like Cary Grant, blond women have sometimes been imagined as having more fun.

Blond is the color of fairy-tale princesses like Cinderella and Rapunzel, not to mention the siren in *Farewell, My Lovely,* of whom Raymond Chandler wrote: "It was a blonde. A blonde to make a bishop kick a hole in a stained glass window."

Jean Harlow was a blonde. So were Carole Lombard and Marilyn Monroe (only their hairdressers knew for sure), who said she liked to "feel blond all over." A dark-haired colleague admits to "blonde anxiety," adding her observation that in California blondes have blonde insecurity. "They don't feel they're blond enough."

Hair-care product companies estimate that in the U.S. 40 percent of women who color their hair choose blond, a choice women also made in ancient Greece. From a biological perspective some researchers say blondness suggests a childlike appearance. Many newborns are blond and darken with time.

What other signals does hair send? In most societies, short hair means restraint and discipline: Think West Point, Buddhist monks, and prison. Long hair means freedom and unconventional behavior: Think Lady Godiva and Abbie Hoffman. Hair says I'm grown-up, and let's get that first haircut. It's the stages of life, from pigtails to ponytail to gray hair.

"This is what I looked like at age five," Noliwe Rooks, a visiting assistant professor of history and African-American studies at Princeton, tells me.

We're at her dining table drinking tea and talking about hair—specifically African-American hair—and how it defines culture, politics, and the tension between generations. The photograph she shows me is of a little girl with a big puff ball of an Afro staring up at the camera.

"My mother was a political activist, and so I wore my hair like this until I was 13," Rooks says, smiling.

"My grandmother had this huge issue with it. I was her only grandchild, and she couldn't stand it. It wasn't cute. It wasn't feminine. You couldn't put little bows in it. Every summer my mother would take me down to Florida to stay with her. As soon as my mother left, my grandmother would take me to Miss Ruby's beauty parlor and straighten my hair. Issues between my mother, my grandmother, and me got worked out around my hair."

While in college Rooks decided to let her hair "lock," or grow into a mass of pencil-thin dreadlocks.

"Before I was able to tell my grandmother, she had a stroke. I found myself on a plane flying to her bedside, rehearsing how I was going to explain the locks. The doctors didn't know the extent of the damage. She hadn't spoken. All she could make were garbled sounds. I couldn't wear a hat to hide my hair. It was Florida. It was 80 degrees. I walked into her hospital room, expecting the worst, when all of a sudden she opened her eyes and looked at me.

"'What did you do to your hair?' she said, suddenly regaining the power of speech."

After her grandmother died, Rooks found herself in front of the mirror cutting her hair in a gesture of mourning.

"When my grandmother was in the hospital, I'd brushed her hair. I pulled the gray hairs out of the brush, put them in a plastic bag, and put it in front of her picture. That was hair for me. There was so much about it that defined our relationship. It meant closeness, and then, finally, acceptance."

Gravity takes its toll on us all. That, along with time, genetics, and environment, is what beauty's archenemy, aging, is about. "The bones stay upright until you go permanently horizontal," says Dr. Linton Whitaker, chief of plastic surgery at the University of Pennsylvania Medical Center. "As the soft tissue begins to sag off the bones, the rosy cheeks of childhood become the sallow jowls of the elderly. What was once jawline becomes a wattle."

Blame the vulnerability of flesh on collagen and elastin—materials found in the second layer of our skin that give it elasticity.

"Collagen under a microscope is like a knit sweater," Whitaker explains. "After the 10,000th wearing and stretching, it becomes baggy, and the same with skin. When the knit of collagen and elastin begins to fragment, skin loses its elasticity." Then gravity steps in.

"If aging is a natural process, isn't there something unnatural about all this surgical snipping and stitching to delay the inevitable?" I ask.

"I guess it's not natural, but what is?" Whitaker sighs. "It's the world we live in. Right or wrong, it's a judgment. But it's doable and makes people happy."

It makes many people happy. According to the American Society for Aesthetic Plastic Surgery, almost three million cosmetic procedures were performed in the United States in 1998. Baby boomers (35 to 50) accounted for 42 percent.

The quest for the perfect look is global. In Russia cut-price plastic surgery lures patients from as far away as London and Sydney. In Australia, where a short-lived magazine called *Gloss* trumpeted the glories of cosmetic surgery, penile enlargements are among the six cosmetic procedures most popular with males, along with nose jobs, eyelid lifts, liposuction, face-lifts, and ear corrections.

In China plastic-surgery hospitals are sprouting up faster than bamboo shoots in spring. Patients can check into a 12,000-square-foot palace of plastic surgery called the Dreaming Girl's Fantasy on Hainan Island.

In Brazil, says Dr. Ivo Pitanguy, a world-famous plastic surgeon, "women get liposuction at 18 and breast reduction at between 16 and 22. They prefer small breasts and big derrieres, whereas Americans want big chests. In the 1970s only 8 percent of my patients were men. Now it's 25 percent. Today society accepts the idea of improving one's image."

The line between self-improvement and neurosis can blur. I hear about a town in Texas where breast augmentations are given as graduation gifts. And how to make sense of singer Michael Jackson with his reported inventory of four nose jobs, a chin implant, eyelid surgery, a face-lift, lip reduction, skin bleaching, and assorted touch-ups?

("Michael designed the way he wants to look," said a source close to the star. "It's no different from choosing your jewelry, your clothing, or your hairstyle.")

"Suppose I'm not so cute when I grow up as I am now?" Shirley Temple is said to have asked with some prescience when she was eight. Fret not. What goes down, comes up. For falling hair, Rogaine. For the drooping face, Retin-A. Prozac for the sagging soul and Viagra for the sagging penis.

"Old age is not for sissies," I say to a friend, quoting one of Bette Davis's favorite lines.

"No, no," she corrects. "Old age is not for narcissists. If you are wrapped up in yourself, you have nothing but the potential for loss."

Even non-sissies have trouble with aging. Martha Graham, a powerful woman and possibly the most influential force in modern dance, grew bitter as she grew old. She would call Bertram Ross, one of her dancers, in the middle of the night. "Die while you're young and still beautiful," she would hiss into the phone, then hang up.

At 48, gravity has taken its toll on me. I look at the mirror and note the delta of wrinkles starting to branch from the corners of my eyes. My chin has begun to blur into my neck. There is a suggestion of jowliness.

Of course I could consult a plastic surgeon like Dr. Sherwood Baxt. On the day I visit his office in Paramus, New Jersey, Baxt, a tall man with a sweep of graying hair, is dressed in a well-cut charcoal double-breasted suit with a pinstripe shirt, yellow silk tie affixed by a gold safety pin, and a pair of black tasseled calf loafers.

You might say that Baxt, who has not one but three different lasers for sculpting, peeling, and taming the bumps and wrinkles of imperfect flesh, offers one-stop shopping for cosmetic surgery. The centerpiece of his office complex is an operating suite that would be the envy of a small community hospital.

"Plastic surgery is exciting," Baxt tells me in calm, reassuring tones. "We're lifting, tightening, firming. We change people's lives."

"How and why?" I want to know.

"Most of my patients work," he says. "I see a lot of high-power women who can't fit into a suit anymore because of hormonal changes and pregnancies. They're in a competitive world. Liposuction is the most common procedure. The face is the next order of business—the eyes, double chins. All of that says to the workforce, 'You look a bit tired. You're a bit over the hill. You're having trouble keeping up.'"

Wondering how I'd fare with nip and tuck of my own, I've asked for a consultation. Thanks to computer imaging, I can get a preview. An assistant takes front and side views of my face with a Polaroid camera and scans them into a computer. As I watch, my face pops up on the screen and then morphs as Baxt manipulates the image. The softness under my chin retracts into firmness; the circles under my eyes disappear; wrinkles smooth out. I'm looking younger—not the hard, stiff, pulled-tight mask-look that screams "face-lift! face-lift!"—but more subtly younger.

"First I did your upper eyelids," Baxt explains, pointing at the screen. "I removed a bit of fatty tissue. I also took off some of the fat pockets over the lower lid, then lasered the skin smooth and tight. Next I did some liposuction on the wad of fat under the chin and brought the chin forward with an implant. You've got two things going for you: good skin and a full face. You age better if you have a full face. You don't need to be lifted and pulled at this point. Maybe in ten years."

The tab? About nine or ten thousand dollars. Of course my insurance would never pay this bill. It's strictly out-of-pocket. No problem. Baxt offers an installment plan.

Back home, I stare at myself in the mirror. I've always scoffed at plastic surgery. Then 50 loomed into view. Now I'm more tolerant. We are living longer. We are healthier. Today the average life expectancy is 76 years. Fifty years ago it was 68. One hundred years ago it was 48. The face in the mirror doesn't always reflect how old or young we feel.

The sad, sometimes ugly, side of beauty: In a 1997 magazine survey, 15 percent of women and 11 percent of men sampled said they'd sacrifice more than five years of their life to be at their ideal weight. Others were prepared to make other sacrifices. One 25-year-old Maryland woman said: "I love children and would love to have one more—but only if I didn't have to gain the weight."

Is life not worth living unless you're thin?

"Girls are literally weighing their self-esteem," says Catherine Steiner Adair, a psychologist at the Harvard

Eating Disorders Center in Boston. "We live in a culture that is completely bonkers. We're obsessed with sylphlike slimness, yet heading toward obesity. According to one study, 80 percent of women are dissatisfied with their bodies. Just think about how we talk about food: 'Let's be really bad today and have dessert.' Or: 'I was good. I didn't eat lunch.'"

In one of its worst manifestations, discontent with one's body can wind up as an eating disorder, such as anorexia, a self-starvation syndrome, or bulimia, a binge-and-purge cycle in which people gorge and then vomit or use laxatives. Both can be fatal.

Today eating disorders, once mostly limited to wealthy Western cultures, occur around the world. "I was in Fiji the year television was introduced," says Dr. Anne Becker, director of research at the Harvard center. "Eating disorders were virtually unknown in Fiji at that time." When she returned three years later, 15 percent of the girls she was studying had tried vomiting to lose weight.

In Japan anorexia was first documented in the 1960s. It now affects an estimated one in one hundred Japanese women and has spread to other parts of Asia, including Korea, Singapore, and Hong Kong. In the U.S., according to the Menninger Clinic in Topeka, Kansas, the proportion of females affected by eating disorders is around 5 to 10 percent.

To say that all women with eating disorders want to look like runway models is to gloss over a complex picture that weaves biology and family dynamics in with cultural influences. One thing can be said: Eating disorders are primarily a disease of women.

"It's easy to be oversimplistic in defining causes," says Emily Kravinsky, medical director at the Renfrew Center in Philadelphia, a treatment center for women with eating disorders. "Some of these women don't know how to cope or soothe themselves. They have low self-esteem. Also, there's increasing evidence that biology and genetics play a role. Finally, the distance between the cultural ideal of what we would like to look like and the reality of what we actually look like is becoming wider. If Marilyn Monroe walked into Weight Watchers today, no one would bat an eye. They'd sign her up."

Late one winter afternoon at Renfrew I sat in what once was the drawing room of an elegant mansion—it is now a space used for group therapy—and had a conversation with two young women who are patients. The subject was beauty and self-image and how that sometimes goes uncontrollably awry. The two sat next to each other on a sofa, occasionally turning to tease or reassure the other, in the easy, bantering way that friends do. One, a former gymnast, was short and compact and very overweight. The other, a former dancer, was tall, and very, very thin.

"My family moved here so I could attend the gymnastics academy," said the former gymnast we'll call Sarah. "I was three years old. Every week they would put us on the scale and call out our weight so everyone could hear. By 13, I was anorexic. And then I started eating and couldn't stop. I became bulimic."

"For me it was the mirrors and being in leotards and tights," said the former dancer we'll call Leah. "It was seeing the parts go to the prettier girls. I thought: 'If only I were thinner.'"

It has been a long struggle and will continue to be so, both said. There are no shortcuts in the search for equilibrium of the soul.

"I want a relationship," Leah said wistfully. "I say to myself: You don't have to be thin. Then I open a magazine and see these gorgeously thin women, and they all have a handsome guy next to them. I tell myself, oh, so you do have to be thin."

And yet, despite setbacks and constant self-vigilance, both could finally begin to see the glimmer of another possibility. There are other ideas of beauty, the two agreed.

"Beauty is all the wonderful creative things that a person is, how they handle themselves and treat other people," Sarah said. "My brother has Down's syndrome, and I judge people by how they treat him. It doesn't matter if you weigh 600 pounds. If you treat him well, you are beautiful."

There is a pause, then a quiet moment of insight offered in a very small voice: "Of course it's a lot easier for me to see beauty in others than in myself." She takes a breath and goes on. "Still, I know more than ever before that there are things about me other than my body. Things that—I can almost say—are beautiful."

The preoccupation with beauty can be a neurosis, and yet there is something therapeutic about paying attention to how we look and feel.

One day in early spring, I went to Bliss, a spa in New York. It had been a difficult winter, and I needed a bit of buoyancy. At Bliss I could sink back in a sand-colored upholstered chair, gaze at the mural of the seashore on the walls, and laugh as I eased my feet into a basin of warm milk. I could luxuriate in the post-milk rubdown with sea salts and almond oil. Beauty can be sheer self-indulgent pleasure as well as downright fun, and it's best not to forget it.

"People are so quick to say beauty is shallow," says Ann Marie Gardner, beauty director of *W* magazine. "They're fearful. They say: 'It doesn't have substance.' What many don't realize is that it's fun to reinvent yourself, as long as you don't take it too seriously. Think of the tribesmen in New Guinea in paint and feathers. It's mystical. It's a transformation. That's what we're doing when we go to a salon. We are transforming ourselves."

Until she was a hundred years old, my grandmother Mollie Spier lived in a condominium in Hallandale, Florida, and had a "standing," a regular appointment, at the beauty salon down the street. Every Friday she would drive, then later be driven, for a shampoo, set, and manicure.

This past year, too frail to live on her own, she moved to a nursing home and away from her Friday appointment.

A month before she died, I went to visit her. Before I did, I called to ask if she wanted me to make an appointment for her at the salon.

"I could drive you, Grandma. We could take your nurse and wheelchair. Do you think you could handle it?"

"Of course," she replied, as if I'd asked the silliest question in the world. "What's the big deal? All I have to do is sit there and let them take care of me."

On a Friday afternoon I picked my grandmother up at the nursing home and drove her to the salon she hadn't visited in more than a year. I wheeled her in and watched as she was greeted and fussed over by Luis, who washed and combed her fine pewter gray hair into swirls, then settled a fog of hair spray over her head.

When he was finished, Yolanda, the manicurist, appeared. "Mollie, what color would you like your nails?"

"What's new this year? I want something no one else has," she shot back, as if in impossibly fast company at the Miami Jewish Home for the Aged.

Afterward I drove my grandmother back to the nursing home. She admired her fire engine red nails every quarter mile. Glancing in the car mirror, she patted her cloud of curls and radiated happiness.

"Mollie," said the nurse behind the desk when I brought her back. "You look absolutely beautiful."

Discussion Questions

1. What is your definition of beauty? Write it down and be specific. Provide at least two examples of something that is beautiful (and why) and something that is not beautiful (and why). Exchange your definition and compare your answers.

2. What are some dangerous or invasive beauty practices that you have engaged in? What were they and what were the risks. How did you rationalize the risks?

4.2
Bottoms Up: Why Butt Lifts Are Big Business in Parts of Africa

Katie Pisa

While some women are doing everything they can to get rid of extra weight, a larger behind is so desirable in some countries that it's fueling a whole industry of creams, surgery and padding.

2015 was called "the year of the rear" by the American Society of Plastic Surgeons.

"In some social circles it's like, 'You haven't had your butt done? What's wrong with you?'", explained Dr.

Stanley Okoro, a plastic surgeon who works in Atlanta, Georgia, and Lagos, Nigeria.

When he's in Nigeria every two months, Okoro said he's able to do four to six butt lifts in a week. Each one usually takes six to eight hours, and Okoro is often booked up until late. "Sometimes I'm in surgery until 1am. It's exhausting," he said.

Why the rear has grown

Dr. Okoro says the biggest contributor to the rise in buttock surgery is without a doubt social media.

"It is a combination of increased popularity of Kim Kardashian, known for her ample backside, as well as increased popularity of social media," said Dr. Matthew Schulman, a plastic surgeon in New York City.

"The pressure to look good is what's driving people," said Okoro. He said in Nigeria, the massive film industry, commonly referred to as Nollywood, has driven the demand for the perfect butt.

A growing middle class has significantly contributed to the growth of cosmetic plastic surgery—once a forbidden industry—in Nigeria and Ghana, added Okoro.

The availability of smartphones in Africa and access to social media has also fuelled the rise in cosmetic surgery, Okoro said.

Over the past three to five years increased economic power and awareness of cosmetic surgery has fueled the popularity of such procedures, said Dr. Ojochide Ebune, a Nigerian surgeon and assistant secretary general of Nigerian Association of Plastic, Reconstructive and Aesthetic Surgeons.

The number of trained and certified plastic surgeons in Nigeria has grown in the last five years, says Ebune, from 70 plastic surgeons five years ago to around 100 now.

"The prosperity of patients is starting to increase. In a few years, it [cosmetic surgery] will be a mainstay in Nigeria and parts of Africa," said Ebune, adding that the demand mostly comes from more cosmopolitan cities such as Lagos and Abuja.

In South Africa, in a suburb in Johannesburg, "Surgeon and Safari" helps clients facilitate their cosmetic procedures, and perhaps go on safari too.

Many clients come from abroad, said owner Lorraine Melvill, who started back in 2000 and told CNN there is an emergence of local Africans that chose to come to South Africa for elective surgery.

"There is quite a big market coming out of Angola, Tanzania, Kenya, Ghana. Their economies are growing and therefore their middle classes are growing and. . . the need increases," she said.

Less invasive options

For those who can't afford surgery, there are cheaper alternatives in the form of pills and creams.

Dr. Okoro advises caution, though, as their contents can be unclear and their effectiveness unproven.

The trend in Africa is definitely on the rise, he said. "The same trend in Nigeria [for butt lifts], we are seeing in other West African countries."

ASPS's report in February showed that 15.9 million surgical and less-invasive cosmetic procedures were performed in the U.S. in 2015, a two percent increase from 2014. Dr. Schulman says he saw the demand for butt lifts start five years ago, and he has patients from all over the world. "I think this trend is here to stay, at least for the near future."

Schulman does warn about choosing an experienced and board certified plastic surgeon, however, as many of his clients come to him for corrective surgeries after bad results from other doctors.

His advice: only select a surgeon who does six to eight of these procedures per week, and can show over 100 of their own before and after photos.

Discussion Questions

1. Why are women more likely to have cosmetic surgery than men?
2. Do you think the reasons for enhancing the buttocks are similar to reasons for enhancing the chest?
3. Is cosmetic surgery deceitful if you don't tell people about it?

4.3
Expanding the Theory of Shifting Erogenous Zones to Men's Tattoos

Andrew Reilly

Tattoos have long been considered to be anti-fashion due to their permanent nature, thus excluding them from the defining feature of fashion which is constant change. Additionally, the theory of shifting erogenous zones has been declared useless in explaining current fashion trends. In this manuscript, I challenge both these assumptions to analyze how the theory can explain fashions in tattoos among men. First I discuss the origins and research on the theory, the debate surrounding the identification of tattoos as fashion, and the erotic nature of tattoos. In order to examine the usefulness of this theory I focused on three types of tattoo locations: the armband, lower back, and sleeve. I examined online blogs as well as interviews and conversations. Interviews were casual and lasted between 5 and 15 minutes. If I saw a man with a one of the three types of tattoos I approached him, explained the nature of my research, and asked if I could ask some questions. Interviews took place in Honolulu, Hawai'i and San Francisco, California. Names were not recorded, so all names that follow of pseudonyms. I also interviewed an employee of a tattoo parlor. Drawing on this data, I then argue how three types of tattoo fashions on the male body—the armband, the lower back tattoo, and the sleeve—are explained by the theory of shifting erogenous zones.

Origins and Research on Shifting Erogenous Zones

Flugel's (1930) assertion that the nudity is anti-erotic influenced Laver (1969) to propose a theory of fashion change based on revealing and concealing body parts. Laver suggested that men were attracted to women's eroticized body parts and women's clothing functioned to eroticize areas of the body by revealing and/or concealing or otherwise emphasizing these. But with the passage of time the featured part lost its erotic value and fashion's function was to provide a vehicle for regenerating eroticism by repeated changing the emphasis of the clothing from one body part to another. Examples that appear to support this theory include hemlines that exposed women's ankles in the Ante-Bellum and Victorian ages, legs in the 1920s when skirts rose dramatically from the prior decade, evening dresses in 1930s when the back was bared, décolleté in the 1950s when plunging necklines were in vogue, mini-skirts in the 1970s, and midriffs in the 1980s.

However, Steele (1985) argued that the theory does not always correlate with what people thought was erotic; Steel cites evidence from the Victorian era, where plump legs were considered sexy but nonetheless they remained covered by long skirts. Perhaps, body areas were not exposed because they were erotic, but exposing them make them erotic. It becomes a question of the chicken or the egg. In addition, Wilson (1993) noted that the theory ignores women's own concepts of their sexuality and sexual identity, and Pilcher, Pole, and Boden (2004) noted that the theory is problematic with regard to children's clothing, given the taboo against viewing children as sexual beings. Additionally, the *Reveal or Conceal?* exhibition at the McCord Museum of Canadian History in 2008–2009 in part demonstrated the concept of shifting erogenous zones. David, (2010) noted that the exhibition "does this by using little black dresses by Lanvin, Balenciaga, Dior, and Nina Ricci from different decades as a barometer for the exposure of new body parts. As a caveat it does state that Laver's theory alone is not sufficient to explain the major shifts in fashion over the last two centuries" (pp. 348–49). The design of the little black has varied during different time periods to reveal, conceal, or otherwise emphasize body parts. Thus, the theory of shifting erogenous zones does not appear to explain *all* fashion changes among *all* people, but it does explain *some* phenomena.

Researchers have noted that erogenous zones play an important role in the development of fashion and

Originally published in Critical Studies in *Men's Fashion* 1(3), 211–221.

style. When blue jeans became fashionable for women in Argentina in the 1960s, "wearing blue jeans . . . involved both constructing and meeting a new ideal of feminine beauty, which encompassed displaying new 'erogenous zones'" (Manzano, 2009, p. 665). Thus, the new blue jeans trend created a new form of erotic femininity by emphasizing the derriere. Likewise, Siami (2011) argued that "samba jeans" from Brazil focused attention on the female buttocks by "concentrating all or any decorations present on the jeans on that body part" (n.p.). Again, the influence of fashion helped to focus and eroticize a new body part. And in an analysis of designer Hussein Chalayan's work, Quinn (2002) noted, "the sensuality associated with revealing and concealing the body is central to Chalayan's work, which challenges the way fashion defines erogenous zones" (p. 367). Quinn identified in particular Chalayan's "remote control" dress, a technology-infused garment that can be electronically altered to expose, enhance, or conceal parts of the wearer's body. Chalayan's dress is thus a commentary on the shifting nature of erogenous zones; that with the touch of a button, a new locus of lust can replace an overexposed site.

The theory of shifting erogenous zones lost favor as an explanation of fashion change by the second wave of the feminist movement begun in the 1960s. Arguments against the objectification of women seemed to destabilize the underpinnings of the theory. In addition, men and their bodies became a focus of the gaze. Therefore, an eye-catching male appearance became a commodity for dating and mating; stylish clothing and a pleasing physique became a portion of what men had to offer women. The theory also did not address same-sex relationships where presumably eroticism and dress were functions of attraction. Additionally, dress scholar Steele (1985) has noted that the premise of the theory excluding men's clothing as erotic is incorrect, as menswear has often had sexual overtones that emphasized body parts, including the derrière and penis.

By the end of the 20th century, the theory of shifting erogenous zone was cast aside in favor of other explanations of fashion change, such as Field's (1970) the trickle up theory which posited that fashions originate in the lower classes and are adopted by subsequently higher social strata, and Polhemus' (1994) idea of style tribes which argued that unique looks of subcultures become the inspiration for new fashion trends. However, the theory of shifting erogenous zones is still a valid explanation for fashion change; it does not explain every fashion nuance or change (what theories do?), but it does explain a phenomenon with tattoos on men. As fashionable clothing has become more revealing and more of the body is now commonly exposed, tattoos have become the new source of erotic appeal. Like apparel, and like exposure, tattoos can be used to highlight and eroticize a body part.

Tattoos as Fashion

Tattooing has been around for at least five millennia with evidence suggesting its first use was for health.[1] Tattoo derives its name from the Samoan word *tatau* and Tahitian word *tatu* which mean *to mark the skin*. Traditional Polynesian tattooing involved pushing ink under the skin with slivers of wood or bone by tapping them repeatedly. In 1891 Samuel O'Reilly modified an invention by Thomas Edison, the electric pen, to draw on skin, and thus invented the tattoo gun. It, and other subsequent variations and intentions, have helped to increase the availability of tattoos to the public and decrease the time needed to create a tattoo.

In the Euro-American world, the 20th century began with tattoos found only among people among the fringes of society but by the end of the century tattoos were found among middle-class housewives, school teachers, doctors, lawyers, stockbrokers, parents, and even Mattel's Barbie© doll. Over the century not only had the people who got tattoos changed, but also reasons for getting tattoos; from modernist iconography imbued with meaning and symbolism to post-modernist motifs highlighting aesthetic design (Negrin, 2007). By the end of the century they also had become fashion.

Tattooing in the West began with contact made between European and Pacific cultures in the 18th century. Sailors adopted the geometric markings they saw on indigenous bodies and helped disseminate tattoos to people in other geographic locations. Tattoos subsequently became fashionable in Europe. In the late 19th and early 20th centuries, tattoos were popular among European aristocracy, including Edward VII of England (Jerusalem Cross on his arm), George V of England (dragon tattoo on his arm), Nicholas II of Russia (dragon tattoo on his arm), and Frederick IX of Denmark (who had several dragon, bird, and anchor tattoos on his arms and chest). By the early 20th century, however, tattoos were no longer fashionable and were only worn by select groups of people who were usually marginalized by the greater society, such as bikers, military, and prisoners (DeMello, 2000), who likely adopted tattoos due to a feeling a lack of control over their

---

1. In 1991 a frozen mummy which dated to the Copper Age (c. 3000–2000 BCE) was found in the Alps. The skin of the mummy was marked with tattoos that corresponded to acupuncture points.

lives (Beynon, 2000; Lentini, 1999). As Negrin wrote, "The adoption of tattoos was predicated on an affirmation of patriarchal conception of masculinity as an antidote to the disempowerment these men [military, bikers] experience in many aspects of their lives" (p. 335). Thus, tattoos were not only a form of asserting masculinity, they were also a form of social identity and social affiliation (Coe, 1993). Tattoos were commonly symbolic and included eagles, hearts, flags, and pin-up girls.

The defining feature of fashion is its constant change. The fashion process is characterized by an introductory phase and an acceptance phase, followed by decline and obsolescence, so it is not surprising that tattoos have long been considered anti-fashion due to their permanent nature (Curry 1993; Pohlmenus 1994). Tattoos "can never be true fashion. . .because tattoos cannot be put on and left off by the season" (Curry, 1993, 13). Yet, Negrin (2007) argued that despite claims to the contrary, today many tattoos are fashion; while the tattoo cannot be changed (and thus, is the antithesis of fashion), there are fashions in the styles and motifs of tattoo. During World War II, the heart, "I Love Mom," the anchor, and pin up girl were popular tattoo motifs among military men. Beginning in the 1970s, tribal tattoos, based on cultural motifs wherein tattooing was common practice, such as among Polynesian Islanders, became popular. By 2010 portrait tattoos were popular (Davis, 2010). Kosut (2006) identified fashionable tattoos as an "ironic fad" because while the popularity for the tattoo will dissipate, the tattoo will nonetheless remain.

Fashionably tattooing the body highlights the trend for transforming the body itself. For men, a fit body became a necessary commodity to attract a mate once women began to find financial independence beginning in the 1960s. As a result, men turned to their appearance as a way to attract someone. Marketing, including Calvin Klein's 1982 advertisement featuring Olympian Tom Hintnaus and 1992 landmark underwear advertisement featuring then-musician Marky Mark (now Mark Wahlberg), helped to usher in a new age where men's bodies became objectified and eroticized. Exercise, working out, and joining gyms became regular features of men's lives as they sought to shed pounds and gain muscle mass.

As tattoos became more popular, so too did the necessity to have a fit physique. Aesthetically, tattoos are perceived to look more pleasing on a toned body. "If you have a tattoo, wherever you get it, you have to be fit," said Joey (2013) during an interview; he continued, "They don't look good on flabby bodies. They get stretched out and they don't look right. You have to stay in shape." This sentiment was also noted by a blogger: "Personally, I think body art can look amazing if it's the right design in the right place. On someone with a ripped abdomen, and a clear, defined, sexy V shape leading to the pubic area, well a good tattoo there can be extremely sexy" (Robert, 2011). Likewise, another blogger noted, "But I do love, love, love a well-placed and well-crafted tattoo on a man—and I will even go so far as to say they can dramatically improve the physique of some guys when done right." (Snow, 2011, n.p.). Snow's comment is particularly intriguing because it implies that the aesthetic nature of tattoos can enhance perceptions of the body. Taken together, these comments suggest that not only do tattoos require a fit body they also echo the sentiment that the body itself is not only a commodity but also malleable and fashionable.

Tattoos as Erotic

In the 1970s new groups of people, including gay men, women and the middle class, began to adopt tattoos. While these groups likely adopted the iconic and symbolic tattoos of the marginalized groups from the early 20th century, they also embraced tattoo motifs common among tribal cultures. Followers of this new type of tattoo motif were called "modern primitives" and their adoption of "primitive" tattoos lead to a new interpretation of tattoos—the eroticization of the body (Lingins, 1983). "Tattoos were adopted as a way of liberating 'repressed' urges and reclaiming the sensual self" (Negrin, 2007, 338).

Tattoos are a sensual experience where sight and touch contribute to the aesthetic enjoyment; my observation has shown that many people automatically extend a hand to feel tattoo on someone else. The primal nature of marked skin adds to the visceral experience. Dimattia, as quoted in Reece (2008), noted, "Ask a tattooed person, and most will say they feel more attractive with their tattoos. . .They bring focus to the beauty of the body at any age. Tattooing can be a positive act of wanting to change the body's look, to feel good about it, and more confident, and thus, sexier." Dimattia's comments about change and feeling sexy underscore the nature of the theory of shifting erogenous zones. Likewise, Steele (1985) noted that tattoos have been a means of highlighting sexual characteristics.

In addition, and in line with the original premise of the theory of shifting erogenous zones, that body parts are used to attract a mate, is Carmen, Guitar, and Dillon's (2012) assessment of the biological nature of tattoos. They based their argument on Darwin's survival of the fittest theory and argued that due to the infection risk associated with getting a tattoo, people with tattoos are demonstrating their superior genes. "By ornamenting one's own body either temporarily (e.g., clothing), permanently (e.g., tattooing), or somewhere in between (e.g., piercing), that individual is using an extension of her or his genes (via behavior) to increase that person's ability to stand out in a sea of possible mates" (p. 135).

Shifting Tattoo Locations

I argue, that based on the concept that tattoo motifs are fashionable, the choice in where tattoos are inscribed on the body is fashionable as well. To illustrate this, I describe men's armband tattoos in the 1990s, lower back tattoos in the 2000s, and sleeve tattoos in the 2010s. I confirmed my assumption that these tattoo styles were in vogue during these timeframes with an employee of a tattoo parlor, who further commented that tattoo locations were made popular by celebrities. Each of these tattoo locations eroticized a particular part of the body and was linked to a particular time. In line with the theory of shifting erogenous zones once the particular style of tattoo became overexposed, men sought new tattoo styles and body locations. The quoted materials that follow were generated from impromptu interviews or were found on Internet websites devoted to tattoos. Names of informants have been changed to protect anonymity although names of bloggers remain unaltered.

The armband tattoo. In the 1990s the tribal armband became fashionable. Its position on the arm was reminiscent of the leather and metal straps worn by Spartan soldiers and Roman gladiators and whispered of more recent S&M aesthetics. Common designs included Celtic knots and barbed wire. The latter was suggestive of prison, which itself is a common theme in sexual role play. Among some gay men, the arm on which the tattoo was etched also denoted sexual behavior. This followed on a long history wherein items such as keys and hankies worn on the left or right signal "top" or "bottom,"[2] respectively. So too do did the armband. These facets highlighted the sexual nature of armband tattoos.

The armband tattoo was aesthetically pleasing on muscular or toned arms. Some men without the desired muscle tone purposefully began to work out to create the desire look. This also coincides with a trend since at least the 1980s of men working out to enhance appearance,

rather than for concerns with health (Silberstein et al., 1989). One informant stated, "I wanted to have an armband tattoo, but I knew I it wouldn't look right with skinny arms. So I started lifting weights" (Alex, 2007); he added that once his biceps were toned he got a barbed wire tattoo. When asked why he chose that particular motif, he said it was popular at the time. Additionally, the vertical line of the armband tattoo helped to make a bicep look visually bigger. "I got mine on the left [bicep] because that one was smaller and I wanted it to look bigger" (Basil, 2009). Basil's statement references knowledge of aesthetic principles and how they can be used to enhance a part of the body, which aligns with the aforementioned statements about tattoos enhancing the physique of the body. Additionally, these statements underscore that the placement of the tattoo was deliberate and aligned with tattoo trends of the time. However, armband tattoos were not to remain popular forever and would soon be replaced by a different form and placement of tattoo.

The lower back tattoo. By the early 2000s the lower back became the fashionable site for a tattoo. Lower back tattoos were mostly scrolling designs but could also include yin/yang motifs, words, or names. The lower back is considered erotic (Fenske, 2007), likely because it is near the buttocks, a site of the body also highly eroticized. Depending upon the clothing worn, the top of the buttocks (including the "crack") might be seen. In addition, the back is highly sensitive to touch likely due to the fact that many people hold tension in their back. When touched, the back releases tension and relaxes the person. The placement of the tattoo on the small of the back coincided with an apparel fashion for low-rise "hip-hugger" pants which provided exposure for the tattoo when worn with a mid-crop shirt or no shirt. Geometric tribal designs and sunbursts were common motifs. Lower back tattoos were so popular that at least one person made a drinking game of them: "drink every time u see someone with a tramp stamp; double if u guess it before you see it; trip[le] for male tramp stamps" (Leto & Bator, 2010, n.p.).

Lower back tattoos were originally popular among women, but were found on men as well. The tattoos on women were despairingly called "tramp stamps," and linked to wanton sexual behavior. Women with lower back tattoos were (and still are) perceived to be promiscuous (Guéguen, 2013; Salinas, 2001). This perception spilled over to men with the lower back tattoos who were viewed as promiscuous, "he-tramps," or "man-whores," according to Internet blogs. In addition, men with the lower back

---

2. Top refers to the penetrator, while bottom refers to the penetrated partner.

tattoos were viewed as following a fashion trend. "I knew a guy in college with a tramp-stamp. He was a real douche" (Clay, 2013). He went on to explain the term "douche," as "someone who blindly follows fashion fads. His tattoo has no meaning; it was just a decoration for him." This statement underscores the postmodern nature of fashion at the end of the 20th century, wherein aesthetics are valued over meaning (Morgado, 1996). Morgado (1996) also cited irony as a characteristic of postmodern fashion, which alludes to one blogger's decision to get a lower back tattoo: "I actually got one at the same time as my friend. . .it was meant to be funny and drove our wives. . .crazy. . .it's a bull's head with icing and candles. . .says beefcake above it." (Getbig, 2010).

The sleeve tattoo. By the 2010s lower back tattoos were no longer in vogue but "sleeves" had become fashionable. Borrowed from Japanese Irezumi[3], or full body art, the sleeves are intertwining designs that covered the shoulder and upper part of the arm. In Japan, these tattoos have a long history with the Yakuza criminal organization, and it is likely the association with the exotic that adds to the erotic nature of the sleeves tattoo among Western men. A tattoo assistant remarked, "The actual tattoo culture (not mainstream) didn't follow these trends too much because sleeves were always popular with them, but they are definitely more popular with everyone now" (Salas, 2013, personal communication).

Some sleeves covered the entire arm and pectoral region as well. This large tattoo style was complimented by the fashion for A-shirts (e.g., tank-tops) which provided exposure for much of the tattoo. One blogger mentioned the shoulder as one of the sexy body parts under the heading "stylish tattoos" in the "fashion" category (Snow, 2011, n.p.), thus reinforcing that tattoos are seen today as fashion accessories. Additionally, I asked three different men who had a sleeve why they chose that particular style of tattoo and each one replied with comments indicating that it was the fashionable things to do: "Everyone gets it there now" (Ellis, 2013), "It's our generation's thing" (Fitch, 2013), and "it's cool" (Greg, 2012). None of them commented on the meaning of the tattoo, which indicates the sleeve tattoo was

---

3. Japanese irezumi has connections to traditional Japan, but more recently to the Yakuza. Yakuza, a type of criminal organization akin to the Mafia, required members to tattoo themselves. By doing so, they were committing themselves to the life of a Yakuza, because tattoos are banned in Japanese society. Thus, once tattooed, the member could never return to polite society. The art of Irezumi was brought to the West by "Sailor Jerry", whose experiences as a sailor in Japan exposed him to the art and technique. After his time in the navy, Jerry opened a tattoo parlor in Honolulu, and irezumi spread residents, visitors, and military.

a trend of the early 2010s as well group aesthetic and further underscore the fashionable nature of sleeves tattoos.

Conclusion

The fashion for tattoos coincided with the fashion for the body, specific to this discussion, fit and toned bodies. In today's culture with an increased emphasis on the musculature of men, the tattoo serves to highlight this aspect. The findings in this article underscore Negrin's (2007) assertion that tattoos are used as accessories in the fashion industry. The three types of tattoos discussed in this article—armbands, lower back, and sleeves—each experienced a rise and decline in popularity over a specific period of time, thus aligning it with the definition of fashion. The three types of tattoo discussed in this article also support the erotic and shifting nature of fashion as described by the theory of shifting erogenous zones. They draw attention to particular parts of the body and add a sensual, textural dynamic to the skin. Comments verified that tattoo motifs/style/location were reflections of fashion. This research has challenged the notion that the theory of shifting erogenous zones is no longer a valid explanation of fashion change, by demonstrating its applicability to three types of tattoos of the male body. In doing so this study has extended the theory to the seemingly, permanent body markings, thus broadening the theory, defending it against critics, and reviving it for future analysis and debate.

References

Alex. (2007). Personal communication. San Francisco, California.

Basil. (2009). Personal communication. Honolulu, Hawai'i.

Beynon, J. (2002). *Masculinities and culture.* Buckingham, UK: Open University Press.

Carmen, R. A., Guitar, A. E., & Dillon, H. M. (2012). Ultimate answers to proximate questions: The evolutionary motivations behind tattoos and body piercings in popular culture. *Review of General Psychology*, 16 (2), 134–143.

Clay. (2013). Personal communication. Honolulu, Hawai'i.

Coe, K, Harmon, M. P., Verner, B., & Tonn, A. (1993). Tattoos and male alliances. *Human Nature*, 4 (2), 199–204.

Curry, D. (1993). Decorating the body politic. *New Formations*, 19, 69–82.

Daniel. (2012). Personal communication. Honolulu, Hawai'i.

David, A. M. (2010). Exhibition review: *Reveal of Conceal? Fashion Theory, 14* (2), 245–252.

Davis, B. (2010). Portraits gaining popularity among choices for tattoos. *The Register-Herald.* March 6, 2010. http://www.register-herald.com/features/x1897229652/Portraits-gaining-popularity-among-choices-for-tattoos

DeMello, M. (2000). *Bodies of Inscription.* Durham, NC: Duke University Press.

Ellis. (2013). Personal communication. Honolulu, Hawai`i.

Fenske, M. (2007). *Tattoos in American Visual Culture.* New York: Macmillan Publishers.

Field, G. A. (1970). The status float phenomenon. *Business Horizons, 8,* 45–52.

Fitch. (2013). Personal communication. Honolulu, Hawai`i.

Flugel, J. C. (1930). *The Psychology of Clothes.* London: Hogarth Press.

Getbig (2010). http://www.getbig.com/boards/index.php?topic=331719.0

Greg. (2012) Personal communication. Honolulu, Hawai`i.

Guéguen, N. (2013). Effects of a Tattoo on Men's Behavior and Attitudes Towards Women: An Experimental Field Study. *Archives of sexual behavior,* 1–8.

Joey. (2013). Personal communication. San Francisco, California.

Kosut, M. (2006). An ironic fad: The commodification and consumption of tattoos. *Journal of Popular Culture, 39* (6), 1035–1048.

Laver, J. (1969). *Modesty in Dress: An Inquiry into the Fundamentals of Fashion.* Boston: Houghton Mifflin Company.

Lentini, P. (1999). The cultural politics of tattooing. *Arena Journal, 13,* 31–55.

Leto, L., & Bator, B. (2010). *Last Night: All the Texts No One Remembers Sending.* New York: Penguin.

Lingis, A. (1983). Savages. In A. Lingis (ed.) *Excess: Eros and Culture* (pp. 18–46). Albany, NY: State University of New York Press.

Manzano, V. (2009). The blue jean generation: Youth, gender, and sexuality in Buenos Aires, 1958–1975. *Journal of Social History, 42* (3), 657–676.

Morgado, M. (1996), 'Coming to Terms with Postmodern: Theories and Concepts of Contemporary Culture and their Implications for Apparel Scholars', *Clothing and Textiles Research Journal,* 14: 1, pp. 41–53.

Negrin, L. (2007). Body art and men's fashion. In A. Reilly and S. Cosbey (eds.) *The Men's Fashion Reader* (pp. 323–336). New York: Fairchild.

Pilcher, J., Pole, C., & Boden, S. (2004). New consumers? Children, fashion, and consumption. Paper presented at "Knowing Consumers: Actors, Images, Identities in Modern History" conference, Universitat Bielefeld, Germany. February 27-28m 2004.

Polhemus, T. (1994). *Streetstyle.* London: Thames & Hudson.

Quinn, B. (2002). A note: Hussein Chalayan, fashion and technology. *Fashion Theory, 6* (4), 359–368.

Reece, P.J. (2008). Erotic Tattoos: Manufacturing Desire. Downloaded January 28, 2013 from http://www.vanishingtattoo.com/erotic_tattoos_3.htm

Robert. (2011). Downloaded March 13, 2013 from: http://emptyclosets.com/forum/chit-chat/78640-what-do-you-think-tramp-stamps-tattoos-gay-men.html

Salas, F. (2013). Interview. September 9, 2013. Honolulu, Hawai`i.

Salinas, Chema (2011). Paul Lester and Susan Ross. ed. *Images That Injure: Pictorial Stereotypes in the Media.* ABC-CLIO. pp. 247–8. ISBN 978-0-313-37892-8.

Simai, S. (2001). Jeans and identity for sale: The case of Brazil. *Americana, 7* (1), n.p.

Silberstein, L. R., Mishkind, M. E., Striegel-Moore, R. H., TImko, C., & Rodin, J. (1989). Men and their bodies: A comparison of homosexual and heterosexual men. *Psychosomatic Medicine* 51(3), 337–346.

Snow, I. (2011). Tattoos women think are sexy on men. Downloaded March 13, 2013 from http://isabellasnow.hubpages.com/hub/Tattoos-Women-Think-Are-Sexy-On-Men

Steele, V. (1985). *Fashion and Eroticism: Ideals of Feminine Beauty from the Victorian Era to Jazz Age.* Oxford: Oxford University Press.

Steele, V. (1996). *Fetish: Fashion, Sex, and Power.* Oxford: Oxford University Press.

Wilson, E., (1993), Fashion and the postmodern body. In J. Ash & E. Wilson [eds.] *Chic Thrills: A Fashion Reader.* Berkeley: University of California Press.

Discussion Questions

1. What areas of men's bodies, other than those discussed in this article, have been eroticized and how were they highlighted?
2. What characteristics of tattoos make them sexy?

CHAPTER 5
APPEARANCE FOR GENDER

Andrew Reilly

After you have read this chapter, you will understand:

- How gender is socially and culturally determined and is a significant component in the study of appearance
- How the Westernized concept of two genders differ from other global concepts of gender

SOCIAL CONSTRUCTION OF GENDER

Gender is a social construction often conflated with sex. **Sex** is a biological category based on genitalia whereas gender is a social construction based on a continuum of masculinity to femininity (Foucault, 1976/1998). Historically, in Euro-American societies, two gender categories dominated: male and female. However, recently, more categories have been acknowledged, including third gender, genderqueer, gender fluid, non-binary, and agender. Genderqueer or transgender are terms used to describe people who do not identify with the male/female dichotomy, and may identify as both male and female, or neither male nor female (agender), or as moving between male and female (gender fluid). Many people who identify as genderqueer, gender fluid, agender, or non-binary may wear clothing that confronts and challenges social gendered expectations. Corwin (2009) has noted that genderqueer presentations of self are not static and may include non-normative presentations of gender that chance depending on context and circumstance.

Early civilizations noted some differences between men's and women's appearance, however for the most part they dressed similarly. Drawings, frescoes, hieroglyphs, and statues have given us clues as to how people dressed. Generally, clothing was of a draped and/or wrapped nature.

For example, in ancient Mesopotamia, the Sumerian men and women both wore skirts and cloaks (c. 3500–1000 B.C.) and Babylonian and Assyrian men and women both wore tunics (1000–600 B.C.). In Egypt, both men and women wore skirts, tunics, and robes (3000–300 B.C.). The men and women of the ancient Minoan civilization (2900–1150 B.C.) both wore loincloths, skirts, and tunics. The men and women of ancient Greek (800–300 B.C.) and Roman (500 B.C.–A.D. 400) civilizations wore a variety of draped and wrapped garments, with some designated specifically for each gender. But it was after the fall of Rome, during the early European Middle Ages (900–1300) that we see significant differences between male and female genders in regard to their dress, with women wearing long gowns and men in tunics and hose. Since then the division between appropriate dress for men and women continued to grow and became somewhat fixed (see Figure 5.1).

Figure 5.1 During the medieval ages, European men and women started to dress in gender-related clothing.

Today's expectations of dress for men and women are rooted in the Industrial Revolution. During this time, a significant portion of labor moved from agricultural fields into buildings. Suits replaced overalls and became the standard for men's office attire. However, at this time, women's responsibilities included managing the home and family. So, whereas men needed to look serious and somber in their business dealings, women had more freedom to follow fashion because their activities were more socially oriented than business oriented. During the 19th century through the 1950s, men followed a restricted code of appearance, limited to angular design lines, neutral and subdued color palettes, bifurcated garments (e.g., pants) for the lower body, natural but not tight silhouettes, sturdy fabrics and shoes, and simple hair and facial grooming. This simple, restricted code helped them to focus on work and accomplishments rather than appearance. Thus, men dressed for the agonic role in society. Women, in contrast, had an elaborate dress code through the 1950s. They could wear some of what men wore, and a lot more. Their unlimited options for fabrics, colors, design lines, and silhouettes gave them a useful treasury for attending to their hedonic role, emphasizing pursuit of beauty and physical being. Their tight or flowing skirts, high heels, and nylons did not facilitate emphasis on physical activity, however. Women were encouraged to spend their time and attention on clothes, hair, weight control, and makeup to render themselves beautiful for men (who would marry and support them).

Though many people do not realistically meet ideal expectations for their gender, they are expected to meet minimum standards. Anyone who defies the minimum expectations is stigmatized. People who fail to meet the minimum expectations historically have been featured as oddities in circuses (e.g., the bearded lady or the she-man; see Figure 5.2). Though today we are more attuned to differences and do not necessarily put people with differences on display, many people are still stigmatized based on failure to reach the minimum expectations. Physical disabilities, extremely thin or overweight bodies, and hair loss are all conditions that can cause a person to be socially stigmatized.

AGONIC AND HEDONIC POWER

Women and men obtain their social power differently. Historically, a woman's power rested in her appearance, a man's in his earning potential. Women needed to look attractive to men in order to gain the attention of (and marry) men who could support them. And men needed to secure a career where they could earn enough money to attract beautiful women. The effect was circular; one was dependent on the other.

What was considered appropriately masculine and feminine has shifted over time and changed according to culture, status, and nationality. Prior to the French Revolution, European men were great followers of fashion and excess. Men's clothing lost its excess after the French Revolution in what has become known as the Great Masculine Renunciation when utility became a virtue and fashion a vice. Women, however, retained their right to aesthetic forms of expression.

Dress scholar Susan Kaiser (1997) refers to the differing forms of power as agonic versus hedonic, or "doing versus being." **Agonic power** is active and direct, whereas **hedonic power** is passive and indirect. Men's power is agonic because it is rooted in doing work, earning a living, and providing for a family. Women's power is hedonic because it is rooted in appearing attractive to others (though one could certainly argue that much work goes into looking attractive). This dichotomy is not all-encompassing and does not apply to all men and women; there are many

Figure 5.2 Women and men are expected to meet certain expectations regarding dress and their gender. When they do not, they are usually labeled as oddities.

women who obtain their power from their careers (e.g., Hillary Clinton and Melinda Gates) and many men who obtain their power from their looks (e.g., model Shermon Braithwaite or 19th-century dandy Beau Brummel).

The agonic/hedonic dichotomy began to shift when women started gaining economic independence. Beginning with World War II when women entered the workforce out of necessity and when some women remained after the war ended, women had started to earn their own living. As women entering the workplace increased with each decade, they no longer needed men to support them. Their goals in a relationship could move beyond simply finding a man with a solid career. Now, good looks were required of men too, and this is when we start to see a change in men's aesthetics and grooming routines. Men were not going to the gym simply because it was healthy, but because they needed to lose a few pounds or tone up in order to compete with other men. Women had known for many decades that their appearance was a commodity, but men are just learning that theirs is too.

GENDER BENDING

One of the clothing hallmarks of the Western male/female dichotomy is that women wear skirts/dresses; men do not. Though the reverse is acceptable—women in pants—and is a common sight today, it was not too long ago that such cross-dressing was seen by some as scandalous and potentially dangerous. Though there were notable exceptions (in the 1920s and 1930s actress Katharine Hepburn eschewed dresses and skirts for pants), it was not until World War II that sweeping changes took effect (see Figure 5.3). Women were working in manufacturing jobs that had previously been held by men who were now in combat on the battlefields. Women's dresses and skirts were not conducive to working with heavy machinery. They needed clothing that was utilitarian, allowed for quick movement, and was not likely to get caught in gears. Women began wearing pants. Though after the war ended, women were expected to return to their former wardrobes (and many did), many women continued to wear pants and were harassed, bullied, and discriminated against for doing so. Today, women in pants—or any variety of "men's" clothing—is ubiquitous.

Occasionally, a designer will produce a men's collection that includes a skirt, but rarely does that become a trend or fashionable. The early 2000s and 2010s saw retailers like H&M, YSL, Jean-Paul Gaultier, Alexander McQueen,

Figure 5.3 It was acceptable for women to wear pants during World War II when they worked in manufacturing plants. However, when the war ended, they were expected to return to wearing skirts and dresses.

Marc Jacob for Louis Vuitton, Craig Green, and Rick Owens offering skirts and dresses to men. Fashion icons and influencers like Jaden Smith, Marc Jacobs, and Kayne West have sported skirts and dresses. It likely will take many more years for men to wear skirts on a regular basis.

Society expects men and women to dress according to their sex. When people wear what is not expected of them they are often discriminated against, bullied, and treated differently. School systems are dealing with these issues as more and more students are challenging traditional gender appearances. When children and adolescents experiment with their clothing as they find their individual identities, sometimes they wear clothes that violate traditional gender norms. Some schools are banning crossdressing and striving to uphold traditional gender appearance norms, while others are trying to foster an atmosphere of tolerance and acceptance (Hoffman, 2009).

When women dress in men's clothing, it is considered a move upward. This is certainly the case in cultures where there is an obvious preference for men. In Afghanistan, dressing as another gender is a necessity to better one's life. Afghani boys are valued over girls, and in order to get an education, hold a job, or walk freely in public, girls dress as boys and assume a male identity. For centuries many parents raised their daughter as a boy, at least until puberty, in order to give her an education and hope for a better economic future, and due to social pressure to have a son (Nordberg, 2012).

While some people prefer to dress either masculine or feminine, others wish to eliminate differences and blend them. The blending together of masculinity and femininity is known as **androgyny**.[1] Despite rigid Westernized, social standards of what is acceptable for men to wear and women to wear, there have been instances where androgynous styling was fashionable. In the 1920s, Chanel's garçonne style for women was an effortless look of tubular silhouettes, loose fit, and cropped hair, giving women a boyish appearance. In the 1960s the androgynous look for women was represented by the model Twiggy. In the early 1980s women began adopting a fair amount of androgyny in business dress in the United States and avidly appropriated the business suit and its corresponding masculine body with motivations similar to their male business counterparts (e.g., to achieve financial and career success; McCracken, 1985). With the current emphasis on skintight clothing in the 2010s, some men are shopping in women's departments that offer tighter fits for jeans and shirts than men's cuts do.

Ben Barry and Andrew Reilly (in press) studied cross-dressing among a sample of men who wear clothes designed for women. They noted that androgynous appearances in the late 2010s had changed from previous iterations of androgyny. Previous androgynous aesthetics seems to unify masculine and feminine elements into one whole; however, the new iteration appears to juxtapose them as if to highlight the differences. Men in their sample, both gay and straight, combined men's apparel, such as military camouflage or basketball jerseys, with women's apparel, such as lace, skirts, and stiletto heels. The men's motivations for combining masculine and feminine signifiers included challenging the social construction of gender, preferring the fit of women's clothing, and enjoying the aesthetics of the fabrics. See Figure 5.4.

Unisex or non-binary clothing, or apparel that lacks any gender designation, is explored in Patrik Steorn's, "Lifestyle and Politics of Fashion and Gender in 1960s Sweden: Unisex Fashion in Theory and Practice." Steorn argues that unisex fashion in Sweden was a politically motivated response that attempted to equalize the genders.

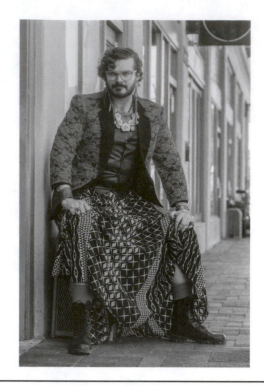

Figure 5.4 The New Androgyny is a configuration of masculine elements such as combat boots, bearded face, and leather vest with feminine elements such as lace jackets and skirts.

The Swedish government in 1972 established a taskforce to address issues of gender inequality and coincided with a public interest in unisex clothing.

Continuing on with the theme of politics and gender, Katalin Medvedev and Lioba Moshi's "Female Tradition in a New Context: The Case of the *Khanga*," explores gender in relation to a garment from Tanzania. The khanga represents not only wealth and ritual life events (e.g., puberty, marriage) but is also a marker of gender. As you read it, note the different meanings related to the female gender, including education, religious restriction of women, and local identity.

As noted in the introductory paragraph to this section, many more gender identities beyond male and female exist. People whose sex assigned at birth does not align with their gender identity often identify as **transgender or transpeople or as third gender**. Unlike in the West, many non-Western societies have multiple gender categories. Native Americans or First Nations people have a third gender called Two-Spirit people, Samoans have fa'afafine, Hawaiians have mahu, Tongans have fakaleiti, Māori have whakawhine, the Maale of Ethopia have Ashtime, and the Mbo of Congo have Mangaiko. In Thailand, there are multiple gender identities based on combination of birth sex, gender identity, sexual orientation, and to whom someone is attracted.

In the final article for this chapter "A Comparative Analysis of Hijras and Drag Queens: The Subversive Possibilities and Limits of Parading Effeminacy and Negotiating Masculinity", Sandeep Bakshi compares the Western drag queen to the Hindu hijra. Hijra is a third gender category; hijaras and are assigned male at birth and later in life remove their sex organs and present as women. Bakshi discusses the gender performance of both hijras and drag queens, but stemming from different motivations: cultural and religious versus social and political. **Drag** queens (and their counterpart, drag kings) lampoon gender by creating an artificial, over-styled version of gender categories. See Figure 5.5.

Figure 5.5 This drag queen performs gender by exaggerating its artificiality.

Summary

Expectations of sex, gender, and sexuality contribute to how and why people dress the way they do. Some people dress in a particular way because it is expected of their gender, while others dress to defy normative expectations or to align their outward appearance with their inward psyche. Sometimes, dressing as one gender is advantageous, and other times it is ostracizing. As society begins to acknowledge multiple gender identities, clothing becomes an important vehicle to perform identity.

Key Terms

Agonic power	Drag	Hedonic power	Transgender or transpeople
Androgyny	Gender	Sex	Unisex

Learning Activity 5.1

PERFORMING GENDER

Watch the film **Paris Is Burning**, a 1990 documentary that examines the drag ball scene in New York City. Take notes on how gender is performed. What types of gender roles (e.g., class, race, style) are created? When you have completed that, identify ways in which you perform your gender and discuss where you learned those rules.

BEYOND THE BINARY

Use your smart phone or computer to look up "third genders." Select one culture and write down the culture and the different gender identities. For each gender identity, find out how the person self-presents (e.g., dress, mannerisms, characteristics). After you have finished, discuss your findings with your classmates. Which culture has the most gender identities? How are they similar? How are they different? How useful is it to have multiple gender identities?

Discussion Questions

1. Which ways do you conform to your gender? Which ways do you violate social gender norms. How many of these are related to dress and appearance?

2. When women wear men's clothing it is considered a move upward, but when men wear women's clothing it is considered a move downward. Why is this?

3. If you were to be reincarnated as another gender from which you are now, what physical characteristics would you want? What type of apparel would you wear? Do you choices demonstrate agonic or hedonic power?

References

Barry, B. and A. Reilly (in press), "The New Androgyny," in A. Reilly & B. Barry (eds.), *Crossing Boundaries: Fashion to Deconstruct and Reimagine Gender*, Bristol, UK: Intellect Books.

Corwin, A. I. (2009), Language and Gender Variance: Constructing Gender beyond the Male/Female Binary," *Electronic Journal of Human Sexuality*, 12. Available online: www.ejhs.org/Volume12/Gender.htm.

Intersex Society of North America (n.d.), Frequently Asked Questions. Available online: www.isna.org.

Hoffman, J. (2009, November 6), "Can a Boy Wear a Skirt to School?" *New York Times*. Available online: http://www.nytimes.com/2009/11/08/fashion/08cross.html?pagewanted=all.

Kaiser, S. B. (1997), *The Social Psychology of Clothing: Symbolic Appearances in Context*, New York: Fairchild Publications.

McCracken, G. (1985), "The Trickle-Down Theory Rehabilitated," in M. R. Solomon (ed.), *The Psychology of Fashion*, 39–54, Lexington, MA: Lexington Books.

Nordberg, J. (2012), "Afghan Boys Are Prized, So Girls Live the Part," in K. A. Miller-Spillman, A. Reilly and P. Hunt-Hurst (eds.), *The Meanings of Dress* (3rd ed.), 189–95, New York: Fairchild.

This introduction is based on a version originally written by Susan O. Michelman and appeared in *Meanings of Dress* editions 1, 2, and 3.

5.1
Lifestyle and Politics of Fashion and Gender in 1960s Sweden: Unisex Fashion in Theory and Practice

Patrik Steorn

In Sweden unisex fashion was a topical issue for about a decade, from the mid-1960s to the mid-1970s. Various media reported on unisex fashion as a new and modern way of organizing everyday life in union with a reorganization of social categories on a structural level. General interest magazines with a left-wing orientation (i.e., *Vi/We*, published by Swedish Cooperative Union) as well as influential design journals (i.e. *Form*, published by Swedish Society for Industrial Design) reported regularly on fashion and included unisex fashion in feature photos, lifestyle reports, published patterns of unisex clothes for home sewing and frequently discussed fashion, especially androgynous models in its reports on Swedish design in the late 1960s. Unisex fashion as a phenomenon brought the political left as well as the art and design community toward the field of fashion as an arena for social and political change.

Unisex fashion was an international phenomenon in the late 1960s, and it seems to be one of these ideas that appear more or less simultaneously in the minds of people in different places. In France, Jacques Esterel designed skirts for men and pants for women, Yves Saint Laurent became famous for pants for women and a unisex Safari-suit. Pierre Cardin's "boy/girl" collection from 1968 (Figure 5.6) is often included as part of this phenomenon. However, French designer Ted Lapidus is considered to be the pioneer of unisex fashion, as his first haute couture shows in 1963 reportedly included "boy/girl" mixes. Austrian-American designer Rudi Gernreich did a collection called UNISEX in 1970 as part of a larger art project that included films and photos (Lobenthal, 1990; Moffitt & Claxton, 1990; Bolton, 2002; Breward, Gilbert, & Lister, 2006).

This paper will study the unisex phenomenon with a focus on Sweden in the 1960s and 1970s and discuss how unisex garments can be related to gender theory and fashion theory, as well as their role as a symbol of opposition to traditional values, such as sex roles.

Figure 5.6 Designer Pierre Cardin's unisex fashions from 1968.

Unisex—Fashion, Gender and Society

Women dressing in men's clothes, fashion design for men inspired by women's wear or clothes designed for men and women alike—what is unisex fashion?

The terminology of unisex fashion is slightly confusing because it refers both to a technical term (to specific garments) as well as to a style. When unisex is used as technical term within the production of ready-to-wear, it refers to a certain category of clothes, comparable to menswear, women's wear and children's wear. However, I think it is important to make a difference between this tailor-related understanding of unisex on the one hand and on the other hand an understanding that implies the creation of fashions that disavow the social categories of masculinity and femininity, not only in cut but also in style. In the 1960s media, the term unisex included both the creation of new types of garments such as the jumpsuit or the monokini, that were not traditionally assigned to men or women, as well as making men's fashion in fabrics, colors and patterns that had been considered to be

Original for this text.

typically feminine, and vice versa. For example, clothes for men were designed in soft fabrics like jersey, and in strong colors and floral patterns. Women dressed in denim and jeans and workers overalls. Unisex fashion can according to my perspective be defined as a set of practices of design and of dressing up that oppose a traditional fashion industry's division between men and women in clothing, and which produce a social and aesthetic symbol of the individual's free choice of lifestyle beyond gender division that can also be used as a symbol of political activism for full gender equality.

Unisex as a general term refers to clothes that are not at all gender specific, whereas androgynous fashion combines feminine and masculine dress conventions in unpredictable ways. Cross-dressing refers to the practice of dressing like the opposite sex, while drag makes this into a performing art—on stage or in everyday life. All of these terms refer to designs and styles or practices that problematize the relation between fashion and gender.

Unisex fashion has been theorized by French sociologists Olivier Burgelin and Marie-Therese Basse as a symbolic end of what they called "vestimentary apartheid," the practice and rule of strict separation of dress that had been prevalent since the 19th century. They point to the women's liberation movement, the rise of youth culture and the appearance of anti-fashion as the main reasons for unisex fashion of the 20th century (Burgelin & Basse, 1987, pp. 285, 296). Women's gradual appropriation of pants in general and jeans in particular is their main example, and some researchers even argue that unisex fashion is all organized around jeans (Burgelin & Basse, 1987, p. 291). They omit to mention the types of garments that were explicitly designed as unisex fashion such as jumpsuits or safari jackets. American sociologist Mark Gottdiener (1995) interprets unisex fashion much the same way but also points out that unisex fashion did have differing implications for men and for women in relation to their respective commercial and professional arenas: for men it marked their entrance as a target group on the fashion market, while it signalled women's strengthened professional position in business and politics. Unisex dress is often interpreted as a consequence of changed social attitudes, which is an important contextualization of this phenomenon. Making unisex dress into vestimentary illustrations of the women's liberation movement however risk disregarding the creative energy that this idea also came to symbolize.

Sociologist Herbert Blumer, in the 1960s, challenged a traditional view that fashion was bizarre, frivolous and irrational and in doing so particularly questioned fashion theorist Georg Simmel's idea that fashion arose as a form of class differentiation: "Fashion appears much more as a collective grouping for the proximate future than a channelled movement laid down by prestigious figures" (Blumer, 2007 [1969], p. 237). In his own empirical research he pointed out that the determination of fashion is a collective process of selection. According to Blumer the role of the designer is to translate themes from the arts, literature, political debates, happenings and the media into dress design and to be oriented toward a certain clientele and to make clothes that this group would adopt.

Blumer's statement that fashion should be understood as a result of collective selection, not class, resonates in many of the comments on fashion in general and on unisex fashion in particular of the 1960s. Instead of simply confirming a bourgeois society order, fashion had the potential of shaping new social orders, based on the process and forming of collective taste. "Fashion is a very adept mechanism for enabling people to adjust in an orderly and unified way to a moving and changing world which is potentially full of anarchic possibilities" (Blumer, 2007 [1969], p. 245). Blumer's words on fashion as a creative driving force in forming a modern world articulates an ideological background of unisex fashion.

Gender was conceived as one of the social conventions that could be refashioned. During the 1960s and 1970s the theorizing of gender was launched and used by activists and scholars all over the western world (Rosaldo & Lamphere, 1974). Recent scholars have noted that sex role theories implies that there is a natural body beyond the gendered masks of "male" and "female" constructions (Butler, 1999, pp. 9–11, 32–33, Connell, 1995, p. 21–17). Unisex fashion was about clothes that in themselves would appear so neutral that the wearer would stand out on own terms. The clothes were supposed to be neutral so that the individual could be expressive in her/himself and be able to perform "man" or "woman" in his or her own way. New and unforeseen versions of sex roles and altered gender structures motivated the unisex vision, but what should these material garments look like, and how should they be worn?

Transgressing Genders— Performing Unisex

Whereas men's fashion had historically been dominated by suits in various and often subtle variations and fashionable detail, this period of the 1960s has been referred to as "the Peacock Revolution" (Frazier, 1968). Integrating traditional signs of femininity into men's dress signalled a new type of masculinity that was socially progressive—or just fashionable. Swedish designer Sighsten Herrgård stressed the role of soft fabric in unisex fashion, and in the following quote he describes its role as more or less able to liberate all gendered bodies from any physical restraint and from a square, polished ideal:

I like jersey, jersey, jersey. . . It is the material for our age. I design for today and tomorrow—not for yesterday and for the space age. I want to make clothes void of gender thinking. Away with men's- and women's buttoning, for example and away with age thinking—it is the environment, the mood and the way of life that decide which clothes we want to wear.1

(Bort med ålderstänkandet, 1969)

The quote also exemplifies how the trope of unisex is established as part of a modern lifestyle through the distinction from allegedly old and stiff gender thinking. In the following quote Herrgård explains how unisex fashion was performed in everyday life (or at least in front of the journalist):

London designer Sighsten Herrgard and his girlfriend, model Ann Jennifer, share almost everything—'pants, sweaters, shirts, belts. We don't worry about what belongs to whom; we just pick out what we want to wear that day'.

(The Genderation, 1968)

This narrative on the total freedom of wearing unisex fashion evokes a fashionable ideal that men and women could share, which marked this era in various areas.

In 1974 feminist psychologist and Professor Sandra Bem introduced the concept of "psychological androgyny" to describe men and women who combined traits from traditionally defined gender roles and she suggested that androgyny could be the solution to a traditional gender division. (Bem, 1974, pp. 155–162) According to platonic myth and spiritual tradition, androgyny is the origin of heterosexual attraction; all the while the idea of *conjuncto oppositorum*, uniting of opposites, has played an important role within alchemy, theosophy, kabbala and other spiritual movements as a symbol of the complete individual: male and female in perfect union (McCleod, 1998). The androgynous appearance is thus based on the primordial existence of two separate sexes that complete each other, physically and spiritually.

From a 1990s queer perspective the American philosopher Judith Butler argues that the division between social and physical gender actually conserves and deepens the understanding of sex and gender according to a fundamental heteronormative structure (Butler, 1999 [1990], pp.162–166). The unisex ideal of indifference to sex roles thus generated fashion ideas in a paradoxical way: sex difference was denied at a theoretical level at the same time as it was emphasized in practice. Looking closer on images of people wearing unisex jumpsuits, it is clear that the tight cut and the soft materials accentuated the physical characteristics of the wearer's body instead of erasing them visually. The tight cut seems to reveal the "natural body within," suggesting that gender difference in fashion is artificial whereas physical gender difference is natural. Herrgård also articulates this side of unisex fashion:

"Unisex clothes don't conceal the sexes" he said, cinching the wide belt black leather belt tighter around the black ribbed sweater which topped a pair of grey tweed trousers. "There is no doubt that even though we are the same size in trousers and in sweaters and though her shoulders are wider than mine, she is a woman and I am a man"

(These Swedes put pants on everyone, 1969)

Social gender difference was questioned to a certain extent, but the division of male and female bodies was taken for granted and a heterosexual attraction between these body types was implied. Sighsten Herrgård and the female models that he was dating in the beginning of his career posed together in magazines all over the world. In his unisex jumpsuit they performed the perfect heterosexual couple—an androgynous union of male and female. At the same time he engaged in same-sex activities in between girlfriends or behind their backs. He could pass both as heterosexual and gay, the unisex jumpsuit being the perfect disguise—gender bending and heterosexual at the same time. Gay and bisexual men and

---

1. (Author's translation) "Jag gillar jersey, jersey, jersey. . . det är materialet för vår tidsålder. Jag formger för idag och imorgon, inte för igår och rymdåldern. Jag vill göra kläder utan könstänkande. Bort med herr- och damknäppning, t.ex. Och bort med ålderstänkandet – det är miljön, humöret och levnadssättet som avgör vilka kläder vi vill ha på oss."

women in the metropolitan areas used unisex fashion to work out social identities of their own during this period (Cole, 2000, p. 89, Lomas 2007, p. 88). Tight colorful clothing was frequently used among gay men to signal non-heterosexual interests in other men.

The emphasis on the adornment of the body accentuates the erotic and sensual potentials of the wearer's physique and the potential agency to subvert traditional sexual orders. However this potential seems only to have been explored implicitly, in private. Rather than dissolving gender categories, unisex fashion during the 1960s seems to have strengthened the belief in men and women as natural categories.

Lifestyle or Politics—Cultural Meaning of Unisex

The intensive gender role debate in Sweden in the 1960s generated a political movement that questioned the male norm within all aspects of society. An institutionalized gender equality politics was established by the Swedish Social Democratic government who appointed a mission for these issues, Delegationen för jämställdhet mellan män och kvinnor (The Delegation for Equality between Men and Women) in 1972. Simultaneously, designers, media and consumers explored new ways of shaping, representing and performing gender with the objective of changing the polarized gender positions of previous eras. The interest in making unisex clothes appeared both in the Swedish art world and in the fashion business.

In the University College of Arts, Crafts and Design (Konstfackskolan) in Stockholm a group of students, young artists whose art was grounded in the 1960s debate on gender roles, formed a collective that designed clothes with soft materials and strong colors and simple, often organic patterns (Eldvik, 1988, pp. 101–120; Hallström Bornold, 2003). The group was called Mah-Jong, signalling their sympathy with Maoist ideology (Figure 5.7). They wanted to make art and fashion more political and social, "closer to the people." According to these thoughts, art should be something that could be used, an everyday object. Posters, happenings and dress collections came out of their creative work. They wanted to create anti-fashion, in opposition to the established fashion world, aiming at empowerment and enabling of women, children and the working class. Their objective was clothes that were primarily functional, clothes that did not necessarily flaunt social status, in opposition to the world of haute-couture. The production was located

Figure 5.7 Family wearing Mah-Jong tights and tunics.

in small-scale industry in a small Swedish town and the clothes were sold in a small boutique in central Stockholm. Mah-Jong clothes are legendary in Sweden today, part of the "political primary scene" of this era.

Designer Sighsten Herrgård's career as a designer started already at the age of 15, when he was announced "Dior of Bromma" (Bromma is an upper-class suburb of Stockholm) after winning a designer contest for girls. In the early 1960s he designed bath-clothes for Jantzen in London and it was in 1968 when Herrgård was employed by House of Worth in London that his career took off (Herrgård & Werkelid, 1989). A unisex-jumpsuit made of jersey was designed for this old fashion house, which got immediate and worldwide coverage that made him and Swedish fashion known all over the world (Figure 5.8). The jersey jumpsuit, in graphic black or discreet beige was designed to fit both women and men and was combined with accessories such as pendant necklaces and long scarves, sandals or high boots and a belt in the waist, in Herrgård's unisex style. Among the clippings in his archive there are several advertisements where unisex fashions appear on models who figure in commercials for example for beer and detergent or in a feature report on buffet food serving (Sighsten Herrgård archive, Nordic Museum, Stockholm). The clothes form part of a change

Figure 5.8 Swedish designer Sighsten Herrgård and his fiancee, Ann Jennifer, model of the designer's unisex belted jacked with wide-legged double-knit trousers.

in social conventions, promoting a new, fashionable and relaxed lifestyle.

There is a very interesting tension between the unisex ideas within the Mah-Jong group that aimed at political change and the unisex ideas held by the commercial designers such as Herrgård. Mah-Jong distributed their clothes themselves through one single shop and consequently did not reach a very large audience. The men's collection was produced in such modest numbers that hardly anyone outside the family and friends of the group could buy it (Hallström Bornold, 2003, p. 139). Herrgård's unisex-jumpsuit was launched and distributed all over the world, not only the western world, but also during fashion weeks in Mexico City and in Teheran in 1970. (Herrgård & Werkelid, 1989, pp. 89–94, p. 114–129) The outreach was incomparable, the political intentions as well, and I suggest that there is a fundamental difference here—Herrgård wanted to change the individual's potential to express personality and identity through fashion while the Mah-Jong group wanted to use fashion as a tool in order to change the relation between individual and society at large. Both sides however imbued these designed garments with the cultural meaning of liberation, in the sense that individual behavior is the foundation of transforming both political and fashionable society.

References

Bem, S. (1974). The Measurement of Psychological Androgyny. *Journal of Consulting and Clinical Psychology*, 2.

Blumer, H. (2007). From class differentiation to collective selection. [1969] In Barnard, M (ed.), *Fashion Theory. A Reader*. New York: Routledge.

Bolton, A. (2002). *Men in skirts*. London: V&A.

Bort med ålderstänkandet. Unisexmode för oss alla. (1969, November 26). Hallands nyheter.

Breward, C., Gilbert, D., Lister, J. (ed.) (2006). *Swinging sixties: fashion in London and beyond 1955–1970*. London: V&A Publications.

Burgelin, O. & Basse, M-T. (1987). L'unisexe. Perspectives diachroniques. *Communications*, 46. Paris: Centre d'études transdisciplinaires.

Butler, J. (1999). *Gender Trouble. Feminism and the subversion of identity*. London & New York: Routledge.

Cole, S. (2000). *Don we now our gay apparel*. Oxford: Berg.

Connell, R. (1995). *Masculinities*. Berkeley: University of California Press.

Eldvik, B. (1988). Mah-Jong. In Kläder. Fataburen. Stockholm: Nordiska museet.

Frazier, G. (1968). The Peacock Revolution. *Esquire*, 10.

Gottdiener, M. (1995) *Postmodern Semiotics. Material Culture and the Forms of Postmodern Life*. Oxford & Cambridge: Blackwell.

Hallström Bornold, S. (2003) Det är rätt att göra uppror: Mah-Jong 1966–1976. Stockholm: Modernista.

Herrgård, S., Werkelid, C. O. (1988) *Sighsten*. Stockholm: Norstedts.

Lobenthal, J. (1990) *Radical rags. Fashions of the Sixties*. New York: Abbeville Press.

Lomas, C. (2007) Men don't wear velvet you know! Fashionable gay masculinity and the shopping experience London 1950 – early 1970's. Oral history, 1.

MacLeod, C. (1998). *Embodying ambiguity: androgyny and aesthetics from Winckelmann to Keller*. Detroit: Wayne State University Press.

Moffitt, P., Claxton, W. (1990) *The Rudi Gernreich Book*. Cologne, Germany, & London: Taschen.

Rosaldo, M. Z. & Lamphere, L. (red.) (1974). *Woman, culture, and society*. Stanford, Calif.: Stanford Univ. Press. The genderation. (1968, August 23). *Womens Wear Daily*.

These Swedes put pants on everyone. (1969, March 14). *Newsday* NY. Archive

Sighsten Herrgård archive Nordic museum, Stockholm, Sweden.

Discussion Questions

1. According to the author, what is the difference between unisex clothing and androgynous clothing?

What are some current styles that fall into the unisex category and the androgynous category, respectively?

2. What are the philosophical ideals of unisex clothing? Did unisex clothing in 1960s Sweden achieve these ideals? Why or why not?

5.2
Female Tradition in a New Context: The Case of the *Khanga*
Katalin Medvedev and Lioba Moshi

All ideologies strive for sartorial expressiveness (Eicher et al.,1995; Baker, 1997; Parkins, 2002); socialist ideology is no exception. Dress was a political issue under socialism primarily because of its potential class implications. As a result, socialist leaders all over the former socialist bloc often personally implicated themselves in the official sartorial discourse. They would go to extreme lengths to inform their subjects about their personal views on issues of dress. They prescribed modesty requirements for their subjects as well as provided them with personal and concrete directives on what they deemed "proper socialist attire." Socialist visionaries, such as Julius Nyerere, Mao Zedong, and Fidel Castro to name a few, tried to set an example with their own sartorial presentation.

Socialist dress had to become a tool of projecting the social and economic values of egalitarianism and serve primarily utilitarian purposes. People's sartorial presentation was also meant to testify to the self-reliance, productivity, and successes of the socialist economy. Furthermore, socialist fashion was expected to be visually distinct and markedly different from Western (bourgeois) fashion (Medvedev, 2008, 2009).

In addition, the official socialist sartorial discourse initiated by the aforementioned statesmen had to ensure that it visually conveyed the basic principles of socialism and superiority of socialist morality, which, at least on paper, included gender equality.

The Khanga: The Garment of the Female Masses

The *khanga* originated from the coastal areas of East Africa (Hanby and Bygott, 1984). It is a rectangle of pure cotton cloth with a border all around it, usually printed in bold designs and bright colors. (Figure 5.9) A khanga is as long as one's outstretched arm and wide enough to cover one from neck to knee, or from breast to toe (Hanby and Bygott, 1984). The *khanga*'s earliest form comes from sewing together 6 kerchief squares that had been brought to Africa by Portuguese traders from the Far East (Green, 2005). The designs at that time included a border and a pattern of white spots on a dark background that had the likeness of the local guinea fowl, hence the name *khanga*, which means guinea hen in Swahili (Figure 5.10).

The *khangas* are a symbol of womanhood. After a girl reaches puberty she begins to receive gifts of *khangas* from her family. *Khangas* change hands several times in wedding rituals as well. For example, the mother of the bride gets several *khangas* from her family and friends, during the send off party of the bride, to thank her for raising her daughter. These gifts are also meant to remind

An extended version of this article appeared in the Paideussis Journal for Interdisciplinary and Cross-Cultural Studies, edited by Linda Arthur and Andrew Reilly. Reprinted by permission of the authors.

Figure 5.9 Detail of a khanga depicting Nyerere. He is referred to as Maliwu, the teacher.

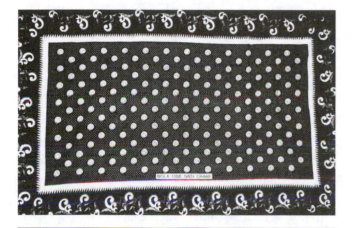

Figure 5.10 This is an ordinary khanga that has the pattern of white spots on a dark background. The white spots are supposed to create a likeness to the local guinea fowl. In this khanga the background is dark blue and the white spots are accentuated by black circles around them.

a mother that even though she will miss her daughter, she will not be alone to cope with her loss because her loved ones will continue to be part of her life. The bride's aunt, who traditionally gives away the bride, is also supposed to get a pair of *khangas* from the bridegroom's family as a way of formally establishing and materially solidifying the relationship with the bridegroom's family. These *khangas* are displayed for the wedding assembly and closely examined by the bride's wedding party. The quality and estimated value of these *khangas* provide a way to evaluate

the wealth and dedication of the bridegroom's family to the bride and her extended family.

After the marriage has been consummated, customarily, the new bride gives a set of *khangas* to her new husband as a sign of belonging, affection and intimacy. In Tanzania *khangas* are always sold in pairs. The young wife will wear one of the set at home as an easily removable wrapper for the upper torso, while her husband will wear the other on his lower torso. However, the man will never be seen in his *khanga* in public, only in the presence of his wife, mostly in the bedroom, which underscores the intimate meaning it carries for the newlyweds. Later, the husband is expected to buy his wife a pair of *khangas* every time he receives a salary. Thus, how many *khangas* a woman possesses indicates her husband's wealth and demonstrates his appreciation for her at the same time.

What Are the Reasons for the Politicization of the Khanga?

The colonial project in many parts of Africa was intimately linked to textiles, so much so that researchers even coined a term, "cotton imperialism," to describe this relationship (Perani and Wolf, 1999). Under cotton imperialism, the goal was the exclusive control of African (and Indian) cotton production. Another aim was to create a market for British finished products made from African (or Indian) raw material. For the same reason, it is logical that textiles played and continue to play a very important role in post-colonial Africa, where the production and control of textiles has been a way to assert economic self-reliance and have become a means and symbol of taking charge of the national economy.

In fact, one of the first instances of women's politicization in East Africa in the 1940s took place through their involvement in the so called *khanga* boycott. During the boycott, coastal women, who were the primary wearers of *khangas*, attempted to put an end to Indian merchants' monopoly of the sale of *khangas* (Mirza and Strobel, 1989). Because these foreign merchants were charging local sellers too much for the privilege of importing and selling *khangas*, East African women began to devise ways to cut out these middle men and order their supply directly from the producers. However, because of the practice of the *purdah*, which is the cultural and religious constrictions of Muslim women and the resulting limitations on their physical mobility, women, after a while, were unable to continue to bring in the shipments from the ports themselves and the boycott ended. Despite the defeat, the boycott made the *khanga* a politically charged dress item already prior to socialism.

How Did the Khanga Change Under Socialism?

Women's socialist sartorial makeover in Tanzania was not as radical as men's. Most women continued to wear *khangas* that had already been popular before Nyerere's ascendance to power. Nyerere's social changes did not affect this dress for a number of reasons. First, the *khanga* had already been embraced by the people before independence. However, as socialist dress, it had to convey new messages. Before independence, written words on the *khanga* expressed social messages or what was going on in the community, together with proverbial and traditional wisdom (Green, 2005). Under socialism, the *khanga* became an important means of communicating political messages (Figure 5.11).

So, khanga texts often served as literal political billboards, commissioned by parties and used in political rallies as means of identification of party affiliations. At political rallies women were either wearing such khangas or threw a *khanga* with a political inscription over their shoulders. The *khanga* has also been used to mobilize people to support public health campaigns as well as

Figure 5.11 This is part of a typical khanga that was used as a political billboard. The background is light blue; the other colors are yellow, dark blue, black, and white. The little images are self-explanatory. They stand for the achievements of the new socialist Tanzanian state, such as its defense, industry, energy production, technical expertise, high-quality produce, telecommunication, transportation, agriculture, information service, as well as its medical system.

creating awareness about particular development projects (Hanby and Bygott, 1984). *Khangas*, thus, were used as a utilitarian, low-cost way of campaigning and convenient means of communicating political content to the masses.

The second reason for Nyerere's support of the *khanga* was that it was the closest any female dress type could come to national dress in the ethnically diverse Tanzania, (there are 129 ethnic groups in Tanzania) so the *khanga* was used as an important "nationalist tool of empowerment and self-expression. The khanga was also more modern than "bark clothes" or animal skins that women used to wear in the past (Ivaska, 2004).

The third reason for Nyerere's approval of the *khanga* may have been that over time it became *the* garment of the female masses because it was utilitarian, multifunctional, versatile and affordable. *Khangas* were made of relatively cheap cotton fabrics and could be re-draped for all types of work—especially agricultural—and social functions. For example, the *khanga* was used as a protective layer over other clothes or to cradle a baby against one's back while working around the house or in the fields (Green, 2005). In addition, *Khangas* were not only imported, but often produced by local manufacturers, which was another important consideration why Nyerere supported it.

The *khanga* was the symbol of Tanzania's educational success as well. Women's education especially was minimal in Tanzania before independence. Therefore, the proverbial, commemorative, and educational messages *khangas* displayed proved that the new, socialist Tanzania was literate and cared about mass education. In fact, when Tanzania gained its independence in 1961, 80 percent of its population was illiterate, but in 1985, at Nyerere's resignation, in marked contrast, 85 percent of adults could read and write, making Tanzania's literacy rate the highest on the continent (Smith, 1986).

The *khanga* remained the visual icon of proper African womanhood under socialism. Other types of female garments, because of their Western and urban associations, seemed to have sparked Nyerere's ideological ire throughout his presidency. For example, on Nov. 1, 1968, *Time* magazine published a short report on Tanzania, titled *Battle of the Minis*, stating that, in the streets of Dar es Salaam, "an angry screaming mob halted buses and dragged off African girls wearing tight dresses and mini-skirts." The report described the phenomenon as a "cultural revolution, African style." What the anonymous reporter refers to is that President Julius Nyerere has decreed that Tanzania shall copy Mao Tse Tung's Great Proletarian

Cultural Revolution, which included the rejection of all things foreign. The "Operation Vijana" to prohibit mini-skirts, wigs, skin-lightening creams and other cosmetics that the journalist refers to was carried out by the TANU Youth League's mostly male members (Ivaska, 2004; Ross, 2008). Although many Tanzanian women, especially university students and young female urban professionals, fought back and staged loud protests, demanding a woman's right to choose what to wear, Nyerere and his followers remained unconvinced and unyielding in their verdict: the "un-African" mini-skirt had to go because it symbolized Western decadence, the "cultural enslavement of the African," and was "antithetical to Tanzania's national culture" (Ivaska, 2004:104). In sum, Nyerere likely left the traditional *khanga* alone, because he might have viewed it as a convenient means of political propaganda, a symbol of educational progress and also a means of reinforcing traditional and new socialist morality and values.

Conclusion

Under socialism, in Tanzania, just like in any other part of the socialist bloc, dress had a metaphorical role. It was an ideologically charged and highly politicized medium. It was a symbol of ideological unity, economic independence and self-sufficiency, as well as national and cultural cohesion. Because of these multiple functions, its control by the highest political leadership seemed to be imperative and had to be absolute.

At first, the Tanzanian socialist subjects subscribed to Nyerere's sartorial policies because they could discern the symbolic role dress played in his nation building efforts and in combating the legacy of colonialism. They embraced the policies also because the prescribed dress was familiar, non-Western, affordable and easily accessible. At the same time, especially young, educated, urban socialist women were not willing to give up their rights to a modern sartorial identity (Ivaska, 2004; Ross, 2008).

The control of sartorial self-expression was key in building socialism. This study in a Tanzanian context supports previous research findings on socialist dress practices in Eastern Europe, and has argued that dress was one of the most important areas where socialism as a world system became constructed, embodied, and articulated. At the same time, sartorial representation was also the area where socialist uniformity became first challenged, revealing the internal contradictions of socialist ideology and social policy.

References

Baker, P. L. (1997), Politics of dress: The dress reform laws of 1920/30s Iran, in: Lindisfarne-Tapper, N. and Ingham, B. (eds.), *Languages of dress in the Middle East*. Richmond, UK: Curzon, 178–191.

Eicher, J. B., Roach-Higgins, M. E., and Johnson, K. K. P. (eds.). (1995), *Dress and identity*. New York: Fairchild.

Green, R. L. (2005), Kanga, in: Steele, V. (ed.), *Encyclopedia of clothing and fashion,* 2. New York: Charles Scribner's Sons, 297–298.

Hanby, J., and Bygott, D. (1984), *Kangas: 101 uses*. Nairobi, Kenya: Ines May Publicity.

Ivaska, A. M. (2004), Anti-mini militants meet modern misses: Urban style, gender, and the politics of "national culture" in the 1960s Dar es Salaam, Tanzania, in: Allman, J. (ed.), *Fashioning Africa: Power and politics of dress*. Bloomington, IN: Indiana University Press, 104–121.

Medvedev, K. (2008), Ripping up the uniform approach: Hungarian women piece together a new communist fashion, in Blaszczyk, R. L. (ed.), *Producing fashion: Commerce, culture and consumer.*, Philadelphia: University of Pennsylvania Press, 250–272.

Medvedev, K. (2009), Divat es Bunozes az 50-es es 60-as Evekben Magyarorszagon. [Crime and Fashion in Hungary in the 1950s and 1960s], in: Simonovics, I., and Valuch, T. (eds.), *Kirakat: Divat a szocializmusban.* [Shopwindow: Fashion under socialism]. Budapest, Hungary: Argumentum, 126–143.

Mirza, S., and Strobel, M. (eds). (1989), *Three Swahili women: Life histories from Mombasa, Kenya*. Bloomington, IN: Indiana University Press.

Parkins, W. (ed). (2002), *Fashioning the body politic*. New York: Berg.

Perani, J., and Wolf, N. (1999), Cloth, dress and art patronage in Africa. Oxford: Berg.

Ross, R. (2008), *Clothing: A global history*. Cambridge, UK: Polity Press.

Smith, W. E. (1986, March 3), A reporter at large: Transition. *New Yorker*, 72–83.

Discussion Questions

1. How do politics and gender play out in the khanga?
2. Why do you think men do not khanga in public?
3. What are some other examples of clothing that combine gender and political views?

5.3
A Comparative Analysis of Hijras and Drag Queens: The Subversive Possibilities and Limits of Parading Effeminacy and Negotiating Masculinity

Sandeep Bakshi

In the following paper I offer a queer reading of the hijra in terms of the subversive possibilities and limits such individuals pose to established modes of thinking about gender binaries. I analyze the hijra alongside that of the much discussed and debated western figure of the drag queen. However, a comparative analysis of the hijra versus the drag queen does not mean advocating the critical meaningfulness of the one over the other. Rather, in this article, I relocate both of these cultural models as potentially destabilizing to contemporary understandings of gendered and sexed identities. The notion of gender as performance as a transcultural "tool" for dismantling rigidities of the masculine/feminine divide is discussed in detail. I make it clear, however, that the hijra figure is not the Indian counterpart of, nor the Indian answer to, the drag queen. The hijra community is an integrated and inseparable part of the Indian social fabric and is "undoubtedly related to the variety and significance of alternative gender roles and gender transformations in Indian mythology and traditional culture" (Nanda, 1999, p. 20).

Hijras and Hindu Culture

Hijras belong to the category of sexually "ambivalent" men–minus man–who dress up as women and perform on auspicious Hindu occasions like weddings and birth ceremonies (O'Flaherty, 1980, p. 297). Official counts of hijras vary significantly from 50,000 to upwards of 1.2 million (Bobb and Patel, 1982; Hall, 1997, p. 431; Jaffrey, 1997, p. 30; *BBC News Online*, 2001). While a few Hijras are born intersexed (which is rare), most are men who undergo voluntary castration and penectomy while "possessed" by the Goddess Bahuchara (Cohen, 1995, p. 276). They consider themselves to be sexually impotent, an important point which I will discuss later in the essay. Hijras have cultural and ritual sanction during wedding and birth ceremonies, and even the colonial rulers in

the nineteenth century had to concede to their rights of property and begging for alms that they had hitherto enjoyed under native rulers (Preston, 1987).

Hijras live in large communities in North India and Pakistan, especially near the city of Ahemdabad (Gujrat, India) where they congregate annually at the Bahuchara Mata Shrine. Every new initiate to the community has a guru (mentor) and becomes a part of the hijra community once he has paid the *dand* (fine) to her guru. The amount of the *dand* is decided by the *Panchayat* (the community elders, a structure replicated from mainstream Indian society). The notion of the community is key to understanding hijra existence, as it is to many marginalized subcultures, which helps them to belong to a hierarchical frame and survive as a "parallel society" (Turner, 1977).

One of the more complicated and difficult tasks that gender and sexuality scholars face when investigating hijras is that there are several, sometimes contradictory definitions of what makes one a hijra. They have been defined as "eunuchs" (Mehta, 1945; Hiltebeitel, 1980, pp. 161–5; Bobb and Patel, 1982; Sharma, 1984; Preston, 1987; Jaffrey, 1997), "hermaphrodites" (Opler, 1960) with a "physical defect, natural or acquired" (Opler, 1961, p. 1331), male or boy prostitutes (Ellis, 1921; Carstairs, 1956, p.130), passive homosexuals (Carstairs, 1957, p. 60; Greenberg, 1988), and as a third gender and/or sex (Herdt, 1996, p. 70; Nanda, 1996; Nanda, 1999) with a cultural and ritual function (Opler, 1961, p. 1331; Hall, 1997; Nanda, 1999). This is further confounded by most hijra representations in the popular press and cinema being "superficial and sensationalist" (Nanda, 1999, p. xvii) and failing to consider their subjective perceptions (for examples of this sort, see Bobb and Patel, 1982, and Bedi, 1994). Moreover, hijras, homosexuals, and jankhas/zankhas (transvestites) are often collapsed in the same category (Bakshi, 2002).

From *Journal of Homosexuality*, April 20, 2004, Volume 46, Issue 3-4/Taylor & Francis Ltd, http://www.informaworld.com

Ultimately, any working definition of hijras must take into account their subjective perception as "neither man nor woman" (Nanda, 1999), and as perceived guarantors of fertility whereby their presence at the marriage and birth rituals is legitimated. They belong to the category of third gender but also to that of third sex (a point not much emphasized in hijra representations). In contemporary India, ritual and religious respect is not given to them per se, rather they negotiate and command this respect in order to empower their marginal identities in "resistance to systematic exclusion" (Hall, 1997, p. 431). Given that hijras do not have children, there is no simple and comprehensive register of genealogy that can give us details on their ancestors. This is partially due to the fact that as "neither men nor women" hijras have few political rights even though in recent times they have been given the right to vote in democratic elections (*BBC News Online*, 2000; *Times of India*, 2002). Thus, the only other source for tracing their beginnings is found in the various myths that have been perpetrated by hijras themselves and other folk literature (songs and chants that are sung during various hijra ceremonies and rituals).

It is interesting to note that transvestism has existed in Hindu mythology even before the conception of humankind and often hijras legitimate their right to existence through a careful decoding of various myths. Almost every hijra has a story of mythological origin relating his/her descendence (Nanda, 1999). For example, most prehistorical myths relate the descent of the hijras from the deity of Shiva (the god of destruction and unparalleled anger), who was also called Ardhanariswar, meaning half man and half woman. For many hijras the quality of being half man and half woman is a source of infinite strength that endows on them the divine power to give a *shraap* (curse), just like Shiva cursed the earth (Hiltebeitel, 1980, p. 159; Nanda, 1999, p. 20).

In yet another famous myth, during the great war of Kurukshetra (*Mahabharata*), the most brave and powerful warriors of the Pandava clan Arjun dressed as and became a woman in appearance called Brihannada (Hiltebeitel, 1980, p. 154; Sharma, 1984, p. 384; Nanda, 1999, pp. 30–1). As Brihannada, he participated in the wedding ceremony of his son Abhimanyu with the princess Uttara (Hiltebeitel, 1980, p. 166). It must be pointed out that Arjun's cross-dressing is read by almost all hijras as an instance of voluntary emasculation that opens up avenues of immaculate physical strength.

All hijras stress the notion of impotence as a prerequisite for joining the community and an eventual surgical emasculation for the attainment of divine and physical power. Castration and penectomy are widely practiced as an inevitable requisite for becoming a hijra. Emasculation is looked upon by the hijras as a source of personal fulfillment. Since such practices are illegal and even criminal under the Indian Penal Code, they take place under strict vigilance away from any outside (police) encroachments. Hijras regard castration as a ritual, a religious offering of their penis to the Goddess and as a source of pleasure which "re/members (it) as a bloody act and takes the violence as central to the representations of thirdness" (Cohen, 1995, p. 277). In a similar vein, the Travesties of Brazil perceive "the injection of industrial silicone into (their) body" as "one of the final steps. . . in (their) transformation into travesty" (Kulick, 1998, p. 46).

I will now further explore English translations of the word "hijra." It is true that for cultural and gender definition purposes, hijras have been relegated to the categories of eunuchs and hermaphrodites, i.e., emasculated biological males and intersexed "males" whose sexual organs are ambiguous at birth or who suffer from a genetical malformation. However, such definitions seem, at best, to be as subjective definitions of the term "hijra" in various Hindi and urdu linguistic codes implies impotence and is stressed by hijras themselves and has been highlighted by Nanda (1996, p. 380; 1999, p. 13). The definitional importance of impotence gains further weight if we consider that most hijras are born with normal male sexual organs and voluntarily undergo surgical castration to become a part of the hijra community. Nevertheless, the term "Hijra" can still be read as a "eunuch" in the broadest sense of the word, which refers "not only to an individual who is physiologically incapable of engendering an offspring but also to one who has chosen to withdraw from worldly activities and thus refuses to procreate," and are a *sanyasi* (to use Hindu terminology), someone who voluntarily renounces the world (Ringrose, 1996, p. 86). As I will demonstrate in a moment, definitional understanding of the hijras is quite helpful in better appreciating what sort of gender performance they undertake.

A Comparative Analysis of Hijras and Drag Queens

In recent years queer theory scholars have increasingly focused on how gender and sexuality is performed.

Judith Butler's works have been influential to the creation and development of critical analyses and emerging understandings of gender as performance (Butler, 1990). She writes about gender identity as a form cultural fiction, that through "a repeated stylization of the body, a set of repeated acts within a highly rigid regulatory frame that congeal over time to produce the appearance of substance, [become] a natural sort of being" (Butler, 1990, p. 33). She also advocates that drag is a parody of fixed and normative conceptualizations of gender. Ultimately, drag for Butler "constitutes the mundane way in which genders are appropriated, theatricalized, worn, and done; it implies that all gendering is a kind of impersonation and approximation" (Butler, 1991, p. 21).

Drag queens, like Hijra performances, often make us think about the various ways in which gender is played out and "naturalized" in society. They help us to realize that gender is a philosophical category and is not "what one is, but more fundamentally, is what one does" (West and Zimmerman, 1987, p. 140). By exaggerating the feminine, drag queens are capable of showing us the fiction of established dichotomous processes of gendering. Stylization of the self by drag can potentially disrupt regulatory notions of the "self" and can subversively reveal the limits of identity. Perhaps notwithstanding a few movie portrayals, however, most drag queens and their subversive potential are largely marginalized from the larger cultural setting, e.g., most perform in gay bars.

Hijras, on the other hand, enjoy religious and cultural legitimacy. The blessings of hijras in Hindu marriage and birth ceremonies are part of a ritual obligation. This means that the potential "denaturalization" of gender binaries that can be seen in the figure of hijras and their presence at various culturally mainstream rituals is part of the larger social framework in which it occurs. In sum, while drag queens operate in private or alternative social spaces (clubs, bars and lesbian and gay prides), hijras, while still culturally marginalized, perform in normative and conventional cultural spaces.

In hijra performances, however, this alternative space is a priori guaranteed and reinforced by religious and social customs even if the presence of hijras is undesired. Unlike drag shows, hijra performances (although seemingly undertaking a similar deconstruction of gender binaries) take place within mainstream institutions like marriage. Almost all Hindu marriages and birth ritual have ceremonies calling for at least one hijra intervention if not more. Sometimes if the hijras are absent from such ceremonies many newlyweds seek the blessings by going to places where they can find the hijra community. As Andrew Whitehead of the *BBC* reports in his personal experiences with the hijras, "an Indian birth (is) hardly complete without the hijras" (Whitehead, 1998).

Let me now explore the relational aspect of hijra shows. The audience of hijra performances usually comprises everyone present at the concerned weddings. It consists of almost all adult male and female relatives, and even children. Unlike the audiences at drag shows, this mainstream public of hijra shows is paradoxically often not fully prepared for a "visible attack" (in the form of a dance-spectacle) on their preconceived notions of rigid gendered and sexed identities. The alternative space which the hijra performs in, and which has the capacity to demythify gender identities, is often negotiated and at times coerced by the hijras in the presence of an involuntary audience who can sometimes refuse that the hijras lift up their *ghagras* (long skirts) or saris.

One of the most fascinating aspects of the audience/hijra interaction is that men in the audience both regulate and control the hijra performance/transgression. Women are relegated to the subordinate rank of mere spectators while the patriarchal figures of the household (father, uncle or a distant male relative) deal with the performers. Men are responsible for negotiating and fixing the boundaries concerning the duration of the shows, the financial compensation of the hijras, and most importantly, the sexual gestures involved in the hijra performance. In this sense, males in the audience (married or otherwise) represent stability and order of gendered identities and are the monolithic guarantors of the continuation of these identities. Nevertheless, they participate in such an exceptional exchange with the hijras (often in a climate charged with sexual dynamics) who represent a challenge to this very notion of normative identity regulation. The hijra performance thus becomes a discursive site of critical negotiations between the symbolic patriarchs and alternatively (inter-)sexed beings. This site reveals the fiction of gendered and sexed realities where gendering and sexualizing forces (in the figure of the patriarchs) play and are played out (in the figure of the hijras, who enact both the feminine and the masculine parts in case the males present in the ceremonies refuse to take part in their song and dance sequences). This dramatic transgression of normativity subsides once the hijra ceremony is over and the males from the audience (who are often the receivers of hijra attention/irony) return to their constructed role of controlling the gender boundaries but not without a sense of pleasure.

Critical commentators on drag have begun to question the attribution of the unproblematic subversion of heteronormative ideals to the figure of drag. Drag, it has been suggested, is not a simple tool of resistance to preexisting gender/sexual dichotomies and, thus, cannot be set up as a uniquely radical and unified category that has the possibility (and the power) to critique identity limits. Even Butler, who proposed drag as a subversive undertaking, has repositioned drag as a potential threat to an exposure of gender fictions rather than being the unquestioned source of resistance to such fictions in itself. In one of her later works she clarifies that drag is never "unproblematically subversive" and it "reflects the mundane impersonations by which heterosexually ideal genders are performed and naturalized." Moreover, she emphasizes that drag has the potential to "reidealize heterosexual norms without calling them into question" (Butler, 1993, p. 231).

Other queer scholars have even inquired into various ways in which discussions on drag in queer theory have significantly centered around "play" and "performance" thus reducing the very "theory of gender" into the "old 'sex roles' framework" (Walters, 1996, p. 854). In the domain of transgender studies scholars have argued that transgender individuals often "reinforce and reify the system they hope to change" and that "female impersonators almost universally present stereotypical and exaggerated images of females" (Gagné, Tewksbury and McGaughey, 1997, p. 478; Tewksbury, 1993, p. 467). Even in studies of third gender, the male/female binary divide is suspected to be reinstated as if it "recuperates social and sexual norms," to borrow a phrase from Garber (Garber, 1992, p. 69; Kulick, 1998, p. 120).

In order to better understand the critical implications of drag in issues of political and social resistance, one needs to (re)view gender and gendering as intellectual sites where the power dynamic of male/female, straight/gay, superior/inferior, original/duplicate is at work. In other words, all contemporary gender relationships are hegemonically structured around the possession of power. Apart from the play and performance that one links to drag, we must also (re-)locate drag in a broader context of the power problematic. I believe that at a non-complex level, drag relies heavily on the ability to shock and scandalize. The techniques for resisting pre-given identity limits used by drag queens mostly consist of an exaggeration and a deliberate overplay of the "feminine." This can certainly be read as an instrument of "male" power so that men can pose as, and seemingly be, "better" women than women themselves. Drag may tell us how gendered identity is constructed by cultural and social conditioning but it also paradoxically often re-legitimates gender as an essential category with its focus on exaggerated forms of the feminine. Drag, as Schacht argues, is often a form of "homosexual embodiment of the heterosexual," whereby a drag performance often fixes and reinstates the gender binary rather than exposing it. Read in this way drag shows "become wholly dependent on the audience's normative expectations about gender and sexuality" and are "frequently more reflective than transgressive of the dominant culture's ideals of gender and sexuality" (Schacht, 2002, p.163).

Thus, while drag is not unconditionally subversive, the hijra paradigm forces us to rethink about the multiplicity of the techniques of resistance to preexisting gender identifications. Shock and scandal are also used in the hijra shows as tools for unsettling gender equations. The audiences are generally involuntary participants in the performances as hijra shows are an unwritten dictate of the cultural context. Once the song and dance sequences are over, the hijras invariably lift up their *ghagras* or saris (unless warned not to do so by the adult male members of the audience), to show that they are male (i.e., possess a male organ) or that they are neither male nor female (i.e., have no sexual organ) as in most cases. This is often done to show that the hijras are "real" hijras (i.e., are castrated), and not fake ones (i.e., men posing as hijras), or just effeminate men, zenanas, for whom the hijra community reserves disdain (Cohen, 1995, p. 276; Jaffrey, pp. 110 and 161; Nanda, 1999, p.11). However, sometimes if the marriage party refuses to pay the desired alms to the hijras, they can use it as a tool to demand their rights. As Cohen puts it, "the sight of the postoperative hole–the seal of the *hijras* impotence–is paradoxically potent, causing impotence in the man who is exposed to it" (Cohen, 1995, p. 296, italics in original).

The lifting of the sari can be accompanied by their *shraap* or other verbal assaults. Various responses can be given to the hijra insults. Some scholars, like Sharma, think that these insults are the result of hijras' "sexual frustration," while others have argued it is a tried and tested technique for extorting money (Carstairs, 1956, p. 130; Sharma, 1984, p. 387). Yet others consider these insults a legitimate replication of societal intimidation and dehumanization

(Mehta, 1945, pp. 47–8; Jaffrey, 1997, p. 241). It should nevertheless be noted that hijra linguistic remarks, though strikingly harsh, form a part of the larger background of their performance. Any drag quarrels remain within closed spaces while the hijra "vituperative banter" is often in the presence of non-hijra males with the aim to "embarrass their male listeners and shamelessly collapse traditional divisions of the secret and the known, private and public, home and market, feminine and masculine" (Hall, 1997, pp. 448–9). Moreover, hijras, like other marginalised and liminal entities, can escape from principal conditions of propriety imposed by social control (Turner, 1977).

Once the hijras lift up their saris, the audience who is seduced into believing that they are witnessing a "female" show often experiences a shock. The myth of seeing a seemingly "female performance" ends abruptly with this gesture. The "incongruity" of sexual and gendered identity that is part of identity politics and identity fiction becomes a "visible" reality. What the audience witnesses and participates in is not only the shock of seeing/not seeing the sexual parts (for many prudish Indians) but also a demonstrative deconstruction of stabilized gender identities.

This effective de-mythification of the "incongruity" of gendered identities becomes all the more meaningful and interesting if we analyze the figure of hijra itself. Unlike many drag queens, many hijras are visible manifestations of the fiction of gender in their person. Some of them do use the masculine attributes when talking of themselves or addressing each other. Some also have masculine names even if this is rare. Almost all of them that I have met or seen always retain their dry and hard masculine voices while at the same time wearing female attires. Even during hijra shows they do not aim at acquiring a high pitched female voice and it is this very disturbing aspect of their appearance that becomes a dynamic tool for resisting the male/female divide and helps them to disrupt in part the semblance of a "female" performance. If the "body" is an essential component of identity through which "we announce our presence to others," then the 'incongruent' hijra body that belongs to third sex poses a real threat to established sexual dimorphism (Gagné and Tewksbury, 1998, p. 85). The fear of this incongruity is pervasive in the film *Darmiyaan*; when Immi the hijra (as a child) unbuttons his trousers to pee, one of the other children remarks: "*Immi ka to nounou hi nahi hai,*" i.e., Immi does not have a penis.

The hijra body and paradigm, so nebulous, can extend anywhere from an emasculated male to a withdrawn or effeminate one right up to a *sanyasi*. It covers the entire spectrum from the holy to the bizarre to the damned! There is so much irony in this spectrum that one form of the hijra is revered as the *sanyasi* and one is marginalised if not always rebuked or ridiculed in the form of the outlandish "eunuch" in urban India. However, in all this irony there lies a grave similarity. In all its forms, the hijra is certainly also feared. In some cases the fear arises out of psychological insecurities, while in some it may arise out of anxiety of the unknown. But it is fear all the same. And yet culturally we tend to associate the archetype of the hijra with the powerless!

Gendered (In)Securities

Studying alternative sex and gender matrices of the Orient involves an unsettling of accepted American and Euro-centric ideas as the only available cultural referent, and debunking sexual and gendered dimorphism across cultures. Transgendered communities found across cultures are suggestive of "a continuum of masculinity and feminin-ity, renouncing gender as aligned with genitals, body, social status and/or role" (Bolin, pp. 447–8). Drag queen and hijras performances open up spaces where we as a larger society "can watch a small group and become aware" of ourselves and understand that all "performance is an illusion . . . and might be considered more 'truthful,' more 'real' than ordi-nary experience" (Schechner, 1988, pp. xiv and 13).

Reading the hijra alongside the drag queen means broadening and enriching the discursive elements of identity (in)congruity and revealing the fiction of all gendering and sexualizing processes of any dominant culture. Gender and sexuality debates, as I have shown, have centered upon drag or hijras as two distinct cultural categories that unsettle our preconceived notions of the masculine and the feminine. Both are subcultural byproducts of Western and Indian societies and have developed in relation to their respective mainstream cultures. The drag queen and the hijra have different modus operandi but both appear to have the same goal of de-legitimizing polarized and normalizing gender categories. While the drag queen typically performs in marginalized settings, hijras have the right to perform in mainstream cultural ceremonies. Yet both have a limited impact on the larger culture. Drag queens are individuals with an acknowledged penis whereas hijras are framed as impotent and eunuchs. Thus, the subversive potential of drag is undermined by limiting their performances to marginalized settings, whereas that of the hijras is limited because of their marginalized status of being impotent and lacking a penis. Ultimately, while both the hijras and the drag queen have a limited subversive impact on the larger dominant culture in which they perform, in practice and image they can forcibly remind us of our own gendered (in)securities.

References

Bakshi, S. (2002). Soupçon d'un Espace Alternatif: Etude de Deux Films du Cinéma Parallèle en Inde. *Inverses*, 2, 9–21.

BBC News Online (2000, March 6). Eunuch MP takes seat.

BBC News Online (2001, March 9). India stages Ms World for eunuchs.

Bedi, R. (1994, April 16). The bizarre and dangerous world of India's eunuchs. *Vancouver Sun*.

Bobb, D., and Patel, C.J. (1982, September 15). Fear is the key. *India Today*.

Bolin, A. (1996). Transcending and transgendering: Male to female transsexuals, dichotomy and diversity. In Gilbert Herdt (Ed.) *Third sex/third gender: Beyond sexual dimorphism in culture and history* (pp. 447–486). New York: Zone Books.

Butler, J. (1990). *Gender trouble: Feminism and the subversion of identity*. New York: Routledge.

Butler, J. (1991). Imitation and gender insubordination. In D. Fuss (Ed.), *Inside/out: Lesbian theories/gay theories* (pp.13–31). New York: Routledge.

Butler, J. (1993). *Bodies that matter: On the discursive limits of "sex."* New York: Routledge.

Carstairs, G.M. (1956). Hinjra and jiryan: Two derivatives of Hindu attitudes to sexuality. *British Journal of Medical Psychology*, 29, 128–138.

Cohen, L. (1995). The pleasures of castration: The postoperative status of hijras, jankhas, and academics. In P.R. Abramson and S.D. Pinkerton (Eds.), *Sexual nature, sexual culture* (pp. 276–304). Chicago and London: University of Chicago Press.

Gagné P., and Tewksbury, R. (1998). Conformity pressures and gender resistance among transgendered individuals. *Social Problems*, 45(1), 81–101.

Gagné P., Tewksbury, R., and McGaughey D. (1997). Coming out and crossing over: Identity formation and proclamation in a transgender community. *Gender and Society*, 11(4), 478–508.

Garber, M. (1992). *Vested interests: Cross-dressing and cultural anxiety*. London and New York: Routledge.

Greenberg, D.F. (1988). *The construction of homosexuality*. Chicago: University of Chicago Press.

Hall, K. (1997). *Go suck your husband's sugarcane: Hijras and the use of sexual insult.*
In A. Livia and K. Hall (Eds.), *Queerly phrased: Language, gender and sexuality* (pp. 430–460). New York: Oxford University Press.

Hiltebeitel, A. (1980). Siva, the Goddess, and the disguises of the Pandavas and Draupadi. *History of Religions*, 20(1-2), 147–174.

Jaffrey, Z. (1997). *The invisibles: A tale of the eunuchs of India*. London: Weidenfeld and Nicholson.

Kulick, D. (1998). *Travesti: Sex, gender and culture among Brazilian transgendered prostitutes*. Chicago: University of Chicago Press.

Mehta, S. (1945). Eunuchs, pavaiyas, and hijaras. *Gujarat Sahitya Sabha Part 2*, 3–75.

Nanda, S. (1996). Hijras: An alternative sex and gender role in India. In Gilbert Herdt (Ed.), *Third sex/third gender* (pp. 373–418). New York: Zone Books.

Nanda, S. (1999). *The hijras of India: Neither man nor woman*. Second Edition. Belmont: Wadsworth.

O'Flaherty, W.D. (1980). *Women, androgynes, and other mythical beasts*. Chicago: University of Chicago Press.

Opler, M.E. (1960). The hijara (hermaphrodites) of India and Indian national character: A rejoinder. *American Anthropologist*, 62, 505–511.

Opler, M.E. (1961). Further comparative notes on the hijara of India. *American Anthropologist*, 63, 1331–1332.

Preston, L.W. (1987). A right to exist: Eunuchs and the state in nineteenth-century. *Modern Asian Studies*, 21(2), 371–387.

Ringrose, K.M. (1996). Living in the shadows: Eunuchs and gender in Byzantium. In Gilbert Herdt (Ed.), *Third sex/third gender* (pp. 85–109). New York: Zone Books.

Schacht, S.P. (2002). Four renditions of doing female drag: Feminine appearing conceptual variations of a masculine theme. *Advances in Gender Research*, 6, 157–180.

Sharma, S.K. (1984). Eunuchs: Past and present. *Eastern Anthropologist*, 4, 381–389.

Tewksbury, R. (1993). Men performing as women: Explorations in the world of female impersonators. *Sociological Spectrum*, 13, 465–486.

The Times of India (2002, June 20). Eunuch elected ward councilor in Bihar.

Turner, Victor W. (1977). *The ritual process: Structure and anti-structure*. Chicago: Adline.

Walters, Suzanna D. (1996). From here to queer: Radical feminism, postmodernism, and the lesbian menace (or, why can't a woman be more like a fag?). *Signs*, 21(4), 830–869.

West C., and Zimmerman, D.H. (1987). Doing gender. *Gender and Society*, 1, 125–151.

Whitehead, Andrew. (1998, August 16). The hijras' blessing. *BBC News Online*.

Discussion Questions

1. What are the differences between hijras and drag queens?

2. How do hijras obtain their power? How do drag queens obtain their power?

3. How do hijras and drag queens challenge heteronormative masculinity?

CHAPTER 6
APPEARANCE FOR SEXUALITY AND SEXUAL IDENTITY

Andrew Reilly

After you have read this chapter, you will understand:

- How the role of modesty contributes to what is perceived as erotic
- How sexual acts have been identified by clothing codes
- How sexual identity is related to aesthetic styles

MODESTY AND IMMODESTY IN DRESS

People—especially women—are stigmatized for dressing immodestly as well as sexually. **Modesty** is enacted by the covering of part of the body that if exposed in public would have a sexual connotation. In the Antebellum period of the United States it was considered erotic for women to show their ankles (though, ironically, plunging necklines and vast décolleté were acceptable); a modest woman therefore kept them covered. In Polynesia, it was acceptable for women to have bare breasts until missionaries arrived in the 18th and 19th centuries and converted them to Christianity. Subsequently, rules of modesty were adopted and Polynesian women began covering their breasts. In the 1960s, Barbara Eden starred in television's *I Dream of Jeannie* and wore a costume that revealed her midriff. Originally, the costume also revealed her navel but that caused too much controversy and the costume was modified. Today, an exposed women's navel is not unusual. See Figure 6.1.

Changes in modesty and eroticism are explained by the **theory of shifting erogenous zones** (Laver, 1969). The theory is based on the principle that complete nudity is anti-erotic. The mind needs to fantasize about what is hidden, and therefore fashion serves to hide and reveal

Figure 6.1 The original *I Dream of Jeannie* costume had to be modified to cover Barbara Eden's navel because it would have been too immodest as originally designed.

different body parts, which are fetishized during different eras. Once the body part becomes overexposed, new styles serve to cover it and reveal a new body part. One reason why the movie *Jaws* was so scary when it was first released is that the shark was rarely seen; a glimpse of a fin here, a shadow there. The mind is highly imaginative and sensitive to suggestion. In the same way, a partially clothed body is more erotic than a nude body—the possibility of what lies underneath is more interesting than the reality. Recall from Chapter 4, The Body, the reading about tattoos ("The Theory of Shifting Erogenous Zones: Tattoos and the Male Body") where the author argued that this theory can support body modifications as well as clothing.

Although there has always been "sexy" clothing styles, punk played a significant role in sexualizing clothing. The punk movement included clothes that were blatantly and unapologetically sexual in nature. Malcom McLaren and Vivienne Westwood opened their store called SEX in 1974 and its assortment of S&M, bondage, and fetish clothes brought the private world into the public domain. Punk style included ripped apparel that revealed the skin underneath, fishnet stockings, chains, metal studs and spikes, dog collars, black leather, plaid bondage pants, body piercings, bras worn as shirts, and anything else that could evoke a sense of sexual liberation. According to Malcom Garrett, who was a prominent figure in the early development of punk in the 1970s and 1980s, "The diverse works of art—embracing music, performance, visual arts, and fashion—all marched to create mixed collectives of people who were bravely exploring identity and with it the potency of sexuality. Sex was forcefully presented and used as a weapon of confrontation. It became a totem of social change" (Garrett & Kettle, 2018, p. 84).

Today, many women are confronted with fashions that are revealing. This becomes a point of contention for women who desire to remain covered (or modest) and look stylish (or immodest). Clothing scholar Annette Lynch (2012) coined the term **porn chic** to describe "fashion and related trend-based behaviors linked to the porn industry that have become mainstreamed in the dress of women and girls" (p. 3). Examples Lynch highlighted include T-shirts with sexually suggestive slogans or *Playboy* insignia, pubic hair shaven to imitate female porn actors, marketing campaigns aimed at tween and teenage girls that advocate a "sexy" lifestyle, and thongs and padded bras designed for tween and teenage girls. Lynch argued that porn chic is the result of the white heterosexual male gaze, sexual objectification, self-objectification, misogyny, and sexual attention as power. This creates dilemmas and concerns for parents as clothing marketing to children and adolescents has become more sexualized. Read more on this topic of sexy clothing "Is Tween Fashion Too Sexy?" by M. B. Sammon.

One example of porn chic is found in the "sex bracelets" of the early 2000s worn by middle and high school girls. The bracelets where colored rubber that were originally popular in the 1980s and known as jelly bracelets. When they began to reappear as a fashion statement two decades later a rumor about their semiotic meaning was attached to them. Colors noted specific sex acts the wearer was willing to perform. School administrators began to ban the bracelets and warn parents. According to the fact-checking website Snopes.com, students were aware of the rumor but did not engage in sexual activity related to the bracelets. "The greatest concern of 'sex bracelets' appears not to be that one is going to engage in any real redeeming, but that children far too young to be entertaining such thoughts are being exposed to them" (Mikkelson, 2014).

Yet, the term porn chic can also be applied to men, where the **spornosexual** body (a combination of the words sports and porno, meaning a man with a fit, trim, and toned eroticized body) is a desired physique to obtain, tight-fitting clothing that reveals chest and bulges, and pubic hair trimmed to replicate male porn actors (see Figure 6.2) (Engle, 2014).

Although many styles of dress are considered sexy or sexual, they do not imply sexual interest. The relationship between dress and sexual interest is complex and fraught with emotion. As you learned in Chapter 3, dress is nonverbal communication and is imbued with coded messages; however, the intended message is not often accurately interpreted. This is the case in sexual assault and sexual harassment cases. Researchers Sharron J. Lennon, Kim K. P. Johnson, and Theresa Lennon

Figure 6.2 An example of spornosexual: the toned, muscular body and skimpy bathing suit eroticize this man's body.

Schulz (1999) documented how survivors' dress was often introduced by the defense as evidence of consent; defense lawyers typically argued that clothing (e.g., short shirt, sheer fabrics, clothing fit, lack of a bra) and makeup indicated interest in sex and implied survivors' responsibility. However, the assumed inferences based on dress are inaccurate (women dress in clothing styles for many different reasons) and since the publication of their article, the U.S. legal system has eliminated the introduction of clothing, except to demonstrate evidence of a struggle.

SEXUALITY IDENTITY

Symbols have frequently been used to signal sexual availability and interest through history. In Ancient Greece, prostitutes wore sandals with the words *follow me* printed on the bottom so that they left a message when they walked the streets (Halpern, 1990). In 17th to 19th-century Japan, courtesans known as *oiran* wore elaborate robes with the obi tied in the front and high-platform shoes with no socks. In 19th-century Europe, courtesans wore a black ribbon tied around the neck. Yet, one need not be a professional sex worker to advertise sexual interest or availability. In the 1970s, gay men used a coded system of handkerchiefs where the color and location in the right or back pocket of one's pants indicated one's sexual interest. And more recently, in the early 20th century, colored rubber bracelets were used in a similar method to indicate sexual interest.

Coded symbols can be also used to signal one's sexual identity/orientation. During the Edwardian era in England, gay men could be imprisoned and sentenced to hard labor for their same-sex attraction. So, in order for gay men to identify other gay men, they used a code: they wore a green carnation in their lapel. Other gay men knew what it signified, and it kept gay men safe from those who did not know the significance of the flower. In the past (and still in some regions today) coded signs were used to remain safe yet covertly identify one's sexual orientation or sexual identity. In recent modern history, other items have been encoded to represent (covertly or not) a lesbian, gay, bisexual, or queer identity, like the pink triangle and the rainbow flag. The inverted pink triangle was originally used by Nazi Germany when that government required all gay men to wear a *rosawinkle* (see Figure 6.3), but the symbol was later adopted as a more affirming emblem. The rainbow flag was introduced to visually depict the

diversity of sexual identities via its many colors. Coding can even occur in the form of pop culture prevalent among lesbian, gay, bisexual, and queer people, for example ruby slippers (from *The Wizard of Oz*) or T-shirts with slogans from films popular among the lesbian, gay, bisexual, and queer population (e.g., "But you are Blanch, you are," from *Whatever Happened to Baby Jane* or "This ain't my first time at the rodeo," from *Mommie Dearest*). Of course, other forms of appearance are more straightforward in relaying sexual identity, like T-shirts with slogans such as "I'm not gay but my boyfriend [girlfriend] is" and "Nobody knows I'm gay."

The categories of gay, straight, bisexual, and queer are relatively recent social conventions, with the term *homosexual* not being coined until the 19th century by psychologists. Foucault (1976/1998) argued that sexuality, like gender, is socially constructed, meaning that society created words and categories for people based on their sexual and romantic behaviors, and people are expected to fit into often-rigid definitions. Lesbian, gay, bisexual, and queer people have often challenged gender norms in their appearance. The clone look was a stylized version of heterosexual masculinity that was popular in the 1970s and incorporated jeans, plaid flannel shirts, mustaches, and cowboy hats. Lesbians could challenge gender norms by dressing in butch styles that incorporated leather jackets, white undershirts, jeans, no makeup and short hair. Frequently, this creates a tension between personality identity and societal expectations. Two articles in this chapter discuss dress associated with gay men and

Figure 6.3 In Nazi Germany, gay men were required to wear the rosawinkle both in public and in concentration camps, as seen in the image from Sachsenhausen Concentration camp in 1938.

lesbians. First, in the article "Queer Women's Experiences Purchasing Clothing and Looking for Clothing Styles" by Kelly L. Reddy-Best and Elaine L. Pedersen write of the aesthetics used among the lesbian women. Second, in "Butch Queens in Macho Drag: Gay Men, Dress, and Subcultural Identity," Shaun Cole documents the varied subcultural aesthetics of gay men and their relationship to concepts of femininity and masculinity.

Summary

Sexuality and sexual orientation/identity, thought two different constructs, are interrelated and connected to dress and appearance. Some people use clothing and coded messages to identify their sexual orientation/identity, as in the case of LGBT people who use appearance as a way to identify similar others and proclaim their identity. Further, some people used clothing and coded messages to indicate their sexual interest or availability, as in the case of the hankie code or rubber bracelets. However, the messages can be misconstrued by the receiver (e.g., viewer) who interprets them differently.

Key Terms

Modesty

Porn chic

Spornosexual

Theory of shifting erogenous zones

Learning Activity 6.1

THE MODESTY CONTINUUM

On the chalkboard, your instructor will create a bipolar scale with "modest" on one end and "immodest" on the other. Review current magazines and advertisements and cut out images of men and women. Tape them along the scale. After the class has completed this, examine the scale to determine where you feel advertisements transform into porn chic. What is the defining feature between modesty and immodesty you notice? Are there differences in gender, age, or race?

Learning Activity 6.2

WARDROBE CONSULTANT

Imagine you are an image consultant hired to speak to teenage girls about developing their wardrobe. The parents have expressed their concerns to you that their daughters are interested in styles that they feel are too sexy or inappropriate for girls. What advice would you give during your speech? Develop an outline of the main topics you would discuss.

References

Engle, M. (2014), "What Is a 'Spornosexual'? It's the New Way of Metrosexuals, Journalist Writes," *New York Daily News*. Available online: http://www.nydailynews.com/life-style/health/spornosexual-article-1.1826983

Foucault, M. (1976/1998), *The History of Sexuality, Vol. 1: The Will to Knowledge*, London: Penguin.

Garrett, M. and A. Kettle (2018), "Flying in the Face of Fashion: How through Punk, Fetish and Sexual Oriented Clothing Made It into Mainstream," in L. Millar and A. Kettle (eds.), *The Erotic Cloth: Seduction and Fetishism in Textiles*, 83–93, London: Bloomsbury.

Halpern, D. M. (1990), *One Hundred Years of Homosexuality: And Other Essays on Greek Love*, New York: Routledge.

Laver, J. (1969), *Modesty in Dress: An Inquiry into the Fundamentals of Fashion*, Boston: Houghton Mifflin.

Lennon, S. J., K. K. P. Johnson, T. L. Schulz (1999), "Forging Linkages between Dress and Law in the U.S., Part I: Rape and Sexual Harassment," *Clothing and Textiles Research Journal*, (17)3: 144–56.

Lynch, A. (2012), *Porn Chic: Exploring the Contours of Raunch Eroticism*, London: Berg.

Mikkelson, B. (2014), "Sex bracelets: Warning about Schoolkids Signaling Their Sexual Availability through the Use of Jelly Bracelets, *Snopes*. Available online: https://www.snopes.com/fact-check/sex-bracelets/.

This introduction is based on a version originally written by Susan O. Michelman and appeared in *Meanings of Dress* editions 1, 2, and 3.

6.1
Is Tween Fashion Too Sexy?

M. B. Sammons

A recent shopping trip to her local mall turned into a jaw-dropping experience for Roxann Reid-Severance. As the Chicago-area mother of two girls, ages 10 and 7, shopped with her oldest daughter for a dress for the tween to wear to a family wedding, she says she discovered rack after rack of low-cut, sequined sheaths.

"I was blown away by how provocative the dresses were," Reid-Severance tells ParentDish. "It was a nightmare. There has to be a balance between fashion fun and good taste. These dresses were skinny straps, lower cut and the fabric had as many sequins as I would have worn on New Year's Eve. It's not age appropriate."

Many moms are agreeing with Reid-Severance, finding themselves on shopping excursions with their young daughters that take them through a Material Girl jungle of animal-patterned, lace, leather and faux fur tween fashions. "Hookers on parade," is how one mom describes the dresses she saw on display during a recent mall visit.

"It's almost as if the fashion world is trying to make preteens look like they are going to the high school prom," Reid-Severance says.

Billions of dollars are on the line in the fashion industry, which targets the 8-to-12 set known as tweens, according to ABC News.

But it's a line increasingly blurred between cute and hot, adorable and sexual. In addition to spending $30 billion of their own money, American tweens hold sway over another $150 billion spent by their parents each year, ABC reports.

"You go into a juniors department, you have a rack of clothing that is appropriate for an 11-year-old next to a rack of clothing that isn't," Alex Morris, who recently reported on tweens and fashion for New York magazine, tells ABC. "It's certainly blurring the lines. . . . It's making it harder for parents to set boundaries."

New research released by the American Psychological Association earlier this year found that sexual imagery aimed at younger girls is harmful to them and increases the likelihood they will "experience body dissatisfaction, depression and lower self-esteem," Morris tells ABC.

Compounding the issue is the fact that tween girls look to celebrity idols, such as 17-year-old Miley Cyrus, who often dresses in daringly sexual outfits, ABC reports. Other teen stars have dressed the sexy party, too: Britney Spears went from a bubblegum pop image morphed to provocateur. Ashley Tisdale left "High School Musical" to "Crank It Up." And former Nickelodeon star Amanda Bynes is now on the cover of Maxim, Morris tells ABC.

"The easiest way for a celebrity to transition from being a child star to an adult star is the pathway through their sexuality," Morris tells ABC. "Children are attracted to this kind of look; it's what they see Miley Cyrus wearing, Demi Lovato wearing, Lindsay Lohan wearing."

It's also what "Gossip Girl" actress Taylor Momsen is wearing on the pink carpet as the face of Material Girl, the recently unveiled clothing line created by Madonna and her 14-year-old daughter, Lourdes, according to ABC.

"I think the reality of the tween fashion market is that the clothes are just more grown up," Michelle Madhok, founder and editor-in-chief of SheFinds.com and MomFinds.com, tells ParentDish. "Whereas a few years ago parents were up in arms about clothes being too revealing (belly shirts, short shorts), the clothes we're seeing now don't show as much skin, but the silhouettes and prints are what you'd normally expect to see an adult wear. No more smiley faces and peace signs, that's for sure."

Critics, such as Washington, D.C.-area mom Michele Woodward tells ParentDish these clothes might work for 20-somethings, but are too racy for girls in their tweens and young teens.

"My daughter and I have had the discussion about what's appropriate just this week, in fact," Woodward, mother to Grace, 14, tells ParentDish. "The new hot trend at her school is wearing tights under a plaid shirt. A shirt which doesn't come down and cover her butt, tunic style, but a short shirt. Nothing is left to the imagination. As we talked about this trend, my daughter leveled her gaze at me and said, 'Mom, if you dress like a 'ho, you get treated like a 'ho.' Precisely."

Discussion Questions

1. Would you interfere with an 11 or 12 year old relative who you thought was dressing too proactive for her age?

2. At what age do you think it is appropriate for young girls to wear "sexy clothes"?

6.2
Queer Women's Experiences Purchasing Clothing and Looking for Clothing Styles

Kelly Reddy-Best and Elaine Pedersen

Individuals in the lesbian, gay, bisexual, and transgender community in the United States have enormous buying power at about $830 billion a year (WITEK Communications, 2013).[1,2] However, many advertisers fear they may lose customers if they appear to support the LGBTQ (lesbian, gay, bisexual, trans, and/or queer) community by using gay and lesbian imagery in advertisements, resulting in many advertisers avoiding any related imagery (Sender, 2003). In some instances, companies advertising to the LGBTQ community in mainstream media have received negative responses from various anti-LGBTQ organizations. For example, One Million Moms attacked JCPenney for their Father's Day advertisement in 2012 that depicted two dads and their children, and warned their followers on Facebook about the ad so they could boycott the company (Zimmerman, 2012). While many companies steer clear of the political topic, some companies reaffirm their stance by displaying support, despite the potential financial risks.

Public and overt discrimination against the LGBTQ community such as the instance described by One Million Moms is not a recent phenomenon as there has been a long history of oppression and discrimination faced by the LGBTQ community. In a survey of over 30,000 people in the United States in the 1970s over 80 percent of the sample stated they preferred not to associate with homosexual individuals (Levitt & Klassen, 1974). However, in a more recent study researchers found that 92% of LGBT adults felt that society is more accepting of LGBT individuals as compared to the last 10 years and that they expect acceptance to increase (Pew Research Center, 2013). Researchers have studied gay men and lesbians' experiences with discrimination and stress related to their sexual identity (Lewis, Derlaga, Bernett, Morris, & Rose, 2001) and heterosexuals' attitudes toward homosexual imagery in the media (Bhat, Leigh, & Wardlow, 1996). However, no researchers have examined queer women's attitudes toward queer imagery in fashion advertisements or queer women's experiences when shopping. The purpose of this study was to explore queer women's experiences when shopping for clothing, looking for styles and examine if they experience any distress or discrimination (overt or subtle) during these processes, specifically in the context of the current

---

Original for this text

1. We recognize the importance of inclusivity and that there are various terms and acronyms (both longer and shorter) for and used by individuals in the lesbian, gay, bisexual, trans, and/or queer (LGBTQ) community. Throughout the article, we use the acronym or terminology that was used by the reference. When not referencing other scholar's work, we will utilize either LGBTQ or in some instances only the term queer. While the term queer can have several definitions and be interpreted or continually re-interpreted in many ways, we utilize the term queer throughout the article as an umbrella term for the LGBTQ community or as a way to describe individuals who are interested in, sexually attracted to, or sexually active with individuals of the same sex or gender or perhaps individuals who do not identify with a particular gender, but see themselves as non-binary.

2. This article is a shorter and slightly revised version of the following article: Reddy-Best, Kelly L. & Pedersen, Elaine L. (2015). Queer women's experiences purchasing clothing and looking for clothing styles. *Clothing & Textile Research Journal. 33*(4), 265–279.

cultural climate when attitudes toward LGBT individuals are thought to be shifting in a more positive direction (Pew Research Center, 2013).

LGBTQ Marketing and Media

A number of companies see the gay and lesbian community as a growing market with excessive buying power (WITEK Communications, 2013); however, as previously mentioned, many advertisers are reluctant to target gay individuals through mainstream advertising (Oakenfull & Greenlee, 2004). One advertising agency explained that they would like to represent a diverse range of sexualities, but "their hands were tied by prudish others on whom they depended for business" (Oakenfull & Greenlee, 2004, p. 344).

Several researchers have studied reactions to LGBTQ imagery in the media. For example, Bhat, Leigh, and Wardlow (1996) found individuals who had a more positive attitude toward homosexuality were much more tolerant toward advertisements with homosexual imagery than those who were not tolerant. Riggle, Ellis, and Crawford (1996) reported that individuals who were exposed to a documentary about a gay politician had a significantly positive change in attitude toward homosexuals. In a more recent study, authors found similar results to those conducted throughout the 1990s that positive portrayals of lesbians and gays in the media increased positive attitudes toward homosexuality (Bonds-Raacke, Cady, Schlegel, Harris, & Firebaugh, 2008).

Distress and Mistreatment of the LGBTQ Community

While there has not been specific work on stress related to experiences shopping for apparel in the LGBTQ community, many researchers have studied sources of stress for the LGBTQ community and have found individuals in the LGBTQ community have unique stressors related to their sexuality. For example, Lewis, Derlega, Bernett, Morris, and Rose (2001) found sources of distress for gay men and lesbian women included visibility, general discrimination, shame or guilt about their sexual identity, and lack of acceptance. More recently, Bowleg, Brooks, and Ritz (2008) revealed that most of their participants were comfortable being out at work. However, they reported still experiencing distress related to their sexual identity due to the dominance of heterosexual conversation in the office. It is important to understand these stressors, because individuals who experience significant stress related to sexual identity are more likely to experience mental distress (Meyer, 2003).

Scholars have also examined treatment of queer individuals and found they experienced varying levels mistreatment from subtle acts of heterosexism to overt hate crimes, and the following studies are just a few of the many examples. Roderick, McCammon, Long, and Allred (1998) studied behavioral aspects of homonegativity and found that heterosexual women frequently or occasionally talked negatively about homosexuals, yelled insulting remarks, told anti-gay jokes, or physically moved away from homosexuals. Huebner, Rebchook, and Kegeles (2004) indicated that, since the 1970s, individuals in the queer community continued to experience everyday acts of heterosexism and discrimination. In a more recent study, Swim, Pearson, and Johnson (2007) found that subtle acts of heterosexism can range from verbal comments and poor service to exclusion.

Heterosexism resulting from verbal comments may stem from everyday language, as suggested by Sedgwick (1990). Sedgwick (1990) discussed the binary oppositions that are created by different speech acts and how this type of language normalizes the binary oppositions, which leads to an oppressive state for individuals who are within those categories. The speech acts Sedgwick refers to are the homosexual and heterosexual notions of sexual identity. She proposed that our language creates an oppressive state because the terms homosexual and heterosexual signify that there are only two categories pitted against each other; however, there is a continuum of identity categories available.

Research Questions

Based on the previously discussed studies it is evident that individuals in the LGBTQ community have historically and still experience various forms of oppression, yet the overall climate is improving. Within the literature, scholars have rarely asked questions about distress or discrimination (overt or subtle) related to shopping experiences or viewing queer imagery in the media by queer women. We sought to understand these experiences; therefore, we asked: (a) Where do queer women look for fashion styles? (b) What are queer women's experiences with shopping for clothing and accessories? (c) Do queer women experience distress or discrimination while shopping or looking for fashion styles?

Method

In order to answer these research question, we conducted interviews with 32 self-identifying queer women. All of the the participants were assigned-female-at-birth, their ages ranged from 18 to 35, and they lived in Colorado, Connecticut, Washington, Oregon, New York, or California. All participants identified as white except for two who identified as mixed race. Fourteen participants were undergraduate students, fourteen were employed full-time, two were unemployed, and two were graduate students.

Each participant completed one in-depth interview and two shorter follow-up interviews. In the first interview, the participants were asked questions related to where they look for clothing ideas, their past shopping experiences, and if they felt any distress or discrimination during these experiences. In the follow-up interviews the participants were asked, in reference to the time period between interviews, if they saw any queer imagery in advertising, if they went shopping, and about their feelings and experiences related to both of these topics. All of the interviews took place in January and February of 2013.

Each interview was analyzed for emergent themes using open, axial, and selective coding (Creswell, 2007). Via open coding, we looked for preliminary codes in the data. Then, during axial coding, we looked for relationships between the preliminary codes. Finally, with selective coding we collapsed codes into larger themes and identified data that fit within these themes. The data were reviewed and re-reviewed in a cyclical fashion until larger themes were defined from the initial coding stage.

Emergent Themes

Four themes surfaced as the participants discussed their shopping experiences and their experiences looking for styles: (a) awareness of or attention to queer styles, (b) frustration with or feelings of alienation with the current apparel marketplace and media, (c) distress or subtle acts of heterosexism related to queer visibility and crossing gender boundaries, and (d) interest in an LGBTQ-friendly shopping environment.

Awareness of or Attention to Queer Styles

We asked participants if they looked for styles, where they looked, and if there were any people they looked to for style ideas. Eighty-four percent of the participants (n=27)

looked for clothing ideas and style trends. Twenty-three participants stated that they looked to family members, friends, or people around them for style ideas. Within these conversations, the participants frequently mentioned that they looked to other queer individuals around them or sought out what other queer individuals were wearing by looking in queer publications.

Twenty participants stated they looked in magazines or followed fashion blogs for current styles; fifteen of these publications or blogs were aimed at a queer audience. Queer publications included *Curve, Lezbehonest, AutoStraddle, Bitch, Bust, Out, Original Plumbing, Tomboystyle,* and *The Advocate*. Micah[3] explained that looking at *Lezbehonest* allowed her to "understand that there weren't just hardcore butches that dressed like men and femmes that always wore lipsticks and heels." She explained that it gave her style ideas that were different from the stereotypical femme/butch presentation.

Fifteen of the 27 participants who looked for style ideas indicated they specifically looked to other queer individuals or men for inspiration. Eleven participants named queer or male celebrities. Queer celebrities included Teegan and Sara, Ellen DeGeneres, the Liz Lemon character on *30 Rock*, and the queer women on the television show *The L Word*. Kayla liked that Ellen DeGeneres is a popular TV host who is openly out about her sexual identity. She described that she will often look to Ellen for style ideas because she is a popular queer celebrity:

> For instance, things that Ellen DeGeneres wears. Occasionally, I might pull in elements from her that I might not do if I were a straight woman. I mean that sounds kind of silly but things that Ellen wears I think about adding to my wardrobe, because she's a queer woman and I look up to her. And I think she does awesome stuff. So why wouldn't you want to emulate people you look up to.

Four other participants also felt that Ellen has a good sense of style that defied traditional gender boundaries and is classic and sporty while still containing hints of femininity. Ellen's signature look, comprised of tennis shoes, trousers, and a well-fit tailored jacket, is a coveted look for many of the women in our sample. Alexa

---

3. Pseudonames are used in place of the participants' actual names to conceal their identites.

loved how Ellen effortlessly combined tennis shoes with a suit and V-neck t-shirt or sweater, vest, and tie. Ellen is a popular style icon for many queer women because she violates gender identity norms in a way that is accessible for women to emulate, and she is accepted in the mainstream through the popularity of her daytime television talk show.

Frustration and Alienation with Current Fashion Marketplace and Media

Most (n=23) participants reported having never seen fashion advertisements specifically targeted at queer women. Five of the nine women who reported having seen advertisements all cited the same JCPenney print and television advertisement featuring two moms that ran in May 2012 for Mother's Day. Participants also indicated having seen queer people featured in fashion advertisements by The Gap, H&M, and American Apparel. A New York City participant remembered a Michael Kors window display with wedding cakes that had same-sex wedding top figurines just after New York passed same-sex marriage laws. Between the interview sessions, none of the participants noted seeing any fashion advertisements with queer imagery.

Almost half of the participants (n=14) had negative reactions to the queer imagery, or lack thereof, in media. Fourteen participants felt frustrated, sad, or alienated by the fashion industry because of the lack of queer images or advertisements. Melissa described her feelings on fashion advertisements by stating:

It's always frustrating where you see more idealized images of what you should do and don't fit into those. . .people always want to see themselves reflected back at them, and want to be able to take cues from that and I feel like because I don't have those sorts of images I sort of have to make it up. It's a blessing and a curse. It's nice to not have those things of what I should do represented back at me because there isn't anyone who really fits that mold. At the same time, it's bothering in a way, where you know you are put on the outskirts.

Kayla related a similar feeling saying, "I kind of feel like I'm missing from them." Riley had a strong reaction to the lack of fashion ads and expressed intense emotion in her response. She stated, "Frankly I feel so utterly alienated by the fashion industry on every possible front that generally what I feel is 'fuck them.'" Avery also experienced a feeling of alienation from the fashion industry. She said, "I mean we're part of society too, we're not just nonexistent and I mean I would love to see more of it, and by more, I mean any."

Thirteen of these 14 participants who felt ostracized by the fashion industry explained that they were not surprised by the lack of advertisements and representation of queer imagery in the media and acknowledged that a lot of groups are missing or not represented. Because these women have become so accustomed to feeling left out or neglected in many areas of their lives, the thought of actually seeing an advertisement that featured queer women seemed like an action that they felt many publishers or advertisers would not take. Eleven of the 14 participants who responded negatively to the lack of fashion ads said they anticipate feeling or felt positive toward fashion advertisements targeting queer women. For example, when Sawyer was walking through lower Manhattan and saw the two wedding cakes with same-sex figurine toppers in the Michael Kors window, she said, "I remember walking and being like 'that's charming' and it stuck in my head."

When asked about their experiences shopping, the participants (n=20) frequently reported frustrations with finding garments that fit. It is important to note that finding garments that fit is a common issue for many women regardless of sexual identity. However, eight of the 20 participants who had trouble finding garments that fit experienced this trouble because they often shopped in the men's department, and it was hard to determine what size to try on and purchase. For example, Debbie felt frustrated looking for plain t-shirts. Even in a simple garment such as the plain white t-shirt, Debbie realized that the slight differences in style and cut between men's and women's garments can cause trouble for her attempt to find a garment that she feels gives her a silhouette that disguises her feminine features without being too baggy.

Distress or Subtle Acts of Heterosexism Resulting from Queer Visibility and Crossing Gender Boundaries

Twenty-four of the participant said that they experienced distress when shopping. Shopping for clothing can cause distress for many women, and the participants in our study experienced some of the typical stressors of shopping such as negative body image. However, these same women experienced additional distress when navigating away from traditional gender norms by shopping in the men's section. Eight participants stated they rarely, if ever, felt distress when shopping, and if they did it was not memorable or it did not have an impact on their shopping experiences.

Shopping or asking for a different size in the men's section resulted in distress for eight of the 18 participants who shopped in this section. Quinn predominantly shops in the men's section, and her high level of distress when shopping on the men's side alters her shopping behaviors. When in the men's section, Quinn is nervous the men in the section are judging her. She explained she gets "really hot and sweaty and especially when other guys are around." The fitting rooms are also a major source of distress for Quinn. To avoid awkward moments with sales associates or negative comments, she usually tries on the garments she wants to purchase outside of the fitting room in a corner of the store. When asked if this makes her uncomfortable she said, "all the time," and when asked if she wore specific outfits in which to go shopping she promptly replied, "Yea, I usually wear a lightweight shirt and a jacket on top." Kelsey described a recent shopping scenario where she attempted to shop in the men's section but felt too embarrassed to try on or buy men's clothing. She said:

> I attempted to find baggy jeans. I didn't know I was really too nervous to ask anybody to help me. The sizing was difficult, and I didn't know about it. I was really worried I was going to be judged when asking for it.

A few of the participants (n=7) explained that when shopping in thrift stores they did not feel as much distress because the distinction of sections was not as concrete as in corporate or mainstream stores. The blurred lines of the gendered sections in these types of stores eased the tension for some women when entering the men's sections, and it allowed for some enjoyment during shopping.

One fourth of the participants (n=9) experienced subtle acts of heterosexism related to their gender or sexuality when shopping. The experiences ranged from salespeople assuming the women were shopping in the wrong section and questioning of garment choices to feelings of mistreatment and poor customer service. About two-thirds of the participants (n=23) stated they had never felt mistreated either overtly or subtly while shopping. When shopping in the men's department, eight participants experienced the salesperson telling them they were in the wrong section or that they had made a mistake and had picked up men's garments. Scarlett explained how she was often corrected when holding men's garments or shopping in the men's section. Additionally, since she has a masculine look, she has also been corrected in the women's sections where people told her she was in the wrong section. Scarlett said she often feels treated differently than other customers in the store and that her service is frequently accompanied by a negative attitude. After explaining her experiences of shopping, she exclaimed, "I can't win!" Participants experienced other subtle acts of heterosexism such as long stares by other shoppers and being neglected by sales staff. Alexa said, "Sometimes salespeople will throw you shifty glares because you are holding hands with your partner in a store and they can act weird." Two participants were not offered shopping assistance or received extremely poor customer service compared to other shoppers in the store. Quinn described that several times when she was in a fitting room, sales associates would knock on the other dressing room doors and skip her. She remembered two stores where sales associates did this to her, and said she reacted by saying, "I don't want their help anyway." Riley also frequently felt mistreated while shopping. When asked if she ever felt as though she was treated differently, she seemed incredulous that I even asked the question. She could not remember any specific stories to tell but stated if she was "looking particularly dyke-y" then she knew she would be treated differently than the other customers.

Interest in an LGBTQ-Friendly Shopping Environment

Some shopping experiences were extremely positive for participants when they felt as though the salespeople were not judging their sexual identity or choice of gendered clothing. When asked if they had any positive, memorable shopping experiences, a few participants recalled some instances. Four participants had positive shopping experiences because they had extremely helpful salespeople who did not judge them for shopping in the men's section, or they felt that the store was openly supporting the queer community. Alexa had an extremely positive experience when shopping for lingerie with her partner. She remembered that the sales associate asked how long she and her partner had been together and that the associate was "not weirded out by anything." Alexa was intimidated at first when going to this lingerie store with her girlfriend because "that's the first place where people would be judging," though when she left she did not feel judged, but rather comfortable and excited. The positive experience made her want to tell other queer individuals about the store.

Avery stated that her best shopping experience was when she was shopping in the men's section and the salesperson did not flinch when she wanted men's jeans. This made Avery comfortable and excited, a feeling she often does not have when searching for new garments. Kayden attributed her positive shopping experience for clothing to the music that was playing in the store. She explained she heard Macklemore, a music artist known for advocating for queer rights, playing in the store while she was browsing. Hearing this music reaffirmed to her that the store was "queer-friendly" and a safe place to let others know that she identified as queer.

After asking the participants about their past shopping experiences, we asked two questions about the likelihood of them shopping in stores that openly support the LGBTQ community and if they would be more likely to shop in a store that does not separate by gender. All but two participants stated they would be more likely to shop in a store that openly and actively supports the LGBTQ community. Melissa immediately responded with "Absolutely." Only one participant stated she might be interested, and one participant stated she would not necessarily shop in a store that supported the LGBTQ community. The participant who indicated she would not be interested was a plus-size participant assumed they would not have her size.

When asked if the participants would be more likely to shop in a store that does not separate by gender but by body size and lifestyle, 28 said yes without hesitation; two participants said maybe, and two said no. Kayla responded, "I think that would be awesome. Yea, I think that would be really awesome." Scarlett responded with an extremely positive attitude by stating, "Oh, that would be awesome. That would be so awesome. I just can't even imagine. It is like what heaven will be like. Not to pick your gender to buy your shirt. YEA!" At the end of the interviews, 17 of the 28 participants who said yes asked the researchers if they were planning to start this company or line of clothing, or they told us we should open this

company. For example, Micah stated with a large smile, "You better email me if you get a clothing line started."

Discussion and Conclusion

Twenty-one participants in this study often looked to other queer individuals or queer publications for style ideas. If the participants looked in fashion magazines or blogs they often looked in alternative media that might feature queer or androgynous women. Almost half of the women (n=14) felt frustrated or ostracized by the fashion industry due to the lack of queer advertisements, yet explained they were not surprised because many groups who have historically experienced oppression are often excluded from media. Eleven study participants, about one-third, stated they would be excited or would react positively toward queerness in advertisements. While these findings are not surprising, it does suggest that queer women who look for fashion styles would appreciate having representation in the media, which is a message to companies that are worried about the possible risk of losing market share as reported by Sender (2003), to think more about their passive stance in LGBTQ politics.

In addition to media, the clothing categories on the market or how they are presented also led to some negative experiences for participants. Sedgwick explained that the categories used in language, which extends to clothing categories, create an oppressive state for individuals who deviate from the normalized categories such as masculine appearing women. Many participants in this study felt as though they were limited by the selections in the women's section of the store, and they felt distress when moving into the *opposite* men's or boy's sections. Not surprisingly, distress related to sexual identity was most often related to shopping for or trying on men's garments. Over the course of this research, one of the first things we came to understand was that many of these women have had negative shopping experiences because many stores employ sales associates who are trained to target people based on appearance and traditional binary gender expressions (feminine versus masculine). Because of their training, these associates direct customer interest toward socially normative gendered clothing. Therefore, hearing that thrift, vintage, and consignment stores served as spaces where some distress over shopping in gendered sections was lessened was not surprising and re-highlights Sedgwick's (1990) point that binaries in our language result in various experiences of oppression and clothing is not an exception.

Queer individuals experience a wide range of distress that is related and not related to their sexual identity. In addition to the common distress of shopping experiences that individuals may feel regardless of their sexual identity, some queer individuals have experiences that are unique to their sexuality; therefore, our research furthers Lewis et al.'s (2001) findings in that that some queer women may experience distress from their sexual identity while looking for clothing styles or shopping for apparel. Similar to many other marginalized groups, close to half of the women (n=14) felt ostracized by the fashion industry due to the lack of queer imagery and representation in media. While many women shopped in mainstream stores, these types of stores caused distress for one quarter of the women (n=8) who were told by the sales associates that they were shopping in the *wrong* department. For some women the experiences of being treated differently were "normal" and did not affect them emotionally because they were part of their everyday life. For others, these feelings of difference caused heightened distress and affected their behaviors. In sum, our findings highlight the continued heterosexism that permeates our society and despite all progress toward understanding, cultural competency, and/or acceptance, there is still work to be done in regards to diversity and inclusion for the queer community.

References

Bhat, S., Leigh, T., & Wardlow, D. (1996). The effect of homosexual imagery in advertising on attitude toward the ad. *Journal of Homosexuality, 31*(1-2), 161–176.

Bonds-Raacke, J. M. B., Cady, E. T., Schlegel, R., Harris, R. J., & Firebaugh, L. (2008). Remembering gay/lesbian media characters: Can Ellen and Will improve attitudes towards homosexuals? *Journal of Homosexuality, 53*(3), 19–34.

Bowleg, L., Brooks, K., & Ritz, S. F. (2008). "Bringing home more than a paycheck": An exploratory analysis of Black lesbians' experiences of stress and coping in the workplace. *Journal of Lesbian Studies, 12*(1), 69–84.

Creswell, J. W. (2007). *Qualitative inquiry and research design: Choosing among five approaches.* Thousand Oaks, CA: Sage.

Huebner, D. M., Rebchook, G. M., & Kegeles, S. M. (2004). Experiences of harassment, discrimination and physical violence among young gay and bisexual men. *American Journal of Public Health, 94*(7), 1200–1203.

Levitt, E. F., & Klassen, A. D. (1974). Public attitudes toward homosexuality: Part of the 1970 national survey by the Institute for Sex Research. *Journal of Homosexuality, 1*, 29–43.

Lewis, R. J., Derlega, V. J., Berndt, A., Morris, L. M., & Rose, S. (2001). An empirical analysis of stressors for gay men and lesbians. *Journal of Homosexuality, 42*(1), 63–88.

Meyer, I. H. (2003). Prejudice, social stress, and mental health in lesbian, gay, and bisexual populations: Conceptual issues and research evidence. *Psychological Bulletin, 129*(5), 674–697.

Oakenfull, G., & Greenlee, T. (2004). The three rules of crossing over from gay media to mainstream media advertising: Lesbians, lesbians, lesbians. *Journal of Business Research, 57*(11), 1276–1285.

Pew Research Center. (2013). A survey of LGBT Americans: Attitudes, experiences and values in changing times. *Pew Research Social & Demographic Trends*. Retrieved from http://www.pewsocialtrends.org/2013/06/13/a-survey-of-lgbt-americans/5/

Riggle, E. D. B., Ellis, A. L., & Crawford, A. M. (1996). The impact of "media contact" on attitudes towards gay men. *Journal of Homosexuality, 21*(3), 55–69.

Roderick, T., McCammon, S. L., Long, T. E., & Allred, L. J. (1998). Behavior aspects of homonegativity. *Journal of Homosexuality, 36*(1), 79–88.

Sedgwick, E. K. (1990). *Epistemology of the closet.* Berkeley, CA: University of California Press.

Sender, K. (2003). Sex sells: Sex, class, and taste in commercial gay and lesbian media. *GLQ: A Journal of Lesbian and Gay Studies, 9*(3), 331–365.

Swim, J. K., Pearson, N. B., & Johnson, K. E. (2007). Daily encounters with heterosexism: A week in the life of lesbian, gay, and bisexual individuals. *Journal of Homosexuality, 53*(4), 31–48.

WITEK Communications. (2013, November 18). America's LGBT 2013 buying power estimated at $830 Billion. Retrieved from http://www.witeck.com/pressreleases/lgbt-2013-buying-power/

Zimmerman, N. (2012, May 31). JCPenney responds to homophobic boycott calls with gay father's day ad. *Gawker*. Retrieved from http://gawker.com/5914527/jcpenney-responds-to-homophobic-boycott-calls-with-gay-fathers-day-ad

Discussion Questions

1. The article mentions fashion brand that targets LGBTQ women. Search online for 2 to 3 brands that might fall into this category.
   a. Create a list of the types of products each brand sells.
   b. After viewing the websites, how do the brands signal to customers that they target LGBTQ women?
   c. Have you ever heard of these or similar brands before? Explain why you think you have or have not heard of them.

2. Pretend you own a fashion brand that was not targeted toward LGBTQ women.
   a. What are some ways you could work toward creating an inclusive store environment for LGBTQ women?
   b. Would you want to publically demonstrate support for the LGBTQ community? Why or why not?

3. Have you ever seen fashion advertisements featuring individuals from the LGBTQ community?
   a. Discuss why you think you have or have not.
   b. If you have seen advertisements, how do you feel about them?

4. Think about past experiences while shopping in brick and mortar stores and when you have tried on garments.
   a. Were any of the fitting room areas separated by gender? Which stores?
   b. Have you ever thought twice about the fitting room areas and if they were gendered?
   c. Discuss the pros and cons of having fitting rooms areas separated by gender and why it might be necessary or not.

5. In this study, most of the participants identified as white. How might identifying as both a woman of color and as queer impact the outcomes of the participant's experiences when shopping or looking for styles?

6.3
Butch Queens in Macho Drag: Gay Men, Dress, and Subcultural Identity

Shaun Cole

Until the 1970s gay men in the United States and Europe were perceived and viewed as one amorphous secretive subculture. In fact, a number of gay subcultures—among them, the "leatherman"—began in the 1960s, each with distinguishing styles of dress or accessories. Nevertheless, gay men's dress until the 1970s was dominated by two choices: adoption of overtly feminine styles or conformity to the accepted masculine dress codes of the day, thus remaining invisible.

Society's emphasis on gender divisions had an overwhelming impact on the development of gay identity and led to effeminacy becoming both the culturally accepted meaning and the stereotype of gay identity. The adoption of female clothing or female-associated attributes, therefore, served as a public announcement of a man's gay sexual orientation and self-identity.

Social and legal climates were such that adoption of an overtly visible gay identity was difficult as it could lead to social ostracism or arrest for most gay men. Dress choice, therefore, followed the conventions of the day and relied on "secret" signifiers to convey a hidden sexual identity to those "in the know" (see Cole 1999). This strategy of passing is the first of three—along with minstrelization, and capitulation—identified by Martin P. Levine that were traditionally adopted by gay men when "managing" their identities. (Levine 1998, 21)

With the advent of gay liberation gay men began to question their position in society and the way in which

Reprinted from *Men's Fashion Reader,* Fairchild Books/Bloomsbury, 2008.

society stereotyped and perceived them. In 1970, this disillusionment and its drive to redefine gay identity was highlighted by gay activist Tony Diaman, who wrote: "The straight world has told us that if we are not masculine we are homosexual, that to be homosexual means not to be masculine . . . one of the things we must do is redefine ourselves as homosexuals" (Diaman 1970, 22). The emergence of a gay liberation movement and the subsequent redefinition of gay identities and self-presentation led to the development of a host of gay subcultures, which took their stylistic leads from both an overt masculinity and an adherence to effeminacy as means of carving out a meaningful and identifiable gay identity.

As a means of questioning the ongoing association of gay identity and effeminacy, and as a continuing means of redefining their identity, gay men have formed several masculine stylistic subcultures that draw on the artifacts and materials found in both their own and broader culture.

Clone

The first recognizably "out" gay male subculture, and the one that informed both gay and straight perceptions and stereotypes throughout the last 30 years of the 20th century, was the "clone." In a move away from traditional effeminate stereotypes, American urban gay men looked toward traditional images of American rugged masculinity for a new image. A plundering of the materials of American culture had led to a preponderance of masculine images of cowboys, bikers, and workmen in the physique magazines of the 1950s and 1960s. They represented a traditional but nonconforming aspect of masculinity and were "used by the media to play up masculinity and sexuality in ways that are understood by the gay populace" (Fischer 1977, 18). These archetypes of masculinity and their clothes, with clear associations of toughness, virility, aggression, and strength, were influential in the development and adoption of "butch" dress styles for men.

The "blue collar" garments that made up the uniform of the clone—Levi's, work boots, plaid shirt, and bomber jacket, worn with short cropped hair and a moustache—were, according to Gregg Blachford, infused with "a new meaning of eroticism and overt sexuality—that is, they [were] used explicitly to make one appear sexy and attractive to other men" (Blachford 1981, 200). The clones were self-consciously styling the elements of an unconsciously masculine wardrobe to create a new, highly sexualized and sexually attractive image or identity. Unlike their "male impersonator" predecessors, clones were not attempting to pass as straight: they were, by stylizing conventional masculine dress, "subverting identity and appearing like 'real men' and yet being the last thing a 'real man' would want to be mistaken for: gay" (Bristow 1989, 70). The appropriation of traditionally "macho" clothes and styles of dress opened up radical and transgressive possibilities. In adopting such an image, clones walked a tightrope between straight imitation and an interpretation that could identify them not only as real men but as real *gay* men. As well as a (homo)sexual signifier, the clone look also initially served as a form of protection. Hostile heterosexuals, used to identifying gay men as effeminate and flamboyant, were unused to the association of homosexuality with archetypical masculinity.

As part of the clone image, gay men developed a set of codes to specify their particular sexual interests. Consequently a man could tell if a potential partner would be sexually compatible just by the position of the keys on his belt or the color of the handkerchief in his back pocket. Along with the sexually loaded codes, specific signifiers were added to the basic look to project an extra butch front, such as boots or hats. They were typically associated with traditional macho icons, such as the cowboy. Many of the men utilizing these butch signifiers did so with a sense of play, inherited from a traditional gay "camp" sensibility, referring to their clone clothes as "butch drag." It was both a self-conscious, almost parodying reference to traditional stereotypical images of masculinity and a self-conscious embracing of that stereotype. "Gay masculinity is not in any simple way, 'real' masculinity," Jamie Gough concludes, "any more than 'camp' is femininity. It is more self-conscious than the real thing, more theatrical, and often more ironic" (1989, 12). Other commentators, however, believed that the advent of overtly masculine images for gay men was not liberating; that, by adopting a super-macho appearance gay men were adhering to the strict binary rules of gender division; and that macho looks and associated behavior were not merely the "new drag" but a return to the closet: "Macho, of course, isn't a new closet; indeed, many have suspected that it's the oldest closet in the house" (Kleinberg 1978, 12).

As the clone image became more mainstream within gay culture, the original proto-clones were quick to move on. By the early 1980s, "strict butch costuming fell out of favour, as clones mixed butch elements for circuit wear and street wear" (Levine 1998, 61). The death of the clones, Andrew Holleran believed, came about once the "boys from Long Island [New York] came into town with their girlfriends on Saturday nights in bomber jackets and plaid shirts, their keys hung on the right side of their belts, like homosexuals looking for a top man" (Holleran 1982, 16). So, as with all subcultural styles the clone image moved from a (gay) minority style to a (gay and straight) majority fashion, following Dick Hebdige's "process of recuperation" in which the clones' subcultural signs of the plaid shirt, Levi's, and work boots were converted into "mass-produced [mass worn] objects," leading to the disavowal of the commercialized subcultures by its originators (Hebdige 1987, 94).

The overt adoption of a hypermasculine image continued into the 1980s despite the dilution of the strictly codified clone image and its rejection as "antiquated" by a younger generation of gay men. The epitome of the hypermasculinized clone was disseminated in the drawings of illustrator Tom of Finland, who created "a blueprint for the appearance of gay men in the latter part of the twentieth century."[1] Clones had favored a physique traditionally associated with weightlifters—"washboard" stomachs, and pumped-up biceps and pectorals—because they felt it was the most macho male build. "Society sees musclemen as more masculine, so I work out putting in long hours in the gym pumping iron," one bodybuilding clone said. "The results make me feel butch" (Levine 1998, 59).

Muscle Boys

The clones' muscular frame was in direct contrast to the traditional stereotype of the gay body—the scrawny frame of the sexless sissy. Weightlifting and bodybuilding had proved popular, from the 1950s onwards, among gay men who had refused to conform to or were desperate to distance themselves from the stereotype of the limp-wristed weakling. In 1963, Donald Webster Cory and John P. Leroy identified that in many gay men the fear of being "less than manly" served as "motivation to overcome and become even more masculine in physical appearance." Cory and LeRoy also posited, "It would be ironic, indeed, if supermasculinity, the cult of the body-builders, the muscle-men and the sports fans, should grow side by side with effeminacy, symbolized by the screaming hairdresser, as the two new stereotypes of the homosexual" (Cory and LeRoy 1963, 91). By the 1990s, far from running alongside

an outward display of effeminacy, the muscular gay body overshadowed it, in what gay activist and journalist Michelangelo Signorile (1997) identifies as the "Cult of Masculinity."

The gym-pumped body was such a common sight in gay areas of cities that it became the new stereotyped gay body. Within this gay subculture the choice of clothes became secondary to the body that those garments displayed or emphasized. Daniel Harris viewed the development of the muscular, hairless, groomed gay body as a means of creating a commonality. He noted that unlike other minorities, gay men have no one geographical place of origin or common physical characteristics, such as skin color or eye shape. Striving to attain a uniform muscular gay body is a means of inventing "those missing physical features that enable us to spot imperceptible compatriots, who would remain unseen and anonymous if they did not prominently display on their own bodies . . . the caste mark that constitutes the essence of gay sensibility (Harris 1997, 35).

The HIV/AIDS pandemic in the early 1980s played a major role in the definitions of body type that gay men were adopting. A common (and visible) way in which HIV/AIDS-related infection manifested itself was through drastic weight loss. As Victor D'Longin, professor of political philosophy at the University of Hartford, observed: "For a long time, outside and inside the [gay] community, the face of AIDS was the emaciated body" (cited in Signorile 1997, 68). Therefore, within the gay community (the one most dramatically and publicly affected by HIV/AIDS in the early 1980s), a fit, muscular body was associated with a healthy body.

Male bodies in gay magazines and pornography in the 1990s offered well-developed musculature with emphasis on shoulder breadth and size of pectorals and biceps, which were almost entirely hairless. This overemphasis on hairlessness is a marker of the continued preoccupation with and primacy of youth on the gay scene,[2] and is highlighted by Michelangelo Signorile in his report and critique of gay male masculinity, *Life Outside* (1997). The regimens (hours at the gym, steroid use or abuse, and even

---

1. This description appears in the film "Daddy and the Muscle Academy," written and directed by Ilppo Pohjola, Filmitakomo Oy, 1991.

2. With the identification of the "teenager" in the 1950s, gay men began to adopt more youthful dress, which became a primary indicator and aspiration of gay men alongside, and eventually overtaking, the leisure-class aesthetic of the first half of the 20th century. Straton Ashley noted in this 1964 article in *One* magazine that "homosexuals in general tend[ed] to dress younger than their years" and that "young and fashionable" attire was essential in New York's gay bars.

cosmetic surgery) undertaken by gay men to replicate these youthful ideals led to an illusion of youth. "Those who buy into 'the look' do so to delay the inevitable aging process," declared journalist Paul Tierney, who concluded that "in reality, this aesthetic leads to a system of body fascism that glorifies and dictates a 'genetically superior' body type at the expense of all others" (Tierney 2001, 34). This led to a form of sexual selection whereby the muscular body became essential (in certain groupings) for sexual attraction and liaison, culminating in the disparaging ethos of "no pecs, no sex."

Even gay men who did not subscribe or aspire to the muscular hairless body were affected, not least because this was, and continues to be, the physical aesthetic that is most frequently projected in advertising and editorial sections of the gay press and in gay pornography. As such it is often perceived as the ultimate ideal. Although advertising and the predominance of the gay "circuit party" scene promoted the muscular masculinity of the contemporary gay man, there was criticism in both the gay community and the gay press (so often responsible for promoting this image) of the importance of the "six-packs and pumping biceps" of the gay "body beautiful." One self-described "punk queerboy" complained: "It's assumed that all gay people look a certain way, and if you don't you start out at a severe disadvantage" (cited in Signorile 1997, 122). Similarly, essays in the book *Anti-Gay* (edited by Mark Simpson, who would later identify and coin the term *metrosexual*) damned "gay culture" with its emphasis on "muscles, gym culture, Calvin Klein underwear and Kylie" (Manning 1996, 106).

Gay men's bodybuilding, which had initially been used as a means to "butch" up, became a new symbol of gay men's obsession with grooming and body image. Despite the striving for a masculine body, Daniel Harris noted an apparently contradictory element, in that the overdeveloped interest in the appearance and body shape is an interest that is perceived as "feminine": "Even homosexuals' strenuous bodybuilding workouts which were first used to butch ourselves up, have ultimately become a sign of the queen's obsessive interest in grooming and self maintenance . . . the gay man's body has become a living, breathing battlefield in which the queen and the [new 1990s circuit queen] clone grapple for supremacy" (Harris 1997, 101).

Bear

Reviling the artificiality of the body type developed by the "buffed baby boys" (Harris 1997, 105), some gay men gloried in what they perceived as "real" masculinity: hairiness, big bulky bodies, work-toned (rather than gym-induced) muscles, and a belly (in direct response to washboard stomachs). The original American "bears"[3] in the 1980s held up miners, loggers, lumberjacks, and Hell's Angels as the paradigm of "real, honest-to-God men," in the same way that the clones had looked to similar icons of American working-class masculinity for their role models.

Bear culture had its origins in informal "chubby and chubby-chaser" networks among gay men in the early 1970s. Its emergence in the 1980s coincided with a moment when the lives of most urban gay Americans had been touched by losses to AIDS and, consequently, losing weight was equated with illness. Bear culture, therefore, operated almost in direct opposition to the cult of youth that permeated gay culture, and in adopting this image men were accepting and glorying in their ageing bodies. The organizer of New York's annual Bearapolooza, Freddy Freeman, highlighted this sentiment: "A bear is what you are meant to look like, not a construct to attract others. Men lose the hair from the top of their head as they age. They grow hair on their bodies. They get a little chubby around the waist. They flab" (cited in Flynn 2003, 68).

As a marker of its masculinity, bear costume drew on the same staples of working-class clothing as that of clones—jeans, plaid shirts, work boots—reflecting (and continuing) the desire to appear to be "real" men. Facial hair and body hair were, and are, important visual signifiers of the bear. Comments and descriptions of bears in books and journals that are not specifically targeted at bears have been criticized for portraying a stereotype of a bear as a fat hairy man in a checked shirt. Philip Locke felt that the descriptions do not "reflect the diversity of men within the Bear community" (Locke 1997, 126). Bears are gay men who knowingly cultivate their bodies (but in a significantly different way from "muscle boys") and select their clothing (not just plaid shirts but Abercrombie and Fitch or rugby shirts) to create the look they find attractive or know others will find attractive.

For many outside the bear community, bears do not "look gay." This is often an intentional move on the part of those involved in the subculture to move away from the stereotypes of what a gay man should look like. The bear image, like that of the original clone, is used in a transgressional way to question the views of both gay and straight societies, acting as a masking device or causing confusion because it appears so "un-gay" to the untrained eye. Folk singer Andy McCarthy noted that straight people "do not like it when they can't tell. I tell people I'm gay and they think 'trucker shirt? Denims? Beard?' . . . It confuses the f—-out of people. They don't know where they stand" (cited in Flynn 2003, 70).

Bear culture stimulated debate both within and outside the bear community. Some gay men have criticized the culture, maintaining that it is a justification or excuse for not taking care of their bodies and becoming fat. Within the American bear community, issues of both class and authenticity have been raised. Accusations have been made that the bear subculture simply fetishizes signs and symbols of lower-class white masculinities. Eric Rofes observed that many of the men attracted to the bear subculture were middle- or upper-middle-class men: "Some insist that Bear sites are populated entirely by middle-class men playing dress-up as working-class men . . . [whereas] others argue that Bear culture is one of the few queer spaces . . . constituted in large part by working-class men" (Rofes 1997, 93–4). In considering the "authenticity" of bear masculinity in 1997, Daniel Harris noted that its "hirsute ideal of rugged masculinity is ultimately as contrived as the aesthetic of the designer queen. While bears pretend to oppose the 'unnatural' look of urban gay men, nothing could be more unnatural, urban and middle class than the pastoral fantasy of the smelly mountaineer in long johns, a costume drama that many homosexuals are now acting out" (Harris 1997, 106; Figure 6.4).

Bear culture spread beyond the United States to the United Kingdom and Europe and utilizing web-based communication, has further embraced diversity of body type and sexualized older men. Writing about the London bear club XXL, British journalist, Laurence Brown

Figure 6.4 The Bear gay subculture takes pride in a natural, hirsute as a sign of "natural" masculinity.

observed, "the proliferation of the bears' movement is about the re-masculinization of gay men, and the eroticization of the chubby body, the hairy body, the body of the older man. It's about men being beautiful & sexy as are, without having to aspire to some unattainable and boyish (or girlish) ideal" (Brown 2002, 52).

In what was perhaps an ironic twist on the original ethos of bear culture, a new sub-subculture emerged, that of the "muscle bear." This development may have reflected the fact that a hairy body was increasingly being regarded as acceptable and desirable among gay men. Or, it may have represented a move by muscle men, as they grew older, to be less constrained by the popular image of the hairless muscle boy and allowed their own natural hair to regrow, spending less time and money on costly hair removal treatments.

Scally

The summer of 2004 saw an explosion of newspaper articles in Britain about a new social subgroup known as the "chav."[4] Many of the articles mocked this subculture, using pejorative descriptions such as "noneducated delinquents" and focusing on the supposed ignorance, fecklessness, mindless violence, and bad taste of its members. The "bad taste" uniform, similar for both male and female chavs, consisted of flashy gold jewelry or "bling" (hooped earrings, thick neck chains, sovereign rings, and heavy bangles), "prison white" sneakers (so-called because they are so clean they look new), clothes in fashionable brands with very prominent logos, and baseball caps, frequently in the soon-to-become-ubiquitous Burberry check.

The descriptions and reporting of the new chav culture assumed the heterosexuality of its constituents (as so many reports on subcultures traditionally have done). However, concurrent with the appearance and reporting of this subculture in the mainstream was an explosion of gay chavs or "scallies."[5] This gay subculture once again looked to the signifiers of working-class masculinity as a means of expressing a masculine male identity and style. Scott, one half of the gay self-confessed "council pop" musical duo Fierce Girl, described the appeal as "really just the latest version of what a bad boy is—and everyone loves a bad boy." He highlighted one of the major dilemmas for identification within gay scally culture: the class makeup of the subculture. "[I]ts like it's always been, it's loads of middle-class people fantasising about a bit of common rough" (cited in Flynn 2005, 71). As with criticism aimed at bear culture, a split existed between real working-class boys and "middle-class" gay men who dressed up because the look was fashionable or perceived as sexy, vis-à-vis a means to achieving sexual liaisons with desirable working class "rough" lads.

Historically, homosexuality had been, for the most part, identified with leisure-class privilege and had been both respected and despised accordingly. Gay academician Alan Sinfield maintained that while on the one hand, "The queer *bricolage* of effeminacy, aestheticism and class stood at an opposite extreme from mainstream working-class values," the association with "posh" culture offered working-class gay men a step away from the confines of hegemonic working class male behavior and a new sense of worth (Sinfield 1994, 138). This association continued with a (media-fueled) presumption that the predominant social class in the gay world is middle class, tasteful, and moneyed, and that all gay men dress with a rare and exquisite elegance. However, this sketch of the fin-de-siècle gay man embedded with the "pink pound," and, by extension the middle classes, was anathema to many gay men's own experience. As gay journalist Paul Flynn noted, "in a culture of high-end aspiration, Scandinavian design and holidaying in Mustique, well, almost any normal gay boy could feel like a true scally" and so "gay scally credentials boiled down to wearing a pair of Umbro tracksuit pants and feeling at home in them" (Flynn 2005, 72).

The gay scally did not appear purely on the back of the appearance of the heterosexual chav. Gay dress had often looked to sportswear for inspiration. In the mid-1990s Britain had been obsessed with "lad" culture, and in gay clubs and on gay pride marches there was a profusion of gay men in sportswear—sneakers, baseball caps, sweatshirts, and tracksuits. Gay commentators dubbed the style "lad drag." Writing in *QX* magazine in March 1996, Paul Hardy identified the "lad-clones" who were "decked out in sweat shirts and baggy jeans" with "a mean and moody dislike of camp and queeniness." Hardy argued that the new gay lad was symptomatic of gay men who weren't stereotypes, who wanted to be who they were rather than fit a clichéd lifestyle, and that "gay men fancy the whole 'lad' image because it represents 'real' masculinity" (Hardy 1996, 23). This look remained on the fringes of the UK gay scene until the explosion of a new gay lad or scally, which coincided with the emergence of the chav.

Those who were (or perceived themselves to be) true working-class scallies were attracted to the look and attitude because, says Thorsten, promoter of the gay scally club Rude Boyz "a lot of guys, including myself, can't really identify with the whole gay scene or don't fit into any typical gay stereotype and are looking for different role models." He continued, "Scallies are associated with roughness, and let's face it, everyone wants a bit of rough. I think it's all about masculinity" (cited in Cary 2005, 22). Like the masculine image of the clone and the bear, that of the scally could offer a form of protection in hostile homophobic environments. The look was "about normal, down to earth lads," said club promoter Tom. "You wouldn't even know they were gay. But that's the point isn't it" (cited in Flynn 2005, 73).

One criticism that was leveled at the gay scally culture was that it fed into a movement among gay men to describe themselves as "straight acting" (Flynn 2005, 72). The straight-acting man accepted that he was gay but desired acceptance by straight society so much that he tried to achieve this by copying straight behavior. Mark Simpson argued that in adopting a straight-acting persona, such gay men are "exaggerating [their] 'masculinity' to "woo the straight man and convince him that not all queers are queer" (Simpson 1994, 52).

However, most gay scallies were *not* attempting to "pass" as straight. They viewed scally identity as a means of reconciling and expressing both their sexuality and their working-class background. They did not want to be tied to society's preconceptions and media stereotypes of what it was to be (or look) gay. The attraction of clubs, such as Rude Boyz, aimed at scallies was that they offered an environment in which these men felt at home and comfortable, away from the more established and commercialized gay scene. Scott, of the pop group Fierce Girl, said that for him being a scally "rude boy is being normal." Greg, his musical partner, summed up the attitude, pointing out that "I'm gay 'cos I fancy men. Boys. Reebok classics & a bit of gold. That ain't pretending to be straight. It's being yourself. I've never dressed to impress. I ain't acting. I'm being myself. I dress normal" (cited in Flynn 2005, 71).

Homothug

The issues surrounding the adoption of a masculine gay image and identity were further complicated for black gay men. African-American culture is traditionally masculine oriented, or macho, and within such cultures gay men may not necessarily have a *moral* problem but often lose social rank and are viewed as "less than a man." Within this community homosexuality has also traditionally been deemed to be a white man's sickness foisted upon people of African descent (Constantine-Simms 2001). This led to what psychiatrist Dr. Frances Cress Welsing established as "the dichotomous identities of race and homosexuality" (cited in McBride 1998, 373). This dichotomy of identity still exists, and "for African-Americans, in a lot of ways we are still in a period of coming out to the black community, to our churches and our families, who are not necessarily accepting of who we are," said Calvin Gipson of the Glide Memorial Church Foundation (cited in Fulbright 2006).

In the late 19th and early 20th century, working-class African-American culture had found a place for the cross-dressed surrogate woman and effeminate "sissy-men" (see Chauncey 1994; Garber 1990). This acceptable feminized face of black homosexuality continued throughout the 20th century. John Campbell recalled that in the 1970s "you were either queens or clones ... On the gay scene you have those that want to be in a uniform and those that are going to say 'I am me' and for me as a black gay man the choice tended towards the queen."[6] Even with the burgeoning of gay rights and increased visibility, the process of identification for black gay men has been difficult, as author Randall Keenan noted: "Too many queer black men and women feel forced to choose whether they are black first or queer first; some even opt to be only one or the other, as best they can" (Keenan 1999).

Such cultural factors, along with the increasing visibility and influence of hip-hop culture, led to a new "gay" identity style that attempted to combine hypermasculinity and same-sex attraction—the homothug. Although this new subculture has been discussed as a gay subculture, this may be an inaccuracy. The club culture of homothugs emerged as a means for African-American men to meet to have sex, but those involved in the culture did not necessarily identify as gay, a practice known as "being on the down-low" or DL.[7]

The cult of masculinity was at the heart of being DL. Homothugs styled themselves both on, and as, prototypes of black manhood. Stylistically, homothugs drew their influence from hip-hop culture, wearing "plaid boxers or Tommy Hilfiger briefs carefully positioned above the waistline of oversized Phat Farm or Fubu jeans that hang low. Large baggy sweatshirts called 'hoodies' or extra long singlets [tank tops] are nonchalantly slipped over smooth muscular abdomens, broad shoulders and chests. The men's heads are wrapped in bandanas or white nylon caps called 'doo-rags'" (Philip 2005). The style was, intentionally, undistinguishable from heterosexual hip-hop style. For homothugs the most effective way to express masculinity was to seem as straight as possible, and any form of typically gay or effeminate behavior was frowned upon. Nathan Kerr, a gay Caribbean American, noted that "Gayness [is] seen as the whole sissy fag thing" (cited in Wright 2001.

One of the categories "performed" in the 1980s voguing "walks"[8] was the "butch-real" competition, in which the participant would "disguise" himself as a heterosexual homeboy so convincingly—in backward baseball cap, baggy pants, and sweatshirt worn with a swagger—that he could walk his neighborhood streets without being found out as gay. This "dragging up" exposed the very unreality of images and lifestyles and reflected what many closeted black gay men were undertaking as a form of self-preservation: "passing" as heterosexual.

For many openly gay men and women, the homothug represented an affront to the gay and lesbian struggle. Criticism of homothugs from "out" gay African Americans centered on the opinion that they were "repackaged closet cases." "It's weird that we'd want to go back into the closet after we worked so hard to come out of it," said Alphonso King, aka DJ Relentless, who played at Escuelita, a gay club catering to black and Latino men. "Everything is switching to Hip-Hop ... I've seen the guys who wear tight t-shirts and vogue at gay bars suddenly switch to baggy clothing and become Homothugs." Much of this criticism was centered on the appropriateness of gay men styling themselves on "homophobic" artists and listening to blatantly homophobic lyrics.

Despite the macho anxiety that underpinned the culture, homothugs could be viewed as part of a new queer presence that employed the macho signifiers of both hip-hop and the society around itself to find an identity and a way out of the closet, a sentiment summed up by American theorist José Esteban Muñoz: "We are so used to white masculinity setting the standard for the closet. Now when we talk about it in relation to communities of colour, it's not so much about the single man on a subway; its about a network of men who recognize each other as DL, and they have this new concept or word to describe it that isn't the closet. It's a way of projecting out a bunch of likes and dislikes, a code of the way you experience the world in relationship to desire and sexuality" (Muñoz 1999, 105).

Conclusion

The history of gay men's dress has been marked by a vacillation between masculinity and effeminacy. Neither masculine nor feminine styles are innate in gay physiology; neither style is genetically encoded, but each represents vital elements of the construction of a gay male identity, utilizing "objects [that] are assimilated into the subjective experience of individuals [or groups of like minded individuals] . . . in the form of culture and production—by appropriating them to human ends" (Slater 1997, 102). The latter part of the 20th century and the beginning of the 21st have witnessed a movement in the positioning of gay men's self-identity. Codes of behavior and styles of presentation that were used by gay men have developed and been cast aside as legal positions and social attitudes have altered. Stereotypes that were formed have been challenged, broken down and replaced by new ones. While there are, and always will be, effeminate gay men, most gay men have (or appear to have) "moved away from seeing [themselves] and being seen by others, as a 'gender invert', a 'feminine' soul in a 'male' body, and towards seeing [themselves] as . . . a complete (that is, 'real') man" (Forrest 1993, 97). However, what separates these masculine gay men from their straight subcultural equivalents is the sense of "knowing" or "camp" with which they select their dress choices or group affiliation.

Notes

1. This description appears in the film *Daddy and the Muscle Academy,* written and directed by Ilppo Pohjola, Filmitakomo Oy, 1991.

2. With the identification of the "teenager" in the 1950s, gay men began to adopt more youthful dress, which became a primary indicator and aspiration of gay men alongside, and eventually overtaking, the leisure-class aesthetic of the first half of the 20th century. Stratton Ashley noted in his 1964 article in *One* magazine that "homosexuals in general tend[ed] to dress younger than their years" and that "young and fashionable" attire was essential in New York's gay bars.

3. The term "bear" first appeared in print in a light-hearted piece of stereotyping entitled "Who's Who In The Zoo: A Glossary of Gay Animals," by the journalist George Mazzei (published in *The Advocate,* July 26, 1979).

4. *Chav* is the most popular term used to describe a white, working-class youth culture, which the *Collins English Dictionary* defines as "a young working class person who dresses in casual sports clothing" (included for the first time in its 2005 edition). The dress style of the chav draws on sportswear and so has stylistic links to hip-hop culture (in its branded tracksuits, ostentatious gold jewelry, and baseball caps). Chav could also be linked to the American terms *white trash* or *trailer trash,* particularly as all have connotations of low social status or poor prospects (i.e., downward mobility), lack of education, and violent or antisocial behavior.

5. The term *chav* is particularly associated with this subculture in the south of England but is synonymous with "ned," "chava," "townie," and "scally" used across other parts of the UK. Use of the term *scally* by gay men may be attributed to the fact that this term was popular in the northeast of England, (particularly Liverpool) before the negative connotations associated with "chav" became widespread.

6. Interview with the author, 1997.

7. DL culture created an enormous amount of debate within the mainstream U.S. media, focusing particularly on the HIV/AIDS epidemic within the African-American community and whether men on the DL were responsible for a rise in the rate of HIV infection.

8. In New York in the late 1980s, groups of black gay men and transvestites bonded in "houses," their own version of gangs or street families. Instead of fighting, as heterosexual street gangs would do, these houses vied with each other in "walks" or house-ball competitions. The competition categories were based on imitations of realities seen not only on television or across white America but also on the streets of the black, primarily heterosexual, ghettos where the participants lived. The most famous event of the house balls was the supermodel walk, in which each drag queen sashayed down the runway as his favorite superstar model, wearing a *haute couture* gown. The competitors struck poses based on those of catwalk models. This was known as "voguing," and was later popularized by Madonna in her song "Vogue."

References

Ashley, Stratton. 1964. The "other" homosexuals. *One* 7 (2).

Blachford, Gregg. 1981. Male dominance and the gay world. In *The making of the modern homosexual*, ed. Kenneth Plummer. London: Hutchinson.

Bristow, Joseph. 1989. Being gay: Politics, identity, pleasure. *New Formations*, no. 9.

Brown, Laurence. 2002. XXL. *axm*, March, 52–4.

Cary, James. 2005. Estate of mind: London Borough of Chav. *Boyz*, 19 March, 20–4.

Chauncey, George. 1994. *Gay New York: Gender, urban culture and the making of the gay male world, 1890–1940*. New York: Basic Books.

Constantine-Simms, Delroy, ed. 2001. *The greatest taboo: Homosexuality in black communities*. Los Angeles: Alyson.

Cole, Shaun. 1999. Invisible men: Gay men's dress in Britain, 1950–70. In *Defining dress: Dress as object, meaning and identity*, eds. Amy de la Haye and Elizabeth Wilson, 143–54. Manchester, UK: Manchester Univ. Press.

Cory, Donald Webster, and John P. LeRoy. 1963. *The homosexual & his society: A view from within*. New York: Citadel.

Diaman, Tony. 1970. The search for the total man. *Come Out,* December–January, 22–3.

Fischer, Hal. 1977. *Gay semiotics*. San Francisco: NFS Press.

Flynn, Paul. 2003. Bear up. *Attitude,* September, 66–70.

———. 2005. Scally fags. *Attitude,* March, 70–3.

Forrest, David. 1993. "We're here, we're queer, and we're not going shopping": Changing gay male identities in contemporary Britain. In *Dislocating masculinity*, eds. Andrea Cornwall and Nancy Lindisfarent, 97–110. London: Routledge.

Fulbright, Leslie. 2006. Black gay pride events grow, reaffirm identity. *San Francisco Chronicle,* June 17. http://sfgate.com.

Garber, Eric. 1990. A spectacle in color: The lesbian and gay subculture of jazz age Harlem. In *Hidden from history: Reclaiming the gay and lesbian past,* eds. Martin Duberman, Martha Vicinus, and George Chauncey, Jr., 318–31. New York: Meridian.

Gough, Jamie. 1989. Theories of sexual identity & the masculinisation of the gay man. In *Coming on strong: Gay politics & culture*, eds. Simon Shepherd and Mick Wallis, 119–36. London: Unwin Hyman.

Hardy, Paul. 1996. Glad to be lad. *QX,* March, 23–25.

Harris, Daniel. 1997. *The rise and fall of gay culture.* New York: Ballantyne.

Hebdige, Dick. 1987. *Subculture: The meaning of style.* London: Routledge.

Holleran, Andrew. 1982. The petrification of clonestyle. *Christopher Street,* 6 (9, no. 69): 14–16.

Keenan, Randall. 1999. Identity: A tricky animal. *The Advocate,* February 16. http://www.advocate.com.

Kleinberg, Seymour. 1978. Where have all the sissies gone? *Christopher Street,* 2 (9, March): 8–10.

Levine, Martin P. 1998, *Gay macho: The life and death of the homosexual clone*, New York and London: New York Univ. Press.

Locke, Philip. 1997. Male images in the gay mass media and bear-oriented magazines. In *The bear book: Readings in the history and evolution of a gay male subculture,* ed. Les Wright, 103–40. New York: Harrington Park.

Manning, Toby. 1996. Gay culture: Who needs it? In *Anti-Gay,* ed. Mark Simpson. London: Cassell.

McBride, Dwight A. 1998. Can the queen speak?: Racism, essentialism, sexuality and the problem of authority. *Callaloo* 21 (2): 363–80.

Muñoz, José Esteban. 1999. *Disidentifications: Queers of color and the performance of politics.* Minneapolis: Univ. of Minnesota Press.

Philip, Matthew. 2005. Homothugs: Hip-hop's secret homo underside. *The Guide,* March. http://www.guidemag.com.

Rofes, Eric. 1997. Academics as bears: Thoughts on middle-class eroticization of workingmen's bodies. In *The bear book: Readings in the history and evolution of a gay male subculture,* ed. Les Wright, 88–89. New York: Harrington Park.

Signorile, Michelangelo. 1997. *Life outside: The Signorile report on gay men: Sex, drugs, muscles, & the passages of life.* New York: HarperCollins.

Simpson, Mark. 1992. Male impersonators. *Gay Times,* August.

Sinfield, Alan. 1994. *The Wilde century.* London: Cassell.

Slater, Don. 1997. *Consumer culture and modernity.* Cambridge: Polity Press.

Tierney, Paul. 2001. Physical attraction. *Attitude,* no. 91 (Nov).

Wright, Kai. 2001. The great down-low debate. *Village Voice,* June 6–12. http://www.villagevoice.com.

Discussion Questions

1. Why does the author use the term "drag" to describe gay subcultures?

2. What are the different motives that each gay subculture described in this reading adopted a particular look?

3. What role does irony play in the subcultural looks described?

CHAPTER 7
RACE AND ETHNICITY
Andrew Reilly

After you have read this chapter, you will understand:

- **That people have culturally constructed categories of race and ethnicity affecting social issues and problems regarding appearance**
- **The relationship of race and ethnicity—particularly as they affect issues of appearance—to gain an appreciation for the experience of those in the minority**
- **The impact that issues of race and ethnicity have on consumer culture**

RACE

The term **race** refers to certain visible and distinctive characteristics that are determined by biology. Along with gender and age, race is one of the first things we notice about another person. Race is also a social construction, meaning that, like gender and sexuality, the concept of race is created artificially, based on physical markers, as a way of grouping people together based on what one particular culture defines as socially significant.

One of the earliest classifications of people into races was created circa 1785 by Christoph Meiners, a German philosopher who believed in polygenism, or that each race has its own unique beginnings, separate from other races. Meiners argued that there were two races: Caucasians and Mongolians (Painter, 2010). Later, Jean-Joseph Virey termed the two groups white and dark (Baum, 2006). German anthropologist Johann Freidrich Blumenback (1752–1840) proposed five races, based on skull size: Caucasian, Mongolian, Malayan, Ethiopian, and American, which became white, yellow, brown, black, and red, respectively (Painter, 2010). However, these categories were not mutually exclusive, and at one point East Asian people and high caste Hindus were considered

"white," and poor Caucasians who worked in the field and had tanned brown skin were not "white." Likewise, other groups of people now considered "white" were "not white" according to the U.S. government, at different times, such as Italian, Greek, Spanish, and Irish. These were likely due to immigration quotas and one could argue were an issue of social class. Today, in the United States there are six government-created categories of race (created for the census): White, Black or African American, American Indian or Alaskan Native, Asian, Hawaiian Native or Pacific Islander, and Other.[1]

The terms "black" and "white" are problematic in that not all cultures understand the terms the same way. In the United Kingdom, the term "black" is used to refer to all people who are not white. In South Africa, the government recognizes four racial categories: black, white, colored, and Indian. An African American person visiting Tanzania is likely to be considered white by the native African black people (Newman, 1995). Hence, racial categories vary among geographic regions as a way of identifying people, based on place of birth and on arbitrary physical characteristics.

In the United States, people of mixed races usually are identified by one race or the other. The United States adheres to the one-drop rule. This applies mostly to black or African American people, coming from a common antebellum law in the South that defined a person as black if he or she had a "single drop of black blood." For example, President Barack Obama had a white mother and African father; however, he is typically referred to as the "first black president." Anthropologists call this a "hypodescent rule," meaning that racially mixed people are always assigned the status of the subordinate group, likely in order to keep the dominant race "pure." Hence, a person with seven out of eight great-grandparents who are white and only one who is black is still considered black.

Racial categories often lead to judgments about beauty and attractiveness (among other characteristics). Historically, dominant groups were considered more attractive than subordinate groups. This has resulted in subordinate groups attempting to change their body aesthetics—skin tone, hair, facial features, body shape—in order to fit in with the dominant version of beauty. African hair has often been altered in texture, and one of the most popular American men's hairstyle in the early and middle 20th century was the conk. The **conk** was created through the use of store-bought or homemade relaxers that used lye and when applied to the head would straighten the hair but also could burn the scalp. The hair was then styled by combing it back or arranging it in a pompadour. Malcom X, who once sported the style, advocated for natural hair in the 1960s in an effort to shed white standards of beauty and celebrate black beauty. See Figure 7.1.

Still today, many women of African descent feel the pressure to modify their hair to fit the white beauty aesthetic of straight hair. Google searches for "professional hair" and "unprofessional hair" yield images of straight and natural hair, respectively (Janin, 2016). Black hairstyles, such as afros and cornrows, have been banned in professional environments and many women fear that their jobs could be at risk if they wear their hair naturally (Sini, 2016; Wilson, 2013).

Even in the fashion and beauty industries, discrimination continues against people of color. At fashion shows, models of color are frequently left to their own devices to style their hair and makeup because professionals who understand "ethnic" hair are not hired.

Figure 7.1 The conk hairstyle, as pictured in this 1956 photograph, was created using relaxers to "straighten" the hair. The style eventually lost popularity as natural African American hairstyles took hold in the 1960s and 1970s.

And, makeup brands seem to cater to lighter skin tones and offer more options for them, while people with darker skin tones are left with fewer choices. Jaleesa Reed further explores this later in the chapter in "Cosmetic Counter Connotations: Black Millennial Women and Beauty."

ETHNICITY

The term **ethnicity** refers to learned cultural heritage that is shared by a group of people. It typically includes a common national origin, ancestry, language, dietary habits, ideology, and style of dress. Ethnicity is different from race yet the terms are frequently, and inappropriately, used interchangeably. For example, Chinese Americans are different ethnically from Chinese people born in China, although their biological background may be identical. Furthermore, people in China may identify by one of 56 officially recognized Chinese ethnicities, including the most populous, the Han. Similarly, India has over 600 officially recognized ethnicities, and Africa, with between 1,000 and 3,000, is the most ethnically diverse continent in the world. Thus, even the concept of grouping people together by country or continent does not truly recognize different individual cultural groups.

Ethnicity plays a significant role in others' perceptions of a person's appearance. Sociologist Paul Starr (1982) found that, in the absence of distinctive skin color and other physical characteristics, ethnicity is judged by others on the basis of many imprecise attributes such as language, residence, and dress (clothing, accessories, and body markings). Dress is an important marker of identity, as **social identity theory** posits (Tajfel & Turner, 1986; also discussed in Chapter 2). According to this theory, people are first categorized into groups; an individual then identifies with one of the groups; groups then compare themselves to other groups and develop group distinctiveness, or note what makes their group different (sometimes better) than other groups. Often, this revolves around dress and adornment to show differences between ethnic groups and affiliation with an ethnic group. In "Dressing the Jíbaros: Puerto Rican Peasants' Clothing through Time and Space," José Blanco F. and Raúl J. Vásquez-López explore a certain style of dress and identity and recount how the dress of peasants in Puerto Rico became symbolic of the nation, even for those who did not identify with the cultures that moved to or colonized the island.

Veena Chattaraman also explores the issue of ethnicity and dress in "Cultural Markers in Dress: Decoding

Meanings and Motivations of College Students." She analyzes how ethnic and ethnic-inspired dress is used to celebrate one's ancestral past and culture, and to show respect to one's heritage.

ETHNIC DRESS

Ethnic dress, sometimes called "folk costume," is the dress of a particular group of people indigenous to a particular area, though one need not have lived in that area to claim ethnic affiliation. Ethnic affiliation might come in the form of color, silhouette, pattern motif, pattern size, or use of a garment. Many ethnicities have unique garments that are immediately recognizable. The Japanese have the *kosode*, with its loose fit and square sleeves. The Scots have the woolen kilt, with each plaid design unique to a particular clan (see Figure 7.2). The Tuareg of North Africa wear indigo-dyed cloaks, leaving their skin blue, giving them the epithet "the blue men." In India, the sari is ubiquitous; made of one long strip of cloth, it is wrapped around and draped over the body, but the specific wrapping, draping, color, and embroidery vary by village or ethnic affiliation.

In addition to cloth garments, jewelry also designates ethnicity. For example, the Navajo, Zuni, and Hopi Native American tribes all wear jewelry, but the style of jewelry is different from each other. Navajo jewelry is made with stones, usually turquoise, in their natural shape. The stones are set in silver that outlines the stone's natural silhouette. In contrast, Zuni jewelry is made from stones that have been precisely cut and placed into mosaics outlined in silver. The Hopi, however, rarely use stones in their jewelry. Their jewelry tends to be polished silver with

Figure 7.2 The Scottish kilt identifies not only a wearer's ethnic origin but also the particular colors and plaid design identify the clan.

Figure 7.3 Body art, such as tattoos, can be markers of ethnic identity. The tattoos on this man's body identify him as Maori.

shapes and symbols carved into the smooth surface. Each of these differences in jewelry is immediately recognizable as being from its respective tribe.

In addition to cloth garments and accessories, altering the body is another way to display ethnic affiliation. Though tattoos in Polynesia are common, the style differs among tribes: traditional Hawaiian tattoos use straight lines and geometric motifs with no curves, traditional Samoan are geometric and linear and cover large portions of the body, traditional Tahitian tattoos are curved, and traditional Maori tattoos look like rope with curved ends (see Figure 7.3).

Although ethnic dress can remain unchanged for generations that does not mean dress never changes. New technologies, new products, and new ideas that are introduced to a culture can be adapted to become "culturally authentic." Cultural authentication is the process whereby a foreign object (e.g., clothing) is incorporated into a culture and becomes authentic to that culture. There are four steps to **cultural authentication** (Eicher & Erekosima, 1980), though Arthur (1997) argues they need not occur in this specific order: selection (adopting an object); characterization (the new culture gives meaning to the object), incorporation (identifying the object to a social group), and transformation (physically altering the object to allow for cultural distinctiveness). By this process, an item that was originally foreign can become synonymous with the culture, as in the case of European ribbon and glass beads that were incorporated into the culture of the Great Lakes Indians of North America (Pannabecker, 1996).

Ethnic dress is often used as a source of inspiration for a designer's collections. Ethnic dress was in vogue in the United States in the 1960s and 1970s when American society was taking a renewed interest in people's origins, news broadcasters were reporting on wars that were being waged in foreign countries, and new trading with countries (such as China) opened doors to new resources and aesthetics. Yves Saint Laurent presented many lines that were inspired by the everyday dress of people in Morocco, Africa, and Russia, and John Galliano took inspiration for various collections from the cultures of Egypt, Indigenous Americans, and Africans (see Figure 7.4).

Yet, at times, the commoditization of ethnic dress as fashion is met with resistance. Some people find the co-opting of sacred or important markers of ethnic identity for a season or two by the fashion industry to be disingenuous. This is called **cultural appropriation**, and it occurs when a person or group of people of one culture profits or uses the cultural creations of another culture. It is argued that it degrades ethnicity into a mere costume and/or that the objects are used inappropriately. Other questions—such as the authenticity of ethnic garments used as fashion items—pose dilemmas such as who has the right to create ethnic fashions or who has the right to profit from ethnic fashions? Christine Beaule explores this issue of ethnic authenticity and fashion in her examination of the indigenous dress of the Andes in "The Modern Chola: Indigeneity, Gender, and Global Fashion in Bolovia."

Figure 7.4 Galliano designed this indigenous-inspired beaded gown during his tenure at Dior, but many would consider this cultural appropriation.

Summary

This chapter focuses on the difference between race and ethnicity and how they are manifested through clothing and appearance. Race is a nebulous term whose purpose is to group people together based on very general appearance terms. Ethnicity, on the other hand, is a term that specifies a person's cultural heritage. Ethnic groups tend to have very specific forms of dress that do not change with the fashions. But when they are used as fashion, conflict between established identity and temporary style may result.

Key Terms

Conk

Cultural appropriation

Cultural authentication

Ethnicity

Race

Social identity theory

ETHNIC STEREOTYPES AND THEIR CONSEQUENCES

Objective

This exercise is a challenging, in-class group activity that helps participants dissect a stereotype, consider the relationships of component parts of a multifaceted phenomenon, and understand consequences of labeling minority groups.

A stereotype is a classification or typing of a group of people that results in applying a set of generalized characteristics to them. Even though the stereotype usually does not completely fit any one individual, all members of the group are typed the same. In this in-class exercise, each student will be asked to verbalize a stereotype in society. Do not be afraid to "speak the unspeakable" and list highly controversial ideas. You are not saying that you hold this stereotype, but that these ideas are held by some people in the United States. We will examine the dangers of stereotypical thinking as we move through the exercise.

Procedure

Form groups of four to seven people. Think of a group of Americans (e.g., Native, Asian, African, or Hispanic) that is stereotyped in U.S. society. List the label given to the group. Next, work as a group to create a written list of characteristics commonly assigned to that group when stereotyped. When listing items, put a star next to those that relate to appearance. Next, identify those parts of the stereotype that are either negative or positive.

Ground Rules

Some essential ground rules for this exercise are:

1. It is OK to feel uncomfortable about writing down a stereotype; we can all learn valuable lessons from the discomfort.

2. It is OK to write socially and politically incorrect thoughts and words during this exercise. You will need to verbalize and understand the components of a stereotype that may seem ugly or even absurd. Laughing about the stereotypes is permissible; this can help to relieve tension about the stereotypes.

3. It is important that no one gets angry at stereotypes that other groups construct; no one in class should be accused of actually holding the verbalized stereotypes. This is a learning exercise, not a statement of personal beliefs. An atmosphere of tolerance and openness is essential for learning.

Discussion Questions

When groups are through recording the stereotypes and noting positive and negative components, each group should:

1. Read to the whole class the stereotype their group chose.

2. Consider whether the appearance components of the stereotype help to trigger the labeling.

3. Read what they consider to be negative about the stereotype and think about what consequences those negative components may have for the people to whom the stereotype is applied.

4. Read what they consider to be positive about the stereotype and think what consequences those positive components may have for the people so labeled.

5. Discuss whether any two or more individuals can have all the components of any of the stereotypes. Is it fair to apply the stereotype before knowing a person, even if the stereotype might fit somewhat?

References

Arthur, L. B. (1997), "Cultural Authentication Refined: The Case of the Hawaiian Holok?," *Clothing and Textiles Research Journal*, 15(3): 129–39.

Baum, B. D. (2006), *The Rise and Fall of the Caucasian Race: A Political History of Racial Identity*, New York: New York University.

Eicher, J. B. and T. V. Erekosima (1980), "Distinguishing Non-Western from Western Dress: The Concept of Cultural Authentication" [abstract]. *Proceedings of the 1980 Annual Meeting of the Association of College Professors of Textiles and Clothing*, 83–84.

Janin, A. (2016), "What the Perception of 'Professional' Hair Means for Black Job Seekers," *Takepart*. Available online: http://www.takepart.com/article/2016/04/13

/what-perception-professional-hair-means-black-job -seekers.

Newman, D. (1995), *Sociology: Exploring the Adventure of Everyday Life*, Thousand Oaks, CA: Pine Forge Press.

Painter, N. (2010), *The History of White People*, New York: Norton & Company.

Pannabecker, R. K. (1996), "Tastily Bound with Riands": Ribbon-Bordered Dress of the Great Lakes Indians, 1735–1839," *Clothing and Textiles Research Journal*, 14(4): 2676–275.

Sini, R. (2016), "Wear a Weave at Work—Your Afro Hair Is Unprofessional," *BBC News*. Available online: http://www.bbc.com/news/uk-36279845.

Starr, P. (1982), *The Social Transformation of American Medicine*, New York: Basic Books.

Tajfel, H. and J. C. Turner (1986), "The Social Identity Theory of Inter-Group Behavior," in S. Worchel and L. W. Austin (eds.), *Psychology of Intergroup Relations*, 33–47, Chicago: Nelson-Hall.

Wilson, J. (2013), Black Women Worry That Their Natural Hair Could Affect Job Employment or Retention, *The Huffington Post*. Available online: https://www.huffingtonpost.com/2013/03/05/black -women-natural-hair-at-the-workplace_n_2811056 .html.

Endnote

1. The U.S. government recognizes Hispanic/Latino as an ethnicity, not a race.

This introduction is based on a version originally written by Susan Michelman and appeared in *Meanings of Dress* editions 1, 2, and 3.

7.1
Cosmetic Counter Connotations: Black Millennial Women and Beauty

Jaleesa Reed

In 1962, Malcolm X, a human rights activist, addressed a crowd gathered for the funeral of Ronald Stokes. Stokes, a Nation of Islam officer, was surrendering during a mosque raid when Los Angeles police shot him in the back (Marable, 2011). In an attempt to call the Nation of Islam to action, Malcolm X delivered a speech focused on the brutalization of Black identity (Marable, 2011). He asked the question: "Who taught you to hate the color of your skin?" (Malcolm X, 1962). Out of context, it is an odd question, considering the occasion. Yet, the question and the speech are still relevant, 55 years later. In 2017, why has the U.S. failed to achieve authentic equality, which in the aftermath of the Civil Rights movement seemed attainable?

Toward the end of his speech, Malcolm X stated "The most disrespected woman in America, is the Black woman. The most unprotected person in America, is the Black woman. The most neglected person in America, is the Black woman" (Malcolm X, 1962). Unfortunately, not much changed since he made the statement. Black women are still disrespected and neglected by America's white beauty industrial complex. Per industry standards, Black women are more beautiful when their skin is light and their hair is straight. In the cosmetics market, cosmetic availability and placement reflect this unsubstantiated belief.

Black women are one of the most disempowered segments of the US population (Bierria, 2014; Pratt-Clarke, 2013). While this fact has been discussed from many angles (Corra & Borch, 2014; Edwards, 2015; Lindsay, 2015; White, 2005), one aspect of their disenfranchisement is rarely investigated: their lack of power in the cosmetics marketplace. Studies on the relationship between Black women and beauty focus on contentious issues of Black women's hair, skin color, and what is deemed appropriate and professional appearance for them (Greene, 2011; Harvey, 2008; Opie & Phillips, 2015; Patton, 2006; Tate, 2007; Thompson, 2009). The fact that they are also enthusiastic participants in the cosmetics market has been overlooked.

The Business of Beauty

Women of all races and ethnicities seek cosmetics that would help satisfy their desires to be beautiful. However, the quest for beauty is an expensive one. In 2015, retail sales of beauty products reached $46.2 billion in the US (Mintel, January 2016). Before, analysts predicted that the beauty industry would be worth $42.5 billion by 2019 (Mintel, January 2015), yet it has already exceeded previous growth predictions. New predictions estimate that US sales of beauty products will reach $51.8 billion by 2020 (Mintel, January 2016).

Mass merchandisers account for 38% of consumer traffic in beauty retailing, down from 41% in 2015 (Mintel, January 2015; January 2016). Yet at a mass merchandiser, Black women experience ongoing difficulties finding products that match their skin color. To be clear, the predicament awaiting Black women in cosmetic aisles is not the hassle of choosing the right foundation shade amongst multiple brand and shade offerings. In fact, having options would assume that cosmetic brands consider Black women as a target market. However, shopping for cosmetics at a mass merchandiser means selection from a tiny number of brands focused on highlighting Black women's beauty. Unfortunately, even amongst products geared toward Black women, variety remains limited.

This unfortunate state of affairs turns perplexing when one considers the fact that Black Americans have a buying power of $1.2 trillion, which amounts to 8.6% of the nation's total discretionary income (The Nielsen Company, 2016). Black buying power reflects Black-Americans' population growth and increasing levels of education and entrepreneurship which in turn, increased their income. Within the personal care category, Black-American's

Original for this text

divide their spending between mainstream beauty brands and brands targeting Black-Americans (The Nielsen Company, 2016). The Nielsen Company consumer report underscores two facts: 1) Black Americans are active participants in the beauty category and 2) Black Americans have the education and income levels necessary to act as well-informed consumers. Considering these points and the primary market for mass merchandisers – the self-described middle class – one would think Wal-Mart, a large retailer which aims to offer affordable products for every American, would offer cosmetic products which meet Black women's needs. But, this is not the case. Black women tend to find the most suitable beauty products at specialty retailers, such as Makeup Art Cosmetics (MAC), Bobbi Brown, or Sephora, where cosmetics retail at a significantly higher price point than their Maybelline and CoverGirl counterparts.

Case in point: Every cosmetics brand at a mass merchandiser will offer a makeup foundation in some variant of White skin, from "ivory" to several shades of beige. But, for women with darker complexions, the array of choice is limited to a couple of shades at the end of the spectrum as if *all* women of color, regardless of their ethnic background, fit into three shades. Having limited options creates a significant disadvantage for women of color, especially for those Black women whose skin color does not fall into the range of "caramel," "cappuccino," or "mocha" (Revlon, 2017). You do not believe me? Count the makeup products and compare the difference in shades in any drug store. Despite external attempts to incorporate more women of color in advertisements, the core offering of foundation shades remains the same. As millennial Black women have expressed, the commercials which highlight popular singers such as Beyoncé and Janelle Monae, are often misleading in relation to actual product choice (Reed, 2015). The lack of choices for Black women is more surprising when one realizes that, of the three colors, "cappuccino," for example, barely matches even the lighter shades of Black skin. In addition, the existing "darker" shades are far from adequate to address the multiplicity of Black women's skin tones.

Several informants for a study on the cosmetics use of African American millennial women (Reed, 2015) reported that, no matter how hard they tried, they could not find a foundation that matched their skin color at a mass merchandiser. While drugstore brands may be ideal for products such as eyeliner, mascara, or eye shadow, these tend to be low-risk purchases because they are relatively inexpensive. In contrast, foundation selection requires knowledge, skin color matching, and can range from $10–$50 for a 4 oz. bottle, depending on the brand. In comparison to eyeliner and mascara, foundation is a high-risk buy. Therefore, after repeated negative experiences with foundations at mass merchandisers, study participants disclosed they no longer even bothered looking for them at such retailers (Reed, 2015). Instead, they migrated to specialty beauty retailers such as MAC and Sephora where knowledge and expertise on black skin is readily available from employees.

A Beauty Standard

Beauty is an age-old topic of interest which has stood the testament of time. Obtaining beauty is more than a self-esteem issue. For better or worse, beauty practices are feminized. While, participating in the beauty industrial complex emasculates men instantly, it sings the praises of women who willingly participate. Yet, protofeminists, such as Mary Wollstonecraft, believed beauty was a weakness and a trivial occupation to appease men's desires and stifle women's ability to reason (Wollstonecraft, 1792). Later, Second Wave feminists also argued that women participate in the beauty industrial complex, not only because they want to, but also because society makes it quite clear that they *have to*. Through personal experience, women learn that a host of benefits and privileges, such as higher salaries and frequent promotions, are associated with beauty (Banks, 2000; Rhode, 2010; Tate, 2009).

It is a fact that many women have used beauty to their advantage and as a means of empowerment. However, beauty as a tool of power is problematic because it is the *only* power women are actively encouraged to seek (Sontag, 2010). Women's access to political or economic forms of power remains controversial, yet daily interactions with the White beauty industrial complex in American media reinforces the aspirational ideal for women. From Instagram models to TV commercials, women are told that obtaining and pursuing beauty is a worthy occupation of time, effort, and money. Even if a woman is an accomplished engineer, high profile lawyer, or even a CEO, to not be lacking, she must be beautiful. As Sontag (2010) states, women are only encouraged to seek beauty as a tool of power, implying that anything a woman achieves professionally is partly due to her looks. If beauty is the only means for a woman to achieve power, she is further isolated from real avenues of empowerment such as education and financial independence. Oppression through beauty affects all women, but those women who are further segregated from mainstream society by race, class, and income are bound to have a different experience. Therefore, for Black women, who have the least power among all groups of women (Bierria, 2014; Pratt-Clarke, 2013), access to appropriate beauty products may be crucial for experiencing at least a slim measure of empowerment. But how, if they do not have the same options as White women?

The tension between Black consumers and White business owners predates today's micro forms of oppression. Exclusionary efforts within White retail spaces during the Jim Crow era allowed the cosmetics business to become an area where "Black consumers showed a preference for products manufactured and marketed by African Americans" (White & White, 1998, p. 185). Though the preference existed, popular media such as *The New York Times* (1909) implied that "Negroes. . .should by all means mask [their features] into some resemblance to the Caucasian race" (White & White, 1998, p. 187). The advertisement referred to by White and White (1998) goes on to imply that when Black people seek to cultivate their culture and looks, they "disesteem" themselves. The popular publications from the early 1900s, as the example shows, created a narrative in which White beauty was placed on a pedestal, and Black women were assumed to be followers. However, in actuality, most Black women who were using cosmetics were not swayed by the White beauty standard. Instead, what they wanted was the "freedom to construct their appearance" (White & White, 1998), the same freedom that White women had. So, the struggle was not about the implied desirability of "whiteness" (White & White, 1998), but that Black women wanted to control the avenues of their own self-actualization.

Beauty is not tied indiscriminately to race. Being born Black or White does not automatically make one beautiful. Yet, the narrative from the 1900s implies that Black women were lacking in beauty, and their usage of cosmetics was a way to increase their beauty potential. Inspired by this narrative, cultural norms supported the idea that physical features were hierarchical. In other words, in the measurement of American beauty – White physical features such as "blue eyes, blond hair, and fair skin" inspired positive connotations, while Black physical features like "thick lips, kinky hair, and dark skin" encouraged negative ones (Haney López, 2006). This byproduct of the social construction of race forced

Black women to cultivate their own beauty standard in opposition to the mainstream White beauty standard. Slogans such as "Black is Beautiful" emerged and helped create a conscious celebration of Black beauty against dominant constructions and understandings of race (Haney López, 2006).

Critics often recommended that Black women embrace their natural beauty (White & White, 1998) as a form of resistance to the beauty industrial complex. This veiled suggestion alluded to the understanding that Black women were better off not caring about their appearance at all. Implicit in this argument is the notion that the beauty industrial complex exists only for White women who are served through representative advertisements and convenient shopping locations. But, where does that leave everyone else? When advertisements repeatedly reinforce race and beauty as dependent, intertwined concepts, this forces women to look at themselves and ask, "Why am *I* excluded?"

Merchandising Beauty

The lack of appropriate cosmetics products affects Black women from all walks of life. During New York's Fall 2015 Fashion Week, Sudanese model Nykhor Paul, voiced her frustration at the absence of makeup artists' preparation for models with darker skin tones. Paul asked: "Why do I have to bring my own makeup to a professional show when all the other white girls don't have to do anything, but show up?" (Andrews, 2016, n.p.). Without a range of foundation options and diversity in models on the runways, makeup artists do not need to learn techniques or stock products for women of color. Through this omission, the market makes it clear that Black women do not belong in this space. Even though the media champions the diversity of the U.S. entertainment industry, a few tokens of visibility mask the fact that mainstream products for Black women are sorely lacking. Even in a professional setting, when a makeup artist is aware of the model's skin tone and hair type beforehand, no one bothers to learn the proper skills or carry the correct arsenal of foundation shades. Therefore, Black women's frustration with the lip service that the industry pays to diversity in the fashion industry is understandable; for every fifteen Black models walking the NYFW runways, there are 150–200 women with pale skin.

For this reason, some makeup artists, such as Fatima Thomas, Senior Makeup Artist, transitioned to using MAC. According to Thomas, when her career took off in the early 90s, "it was rare for any one brand to have a universal offering of products for light and dark skin tones, especially foundations. But MAC did" (Andrews, 2016). MAC, in addition to other brands such as Bobbi Brown and Iman Cosmetics, has become known for its attention to women of color's needs in professional makeup artistry. MAC's serendipitous, but profitable, realization has helped the brand to continue to be at the forefront of Black Millennial women's minds and wallets.

There are two standards that Black women can measure themselves against – the mainstream (White) standard of beauty or their culturally-specific standard. In the case of young Black women, personal fulfillment within their cultural group appears to be more important than obtaining the mainstream society's approval. Part of this stems from the realization that Black women can never measure up to the White beauty standard, and thus, are not the target market for most beauty products. Measuring Black women against a White "norm" provides a narrative of disempowerment. Yet, finding products that work allows Black women to tilt the status quo in their favor.

Black women will increasingly influence and shape the marketplace. Today, if a Black woman has a bad experience at a makeup counter, she has options that did not exist even 25 years ago. It is a known fact to industry insiders that cosmetic choices for Black women continue to be limited. Still, very little is being done to improve the situation. Therefore, when Black women find cosmetics that fit their needs and help them actively shape their self-expression and help them reach their goals in self presentation, they are a step closer to where they want to or should be in terms of social recognition and inclusion.

Cultural and ethnic groups have their own standards of beauty that exist alongside mainstream beauty standards. Acknowledging this illuminates the reasons behind Black women's cosmetics purchase decisions and motivations. Black Millennial women's identification with MAC demonstrates that a brand can be successful in appealing to mainstream consumers as well as minorities. In a multicultural society, where the population is getting increasingly browner through migration, interracial marriages, or relationships, embracing several types of beauty standards is not only the ethical but also most likely the most profitable way to move forward.

Brands such as MAC are mainstream, but minor changes in their marketing philosophy have allowed them to operate as gatekeepers for young Black women interested in using makeup. Because women remain loyal to beauty brands over the course of their lifetime (Mintel, December 2013), this relationship can be significant for attracting their buying power and retaining it. The relationship between Black Millennial women and MAC products exemplifies the importance young women place on self-presentation, the need for social inclusion, and communal acceptance.

The fact that Black Millennials cannot find culturally appropriate cosmetics in mainstream stores suggests that the beauty industry is still not inclusive. When Millennial Black women remedy this situation giving their patronage to stores that cater to their specific requirements, they empower themselves and gain importance as consumers. In addition, they achieve their beauty goals, which earn them admiration in their community. Black Millennial women's experiences in the cosmetic marketplace also demonstrate that a brand can thrive by simply embracing *all* races and *all* beauty standards. The problem is not that Black Millennial women are not interested in cosmetics, but rather that the roots of the problem lie in the historical repudiation of Black women's femininity, which continues to this day. Mainstream brands still appear to believe that Black women's beauty aspirations are not important enough to invest in. What they have failed to acknowledge is that Black Millennial women merely demand a level playing field: appropriate beauty products and value for their money.

References

Andrews, J. C. (2016, March). How Black models are fighting discrimination backstage at fashion shows. *Teen Vogue*. Retrieved from http://www.teenvogue.com/story/black-models-diversity-backstage-fashion-week

Banks, I. (2009). Hair matters: Beauty, power and Black women's consciousness. New York: NYU Press.

Bierria, A. (2014). Missing in action: Violence, power, and discerning agency. *Hypatia*, 29(1), 129–145.

Corra, M. K., & Borch, C. (2014). Socioeconomic differences among Blacks in America: Over time trends. *Race and Social Problems*, 6(2), 103–119.

Edwards, K. T. (2015). Perceptions of power and faith among Black women faculty: Re-thinking institutional diversity. *Innovative Higher Education*, 40(3), 263–278.

Greene, W. D. (2011). Black women can't have blonde hair . . . in the workplace. *Journal of Gender, Race & Justice*, 14(2), 405–430.

Haney López, I. (2006). *White by law: The legal construction of race.* 2nd ed. New York: New York University Press.

Harvey, A. M. (2008). Personal satisfaction and economic improvement: Working-class Black women's entrepreneurship in the hair industry. *Journal of Black Studies*, 38(6), 900–915.

Lindsay, K. (2015). Beyond "model minority," "superwoman," and "endangered species": Theorizing intersectional coalitions among Black immigrants, African American women, and African American men. *Journal of African American Studies*, 19(1), 18–35.

Malcolm X. (1962). Who taught you to hate yourself? Retrieved February 1, 2017 from https://genius.com/Malcolm-x-who-taught-you-to-hate-yourself-annotated

Marable, M. (2011). Malcolm X: A life of reinvention. London: Penguin Books.

Mintel Group Ltd. (2013). Shopping for beauty products – US –December 2013.

Mintel Group Ltd. (2015). Beauty retailing – US – January 2015.

Mintel Group Ltd. (2016). Beauty retailing - US - January 2016.

Mintel Group Ltd. (2016). The beauty consumer - US - March 2016.

Opie, T. R., & Phillips, K. W. (2015). Hair penalties: The negative influence of Afrocentric hair on ratings of Black women's dominance and professionalism. *Frontiers in Psychology*, 6(1311), 1–14.

Patton, T. O. (2006). Hey girl, am I more than my hair?: African American women and their struggles with beauty, body image, and hair. *NWSA Journal*, 18(2), 24–51.

Pratt-Clarke, M. (2013). A radical reconstruction of resistance strategies: Black girls and Black women reclaiming our power using transdisciplinary applied social justice©, Ma'at, and rites of passage. *Journal of African American Studies*, 17, 99–114.

Reed, J. (2015). The beauty gap: Black women and the relationship between beauty standards and their decision to purchase MAC cosmetics. (Unpublished master's thesis). The University of Georgia, Athens.

Revlon Photoready Airbrush Effect Makeup. (2017). Retrieved February 1, 2017, from http://www.revlon.com/products/face/foundation-makeup/revlon-photoready-airbrush-effect-makeup#309975397109||0

Rhode, D. L. (2010). The beauty bias: The injustice of appearance in life and law. New York: Oxford University Press.

Sontag, S. (2010). A woman's beauty: Put-down or power source? In R. DiYanni (Ed.), Fifty Great Essays (pp. 643–645). Longman.

Tate, S. (2007). Black beauty: Shade, hair, and anti-racist aesthetics. *Ethnic & Racial Studies*, 30(2), 300–319.

Tate, S. (2009). Black beauty: Aesthetics, stylization, politics. Aldershot: Ashgate.

The Nielsen Company. (2016, October 17). Young, connected and Black: African-American millennials are driving social change and leading digital advancement. Retrieved from http://www.nielsen.com/us/en/insights/reports/2016/young-connected-and-black.html

Thompson, C. (2009). Black women, beauty, and hair as a matter of being. *Women's Studies*, 38, 831–856.

White, S.B. (2005). Releasing the pursuit of bouncin' and behavin' hair: Natural hair as an Afrocentric feminist aesthetic for beauty. *International Journal of Media and Cultural Politics*, 1(3), 295–308.

White, S. & White, G. (1998). Stylin': African American expressive culture from its beginnings to the Zoot Suit. Ithaca: Cornell University Press.

Wollstonecraft, M. (1792). A vindication of the rights of woman. Minneola, New York: Dover Publications, Inc.

Discussion Questions

1. How have Black women and White women experienced and interacted with beauty standards differently?

2. How have beauty standards impacted social recognition and inclusion for Black women?

7.2
Dressing the Jíbaros: Puerto Rican Peasants' Clothing through Time and Space

José Blanco F. and Raúl J. Vázquez-López

The *jíbaro* is arguably one of the two most important symbols of Puerto Rican national identity. The term refers to the nineteenth-century, mountain dwelling Puerto Rican white peasant of Spanish descent. Jíbaros were farmers; men worked in coffee and later sugar cane plantations while women—besides doing agricultural work—tended to the family and did laundry for pay. The image and dress of the jíbaro has undergone changes since the term first appeared in print on June 17, 1814 in *El Diario Económico* (Pedreira as cited in Babín, 1963, p. 61). It quickly secured an important place in Puerto Rican cultural and political production and has been ascribed a variety of meanings over the last two centuries. Literature professor Carmen L. Torres-Robles (1999) states: "for many critics and Puerto Ricans in general, the image of the jíbaro represents the essence of Puerto Rican nationality" (our translation of Torres-Robles, 1999, p. 241).

The jíbaro, it can be argued, became the locus of Puerto Rican identity as a response to socio-political and economic uncertainties on the island during the turn of the twentieth century. Historian Lillian Guerra (1998) presents an account of the appropriation of the image of the jíbaro as resistance against hegemony and American colonialism. Guerra—referring to Puerto Ricans living in New York—explains: "By invoking the jíbaro as the symbolic habitus of the Puerto Rican soul, Puerto Rican migrants and their descendants actively and consciously locate the roots of their identity in the history of the island" (Guerra, 1998, p. 5). The jíbaro provides a point of reference to many Puerto Ricans who do not fully identify themselves with native Taino culture, African culture, or even the cultures of the two powers that have colonized the island: Spain and the United States. It is through the jíbaro that many see the history of the island as a constant movement from one region to the other in search of progress and a better life. Identifying oneself as a jíbaro is a claim to a connection with a group of people that has

struggled to find a place within the history of an island facing social, political, and economic challenges that spun in part from the fact that Puerto Rico has never been an independent nation. The term jíbaro, though, has a variety of connotations. It may be used pejoratively in reference to a person who—allegedly similarly to the peasants—lacks proper education and social manners, or, as previously discussed, it can be appropriated as an honorary title as one claims a connection to the struggling working peasant class and their association with agricultural productivity and the land. It is in this second use that many see the essence of Puerto Rican identity, in a state of romantic freedom connected to nature.

Coquí or the Jíbaro out of Context

The jíbaro, however, is not the only symbol of Puerto Rican national identity. Its role as central locus of this identity is equally shared by the coquí. The coquí, or Eleuterodactilus coquis, is a small brown frog that makes the distinctive sound "co-ki." Puerto Ricans are often taught that the coquí is unable to survive outside of Puerto Rico.[1] The idea of the coquí not being able to survive outside of Puerto Rico is parallel to the image of the Puerto Rican jíbaro struggling to survive the Puerto Rican Diaspora of 1950s.[2] Puerto Rican literature often portrays the jíbaro as a struggling individual when placed outside of his context as in the collection of vignettes *Spiks* by Pedro Juan Soto and implied in the poem *Boricua en la luna* by Antonio Corretjer. Doris Troutman Penn presents a diasporic coquí, named Pepe Coquí, in *La canción verde* (The Green Song.) In this short novel Pepe Coquí travels by plane to New York (where he even gets the key to the city) only to find out that he can only live in Puerto Rico. The coquí becomes then the zoomorphic representation of Puerto Ricaness, and, as in the case of the jíbaro, "the coquí forms part of an iconography of puertorriqueñidad. . .a symbol of cultural pride and nostalgia" (Goldman, 2004, p. 378).

Original for this text

Furthermore, tourists visiting Puerto Rico can purchase souvenirs of the tiny tree frog dressed as a jíbaro. When recognizing fellow Puerto Ricans outside the island—and occasionally inside the island—it is not uncommon to hear the phrase "yo soy de aquí como el coquí" (I'm from here, like the coquí).

Dressing the Jíbaro in Puerto Rican Literature

The first Puerto Rican authors to employ the term "jíbaro" were Antonio Vidarte with his 1844 poetry book *Aguinaldo puertorriqueño* (Puerto Rican Carol), and Miguel Alonso with his 1880 collection of vignettes *El gíbaro*. According to Antonio Pedreira (1970) there are two cycles of cultural production related to the jíbaro. In the first cycle of the nineteenth and early twentieth centuries the jíbaro emerges as the locus of Puerto Rican identity. The end of the nineteenth century marks a period of transition in Puerto Rico as the former Spanish colony is ceded to the United States as a result of the Spanish-American War of 1898. The jíbaro of this period was romanticized and "traditionalized" in Puerto Rican cultural production in part because of the dominant romantic zeitgeist of the nineteenth century. This appropriation can be traced to Puerto Rican intellectual elites. As Mary Cannizzo suggests (1955, p. 472) "[s]ince the nineteenth century, Puerto Rican writers have focused their creative interest on local and national manners and customs," the jíbaro being the subject of most of these writings. The focus on the peasant in the literary production of this period is neither accidental nor exclusive to Puerto Rican cultural production. Peasant life, after all, plays an integral part on the literature of the period internationally. The nineteenth century is the time of *costumbrismo*[3] and naturalism. In 1894 Manuel Zeno Gandía published the quintessential naturalistic novel *La charca* (The Pond), one in a series of four novels titled *Crónica de un pueblo enfermo* (Chronicle of a Diseased People). The naturalistic style of the work bluntly portrays the tragic life of the peasants and their dire conditions and total marginalization. It shows jíbaros as a group without cohesion, unable to act, and merely at the mercy of nature and an established social structure (Beauchamp, 1976, pp. 50–51). The jíbaros of La charca are described as physically drained, skinny and emaciated, with a languid appearance. The author makes it clear that their pain—a result of social injustice and abuse—is reflected on their faces and their bare feet, hardened by contact with the ground. Far from following dress

Figure 7.5 Wife and child of a jíbaro tobacco worker near Cidra, Puerto Rico. January 1938.

practices of those in Puerto Rico's urban areas, the jíbaros wore functional clothing to pick coffee beans. Women are described as wearing loose skirts with baskets attached to their waists and loose peasant-style blouses (see Figure 7.5). Men wore simple trousers and worked shirtless or wore sleeveless shirts and straw hats known as *pavas*.

These elements of jíbaro dress are essentially descendants of European peasant clothing. The jíbaro wardrobe shows very little influence from native pre-Columbian cultures such as the Tainos or from material creations of African slaves and their descendants.

The jíbaros dressed up for special occasions such as a dance. In *La charca* Zeno Gandía describes women wearing linen dresses in yellow or red with colorful ribbons, flowers or hairpins in their loose or braided hair. Men wore white shirts, working pants, starched white jackets, wide brimmed straw hats, and carried machetes in their hands, which the author indicates was used for labor, as support, and as a weapon—all in one. (See Figure 7.6.) An extraordinary luxury for the peasants was the use of any type of shoes; wearing them required an effort on their part due to the damaged conditions of their feet as a result of constantly walking barefoot. The author explains that they would carry their shoes to the dance and put them on upon arrival, not only to be comfortable during their walk but also as a way to protect the shoes from additional wear and tear as they were considered a special commodity.

Figure 7.6 Old jíbaro, patriarch of a clan of twenty-one tobacco hill farmers, Puerto Rico. January 1938.

A second cycle in literary production related to the jíbaro extended from the 1930s to the early 1950s. The early cycle had shown the effects of American colonization and the struggle of the *hacendados* (land owners) trying to maintain coffee plantations competitive against the American controlled sugar plantations. The second cycle emphasizes Puerto Rico's move toward industrialization and away from agriculture and in turn the burden on peasants struggling with the decision of staying in the countryside or emigrating to the city—first San Juan, then New York City—unprepared for either environment. Important literary creations of the period portraying jíbaros include *Terrazo* (1947) by Abelardo Díaz Alfaro, a collection of short stories, some dramatic and others comedic, describing the life of peasants in the mountain and sugar cane plantations; and René Marqués' *La carreta* (1951), a play about a peasant family dealing with the consequences of moving first to the capital San Juan and then to New York City. The most striking image of the jíbaro portrayed during this cycle, however, is in the 1937 song *Lamento borincano* (A Puerto Rican Peasant's Lament, also known *as El jibarito*) by Rafael Hernández. The lyrics capture "[the] island's socioeconomic plight during the Great Depression, the dismal conditions of the poverty-stricken jíbaro" (Acosta & Santiago, 2006, pp. 57–58). The song narrates the tale of a young peasant riding his mare to the city market, hopeful that he could sell his scant agricultural produce in order to support his family and buy a dress for his mother. The jibarito returns home empty handed, overwhelmed by sadness and hopelessness, lamenting his fate, and wondering what the future would bring to the country.

The most important change in jíbaro wardrobe during this cycle is the wearing of shoes on a daily basis, an indication of adapting to urban life and the abandonment of traditions. As the jíbaro peasants face further discrimination and challenges in the urban landscape due to their lack of preparation for the new environment, their clothing becomes a clear visual marker of their status as peasants, an image interpreted by the urbanites as reflecting a lack of education and manners. Dress functions as an indicator of the perceived and actual inequality of the jíbaro. These "urban" peasants learn quickly that in order to fit into their new landscape and avoid being labeled as "others," they must change their wardrobe and adapt their appearance to match the clothing styles of those in the city.

The Image of the Jíbaro as a Political and Cultural Commodity

It is during this second cycle of literary production that the jíbaro emerges as a political image in the logo of the Partido Popular Democrático de Puerto Rico (Democratic Popular Party of Puerto Rico). Founded by Luis Muñoz Marín in 1938, the party supports Puerto Rico's current political status as a commonwealth—some will argue, a colony—of the United States. The logo, designed in 1938 by Antonio I. Colorado, reads "Pan, Tierra y Libertad" (bread, land, and liberty) and includes the red silhouette of a jíbaro, wearing the pava, against a white background.[4] Although somewhat modernized, the logo is still in use. In the 1940s, Luis Muñoz Marín used a political campaign photo with a superimposed image of a jíbaro. The populist leader made the countryside his stomping ground and was in direct contact with poor peasants, emphasizing his connection with them. The image of the disadvantaged, impoverished jíbaro became—in the hands of politicians—a tool to denounce class inequality in Puerto Rico. The clothing of the jíbaro, by extension, acquires a new meaning in the political arena, becoming a symbol of inequality.

There are also canonic representations of the jíbaro in visual arts. *El velorio* (The Wake) (1893) by Francisco Oller is an oil on canvas painting depicting the wake of a child or *baquiné*. The scene shows the interior of a jíbaro mountain house where children and adults attending the wake join in dance, song, and prayer. The child's corpse rests on top of a table covered with white linens and wears a crown made out of flowers. Men are depicted barefoot, wearing long pants, and long sleeve shirts. Women are painted wearing solid color long dresses cinched at the waistline with full skirts and blouses with short sleeves and low necklines. The 1905 painting, *El pan nuestro* (Our Bread), by Ramón Frade, depicts an old jíbaro man on a mountain trail carrying a plantain cluster. The iconic character wears mid-calf mustard color trousers, a white collarless long sleeve shirt, and a wide-brim straw hat. Like any other typical jíbaro depiction, the painting would not be complete without the traditional machete tied around the waist. These quintessential paintings have become the most widely accepted visual images of jíbaro dress. It can be assumed that the pieces do depict some basic elements of jíbaro clothing observed firsthand by the artists, just as the literary cannon probably contains descriptions based on the authors' observation of primary sources.

Jíbaros depicted in these two paintings or described in literature, however, have little in common with the modern costumes used in folkloric performances where men wear bright white ensembles with colorful sashes and handkerchiefs around their necks and women use low-cut peasant blouses and full flounced skirts in bright solid colors or prints with lace embellishments. This cleaned-up, colorful version—partially inspired by both European peasant and fashionable dress—romanticizes jíbaros and ignores the poverty conditions that dominated their lives. As a matter of fact, jíbaros never had a characteristic form of dress and did not imitate Spanish dress. As in many similar cases in Latin America and around the world, a romanticized version of the peasantry has been frozen in time and adopted as a national symbol. In the case of dress traditions, this version of the peasants' appearance has been turned into the national costume of several countries. This adoption of appearance often ignores the lower status of the population that purportedly originated this dress and pays little attention to the inequalities of which they were or are still victims. Dress practices that were born out of a struggle for survival and a necessity for hard labor are cleaned up, embellished with some elegant detailing and brighter colors, and proudly claimed as authentic national dress. The Puerto Rican government actually created Law No. 21 in 1983, defining parameters for representative dress of Puerto Rico. The law provides guidelines for materials, silhouette, construction, color, embellishments, and accessories of female dress. There

are no penalties for not constructing a garment accurately except that it shall not be considered representative.

Rebecca Earle explains: "In Europe, national dress, and 'national culture' more broadly, often derived from a romanticized vision of a folk culture rooted in the land and exemplified by the peasantry" (2007, p. 64). In nineteenth-century Spanish America, according to Earle, national dress played a part in the process of nation-formation. The elites did not trust indigenous and mixed-race populations but considered peasant culture acceptable. They regarded peasant dress as the basis for national dress as it held connections to white European groups even though indigenous dress was widely seen as the clear marker of regional variations (Earle, 2007, p. 68).

Mattel's 1997 Puerto Rican Barbie also features the approved national dress. The doll is a light-skinned mulatta with long, dark, and wavy hair and brown eyes. She wears a white cotton dress with lace ruffles and a pink ribbon. Her features and dress were criticized for the lack of representation of Puerto Ricans as a mixed race, including the pale and tattered historic jíbaras. The box describes the dress in the doll's voice asking: "Like the special white dress I am wearing? It is very typical of a dress I might wear to a festival or a party." The elaborate costume was never worn by a peasant in any visual record and it resembles more a Spanish colonial dress than any other style ever worn in Puerto Rico. It includes lace—a very expensive material that only wealthy women could purchase during the first part of the century—and accessories such as white high heels, earrings, and a ring, none of which would have been worn by the impoverished white peasants.

As discussed earlier, most traditional costumes in Latin America are creolized variations of Spanish dress and are a product of fantasy and aesthetic synthesis. Thus the dress that should reflect the misfortunes and pain of the working rural classes is transformed into a symbol of national pride, ignoring the historic disadvantaged conditions of the groups that purportedly originated it. The romantic nationalism of the nineteenth century idealized peasant life as genuine and invented a timeless context where unchanging "traditional" dress was said to come from, making it "authentic." Already in 1953, after a competition to select a representative Puerto Rican "regional dress," the cultural critic Nilita Vientós Gastón denounced the existence of any such costume and argued that any creation could only be a product of fantasy. Through time, however, this dress has come to be known and accepted not only as authentic but also as unchanging. The connection with the dress of jíbaro peasants is rarely questioned and the "national costume" has contributed to the elaboration of a national myth that ignores the political and economic struggles of peasants in Puerto Rico. Negrón-Muntaner adds: "The main irony of this identification, particularly for future generations, is that the elites fashioned national identity as a simulacrum—technically dead but symbolically alive, like a doll" (2004, p. 219).

The Cyber-jíbaro: Another Cycle, Another Migration

Digital manifestations of the jíbaro abound on the World Wide Web. Zeno Gandía, Frade, Laguerre, and other authors and painters worked toward a representation of the jíbaro on the page, the canvas, and the stage but they did this from the point of view of an observant; they did not consider themselves jíbaros. They wrote or painted the Other. The latest representations of the jíbaro—those in cyberspace—differ in one significant element: the cyber-jíbaros are individuals who choose to represent themselves through the image of the jíbaro regardless of their respective agendas. These cyber-jíbaros construct a postmodern identity from a pastiche of possibilities using elements of dress—whether jíbaro or not—to create said identity.

Orlando Vázquez, for instance, hosts and writes the website Don Jíbaro, the purpose Vázquez explains, is to celebrate "the humble Puerto Rican campesino [sic], the one that makes mistakes but seeks resiliently to bounce back without missing a beat. He learns from his errors and will not allow history to repeat itself on him." He further explains that Don Jíbaro Barbanegra is his nom de plume, adopted to conceal his civil identity, presumably not his physical identity as the website has multiple pictures of Vázquez, sometimes of him as a twenty-something-year-old musician, and other times posing as Neo, the lead character played by Keanu Reeves in the blockbuster movie franchise The Matrix or, thanks to digital manipulation, flanked by iconic figures such as Alfred E. Neuman (the kid from MAD magazine).

Throughout the website Vázquez usually sports a guayabera and occasionally a Panama hat, clothing items associated with a landowner, the historic antagonist of the jíbaro. As it was told by the costumbrista writers, the relationship between landowners and jíbaros was similar to feudalism; peasants were allowed to live in the

hacendados land in exchange for labor. Eventually, with the distancing powers of time, many Puerto Ricans—including people who could perhaps be considered jíbaros—adopted the guayabera. The guayabera, the official Cuban national costume since 1935, is one of the most important symbols of cultural heritage among Cuban expatriates around the world. Once more, a piece of clothing not related historically or socially to the jíbaro is appropriated to create a recognizable image. Don Jíbaro, writing from exile, maintains a physical appearance somewhat associated with the traditional jíbaro, but uninformed readers of his website might assume that Don Jíbaro looks and acts like an "actual" jíbaro.

Another example of a cyber-jíbaro is that of Genoveva Baños, the character name of an actress for hire at www.lajibara.com. She wears a costume associated with the jíbara—a full skirt made out of a vivid flower print, a flounced bright red or white top, a purple bead necklace, gold bracelets, a flower on her hair, and occasionally, a red-hair wig—but it differs from the guidelines stipulated by Law 21 of 1983 which calls for white fabric and little embellishment. Her cyber-identity is built using imagery popularly acknowledged and accepted as jíbaro. Like Vázquez she appropriates an image that does not correspond to her reality outside from her acting. For Don Jíbaro and Genoveva Baños the jíbaro solidifies a connection with Puerto Rico and their own national selves. Both individuals adopt visual elements closely related to the jíbaro; yet at the same time they both distance themselves from the jíbaro characters of the Puerto Rican literary canon. Unlike Silvina, the tragic heroine of La charca, Genoveva is in charge of her time, space, and business.

The cyber-jíbaros are urban and/or write from exile, they do not handle the tools of the farm, but can handle the tools of the Web. Their wardrobe is postmodern and may include elements of the original jíbaro wardrobe (a straw hat) but also may appropriate symbols of other cultures (Cuban guayabera), objects from completely unrelated worlds (the Matrix coat), or as with Genoveva alterations of a sanctioned traditional dress.

Conclusion

Jíbaro culture remains intrinsic to Puerto Rican identity. Jíbaro traditions are continued in a number of ways. The image of the jíbaro is a malleable commodity responding to the cultural, social, and political context in which it is framed. Jíbaro dress has been used in different ways throughout history to communicate changing ideas of identity and ethnicity. The meaning and material culture of jíbaro dress, therefore, has been reinvented and appropriated in different ways, as needed, by singular groups including intellectuals, politicians, and diaspora emigrants. The social reality of the deprived jíbaros can be embraced or ignored while appropriating jíbaro dress. At any rate, jíbaro identity seems to be a process, not an essential characteristic. Stuart Hall (1994) believes that cultural identity is a matter of "becoming" not "being." The cultural identity of the jíbaro is an example of what Hall argues is a cultural product in constant transformation, an identity that belongs to the future as much as to the past, transcending place, time, history, and culture. Material culture objects associated to ethnic identity—such as "traditional" or "national" dress—can be traditions that are invented or re-invented by those belonging or claiming to belong to an ethnic group—even in the case of Puerto Rico where a traditional dress (at least for women) is sanctioned by law. Michael Fischer (1986), among others, sees ethnicity as reinvented and reinterpreted in each generation by each individual and not simply passed from one generation to another. Jíbaro dress, although regarded as traditional and authentic by many or even by law is susceptible to forces that have changed—and will continue changing—not just its form but also its meaning.

Notes

1. Ironically, the frog was able not only to survive, but also to proliferate on some Hawaiian Islands where it has no romantic meaning and is considered a nuisance. It is believed that the coquí was accidentally transported to Hawaii from Puerto Rico on plants and soil and there are concerted efforts to eradicate the species.
2. The Puerto Rican diaspora refers to the mass migration of Puerto Ricans to the United States. It is popularly associated with migration to New York but as Carmen Teresa Whalen and Víctor Vázquez-Hernández (2005) point out, the Puerto Rican diaspora reached as far as Hawaii and included the cities of Boston, Chicago, and Philadelphia, among others. This mass migration was facilitated by the colonial relationship between the United States and Puerto Rico and it was, at times, sponsored by the U.S. government.
3. *Costumbrismo* refers to a nineteenth-century literary tradition in which artists paid close attention to the costumes and manners of a region and/or social group, often from a Hispanic country. It is closely related to realism and tends toward a faithful representation of the folkloric without interpretation.
4. "Historia del Partido Popular Democrático," Partido Popular Democrático, accessed February 16, 2011, http://ppdpr.net/info/. It should also be mentioned that The Partido Popular Democrático de Puerto Rico is also known as the PPD and as "La pava," in direct reference to its logo.

References

Acosta-Belé, E. & Santiago C. E. (2006). *Puerto Ricans in the United States: A contemporary portrait*. Boulder, CO: Lynne Rienner Publishers.

Babín, M. T. (1963). Prologue to R. Marqués *La carreta*. Río Piedras, Puerto Rico: Editorial Cultural.

Beauchamp, J. J. (1976). *Imagen del puertorriqueño en la novela*: En Alejandro Tapiay Rivera, Manuel Zeno Gandía y Enrique A. Laguerre. San Juan, Puerto Rico: Editorial Universitaria.

Brameld, T. (1959). *The remaking of a culture: Life and education in Puerto Rico*. New York: Harper & Brothers.

Cannizzo, M. (1955). The article of manners and customs in Puerto Rico. *Hispania*, 38(4), 472–475.

Coquigrams Inc. (2007). La jíbara. Retrieved March 20, 2010, from http://www.lajibara.com

Earle, R. (2007). Nationalism and national dress in Spanish America. In M. Roces & L. Edwards (Eds.), *The politics of dress in Asia and the Americas* (pp. 63–81). Brighton, Australia: Sussex.

Fischer, M. M. J. (1986). Ethnicity and the post-modern arts of memory. In J. Clifford & G. E. Marcus (Eds.), *Writing culture: The poetics and politics of ethnography* (pp. 194–233). Berkeley: University of California Press.

Goldman, D. E. (2004). Virtual islands: The reterritorialization of Puerto Rican spatiality in cyberspace. *Hispanic Review*, 72(3), 375–400.

González, J. L. (1987). *El país de cuatro pisos y otros ensayos*. Río Piedras, Puerto Rico: Ediciones Huracán.

Guerra, L. (1998). *Popular expression and national identity in Puerto Rico: The struggle for self, community, and nation*. Gainesville, FL: Univ. Press of Florida.

Hall, S. (1994). Cultural identity and diaspora. In P. Williams & L. Chrisman (Eds.), *Colonial discourse and post-colonial theory: A reader* (pp. 392–401). London: Harvester Wheatsheaf.

Negrón-Muntaner, F. (2004). *Boricua pop: Puerto Ricans and the Latinization of American culture*. New York: New York Univ. Press.

Pedreira, A. S. (1970). La actualidad del jíbaro. In L. F. Negrón García & C. López Baralt (Eds.), *Obras de Antonio S. Pedreira* (pp. 652–703). San Juan, Puerto Rico: Instituto de Cultura Puertorriqueña.

Rak, J. (2005). The digital queer: Weblogs and Internet identity. *Biography*, 28(1), 166–182.

Silén, J. A. (1971). *We, the Puerto Rican people: A story of oppression and resistance* (C. Belfrage, Trans). New York: Monthly Review Press.

Torres-Robles, C. L. (1999). La mitificación y desmitificación del jíbaro como símbolo de la identidad nacional puertorriqueña. *Bilingual Review*, 24(3), 241–253.

Vázquez, O. (2001). Don Jíbaro's Jibaros.com. Retrieved March 20, 2010, from http://www.jibaros.com

Vientós Gastón, N. (1962). El traje típico puertorriqueño. *Indice cultural* (Vol. 1). Río Piedras, Puerto Rico: Ediciones de la Universidad de Puerto Rico.

Whalen, C. T. & V. Vázquez-Hernández (Eds.). (2005). *The Puerto Rican diaspora: Historical perspectives*. Philadelphia: Temple University Press.

Discussion Questions

1. What does the term jíbaro mean?
2. What aspects of their dress represents ethnic identity?
3. How did the dress evolve into a nation costume for Puerto Rico? Can you think of other items of dress that have made similar transitions?

[handwritten note: Barbie did not portray Puerto Rican dress accurately]

7.3
Cultural Markers in Dress: Decoding Meanings and Motivations of College Students
Veena Chattaraman

The millennium began with talks about the changing ethnic and racial composition of the United States and how cultural diversity will increase over the coming decades. A decade into the millennium, and these predictions are revealed as facts. U.S. demographic evidence from cities, towns, and even rural areas documents that cultural pluralism is an all-pervasive phenomenon in the U.S. and is here to stay. Within this pluralist context, where racial and ethnic differences vary in their external visibility, due to color of skin, language, neighborhood, and other factors—dress serves as an important visibility factor in externalizing cultural pluralism. Beyond externalizing ethnicity, dress as visual communication also facilitates the construction and maintenance of cultural identities among diverse subgroups in the populations and becomes the critical locus for realizing the cultural self. The purpose of this paper is to decode the social meanings and motivations attached to the use of cultural markers in dress among college-aged multicultural students.

The paper employed a qualitative strategy of inquiry through an open-ended survey conducted among a convenience sample of 106 male and female students belonging to minority ethnic groups, who were enrolled at a large Midwestern university. A college campus provided the right setting for the research questions examined in this paper since it represents a truly diverse and pluralist environment, where self-expression in thought, dress and appearance is encouraged, and where a diversity of clothing styles coexist. Four ethnic groups were represented in the sample: Asian or Asian American (55.7%); Black or African American (20.8%); Hispanic or Latino (5.7%); American Indian (1.9%); and Others, chiefly biracial (16%). The mean age in the sample was approximately 25 years and a majority of the participants

---

Original for this text.

was female (77.4%). A majority of the participants, reported owning cultural dress (69.8%), of which 67% reported wearing cultural dress in casual occasions, 79% reported wearing cultural dress for ethnic celebrations and festivals, and 64.8% reported wearing cultural dress for non-ethnic special occasions. The open-ended data provided by the respondents addressed two questions: (1) what does wearing ethnic or ethnic inspired items of dress mean to you? (2) when you use ethnic or ethnic-inspired items of dress, what emotions do you tend to feel? Participant responses were content-analyzed to identify underlying thematic meanings and motivations in the use of cultural dress.

Cultural Dress: Themes

Cultural Connection and Belonging

This was an important theme that repeatedly surfaced in participant responses while identifying the meanings ascribed to wearing cultural dress. The college students articulated that they used cultural dress to form, express, or sustain cultural connections and belonging to the culture, ancestry, or the ethnic group. Some students expressed using cultural dress for both the self and for communicating to others. The following statement articulates this theme:

"It shows that I have a sense of culture that I enjoy and am willing to share with others."

Others expressed using cultural dress to showcase cultural support:

"Belonging to my culture. . .showing support for Asian Awareness."

Some students used phrases such as "feel rooted" and "sense of nativeness" when discussing their relationship with cultural dress. A majority perceived that they could create a meaningful bond with their culture by wearing cultural dress:

"It creates for me a strong sense of belonging and a closeness to my people and culture."

"It makes me feel as if I belong. I belong to a specific group that no one else does."

"Going back to my roots, gives me that connection with my ethnicity which is not there in daily life."

"Culturally connected to my ancestors."

"I feel good, and comfortable. Especially when I go to certain events involving people from my ethnic group, I feel like that is where I belong."

Cultural Pride and Celebration

A closely related theme to the above and one that was equally mentioned by the multicultural participants was the demonstration of cultural pride through wearing cultural dress. Respondents emphasized pride in the accomplishments of the culture, their nationality, and respect for the struggle of their ancestors. The following quotes illustrate this theme:

"Adorning the cultural dress reminds me of my heritage and the pride of all the accomplishments made and the ancestors who made it possible. This gives me great PRIDE!"

"I respect my own country, pride."

"I feel very prideful, to think of what my ancestors went through so that I could live here in America. . . .I also, hold on to the past, and link it to the future. . . .I feel, proud, happy, strong."

Respondents also remarked on their feelings of pride or moderated pride in their cultural dress. One of the respondents interestingly noted that he/she did not feel too proud, rather grateful that his/her ethnicity "has decent traditional clothes." Others were more emphatic in their expression of pride in their dress:

"Proud and beautiful, truly like a nubian queen—from earrings to a formal, dress."

"I feel pride in the ethnic-dress of my country. . . .It gives me a sense of belonging to a rich heritage and tradition."

"My ethnic dress is the most beautiful in the world. . . .I used to feel that I became a special person. I try to behave very calm and elegant when I wear my ethnic costume."

Some respondents linked the sense of pride in cultural achievement to external celebration of the culture represented through cultural dress. For example, participants used phrases such as the following in discussing their emotions on wearing of cultural dress: "special, joyous, celebrated."

Identity, Expression, and Distinctiveness

Stryker and Serpe (1982) define identities as "reflexively applied cognitions in the form of answers to the question 'Who am I?'" (p. 206). This definition applies to personal or role identities. Ethnic identity on the other hand, is a group identity, and has been defined as the shared identity of a group of people based on a common historical background, ancestry and knowledge of identifying symbolic elements such as nationality, religious affiliation and language (Forney & Rabolt, 1985–86). Respondents voiced that cultural dress serves to express both their personal identity and group identity. The following statement from a respondent well-reflects both these dimensions of identity: "It means knowing WHO I am and WHO I represent."

"It means respecting my heritage and background. I do not usually wear ethnic dress, so when I do, it is a special occasion and I feel that I should remember where I came from because it is part of who I am."

"That identify with the traditions and customs of my culture."

"It's a representation of who I am."

Some respondents perceived that wearing cultural dress went beyond personal self-expression and expressed stories of the group's cultural history, and served to initiate cultural education. The following quotes illustrate these complex themes of identity and expression:

"It tells a story of all the goals accomplished and the trials and tribulations they had to go through for us."

"I feel that it is a good way to inspire others to learn about other cultures and ask questions."

Another important sub-theme that emerged in the context of identity is distinctiveness. Distinctiveness is defined as an individual's numeric (minority status) or social traits that are distinct in relation to the environment (McGuire, 1984). Being persistently different from the reference group's ethnicity, makes the ethnic identity salient or important in a person's self-concept (McGuire & McGuire, 1981). Numerous respondents voiced the theme of distinctiveness either from a personal or a group perspective in using cultural dress to externalize differences from the mainstream. To some respondents, this externalization of ethnic difference was a way to reject assimilation into the mainstream culture and maintain and strengthen linkages with the ethnic culture. The following quotes from two respondent capture the deep personal and social struggles involved with their display of cultural distinctiveness through dress:

"It means to me that as an African, wearing clothing that can allow others to identify me as an African even if it is just one article of clothing sets me apart from other people. I feel complete and whole as an

individual but I also become alienated from others and I become categorized and classified in negative ways. I have been discriminated against because my clothes made my ethnicity identifiable to others. Ethnic inspired items are also a way of expressing my rejection of assimilation and maintaining my own unique ethnic identity."

"When I wear ethnic clothing/items I feel complete, whole and satisfied. When I dress in clothes that are too mainstream and not ethnic, I feel distressed, dissatisfied and uncomfortable. I am so used to standing out and being recognized because of my ethnic dress that when I wear mainstream clothing I feel like I am betraying my identity and myself. Also, when I do not wear ethnic dress I become alienated and feel unwelcome in my own ethnic community. After living in a non-ethnic relatively homogenous environment and having to make the difficult choice of assimilating or not I had to make a choice and I chose not to assimilate by wearing my ethnic dress. Living in an environment where I felt alienated caused me to have emotions such as feeling shame about my culture because it was not 'normal' and dressing in ethnic inspired dress solidified my status in society as alien and not 'normal' and that I can never possibly be 'normal' because of my ethnic dress. I believe this has emotionally caused me to become a stronger person and has allowed me to make a clear definition of what my identity is."

Some respondents experienced feelings of enjoyment in being distinct for more personal and hedonic reasons. They enjoyed being able to "show off" their distinctiveness and the attention it brought them. The following quotes illustrate these perceptions:

"I like feeling unique and having a sense of heritage, while knowing I can be fashionable because I accept what I wear."

"I have some cute items that I picked up when I was in China and Hong Kong a couple of summers ago, and I think it's kind of cool to have something obviously from another country. They're kind of like souveneirs that I can show off."

"I love wearing them. It's fun and different from everyday jeans and t-shirts."

Other respondents experienced feelings of pride in the distinctiveness they achieved through cultural dress:

"I'm proud of being dressed differently than others"
   "I feel that I am unique and it shows a side of me that I am very proud of."

There was also a small group of respondents who did not want to externalize their distinctiveness from the mainstream culture due to lack of attachment with cultural dress, discomfort and self-consciousness:

"I am not really attached to our ethnic costume. When I wear the costume, I feel differently. but it is not because I am really proud of my culture or something. I like it and think it is pretty, nothing more than that."
   "Distinctive. Uncomfortable for having to wear something that I never wear."
   "More self-conscious."

Thus, distinctiveness revealed itself as a complex theme, laden with emotion, and reflecting both the positive and negative voices of respondents. Since cultural dress serves as a visible marker of ethnicity, the maintenance of a distinctive cultural identity lies at the heart of understanding multicultural college students' motivations to wear cultural dress.

Conclusion

This study suggests that a majority of multicultural college students own and wear cultural dress, and also associate deep, positive meanings and emotions with this act of dress. The qualitative strategy of enquiry employed in this study revealed three important themes reflecting the social meanings and motivations attached to the use of cultural markers in dress among college students. The first theme labeled "cultural connection and belonging" addressed the use of cultural dress to form, express, or sustain meaningful bonds with the culture, ancestry, and the ethnic group. The motivations behind this expression through dress were for both, the "cultural self" of the individual, and for communicating the "cultural self" to others. This communication was perceived as a form of in-group support. The second theme labeled "cultural pride and celebration" addressed the use of cultural dress to demonstrate pride in the accomplishments of the culture, nationality, and respect for the struggle of ancestors. This theme also addressed pride in the beauty and uniqueness of the cultural artifact of dress, which was recognized for its ability to transform the wearer. The third theme labeled "identity, expression, and distinctiveness" was a critical theme in understanding the deeper motivations

underlying the use of cultural markers in dress. This theme addressed the use of cultural dress to express both personal and group identity. With respect to the latter, cultural dress was viewed as expression of the group's cultural history, and as a facilitator of cultural education. This theme also addressed the use of cultural dress as an externalization of ethnic difference. For some, this was a way to reject assimilation into the mainstream culture and maintain and strengthen linkages with the ethnic culture. For others, ethnic distinctiveness was either a source of enjoyment and pride, or a source of self-consciousness and discomfort.

In summary, social meanings and motivations attached with the use of cultural markers in dress are thematically similar and yet varied with respect to the undertones and perspectives that the respondent raised. Decoding these meanings and motivations is important in a multicultural society to better understand, communicate and uphold cultural pluralism.

References

Forney, J. & Rabolt, N. (1985–86). Ethnic identity: Its relationship to ethnic and contemporary dress. *Clothing and Textiles Research Journal, 4*(2), 1–8.

McGuire, W. J., & McGuire, C. V. (1981). The spontaneous-self-construct as affected by personal distinctiveness. In M. D. Lynch, A. A. Norem-Hebeisen, & K. J. Gergen (Eds.), *Self-concept: Advances in theory and research* (pp. 147–171). Cambridge, MA: Ballinger.

McGuire, William (1984). Search for the self: Going beyond self-esteem and the reactive self. In R. A. Zucker, J. Aronoft, & A. T. Rabin (Eds.), *Personality and the Prediction of Behavior* (pp. 73–120). New York: Academic Press.

Stryker, S., & Serpe, R. T. (1982). Commitment, identity salience, and role behavior: Theory and research example. In W. Ickes and E. Knowles (Eds.), *Personality, Roles and Social Behavior* (pp. 199–218). New York: Springer-Verlag.

Discussion Questions

1. Of the themes the author identifies, which one do you identify with, if you wear ethnic or ethnic-inspired clothing?

2. What does the author mean when she writes "social meanings and motivations attached with the use of cultural marker sin dress are thematically similar yet varied"?

7.4
The Modern Chola: Indigeneity, Gender, and Global Fashion in Bolivia

Christine Beaule

Scholars have written extensively about gender as a socially constructed identity (Butler 2003; Joyce 2005). Joyce writes of the body as a scene of display, where gender and other identities are enacted and performed by agents who choose to adopt, modify, or subvert their societies' norms through bodily modification and dress. Clothing is one common way in which one's identity is created and enacted by individual agents, and gender identification within a person's cultural context is reflected through clothing choices. This chapter contributes to a more complex understanding of how clothing embodies gender, by exploring the related social axes of indigeneity, race and class in the globalized contexts of international tourism and high fashion by analyzing Peruvian women's pollera, Andean market women's ethnic dress, and high-end versions of these found on runways. These examples illustrate Butler's point that gender 'is an identity tenuously constituted in time' (2003: 97). The examples included in this chapter, taken from various cultural contexts and periods of Andean history, collectively suggest that ethnic and other social identities (e.g., Aymara, wealthy tourist, or global elite) intersect with the construction of gender in ways that are historically and culturally constituted.

Beautiful Indians

On a cold winter evening in July 2016, I stood on a sidewalk fronting the historic Plaza de Armas in Cuzco, Peru chatting with an indigenous Quechua *chola* (urban market vendor) selling candy, cigarettes and water. I asked *Señora* Josefina (a pseudonym) about the store across the street from her cart, which marketed high-end llama and alpaca scarves, shawls, and sweaters to the thousands of international tourists that visit Cuzco each year, usually as part of a Machu Picchu tour. This particular store featured a series of eye-catching and colorful posters depicting indigenous women wearing the clothing that identifies them as members of the indigenous Quechua

ethnicity (Figure 7.7). Photos of Quechua women wearing colorfully embroidered *polleras* (multi-layered skirts), lacy *mantillas* (shawls) over blouses, and ethnically diverse hat styles appear on postcards, prints, mugs, small figures and dolls, and countless advertisements luring tourists from abroad to the highland Andes. Indeed Josefina wore exactly the same set of garments that made her a living symbol of indigenous Peru: for the foreigners around her, she was both a symbol of the living Inka (via their Quechua descendants) and an exotic 'other' with whom they could buy a bit of cross-cultural interaction.

Figure 7.7 Poster advertising Quechua indigenous heritage in Cuzco boutique that sells alpaca clothing to tourists (left); Aymara chola in Oruro, Bolivia open-air market (right).

Original for this text

As an anthropological archaeologist who has worked in the central and southern Andes for two decades, the contrast between a *chola* making a living by selling small sweets on the street, and the sanitized and professionally produced advertisements in the adjacent storefront, was quite striking. Highland Andean indigenous peoples have had a long and complex history in nations such as Peru since conquest and incorporation by the Inka Empire (ca. AD 1425–1533) then under the Spanish as part of the construction of a far flung colonial empire. Since achieving independence from Spain in the 1820s, Latin America has struggled to build coherent nation-states that integrate people of vastly different linguistic, cultural, and socioeconomic backgrounds. For centuries, indigenous peoples in the Americas were lumped together as *indios* (Indians), a term dating back to Christopher Columbus' mistaken conclusion that the inhabitants of Hispaniola (now Haiti and the Dominican Republic), were actually part of India. *Indio* is a derogatory term in the Andes associated with dirtiness, stupidity, and laziness (Van Vleet 2005: 109). Although the Bolivian state, for example, has not used the term since the 1952 national reforms, replacing *indios* with *campesinos* (peasants), there persists 'an ideological and institutional separation between the "modern nation" and the "indian nation"' (Van Vleet 2005: 111).

The last century has seen a boom in domestic and international tourism that has been especially influential in Peru, where a series of civilizations culminating in the Inka left magnificent archaeological sites, now exploited by a well-developed tourism infrastructure throughout much of the highlands and Pacific coast, as well as the Amazonian lowlands to the east. Many indigenous communities have found ways to take part in the economic opportunities offered by tourism, from street vendors to owners of tour agencies. But for Quechua women in particular, they sometimes serve as both agents and subjects of international tourism – some dress in brightly colored versions of indigenous clothing and, together with a lamb or llama, offer to take photos with tourists for a small fee. Others dress *de pollera* (in the clothing described above) in order to attract customers because they know that foreigners have come to expect 'real Indians' to dress accordingly.

The irony lies in the contradiction between the 'real Indian' selling candy from a sidewalk stall and the counterpart depicted in the boutique's advertisements. Both are *de pollera* but a closer look reveals the deceptive nature of the latter. As Van Vleet (2005:111) writes, 'hands and feet as well as clothing and shoes, are signifiers of class and race as well as gender.' Josefina's wind-chapped cheeks, hands and dirty fingernails, as well as calloused feet clad in rubber sandals, belie her poverty. The indigenous women in the store's advertisements, in contrast, have pale complexions, smooth skin, and well-cared for, white smiles (when their faces are visible at all). They, and the alpacas also featured in the posters, were posed in beautiful mountain locations or clean rooms in cottage-industry or factory spinning and weaving facilities, empty of people and trash alike. These were the sanitized, idealized, and romantic locales that make for the ideal photographic memento, free of obvious signs of poverty, racism, and pollution, all social problems that fall disproportionately on indigenous communities' shoulders.

During our conversation, I asked Señora Josefina about how she felt about the use of indigenous Quechua women as exotic symbols of Peru's past. She replied that it made her happy that her country thought Quechua women like her were beautiful, and it helped bring many tourists to places like Cuzco to visit the sites once inhabited by her Inkan ancestors (she made the direct genealogical connection). She added that the tourist who bought bottled drinks, candy, and cigarettes from her helped her to cover the compulsory costs associated with sending her children to a public school in Peru, including uniforms and school supplies. But when I pointed to the posters in the windows of the high-end boutique in front of us selling expensive versions of clothing more suited to Americans' and Europeans' urban tastes, her response shifted. Señora Josefina indicated that these fashionable re-imaginings of indigenous women's clothes were unimportant ('A nosotras no nos importan'). The women in those advertisements were not *runa* (a Quechua term of self-identification as indigenous or, literally, real person), she insisted, because their skin, hands, and teeth were those of white women. For this Cuzqueña *chola*, she felt greater cultural affiliation with the Inka of 500 years ago than the women in the advertisements.

Cholas as Racial and Gendered Citizens

The term 'cholas' describes vendors in a wide range of circumstances, from the poorest unlicensed *ambulantes* walking the streets with their small wares, to wealthier women with permanent stalls in open-air markets, and even those successful enough to inhabit an urban storefront. Although many wear familiar Western dress (straight skirts or sweatpants, t-shirts or blouses, and low pumps or canvas slip-on sneakers), dressing *de pollera* imparts a colorful atmosphere to Andean cities. In Cuenca, Ecuador, cholas wear white straw hats and huge felt skirts in brilliant shades of orange and pink. Cuzqueña *cholas* wear 'tall white hats, big skirts, and flashing earrings, while Bolivians recognize a *chola paceña* (from La Paz) by the little bowler hat that sits rakishly atop her head' (Weismantel 2001: xxv).

But *cholas* are far from universally treasured. The label describes a racial category between Indian and white; *cholas* are considered racially inferior by elites, vulnerable to sexual harassment and even rape, and associated with racial connotations of dirtiness, laziness, promiscuity and stupidity. First, precisely because they inhabit urban markets and sidewalks, *cholas* are Indians out of their place (rural indigenous villages and towns). Indeed the widespread linguistic replacement of *indio* with *campesinos* cemented this association of indigenous peoples with rural peasants. Secondly, precisely because they are businesswomen working outside the home, they fall far short of the Colonial social ideal of *marianismo*. *Marianismo* is an imposed Spanish Colonial ideal stemming from the Catholic Virgin Mary, 'with all the accompanying expectations of motherhood and protection of feminine honor' (Bigenho 2005: 65–66). Chaste, self-sacrificing mothers do not profit by selling vegetables, unaccompanied by husbands, in a public city market.

Weismantel (2001: xxvii) writes, 'With its power to slander, the word *chola* is not a careless pleasantry, as local men pretend; nor is it just a colorful phrase when used by poets, or a value-free ethnic category when employed by social scientists.' The label *chola* redirects attention from women's economic activities (as market vendors) onto their bodies, and this in turn shapes the state's position toward them. Politicians who promise to 'clean up the markets' rarely do so through infrastructural improvements to modernize these areas where most city residents buy food and other household sundries. Instead, the ever-present trash, half-starved dogs, rotting food scraps, and petty crime are thought to emanate directly from the 'dirty Indians who work there, rather than from systematic neglect of these critical centers of everyday commerce' (2001: xxvii). To return to Señora Josefina in Cuzco's Plaza de Armas, her dirty hands and feet are thought to result from her innate unwholesomeness, rather than from the absence of facilities where she might use the restroom, wash up, or seek shelter from the biting cold highland winds. The women depicted in the boutique's posters, on the other hand, suffer no such indignities. They are photographed outside their homes and without their children, but in their 'proper place' (the open countryside). Their morality is communicated effectively through clean hands, faces and clothing. They, unlike Josefina, can represent the nation and symbolize national pride in Peru's glorious Prehispanic past.

Dressing the Part

Unlike the wearer's gender or race, clothing is something that can be put on and taken off. Fashion is, in this sense, performative (Van Vleet 2005: 119). Two brief examples illustrate how indigenous Andean women themselves make use of the performative nature of the *pollera*. Marisa is a teenager who buys *polleras* for the week-long celebration of Carnavál in Bolivia that takes place each February, even though she wears pants on a daily basis. She is one of thousands of *cholitas* in Bolivia, teenage girls who migrate for work or school to the cities, who return to their families' villages for this iconic national holiday. Although new *polleras* can cost $60 to $80 each, Marisa will try to purchase or borrow a new one for each of the seven days of dancing, along with the eyelet blouses, lace slips, bowler hats, shawls and slip-on shoes that are necessary elements of a complete *runa p'acha* (Quechua for human or Indian dress) outfit. Van Vleet (2005: 116–119) argues that conspicuous consumption demonstrate Marisa's belonging to the modern Bolivian nation through the consumption and display of commodities. Along with speaking Spanish, getting more education, and living in an urban environment with electricity, running water, and cement floors, new *pollera* outfits communicate one's material success. The consumption of clothing, she asserts, is one way that Sullk'ata (Marisa's indigenous community) youths 'experience the possibilities and constraints of their own "belongingness" in Bolivia at the turn of the 21st century' (2005: 108). As a young woman, Marisa grew up seeing images of idealized *cholas* everywhere, those symbols of national motherhood, chastity, a glorious Inkan past, and nationally treasured beauty. Although she may not experience the reverence afforded idealized *cholas* in postcards and tourist brochures, she enjoys the relationships that come from sometimes dressing *de pollera* and sometimes in secondhand Western clothing (2005: 118). Both are performative practices that allow her to mimic either a successful Bolivian indigenous woman, or a modern, middle-class, educated and thoroughly Westernized urban teenager.

Zorn (2005: 115–116) argues, moreover, that dressing *de pollera* is critical to the maintenance of ethnic identity. Her work with the Sakaka *ayllu* (indigenous community) of northern Potosí, Bolivia indicates that the nearly 21,000 Sakaka who wear distinctive daily dress that is both handmade and hand embroidered do so to consciously mark 'a division between clothed indigenous humans, or *runa*, and naked foreign outsiders, *q'ara*. (This interpretation coincides with but reverses ethnocentrism between Indians and non-Indians.)' The term *q'ara´* translates as 'peeled', as in a bare animal hide; those not dressed in *runa p'acha* are, by definition, not indigenous and, in this sense, not fully human. Zorn continues, 'To dress is to be: *de pollera* (Indian or *cholita*) versus *de vestido* (*mestiza* [mixed-blood] or white)' (2005: 118). Displaying and reinforcing one's belongingness in an indigenous community in the highland Andes is to continue a millennia-old tradition in the region that values expertly handwoven and decorated textiles as the highest art form. Indeed, *chola* dress is among the most expensive in the Andes. Dressing *de pollera* is thus an investment of time and scarce resources, and a statement about the value of being *runa*.

A second example comes from Bigenho's research on single female folklore singers in La Paz in the 1940s. *Peñas* are folklore shows popular with both urban Bolivians and tourists, where the audience is treated to a variety of traditional ethnic music and dances. In the 1940s, it was socially acceptable for single women to perform only in specified contexts (*peñas* and programs broadcast on Radio Illimani, the national radio station), and their careers were commonly cut short by marriage and children. The subjects of Bigenho's work called themselves 'pioneers', a concept tied to both rural landscapes and being agents that helped to transform something marginalized and despised (indigenous music and bodies) into something today treasured by urban *mestizo*-creoles (people of mixed indigenous and Spanish blood, as many Andeans conceive of their national identities) (Bigenho 2005: 66). For the *peña* singers themselves, their *pollera* costumes symbolized material success. However in the 1940s, 'this form of dress represented the indigeneity they were bringing into the service of a mestizo-creole nationalist culture' (2005: 73). Older women might return to the stage wearing ponchos, an item of clothing strongly associated with men on horseback, and so scandalous for an unmarried young woman to wear (2005: 73). Together with their use of the indigenous languages of Quechua and Aymara in their performances, these *mestiza* (mixed-blood and urban) singers identified strongly with the Indian costumes, music, and the landscapes about which they sang in 'a multisensorial portrayal of indigeneity.' The picture of mixed-blood urban young women performing (rural) indigeneity in shows meant to evoke nationalist pride in their mestizo-creole audiences is a fascinating one. Bigenho is right that these singers' stories 'signal the incredible degree to which indigeneity has become the lens through which many mestizo-creoles feel themselves to be Bolivian' (2005: 75).

In both of these examples, we see a performative process of donning a specific set of clothing in order to foster national pride and unity around a socially constructed idea about Bolivia's indigenous heritage. Whether in *peñas* or to dance in Carnavál, indigenous and *mestiza* women alike read the *pollera* in distinct ways: as signs of material success, and as conscious attempts to evoke feelings of pride in Bolivia's prehistoric past and its rich cultural tapestry today. But both folklore shows and Carnavál represent tightly controlled contexts for performing indigeneity, ones that are in many ways far removed from the daily struggles of *cholas* like Señora Josefina selling candy in Cuzco.

International Fashion

The cultural appropriation of indigenous clothing and art in modern designers' collections is nothing new, but the examples in this section offer an important contrast in the ways that indigeneity impact and are impacted by that appropriation. The first example comes from designer Prabal Gurung. Inspired by the Mustang region of Nepal where he comes from, Gurung's fall 2014 collection used deep oranges and reds to deliberately evoke the saffron-hued robes of Buddhist monks (see slideshow at mobile. nytimes.com/slideshow/2015/09/13/t-magazine/prabal-gurung-spring-summer-2016/s/13tmag-sceneprabal-slide-U5VU.html?_r=0&refer=). Cashmere wraps, high-necked and long-sleeved gowns, and flowing chiffon skirts marry Nepalese cultural inferences with thoroughly modern garment forms for elite First World customers (jugnistyle.com/fashion/prabal-gurungs-nepal-inspired-fall-2014-collection-is-beautiful/). This designer has had his work worn by the likes of Michelle Obama and Kate Middleton, but only first showed it in the Indian subcontinent in 2016 because, in his words:

'[India] wasn't ready for anyone's clothes. Let's be honest. India as a market is extremely price conscious. . .the market for high-end luxury designers is only really starting to take off now. As a result, patrons too are evolving. They're no longer seeking validation by the brands they're carrying. It's no longer about loud logos, but rather, a more muted, understated display of luxury' (elle.in/fashion/news/prabal-gurung-talks-to-us-before-his-first-trunk-show-in-india/).

Prabal Gurung's cultural inspirations give way to the expectations of an international luxury fashion market, in which everything from the settings (e.g., Mumbai's Le Mill, New York's Fashion Week) to the models (none of whom appear to be Nepalese peasants or Buddhist monks) fit the socially-constructed expectations of a global elite.

Elite consumers in the Andes travel to those same meccas of fashion, but trunk shows of less-pricey versions are starting to appear in Latin American capitals as well. Eliana Paco Paredes is a Bolivian designer of indigenous Aymara descent whose collection was recently featured at both Bolivia's Fashion Week and New York's Fashion Week. Unlike Gurung, Paco Paredes' outfits retain traditional garment forms, including *polleras*, derby or *bolero* hats, *mantilla* shawls, and blouses (Figure 7.8). But the materials, colors, and embroidered designs on the skirts and shawls are less traditional. For example, fitted blouses and skirts are of a single shade, while lace and jewels may adorn the blouse's neckline and shawl. Thus the combination of garments and their basic forms are wholly indigenous. An article published by Agencia EFE (www.efe.com/efe/english/life/the-elegance-of-bolivian-cholitas-reaches-big-apple/50000263-2940765) notes La Paz's municipal 2013 law recognizing the *chola* as 'an intangible cultural heritage,' and the Aymara woman as 'the most comprehensive personification of the Indian-mestizo amalgam, which since colonial times has maintained indestructible components of identity and individuality.' Paco Paredes has sold her designs to indigenous women in her La Paz store Diseños Esmerelda for many years, but her inclusion in New York's Fashion Week introduced the *chola* to new international audiences. It remains to be seen whether her designs' strict adherence to form is maintained for a non-Bolivian audience, or whether those indigenous and nationally-treasured cultural references become more subtle, as they are in Prabal Gurung's designs. The contrast between the two collections – one

employing color and drape lifted from a region of Nepal, and the representing high-end but more literal borrowings from indigenous Bolivia – serve as two ends of a continuum of indigenous cultural influences in high fashion collections. Paco Paredes' indigenous Aymara heritage, and the national pride expressed in the Bolivian media over her participation in New York's Fashion Week, will likely counteract pressure to experiment too freely with the *pollera/mantilla/bolero* combination or garment forms in the same ways that Gurung does.

Gurung and Paco Paredes are two designers whose participation in the high-end fashion industry reflect a peculiar brand of global modernity. Slade's (2009: 12) examination of Japanese modernity and fashion theory illuminates the relationship between sartorial borrowing from the past in a thoroughly modern form of conspicuous consumption. He characterizes this borrowing from the past as 'a type of exoticism, replacing the appeal of the geographically far away with that of the temporally far away. Resurrecting old forms and investing them with fresh significance and value as emblems of a past whose worth and moment has been newly clarified and

Figure 7.8 Eliana Paco Paredes, a Bolivian Aymara designer, brings "cholita fashion" to an international community (Bolivia Fashion Week 2016, photos by Andrés Herbas).

acknowledged is an essential, though mainly reactionary, facet of fashion.' Much of the Japanese civil war period predating the Restoration was, Slade writes, 'a violent manifestation of the difficulty of accepting a new means of identity-framing' (13), one based on time (modern versus feudal Japan) rather than region. This closely parallels the inherent conflict in the sartorial presentation of *de pollera* at New York's Fashion Week or, to a lesser extent, baby alpaca shawls as modernized *mantillas*. Eliana Paco Paredes, more than her counterparts in Cuzco's high-end tourist boutiques, offers some cultural context (albeit superficially and sanitized) for her collection.

Framed as 'an astonishing debauchery of efforts to produce a minimum of garments' (Slade 2009: 11), fashion's ability to take consumption to new heights of effort and expense signify both the luxurious excesses of a global elite and the extent to which modernity highlights continual efforts to remake the past and/or present into something new and exciting. Efforts to counteract the need for continual reinvention, sometimes spearheaded by the very states whose capitalist economic structures made vast wealth inequalities possible, are almost inevitable. In pedagogical manuals for rural and urban Bolivian girls' schools in the 1920s and 1930s, the state saw the fashion industry as epitomizing 'the negative side of modernity because it appealed to women's "irrational" nature to consume voraciously' (Stephenson 1999: 6). Bolivian girls were instead encouraged to focus on personal hygiene as a way to instill patriarchal values based on bodily and household management. Similarly, the *bunad* is a closely controlled festive folk costume that symbolizes rural Norwegian identity (Hylland Eriksen 2012: 258). Although it was invented by nationalist activist Hulda Garborg in 1905 just after Norway gained independence from Sweden, the *bunad*'s specific decorative reference to the wearer's particular regional origins or place of residence is 'an important, traditionalist symbol of modern Norwegianness.' The Bunad and Folk Costume Council and strong public opinion limit the wearer to particular *bunad* styles associated with her place of birth, childhood or current residence. In doing so through a folk costume however, the *bunad* 'confirms Norwegian identity as an essentially rural one, where personal integrity is connected to roots and rural origins' (Hylland Eriksen 2012: 258).

Both the formal Bunad and Folk Costume Council and the Bolivian pedagogical manuals emphasizing social restrictions on sartorial experimentation by women are examples of the social construction of gendered norms. Both also illustrate a pushback against the playfulness inherent in the vast choices available to wealthy elite women. Although it would be highly unlikely that elite Norwegian and Bolivian women would choose expensive *bunads* or *polleras* for everyday wear, their wealth allows them to purchase clothing with playful references to other cultures that are simultaneously divorced from the violent, racist histories experienced by the 'real' women in those cultures. The clothing choices available to Gurung's and Paco Paredes' clients represents, in this sense, the essence of modernity.

Moreover, it is unsurprising that the targets of Norway's and Bolivia's social and state-supported control over dress should be women. Van Vleet (2005: 113) explains that because of indigenous Bolivian men's seasonal migration to the cities or eastern lowlands (as seasonal agricultural laborers), men have greater access to commodities, including cash, and so are considered 'more advanced' than their wives. Women, because of their more limited mobility, are thus considered more indigenous, and so it is women who are both the subjects of romanticized depictions of the Andean countryside and the subjects of campaigns to control their clothing choices. Like the Norwegian *bunad*, dressing *de pollera* is a statement of ethnicity and adherence to tradition for urban *cholas* and rural indigenous women. They wear *polleras* as 'a visible symbol of resistance that exemplifies the many struggles lived out each day for indigenous and *chola* women who deliberately refuse to be "refashioned"' (Stephenson 1999: 5). For a wealthy New Yorker or Parisian consumer, in contrast, costly versions of these garments are potentially exciting additions to one's wardrobe that signal one's global modernity. Elements of indigenous clothing from Bolivia, Norway and elsewhere can thus be recycled and reimagined in the continually shifting world of international fashion.

Discussion

How does such refashioning impact indigenous women themselves? Standing outside the Cuzco boutique advertising a romantic Peruvian countryside but selling alpaca wraps and straight skirts, Señora Josefina dismissed it as unimportant to her sense of identity. This is probably because the shop's wares bear little resemblance to real *cholas*' outfits, instead more closely resembling Prabal Gurung's saffron-hued gowns and wraps. On the other hand, Eliana Paco Paredes's collections, like Norwegian *bunads*, aim to celebrate and preserve distinctive local cultural traditions. Even when marketed to an international audience, they maintain local guidelines of garment construction, decorations and combinations of clothing items. Local celebrations of Bolivian and Norwegian cultural heritage do shape outsiders' ideas about 'authentic' cultural traditions, but there seems to be little demand to take home a *bunad* or *pollera* for everyday wear.

The *pollera* does, however, offer indigenous women a strong political and economic statement. Despite its association with Indians, Andean women wear them as 'a visible symbol of resistance' to real daily struggles for upward mobility and respect (Stephenson 1999: 5). Dressing *de pollera* also offers savvy vendors a tool to attract potential customers. Increasing numbers of young *cholas* who achieve upward mobility through a university education choose to dress *de pollera* in the markets because these have long been the domain of indigenous women. Thus the *chola* outfit becomes a statement of ethnic identification that may simultaneously serve the women's entrepreneurial strategies in building successful small business (Scarborough 2010). Even in contexts in which wearing a bulky layered skirt might hinder their movements, *cholas* choose to dress *de pollera* instead of *de vestido*. Tourists in Bolivia's capital are invited to attend Cholita Wrestling matches in the vast black market of El Alto, the Aymara capital city perched on the cliff overlooking La Paz. Modeled after the U.S.'s World Wrestling Foundation and Mexico's *lucha libre* ('free fight'), Cholita Wrestling features Aymara women in *polleras* wrestling each other and their male counterparts clad in spandex wrestling costumes and face masks (www .lapazlife.com/places/cholita-wrestling-in-la-paz). Clearly the *pollera* is fundamental to Andean indigeneity and women's ethnic identities.

Perhaps this is why it would take more than the availability of cheaper Western-style straight skirts and dresses to lure *cholas* away from the *pollera*. The *pollera* may retain strong associations with motherhood and colonial social ideals of *marianismo*, but real *cholas* also associate it with business opportunities and cultural pride. The latter is supported by national media's celebration of the *chola* as a cultural treasure, whether depicted on postcards or fashion shows. Although the bulky layered skirts and otherwise unfashionable *bolero* hats generally do not appeal to the globalized elites of the fashion industry, there is little sign that Andean consumers prone to dress *de pollera* will switch to the slimming straight skirts of Westernized elites. Similarly, lacy *mantilla* shawls only seem to appeal to tourists when transformed into a cashmere or alpaca wrap.

The widespread availability of these garments in both high-end boutiques and in city markets may offer *cholas* a chance to modernize their images. But even when given the choice to dress *de vestido* in straight skirts and Western tops, indigenous Andean women often choose the more costly *pollera* outfit as a political statement or to dress the part in the indigenous-dominated world of Latin American markets. Participating as business women, as an internationally-featured fashion designer, or even as a professional wrestler, these thoroughly modern women use *polleras* to help redefine the modern *chola*. Their choices support academic arguments that clothing is one way that agency is embodied within specific cultural and historical contexts, and that ethnicity, race, class and gender are performed by social agents through their bodies and dress. *Señora* Josefina was correct: expensive alpaca wraps marketed to tourists using photos of *cholas* in *polleras* do not seem to matter much to women like her. Rather, whatever independence, status and power she may achieve within her community stem from her success as a business woman with a stall in the prestigious Plaza de Armas, not from her ability to choose to dress *de vestido*. In fact, choosing to dress *de pollera* reinforces the modern *chola*'s educational and business successes, and thus her femininity.

References

Bigenho, Michelle (2005), 'Making music safe for the nation: Folklore pioneers in Bolivian indigenismo,' in Andrew Canessa (ed.), *Natives Making Nation: Gender, Indigeneity, and the State in the Andes*, Tucson: University of Arizona Press, pp. 60–80.

Butler, Judith (2003), 'Perfomative acts and gender constitution: An essay in phenomenology and feminist theory,' in Philip Auslander (ed.), *Performance: Critical Concepts in Literary and Cultural Studies* (Volume IV), London: Routledge, pp. 97–110.

Canessa, Andrew (2004), 'Reproducing racism: Schooling and race in highland Bolivia,' *Race, Ethnicity and Education*, 7:2, pp. 185–204.

Hylland Eriksen, Thomas (2012), 'Dress between the sacred and the commercial: The case of the Norwegian bunad,' in Kimberly A. Miller-Spillman, Andrew Reilly, and Patricia Hunt-Hurst (eds.), *The Meanings of Dress* (3rd edition), New York: Fairchild Books, pp. 257–264.

Joyce, Rosemary (2005), 'Archaeology of the body,' *Annual Review of Anthropology*, 34, pp. 139–158.

Scarborough, Isabel M. (2010), 'Two generations of Bolivian female vendors,' *Ethnology*, 49:2, pp. 87–104.

Slade, Toby (2010), *Japanese Fashion: A Cultural History*, New York: Bloomsbury Academic.

Stephenson, Marcia (1999), *Gender and Modernity in Andean Bolivia*, Austin: University of Texas Press.

Van Vleet, Krista (2005), 'Dancing on the borderlands: Girls (re)fashioning national belonging in the Andes,' in Andrew Canessa (ed.), *Natives Making Nation: Gender, Indigeneity, and the State in the Andes*, Tucson: University of Arizona Press, pp. 107–129.

Weismantel, Mary (2001), *Cholas and Pishtacos: Stories of Race and Sex in the Andes*, Chicago: The University of Chicago Press.

Zorn, Elayne (2005), 'Dressed to kill: The embroidered fashion industry of the Sakaka of highland Bolivia,' in Regina A. Root (ed.), *The Latin American Fashion Industry*, New York: Berg Publishers, pp. 114–141.

Discussion Questions

1. Do you believe an item can only be ethnically authentic if it is produced by its own people?
2. How can culture be copyrighted?
3. Is glamorizing a culture (as in the case of the tourist ads in this article) an acceptable form of practice?

CHAPTER 8
DRESS AND RELIGION
Kimberly A. Miller-Spillman

After you have read this chapter, you will understand:

- **Examples of dress in different religions**
- **How ideology in religion may be reflected through dress**
- **How morality and sexuality are reflected through religious dress**
- **Dress as a material artifact that mirrors change in religions**

This chapter focuses on the meanings of dress within several religions. Specifically, the readings at the end of this chapter address issues of dress in Christianity (including Amish and Latter Day Saints), Judaism, Islam, and Sikhism.

Membership in a religious group is not always associated with a particular style of dress. For example, in the United States, many Roman Catholics and Protestants wear the equivalent of work dress to worship at church. Other religious groups use dress to differentiate and set themselves apart from others in the larger society or surrounding world. The readings for this chapter have been chosen to illustrate how and why religious dress symbolizes the values and beliefs of religious organizations. Dress is examined for its ability to promote social stability within religious organizations and resist the rapid style changes associated with the contemporary fashion process of materialistic society.

IDEOLOGY AND DRESS

To understand religious dress, the cultural context of a religious group must be considered. For example, each of the religions included in this chapter has dominant ideologies that guide decisions about dress. Ideology is a set of ideas that do not hold up under the rigors of scientific investigation and that support the interest of dominant groups (Ferrante, 1995). For instance, dress within Christianity is based in large part on the story of Adam and Eve in the Garden of Eden; therefore, modesty should be a goal in dress. Judaism is based on the philosophy that individuals exist to glorify God; therefore, to be well-dressed is a religious duty. Islamic philosophy promotes the separation of the sexes, as do Mennonite beliefs. Sikhism is a monotheistic religion originally from India. Sikhs (pronounced seeks) emphasize faith and meditation, unity of all mankind, and engaging in selfless service. Male Sikh dress is similar to the dress of Islamic men who wear a turban and a long beard (see Figure 8.1) resulting in sporadic hate crimes toward

Figure 8.1 Sikh man wears a turban and beard which correspond to Sikhism articles of faith.

Sikhs mistaken as Muslims (see reading "Sikhs: Religious Minority Target of Hate Crimes"). Amish have distinct clothing for the purpose of keeping them separate from the larger society. Latter Day Saints (Mormons) wear a temple garment under their clothing to remind them of their special commitments to their faith. In many religions, women's bodies must be covered in public and their movements within society are highly restricted and carefully controlled by male family members.

WHAT IS RELIGION?

Religion is a set of beliefs, symbols, and practices that is based on the idea of the sacred and unites believers in a socioreligious community (Marshall, 1994). **Sacred** refers to that which people define as extraordinary, inspiring a sense of awe and reverence. Contrasted to the sacred is the **profane** or that which is considered an ordinary element of everyday life. **Monotheism** is a belief in a single God (e.g., Islam, Judaism, and Christianity), whereas **polytheism** is a belief in many gods (e.g., Buddhism, Hinduism, Confucianism, Taoism, and Shintoism) (Marshall, 1994). Christianity, Judaism, and Islam are often referred to as world religions.

Monotheistic Religions

Christianity, which includes Catholicism, Protestantism, and the Anabaptists (including the Amish and Mormons), handed down a code of morals from early times, including strict rules about clothing. Early Christian teachings stress the link between the outward appearance of the body and the state of the person's soul (Ribeiro, 1986). One reading in this chapter examines the influence of Christian religious beliefs on appearance. For example, the Amish wear garments that keep them separate from the larger world while Mormons wear an undergarment (called a temple garment) so they may influence those in the larger society (see reading "Amish and Mormon Sacred Dress").

Islam is based on the principle of submission to Allah, or God. Its holy texts are the Koran and the Hadith (or sayings of the Prophet). Islam pays special attention to the status and clothing of women (Marshall, 1994). Although there are no specific injunctions or rules in the Koran regarding veiling, women are believed to have sexual powers that may tempt males (Ribeiro, 1986). Therefore, many Islamic women veil their faces and cover their heads, hair, necks, and bodies to a greater or lesser extent. Some Islamic women do not veil at all and are indistinguishable in a group of Western women. The type and extent of veiling of women varies greatly from one Islamic nation and from one group to another, depending on the nature of their beliefs and the political context in which they live (see Figure 8.2). For example, in the reading "Fashion and Gender in the Middle East," Christina Lindholm describes Islamic men's and women's interest in fashion and the difficulty in defining the Middle East. It may come as a surprise to some that there is a lot of ambiguity in Islam, including a lack of consensus on which countries are included in the Middle East and which countries are not. However, after reading this article, you will understand men's and women's interest in fashion and why Lindholm says there is no "one size fits all" in this area of the world.

Judaism originated in prophesies about the God Yahweh. Jewish religious knowledge is founded in the Torah, the first five books of the Hebrew Bible (corresponding to the Christian Old Testament; Macionis, 1996). As with other religions, Jewish beliefs vary from liberal to highly conservative interpretations.

Figure 8.2 Young Muslim women dress stylishly while remaining true to their faith.

Figure 8.3 Orthodox Jewish men in traditional dress.

"Conservative" Jews are actually less strict than Orthodox (although more so than Reformed). For instance, men who follow Orthodox tradition wear black hats, trousers, and jackets and white shirts (see Figure 8.3).

Women who follow Orthodox Jewish tradition wear wigs in public from the time of their marriage. Covering their head with wigs ensures their modesty under Orthodox interpretation of Jewish law, while allowing them to visually fit into mainstream U.S. culture (Hayt, 1997). This desire of Jews to assimilate into U.S. culture was undoubtedly colored by the French government's decision in October 1940 to enforce the Nazi order that all Jews wear the Jewish star on their outer clothing. Given the history of Jewish persecution by Nazi Germany, it is little wonder why Jews want to blend in rather than stand out and be identified as Jews.

Polytheistic Religions

Two examples of polytheistic religion include Buddhism and Hinduism. **Buddhism** is an Indian religion that originated 2,500 years ago. *Buhdi* means "to awaken" and Buddha, the founder of the religion in 566 B.C., was enlightened (to receive spiritual or intellectual insight) at the age of 35. Buddhism is an old and complex religion that includes the concept of karma. Karma is the law that every action has an effect on the self and on others. Buddhism stresses mindfulness of one's actions and effects of those actions. Buddhism also stresses that material possessions do not bring happiness; happiness can only come from within.

Hinduism, also an Indian religion, is unique from Christianity, Judaism, and Islam in that it does not have a founding member, nor is there one text or scripture that unites its members. Rather, Hinduism is a combination of South Asian and Western beliefs. Prominent themes in Hindu beliefs include (but are not restricted to) dharma (morals/ethics/duties), samsara (the continuing cycle of birth, life, death, and rebirth), and karma (action and subsequent reaction). In Hinduism, a sadhu or holy man is a wandering monk whose lifestyle is characterized by abstinence from worldly pleasures in order to pursue the fourth and final stage of life. A sadhu's life can include meditation, yoga, and body painting.

Dress and Religious Fundamentalism

Fundamentalism is a conservative religious doctrine that opposes intellectualism and worldly accommodation in favor of restoring traditional, otherworldly religion (Macionis, 1996). Fundamentalism is a more complex phenomenon than popular conceptions would lead people to believe. First, a fundamentalist cannot be stereotyped by gender, age, race, ethnicity, social class, or political ideology. Second, fundamentalists are characterized by a belief that a relationship with God, Allah, or some other supernatural force provides answers to personal and social problems (Ferrante, 1995). Third, fundamentalists do not differentiate between the sacred and the profane in their everyday lives. All areas of their lives, including work, family, and leisure, are governed by religious principles.

Fourth, fundamentalists want to reverse the trend toward gender equality, which they believe is symptomatic of a declining moral order (Ferrante, 1995). Fundamentalists often believe the correct ordering of priorities in life requires subordinating women's rights to the concerns of the larger group and the well-being of the society, such as the "traditional" family.

Readings in this chapter discuss dress and religious fundamentalism because it is often within these groups that dress practices widely diverge from the majority. Why is control of dress, particularly for women, frequently a component of fundamentalist beliefs? Fundamentalist religious groups have often emerged after a perceived threat or crisis—real or imagined. Any discussion of a particular fundamentalist group must include some

Figure 8.4 The Amish are an example of a group that was persecuted and maintains dress that encourages separation from mainstream society.

reference to an adversary. Dress, then, can be linked to a way of expressing group solidarity as well as indicating opposition to the general culture. See Figure 8.4.

Dress acts as a visible symbol for the precepts of fundamentalism, including the fact that religious principles govern all aspects of the fundamentalists' lives (including dress) and that women's roles are frequently more "traditional" with individual needs and beliefs relinquished to the greater good of the family and religious group. This leaves fundamentalists open to criticism by feminists regarding the oppression of women by the patriarchal nature of many fundamentalist groups.

Patriarchy refers to cultural beliefs and values that give higher prestige to men than to women (Newman, 1995). Women's roles as wives, mothers, and supporters of the faith may be seen as important, but men are given priority or exclusive rights to govern and hold power in the group. Patriarchy has been regarded as a form of social organization and has been considered, particularly by feminists, as an undifferentiated theory to explain the whole of human history (Grimshaw, 1986):

> Patriarchy is itself the prevailing religion of the entire planet. . . . All of the so-called religions legitimating patriarchy are mere sects subsumed under its vast umbrella/canopy. . . . All—from buddhism and hinduism to islam, judaism, christianity—to secular derivatives such as freudianism, marxism and maoism—are infrastructures of the edifice of patriarchy (Daly, 1990).

Agency is a concept used by feminists to describe the resistance women use to combat patriarchy. Boynton-Arthur (1993) describes the agencies (i.e., the various forms of resistance) women in one Holdeman Mennonite community use in subverting the strict dress codes dictated by male ministers and deacons. Boynton-Arthur describes the daily process of subtle changes in dress that give women an opportunity to express themselves creatively. Agency can be found in the reading "Amish and Mormon Sacred Dress" (at the end of this chapter). For example, breaking the rules where clothing is concerned is often the first step in changing the rules for women's dress.

Dress, Religion, and Morality

Common themes can be identified among the articles included in this chapter. One theme is **modesty** and its relationship to morality in religious beliefs. Some Christians, Jews, and Muslims have rules about covering parts of the body that might be seen as having sexual connotations, such as hair, neck, breasts, arms, and legs. Women are frequently targets of modesty rules, and certain religious groups feel that **morality** is maintained through the behavior of women, including their dress. Although not part of all religions, beliefs are held by some religions that regard female sexuality as dangerous if left unharnessed and uncontrolled (Fernea & Fernea, 1995). These beliefs lead to the religious practice of prescribing modest and proper dress for female members.

For an Orthodox Jewish woman to be properly dressed, she must cover her hair after marriage (Hayt, 1997). This practice helps women to avoid expressing sexuality outside marriage. Holdeman Mennonite women must also cover their head and hair (Boynton-Arthur, 1993). The starched cap represents an Amish woman's humility to God and her resistance to worldly possessions. Submissiveness to her God, her community, and her husband is also symbolized by her head covering. Among Muslim women, the burka covers the entire body (with a mesh area for the eyes) (see Figure 8.5).

Covering body curves appears to be somewhat less of an issue for Mennonite women than for Islamic women. Compare Figures 8.5 and 8.6 and examine the differences in Mennonite (Christian) and Islamic dress for women. The evolution of silhouettes shown in Figure 8.6 indicates that an unmarried Mennonite woman can emphasize body curves more than an Orthodox woman.

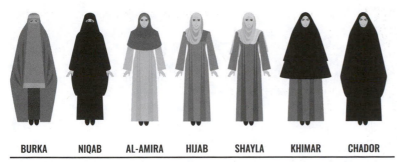

| BURKA | NIQAB | AL-AMIRA | HIJAB | SHAYLA | KHIMAR | CHADOR |

Figure 8.5 Islamic women's dress choices that communicate modesty.

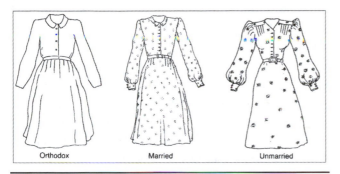

Orthodox   Married   Unmarried

Figure 8.6 Dresses worn by Holdeman Mennonite women express both a religious affiliation and status (i.e., orthodox, married, and unmarried) within the group.

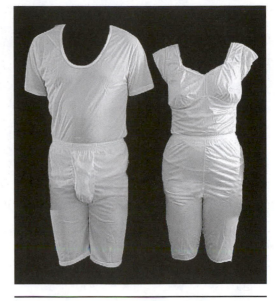

Figure 8.7 A temple garment is worn by both male and female Mormons to prompt them to remember the commitments they have made to their faith.

Religious Dress and Social Change

Although changes in dress occur with much less frequency among the religious than the general population, forces of social, economic, and political change do influence sacred dress, as discussed in this chapter. Among the Amish, change most often occurs when church governance fails to take action when a suspected violation is reported. Amish teenage girls experiment with dress by dressing *English* when traveling in a group to a bar (see "Amish and Mormon Sacred Dress"). Mormons report that the temple garment has undergone changes over time (see Figure 8.7). The temple garment began in 1843 as an unbleached muslin garment with sleeves to the wrists and legs to the ankles. Today the temple garment covers the leg to the top of the knee and covers the top of the upper arm (see reading "Amish and Mormon Sacred Dress" at the end of this chapter).

Social class can also be expressed through religious dress. For example, Mormons wear a temple garment so they may easily interact with others in the greater society. Mormons want to influence society and understand that any clothing that stands out may hurt their chances of achieving this goal.

Summary

This chapter covers examples of dress in different religions. Specifically, the articles in this chapter address issues of dress in Christianity (including Amish and Latter Day Saints), Islam, and Sikhism. Ideology reflects the beliefs of cultures that justify particular social arrangements (Marshall, 1994); these beliefs are reflected in religious dress. Several themes (e.g., morality, sexuality, patriarchy, and agency) were identified in this discussion of religious dress. Lastly, religious dress as a material artifact mirrors changes in religion that often coincide with changes in the greater society or culture. Dress within religious groups illustrates an apparent relationship between social stability and resistance to rapid style changes associated with fashion.

Key Terms

Agency	Hinduism	Modesty	Polytheism
Buddhism	Ideology	Monotheism	Profane
Christianity	Islam	Morality	Religion
Fundamentalism	Judaism	Patriarchy	Sacred

Learning Activity 8.1

RELIGIONS' RULES FOR DRESS

Objective

To learn about dress within a previously unfamiliar religion

Interview

Interview someone who believes in a religious ideology with which you are unfamiliar. Consider religions (or faiths) of which you have little or no knowledge. Use the internet to determine whom you could interview. Depending on your background, you may want to consider interviewing someone belonging to one of the following faiths:

- Amish
- Buddhist
- Catholic priest or nun
- Greek orthodox priest
- Hindu
- Jewish rabbi (or layperson)
- Mennonite
- Mormon
- Muslim

Develop five or six questions about religion and dress for your interview. You may want to know about specific dress items you have seen in the media but did not understand. You may want to ask general questions about how dress is used during formal ceremonies (and by whom) compared to how a religious observer might dress on a daily basis. Other possible questions include: How is dress used in rituals of the faith? How does the dress of clergy (or religious leaders/teachers) compare to the dress of the worshipper?

After conducting the interview, share your information in small groups or during a class discussion. Or invite those interviewed to serve on a "religion panel" during class. Each speaker could be allowed 10 to 15 minutes to discuss dress within his or her own religion.

Learning Activity 8.2

TEACHERS AND RELIGIOUS GARB

Objective

To learn about rules that apply to teachers who want to wear religious dress to work.

Procedure

In the United States, the focus in schools is proper attire for students. But what about teachers who want to wear religious garb to school? Read the following article:

Kiracofe, C. (2010). "Can Teachers Really Wear That to School? Religious Garb in Public Classrooms." *The Clearing House*, 83: 80–83.

After reading the article, have an online or a face-to-face discussion with your classmates about the article and its primary points.

CASUAL DRESS IN CHURCH

Objective

To learn about the reasons people give for dressing casually to go to church/worship.

Procedure

In the United States, churchgoers have begun dressing casually for church. Does this type of dress behavior have something to do with a person's lack of respect for the church and for God? Or, is it better to be at church in casual dress than not going to church at all?

Read the following article:

Blake, John. (2014, April 19). *Stop Dressing Tacky for Church*. Retrieved on April 15, 2018, from religion.blogs.cnn.com/2014/04/19/stop-dressing-so-tacky-for-church/.

After reading the article, address these questions:

1. What are the reasons given for dressing casually for church?
2. What reasons are given for dressing up for church?
3. Who are the two groups of people mentioned in the article that still dress up?
4. Do you agree that casual dress is an indication of a lack of respect for the church and the God you worship?

Have an online or a face-to-face discussion with your classmates about the article and its primary points.

References

Boynton-Arthur, L. (1993), "Clothing, Control, and Women's Agency: The Mitigation of Patriarchal Power," in S. Fisher and K. Davis (eds.), *Negotiating at the Margins*, 66–84, New Brunswick, NJ: Rutgers University Press.

Daly, M. (1990), *Gyn/ecology: The Metaethics of Radical Feminism*, Boston: Beacon Press.

Fernea, E. W. and R. A. Fernea (1995), "Symbolizing Roles: Behind the Veil," in M. E. Roach-Higgins, J. B. Eicher and K. K. P. Johnson (eds.), *Dress and Identity*, 285–292, New York: Fairchild Books.

Ferrante, J. (1995), *Sociology: A Global Perspective*, Belmont, CA: Wadsworth Publishing Co.

Grimshaw, J. (1986), *Philosophy and Feminist Thinking*, Minneapolis: University of Minnesota Press.

Hayt, E. (1997, April 27). For Stylish Orthodox Women, Wigs That Aren't Wiggy. *New York Times*, 43, 48.

Macionis, J. J. (1996), *Society: The Basics* (3rd ed.), Upper Saddle River, NJ: Prentice Hall.

Marshall, G. (ed.) (1994), *The Concise Oxford Dictionary of Sociology*, Oxford: Oxford University Press.

Newman, D. (1995), *Sociology: Exploring the Architecture of Everyday Life*. Thousand Oaks, CA: Pine Forge Press.

Ribeiro, A. (1986), *Dress and Morality*, London: Batsford Press.

8.1
Amish and Mormon Sacred Dress
Jana M. Hawley and Jean A. Hamilton

Introduction

Amish and the Mormons both wear sacred everyday dress, yet both have distinctly unique belief systems that affect how they interact with outsiders which then influences the sacred dress they have adopted. Both the Amish and the Latter Day Saints (LDS or Mormons) are commonly misunderstood minority groups who have been persecuted throughout their histories. To understand their sacred dress, we must explain the history, theory, and culture of each group.

Amish and Mormon Cultural Contexts

Amish History, Theology, and Culture

The Amish are a Christian-based group whose core values focus on being separate from the world with commitment to tradition, family, and community. As an outgrowth of the 16th century Swiss Anabaptist movement, the Amish began migrating to the United States in the early 18th century, and settled initially in the area of Lancaster County, Pennsylvania. By the 19th century, disagreement regarding the issue of *strict* verses *loose* discipline resulted in small groups of Amish leaving Pennsylvania and establishing new communities across the United States (Hostetler, 1980). The Amish population has doubled every 22 years and now number approximately 308,000 across 31 states, three Canadian provinces, and in South America (Amish Studies: The Young Center, 2016).

Amish theology. The Amish favor a number of principles grounded in particular scriptures. These include:

a) the authority of scriptures in matters of faith as well as action;
b) the rejection of violence, and
c) the separation of the Amish from the dominant society in which they live.

Additionally, the Amish adopted the use of plain clothes, headcoverings, and beards for adult men.

Particular scriptures from the Bible shaped Amish perspective. Romans 12:2, "Be ye not conformed to this world," and Corinthians 6:14, "Be you not unequally yoked together with unbelievers: for what fellowship hath righteousness with unrighteousness?" provide context that have informed Amish culture. Additionally, the *Martyr's Mirror,* while not scripture *per se,* continues to hold a place of honor in most Amish homes. It contains chronicles, memorials, and testimonies of the persecutions suffered by Amish forbearers and serves as a constant reminder of the days of their most severe persecution.

Amish Culture. Fundamental to Amish culture is a commitment to family and community, a reliance on the authority of local Church leaders for regulating individual behavior, high value on individual humility (as opposed to pride), and stewardship (rather than greed). Other Amish values include a strong work ethic, thrift, a reverence for longstanding tradition, a willingness to share resources with those who have more need, and a commitment to an agricultural lifestyle. These values promote community and family togetherness and oppose acceptance of the dominant cultural system. Their work patterns become a ritual part of their daily lives; thus they view labor-saving technologies as threats to their cultural system (Kraybill, 1989).

The fundamental rules that operate within each Amish community are contained within the *Ordnung,* which details the way in which the Amish structure their daily lives—from whether or not community members may use diesel-powered milking machines, to whether or not women are allowed go outside their home without their traditional black stockings in the heat of summer. Across Amish communities, these rules range along a continuum from orthodox to progressive, or, as the Amish would say,

---

Adapted from an article that originally appeared in *Religion, Dress, and the Body*.

from *lower to higher*. Low Churches are those that observe strict discipline, practice social avoidance, and are the most technologically conservative. At the other end of the continuum are the high churches that are generally more relaxed about the rules.

Amish families are organized around traditional age/sex roles with power lying in the male gender and increasing with age. The Amish husband is responsible for the spiritual welfare of the household. Women are expected to carry out domestic chores, care for the young children, and submit to the authority of the husband. Amish children are a much-wanted asset who provide labor on the family farm or in the family business and thereby perpetuate the Amish values of hard work and strong family ties. Except for a few areas in which they are unavailable, Amish children attend Amish schools through about the 8th grade. These schools emphasize basic skills, traditional Amish values and beliefs, and community commitment (Hostetler & Huntington, 1989).

Mormon: History, Theology, and Culture

Mormons claim that the true Church, which Christ had established, became corrupted and was lost from the earth shortly after Christ's death; thus, the true gospel of Christ was restored to the earth through Joseph Smith by divine revelation from God between 1820 and 1830. Like the Amish, early members of the LDS Church were severely persecuted. After Joseph Smith's martyrdom, Brigham Young led many Church followers to Utah in the late 1840s. After a number of skirmishes with the federal government, the Mormons found relative security in Utah. Committed to proselytizing, the Mormon Church currently has a world membership of nearly 16,000,000 (Mormon Newsroom, 2017).

Mormon theology. Mormons are genuinely dumfounded when they are occasionally accused of not being Christians. To them, Jesus Christ is the center of their religion and His mission is described in both the *Bible* and the *Book of Mormon*, the latter of which they describe as a second witness to Christ's ministry. This additional understanding of Christ, combined with their convictions regarding the appropriate use of temples, sets Mormonism apart from other Christian religions.

Mormon Church buildings serve as the locus for weekly worship services and ancillary activities. Temples, by contrast, are viewed as more sacred than churches and have a special two-fold function. First, they are a place where an individual may do his or her own *endowments*,

certain covenants made with God regarding one's behavior and commitment. While children who are born to members of the Church are normally baptized near their 8th birthday, going to the temple for one's temple endowments is seen as a more intense commitment to the beliefs members hold, one entered into at a more mature age and after more careful study of the gospel. Second, temples are the locus of rituals for oneself and one's ancestors, including baptisms and *sealings*, ceremonies in which families are sealed together for eternity, a belief illustrated in the *Bible* (see Genesis 25:8, Ecclesiastes 3:14, Malachi 4:6, and Matthew 18:18 and elaborated in Mormon scriptures). Thus, the belief that families can be united after death is a cornerstone of LDS faith. Mormons believe they are commanded to teach the gospel to the world and missionary efforts are increasingly successful in all parts of the world.

Mormon culture. Mormon culture and theology are closely linked. Among its hallmarks is a commitment to family and the strengthening of family life. Mormons also exhibit a strong reliance on authority, a result in the belief that they are led by living prophets of God. Importantly, there are no paid Mormon clergy; rather, all offices in the Church are lay offices. Consequently, responsible Mormons expect to be active in their local congregations leading to a strong sense of responsibility for the welfare and functioning of the entire congregation.

Like the Amish, Mormons place a high premium on personal moral responsibility, including honesty, chastity, fidelity in marriage, and the establishment of family-centered homes in which to raise children. Church members are expected to refrain from tobacco, alcohol, tea, and coffee. They are regularly encouraged to keep the Sabbath day holy by attending Church meetings, spending time with their families, and studying the Scriptures. Church authorities encourage personal thrift and modesty, in dress and in lifestyle, but individual behavior is not monitored with nearly the same intensity as it is among the Amish, due largely to the value Mormons place on individual agency.

The LDS Church is headquartered in a twenty-eight-story office building in Salt Lake City, Utah. Locally, Church members are organized into congregations (wards), which combine to comprise larger membership units (stakes). Missionary work, something that has no role in an Amish community, is central to the culture of LDS families and to the Church's value system. Many parents save from the time their children are young to be able to send their children on missions for the Church. This generally occurs between the ages of 19 and 22, and young people serve for 1 1/2 to 2 years. As a result of this commitment to proselytizing, the Church currently has over 30,000 organized congregations worldwide.

Relevant Amish-Mormon Cultural Differences

LDS and Amish theology and culture are different in a number of ways, four of which are important to this topic:

1. Mormons have been enthusiastic supporters of the Constitution of the United States and seek to influence political life, rather than be separate from it as the Amish claim to do.

2. Mormons place a high value on education, both secular and spiritual. The Church encourages members to obtain as much secular education as possible. The Church owns and operates three universities, one of which, Brigham Young University in Provo, Utah, the largest church supported university in the United States.

3. Mormons are committed to the use of modem technology to facilitate the Church's missions and agenda. Moreover, the LDS Church relies heavily on sophisticated technology to facilitate genealogical record keeping and information transmittal, for running both the central and local Church bureaucracies, and for facilitating the Church's overall programs.

4. LDS culture is different from Amish culture in that while the Amish actively seek to be separate from the external world, Mormons seek to be active and influence the external world. The LDS Church's enormous bureaucracy and its ancillary activities including a motion picture production studio, television studios and satellite broadcasting facilities, and publishing facilities that provide a variety of books, newspapers, and multi-language periodicals and digitized services facilitate this very different goal. It also includes a welfare program with farms, canneries, and storehouses around the country that cooperate with international relief agencies to provide food, clothing, shelter, and medical supplies as needed throughout the world (Derr et al. 2016).

Amish and Mormon Sacred Dress

Amish Sacred Dress

Amish dress, like other aspects of their material world, is plain, functional, economical to produce, and relatively uniform among wearers who belong to the same community. Because of the way they dress, it is easy to identify an Amish person. Amish dress has changed little since the mid-20th century, but change has occurred. While the rate of change is much slower than it is in the dominate culture Amish dress is clearly influenced by the dress of the dominant society.

Description. In the Amish community studied for this paper, the dress style is an open front bodice, elbow-length sleeves, and a fitted bodice with a narrow band-style collar. The bodice is attached to a same-fabric belt of about 2" in width to which the dirndl type, center-front-opened skirt is attached with a wide lap. The bodice is held closed by straight pins inserted horizontally down the front to the bottom of the belt. The skirt always comes to just below the knee on young girls and unmarried women, but tends to be anywhere from 2–6 inches below the knee for married women, depending on their age. Colors vary, but those prescribed for married women are quite dark in value and dull in intensity, in hues of burgundy, brown, navy blues, and blacks. Unmarried girls are permitted to choose much lighter values of rose, greens and blues.

Around the house women are expected to wear the white organza cap; outside the house, they are expected to don the traditional black bonnet over the cap. Women also wear sweaters and capes, always dark in color, and they are expected to wear black hose and black shoes; however, unmarried girls are seen wearing sneakers. Amish women are expected to use no makeup.

Amish men wear heavy denim and a commercially manufactured man's dress shirt with sleeve length depending on the season, leather braided suspenders, a felt or straw hat depending on the season, and work boots. Amish adult men wear full beards and no mustache. For church, men appear in black suits.

Acquisition. Except for head coverings, women sew most of the family's clothing. Shoes, hats, stockings, items of underwear, and men's everyday work shirts are purchased in the local dry goods store or a nearby market town. Dresses are made of purchased lightweight polyester knit. This illustrates one way in which changes in Amish clothing are dependent on their willingness to embrace the technological advantages of the dominant culture they claim to reject.

Shopping in a Wal-Mart in a nearby market town is something of an adventure and looked forward to with great anticipation. The Amish are very resourceful in tailoring commercially available products to their own needs, buying, for example, black and white sneakers at Wal-Mart along with a can of black paint to cover any ornamentation or logos.

Rules and stretching the limits. The rules of dress in an Amish community apply to outwardly visible dress and are enforced by social coercion of the group. Whereas underwear is open to personal touch. For example, when collecting data, one of the authors was asked to go to the basement to get a jar of peaches. There, drying on a clothesline were several pairs of bright, colorful men's underwear, decorated with such worldly icons as Disney™ characters and SMAK lips. The wife acknowledged that her husband wore them and the church allowed whatever they liked in the way of underwear.

As in any socially-controlled community, there is always an individual who acts as self-appointed moral police. They report to church leadership when someone has broken the dress-code. If the church leaders agree, they will have a quiet talk about the matter with the person who has been accused of stretching the limits too far. If the behavior is not corrected in a reasonable period, the church leaders will visit again, likely accompanied with a bishop or other male church officer. Interestingly, the failure of the church leadership to take action when an alleged infringement is reported constitutes the mechanism by which change most often occurs in an Amish community.

From the time a young person turns 16 years until marriage, Amish children are given considerable license to run amok while their parents sigh and fret. This practice, known as *rumspringa*, generally gives more freedom to male teenage children than to female children, and the period of license normally lasts longer for males than females. This newfound freedom is commonly expressed through some experimentation with smoking, drinking, and bar behavior. Some young Amish even leave the Amish community for a period to live *English*, while the family hopes the episode will be short-lived. **Amish** females usually explore this liminal status in somewhat less egregious ways, but experimentation with dress is a common mode of expression. For example, about 3 months into the field work experience, the researcher was interrupted at her house in town about 9:00 one night by 3 unmarried Amish girls ranging in age from 17–20. They wanted the researcher to drive them 25 miles to a bar in a nearby market town. The young women were wearing makeup and were dressed in *English,* destination-appropriate dress. Only their Dutch accents would have given them away.

Mormon Sacred Dress

Fundamental to LDS culture and theology, and fundamental to the LDS manifestation of sacred vestments, is the institution of sacred temples. Currently, the Church has 155 operating temples (Mormon News, 2017). Mormons associate their *endowments,* the covenants made in temples, and the undergarment, *or garment,* worn thereafter, with the symbolic connection between dress and faith. This is illustrated in Isaiah 61: 10: "I will greatly rejoice in the Lord, my soul shall be joyful in my God; for he hath clothed me with the garments of salvation, he hath covered me with the robe of righteousness" (The Holy Bible, 1948, p. 831). During visits to a temple, members wear special white temple clothes. Outside the temple, however, what is referred to as one's *garments* is an undergarment that is hidden by one's street clothes. Once endowed, a faithful Church member wears the *garment* for the rest of one's life as one would wear any undergarment.

Mormons explain that because they have no professional clergy, but rather subscribe to a system in which all faithful members of the church share ecclesiastical responsibilities, the garment serves to remind the wearer of their special commitments. "It is an outward expression of an inward covenant to the gospel principles of obedience, truth, life, and discipleship in Christ, and "it symbolizes Christ-like attributes in one's mission in life." (Marshall, 1992, p. 534).

Description. For both men and women, the everyday *garment* is a one- or two-piece bifurcated garment that covers the body from just above the knees to above the chest and upper part of the arm. There is some variation in neckline style and in the fullness of the legs. That the design of the garment has changed over time is confirmed both by informants and secondary sources. Joseph Smith initiated the existence of a temple garment about the time the Nauvoo Illinois temple was nearing completion in 1843. Then the garment consisted of unbleached muslin with sleeves to the wrists and legs to the ankles. In 1923, the Church authorized a new design that included sleeves to the elbows and legs to just below the knee (Buerger, 1994). Since then, minor design changes have been initiated, usually in consultation with LDS designers. While the one-piece garment is still available and commonly worn, since 1979, the Church has manufactured a two-piece garment which, according to informants, was accepted with enthusiasm.

Today, both one-and two-piece styles for both men and women, are available in a wide variety of fabrics, and sizes. Regardless of style, the leg length is intended to come to the top of the knee. Women's garment tops are available in a rounded-neck and a sweetheart-neck style that generally correspond to bra line. Men's tops are also available in two different tee-shirt necks. All garments have a sleeve, short for men and cap-style for women. Other undergarments such as bras are worn over the garment. Regardless of style of garment selected, wearing the garment ensures that the wearers are modest in street dress as well.

Acquisition. Prior to the 1930s, there was no standardized garment *per se*. One elderly woman who lived in Virginia reported going to Salt Lake City in the mid 1920s for her endowments. Returning to Virginia, she visited her local department store where she purchased several *silhouettes*, an undergarment available for sale during that period. These she *defined* as her temple garments. She described it as a modest sleeveless, bifurcated one-piece undergarment with wide legs coming nearly to the top of the knee and a bosom top with thin straps over the shoulder. This woman and other elderly informants who lived long distances from Salt Lake City indicated some pressure to substitute this for what at the time was commonly used in Utah and was more similar to a long legged union suit. The intent was to substitute something that would require fewer adjustments in street dress, rather than subject themselves, and, therefore, their religion, to ridicule. Others recalled making their garments, which in those days were supposed to cover most of the arms and legs.

By the mid 1930s, the Church established a manufacturing plant, Beehive Clothing Mills, to produce garments to sell to endowed Church members. For women, the "authorized pattern" consisted of a full-legged one-piece garment that came to just above the knee with a cap sleeve, designed so that regular street clothes of the time easily covered the garment. Then, in mid 1970s, the Church approved a two-piece garment style for both men and women. Today, the LDS Church continues to operate Beehive Clothing Mills which manufactures garments for endowed Church members. Garments are produced in a variety of *authorized* patterns in a variety of fabrics for both men and women. Prices of garments range from about $3–$7, depending on the style and fabric. Church members assume these are sold at or near cost. The prices suggest this is so. One can purchase garments at distribution centers, usually located near temples throughout the world. In locales with a high Mormon population, retail distribution centers can be found in shopping mall settings as well. Beehive Clothing Mills

also has an 800 number that members may use for placing mail orders and garments can also be ordered online.

Rules and stretching the limits. Endowed members of the LDS church are expected to wear their garments all day, every day, for the rest of their lives. "How [the garment] is worn as an outward expression of an inward commitment to follow the Savior." Interestingly, the lack of detailed instructions about wearing them is consistent, as one informant explained, "with how the gospel operates." A monthly Church magazine explains: "This sacred covenant is between the member and the Lord. Members should be guided by the Holy Spirit to answer for themselves personal questions about wearing the garment" (*Ensign*, March 1989, p. 6).

Informants expressed the belief that the garment represented the covenants they had made in the temple to live a certain way and that the garment had the power to protect them. One married woman in her mid-20s explained, "Well, it's never real clear what kind of protection they provide, but . . . if all else failed, just having your garments on would discourage you from getting too intimate with another man. . . [I mean,] how would you explain them to anyone else." Other informants indicated that the garment could protect one from being tempted to do things one should not do. Still others indicated that a major reason for the garment was to encourage modesty. "It's hard to run around half naked with your garments on," explained one informant. Indeed, modesty is an important theme for church authorities who encourage church members to dress modestly. "The principles of modesty and of keeping the body appropriately covered are implicit in the covenant and should govern the nature of all clothing worn. Endowed members of the Church wear the garment as a reminder of the sacred covenants they have made with the Lord and also as a protection against temptation and evil," (Monson, 1997).

Still, it is not difficult to find examples of individuals who stretch the limits, and of others that are judgmental about it. Informants were quick with stories of women who tuck the cap sleeve of the garment under their bra strap so they can wear sleeveless blouses or dresses, or of men who wear only their garment tops with biker shorts. The most frequently mentioned infraction concerned younger endowed adults who wear Bermuda shorts that fail to be quite long enough, which was judged by many not only as a breech of instruction regarding how to wear the garment, but as the ultimate in tasteless appearance.

Discussion

For both the Amish and Mormons, everyday sacred dress fulfills and reflects both micro and macro (Ritzer, 1991) objectives. The form and function of both Amish and LDS sacred dress are related to the belief systems and ideological commitments held by both groups. While Mormons find the distinction of *sacred* appropriate for their dress, the Amish find the distinction a bit awkward, generally noting that they never think about it that way. "It's just what we wear because we're Amish." This is likely because Amish theological and community commitment is so intimately connected. With only a bit of probing, however, Amish informants easily acknowledge that they ground their distinctive dress in their religious ideology.

At the micro-level, one's sacred dress serves as a constant symbolic reminder to the wearer of personal spiritual commitments he or she has made and as a reminder of church organization/community. Thus, it is not enough merely to note the existence of the *form* of everyday sacred dress represented by these two religious groups. Members of other Western Christian religions use accessories to suggest messages of affiliation or commitment, e.g., head coverings or jewelry. However, the Amish and Mormons are unique in that faithful adult members literally clothe themselves daily in items of apparel that represent their spiritual commitment and organizational affiliation as they engage each day in the external world.

Sacred dress serves, to members of both groups, as a *daily* reminder of commitments. Interestingly, members of both groups reported feeling "naked," "undressed," and uncomfortable functioning in the public world without it. Even those willing to push the limits and break the rules reported being uncomfortable in doing so. While the principle of individual agency is an important doctrine for Mormons, social expectations and group coercion are powerful tools in regulating behavior. For the Amish, by contrast, *tattletale* enforcement is an efficient and direct way to correct an individual's inappropriate behavior. Interestingly, pushing the rules in an Amish community is a legitimate way to encourage change.

At a more individual level, the sacred dress of both groups is believed to provide a kind of protection to the wearer. This is an explicit point of doctrine for Mormons (Asay, 1997). Exactly what sort of protection the garment provides, however, is unclear. While virtually all informants expressed the belief that the garment provided spiritual protection and encouraged them to keep the covenants they had made, some asserted that the garment also provided a physical protection. Most of the Mormon informants showed that they would feel vulnerable without wearing them, something that they must negotiate, for example, when going to the doctor or during hospitalizations.

The Amish, by contrast, suggested no supernatural advantage through wearing their unique dress. Rather, expectations from childhood and the rules of the *Ordnung* make their unique dress *de rigueur* for baptized Amish adults. Yet in a literal sense, Amish dress provides a very real protection from that which they fear most—contamination from the outside world. Their dress announces who they are and suggests that outsiders maintain social distance. In that sense, it works to keep them separate from the world and to protect them from worldly influences.

A garment-wearing Mormon is not obvious to an observer. Hidden by street clothes, the benefits of wearing one's garments, from the view of most members, are spiritual. However, as an unseen undergarment, they also facilitate the individual's immersion in, and influence on, the dominant social world. This is consistent with LDS institutional goals. Mormons are proselytizing people. They wish to convert others to their religion and are successful in doing so as evidenced by their ever-increasing membership. Moreover, they wish to have influence in the world and over the social agendas of the dominant world. Garment-wearing Mormons include people from all social classes. The LDS church's emphasis on education for its members positions them for activity in most professions and occupations, an achievement that would be difficult if they looked funny, unapproachable, or strange.

The Amish appear unique, unapproachable, and strange to most casual observers. As people who seek to be separate from the outside world and to maintain a commitment to a low-technology agricultural existence, their dress serves those ends. By any assessment, Mormons have more interaction with the public world, are more secular regarding daily concerns and activities, and use virtually *invisible* dress symbols that facilitate their secular participation with the public world. This, in turn, facilitates their ability to influence it. The Amish, with no interest in influencing the external world, use *visible* dress as a boundary maintenance mechanism.

The sacred dress of both groups restrains one's behavior in the social world albeit in different ways. However different the Amish and Mormons cling to their social and ideological agenda, their sacred dress serves their worldviews at the same time it mediates being both in and of the world.

References

Amish Studies: The Young Center (2016). Amish Population Profile. Retrieved April 25, 2017 from https://groups.etown.edu/amishstudies/statistics/amish-population-profile-2015/.

Asay, C.E. (1997, August). The temple garment. Ensign, 19–23.

Buerger, D. J. (1994). *The Mysteries of Godliness: A History of Mormon Temple Worship.* San Francisco: Smith Research Associates.

Derr, J. and Madsen, C., Holbrook, K. and Grow, M. J. (Eds) (2016, Feb. 29). *The First Fifty Years of Relief Society: Key Documents in Latter-Day Saint Women's History.* Church Historian's Press.

The Holy Bible (1948). (King James Version.)

Hostetler, J.A. (1980). *Amish Society.* Baltimore: The Johns Hopkins University Press.

Hostetler, J.A, & Huntington, G. E. (1989). Children in Amish Society: Socialization and Community. Baltimore: The Johns Hopkins University Press.

Kraybill, D.B. (1989). The *Riddle of Amish Culture.* Baltimore: The Johns Hopkins University Press.

Marshall, E. T. (1992) Garments. In D.H. Ludlow (Ed.), *The Encyclopedia of Mormonism (Vol 2)* New York: Macmillan.

Monson, T.S. (1997, June). Our brother's keeper. Ensign, pp. 32–39.

Mormon Newsroom (2017). Worldwide Statistics. The Church of Jesus Christ of Latter Day Saints. Retrieved April 25, 2017 from http://www.mormonnewsroom.org/facts-and-statistics.

Ritzer, G. (1991). *Metatheorizing in* Sociology. Lexington, MA.: D.C. Heath and Co.

Discussion Questions

1. According to Hawley and Hamilton, both the Amish and Mormons wear sacred dress to remind them daily of their commitments to their religion. Describe what the Amish wear and how they acquire their clothing and what Mormons wear and how they acquire their clothing.

2. According to this reading, the Amish have a goal of not being affected by the outside world. How does their dress help this goal?

3. Also, according to the reading, Mormons have a goal of acquiring as much education as possible in order to influence political power. Describe the dress worn by adult Mormons and how it helps them to reach their goal.

Article is adapted from Hamilton, J.A. and Hawley, J.M. (1999). Sacred dress, public worlds: Amish and Mormon experience and commitment. In L. Boynton-Arthur and J. Eicher (Eds.) *Religion, Dress and the Body, 31–51.* Berg Publishing, Inc.: New York.

8.2
Fashion and Gender in the Middle East
Christina Lindholm, PhD

The region commonly referred to as the Middle East is situated at the crossroads between Europe, Asia and Africa. In the late 1950s John Foster Dulles, then US Secretary of State defined it as 'the area lying between and including Libya on the west and Pakistan on the east, Syria and Iraq on the north and the Arabian Peninsula to the south, plus Sudan and Ethiopia.' In 1960 historian Roderic

Davison stated clearly 'the fact remains that no one knows where the Middle East is. . .There is no accepted formula, and serious efforts to define the area vary as much as three to four thousand miles east and west. There is not even an accepted core for the Middle East.' (Davison 1960:665). Confusion persists today in what countries are recognized as Middle Eastern. Organizations such as the United

Original for this text

Nations exclude Algeria, Libya and Morocco, while the Washington Institute for Near East Policy includes them and does not recognize Cyprus in the group. Tunisia is included by the US State Department, but excluded by several other agencies. Various governmental agencies and organizations definitions vary anywhere from 18 to 24 countries.

Known as the Near East until after World War II, the area is the subject of myths, mysteries and misconceptions. Perhaps the most significant of these is the notion that the region is united by race, religion, culture, tradition, governance, climate and economics. Nothing could be further from the truth.

History of Dress in the Middle East

Long, loose flowing robes have been worn by all people in the region since pre-history, regardless of age, gender and social station. These garments covered the body from the neck to the ankles and often head covers were worn by both men and women. Facial covers or veils were worn in various forms, and in some societies they identified respectable women. The penalty for a slave caught wearing a veil was severe. Facial veiling for women became accepted practice in the areas where Islam was prevalent in the early to mid 600s. Initially, only the Prophet Mohammed's wives covered their faces in public. They did this for anonymity to avoid people who wished to curry favor with the Prophet, and for protection from harassment from non-believers. The custom was adopted by many women seeking to express their piety and became conflated with Islam as a sartorial requirement.

In the 1400s, the religious leaders of Islam became concerned about the increasing secularism and interaction with the science and technology of the west among Muslims. They initiated a rejection of westernization and any ideas and practices that did not revolve around a religious life that adhered closely to the teachings of the Qur'an. This effectively kept residents of much of the region in the Middle Ages while the west moved forward in terms of scientific and technological discovery. Dress changed very little during this time, thus the survival of the all covering robe and head cover.

Women

The range of fashionable dress in the Middle East is simply astounding. What is worn, when, where and by whom is determined by many factors including the laws and customs of the specific country, the religiosity of the wearer and the occasion to name only a few. Adding to this is the history of various western occupation and the legacy of those situations. For example, Lebanon was under French control from the collapse of the Ottoman Empire until the end of World War ll. The style and love of high fashion is one of the many things that remain. While covered women are occasionally seen in Beirut and more often in smaller towns in the country, current western fashion is far more the norm as evidenced by the thriving fashion industry. Known for their use of gorgeous textiles, Lebanese designers Elis Saab, Reem Akra and Zuhair Murad have gained international success and are avidly collected and worn by Hollywood celebrities.

Other countries, such as Kuwait are home to western style shopping malls that host international chain clothing stores like Zara, H&M, Pull and Bear, and Mango. Traditional covering dress is worn on formal or religious occasions, but western dress suffices for most days for the middle aged and young (Kelly 2010:221). Kelly reports 'Kuwaiti women shop internationally, combine elements from several cultures and, should they not find what they want, have it custom-made to suit their taste.' (Kelly 2010:217).

Jewish women in Israel range from dressing in entirely western dress such as jeans and T shirts, to the ultraconservative who wear very modest dress. This is usually a long skirt and loose top, thick stockings and either a headscarf or a wig over their natural hair. Like Muslims, they feel that a woman's hair is her crowning glory and should be reserved for only the eyes of her husband and immediate family.

At the other end of the fashion spectrum are the Arabian Gulf states where the all black shayla and abaya are the usual dress worn in public by Muslim women. The abaya is a long sleeved floor length robe worn over another set of clothing- either a traditional caftan like dress, also long sleeved and floor length, or often among the young, western attire. These garments, holdovers from prior eras, were largely abandoned after World War ll. Oil revenues launched Saudi Arabia and Qatar into unimaginable wealth and one of the best ways to express that was traveling Europe and commissioning haute couture fashion from the most exclusive houses in Paris, Milan and other fashion capitals. While less wealthy, some of the other Arab states followed suit and traditional dress was put aside for decades as residents eagerly adopted Euro-American fashion.

The reemergence of religious dedication occurred in the Arab Spring movement in the 1970s, triggering a new round of rejection of western culture. At this time, young Egyptian women were leaving small towns for education in larger cities and by adopting conservative, concealing dress, they visually communicated that they were observant Muslims and not to be approached or harassed by male strangers. New found pride in Islam spread throughout the Gulf States and many women found it desirable to literally wear their piety by adopting the all black shayla and abaya. There is debate whether this was legally decreed everywhere in the region. Saudi Arabia and Iran did and currently do have legal requirements for women to cover, albeit in very different ways. While the Saudis wear an all black robe and scarf, the Iranians wear a headscarf, trousers or long skirt and long, loose coat, covering their hair and bodies completely. In Qatar and the United Arab Emirates, women are theoretically free to wear what they please, but the social and familial pressure to cover is so strong that nearly all women wear abaya when out of the home. In Turkey, veiling practices by observant Muslim women have been on the rise since the turn of the 21st century. Gökariksel and Secor report that the practice is 'rife with ambivalence' and is 'caught between its function as modest covering' but as fashion consumption 'works as part of an ever-shifting economy of taste and distinction.' (Gökariksel and Secor 2012:847).

Nowhere in the world is gender so definitively expressed by dress as in the Arabian Gulf region. Because of the universally worn traditional garments, there is simply no mistaking one gender for the other, nor is there acceptable social room for anyone who is not clearly male or female. Cross-dressing is an anathema and forbidden by both culture and the Qur'an. Curiously, many Muslims support this view by referring to the Bible verse Deuteronomy 22:5 which says:

A woman shall not wear a man's garment, nor shall a man put on a woman's cloak, for whoever does these things is an abomination to the Lord your God.

It is interesting to note that men's and women's gowns are very similar in cut. The major difference is that the men's robe is generally white while the woman's is a black over garment, worn over another complete set of clothes. Both are long sleeved and ankle length. While neither gender would wear the others robe, Sheikha Mozah bint Nasser Al Misned wore a man's checkered head scarf as a shawl at an international women's meeting, along with a pair of loose pantaloons.

Enormous confusion exists over covering garments terminology. Veil is often widely and inaccurately used interchangeably as both head and face cover. The khimar is a long hood like scarf that goes over the head and hangs down the back, while the shayla is a large rectangular scarf that is wrapped around the head and neck and usually worn with a matching abaya. An Iranian chador is an enormous half circle that is positioned at the top of the head and wrapped around covering the body to the ankles. The burqa comes from Afghanistan and consists of a small pillbox cap with the equivalent of a tent attached to it that completely surrounds the body. It has a small embroidered screen in front for vision. Hijab has emerged as the general and most frequently used term applied to head covers. This is often a large square scarf that covers the head and neck, completely concealing hair and ears. The term hijab actually translates to curtain, partition or screen (Kahera 2008: 130). A hijab (screen) was and still remains in many traditional Arab homes to divide the public area, primarily for men, from the private domain and allowed women to observe activities without having to interact with or be seen by unrelated males.

The Qur'anic verse that are most often quoted regarding dress are Sura 24/31.

And say that the believing women that they should lower their gaze and guard their modesty that they should not display their beauty and ornaments except what (must ordinarily) appear thereof; that they should draw their veils over their bosoms and not display their beauty except to their husbands, their fathers, their husband's fathers, their sons, their husbands' sons, their brothers or their brothers' sons, or their sisters' sons, or their women, or the slaves whom their right hands possess, or male servants free of physical needs, or small children who have no sense of the shame of sex; and that they should not strike their feet in order to draw attention to their hidden ornaments.

While interpreted many ways, the basic directive is to dress modestly so as not to attract attention and lead men into impure thoughts and actions. Muslims believe that men are helpless in the presence of a woman's sexual allure and that they must be protected. Ayatollah Motahari believed that 'women's sexuality can lead to fitna (social chaos), unless it is properly controlled. According to Motahari, the hijab provides a barrier between the sexes and thus serves to uphold the social order.' (Shirazi 2001: 92).

The advent of the decorative abaya, which began in the 1990s, was not lost on international haute couturiers. In 2008 British designer Bruce Oldfield designed a diamond encrusted abaya, valued at $365,000 for the Saudi Gulf Luxury Trade Fair. As the ultra-wealthy, European couture clientele was ageing and dying off, fashion houses gained new customers from the Middle East. After Oldfield's abaya created a sensation, houses like Nina Ricci, Jean Claude Jitrois, Italian Blumarine, Alberta Feretti and American Carolina Herrera realized that they were ignoring a vital part of their Middle Eastern clientele's wardrobe needs. The designer dress that their clients were wearing was almost always covered by locally made abayas. Working with the Saks Fifth Avenue in Riyadh, a fashion show of luxurious abayas and shaylas from the afore mentioned couturier was produced at the Parisian George V hotel in 2009. While the show included an Arabian stallion on the catwalk, the models were otherwise westerners. Since then, many other well know designers such as Dolce & Gabbana and Donna Karan have offered clothing designed specifically for the Middle Eastern consumer.

The abaya has now joined the ranks of other fashion garments and entered the fashion cycle with seasonal offerings and trends carefully culled from world fashion. Out of date abayas are usually given to the less fortunate, be that maids, less wealthy relatives or charity. Previously, all abayas were custom made and would require a few days to complete. In the last decade, name brand abaya shops have sprung up in the Gulf region. They offer fashionable, well designed and constructed robes for immediate purchase, much like shopping in Europe or America. Like western designer clothing, many have distinctive logos that are often visible on the outside of the garment so there is no mistaking the prestige—and price points—of the robe.

The adoption of the fashion abaya has resulted in two important considerations. First, it allows a woman to express her individuality and personal sense of style and status while adhering to the dictates of her culture and religion. Many Muslims are proud of their country and religion and do not feel the need to completely abandon traditions in favor of Euro-American dress. Secondly, and more puzzling is that a fashion abaya has largely removed the anonymous aspect that wearing a plain black abaya achieved. In the 1990s, an abaya wearing woman, often with a face veil, could slip through public places almost invisibly. Her identity was unknown, she was not noticed and she was protected from unwanted attention by male strangers. Children recognized their abaya clad mothers

by their handbag or shoes. The fashion abaya is now so highly embellished and individualized that it attracts attention, rather than deflecting it. While religious leaders have decried the fashion abaya, recognizing that it has evolved in a manner far from its original purpose, it shows no sign of disappearing any time soon (Figures 8.8 and 8.9).

Figure 8.8 Subtle black embroidery on abaya sleeve. Richard Harris Photography.

Figure 8.9 Fashion abaya. Laurence Koltys, photographer.

Men

Men's dress is similar to women's in the Middle East in the aspect that many men wear Euro-American styles in the form of westernized shirts, trousers and jackets. In fact, in many areas they have often given up traditional dress years before women have. Some societies have found a way to combine modern and traditional dress. Conservative Jewish men in Israel wear Euro-American male attire with the traditional yamaka (skull cap) and a tallit katan. This is a small poncho type garment that fits under a shirt. The tallit has tzitzit, braided fringes, dangling from each of the four corners to remind the religious of the Torah's 613 do's and don'ts.

The only place where traditional men's dress worn by most of the population is likely to be found is in the Arabian Gulf States. Like observant Muslim women, Muslim men adhere to the Qur'anic directive to dress modestly.

> Sura 24/30: Say to the believing men that they should lower their gaze and guard their modesty: that will make for greater purity for them: And Allah is well acquainted with all that they do.

In the Gulf, most Arab Muslim men wear the sparkling white thobe (or thawb) and ghutra (headscarf) when present in the region. The thobe, also called a dishdash, is designed like a westernized dress shirt that extends to the ankles. Small details differ in each country allowing those familiar with the region to identify a Saudi from a Qatari or an Omani. In Saudi Arabia, the thobe has a stiff, standing band collar often with 2 buttons, a front placket, usually with concealed buttons and set in sleeves that may or may not have cuffs, or French cuffs. The Qatari and UAE thobe generally has a 2 piece fold over collar like a western dress shirt. It has the same placket as the Saudi robe and usually has a breast pocket. Cuffs are almost always present. Omani thobes are distinctive for lacking a collar and having a round neckline instead. A small, triangular cloth tab folds over the front neckline and has a braided tassel attached to it, hanging down over the placket. Cuffs are seldom seen on Omani thobes. Another distinction is that Omani male thobes are worn in a variety of colors.

High quality thobes are usually custom made, although, like women's dress, that is changing as well with name brand thobes entering the marketplace. A typical thobe shop has rolls upon rolls of white cloth. There is a huge variety in the quality of fiber, weight, and weave and the resulting thobe will be the product of consultation with the tailor on cloth, cut and fit. As it is daily dress, and a matter of personal and cultural pride to wear a spotless white thobe, most men own many.

Children

Children's dress has largely mimicked western children's wear. In the Arabian Gulf region, young children wear traditional dress for special occasions or as 'dress up' to ready them for the eventual adoption of the thobe or abaya and shayla. Girls adopt the abaya and shayla at the onset of puberty while there is no specific time for young men to don the thobe. Children's clothing stores featuring Euro-American styles abound. For the economically disadvantaged, enormous amounts of used western clothing is shipped internationally and available in traditional marketplaces.

Conclusion

Depending on the Middle Eastern country, it may be difficult, if not impossible to determine ethnicity, citizenship or religious preference, but it is never hard to tell the men from the women. Gender roles in the region are changing, with a growing number of women pursuing education and careers, but there remains a strong sense of gender identity. All forms of covering dress signal that a woman is an observant Muslim who expects be treated with respect.

Traditional dress is absolutely gender specific, and cross dressing is simply not done. I discovered this on a visit to Fez, Morocco in 2003. It was much colder than anticipated, so I stopped in the market for a warm garment. My choices were a thin, silky polyester jellabiya- a woman's garment, or a hooded rough wool djellaba- a man's garment cut almost identically to the jellabiya. Choosing comfort over beauty, I had no idea of the amusement that I would be causing. While the shop keepers did try to dissuade me from wearing the djellaba, as a westerner, it did not cause nearly the issues that it would have had I been a Middle Eastern woman. I endured nothing more than a great deal of good natured teasing and astounded stares.

Along that same line of reasoning, there is no cultural issue with Middle Eastern women donning Euro-American male or unisex clothing, and it is common to see jeans or trousers peeking out below the hem of an abaya. Many Middle Easterners don western fashion when going to Europe or America. Unless the women retain a head covering, they are indistinguishable from everyone else.

References

Davison, Roderic H. (1960), "Where is the Middle East?". *Foreign Affairs* 38 (4): 665–75.

Gökariksel, B. and Secor, A., (2010), 'Between Fashion and Tesettur', *Journal of Middle Eastern Women's Studies*, 6:3, pp.118–148.

——(2012) "Even I was Tempted" The Moral Ambivalence and Ethical Practice of Veiling-Fashion in Turkey", Annals of the Association of American Geographers, 102:4, pp. 847–862.

Kahera, A. (2008), Deconstructing the American Mosque: Space, Gender and Aesthetics, Austin: University of Texas Press.

Kelly, M. (2010), 'Clothes, Culture and Context: Female Dress in Kuwait.' *Fashion Theory*, 14:2, pp. 215–236.

Shirazi, F. (2001), *The Veil Unveiled*, Gainesville: University Press of Florida.

Discussion Questions

1. How did the practice of covering faces in public begin? Why do Muslim women (similar to Jewish women) wear a wig or headscarf?
2. After WWII, what did women do to express their wealth when oil revenues propelled Saudi Arabia and Qatar into wealth beyond imagination?
3. Since men and women of the Arabian Gulf region wear garments very similar in cut, how can you tell men from women?
4. Why and how was European haute couture saved by Middle Eastern fashion?

Chador: large piece of cloth, wrapped around head + upper body, leaves only face exposed – muslim women

8.3
Sikhs: Religious Minority Target of Hate Crimes
Manveena Suri and Huizhong Wu

New Delhi (CNN) The victim of a possible hate crime in Washington state Friday would not be the first Sikh to be targeted.

Since 9/11, Sikh-American groups say members of their religion have faced discrimination and abuse because their long beards and turbans make them more visible than other minority groups (Figure 8.10).

According to the FBI, anti-Muslim hate crimes in the US surged 67% last year, to levels not seen since 2001.

Highly Visible

In a statement, the Sikh Coalition, America's largest Sikh civil rights group, said that Sikhs are often targeted for hate crimes in part "due to the Sikh articles of faith, including a turban and beard, which represent the Sikh religious commitment to justice, tolerance and equality."

In 1699, Guru Gobind Singh commanded all Sikhs to wear the "Five Ks" in order to identify themselves as a member of the Khalsa Panth, an army of the devout.

The "Five Ks" are: Kesh (uncut hair), Kara (a steel bangle), Kanga (a wooden comb), Kaccha (cotton underwear) and Kirpan (a steel sword).

Figure 8.10 Young Indian Sikhs participate in a turban tying competition in 2014.

Devout Sikh men don't cut their hair or shave because they believe you must maintain your body in the way that God created you. Turbans are worn as a way to keep heads covered out of respect when in public and in religious spaces.

Sikh women often cover their heads with a long scarf called a chunni or dupatta.

For Sikhs, the turban is not about culture, it's an article of faith that is mandatory for men. The turban is also a reason why Sikh men have been targeted and attacked in America, especially after 9/11. Turbans were featured in "The Sikh Project," a 2016 exhibition that celebrated the Sikh American experience. British photographers Amit and Naroop partnered with the Sikh Coalition for the show. This photo (see Figure 8.1) is of New York actor and designer Waris Singh Ahluwalia, who was kicked off an Aero Mexico flight in February after refusing to remove his turban at security.

Hate Crime

In the first month following 9/11, the Sikh Coalition documented more than 300 cases of violence and discrimination against Sikhs in the US.

Last year, multiple Sikhs told CNN that they felt no safer, 15 years after the terrorist attacks.

"The threat of hate and racism has become a part of our daily lives," lawyer and activist Valarie Kaur said.

In 2012 a gunman walked into a gurdwara, a Sikh place of worship, in Wisconsin and killed six people.

Sikhs have also been subject to racial profiling outside the US. Last year, designer and actor Waris Ahluwalia spoke out after he was prevented from boarding an airplane in Mexico by local security agents after he refused to remove his turban during a security screening.

Ahluwalia said Aeromexico staff and security screeners told him to buy a ticket for a different carrier after he refused to remove his turban.

"I was upset, I had anxiety, I was shaking, I did not speak. And then I realized, clearly, they have not been trained properly. I knew yelling will not do anything. It is about education and the policy," Ahluwalia told CNN at the time.

Climate of Fear

According to the Southern Poverty Law Center, which tracks hate crime, there has been an uptick of incidents targeting Muslims and other religious minority groups since the election of President Donald Trump.

While the White House condemned the recent shooting of two Indian men as "an act of racially motivated hatred," some commentators have blamed Trump for not doing enough.

During his first address to Congress last week, Trump said the violence was a reminder that "while we may be a nation divided on policies, we are a country that stands united in condemning hate and evil in all its very ugly forms."

But it's not enough for some.

"A few words of condemnation cannot erase months of President Trump's own divisive rhetoric and his administration's policies targeting and stigmatizing the very communities most vulnerable to hate violence," civil rights lawyer Deepa Iyer wrote last week for CNN Opinion.

Sikh-American leaders have called on the President to address the attack in Washington, while others have warned that his words may lead to violence.

"What (Trump) says goes short of being defined as hate, but in the hearts and minds of the lay person is translated as hate," Mejindarpal Kaur, international legal director of global advocacy organization United Sikhs, told CNN.

"They've targeted their hate toward anyone who looks Middle Eastern."

Discussion Questions

1. Watch the video 'Sikh actor Waris Ahluwalia: This is about education' at https://www.cnn.com/2016/02/09/travel/aeromexico-sikh-turban-waris-ahluwalia/index.html 05: 05. After watching the video, what surprised you the most? Or what did you notice about this video?

2. The incident was about Ahluwalia refusing to take off his turban. The turban for Sikhs is part of the "Five Ks". What are these?

3. Sikhs are often mis-identified as Muslims. What happened to the Sikhs after 9/11?

CHAPTER 9
DRESS IN THE WORKPLACE

Kimberly A. Miller-Spillman

After you have read this chapter, you will understand:

- **How dress facilitates or hinders human interaction in the workplace**
- **Why dress helps individuals acquire, learn, and perform job roles**
- **How dress affects and reflects specific jobs in business, sports, and the military**
- **How to present oneself in a professional setting to the best advantage**

As you sit in your college classes, you may notice the very different ways that your professors dress for work: one professor might always wear suits and heels; another always wears blue jeans, a plaid shirt, and cowboy boots; another wears a suit and tie; still another wears clothing that reflects his African heritage. Academia is often regarded as a career for which appropriate dress is not clearly defined. Professors may choose to reflect their individuality through their dress rather than to follow a strict professional dress code (Figure 9.1). On the same college campus you will find employees who must follow the prescribed dress code of a uniform (campus police, for example). Therefore, college campuses are a good place to start the examination of dress in the workplace.

Working takes up a large portion of adult life. Spending 40 to 60 hours a week at work, in addition to commuting time and getting ready for work (including dressing), makes our time devoted to work-related activities substantial. Work dress becomes one of the most frequently used parts of the wardrobe and, for many individuals, the part of the wardrobe on which they spend the most money. Because work provides money for family and self-support, work tends to be highly valued by most individuals. In addition, many people prepare for careers through long years of education, training, and building a

professional reputation and accomplishments. For many adults, work roles define much of one's self-identity.

This chapter describes how dress affects work. Dress is a powerful communicator, especially when people interact at work. Clothing researchers have attempted to unravel the role that dress plays in the work environment, but more research is needed to fully understand the phenomenon. For instance, researchers have examined body type (Thurston, Lennon, & Clayton, 1990), the wearing of masculine dress by women (Johnson, Crutsinger, & Workman, 1994), and the impact of ideal business image (Kimle & Damhorst, 1997) on a woman's success in the workplace. The readings for this chapter address both men's and women's dress at work to demonstrate the importance of appropriateness of dress in the workplace.

Knowing how to dress for work has been a concern for a long time (see Figure 9.2). Dress historians Sara Marcketti and Jane Farrell-Beck (2008–2009) found that during the 20th century, American women received an excess

Figure 9.1 College professors dress in a range of outfits for work. Some days may require a suit while other days it is acceptable to wear blue jeans.

Figure 9.2 Jackets are often regarded as a symbol of authority. The blouse, jewelry, and simple hairstyle also add to a professional look in the office.

of advice about how to dress correctly for the workplace. Their research explores advice women received about how to dress for work between 1970 and the early 2000s. In the 1970s women had difficulty finding clothing for middle management positions. But by the 2000s, women in corporate management positions had more choices for dress in the workplace.

Since 2017, there are several new choices for acquiring work dress, including subscription clothing services. Emily Gould and Rumaan Alam subscribed to several of these services (e.g., Trunk Club for women and Stitch Fix for men) to see what they offered (Gould & Alam, 2017). The authors determined that the service can be convenient especially if you are in a new job or your schedule doesn't allow long shopping sessions and trying on clothes. However, subscription services vary and you might get inappropriate clothing for your lifestyle, or the quality of the garments may not necessarily warrant the high prices.

Many companies have a formal **dress code** policy, meaning that a suit and tie are required for men, suit and skirt or pants for women. Some companies have a business-casual dress code or require employees to wear a specific outfit that represents the overall branding of the organization. Examples of this strategy include Target's red shirt and khaki pant, Best Buy's blue shirt, and Walmart's blue vest. This kind of dress has become especially important to promote company cohesiveness and identity (it makes it easy to find a sales associate if customers know how they dress). Other companies may not have

specific dress regulations but may instead encourage employees to show good taste. Good taste typically means no skimpy tops, short-short skirts or shorts, and no flip-flops. Appearance is important, and this is directly tied to clothing as well as other aspects of dress in the workplace.

Many years ago, some employers prohibited women from wearing pants to work for white-collar jobs and for teaching. It took the women's movement of the 1970s for this option to become available, and then, as dress historian Patricia A. Cunningham (2003) notes, even after the 1970s it remained "a struggle" (p. 221) since many male employers were not receptive to the change. Fortunately, most companies revised these dress codes in the late 20th century to correspond to contemporary ideas of appropriate dress for the workplace.

Since women were singled out by this policy, to disallow female employees from wearing pants, the policy was a form of discrimination. Another example of discrimination appeared in the United Kingdom when a Muslim teaching assistant refused to remove her veil in the classroom, and a British Airways employee was fired for wearing a visible cross. A more recent controversy has emerged about piercings and tattoos: these body modifications are considered to be in "bad taste" by some employers, so an employee might be required to remove piercings and cover tattoos during the work day.

Another form of discrimination—racism—continues into the modern workplace. Skin color can exclude a person from a position or make it difficult to advance in the corporate hierarchy, although this is illegal in the United States and in violation of laws enforced by the Equal Employment Opportunity Commission. Edwards, in "How Black Can You Be?" describes how dress can increase the comfort factor for whites—one of the main challenges blacks have to face when working in an executive position (Edwards, 2000). Edwards reminds black professionals that others in the office (often white coworkers) may wonder if minority executives value black culture more than corporate culture. All professionals must assume responsibility for the work culture they have chosen to inhabit. There are many behaviors (e.g., sexual harassment) and dress items (e.g., dirty T-shirts) that are not acceptable to employers.

In the late 1990s, the topic of casual dress received attention from corporations and clothing scholars. The casual-dress trend was interesting from several perspectives. One explanation is that following the turbulent late 1980s and early 1990s, when downsizing was prevalent in business, employers wanted to give employees a perk, especially one that did not cost money. So casual dress days (and casual Fridays) became a cost-effective way to raise morale among apprehensive employees. Another possible reason for the development of casual-dress policies was to minimize distinctions between employees, no matter the person's rank, salary, or position in the corporation. Some college campuses and corporations instituted a "casual" Friday during which staff could dress down and wear blue jeans or khakis to work rather than dress slacks and suits. Over the years of this practice in business, industry, and academia, some employees took casual dress to an extreme, and employers got tired of employees showing up for work looking as though they had just woken up.

An example of casual dress worn in the tech world are the executives at Facebook: Mark Zuckerberg and Sheryl Sandburg (see "Sheryl Sandberg's Shoes Perfectly Illustrate the Hypocrisy of Tech's 'Casual' Dress Code" at the end of this chapter). Zuckerberg is known to wear his trademark gray T-shirt with jeans and tennis shoes while Sandberg wears power suits with stiletto heels. This example is especially ironic given that casual dress days began in the tech world.

Today "dress for success" is linked to the desire to get ahead. Women are particularly encouraged to dress better than their peers to present a professional image, even on casual Fridays.

DRESS FOR A JOB INTERVIEW

People often make judgments about others in just a few seconds. The term **person perception** refers to the way we learn and think about others and their characteristics, intentions, and inner states (Taguiri & Petrullo, 1958). Forming an initial impression is the first step in person perception (Figure 9.3). A job interview is one situation in which a **first impression** can determine one's future earning capacity; appropriate dress for an interview is therefore crucial. Magazines and professional journals provide up-to-date information on how to dress appropriately in the workplace and for job interviews. Not surprisingly, clothing researchers have studied the effect of dress during a job interview (Damhorst & Pinaire Reed, 1986; Damhorst & Fiore, 1999; Johnson & Roach-Higgins, 1987; Rucker, Taber, & Harrison, 1981). More recently,

Figure 9.3 Career coaches often recommend that we dress conservatively for job interviews.

researchers have surveyed potential employees about their beliefs and attitudes regarding clothing for the corporate workplace (Blalock, 2006; Peluchette, Karl, & Rust, 2006). Some of this research reveals that college students are very aware that how they dress for job interviews is important and that specific requirements may differ from one type of job to another.

For example, if you are interviewing for a job with a company that specializes in apparel for surfing and other water sports, they may expect you to show up for your interview in something more casual than a typical suit. However, researchers indicate that if in doubt, one should dress conservatively for a job interview; it is better to overdress than underdress.

Today most college career center websites continue to provide guidance on appropriate dress for interviews and work. It would not be surprising in the second decade of the 21st century to learn that a conservative suit continues to remain the basis of professional dress. Dressing appropriately for interviews is even more important in today's economy than in the past. Numerous websites give advice on how to dress for job interviews; college career center websites are an excellent place to start.

DRESS AND HUMAN INTERACTION AT WORK

Why is the discussion about appropriate dress in the workplace important? Dress at work provides visual cues to a person's role and guides an understanding of the value of being appropriately dressed for the workplace. Workplace roles typically give structure and guidance to clothing on the job; many roles require a specific type of dress. For example, a farmer needs overalls, a lawyer needs a business suit, and a judge needs a robe. To a large extent, one who looks the part through appropriate dress can be confident that others will assume he or she legitimately holds the claimed position. The reading "How Your Physical Appearance Impacts Your Career" (at the end of this chapter) relates a story in which a young man who worked in a manufacturing plant was dressing as an individual. He had aspirations of becoming a supervisor but he had not yet begun to dress like one. This article focuses on conforming at the workplace so you can reach your goals versus dressing for comfort as an hourly worker. Even though we believe that people who do well at their job should be promoted regardless of their dress, the real world does not always work that way.

Because dress is such a powerful communicator, appropriate clothing in the workplace conveys the idea that individuals understand their work roles and perform them effectively; dress also cues workers into the roles of other employees in the workplace. However, in some corporations a relaxed dress code is practiced by the CEO of the company as well as the designer, the logistics manager, and the shop foreman. In fact, some clothing companies may expect only that the employees wear a T-shirt or sweatshirt that bears the company logo, and the rest (a pair of khakis, jeans, or shorts) depends on the employee. So what is appropriate for one company is often not okay for another. Therefore, it is important for job seekers to learn about an employer's dress codes. This information is often available via a company's website or human resource office.

Roles within a society can be either achieved or ascribed. **Achieved roles** are those that we work to earn. College degrees, work skills, even marriages are roles that people must strive to attain. A wedding band and an academic robe are examples of achieved roles expressed through dress. An **ascribed role** is a position that people acquire through no fault or virtue of their own. Age, gender, skin color, and birth order are examples of ascribed roles. These roles have an immense impact on individuals because they are so visible and, with the exception of gender, they can rarely be changed. Age, gender, and skin color are difficult to hide in everyday interactions with others, and therefore their impact is very great. Both achieved and ascribed roles are expressed through dress at work. A good example about how ascribed and achieved roles may merge and are reflected in one's dress comes from Ghana, West Africa. A young lawyer (achieved role) in Ghana may be chief of his traditional Asante village (ascribed role), which is inherited through female lineage of his family. As a lawyer, he wears a suit and tie to work each day; however, on the weekends or for traditional Asante ceremonies, he wears the traditional kente wrap that signifies his ascribed role as a village chief (Figure 9.4).

Because ascribed roles can rarely be changed, using dress to offset stereotypes becomes a useful tool in the workplace. Age, gender, and skin color—in certain situations—may be perceived by some as a negative (e.g., female firefighter or young-looking college professor or neurosurgeon). Presenting oneself appropriately through dress can often help to offset negative stereotypes. For example, one might be perceived as too young to do a job if one's dress is not appropriate. A person with a youthful appearance may be read as too inexperienced,

Figure 9.4 In some countries ascribed roles may be expressed by wearing traditional dress and fabrics.

too naive, or too avant-garde to be trusted to do a good job. The reverse is also true. An individual with an older appearance may be read as too old-fashioned, too conservative, or possessing a skill set that is too outdated. Dressing "older" or "younger" might help to overcome these misperceptions.

Gender becomes an issue in the workplace when a professional woman is pregnant. It can be difficult to convince bosses and colleagues that her work will not suffer or that she doesn't secretly plan to quit her job soon after the baby is born. Although many women are now postponing pregnancy until careers are well established, negative perceptions about pregnant women in the workplace still persist. Apparel companies are providing many more options for styles of professional dress for pregnant women than in previous years and at a variety of price points. Therefore, an expectant mother can continue to dress professionally for her job throughout her pregnancy. Other issues may arise after the baby is born based on company policies. Expectations that a woman will be back to her pre-pregnancy size just six weeks after giving birth, even if nursing, can cause stress for some employees. As industries become more service-oriented and image-conscious, more and more employers may require that employees meet these kinds of specific appearance standards.

Gender can often shape work so that the work it takes to be a successful entrepreneur is hidden. Fashion blogging is one example of the traditionally feminine domains of fashion, beauty, domesticity, and craft. In the reading "'Having It All' on Social Media: Entrepreneurial Femininity and Self-Branding among Fashion Bloggers" (at the end of this chapter), authors Erin Duffy and Emily Hund remind us of the feminist era rhetoric of Helen Gurley Brown's time as editor of *Cosmopolitan* magazine. Yes, you can "have it all" but you may not enjoy being pulled from one area of your life to other areas or having to multitask to the extent of not remembering why you chose to have it all. See the reading for a discussion of how female entrepreneurs' preferences as bloggers are actually hiding social inequalities.

Dress and Status at Work

If roles are special tasks that a person performs in a society, **status**, or **prestige**, is the social stratification with which groups and individuals are ranked and organized by legal, political, and cultural criteria (Marshall, 1994, p. 510). In addition, a status hierarchy reflects the value society places on certain roles or groups of roles (Storm, 1987). The presence (or absence) of a status symbol is one way the perceptions regarding status are formed. A Rolex watch, for example, is a major status symbol in U.S. culture. If a doctor or lawyer wears a Rolex watch, others may assume that he or she has not only the financial means to purchase such an item but also the skills required to achieve occupational success in his or her field. Status is readily evident by men and women in the U.S. military, where dress codes are strict. Men and women in the U.S. Army wear the same type of uniform with a universal digital pattern, no matter their rank. However, it is the insignia on the uniforms that denotes a person's rank (and status) within the army; these emblems are visual cues, well understood by men and women of the military. Thus, a military uniform is a very good example of how dress at work functions to visually express status distinctions in the workplace (Figure 9.5).

Social class is a concept that is related to and greatly defined by one's occupation. Although social class distinctions are blurry, in the United States individuals are generally divided into three classes: upper, middle, and lower. Social class is a complex issue involving a person's social background, education, occupation, and income. When social class and dress become a concern in the workplace, it is typically because an individual does not adopt dress appropriate to the position. For example,

Figure 9.5 Badges, pins, and stripes identify a military person's rank while in uniform.

a woman who is promoted to management but continues to wear dress similar to what a secretary wears in her firm may hit the "glass ceiling," preventing further promotion or even causing demotion (cf. Form & Stone, 1957).

The terms **white-collar dress** and **blue-collar dress** refer to types of occupations. These terms imply the social classes historically associated with white-collar and blue-collar occupations. Management and labor jobs have typically reflected their status in dress: a man's white shirt worn with a suit for a management role, but a denim shirt or uniform worn by a laborer. Some presidential candidates have borrowed the traditional symbolism of blue-collar and white-collar dress. These candidates have worn a blue shirt while campaigning in parts of the country that have organized labor unions. The message of the blue shirt is "I may be running for president, but I know what it means to physically work hard." Wearing a blue shirt is meant to establish connections with constituents and gain voter support. Wearers of white-collar dress are perceived as professional. Awareness of different environments and expected dress is often half the battle when dressing for work. One way to ensure appropriate work dress is to observe others at work and adopt their dress codes.

Dress and Specific Occupations

Whereas it might be difficult to describe the dress of a mother in U.S. society (a role that has undergone significant changes), most people have a clear picture of what a police officer should wear. A police uniform is an example of **role-related dress**, that is, dress that has become inextricably tied to a particular occupation. Police uniforms communicate ideas such as power and authority. Research confirms that clothing such as uniforms can legitimize and convey power (Bickman, 1974). In order for police officers to successfully do their job, they must be perceived as legitimate and authoritative. Another example would be the robes that judges wear in the U.S. judicial system. The black robe signifies a judge's authority over the court proceedings and reflects his or her position of respect. The appropriate clothing symbols help make this perception possible.

As jobs become more specialized, clothing for specific needs becomes important. With the advancement of technology, some workers are required to wear clothing that protects the product (e.g., sensitive computer equipment, electronics) from the worker (e.g., hair, lint, tobacco smoke). There are many other types of jobs that require a uniform. In some cases, the uniforms are required to provide protection against injury and illness. This includes protective clothing for agricultural workers, bullet-proof vests for police officers, and cooling vests for firefighters. Researchers continuously work to develop gear for athletes to better protect them from injury while the athletes engage in physically demanding and dangerous sports.

Summary

Dress in the workplace is important because most working people spend 40 to 60 hours a week at their jobs. That is a lot of time and a lot of human interaction to consider. Appropriate dress can make the difference in receiving a job offer, appearing effective in a job role, and receiving a promotion. Understanding how dress can facilitate or hinder human interaction in the workplace can help employees make favorable impressions at work. Most important, dress is a powerful communicator—especially in the workplace.

Key Terms

Achieved roles

Ascribed roles

Blue-collar dress

Dress code

First impression

Person perception

Role-related dress

Status or prestige

White-collar dress

VISIT A CAREER CENTER WEBSITE

Procedure

To gain information from your college/university website about dressing for a job interview, visit its career center website. What do's or don'ts does the website provide? Were you surprised by any of this information? Do you agree with the advice? Why or why not?

INTERVIEW A PROFESSIONAL

Objectives

- To observe and interview a professional about his or her work dress, including casual dress policies and personal preferences.
- To form an opinion about dress in the workplace based on an interview with a professional in a field of personal interest.

Procedure

Choose a profession that's interesting to you. Talk to a professional in that field for a minimum of 20 minutes about his or her dress for work. Ask the person if you can meet him or her at work, so you can see that person in a professional setting. Ask as many of the following questions as time allows.

1. Does your company have a dress code? Formal or informal? If so, what are some specifics?
2. What do you wear to work on most days? Do you vary your dress according to activities you have planned for that day?
3. How much time and energy do you spend on dress for work?
4. Does your company allow casual dress? If so, why? If not, why not?
5. Is casual dress allowed every day or just on certain days of the week or month?
6. How do you feel about the company's casual-dress policy? Do you like it? Why or why not?
7. How do you prefer to dress at work?
8. Have you seen a difference in your performance when dressed in formal dress versus casual dress?

Discussion Questions

1. What did you learn about dress at work that surprised you?
2. Are you still interested in this profession after completing this assignment? If so, why? If not, why not?
3. How do you want to dress when you begin your career?

Writing Activity

1. Write two or three paragraphs about your thoughts on casual dress in business.
2. Do you think that casual dress was a fad that has passed? Or do you think that casual dress will be a part of business dress in the future?
3. What effect (if any) do you think that dress that emphasizes status distinctions will have on the effectiveness of teamwork? Explain the reasons behind your position.

References

Bickman, L. (1974), "The Social Power of a Uniform," *Journal of Applied Social Psychology*, 4: 47–61.

Blalock, E. C. (2006), "African American College Students' Perceptions of Professional Dress." Unpublished master's thesis, University of Georgia, Athens, Georgia.

Cunningham, P. A. (2003), *Politics, Health, and Art: Reforming Women's Fashion, 1850–1920*, London: Kent State University Press.

Damhorst, M. L. and A. M. Fiore (1990), "Women's Job Interview Dress: How Personnel Interviewers See It," in M. L. Damhorst, K. A. Miller and S. O. Michelman (eds.), *The Meanings of Dress*, 92–97, New York: Fairchild Publications.

Damhorst, M. L. and J. A. Pinaire Reed (1986), "Clothing Color Value and Facial Expression: Effects on Evaluations of Female Job Applicants," *Social Behavior and Personality*, 14: 89–98.

Edwards, A. (2000, March), "How Black Can You Be?" *Esquire*, 30(11): 96.

Form, W. H. and G. P. Stone (1957), "The Social Significance of Clothing in Occupational Life" (Technical Bulletin 262), East Lansing: Michigan State University, Agricultural Experiment Station.

Gould, E. and R. Alam (2017), "You'll Wear What They Tell You to Wear," October 24, *The New York Times*. Available online: https://www.nytimes.com/2017/10/24/style/bombfell-stitch-fix-litotes-clothing-subscription-boxes.html.

Johnson, K., C. Crutsinger and J. Workman (1994), "Can Professional Women Appear Too Masculine? The Case of the Necktie," *Clothing and Textiles Research Journal*, 12: 27–31.

Johnson, K. and M. E. Roach-Higgins (1987), "Dress and Physical Attractiveness of Women in Job Interviews," *Clothing and Textiles Research Journal*, 5: 1–8.

Kimle, P. A. and M. L. Damhorst (1997), "A Grounded Theory Model of the Ideal Business Image for Women," *Symbolic Interaction*, 20(1): 45–68.

Marcketti, S. B. and J. Farrell-Beck (2008–2009), "'Look Like a Lady; Act Like a Man; Work Like a Dog': Dressing for Business Success," *Dress*, 35: 49–67.

Marshall, G. (ed.) (1994), *The Concise Oxford Dictionary of Sociology*, Oxford: Oxford University Press.

Peluchette, J. V., K. Karl and K. Rust (2006), "Dressing to Impress: Beliefs and Attitudes Regarding Workplace Attire," *Journal of Business and Psychology*, 21(1): 45–63.

Rucker, M., D. Taber and A. Harrison (1981), "The Effect of Clothing Variation on First Impressions of Female Job Applicants: What to Wear When," *Social Behavior and Personality*, 9: 53–64.

Storm, P. (1987), *Functions of Dress: Tool of Culture and the Individual*, Englewood Cliffs, NJ: Prentice Hall.

Taguiri, R. and L. Petrullo (1958), *Person Perception and Interpersonal Behavior*, Stanford, CA: Stanford University Press.

Thurston, J., S. Lennon and R. Clayton (1990), "Influence of Age, Body Type, Fashion and Garment Type on Women's Professional Image," *Home Economics Research Journal*, 19: 139–50.

9.1
Sheryl Sandberg's Shoes Perfectly Illustrate the Hypocrisy of Tech's 'Casual' Dress Code

Emily Peck

The rules for dressing for the office are completely different for men and women.

Perhaps no two people better exemplify the double standard than the most well-known executives working at Facebook: cofounder and Chief Executive Mark Zuckerberg, known for wearing the same grey T-shirt and jeans every day, and Chief Operating Officer Sheryl Sandberg, who is typically seen perched atop towering high heels.

Sandberg is arguably the most influential female executive in Corporate America, inspiring (or pissing off) many women with her book *Lean In*. Her frank openness about dealing with the sudden death of her husband last year was both heartbreaking and admirable. She's incredibly successful by every measure.

Yet on Wednesday, while watching her talk to Recode's Kara Swisher and Facebook Chief Technology Officer Michael Schroepfer, I caught myself staring at her shoes.

Facebook/Recode

I couldn't help but marvel at the fact that while Zuckerberg slumps around in super-casual clothes every day, Sandberg is smartly decked out in full corporate power garb: towering, patent leather, red peep-toe heels.

To be sure, these two are an extreme example. Sandberg, who holds an MBA from Harvard, is a seasoned executive and considered to be the "adult" in the room who brings balance to Zuckerberg's more introverted personality. And of course, nobody is forcing Sandberg to wear her (extremely stylish) stilettos.

Still, their case highlights the fact that even in the tech world, where the concept of dressing down was invented, and even at Facebook, a progressive company run by a guy in jeans, women and men don't quite play by the same rules.

Women can't just roll out of bed, toss on yesterday's jeans, brush their teeth and do well at work. If they do,

Figure 9.6 Here's a pair of shoes Sandberg wore to the World Economic Forum in Davos.

they'll struggle in the professional world. One woman I spoke with recently, who works at a private equity firm, told me that she wasn't taken seriously at work until she started wearing stilettos.

In fact, women who spend more time grooming—including efforts like putting on makeup—are promoted more often and make more money than their bare-faced colleagues, according to one recent study.

"Although appearance and grooming have become increasingly important to men, beauty work continues to be more salient for women because of cultural double standards with very strict prescriptions for women," the paper says.

So if you're looking to be the next Sheryl Sandberg, better bust out that lipstick and heels. You'll be spinning your wheels without them.

Discussion Questions

1. What is your opinion of how Facebook executives Mark Zuckerberg and Sheryl Sandberg dress for work?

2. How do you feel about casual dress at work? Some groups embrace casual dress at work while others do not.

3. What do you think of women who spend more time grooming make more money and are promoted more often than women who do not spend time grooming?

9.2
How Your Physical Appearance Impacts Your Career

Jeff Haden

Years ago I worked on the shop floor of a manufacturing plant. I had worked my way through school at another plant so I definitely identified more with the hourly workers than the "suits." (Even though most of the guys referred to me as "college boy.")

One day the department manager stopped by. He asked about my background. He asked about my education. He asked about my career aspirations.

"I'd like to be a supervisor," I answered, "and then someday I'd like your job."

He smiled and said, "Good for you. I like a guy with dreams." Then he paused.

"But if that's what you really want," he said, looking me in the eyes, "first you need to start looking the part."

I knew what he was saying but decided to play dumb. "What do you mean?" I asked.

"Look around," he said. "How do supervisors dress? How does their hair look? How do they act? No one will think of you as supervisor material until they can actually see you as a supervisor—and right now you look nothing like a supervisor."

He was right. I was wearing ratty jeans with a couple of holes. (Why wouldn't I? I worked around oil and grease all day.) I was wearing a cut-off t-shirt. (Why wouldn't I? It was the middle of the summer and the air wheezing through the overhead vents was far from conditioned.) And my hair was pretty long, even for the day. (No excuse for that one, as is obvious from this photo.)

"But shouldn't how well I do my job matter more than how I look?" I asked.

"In a perfect world your performance *is* all that would matter," he said. "But we don't live in a perfect world. Take my advice: if you want to be promoted into a certain position. . . *make sure you look like the people in that position.*"

I've thought about that conversation a lot over the years.

I've hired and promoted people who looked the part. . . and they turned out to be all show and no go. I've hired and promoted people who didn't look the part at all. . . and they turned out to be superstars. I'm convinced that how you look and, at least to a large degree how you act, has nothing to do with your skill and talent and fit for a job.

LinkedIn Influencer Jeff Haden published this post originally on LinkedIn.

Figure 9.7 Looking the part will help you get the promotion you want.

Still, he's right: the world isn't perfect. People still make assumptions about us based on irrelevant things like clothing and mannerisms. . . and height and weight and age and gender and ethnicity and tons of other qualities and attributes that have absolutely no bearing on a person's performance (Figure 9.7).

So Are You Better Off Trying to Conform?

Unfortunately, probably so. The people doing the hiring and promoting are *people*—and people tend to be biased towards the comfortable and the familiar. People tend to hire and promote people who are much like themselves. (If you remind me of me. . . then you must be awesome, right?)

Besides, highly diverse teams are like unicorns—we all know what one should look like, but unless you're NPH you rarely encounter one in the wild.

And don't forget that hiring or promoting someone who conforms, even if only in dress and deportment, makes a high percentage of the people making those decisions feel like they're taking a little bit less of a risk. I know I was viewed—admittedly with good reason—as a wild card, and I'm sure that impacted my promotability.

But still: are you better off being yourself and trusting that people will value your skills, experience, talent. . . and uniqueness?

Sadly I think that's a move fraught with professional peril. If your goal is to get hired or promoted then expressing your individuality could make that goal much harder to accomplish. (Of course if being yourself in all ways is what is most important to you, by all means let your freak flag fly. Seriously.)

I have no way of knowing for sure, but changing how I dressed—and in a larger sense, tempering some of the attitude I displayed—would likely have helped me get promoted sooner. For a long time I didn't look the part, didn't act the part. . . and I'm sure that made me a less attractive candidate.

But that's just what I think; what's more interesting is what *you* think about fitting in and conforming.

Has the way you look affected your career? Have you ever decided to conform. . . or not to conform. . . and what difference did that make?

Discussion Questions

1. Have you ever thought about how you will dress once you leave college? Have you been known to say things such as 'When I go to work I'm going to dress the way I want to dress' or 'I'm in fashion so I should dress stylishly and get that pink briefcase I have always wanted'.

2. How do you feel about the imperfect world where how you look and act means as much as how well you do the job?

3. Has the way you look affected any job you have held?

9.3
"Having It All" on Social Media: Entrepreneurial Femininity and Self-Branding among Fashion Bloggers

Brooke Erin Duffy and Emily Hund

Abstract

Against the backdrop of the widespread individualization of the creative workforce, various genres of social media production have emerged from the traditionally feminine domains of fashion, beauty, domesticity, and craft. Fashion blogging, in particular, is considered one of the most commercially successful and publicly visible forms of digital cultural production. To explore how fashion bloggers represent their branded personae as enterprising feminine subjects, we conducted a qualitative analysis of the textual (n =38 author narratives) and visual (n=760 Instagram images) content published by leading fashion bloggers; we supplement this with in-depth interviews with eight full-time fashion/beauty bloggers. Through this data, we show how top-ranked bloggers depict the ideal of "having it all" through three interrelated tropes: the destiny of passionate work, staging the glam life, and carefully curated social sharing. Together, these tropes articulate a form of entrepreneurial femininity that draws upon post-feminist sensibilities and the contemporary logic of self-branding. We argue, however, that this socially mediated version of self-enterprise obscures the labor, discipline, and capital necessary to emulate these standards, while deploying the unshakable myth that women should work through and for consumption. We conclude by addressing how these findings are symptomatic of a digital media economy marked by the persistence of social inequalities of gender, race, class, and more.

Keywords

fashion blogging, self-branding, post-feminism, social media, Instagram

Introduction

From mommy blogs and beauty vlogs to craft micro-economies associated with do-it-yourself (DIY) sites like Etsy and Artfire, the last decade has witnessed a proliferation of socially mediated cultures of creative production located in the traditionally feminine domains of fashion, beauty, parenting, and craft. Popular discourses about the role of these platforms in economically empowering women can be ascribed to assumptions about the merits of highly individualized, flexible employment conditions, especially for female workers aspiring to combine professional and domestic responsibilities. Although findings about the persistence of gender inequalities in digital media industries have productively challenged this myth of technologically enabled empowerment (Gill, 2008; Gregg, 2008), independent employment continues to be valorized through such hybrid neologisms as mom-preneur, etsy-preneur, and blogger-preneur.

These modes of creative self-enterprise are symptomatic of labor in the post-Fordist era, which is characterized by destabilized employment, the concomitant rise of casualized and contract-based work, and the logic of flexible specialization. Indeed, the number of independent workers[1] has grown explosively in recent years; in 2013, there were more than 17 million, up 10% from two years prior (MBOPartners, 2013). Labor experts project that by 2020, 45% of the US workforce will be independent (Pofeldt, 2012). While worker independence is validated in the popular imagination through the ideals of freedom and flexibility, scholars and policy-makers highlight the extent to which employment conditions emblematic of the so-called "new economy" shape the psychological, cultural, and financial experiences of workers. For instance, workers assume the responsibility for benefits previously shouldered by organizations, including steady pay, occupational training, health care, and pension (e.g. Gill, 2010; Neff, Wissinger, & Zukin, 2005; Ross, 2009). Moreover, individuals are encouraged to invest time, energy, and capital in an imagined future as part of what Neff (2012) conceptualizes as "venture labor."

Critical debates about worker independence are especially pertinent to the culture industries, fields that overwhelmingly rely upon freelance and project-based labor. In examining the dialectic between the ostensible rewards of a career in the culture industries—including the prestige, autonomy, and "coolness" of the job—and the very real risks of flexible employment, Neff et al. (2005) underscore the progressively entrepreneurial nature of creative labor. The rhetoric of self-investment is emphasized as cultural workers are compelled to internalize, and even glamorize, various employment risks (pp. 317, 331). To this end, entrepreneurialism has become a much-vaunted ideal in the creative and digital media industries as reconfigured organizational and economic structures command content creators to understand themselves through "the values and qualities of enterprise" (Storey, Salaman, & Platman, 2005, p. 1049; see also Gill, 2010; Neff, 2012). Against this backdrop, it is perhaps not surprising that there exists a booming market for how-to resources aimed at aspiring creative industrialists, including The Creative Entrepreneur: A DIY Visual Guidebook for Making Business Ideas Real and Make Your Mark: The Creative's Guide to Building a Business with Impact among countless other titles (see also Duffy, 2015).

These discourses often encourage entrepreneurial aspirants to engage in self-branding practices, which draw upon the codes, processes, and market logics of mainstream culture industries (Hearn, 2008). This is not to suggest impression management is a distinctly modern social imperative; rather, efforts to manage one's reputation have deep antecedents in Western culture (Pooley, 2010). Yet structural transformations associated with the neoliberal ideologies of individuality and self-governance have instigated more calculated strategies to brand the self. Marwick (2013a) explores the rise of these imperatives in the context of web 2.0, revealing how socially mediated entrepreneurialism gets articulated through attention-seeking and status-enhancing behaviors.

Despite the veritable groundswell of research published on creative workers and digitally enabled entrepreneurialism, we have argued elsewhere (Duffy, 2013, 2015) that the implications of this system for gendered subjectivities have yet to be fully realized. Fashion blogs, we contend, are an ideal site to explore how (mostly) female social media producers represent their branded personae given the extent to which personal style bloggers negotiate codes of heteronormative femininity with discourses and practices of masculine entrepreneurialism (Lewis, 2014; Marwick, 2013a). Indeed, mainstream media depict fashion bloggers as a particularly visible and self-enterprising class of digital cultural producer; this perspective can be summed up by a recent Wired (UK) feature, which opened, "rarely are fashion bloggers just hobbyists these days—increasingly *they are entrepreneurs with business plans and revenue*" (Epstein, 2015, italics added). Accordingly, this article explores fashion bloggers through the lens of what Gray (2003) termed "enterprising femininity," a subjectivity formed through the characteristics of flexibility, valuable skills, informal knowledges, and modes of self-fashioning rooted in the consumer marketplace (pp. 492–493).

To examine how fashion bloggers represent their personae as enterprising feminine subjects, we conducted a qualitative analysis of textual (n = 38 author narratives) and visual (n = 760 Instagram images[2]) content published by top-ranked US fashion bloggers; we supplement this with in-depth interviews with eight full-time fashion/beauty bloggers. Drawing on this data, we argue that well-known bloggers utilize a series of interrelated tropes—predestined passionate work, staging the glam life, and carefully curated social sharing—to depict an updated version of the post-feminist ideal of "having it all." These tropes articulate a form of entrepreneurial femininity that obscures the labor, discipline, and capital necessary to emulate these standards, while deploying the unshakable myth that women should work through and for consumption. We close by tying these findings to more widespread trends in a creative economy marked by social inequalities of gender, race, class, and more.

Creative Work in the New Economy

Studies of creative laborers and their employment conditions have flourished over the last decade, offering key insight into the shifting positioning of worker subjectivities within various technological, political-economic, and regulatory contexts. This mushrooming body of literature encompasses various theoretical frameworks and subfields, including political economy of communication, sociologies of work, critical theory, and policy research (e.g. Blair, 2001; Deuze, 2007; Duffy, 2013; Hesmond-halgh & Baker, 2011). Despite significant variance in their conceptual approaches and sites of analysis, these scholars collectively highlight key features of labor in contemporary media and cultural industries, including high barriers to entry, unstable employment, occupational flexibility, and the pervasive mentality that "you're only as good as your last [TV script, novel, magazine article]" (Blair, 2001). Of course, these characteristics are offset by the perceived glamour and independence associated with a creative career. As Hesmondhalgh and Baker (2011) explain, "good work" in the culture industries is ascribed to assumptions about compensation, involvement, autonomy, and the production of high-quality creative products (pp. 17, 39).

More recently, scholars have shifted their attention to the nature of creative work across the information and technology sectors (e.g. Gill, 2010; Gregg, 2011; Neff, 2012). Using a Foucauldian lens, Gill (2010) characterizes the new media work environment as one wherein traditional power hierarchies are supplanted by a new worker-subject tasked with "managing the self in conditions of radical uncertainty" (p. 249, italics original). This technologically mediated worker must constantly perform the labor of the self as her "entire existence is built around work" (Gill, 2010). Not only does this mode of self-governance shift the burden of management from formal structures onto the individual, it also testifies to the further encroachment of commercial discourses into all realms of social life (Banet-Weiser, 2012; Hearn, 2008).

For creative aspirants seeking employment in fashion and magazine journalism, online resources such as Ed2010 and the Independent Fashion Bloggers (IFB) Coalition advocate crafting a personal brand "to set yourself apart from the competition and highlight what makes you special" (Foresto, n.d.). Noting that blogs, in particular, are assumed to be "an extension, or representation, of [yourself]," IFB positioned self-branding as "the most important way to proactively control your career development and how the market perceives you" (Noricks, 2013). Furthermore, an expert advised Ed2010 readers, "If you're passionate about something, that's going to shine through . . . but if you're being inauthentic or trying to sound like you're someone you're not when you're online, people are going to pick up on this really fast" (Foresto, n.d.). These requirements for personal branding rely upon participants' emotional labor, which "requires one to induce or suppress feeling in order to sustain the outward countenance that produces the proper state of mind in others" (Hochschild, 1983, p. 7). The gendered nature of "emotional labor" is part of a long history of "women's work" comprising activities that are undervalued and unpaid—despite their central role in maintaining the capitalist circuit of production. As Jarrett (2014) compellingly argues of contemporary modes of digital labor, "the uncanny, ghostly presence of women's labor can provide a framework to reinvigorate analysis of specific qualities of the laboring involved in the digital economy" (p. 26). The success of fashion bloggers and other cultural producers who make their living by sharing their "passions" and connecting with readership makes clear that a substantial (and ever-increasing) amount of value and capital is generated by this type of work.

Post-Feminism, Self-Branding, and Social Media Production

The infectious rhetoric of personal branding has been linked to gendered discourses and, more specifically, the contemporary logic of post-feminism, which celebrates individual choice, independence, and modes of self-expression rooted in the consumer marketplace (Banet-Weiser, 2012; Gill, 2007; McRobbie, 2004). Gill (2007) identifies the similar injunctions of post-feminism and neoliberalism, compelling subjects to "render one's life knowable and meaningful through a narrative of free choice and autonomy" (p. 154). Exploring the imbrication of this narrative to various shifts associated with emergent digital technologies, Banet-Weiser (2012) notes how post-feminism and interactivity are constitutive of a "neoliberal moral framework," that calls for the cultivation and regulation of a self-brand (p. 56). This post-feminist self-brand is constructed through girls' and young women's bodily display, cultivation of affect, and narratives of authenticity. What is especially problematic about digital expressions of the post-feminist self-brand is the extent to which visibility gets articulated through normative feminine discourses and practices, including those anchored in the consumer marketplace (p. 64).

The contemporary ideals of individualism, creative autonomy, and self-branding provide the necessary backstory for understanding forms of gendered social media production that have emerged in recent years: mommy blogs (e.g. Lopez, 2009), hauler videos (Banet-Weiser & Arzumanova, 2012), DIY craft sites (Gajjala, 2015; Luckman, 2013), and fashion blogs (Duffy, 2013;

Luvaas, 2013; Marwick, 2013b; Nathanson, 2014; Rocamora, 2012), among others. Of these, we argue that fashion blogs occupy a particularly prominent place in the popular and scholarly imaginations. Mainstream media coverage of fashion bloggers is ubiquitous with top-ranking personal style bloggers making deep inroads into the book, magazine, television, and retail fashion industries, among others. Scholars, too, have studied personal style bloggers as part of critical inquiries into the commercial logic of authenticity (Duffy, 2013; Marwick, 2013b), post-feminist commodity culture in an age of thrift (Nathanson, 2014), emergent global fashion ecologies (Luvaas, 2013; Pham, 2013), and the relationship between "traditional" and "new" sources of fashion journalism (Rocamora, 2012), among others. While much of this research addresses the promotional nature of blogger activities—including what Nathanson (2014) describes as the dual-level production of the self and of the career—scholars have not yet examined fashion bloggers through the lens of entrepreneurial femininity, which we argue is a key theoretical context. Furthermore, as these critical studies tend to draw on a few paradigmatic exemplars, systematic studies of fashion blogging are lacking. Moreover, by looking only at media texts, they ignore the value of understanding the production of the fashion blogger subject in her own voice. In this article, we attempt to address these gaps in the literature by providing a broad analysis of bloggers' digital self-brands as well as a look at the lived experiences behind these socially mediated personae.

Method

In order to examine the self-presentation strategies of well-known bloggers, we conducted a qualitative analysis of the textual and visual content of the top 38 US fashion blogs, drawn from a list of the highest ranked bloggers in this category published on Bloglovin, a website used for following and discovering new blogs. Because our focus was on individualized self-production and self-promotion, we eliminated those with more than 10 employees; two others in our original sample were eliminated as they were either defunct or had since been bought by corporate blog networks. Most of the bloggers we studied were between the ages of 18 and 35; the majority were either Caucasian (30) or Asian-American (5).[3] To this end, we found that the bloggers overwhelmingly conformed to a Western, heteronormative beauty aesthetic (young, thin, light-skinned).[4]

The textual and visual elements of each blogger's "About Me" section were coded or, in the cases where none was included, we selected a media interview in which the blogger spoke about the creation of her blog. Indeed, we found it important to retain a sense of what Banet-Weiser and Arzumanova (2012) call "creative authorship," wherein the curated authorship of the self is done against the backdrop of feminine confessional culture (p. 164).[5] We also gathered a strategic random sample of 20 Instagram photos of each blogger (n =760 images),[6] using the Instagram account linked to the blog; both visual and textual elements of blogs were coded. The coding sheet was guided by a preliminary review of the data and further refined inductively. The categories that emerged included expressions of authenticity/ relatability, passion/creative autonomy, self as brand, American Dream, education/experience, personality, commercial affiliations, and travel, among others.

We supplemented this data with information gleaned from in-depth interviews with eight professional bloggers, including two in our original textual/Instagram sample.[7] Although these interviews were conducted as part of a separate project on women, creativity, and social media, they nonetheless helped to provide a more reflexive account of the production of the socially mediated self. Interviews were conducted in person or over the phone and lasted approximately 45 minutes to an hour. Topics included participants' background and/or expertise, narratives of "getting started" and aspirations, creative production and promotion processes, reflections on branding and entrepreneurship, and relationships to advertisers, audiences, and other bloggers.

Entrepreneurial Femininity Among Fashion Bloggers

Our analysis of blogger narratives and Instagram images revealed that bloggers utilized three interrelated tropes:

1. The Destiny of Passionate Work;
2. The Glam Life; and
3. Carefully Curated Social Sharing

To articulate a form of "entrepreneurial femininity" that draws upon post-feminist narratives of individual choice, independence, and self-fashioning; yet, bloggers tended to downplay the discipline and investments that go into this mode of self-production. Our interview participants, meanwhile, brought the labor of social media creation, distribution, and promotion into stark relief; the project of the fashion blogger, they assured us, requires significant reserves of time and energy.

The Destiny of Passionate Work

Discourses of "passion" have been used to rationalize un- or under-compensated labor in both the fashion and new media sectors, illuminating how producers derive value from their creative activities irrespective of monetary compensation or material rewards (Arvidsson, Malossi, & Naro, 2010; Postigo, 2009). The bloggers in our sample also invoked the narrative of career passion, despite the fact that they *also* earn a presumably sizable income from their digital media brands. For instance, while one blogger articulated her site as a forum to "share her passion for life, art, and all things style" (eat.sleep. wear), another described her blog as "a creative outlet fueled by a passion" (Happily Grey). Similarly, recalling what inspired her to launch Late Afternoon, Liz C. wrote, "I started out when I was still in college working on my degree in social psychology. I was drowning in lab work and needed a creative outlet." These narratives of passion and creative expression suggest individuals came upon blogging unintentionally, as an escape from the banality of unrewarding professional lives. By downplaying calculated entrepreneurial aspirations, these bloggers reaffirm the post-feminist ideal of individual success obtained through inner self-discovery.

Indeed, the version of passionate work offered by the bloggers in this study is noteworthy for its seemingly destined nature, which deflates the notion of masculine self-enterprise. For instance, on her "About Me" page, Garance Doré encouraged readers to look at "the five part story that explains *how I came to find my calling,* [. . .] and then finally, start the blog that you're reading right now" (emphasis added). Geri's (because I'm addicted) personal narrative invoked the "creative outlet" rhetoric while calling attention to the successes that seemingly unfolded at her feet over the years:

> *I started this blog in 2005 chronicling fashion, music, food (including a culinary school stint!) and art as a creative outlet while miz [miserable] at my full time job and over the years it has been named a favorite by Women's Wear Daily, Vanity Fair, Lucky Magazine, Refinery 29 and WhoWhatWear. This bloggy [sic] has afforded me all sort of incredible opportunities like launching a capsule collection clothing line with Lovers + Friends, starring in national commercials,*

> *traveling the world for all sorts of rad things . . . I can't imagine what life would have been like if I hadn't clicked over onto blogger and hit the "create blog" button.*

By emphasizing an almost mystical inevitability of their fashion blogging careers (borne out of following their hearts and experimenting with digital technology), bloggers demonstrate what happens when the self is a project of continuous labor (Gill, 2010) matured into the social media age. Passion is no longer just a driver or a byproduct of new media work, but also a means of rationalizing individualized success. Implicit in this narrativization, however, is the notion that one need only to look inward and fuel oneself with passion to find success; those who are not successful are simply not passionate enough.

Bloggers' profiles and Instagram feeds were also spaces to reconcile the contradiction between production and consumption. Indeed, despite the central role of consumerism in providing fodder for blog and Instagram content, those we analyzed were meticulous in their efforts to show what they were doing was indeed work, albeit a highly pleasurable form. On Instagram, bloggers included images of DSLR cameras, smartphones, and laptops to reveal the technologies of creation that were a regular part of their daily work routines. Often, these images depicted a well-organized, inspirational working environment, instances of what Pinterest and Reddit users have dubbed "workspace porn." Wendy (Wendy's Look Book) posted a photo on Instagram of her sitting on a window seat, propped up by a white pillow with an Apple laptop resting on her outstretched legs. Her clothes are casual-chic, and she is wearing light makeup with a headband in her long, wavy hair. The image is captioned, "Favorite spot in the room! Typing away and working on tomorrow's blog post." This image was not an impulsive "selfie," but carefully staged to ensure adequate lighting and a clean aesthetic, underscoring the labor required to display the working subject.

In other instances, bloggers implicitly and explicitly defined their practices as productive labor rather than leisurely consumption; of course, the boundaries between these are—and have been—muddled in the feminine realm (Gregg, 2008). In one of her Instagram posts, Olivia Palermo is posed in the foreground of a retail space captioned, "popping by this morning for my monthly meeting @piperlime" followed by a string of emojis. While the visual display locates her in the consumer sphere, the textual referent clarifies that she is there on business, as a cultural producer. Mary (Happily Grey) posted a similar photo outside the British high-street shop Whistles, noting, "Thanks for an amazing afternoon to my new friends at @thisiswhistles #hgxlondon." Travel images, which we discuss in the following section, were also framed as a pleasurable yet necessary part of the job. For instance, Aimee's (Song of Style) image of the sun setting over a hillside is captioned, "Working on a Saturday evening at the job site but not complaining with a view like this and the coolest clients. #ilovemyjob #hustlin." Although she justifies the incursion of work on her leisure time with acknowledgments of an enviable location, her comments speak to the "always-on" lifestyle of the social media entrepreneur.

And, accordingly, our interview participants brought the less glamorous aspects of this lifestyle into sharp focus. As personal style blogger Jenn explained, "I do it all. I do styling, I write for my site . . . I do TV segments . . . I have a weekly syndicated radio segment, and I just started a vintage jewelry business." Then, identifying one of the main challenges involved with this mode of entrepreneurialism, she added, "we all have to work really, really hard to build up our own [audience] numbers."

Figure 9.8 Instagram image of Aimee Song (Song of Style) on a trip to Morocco sponsored by fashion brand Diane von Furstenberg.

Similarly, in explaining why she recently hired an intern, couture fashion blogger Joy explained,

It is getting harder and harder to handle everything. And people don't understand that a blog is like . . . a company, and you need people to help you out, to keep growing. Because it's a lot of work doing everything . . . I used to do photographing by myself, going to the event, tweeting at the event, coming back home and blog, edit the pictures, I did the videos too, like, it's too much for one person.

Although this honest self-appraisal of blog labor was omitted from most "About Me" statements, Blair Eadie (Atlantic-Pacific) was an exception who acknowledged the level of self-discipline required to manage her blog:

During busy weeks and sometimes busy months it feels daunting to keep up both a day job and the blog, but I have so many lovely readers and supporters who make it all worth it . . . I went to a big state school that taught me very early on the importance of self motivation. There is no one there to make sure you came to class or check in on you if you haven't turned in your homework in a while. You have to be disciplined and motivated to push yourself, knowing there is no one else there to do it for you.

Eadie's comment directly invokes the neoliberal ideal of the enterprising worker-subject; yet her acknowledgment of her "lovely readers and supporters" reveals the calculated nature of this post (i.e. compare this description with Jenn's comment about "numbers"). Taken together, bloggers' spectacular images of "predestined passionate work" romanticize the project of the fashion blogger while concealing the less dazzling aspects of production: flexibility, self-management, and the "always-on" persona, all of which represent the kinds of immaterial labor that increasingly characterize cultural work in an era of advanced capitalism (Lazzarato, 1996).

The Glam Life

A separate yet related way that fashion bloggers unsettle the binary between labor and leisure is through their staging of "the glam life," characterized by global travel, invitations to exclusive events, and access to luxury goods and swag. By depicting this lifestyle on their Instagram accounts, the bloggers in our sample engaged in what Marwick (2013a) has described as "aspirational production," an attention-seeking practice whereby an individual presents herself in a high[er].status social position (pp. 122–123). For example, Fashion Squad's Carolina Engman shared a photo of herself sandwiched between actress/writer Lena Dunham and musician Taylor Swift, ostensibly an attempt to elevate her standing in the imagination of readers and advertising partners. Casually dressed, the three women smile for the camera in what appears to be a café or shop, indicating that they are peers rather than individuals encountering each other in some other situation (e.g. a fan meet-and-greet) that would imply a status differential. Similarly, Natalie Off Duty posted a photo with model Kate Upton at an Express jeans event for which they collaborated: "Thanks to my girls for coming out to meet me and #KateUpton for @expressrunway #expressjeans night!" By aligning their personas with established celebrities, these bloggers situate themselves within what Mears (2011) described as the glamorous aura of elite work, wherein prestige becomes a vital form of social currency.

It is perhaps not surprising that designer goods are also central to bloggers' staging of "the glam life"; the blogs and Instagram feeds we analyzed displayed a compendium of Valentino pumps, Chanel handbags, and Céline sunglasses, luxury goods offset by the occasional thrift store purchase or product identified with a discount retailer such as Kohl's or Old Navy. In many cases, these products were "gifted" from designers and publicists as part of a mutual incentive structure that mobilizes the activities of social influencers in the aptly named "attention economy." The practice of "tagging," or linking to a branded product in one's blog or Instagram feed, stands as public recognition of a commercial gift; for instance, the bloggers we analyzed posted: "Collecting sorries. Thanks @monicavinader #monicavinader" (The Man Repeller); "Sharing my favorite @gorjana pieces today on Happily Grey. Head over to www.gorjana-griffin.com to shop my special curated section" (Happily Grey); "Oh how I love a classic black boot with a Cuban heel . . . Thanks @senso" (Ring My Bell); and "the prettiest flowers thanks to #highcampsupply" (Atlantic-Pacific), among others. Comments such as these tended to generate substantial feedback, an indicator of the gendering of the "social media audience commodity" whereby (female) consumer-audiences provide valuable data that can be harnessed by marketing institutions (Shepherd, 2014).

To this end, "the glam life" is a continually reiterated lifestyle that primarily exists through the aesthetics and language of commercial brands. For Aimee Song, a trip to Morocco is an extended marketing opportunity sponsored by Diane Von Furstenberg [see Figure 9.8]. The caption for this image reads, "All about my rug shopping tips in Morocco on #songofstyle today! Wrap romper by @dvf. #journeyo.fadress http://www.songofstyle.com." Travel photos were a habitual presence on the blogs and Instagram feeds of those in our sample; the cityscapes or beaches of Greece, Morocco, Korea, France, Spain, and Thailand thus provided stunning backdrops for blogger photo-shoots. Bloggers also posted artfully arranged food photos ("Winding down over fig crostini straight out of the oven and a glass of wine," from Late Afternoon), and restaurant location check-ins were common (Viva Luxury posted of her "Late lunch at @ivyrestaurants with my girl @sydnesummer"). While these check-ins testify to the ubiquitous culture of sharing that structures social media activity, the act of "tagging" particular restaurants also speaks to the extent to which leisure activities (if we presume not all of these events are sponsored) become another opportunity to shape the contours of one's personal brand.

Navigating this paradox of the personal brand— translating the self into a consistent yet distinct visual aesthetic, written voice, and potential partner for commercial brands—requires a tremendous amount of self-discipline. Our interviewees illuminated the work that goes into crafting this visage. Jenn remarked that bloggers can end up as "a flash in the pan," because they underestimate the work it entails. "They think that it's going to be really glamorous," she said. "And so they see other bloggers maybe working at brands or getting free things and they only see . . . everything that's through an Instagram filter that looks so fabulous." As Jenn's comment suggests, a key factor in the "glam life" is its effortless aesthetic. This lifestyle that includes networking, global travel, and frequent event attendance (on top of regularly creating blog content) is artfully displayed on social media, obscuring the work that goes into obtaining and maintaining the production of the self-brand.

Interview participants were also quite candid about the challenges of working with corporate sponsors that failed to resonate with their own brand image, lest they be accused of *doing it just for the money*. As Los Angeles–based blogger Eliza confessed,

If a brand comes to you and is like, "We'll give you [a] paycheck to write two blog posts" . . . it is obviously

hard to say no to things that come along because it is such a feast-or-famine kind of lifestyle . . . I think it can be a little bit scary that at the first of every month you're like, "alright, how am I gonna make money this month . . ."

Karina, too, explained that if she had one regret, it would be her lack of selectivity with advertisers in the early days of blogging. Now, she continued, "because my site has become a business, and it is its own brand, and so now I have to be more selective because my readers expect a certain level of quality from me." As such narratives make clear, the presentation of the self must be carefully managed in a way that still enables brand partners to communicate meaning *through* the blogger. Furthermore, since commercial brands are unlikely to partner with bloggers lacking a commodifiable ("glam") social media image, the codes, aesthetics, and subjectivities of mainstream fashion culture get reaffirmed.

Carefully Curated Personal Sharing

Despite their vigilant presentation of "the glam life," most of the bloggers in our sample shared elements of their personal lives with readers, ostensibly an attempt to depict themselves as "authentic" (for a discussion of authenticity in the blogosphere, see Duffy, 2013; Marwick, 2013b; McQuarrie, Miller, & Phillips, 2013). The gendered nature of this intimate social sharing must be historically contextualized, as Victorian era demarcations between public and private were guided by assumptions about masculine and feminine realms, respectively. However, the twentieth century saw the progressive unfolding of a "sentimentalization of the public sphere," a manifestation of what Illouz (2007) terms emotional capitalism. While Illouz contends that the axioms of emotion and communication that infiltrated bureaucratic work cultures effaced traditional gender norms, feminist media scholars have explored contemporary expressions of a gendered "confessional culture" that compels the private worlds of young women into the public sphere (Harris, 2003). The recent ascension of social media has coincided with renewed emphases on feminine self-expression and visibility that exist within consumer spaces (Banet-Weiser, 2012; Banet-Weiser & Arzumanova, 2012). The bloggers we studied performed visibility according to scripts that made them simultaneously relatable and aspirational.

In their "About Me" statements, bloggers frequently shared personal details by, for example, acknowledging the support of parents or partners (e.g. boyfriends, fiancés, or husbands; none of the bloggers in our sample explicitly identified as lesbian, gay, bisexual, and transgender [LGBT]) or offering up brief statements of faith. Children, friends, and pets made consistent appearances in their Instagram feeds; eat.sleep.wear shared "date night . . . with my boo"; See (anna) Jane shared an image of her sleeping husband and infant, "Happy first Father's Day to this guy. He's already the best dad ever," and The Glamourai uploaded a photo of her pet toy spaniel next to a hairdryer, "Someone is in a fight with the blow dryer."

In other instances, bloggers shared more candid images of their lives, seemingly letting their guard down and presenting themselves as "authentic" in ways that temper the glamour lifestyles discussed above. For instance, in the "About Me" section of her blog, Brooklyn Blonde confesses, "I grew up in a fairly bad neighborhood, but wouldn't change it for the world. It made me, what I think, such a well-rounded person." Damsel in Dior posted an image of herself looking fashionable albeit distraught with the caption: "'crap my wallet is gone' look of the day." Similarly, Kendi's "Blurry Selfie; Messy House," reveals a table scattered with papers as the backdrop for a full-length shot of her in a summer outfit. These images do little to disrupt the overall aesthetic but, instead, offer representations of life that would not appear in the pages of a fashion magazine. Others offered individual expressions of quirkiness or wit. For instance, That's Chic's Instagram feed included the blogger in front of neon sign for "Flo's V8 Café" wearing Minnie Mouse ears and a black sweatshirt with the caption: "If you are looking for a good time, just take some smart ass to Disneyland and listen to their commentary." Leandra Medine of The Man Repeller is particularly well known for a mode of frank personal sharing that doubles as entertainment; she wrote a clothing-based memoir in which she notoriously recounted her first sexual encounter, during which she wore white athletic socks.

Behind the scenes, though, bloggers reflected on the challenge of trying to seem "authentic" in the minds of readers. As Fashion Toast author Rumi confessed to a writer from Into the Gloss: "It's hard not to think of things in terms of the last post on your blog." She added that she constantly asks herself, "What's next, what's going to look better? What else can I do with photography? Is my clothing too inaccessible? Am I not affordable, am I not relatable?" Her invocation of the term "relatable" nods toward the popular construction of fashion bloggers as "real people," a pervasive myth that has been challenged by findings that the blogosphere is heavily imbricated with markers of existing social and economic capital (Duffy, 2015). The bloggers we interviewed also acknowledged the personal demands of being a social media brand. As Liv reflected,

> It's hard to not have [your blog] be a personal reflection of yourself. And you like to think that everyone likes you, and everyone likes what you have to say, [But] . . . we're human, we can't help but change and so, as I go on in life, I might be interested in different things, or need different things, you know, maybe I'll have a baby, I don't know if I'll blog about that, I don't know if that's on brand for me or if I'd want to keep it private.

Liv's comment about being "on brand" indexes the blurring of separate spheres associated with context collapse, which makes it "impossible to differ self-presentation strategies" in social media environments (Marwick & boyd, 2010). Meanwhile, Karina explained her desire to make her blog more "personal," adding,

> And just being real with readers and not just, "Oh, here's another pretty picture of me in a cute outfit." But, you know, it's really what's going on. You know, everybody has difficulties in their life. And I think it would almost be a disservice to my readers if I wasn't honest because that's very relatable, you know, when you share those things that maybe are a little bit more personal, more guarded.

While Karina's comment underscores how important considerations of the audience are to bloggers, other interview participants similarly explained how cultivating a relatable persona involves interactions with audiences.

Full-time blogger Claudia emphasized the imperative to be responsive to her readers, explaining,

> I try to keep on top of comments. If I get a question I try to respond right away . . . when I first started I would get, like, 80 to 150 comments every time I did a post and it was crazy trying to write back.

Her reference to responding "right away" prompted us to ask about how much time she devotes to the blog. She clarified, "I try not to do stuff on the weekends and if I do it's just taking photos, but I try not to be on the computer too much to get a break and be with my family." Claudia was unique in demarcating labor and leisure time, although she too admitted to "just taking photos" on the weekends. Other full-time bloggers, such as Crystal, said she "doesn't really differentiate" between labor and leisure. Not only does this comment describe "presence bleed," which Gregg (2011) defines as the blurring of work and nonwork time into one another, but it also offers another explanation of why bloggers' personal images and anecdotes seep into professional spaces.

Discussion and Conclusion

The sustained growth of the independent workforce, which marks a rupture with the so-called "era of big work" (Horowitz, 2014), has coincided with a pervasive rhetoric about the merits of social media platforms as vehicles for "getting discovered" and "making a living from one's passion project." Against this backdrop, genres of social media production that focus on traditionally feminine domains—mommy blogging and micro-economies of DIY craft, for example—have been positioned as conduits to financial independence and female empowerment. Despite important findings on these genres, including those that productively problematize these narratives of "empowerment" (e.g. Luckman, 2013), this research has little import for social media contexts where the enterprising self is made visible through personal branding strategies. By analyzing fashion bloggers, however, we can assess how social media producer-brands negotiate codes of hetero-normative femininity with discourses and practices of masculine entrepreneurialism.

The bloggers in our sample, who have translated their voices of authority into lucrative and seemingly fulfilling careers, use social media to depict an updated version of the post-feminist ideal of "having it all." And in contrast to the images of "having it all" that circulated in the analogue era—in the pages of *Cosmopolitan* under Helen Gurley Brown's editorship or, alternatively, through the fictional characters of Ally McBeal, Carrie Bradshaw, and Elle Woods, among others[8]—these socially mediated versions are ostensibly women just like us. Yet, just as this rhetoric of "real" obscures hierarchies of age, race, class, sexuality, and body type (as we discuss below), the codes by which top-ranked fashion bloggers represent themselves veil the labor, discipline, and capital that go into the production of the digital self.

Through discourses of passion, bloggers create a notion of work that doesn't seem like work as labor and leisure blend seamlessly together: meetings in shopping spaces, photo-shoots in exotic locations, and the ability to work from home. Under this shiny veneer are very real disadvantages of an always-on, 24/7 workstyle. For instance, nuancing the much-vaunted ideal of "flexibility," Gregg (2008) illuminates how the ability to work from anywhere translates into "constant contactability and the ever present possibility, if not the outright expectation, of work" (p. 290). Moreover, by articulating passion through the language of destiny, bloggers encourage the kinds of individualistic, self-discovery characteristic of the post-feminist self. Next, depictions of the "glam life" create the spectacle of a lifestyle flush with celebrities, designers, and fellow social influencers who attend parties and other social events in between international jet setting. Yet, these socially mediated representations of affective pleasure and compulsory sociality must be understood within a long history of gendered emotional labor (Hochschild, 1983). An element of "deep acting" (ibid) is no doubt necessary for the blissful countenance in photos, the gracious interactions with readers across various social media sites, and the witty expressions that enable them to rise above the din of the legions of other aspiring taste-makers. Finally, given that "authenticity" and "realness" are governing logics in the fashion blogging community (Duffy, 2013; McQuarrie et al., 2013; Marwick, 2013b), it is perhaps not surprising that bloggers moderate representations of the "glam life" with images that make them seem just like us. The latter depictions serve as a kind of aesthetic foil to images of artful perfection that circulate in women's magazines. Of course, even these seeming moments of candor—with family, friends, and pets included—do not disrupt bloggers' well-crafted social media personae.

Despite their seemingly effortless nature, bloggers' online presentations were paragons of discipline in their displays of passionate work, glamorous lifestyles, and selective social sharing in their construction of blogging as a way to "have it all"; the interviews revealed the significant amount of time and energy required to achieve this. Many bloggers described navigating uncertain economic environments and diversifying their work beyond that of maintaining a blog to having clothing/jewelry lines, doing media appearances, even teaching. "Having it all" is thus part of the carefully constructed, deftly managed, and constantly renegotiated self-brand.

While the articulation of entrepreneurial femininity we explored may at first blush seem to challenge conventional assumptions about male-dominated entrepreneurialism (e.g. Lewis, 2014; Marwick, 2013a), we do not believe these bloggers' achievements should be read as wholly optimistic accounts of female empowerment in an age of social media. In fact, our findings suggest that these representations do little to resolve widespread gender stereotypes and social inequalities in the digital industries. For one, those in our sample adhered to what Banet-Weiser (2012) describes as "preexisting gendered and racial scripts and their attendant grammars of exclusion;" that is, they were overwhelming young, thin, and white (p. 89). The underrepresentation of women of color, LGBT, and plus-size models reveals how the playing field for "top-ranked" bloggers is highly uneven— even despite the outward countenance of "real women." Moreover, the aesthetic that was represented in the blogs and Instagrams suggests a level of disciplining the body or physical maintenance that is often discussed in theories of aesthetic labor (Entwistle & Wissinger, 2006).

In closing, we must acknowledge that fashion bloggers and their content are bound to a capitalist system that reifies particular conceptions of femininity. The form of self-creation and brand-laden promotion they engage in ensures that they do not deviate too far from their traditional roles as consumer; in so doing, it privileges those with existing economic capital and/or individuals that conform to the aesthetic standards celebrated by mainstream media. These depictions of entrepreneurial femininity are thus inscribed within a culture that constructs women as feminine subjectivities, emotional laborers, and above all, consumers.

Declaration of Conflicting Interests

The author(s) declared no potential conflicts of interest with respect to the research, authorship, and/or publication of this article.

Funding

The author(s) received no financial support for the research, authorship, and/or publication of this article.

Notes

1. Defined as those who work in nontraditional environments and identify as freelancers, contractors, and/or self-employed.
2. The images used in this article have been made available to the public and are included as third-party material in a new work for the purpose of criticism and/or review. The images are directly referenced and critiqued, thus fair dealing applies, and their use falls under this copyright exception.
3. The others were Latina (2) and multi-ethnicity (1).

4. Based upon images on their blog including textual and visual data.

5. We acknowledge that some of these individuals may have managers/agents that help to construct their persona.

6. We gathered this dataset in July 2014, starting with each blogger's most recent Instagram post and collecting every 10th image until we had collected 20 images per blogger.

7. Interview informants are given pseudonyms, including those in our original sample.

8. See, for example, Moseley and Read (2002).

References

Arvidsson, A., Malossi, G., & Naro, S. (2010). Passionate work? Labour conditions in the Milan fashion industry. *Journal for Cultural Research*, 14, 295–309.

Banet-Weiser, S. (2012). *Authentic™: The politics of ambivalence in a brand culture*. New York, NY: NYU Press.

Banet-Weiser, S., & Arzumanova, I. (2012). Creative authorship, self-actualizing women, and the self-brand. In C. Chris & D. Gerstner (Eds.), *Media authorship* (pp. 163–179). New York, NY: Routledge.

Blair, H. (2001). "You're only as good as your last job": The labour process and labour market in the British film industry. *Work, Employment & Society*, 15, 149–169.

Deuze, M. (2007). *Media work*. Cambridge, UK: Polity Press.

Duffy, B. E. (2013). *Remake, remodel: Women's magazines in the digital age*. Champaign: University of Illinois Press.

Duffy, B. E. (2015). The romance of work: Gender and aspirational labour in contemporary culture industries. *International Journal of Cultural Studies*. Advance online publication. doi:10.1177/1367877915572186

Entwistle, J., & Wissinger, E. (2006). Keeping up appearances: Aesthetic labour in the fashion modeling industries of London and New York. *The Sociological Review*, 54, 774–794.

Epstein, S. (2015, February). Meet the fashion mavens making big bucks from style musings. *Wired*. Retrieved from http://www. wired.co.uk/magazine /archive/2015/02/start/wear-blog-earn

Foresto, A. (n.d.). *It's all about me: How to brand yourself online*. Retrieved from http://ed2010.com/generic/its -all-about-me.how-to-brand-yourself-online/

Gajjala, R. (2015). When your seams get undone, do you learn to sew or to kill monsters? *The Communication Review*, 18, 23–36.

Gill, R. (2007). Postfeminist media culture: Elements of a sensibility. *European Journal of Cultural Studies*, 10, 147–166.

Gill, R. (2008). Culture and subjectivity in neoliberal and postfeminist times. *Subjectivity*, 25, 432–445.

Gill, R. (2010). Life is a pitch: Managing the self in new media work. In M. Deuze (Ed.), *Managing media work* (pp. 249– 262). London, England: SAGE.

Gray, A. (2003). Enterprising femininity: New modes of work and subjectivity. *European Journal of Cultural Studies*, 6, 489–506.

Gregg, M. (2008). The normalisation of flexible female labour in the information economy. *Feminist Media Studies*, 8, 285–299.

Gregg, M. (2011). *Work's intimacy*. Cambridge, UK: Polity Press.

Harris, A. (2003). *Future girl: Young women in the twenty-first century*. New York, NY: Routledge.

Hearn, A. (2008). Meat, mask, burden: Probing the contours of the branded self. *Journal of Consumer Culture*, 8, 197–217.

Hesmondhalgh, D., & Baker, S. (2011). *Creative labour: Media work in three cultural industries*. London, England: Routledge.

Hochschild, A. R. (1983). *The managed heart: Commercialization of human feeling*. Berkeley: University of California Press.

Horowitz, S. (2014, August 26). America, say goodbye to the era of Big Work. *Los Angeles Times*. Retrieved from http://www. latimes.com/opinion/op-ed/la-oe -horowitz-work-freelancers.20140826-story.html

Illouz, E. (2007). *Cold intimacies: The making of emotional capitalism*. Cambridge, UK: Polity Press.

Jarrett, K. (2014). The relevance of "women's work": Social reproduction and immaterial labour in digital media. *Television & New Media*, 15, 14–29.

Lazzarato, M. (1996). Immaterial labour. In P. Virno & M. Hardt (Eds.), *Radical thought it Italy: A potential politics* (pp. 133– 150). Minneapolis: University of Minnesota Press.

Lewis, P. (2014). Postfeminism, femininities and organization studies: Exploring a new agenda. *Organization Studies*, 35, 1845–1866.

Lopez, L. K. (2009). The radical act of "mommy blogging": Redefining motherhood through the blogosphere. *New Media & Society*, 11, 729–747.

Luckman, S. (2013). The aura of the analogue in a digital age: Women's crafts, creative markets and home-based labour after Etsy. *Cultural Studies Review*, 19, 249–270.

Luvaas, B. (2013). Indonesian fashion blogs: On the promotional subject of personal style. *Fashion Theory: The Journal of Dress, Body & Culture*, 17, 55–76.

Marwick, A. (2013a). *Status update: Celebrity, publicity, and self-branding in web 2.0*. New Haven, CT: Yale University Press.

Marwick, A. (2013b). "They're really profound women; they're entrepreneurs": Conceptions of authenticity in fashion blogging. Presented at the International Conference on Web and Social Media, Cambridge, MA, 8 July.

Marwick, A. E., & boyd, D. (2010). I tweet honestly, I tweet passionately: Twitter users, context collapse, and the imagined audience. *New Media & Society*, 13, 114–133.

MBO Partners. (2013). *The state of independence in America*. Herndon, VA: Author.

McQuarrie, E. F., Miller, J., & Phillips, B. J. (2013). The megaphone effect: Taste and audience in fashion blogging. *Journal of Consumer Research*, 40, 136–158.

McRobbie, A. (2004). Post-feminism and popular culture. *Feminist Media Studies*, 4, 255–264.

Mears, A. (2011). *Pricing beauty: The making of a fashion model*. Oakland: University of California Press.

Moseley, R., & Read, J. (2002). "Having it Ally": Popular television (post-)feminism. *Feminist Media Studies*, 2, 231–249.

Nathanson, E. (2014). Dressed for economic distress: Blogging and the "new" pleasures of fashion. In D. Negra & Y. Tasker (Eds.), *Gendering the recession: Media and culture in an age of austerity* (pp. 192–228). Durham, NC: Duke University Press.

Neff, G. (2012). *Venture labor: Work and the burden of risk in innovative industries*. Cambridge, MA: MIT Press.

Neff, G., Wissinger, E., & Zukin, S. (2005). Entrepreneurial labor among cultural producers:

"Cool" jobs in "hot" industries. *Social Semiotics*, 15, 307–334.

Noricks, C. (2013, November 13). How a personal brand pyramid can help define your blog's direction. *Independent Fashion Bloggers*. Retrieved from http://heartifb.com/2013/11/13/ how-a-personal-brand-pyramid-can-help-define-your-blogs-direction/

Pham, M. T. H. (2013). Susie Bubble is a sign of the times: The embodiment of success in the Web 2.0 economy. *Feminist Media Studies*, 13, 245–267.

Pofeldt, E. (2012, April 3). What you'll need to know to be the boss in 2020. *Forbes*. Retrieved from http://www.forbes.com/sites/ elainepofeldt/2012/04/03 /what-youll-need-to-know-to-be-the-boss-in-2020/

Pooley, J. (2010). The consuming self: From flappers to Facebook. In M. Aronczyk & D. Powers (Eds.), *Blowing up the brand* (pp. 71–89). New York, NY: Peter Lang Publishing.

Postigo, H. (2009). America online volunteers: Lessons from an early co-production community. *International Journal of Cultural Studies*, 12, 451–469.

Rocamora, A. (2012). Hypertextuality and remediation in the fashion media: The case of fashion blogs. *Journalism Practice*, 6, 92–106.

Ross, A. (2009). *Nice work if you can get it: Life and labor in precarious times*. New York, NY: NYU Press.

Shepherd, T. (2014). Gendering the commodity audience in social media. In C. Carter, L. Steiner, & L. McLaughlin (Eds.), *The Routledge companion to media and gender* (pp. 157–167). New York, NY: Routledge.

Storey, J., Salaman, G., & Platman, K. (2005). Living with enterprise in an enterprise economy: Freelance and contract workers in the media. *Human Relations*, 58, 1033–1054.

Discussion Questions

1. The stated purpose of this reading is:

    To explore fashion bloggers through the lens of "enterprising femininity"; a bias (or prejudice) formed through flexibility, valuable skills, informed knowledges, and modes of self-fashioning rooted in the consumer marketplace.

    Work in groups of four with your classmates to re-write the purpose statement in everyday language. For example, what do you think the authors meant by 'self-fashioning rooted in the consumer marketplace'?

2. This article brings to light the large amount of work that goes into the image of "Having it All" as a female fashion blogger. Why do women hide the amount of work it takes to be a successful blogger? Does she want people to believe that to run a blog is easy and takes little time, money, or effort? Are there any stereotypes that fit the female blogger?

3. Several articles on the topic of "Having It All" can be found on the internet including Jennifer Szalai's January, 2015 essay on the history of "Having It All" (https://www.nytimes.com/2015/01/04/magazine/the-complicated-origins-of-having-it-all.html) . Read Szalai's short essay about the history of "Having It All" and compare the essay to the reading in your text.

CHAPTER 10
DRESS AND MEDIA

Kimberly A. Miller-Spillman

After you have read this chapter, you will understand:

- How fashion images can create anxiety for viewers
- How magazines retouch photographs to create idealized images
- How media images impact body image
- How media includes ads of violence toward women as a selling tool

Fashion is at our fingertips. With easy access, we can click on an icon and journey into our favorite fashion magazine, television show, blog, or website. These venues treat us to our favorite designer's latest runway show, a critique of red carpet dresses, an article about how to lose 10 pounds, and how to dress appropriately for a job interview. This information and its accompanying images are often infused with views of flawless human bodies and faces or what we refer to as **Western idealized images** or **Euro-American idealized images**. We refer to idealized images rather than perfect or flawless images since most images are retouched (i.e. **retouched digital images** can be airbrushed or photoshopped) to the extent that it no longer resembles the actual model. Therefore the image is idealized beyond what the live model actually looks like. Fashion media can be helpful in the information it dispenses, but the information can also create anxiety. This chapter discusses the multifaceted aspect of dress and media: the good, the bad, and the ugly.

Fashion media, including magazines, television, websites, Facebook, Twitter, and blogs, gives us the latest fashion information. For example, **influencers** (or bloggers) are a relatively new type of social media that did not exist until the ubiquitous cell phone was part of everyone's wardrobe. Now, Instagram and Facebook are common avenues for influencers to tell you what is hot and what is not.

Social media sites expand viewership beyond Lincoln Center and the Paris runways. A student can sit in a dorm and watch live streams of Marc Jacobs's runway show. Some designers utilize the live streaming option as a selling tool, giving shoppers 24 hours to preorder items straight from the runway. Some retailers have taken social media to a new level by listening to what customers are saying about products they want. In one example, American retailer The Loft posted photos of a new pair of pants on a skinny model. Customers responded with negative comments like "Sure, they look great, if you're 5'10" and a stick like the model in the photo." The retailer quickly reacted with new photos, this time of employees from sizes 2 to 12 wearing the same pair of pants. After this change, The Loft received positive comments about the pants and the realistic models. This is an example of how the fashion industry is utilizing technology changes in the media.

The tall, thin models that walk the runway, adorn fashion magazine pages, and decorate retailers' websites are not what most women look like (see Figure 10.1). **Western cultural ideals** of beauty and appearance are constant throughout media and have been for as long as practices of adornment have been recorded. Fashion publications have been around since the 18th century when Paris and London printed journals to disseminate the latest fashions in men's and women's clothing, accessories, and hairstyles. These early publications included drawings and color illustrations of dresses, hats, carriages, and much more. The use of illustrations continued into the 20th century when magazines' drawings and illustrations documented the newest styles and promoted the ideal figure for the time. For example, the **Gibson Girl** personified the ideal woman of the early 20th century with her large bust, tiny waist, and rounded hips, supposedly perfected by the "S" corset (Figure 10.2). The **Flapper** epitomized the flat-chested, straight figure of the 1924 to 1928 period, while bust, waist, and hips in a slender form prevailed in the 1930s. The ideal figure of the 1940s included broad shoulders with the noticeable curves of the breasts, waist, and hips; these curves were further accentuated in the 1950s with a noticeably smaller waist. This ideal was replaced in the late 1960s by a thin, androgynous figure made famous by **Twiggy**. Non-European models appeared for the first time in the 1960s, including the first African American model in a major fashion publication. All these changes in cultural ideals were reflections of changes in society as a whole during each period. A 2009 exhibition called "The Model as Muse" at the Metropolitan Museum of Art in New York showcased these ideals and more through fashion's famous faces from the 1950s to the present, supporting the notion that the models from each period represented the ideals of beauty for that particular time. Today fashion magazines continue to promote idealized images. Currently, thinness continues to fill pages and websites, indicating that it is valued. Yet, actresses such as Christina Hendricks, Sophia Vergara, and Jennifer Lopez provide an alternative to thinness as a beauty image (Figure 10.3). Some retailers are responding. For example, Talbot's uses curvy models in its catalogs and in 2011 hired Ashley Falcon as style advisor for Talbot's Woman and Woman Petite fashions. Ashley Falcon is known for her curvy, full figure and for the style advice she gives plus-size girls and women through her *Marie Claire* columns. This is a move in the right direction for designers and retailers.

It will be interesting to see if other retailers, magazines, and advertisers take notice and refocus to include the vast majority of women and their needs.

MAKING THEM PERFECT

Images of actresses, singers, and other entertainers, whether male or female, appear flawless and blemish-free in magazines. The results of using a model's photo to then create an **airbrushed image** or a **photoshopped image** leads to images that bear only a resemblance to the model who was photographed. Research has found that media images impact how girls, boys, men, and women feel about their own bodies, particularly if they don't match the idealized standard: muscular build; thin body; small hips and breasts; long blonde, straight hair; and pore-free skin. Along with the ideal body, celebrities and models are depicted with perfect, blemish-free faces. In reality, these images are retouched digitally. In a reading at the end of the chapter, the famous 1960s fashion model Twiggy, now in her late 50s, appears in an airbrushed skin-care advertisement in which she looks 30 years younger. The article also includes an untouched photograph of how she really looked at age 59. Richard Simpson states in "The Two Faces of Twiggy at 59: How Airbrushing in Olay Ad Hides Truth of the Skin She's In" that the real Twiggy looks good for her age but does have the typical signs of

Figure 10.1 Models show us the latest runway styles that represent the contemporary image of beauty.

Figure 10.2 Early 20th-century fashions presented a curvy figure: large bust, tiny waist, and curving hips.

Figure 10.3 Actresses like Christina Hendricks provide an alternative to thinness as a beauty image.

aging (e.g., wrinkles). Do these idealized cultural images of men and women in the 21st century matter?

All people are adversely affected by fake images (Bordo, 2004), and young girls are especially vulnerable. To show that models and actresses are perfect and flawless is deceptive and encourages women and girls to believe that something is wrong with them because they have wrinkles, blemishes, and cellulite.

Outside of the United States, the public in some instances is beginning to protest the retouching of images and even believe that it is the media's **social responsibility** to notify its readers of the retouched photos. A protest organization in the United Kingdom started a campaign called "Real Women" with the goal of encouraging companies to include realistic images of women in advertisements. The group is working toward a warning system or symbol that notifies the reader (and/or viewer) about whether an image has been digitally modified and to what degree. A consumer group in Australia want to see voluntary programs that, among other things, encourage companies not to use retouched images or, if they do, to notify readers (and/or viewers) that an image has been retouched. These are small steps in the movement away from the falseness of retouched bodies and faces.

Research: Objectification and Impact

Objectification refers to a phenomenon of regarding people as "things" or "objects" by focusing on one part of the body rather than considering the whole individual. One long-standing cliché in the advertising industry is "sex sells." This belief is a matter of concern in regard to how men and women are represented in magazines. Research has indicated that since the 1960s fashion advertising has become more sexually overt in that women are shown nude or partially nude to help sell products. Dress scholar Mary Thompson (2000) studied the sexual portrayal of both male and female models in advertising from 1964 to 1994 in two magazines: *Vogue* and *GQ*. Not surprisingly, she found that there was an increase in sexually overt images of women between 1964 and 1994. However, the first sexually explicit imagery involving men's bodies appeared in 1984. The overall number of images was higher in the women's category than for the men's, yet men were also objectified after 1984.

Jung and Lee (2009) conducted **cross-cultural research** of women's fashion and beauty magazines in the United States and Korea. One component of their research included an examination of women as sex objects in advertisements. The researchers wanted to find out if there were differences or similarities between how female models were portrayed in advertisements in the United States and Korea. The authors of the study indicated that:

> When objectification occurs, the female body is seen as a decorative object that is used as part of the scene for the advertised products/services. Sexual objectification often occurs when the focus is on isolated body parts, such as a bare stomach, cleavage, or buttocks, and it is not unusual that isolated body parts are being used in ads as part of or in comparison to product features such as shape, weight, and texture (2009, p. 277).

Jung and Lee also found that female models were mostly represented as sexual objects in both the U.S. and Korean magazines, with more in the Korean than in the U.S. fashion and beauty publications. In addition, they found that more models were shown in partial or full nudity in advertisements in the U.S. magazines, and more faces were hidden, indicating greater frequency of female objectification in the U.S. magazines. They also found that the traditional Korean concept of female attractiveness that concentrates on the face rather than on the body was maintained. In addition, Jung and Lee found a standardized ideal of beauty based on the Western concept of thinness and noted that the Korean traditional concept of female beauty that included mild plumpness with a round face was replaced by models who followed the U.S. standard of thin bodies and prominent facial features. Another finding in this study was the fact that magazines from both countries were primarily using Caucasian models, thus moving toward a Western standard of beauty rather than a focus on the unique and differing features of women's bodies and faces.

Taking the view of body-as-object to its ultimate conclusion are ads and editorials that include violence to female models or, in some instances, death. Some advertisers and shop window designers developed images to literally fit the "to die for" adage. That beginning gave birth to other instances of mixing fashion with violence and death (see the reading "Why Do Ads and Editorials Depicting Violence Keep Happening?" at the end of this chapter). The most remembered images from designers Dolce & Gabbana's "gang rape" ad along with other images of lifeless women in the trunks of cars are disturbing.

These ads portray women as helpless victims while simultaneously selling this demented view of "fashion" to women. The author suggests that it would help if there was a critical discussion about such ads but that never seems to happen. The "disturbing media" tends to get a lot of attention initially but then gets pulled by the advertiser without any context or critical analysis. However, violent ads continue to pop up randomly again and again without warning.

Over the years researchers have studied the effects of media on **self-esteem**, **body image**, and **body dissatisfaction**. This research focused on the impact that advertisements and photographs of thin models in magazines and on television have on young women (Ju & Johnson, 2010; Jung, 2006; Jung & Lee, 2009; Kim & Lennon, 2007). The **social comparison theory** often serves as a theoretical framework for analysis of the impact of media. This theory, developed by social psychologist Leon Festinger, indicates that humans compare themselves with others, particularly in regard to appearance "for purposes of self-evaluation" (Kaiser, 1997, p. 171). Comparing ourselves to celebrities, models, and others in the media is typical; it is how this comparison affects us that makes it a controversial topic. Kim and Lennon (2007) found that there is a connection between looking at ideal images in fashion or beauty magazines and dissatisfaction with one's appearance, as well as with a propensity to develop eating disorders. Jung (2006) studied the impact of media on mood and body image. She found that advertisements in fashion magazines may negatively affect the mood of research participants rather than their perception of body image. Jung found that exposure to media images in magazines decreased "a positive mood and elevated depression and anxiety" (p. 341). These findings confirm the alienation that people can feel if their bodies and other aspects of their appearance (hair color and texture) do not match cultural standards.

Adolescents are also surrounded by media images of thin and perfect bodies and tend to be more susceptible to believing that those impossible norms are attainable. Recent research found that greater involvement with visual media such as TV and fashion magazines correlates with greater body dissatisfaction and desire to achieve thinness norms.

Lisa Duke (2002) studied African American and European-American girls' assessments of their favorite teen magazines. She found that the African American girls were often critical of the lack of representation of real girls like themselves in the magazines (see Figure 10.4).

Figure 10.4 Fashion publications often provide us with homogenous images of beauty rather than the real diversity of beautiful faces.

Even though they often liked the articles in mainstream teen magazines, they wanted to see more representation of girls who weren't so thin, so perfectly and unrealistically made up, and so white. The white girls in the study did not tend to notice the limited representation of diversity and were less critical consumers of the magazines.

Men and boys are likewise not immune to cultural ideals. If boys are too thin or overweight, they are often teased, a problem that starts as early as elementary school. Due to the influence of the media, men are paying more attention to their appearance (Rohlinger, 2002) (Figure 10.5). Today, doctors and medical media warn about the dangers of steroids, bodybuilding, and weight loss, a combination that many boys and men use to change their appearance and better fit the idealized body image. Jones (2001) found that boys, like girls, make social comparisons of themselves to media celebrities and models. A study on body image among adolescents found that there has been an increase in male body image concerns due to changes in media portrayal of men. In addition, children are not immune to ideal images of thinness as attractive. Researchers are finding that girls as young as *four years old* express concern about their weight and mimic dieting behaviors and restrict their food intake (Smolek & Levine, 1994). Many girls in middle childhood talk about their

Figure 10.5 Many young men also give attention to their body image by working out and exercising daily.

need to diet, indicating that socialization to weight control is learned at an early age. The reading "Do Thin Models Warp Girls' Body Image?" (at the end of this chapter) discusses the current standard of even thinner models on the runway, how this perception is affecting girls, links to eating disorders, and what some fashion professionals are doing to move away from extreme thinness.

GLOBAL VIEWS

The discussion of idealized images also reveals the fact that most models and celebrities do not represent Western society as a whole. By 2025, one-fifth of the U.S. population will be age 65 and older. It is well known that baby boomers spend more money on consumer goods than Generation X or Y, so this demographic fact indicates that the fashion industry and fashion publications should already be preparing for these changes (Underhill, 2009).

There is a relationship between an advertising image and a consumer's attraction to the image (Solomon, Ashmore, & Longo, 1992; Hornick, 1980). Research findings in a cross-cultural study by Bjerke and Polegato revealed that women in five different European cities had differing images of what they considered healthy and beautiful. They showed women in five European cities (London, Hamburg, Paris, Madrid, and Milan) a black-and-white photograph of two different women's faces: a woman with (A) light hair and eye color, and (B) dark hair and eye color. The researchers asked, "If you want to look more healthy (or beautiful), which of these women would you prefer to look like?" Respondents could answer A, B, or neither. They were also asked to respond to eye and hair color. The findings revealed that there were differences in preference for one over the other, indicating that images of health and beauty are not the same across the five cultures. Woman B, however, was most preferred across the five cultures; therefore, Woman B can be "considered more cross-culturally acceptable" as an ideal image of beauty and health (Bjerke & Polegato, 2006, p. 874). This finding has implications for advertisers and others in the fashion industry to value multicultural and multi-ethnic features instead of cookie-cutter, blemish-free, tall, thin, and young models.

Summary

This chapter explores the topic of dress and the media, particularly the negative impacts that idealized images in the media can create in the minds of consumers. Articles relate industry methods to disguise flaws and create idealized images of celebrities and models in advertisements, fashion layouts, and articles, as well as discuss the results of fashion's fascination with thinness. Although some magazines, advertisers, and retailers use models that represent different ethnicities, ages, and body sizes to model clothing and other products, this is not a major trend in the fashion industry.

Key Terms

Airbrushed image
Body dissatisfaction
Body image
Cross-cultural research
Cultural ideals

Euro-American idealized images
Flapper
Gibson Girl
Idealized images

Influencers
Objectification
Photoshopped image
Retouched digital image
Self-esteem

Social comparison theory
Social responsibility
Twiggy
Western cultural ideal
Western idealized images

Learning Activity 10.1

FASHION AD ASSESSMENT

Review recent issues of your favorite fashion magazines and count how many advertisements you see that represent only (1) faces, (2) bodies with no head, (3) heads and bodies, and (4) nudity or partial nudity. This exercise can also be done with a menswear magazine. What did you find? Share with the class.

Learning Activity 10.2

BEAUTY DEBATE

Create a team of students who can debate in support of a homogenized standard of beauty in the United States or globally. Also create a team with the opposite position. Think about your arguments for and against, research your position, and have a debate in class.

Learning Activity 10.3

1950S BEAUTY IDEALS

If you can find a copy at your college library of a *Vogue, Essence, Ebony, Harper's Bazaar*, or other fashion publication from the 1950s, try this activity. Examine body types, faces, hair, and body size in the 1950s. What do you find in comparison to one of these magazines today? Are you finding differences? Similarities? What do you think are the reasons for the differences and similarities? Write up your findings; include photos of the images to back up your findings and analysis.

References

Bjerke, R. and R. Polegato (2006, October), "How Well Do Advertising Images of Health and Beauty Travel across Cultures? A Self- Concept Perspective," *Psychology & Marketing*, 23(10): 865–84.

Bordo, S. (2004) *Unbearable Weight: Feminism, Western Culture, and the Body*, Berkeley: University of California Press.

Duke, L. (2002), "Get Real!: Cultural Relevance and Resistance to the Mediated Feminine Ideal," *Psychology & Marketing*, 19(2): 211–33.

Hornick, J. (1980) "Quantitative Analysis of Visual Perception of Printed Advertisements," *Journal of Advertising Research*, 20: 41–48.

Jones, D. (2001), "Social Comparison and Body Image: Attractiveness Comparison to Models and Peers among Adolescent Girls and Boys," *Sex Roles*, 45(9/10): 645–63.

Ju, H. W. and K. K. P. Johnson (2010), "Fashion Advertisements and Young Women: Determining Visual Attention Using Eye Tracking," *Clothing and Textiles Research Journal*, 28(3): 159–73.

Jung, J. (2006), "Media Influence: Pre- and Post-Exposure of College Women to Media Images and the Effect of Mood and Body Image," *Clothing and Textiles Research Journal*, 24(4): 335–44.

Jung, J. and Y. J. Lee (2009), "Cross-Cultural Examination of Women's Fashion and Beauty Magazine Advertisements in the United States and South Korea," *Clothing and Textiles Research Journal*, 27(4): 274–86.

Kaiser, S. B. (1997), *The Social Psychology of Clothing: Symbolic Appearances in Context* (2nd ed.), New York: Fairchild Publications.

Kim, J. H. and S. J. Lennon (2007), "Mass Media and Self-Esteem, Body Image, and Eating Disorder Tendencies," *Clothing and Textiles Research Journal*, 25(1): 3–23.

Rohlinger, D. (2002), "Eroticizing Men: Cultural Influences on Advertising and Male Objectification," *Sex Roles*, 46(3/4): 61–74.

Smolek, L. and M. Levine (1994), "Toward an Empirical Basis for Primary Prevention of Eating Problems with Elementary School Children," *Eating Disorder: The Journal of Treatment and Prevention*, 2(4): 293–307.

Solomon, M. R., R. D. Ashmore and L. C. Longo (1992), "The Beauty Match-Up Hypothesis: Congruence between Types of Beauty and Product Images in Advertising," *Journal of Advertising*, 21: 23–34.

Thompson, M. J. (2000), "Gender in Magazine Advertising: Skin Sells Best," *Clothing and Textiles Research Journal*, 18(3): 178–81.

Underhill, P. (2009), *Why We Buy: The Science of Shopping*, New York: Simon and Schuster.

10.1
The Two Faces of Twiggy at 59: How Airbrushing in Olay Ad Hides Truth of the Skin She's In

Richard Simpson

It recently emerged that Twiggy was again to be the face of anti-ageing cream Olay, 25 years after she first won the job to become the fresh new face of one of the biggest beauty brands. Yet pictured in a natural state a few weeks shy of her 60th birthday, Twiggy, who is often referred to as the original supermodel, showed she does in fact age just like the rest of us.

Out on a grocery shop to her local London Marks and Spencers, a brand she also promotes, she appeared to be the age of, well, a woman of 59. Twiggy in her Olay ad looks a far cry from her more natural appearance on a trip to the supermarket. With slight jowls and only hairline wrinkles around her eyes and mouth, Twiggy does indeed look good for her age. However she bares very little resemblance to pictures, apparently of her, recently distributed to advertise Olay, whose catchphrase is 'Love the skin you're in.'

Airbrushing expert Michelle Facey of Facey Media said the amount of work done to wizard away the signs of aging in the advert picture was "a sham" and "totally misleading to the customer." (Figure 10.6) She said: "I think they have really gone overboard. It's a sham. I did not realize she looked so different in real life. She always seems so youthful. What I can see from the picture is that she has plenty of age spots all over face, neck and decolletage. I would say she has had lip filler too. I am shocked by how much airbrushing has been done. She looks like a woman in her late 20s or 30s. This has to be the worst airbrushing I have ever seen in terms of making someone look younger it's completely unnatural and untrue. In my opinion, it's totally misleading to the customer."

Almost a quarter of a century after she first became the face of Olay, Twiggy has been chosen to star in its latest advertising campaign. She has signed up for a 12-month stint as the face of Olay Definity the brand's anti-ageing range. Twiggy first promoted the Olay range back in 1985, when it was known as Oil of Ulay.

She became one of the most recognized faces of the Sixties after modeling boss Nigel Davies spotted her as a 16-year-old schoolgirl called Lesley Hornby. Her waif look, which gave her a new name, was an immediate hit with the British public and within weeks she became the

Originally published in the Daily Mail. Reprinted by permission of Solo Syndication.

Figure 10.6 Two photos show Twiggy without retouching (a) and Twiggy with retouching (b). Which photo looks best to you?

"Face of 1966." A year later pictures of Twiggy, complete with gamine haircut, long eyelashes and Mary Quant clothes, were adorning billboards in New York. Her enduring appeal has seen her take a central role in the highly successful Marks & Spencer advertising campaign.

Sarah Clark, spokesman for Olay Definity, would not say how much the new deal was worth, but said: "We were thrilled to welcome Twiggy back to the brand. She is a true beauty icon who continues to be an inspiration to millions of women across the UK."

The stunning new pictures of Twiggy were taken by Karan Kapoor, the 1980s Bollywood actor turned photographer. In the past Twiggy has spoken of her desire to maintain a natural look as she gets older. "I'm grateful for my lines of wisdom," she said. "Of course, there are days when I think: 'Oh my gawd, I look a bit tired.' But I can pull it together if I have to."

Discussion Questions

1. Do you think it's OK for magazines to retouch wrinkles, sags, and other signs of aging? Why or why not? Why do magazines find this necessary?

2. What aspects of American society make this approach to picturing women (or men) acceptable?

10.2
Why Do Ads and Editorials Depicting Violence Keep Happening?

The Fashion Law, Julie Zerbo

Interview magazine's November 2014 issue included an interesting editorial. Entitled "Pretty Wasted," the spread – which starred with models Anja Rubik, Andreea Diaconu, Lily Donaldson, Daria Strokous, and Edita Vilkeviciute looking less-than-alive – was nothing if not a thought-provoking one, both when it came out in 2014 and now,

when mass shooting happen in the U.S. on an alarmingly regular basis.

While it may not have *explicitly* promoted violence, it does depict women as helpless victims, and given its inclusion in a mainstream(ish) magazine, we can assume that it sells magazines and/or clothes. Moreover, if taken

Julie Zerbo/The Fashion Law (www.thefashionlaw.com)

out of context, as images are often portrayed and shared online – and especially on social media – the alcohol-infused editorial takes a markedly darker turn.

Interview's spread and other ones just like it are confusing if we consider who, exactly, fashion caters to – most immediately – and who it is largely dependent on. **Fashion is an industry that thrives on and thus, caters to, women - and yet, it continues to victimize them.** A few figures: As of 2016, the womenswear industry was worth a total of $621 billion dollars, compared to the men's fashion industry's revenue of $402 billion. As for the individuals within its ranks: Male models make about 1/10 of what females do. And save for many of the top positions, including chief executive and creative director roles, fashion is an overwhelmingly female-run industry.

Even with these stats in mind, fashion appears to be skewed against women quite a bit, and finds it to be rather "edgy" – or artistic even? – to depict women as the victims of violence.

More Than Just One Editorial

We cannot merely rely on a single editorial. Let us consider a few recent ad campaigns (Note: There are far too many editorials – such as Bulgaria-based *12 Magazine*'s "Victims of Beauty" spread and *Pop magazine*'s editorial featuring then-16-year-old model Hailey Clauson being choked by a man – to take into account).

On the advertising front: There was Dolce & Gabbana's controversial campaign, which has since been coined the "gang rape" ad. There was the similarly rape-themed ad that Calvin Klein ran for its jeans collection in 2010. There was also The Standard's 2013 ad, which featured a women strewn on the floor and according to commentators, served to trivialize violence against women.

There is more, though. Do you recall Jimmy Choo's Fall/Winter 2006 ad starring a dead Molly Simms in the trunk of a shovel-wielding Quincy Jones' car? What about Marc Jacobs' Spring/Summer 2014 campaign with Miley Cyrus, who was posed amongst what appeared to be a number of dead women?

Ah, and do forget the short film released in coincidence with Louis Vuitton's Fall/Winter 2013 collection, which sparked controversy for allegedly promoting prostitution. Still yet, there was the uber-controversial windows that Barneys New York debuted in 2009. With red paint splattered all over the windows and mannequins posed as

though they were (unsuccessfully) fending off attackers, the display – entitled, "Dressed To Kill" – was met with fury before it was nixed entirely.

Speaking at the time, Barneys' creative director, Simon Doonan, said, "We encourage our display people to be creative. We give them a lot of latitude, but this clearly crossed the line. It's as if someone saw a bad Hitchcock movie."

Fashion or Art?

One thing these campaigns (and in Barneys' case, windows) all have in common is that they portray women in unfavorable positions – whether they are dead, beaten up, about to be raped, or some variation thereof. What these campaigns also share is the fact that such treatment is being passed of as "Fashion," which is unfortunately nothing new.

Photographers, such as Helmut Newton (who was behind the 1997 ad for Redial handbags, which featured a model holding a handbag in front of her face to shield it from a gun, for instance) and Guy Bourdin, just to name a couple, have long used violence as a theme.

Nowadays, the violent depictions appear to be occurring with marked frequency as a catalyst for selling pricey garments and accessories.

There is an array of popularly-cited explanations for why the fashion industry has an enduring fascination with violence. Put simply, some of these campaigns are opting for shock-value as PR. They are ads designed to shock and create controversy in order to gain traction and get you to remember them. Oftentimes, this is achieved by using violence or sex.

Others seem to simply confuse – or perhaps overlook – the distinction between art and advertising. Yes, there is a distinction, and it stems from the fact that the latter is a far more commercial medium. In relying on the fashion-as-art argument, the so-called guilty party (the fashion figure) is essentially saying he/she expects to be held to the same standards as art, where political correctness is not expected, let alone demanded.

This is the excuse The Standard looked to when it was called out for its violence-centric ad campaign. The trendy hotel chain said its campaign was simply making use of the photographs of Austrian artist Erwin Wurm. But unlike art, fashion is – first and foremost – a consumer-facing industry, and the quantities of its products that are sold are markedly greater than those of even your most esteemed or in-demand artist.

With such facts in mind, it is not difficult to see why arguments are made to the effect that fashion should be held to slightly different standards than art.

A Reflection of the World?

More interestingly, however, is that others' uses of violence in fashion are likely a reflection of what is going on in the world right now, as fashion – whether it be in the form of an advertisement, editorial and/or garment – is known to do.

Jeremy Scott, for instance, looked to current events as inspiration for Spring/Summer 2013. Entitled, "Arab Spring," the collection – which included "riffs on Middle Eastern themes," per Vogue – came on the heels of the series of the deadly protests and demonstrations across the Middle East and North Africa that commenced in 2010.

Raf Simons is also famous for tapping into the cultural zeitgeist ahead of America's war on terror, which closely followed the 9/11 attacks. In a couple collections around that time, Simons made use of militant and rebel themes, including camouflage bombers and models whose faces were wrapped in balaclavas and/or covered in hoodies. As noted by Vice, Simons' "Woe onto Those Who Spit on the Fear Generation . . . The Wind Will Blow It Back" collection, "conceived before the 9/11 attacks and the subsequent war on terror, and pre-dating the murder of Carlo Giuliani at the G8 Summit, was apt for a time of international unrest and angst."

Similarly, violence against women is an unfortunate but undeniable reality. So, there is, of course, a chance that some of the aforementioned ads have served to portray an observation of the time in which we live.

If that is the case, it leads us to yet another inquiry: Does that make it alright?

The Guardian touched on the topic of the "fashion-forward" depiction of female corpses on the heels of the release of Marc Jacobs' Spring/Summer 2014 campaign. The publication's analysis of the matter, read, in part: "This obsession with death isn't so surprising, when you consider it as the obvious and ultimate end point of a spectrum in which women's passivity and silence is sexualized, stylized and highly saleable."

The Guardian's Kira Cochrane went on to make another point: "There's a reason these images proliferate. If the sexualised stereotype of a woman in our culture is passive and vulnerable, the advertising industry has worked out that, taken to its logical conclusion, there is nothing more alluring than a dead girl."

Death Sells

Following from this are some dark implications about our norms and motivations as a society but what may be worse is that brands are pushing off these images as fashion, as "edgy" fantasy scenarios, *in order to sell stuff.*

The backlash that followed Louis Vuitton's Fall 2013 "prostitution-promoting" video sheds some additional light on this industry practice. Inna Shevcenko, the leader of women's rights group, Femen, spoke out about the video, suggesting that it was a mix of PR stunt and sex-sells advertising. Femen told the Huffington Post: "Once again, naked women are used to create a buzz or sell clothes."

A piece in France's Libération, on the other hand, said Vuitton's video essentially relied on the ignorant glamorization of something that is not glamorous at all. "What indecency, ignorance and indifference to play with the fantasy of porn chic: the social condition of the vast majority of prostitutes has nothing enviable, nothing fancy, nothing happy about it.'"

Coupled with this is the underlying nature of the fashion creator vs. fashion observer dynamic. Most designers prefer that their clothes speak for themselves and in this same vein, editorials speak for themselves, as well, save for the accompanying text – which almost never explicitly takes on social causes. It is largely up to the audience to decide what to make of what they have seen.

But what about when the messages (inherent or completely obvious) are harmful? Does this change the "We Show, You Interpret" relationship between fashion's creators and fashion's observers? While it feels as though it potentially should, it probably does not, and so, in this way, these ad campaigns and editorials may aim to open the door for discussion amongst their viewers.

On the other hand, they may just be glamorizing violence against women as a way to sell more bags.

Discussion Questions

1. Explain how the fashion industry can target women, who are the industry's target market, while simultaneously degrading those same women as helpless victims.
2. What is sexy or alluring about violence? Why have some brands taken this approach to sell to their target market?

3. Why does violence against women get interpreted as "fashion"?
4. Do you agree that the fashion industry is somehow "above" other general commercial industries and can get away with much more than other industries?

5. Why do you think there is a lack of critical engagement after the violence or prostitution ads are released?

10.3
Do Thin Models Warp Girls' Body Image?
Nanci Hellmich

When Frederique van der Wal, a former Victoria's Secret model, attended designers' shows during New York's Fashion Week this month, she was "shocked" by the waiflike models who paraded down the catwalk. They seemed even skinnier than in previous years.

"This unnatural thinness is a terrible message to send out. The people watching the fashion shows are young, impressionable women," says van der Wal, host of *Cover Shot* on TLC.

Psychologists and eating-disorder experts are worried about the same thing. They say the fashion industry has gone too far in pushing a dangerously thin image that women, and even very young girls, may try to emulate (Figure 10.7).

"We know seeing super-thin models can play a role in causing anorexia," says Nada Stotland, professor of psychiatry at Rush Medical College in Chicago and vice president of the American Psychiatric Association. Because many models and actresses are so thin, it makes anorexics think their emaciated bodies are normal, she says. "But these people look scary. They don't look normal."

The widespread concern that model thinness has progressed from willowy to wasted has reached a threshold as evidenced by the recent actions of fashion show organizers.

The Madrid fashion show, which ended Saturday, banned overly thin models, saying it wanted to project beauty and health. Organizers said models had to be within a healthy weight range.

Figure 10.7 Many experts feel that excessively thin models promote an unrealistic image of the female body.

That means a 5-foot-9 woman would need to weigh at least 125 pounds.

Officials in India, Britain and Milan also have expressed concerns, but some experts say consumers in the USA will have to demand models with fuller figures for it to happen here.

"The promotion of the thin, sexy ideal in our culture has created a situation where the majority of girls and women don't like their bodies," says body-image researcher Sarah Murnen, professor of psychology at Kenyon College in

Gambier, Ohio. "And body dissatisfaction can lead girls to participate in very unhealthy behaviors to try to control weight."

Experts call these behaviors disordered eating, a broad term used to describe a range of eating problems, from frequent dieting to anorexia nervosa (which is self-starvation, low weight and fear of being fat) to bulimia nervosa (the binge-and-purge disorder).

Girls today, even very young ones, are being bombarded with the message that they need to be super-skinny to be sexy, says psychologist Sharon Lamb, co-author of *Packaging Girlhood: Rescuing Our Daughters from Marketers' Schemes.*

It used to be that women would only occasionally see rail-thin models, such as Twiggy, the '60s fashion icon. "But now they see them every day. It's the norm," Lamb says, from ads, catalogs and magazines to popular TV shows such as *America's Next Top Model* and *Project Runway.* "They are seeing skinny models over and over again."

On top of that, gaunt images of celebrities such as Nicole Richie and Kate Bosworth are plastered on magazine covers, she says.

What worries Lamb most is that these images are filtering down to girls as young as 9 and 10. Some really sexy clothes are available in children's size 6X, says Lamb, a psychology professor at Saint Michael's College in Colchester, Vt. "Girls are being taught very young that thin and sexy is the way they want to be when they grow up, so they'd better start working on that now," she says.

Lamb believes it's fine for girls to want to feel sexy and pretty when they are teenagers, but that shouldn't be their primary focus. "If they are spending all their time choosing the right wardrobe, trying to dance like an MTV backup girl and applying lip gloss, it robs them of other options."

Some girls don't want to participate in sports because they're afraid they'll bulk up. Some won't try to play an instrument such as a trombone because it doesn't fit their image of what a "girly girl" should do, she says.

It Begins in Youth

There's no question younger girls are getting this message, says Murnen, who has studied this for 15 years. "We have done studies of grade-school girls, and even in grade 1, girls think the culture is telling them that they should model themselves after celebrities who are svelte, beautiful and sexy."

Some girls can reject that image, but it's a small percentage: 18% in Murnen's research. Those girls were shown to have the highest body esteem. Murnen and her colleagues reviewed 21 studies that looked at the media's effect on more than 6,000 girls, ages 10 and older, and found those who were exposed to the most fashion magazines were more likely to suffer from poor body images.

Societies throughout the ages have had different ideals for female beauty, says Katie Ford, chief executive officer of Ford Models, whose megastar models include Christie Brinkley and Rachel Hunter. "You can look as far back as Greek statues and paintings and see that. It's part of women's fantasy nature," Ford says. "The question is: When does that become destructive?"

She doesn't buy into the idea that fashion models are creating a cult of thinness in the USA. "The biggest problem in America is obesity. Both obesity and anorexia stem from numerous issues, and it would be impossible to attribute either to entertainment, be it film, TV or magazines."

Anatomy of a Runway Model

This year's fashion shows in New York featured a mix of figure types, some of them a little more womanly and some thin, says Ford, whose agency had about 20 models in shows of top designers, including Ralph Lauren, Bill Blass, Marc Jacobs and Donna Karan. "Our models who did very well this season were not super-skinny. However, there were some on the runway who were very thin."

Cindi Leive, editor in chief of *Glamour* magazine, says some models were teens who hadn't developed their curves yet, which is one reason they appeared so thin. "You do see the occasional model on the runway looking like she should go from the fashion show to the hospital. You hear stories of girls who come to model and are collapsing because they haven't eaten in days. Any responsible model booker will tell you they turn away girls who get too thin."

Runway models have to have a certain look, says Kelly Cutrone, owner of People's Revolution, a company that produces fashion shows around the world. Her company produced 16 fashion shows in New York, including one for designer Marc Bouwer.

The runway models this year were no thinner than years before, she says. "I didn't see any difference in the girls at all. When they bend over, are you going to see the rib cage? Yes, they are thin naturally."

Women shouldn't be comparing themselves with these girls, she says. "These girls are anomalies of nature. They are freaks of nature. They are not average. They are naturally thin and have incredibly long legs compared to the rest of their body. Their eyes are wide set apart. Their cheekbones are high."

Most runway models are 14 to 19, with an average age of 16 or 17, she says. Some are older. Many are 5-foot-10 or 5-foot-11. They average 120 to 124 pounds. They wear a size 2 or 4. "If we get a girl who is bigger than a 4, she is not going to fit the clothes," Cutrone says. "Clothes look better on thin people. The fabric hangs better."

Stephanie Schur, designer of her own line, Michon Schur, had her first official runway show in New York a few weeks ago. When she was casting models, she looked for women who had "a nice glow, a healthy look."

She encountered a few models who looked unhealthy. "They tend to be extremely pale, have thin hair and don't have that glow."

But many of today's runway models look pretty much alike, Schur says. "They are all pretty girls, but no one really stands out. For runway it's about highlighting the clothes. It's finding the girls that make your clothes look best."

Schur says she doesn't believe many young girls today are going to try to imitate what they see on the fashion runways. She says they are more likely to look to actresses for their ideal body image.

It's not surprising that women want to be slender and beautiful, because as a society "we know more about women who look good than we know about women who do good," says Audrey Brashich, a former teen model and author of *All Made Up: A Girl's Guide to Seeing Through Celebrity Hype and Celebrating Real Beauty*.

For several years, Brashich worked for *Sassy* and *YM* magazines and read thousands of letters from girls and teens who wanted to become a famous model, actress or singer.

And no wonder, she says. "As a culture, we are on a first-name basis with women like Paris Hilton or Nicole Richie," she says. "The most celebrated, recognizable women today are famous primarily for being thin and pretty, while women who are actually changing the world remain comparatively invisible. Most of us have a harder time naming women of other accomplishments." The idolizing of models, stars and other celebrities is not going to change "until pop culture changes the women it celebrates and focuses on."

Women Come in All Sizes

Glamour's Leive believes the media have a powerful influence on women's body images and a responsibility to represent women of all sizes. "We do not run photos of anybody in the magazine who we believe to be at an unhealthy weight. We frequently feature women of all different sizes. We all know that you can look fabulous in clothes without being a size 2."

Ford believes the trend next year will be to move toward more womanly figures. Model van der Wal agrees and says she's trying to include women of varying figure types in *Cover Shot*. "Women come in lots of different sizes and shapes, and we should encourage and celebrate that."

Cutrone says models will become heavier if that's what consumers demand. "If people decide thin is out, the fashion industry won't have thin models anymore. Have you spent time with fashion people? They are ruthless. They want money."

"And the one thing they know is people want clothes to cover their bodies," Cutrone says. "Unfortunately, most people aren't comfortable with their bodies."

Discussion Questions

1. Why is thinness regarded as beautiful? The author states, "The widespread concern that model thinness has progressed from willowy to wasted has reached a threshold as evidenced by the recent actions of fashion show organizers." Will thinness continue into the future? If not, what do you think the next ideal image will be?

2. What could fashion magazines or designers do to counterbalance the thinness craze?

CHAPTER 11
FASHION AND FANTASY
Kimberly A. Miller-Spillman

After you have read this chapter, you will understand:

- **How fantasy and fashion are interrelated**
- **Public, private, and secret levels of fantasy and dress**
- **How fantasy occurs in almost every aspect of fashion**
- **How escapist fantasies and fantasy bodies can help individuals temporarily escape challenges of everyday life**

Fantasy can be found in many aspects of fashion. Actually, it is sometimes difficult to separate fashion from fantasy or vice versa. In this chapter, we will limit our discussion of fashion and fantasy to the following: advertisements, shopping, designer runway shows, gender identity, the body, costuming, fashion design, historic and futuristic reenactments, and video game attire. Is fantasy a tangible commodity we purchase—or is it an idea that cannot be bought? Merriam-Webster's dictionary defines **fantasy** as follows: (n.) the free play of creative imagination and (v.) to indulge in reverie: create or develop imaginative and often fantastic views or ideas. For our purposes, fantasy is both the product (an apparel design) and the process (daydreaming/images in the mind).

THE PUBLIC, PRIVATE, AND SECRET SELF MODEL

To assist in this discussion of fantasy and fashion, we will use the public, private, and secret self model as an organizational tool in this chapter (see Table 11.1). Fashion and fantasy will be explored on three levels as indicated by the shaded cells in the table: a) a public level (cell #3), b) a private level (cell #6), and c) a secret level (cell #9). The **public, private, and secret self (PPSS) model** was developed by dress scholar Joanne Eicher (1981), who built on sociologist Gregory Stone's (1965) ideas of appearance and the self. Later, Eicher and Miller-Spillman collaborated on an expanded version (Eicher and Miller, 1994) of her original model. Still later, historic re-enactor's experiences were added to the model (Miller-Spillman, 2008).

The PPSS model connects types of dress (reality, fun/leisure, fantasy) with parts of the self (public, private, and secret). The public part of the self (row 1) is the part we let everyone see. The private part of the self (row 2) is the part we let family members and friends see, and the secret self (row 3) is the part we let no one or only close intimates see. Reality dress (column 1) is the dress that is seen weekdays at work between 9:00 a.m. and 5:00 p.m., for running errands and attending religious observances. Fun/leisure dress (column 2) is the dress worn when relaxing after 5:00 p.m. on work days and on weekends with family and friends. Fantasy dress (column 3) is dress that helps us articulate and express our fantasies and secret desires. In this chapter we focus on the highlighted column labeled fantasy dress.

Public Level

On a **public level**, fashion is a multibillion-dollar business that very deliberately offers fantasies to consumers via dress. Fashion is a public expression that everyone can see and a collective fantasy on a societal level. This collective fantasy called fashion is a creative outlet; it allows consumers to have fun in a culturally sanctioned way. How can fashion students use this collective fantasy called fashion to create a profitable career? One way is to help consumers connect their fantasies to products. One example is the Ralph Lauren polo look of traditional polo-style clothing and weathered leather and denim. Very few people actually play polo, but you can still live the fantasy of being a wealthy person who plays polo for leisure while your investments make money by purchasing

TABLE 11.1

THE PUBLIC, PRIVATE, AND SECRET SELF MODEL (MILLER-SPILLMAN, 2008) BASED ON PREVIOUS COLLABORATION WITH JOANNE EICHER (EICHER & MILLER-SPILLMAN, 1994)

	Reality Dress	Fun/Leisure Dress	Fantasy Dress
Public Self	Gender Uniforms Business wear Reenactors' love of history	Office parties Dating Sports events Reenactors' public performances	Fashion as a collective fantasy Halloween costuming Living history first-person interpretations Festivals
	(1)	(2)	(3)
Private Self	Housework Gardening Novelty items	Home Exercise Reenactors' interests shared with family and friends	Childhood memories Sensual lingerie Drag shows
	(4)	(5)	(6)
Secret Self	Tight Underwear	Some tattoos Novelty underwear	Sexual fantasies Assume another persona Reenactors' magic moments
	(7)	(8)	(9)

Sources: Miller-Spillman, K. A. (2008). "Male Civil War Reenactors' Dress and Magic Moments," in A. Reilly & S. Cosbey (eds.). *The Men's Fashion Reader*, 445–63. New York: Fairchild.

Eicher, J. B. & K. A. Miller-Spillman. (1994). Dress and the Public, Private, and Secret Self: Revisiting a Model. *ITAA Proceedings*, Proceedings of the International Textiles & Apparel Association, Inc., 145.

Ralph Lauren clothing (see Figure 11.1). Public examples of fantasy and dress often consume the majority of information in the research literature because they are the easiest to observe and study. This does not mean that private and secret fantasies are less important. They are just harder to observe than public fantasies.

Private Level

Second is the **private level**. Private fantasies can include memories of playing dress-up as a child, or, as an adult, dressing in Victoria's Secret (VS) lingerie for private fantasies among family members and close friends. Most people would agree that VS is a successful business, and part of that success comes from its ability to tap into a culture-wide fantasy for consumers in a socially acceptable

Figure 11.1 Live the fantasy of Ralph Lauren Polo even if you don't play polo or live off of the interest from your inheritance.

Figure 11.2 Victoria's Secret lingerie can be a part of personal fantasies.

manner (see Figure 11.2). The same can be said of the Halloween costume market for children, a successful business that is socially acceptable.

Not all examples of public or private fantasies are easy to distinguish. For the purposes of this chapter, I will categorize examples of public fantasy as dress worn in public that everyone can see, such as costumes worn in parades, for festivals, or other events that take place between 9:00 a.m. and 5:00 p.m. Examples of private fantasy are those where dress is worn in limited venues or after 5:00 p.m. For example, shopping in a store is a public activity and takes place during business hours. When you enter a Victoria's Secret store in the mall you are participating in a public fantasy. Conversely, once you take the Victoria's Secret items home to wear or give to an intimate, the dress items are then considered dress for a private fantasy. Likewise, venues that are reserved for a select group pare down a public event to a private one. Examples include couture shows—which may be covered by the media but attended by a select group—and costuming at conference hotels or in remote locations suitable for the event in which only those with a specific interest will attend.

Secret Level

Lastly, the **secret level** of fashion and fantasy is usually held close and not easily revealed. If no one knows the secret or only an intimate knows, this makes a fantasy difficult to document. However, it is safe to say that some individuals have sexual fantasies that involve dress. One example would be heterosexual male cross-dressers. Often these are married men who would not want their secrets known. Another example are "magic moments" for historic reenactors who feel as though they have stepped back in time to experience the actual moment in history they are reenacting (see Figure 11.3). This level of fantasy fuels historically accurate dress purchases in order to make the fantasy successful.

To illustrate the many different forms fantasy can take, consider this scenario. A woman has a secret fantasy to be a rock 'n' roll star. Although this fantasy is not likely to come true, she can at least "dress out" her fantasy on weekends or choose rock-star dress for Halloween. Unless she tells others of the fantasy of being a rock star (making the fantasy public), only she knows her secret desire (secret fantasy). Others may view her rock 'n' roll dress only as an indulgence into "fashion" (public level) rather than associating her dress with a fantasy (secret level). In addition to wearing dress to express the fantasy, she enjoys shopping for and assembling the pieces for her rock 'n' roll appearance. She can also own the clothing for

Figure 11.3 Having historically correct clothing can lead to a "magic moment" among reenactors while reenacting an event.

this fantasy and never wear it, experiencing pleasure from simply having it (Eicher, 1981).

Consequently, fantasy in fashion can be found almost everywhere; whether it appears in consumers' fantasies, popular culture, gender socialization, or couture runway shows, fantasy in fashion offers individuals an outlet for fun and play. Fashion also offers society a collective mechanism to facilitate change. **Collective selection theory** is a term that Herbert Blumer (1969) devised to describe the collective experience of following fashion. When viewed in this way, fantasy in fashion can help individuals relax, escape the responsibilities of everyday life, and prepare for future societal changes.

THEORY, RESEARCH, AND PPSS MODEL

Stone (1965) identified two types of socialization through dress: anticipatory and fantastic socialization. **Anticipatory socialization** through dress is described by Stone as dressing for a job or a position one could realistically hold in the future. **Fantastic socialization** through dress is described as dressing in roles that could not be realistically played in the future, such as Wonder Woman or Superman. Both types of socialization through dress are essential for the social development of children and adults. According to Stone, all individuals benefit when they dress in roles to prepare for the future and use their imagination to dress as an unrealistic character. Our dress choices may receive positive feedback from others (e.g., a smile) or we may receive negative feedback (e.g., someone scoffing at our outfit).

Eicher's ideas about dress and the public, private, and secret self have been used by researchers Kim & DeLong (1992) in a **cross-cultural research** study about the design effects of garments between 1890 and 1927. These researchers found that Sino-Japanism (a renewed enthusiasm for Far Eastern, mostly Chinese and Japanese, art and culture) dress elements were adopted in Western fashionable dress for both public and private situations. In the earlier periods studied, the adoption of Sino-Japanism in Western dress was found in dress for the **private self**, such as a negligee, dressing jacket, or bathrobe. Later, the adoption of Sino-Japanism in Western dress was found in dress for the **public self**, such as a frock (dress) or a wrap (outer garment). The researchers also noted the cultural authentication (see Chapter 1) of Asian dress elements into Western dress, such as an asymmetrical closure and a Mandarin-style collar.

PUBLIC FANTASY: FASHION AND CONSUMERS

Retailing and Marketing

When consumers enter a store, there are many possibilities for creating a personal "look." The shopping experience can be one of creatively imagining oneself in all sorts of dress styles for many different roles, for example, employee, jogger, religious observer, etc. "**Show royal blue, sell navy blue**" was once a slogan used by retailers to indicate how to market and sell clothing successfully. In other words, display royal blue clothing in a store window to attract customers into the store, but once the customer is in the store, he or she will probably forgo the royal blue clothing for the more practical navy blue.

A theory that helps to explain the reasoning behind this slogan comes from sociologist George Herbert Mead (1934), recognized as the father of symbolic interaction theory. Mead identified parts of the self as the "I" and "me." The **"I"** is the impulsive and unpredictable part of the self that engages in impulsive actions or behaviors (such as impulse buying). Coexisting with the "I" is the "me" or the social conscience part of the self that considers what is socially acceptable. The "I" part of the self is attracted to royal blue pants as a vibrant, bright, and, for some, daring wardrobe choice. Once in the store, the **"me"** part of the self emerges as a voice in your head that asks, "But where would I wear this?" or "What would my friends think of me in this color?" therefore causing the individual to reconsider and purchase the more practical navy blue pants.

Marketers often use fantasy in advertising campaigns. Lyons (2005) analyzed a Maidenform advertising campaign between 1949 and 1970. The slogan "I dreamed I . . . in my Maidenform bra" featured a glamorous young model doing anything imaginable (see Figure 11.4). She was influencing juries, on safari, or working as an editor conspicuously wearing a Maidenform bra. The ads appeared to connect with women's discontent in the 1950s and were interpreted as a classic example of **wish fulfillment psychology** (Lyons, 2005). The ads struck a psychological chord with women who capably managed homes and finances during World War II. Following the war, many women took on more traditional roles of housewife and mother. The Maidenform bra ads fed women's secret fantasies for independence, power, and influence. An unexpected result of the campaign was the large number of customers' photos sent to Maidenform of themselves in scenes of "I dreamed I . . . in my Maidenform bra." An interesting twist is that a bra is considered a private item of dress; however, this ad turns the bra into a very visible, public item.

Designers and Inspiration

Designers need inspiration from a variety of sources in order to create fresh and new designs. Sometimes inspiration for design comes from dreaming up ideas just for fun. When we allow ourselves to brainstorm the most far-fetched and ludicrous ideas, those ideas often lead to workable design solutions or one-time exercises in excess such as Lady Gaga's "meat" dress worn to an awards show. Inspiration to create new designs can also come from movies, plays, concerts, nature walks, museum exhibits, or current events.

Figure 11.4 Through this popular ad campaign between 1949 and 1970 American women could picture themselves doing anything imaginable, all in their Maidenform bra.

Since designers work with fashion figures, there is a certain amount of fantasy incorporated into their job. Given that most women do not have the ideal figure shape (Danielson, 1989), fashion figures or *croqui* represent models on the runway rather than actual customers. In view of the fact that these idealized figures reflect our fantasies or desires rather than reality, the element of fantasy is at work as a designer creates the next apparel line.

Halloween and Identity

Halloween, especially for children, is a public fantasy. American children look forward to dressing in costume and collecting candy each year at Halloween. Child development scholar Jeanne Iorio shares her experience in dressing her daughter for Halloween in the reading "'What Disney Says': Young Girls, Dress, and the Disney Princesses" (at the end of this chapter). Iorio uses the popularity of princess merchandise to pose questions regarding society's expectations of girls. Iorio also questions the effect large corporations have on a girl's view of her own individual identity. In other words, will girls be passive consumers and buy what all their friends are buying or will girls become critical thinkers and creators of their own identity by purchasing items counter to their friends' choices? And lastly, who will help girls navigate these choices that affect their identities? The peer group? Large corporations? Parents?

Dressing in costume to attend an event not only occurs among children in Halloween costumes but is practiced by adults as well. Consider the following examples: Harry Potter fans who dress as their favorite book character to see the latest movie or buy the latest book; midnight screenings of the cult favorite *Rocky Horror Picture Show* attended by fans with newspapers, umbrellas, and water guns (props appearing in the film); and lastly, the royal wedding of Prince Harry and Meghan Markle in 2018, which inspired some U.S. party guests to dress as members of the wedding party. Many Americans are fascinated by European royalty and fantasize about being an English royal or a royal descendant.

Runway Shows and Fantasy

The design house of Alexander McQueen is known for dramatic and fantastic runway shows, such as the October

2006 show in an uncharacteristic environment—the *Cirque d'Hiver* (a show staged in the round runs counter to the typical designer show, which has a straight runway). This show included unusual set designs, a chamber orchestra, and exquisite clothing (Horyn, 2006). McQueen created a fantasy through clothing, environment, and music that was unique among runway shows. This uniqueness made his shows irresistible to customers who wanted an exclusive experience. Two examples of McQueen's fantastic shows include his spring 2010 collection with controversial armadillo shoes (see Figure 11.5) inspired by Charles Darwin's *Origin of the Species* and his 1998 collection with Marie Antoinette-style designs (Rawi & Abraham, 2010). McQueen's runway shows were covered in the public media; however, his ability to create a private fantasy among those who could attend made him a success.

Ames (2008) points out that runway couture shows often feature a **showpiece** that produces feelings of nostalgic and escapist fantasy; these showpieces are also usually unwearable and non-saleable. Ames states that the purpose of the runway showpiece is to be noticed, not to sell—to create an image of the design house as confident and bold (p. 104). As such, couture is considered a creative laboratory for the development of fantastic items; not necessarily for the sale of their showpiece items. However, if the showpiece is successful it will generate sales for the designer's ready-to-wear line. This is a good example of how fantasy (runway showpieces) can indirectly fuel sales (ready-to-wear).

Next are examples of fashion and fantasy on a private level.

PRIVATE FANTASY: CONSUMPTION TO CREATE A FANTASY

Costuming and Identity

Since clothing enhances one's imagination, then costuming is an ideal pastime for those looking to experience a fantasy. A **costume** is defined as body supplements and modifications that indicate the out-of-everyday social role or activity. Therefore, the word costume is reserved for use in discussions of dress for the theater, folk and other festivals, ceremonies and rituals (Roach-Higgins & Eicher, 1992, p. 10). There are several opportunities to dress in costume in American culture, such as Halloween, reenactments, science fiction conventions, and theater productions. While there are costuming opportunities, most would hesitate to publicly announce they love to costume. So, there may be real or perceived stigma with those who openly embrace costuming on a regular basis. However, the experiential benefits of costuming may outweigh the risks.

Costume is one way that reenactors of earlier times embrace their fantasies and communicate their level of historical authenticity. Members in the Society of Creative Anachronism (SCA) often provide the characters (jousters, blacksmiths, etc.) for medieval festivals. Decker (2010) used ethnographic methods (**participant observation**) to query SCA members to determine how a large membership with many diverse interpretations of authenticity could continue to survive. Wearing tennis shoes to an event (often referred to as a "rendezvous") because one has forgotten their period boots (p. 283) or having to wear Birkenstocks because it is one's first year in reenacting (p. 290) and there hasn't been time to invest in all of the necessary clothing items creates a confusing picture for those attending the event (often called spectators).

Figure 11.5 Fantasy on the runway. Alexander McQueen's spring 2010 collection including armadillo shoes.

What causes one person to embrace costuming while others actively avoid any activity that involves costume? Since many people associate a person's dress with their personality, perhaps personality differences could help explain the difference. Johnson, Francis, and Burns (2007) researched this intriguing possibility using the Five Factor Model of Personality (McCrae & John, 1992) and a questionnaire about appearance. The five factors are neuroticism, extraversion, openness to experience, agreeableness, and conscientiousness. Of particular interest here is **openness to experience**, which includes fantasy, aesthetics, feelings, actions, ideas, and values. Persons who score high on openness to experience are curious; have broad interests; and are creative, original, imaginative, untraditional, artistic, perceptive, and insightful. The results of this study indicate that openness to experience had a significant negative relationship with appearance, meaning that if an individual is open to experiences, he or she is not overly concerned with appearances but is more experientially oriented. This leads us to believe that those who enjoy the experience of being in costume are less concerned with public appearances and more focused on their experiences.

A **consumer consumption fantasy** is described by marketing researchers Belk and Costa (1998) as one way that consumers participate in fantasy through shopping. These researchers use the example of mountain men reenactors purchasing items needed for a successful reenactment or production of their fantasy as historic mountain men. These men must purchase items such as tents, cooking equipment, buckskin pants, boots, shirts, and guns. Through their online and event purchases they are building a fantasy.

Feeling membership with a group has motivated a select group of North American and Japanese individuals to participate in anime and manga (hardcore) costuming. Theresa Winge's article "Costuming the Imagination: Origins of Anime and Manga Cosplay" (at the end of this chapter) delves into the social benefits for those who attend costume conventions where anime and manga costuming are featured. Since this type of costuming involves two cultures (Japanese and North American), Winge explored the origins of **cosplay** (combination of "costume" and "play"). Cosplay merges fantasy with reality into **carnivalesque** environments where people are not themselves but instead are transformed into robots, part-robot-part-man, and Lolitas. Cosplayers who are considered geeks or social outcasts in everyday life get a chance at the spotlight and interact with others with similar interests at cosplay venues.

SECRET FANTASY: ASSUMING ANOTHER PERSONA

Costuming for Fantasy

Individuals experience fantasy in a variety of ways: through reading, research daydreaming, watching movies, and searching for information on the Internet. Some individuals want an actual experience in which they "become" a character in a book, movie, or online game. Examples can include people with long-held interests in topics such as science fiction or history. A *Star Trek* enthusiast is one example of someone who has watched all the TV shows but now wants to actually portray a *Star Trek* character. He or she decides to attend a Costume Convention (or Costume Con) to participate in a costume contest of his or her favorite *Star Trek* character. There are also many historic examples, such as The Jane Austen Society (individuals who reenact the time period of Jane Austen books); Civil War reenactments (American Civil War period); the previously mentioned Society of Creative Anachronism (Medieval); Buckskinners or Fur Traders (Daniel Boone era); and dance organizations such as English country dancers, Morris dancers, and Scottish country dancers. People in these groups want to experience another time and place by making or buying period-correct costumes/accessories, attending events in costume, and meeting others with similar interests. (For more information, see Miller-Spillman, 2008.) These individuals also share a desire for an **escapist fantasy**: a way to temporarily escape day-to-day problems or boredom. Two dress researchers have examined dress for those who reenact earlier times (Miller, 1997 and 1998; Strauss, 2002 and 2003). In addition, there are many fantasy sports/music camps now available to those who want that type of experience.

Authors Dina Smith and Casey Stannard examined how women handle problems while making dresses from the Jane Austen period (see Figure 11.6). Many hobbyists aspire to making their historic style of dress authentic to the period but often run into challenges that are difficult to overcome. Therefore, Smith and Stannard decided to research blogs of female designers who post information about problems encountered while making Jane Austen dresses. (See reading "Balancing Personal Needs and Authenticity When Designing Historic Styles of Dress" at the end of this chapter).

Miller-Spillman (2008) examined male Civil War reenactors' dress and their experience of magic moments

Figure 11.6 Regency dress that is worn to reenactment events such as balls or teas.

or time travel during reenactments. **Magic moments** are times when reenactors feel as though they are actually participating in an historical event. They are no longer reenacting but are experiencing time travel in the actual moment in history. Wearing historically accurate clothing as well as being surrounded by others in accurate historic dress can set the stage for a magic moment to occur.

Researchers in the field of psychology have identified a fantasy-prone personality (Wilson & Barber, 1983). **Fantasy proneness** has been studied in relation to childhood memories and imaginings (Rhue & Lynn, 1989), hypnosis (Green & Lynn, 2011), excessive daydreaming (Schupak and Rosenthal, 2008), creative experiences (Merckelback, Horselenberg, & Muris, 2001), and extreme celebrity worship (Maltby et al., 2006). One researcher found evidence connecting fantasy proneness to dress and the public, private, and secret self model

(Miller, 1998). Miller found in a sample of historic and futurist reenactors that female respondents were more fantasy prone than male respondents.

Eicher (1981), in her original framework of dressing the public, private, and secret self, notes that we often find pleasure in garments we own but never wear. This suggests that there may be a part (or parts) of the self that is pleased just knowing the item is in our closet. This unworn item reminds us that we could be that other person if we wanted it badly enough.

Fantasizing about having a body different than the one we were born with can be supported by our clothing choices. The desire to fantasize about a different body can be triggered in several ways. For instance, a teenager who reads magazines realizes he or she doesn't look like the models featured. This perceived physical limitation because of comparing oneself to air-brushed models can cause a person to fantasize about having the "ideal" body. Another way a person can fantasize about a different body is because of an actual physical condition or illness. For example, one study respondent gave this example: "I had eczema as a child and could not wear the frilly sundresses or shorts that other young girls wore" (Miller-Spillman, 2005, p. 278). Lastly, one could feel constrained by society's limited gender expectations (Jacob, 2012). For example, many transgendered individuals feel as though society expects people to fit into strictly limited categories of either male or female with no mixing of the two in appearance.

Since most everyone has access to the Internet, the creation of a character or avatar as a representation of the self is a commonly understood concept. Merriam-Webster's online dictionary defines *avatar* as an electronic image that represents and is manipulated by a computer user (as in a computer game). Creating a body double to virtually try on clothing and hairstyles is another example. There is a lot of freedom of expression offered through computer representations of oneself. Images can range from realistic to fantastic.

Summary

Fashion and fantasy appear to go hand in hand. Fashion is a serious multibillion-dollar business and it provides a fun outlet that can support individuals' fantasies. Given the part that fantasy and dress may play to a larger or smaller degree in a person's life, this area is relevant to fashion adherents worldwide. Several theoretical approaches can be used to study fantasy in dress. Examples include carnivalesque in cosplay, wish-fulfillment psychology in advertisements, gender socialization in girls' Halloween costumes, collective selection theory in which fashion (and by association fantasy) offers society a mechanism to tolerate change, personality traits such as openness to experience and fantasy-prone personality, and consumer consumption fantasies among historic reenactors.

Key Terms

Anticipatory socialization
Carnivalesque
Collective selection theory
Consumer consumption
    fantasy
Cosplay
Costume
Cross-cultural research

Escapist fantasy
Fantastic socialization
Fantasy
Fantasy proneness
Five factor model of
    personality
"I"
Magic moments

"Me"
Openness to experience
Participant observation
Public, private, and secret self
    (PPSS) model
Private level
Private Self
Public level

Public Self
Secret level
Secret Self
Showpiece
"Show royal blue, sell navy
    blue"
Wish fulfillment psychology

Learning Activity 11.1

USING COSTUME TO ENCOURAGE FANTASY PLAY

These questions are for students in dress and culture courses. Have students make a list of the costumes they have worn (and may still wear) then have the students talk in groups of two, then groups of six, and so on. Ask for volunteers to share their costume experience with the class:

1. Do you remember any of the costumes you had for Halloween as a kid? Were your childhood Halloween costumes store-bought or handmade? Write down as many costumes as you can remember and any detail of the costume that you can remember.

2. Have you acted in a play or music performance that required a costume?
    Write down descriptions of the costumes and the basic theme of the play or performance.
3. Do you costume now? In what situations?
4. What feelings do you remember having while in costume? These can range from a Halloween mask that makes it difficult to see, or a costume fabric that is scratchy, to feeling empowered or special while in a costume. Record those feelings as well and share in small groups and to the entire class.

References

Ames, A. (2008), "Fashion Design for a Projected Future," *Clothing and Textiles Research Journal*, 26(2): 103–18.

Belk, R. W. and J. A. Costa (1998), "The Mountain Man Myth: A Contemporary Consuming Fantasy," *Journal of Consumer Research*, 25(3): 218–40.

Blumer, H. (1969), "Fashion: From Class Differentiation to Collective Selection," *Sociology Quarterly*, 10: 275–91.

Danielson, D. R. (1989), "The Changing Figure Ideal in Fashion Illustration," *Clothing and Textiles Research Journal*, 8(1): 35–48.

Decker, S. K. (2010), "Being Period: An Examination of Bridging Discourse in a Historical Reenactment Group," *Journal of Contemporary Ethnography*, 39(3): 273–96.

Eicher, J. B. (1981), "Influences of Changing Resources on Clothing, Textiles, and the Quality of Life: Dressing for Reality, Fun, and Fantasy," *Combined Proceedings, Eastern, Central, and Western Regional Meetings of Association of College Professors of Textiles and Clothing*, 36–41.

Eicher, J. B., and K. A. Miller (1994), "Dress and the Public, Private, and Secret Self: Revisiting a Model," *ITAA Proceedings*, Proceedings of the International Textile & Apparel Association, Inc., 145.

Green, J. P. and S. J. Lynn (2011), "Hypnotic Responsiveness: Expectancy, Attitudes, Fantasy Proneness, Absorption, and Gender," *International Journal of Clinical and Experimental Hypnosis*, 59:103–12.

Horyn, C. (2006, October 9), "Two Madmen in Paris, Maybe Just a Little Bit Lost," *New York Times*. Available online: http://query.nytimes.com/gst/fullpage.html?res=9907E1DE1330F93AA35753C1A9609C8B63.

Jacob, J. (2012), "A Drag Experience: Locating Fantasy in the Construction of Alternative Gendered Appearance," in K. A. Miller-Spillman and A. Reilly (eds.), *The Meanings of Dress* (3rd ed.), 508–13, New York: Fairchild.

Johnson, T. W., S. K. Francis and L. D. Burns (2007), "Appearance Management Behavior and the Five Factor Model of Personality," *Clothing and Textiles Research Journal*, 25(3): 230–43.

Kim, H. J. and M. R. DeLong (1992), Sino-Japanism in Western Women's Fashionable Dress in Harper's Bazaar, 1890–1927," *Clothing and Textiles Research Journal*, 11(1): 24–30.

Lyons, N. N. (2005), "Interpretive Reading of Two Maidenform Bra Advertising Campaigns," *Clothing and Textiles Research Journal*, 23(4): 322–32.

Maltby, J., L. Day, L. E. McCutcheon, J. Houran, and D. Ashe (2006), "Extreme Celebrity Worship, Fantasy Proneness and Dissociation: Developing the Measurement and Understanding of Celebrity Worship within a Clinical Personality Context," *Personality and Individual Differences*, 40: 273–83.

McCrae, R. R. and O. P. John (1992), "An Introduction to the Five Factor Model and Its Applications," *Journal of Personality*, 60(2): 175–215.

Mead, G. H. (1934), *Mind, Self and Society: From the Standpoint of a Social Behaviorist*, Chicago: University of Chicago.

Merckelback, H., R. Horselenberg and P. Muris (2001), "The Creative Experiences Questionnaire: A Brief Self-Report Measure of Fantasy Proneness," *Personality and Individual Differences*, 31: 987–95.

Miller, K. A. (1997), "Dress: Private and Secret Self-Expression," *Clothing and Textiles Research Journal*, 15(4): 223–34.

Miller, K. A. (1998), "Gender Comparisons Within Reenactment Costume: Theoretical Interpretations," *Family and Consumer Sciences Research Journal*, 27(1): 35–61.

Miller-Spillman, K. A. (2005), "Playing Dress-Up: Childhood Memories of Dress," in M. L. Damhorst, K. A. Miller-Spillman and S. O. Michelman (eds.), *The Meanings of Dress* (2nd ed.), 274–83, New York: Fairchild Books.

Miller-Spillman, K. A. (2008), "Male Civil War Reenactors' Dress and Magic Moments," in A. Reilly and S. Cosbey (eds.), *The Men's Fashion Reader*, 455–73, New York: Fairchild Books.

Rawi, M. and T. Abraham (2010, February 25), "A Life in Fashion: How Alexander McQueen Became 'the Most Influential Designer of His Generation.'" Available online: http://www.dailymail.co.uk/femail/article-1250252/Alexander-McQueen-A-life-fashion.html.

Rhue, J. W. and S. J. Lynn (1989), "Fantasy Proneness, Hypnotizability, and Absorption—A re-examination," *International Journal of Clinical and Experimental Hypnosis*, 37: 100–06.

Roach-Higgins, M. E. and J. B. Eicher (1992), "Dress and Identity," *Clothing and Textiles Research Journal*, 10(4): 1–8.

Schupak, C. and J. Rosenthal (2008), "Excessive Daydreaming: A Case History and Discussion of Mind Wandering and High Fantasy Proneness," *Consciousness and Cognition*, 18(1): 290–92.

Stone, G. P. (1965), "Appearance and the Self," in M. E. Roach and J. B. Eicher (eds.), *Dress, Adornment and the Social Order*, 216–45, New York: John Wiley.

Strauss, M. D. (2002), "Pattern Categorization of Male U.S. Civil War Reenactor Images," *Clothing and Textiles Research Journal*, 20(2): 99–109.

Strauss, M. D. (2003), "Identity Construction among Confederate Civil War Reenactors: A Study of Dress, Stage Props, and Discourse," *Clothing and Textiles Research Journal*, 21(4): 149–61.

Wilson, S. C. and T. X. Barber (1983), "The fantasy-prone personality: Implications for Understanding Imagery, Hypnosis, and Psychological Phenomena," in A. A. Sheikh (ed.), *Imagery: Current Theory, Research, and Application*, 340–90, New York: Wiley.

11.1
"What Disney Says": Young Girls, Dress, and The Disney Princesses

Jeanne Marie Iorio

With a wave of the wand ($10.99 at Target, tiara included) they were all elevated to royal status and set loose on the world as an imperial cabal, and have since busied themselves achieving global domination. Today, there is no little girl in the wired, industrial world who does not seek to display her allegiance to the pink- and purple-clad Disney dynasty.

Ehrenreich, 2007

Recently I was visiting a preschool to observe one of my early childhood teaching students. During the visit, two four-year old girls began a conversation with me. It moved quickly from "Who are you?" to "Would you like to play with us?" I agreed and inquired about what they were playing. The response was one word, "Princesses." I then asked, "What is a princess?" Without hesitation, the same girl replied, "What Disney says."

As I reflected on the conversation over the next few days, I was disturbed by how these young children were creating what it means to be a girl in terms of a large corporation. This is not surprising as the marketing strategy for the Disney Princesses is targeted at girls as young as two years old (Strauss, 2004). In 2006, there were over 25,000 different princess-related merchandise, including clothing, available for purchasing, moving profits into the billions (Orenstein, 2006) (Figure 11.7).

After my experience with the preschoolers, I spent time online viewing Gymboree, a children's clothing site, looking at Halloween costumes for my daughter (at the time, she was about to turn one year old). The first costume I saw was a pumpkin princess, right next to a peacock princess. The trend initiated by Disney has moved beyond one corporation and is part of the young girl's clothing culture as being a pumpkin is left behind for the pumpkin princess. Observing the princess phenomenon in another company besides Disney brought up questions for me, as an early childhood educator and mother—How

Figure 11.7 Princess-related merchandise is a billion-dollar industry.

do the "princess" clothes of a specific marketing strategy determine how girls are constructed in society? How do these corporate constructions of "princess" influence girls in constructing their identity? It is with these questions in mind and an understanding that one of the foundational purposes of dress is to define identity (Reilly & Cosbey (Eds.), 2008), I began my own journey exploring the presence of princess and its marketing impact on retail.

For six months, I visited several stores and their websites including (but not limited to) The Disney Store, Gymboree, The Gap, and Old Navy—all large clothing stores for young girls. I also collected various catalogs delivered to my home with a targeted audience of children. Observing both, the clothing and marketing offered views on my questions as well as the space for other questions and observations to emerge.

Framing my exploration are ideas of philosopher Michel Foucault (1972, 1995), in particular surveillance,

Original for this text.

technologies of power, and ethics. From this perspective, "princess" clothing and marketing function as a means to impose homogeneity and conformity on what it means to be a girl in our current society. Further, Foucault's ideas imply as larger corporations perpetuate a discourse like "princess," children police themselves, ostracizing those who may not follow the "princess" ideals, terms, or wear the clothing. I also consider how gender identities develop for young children in the presence of corporate marketing strategies. Construction of identity is dependent on the relationship between self and society (Reilly & Cosbey (Eds.), 2008) creating identity through experiences and navigation through the discourse presented and utilized (MacNaughton, 2000; MacNaugton & Hughes, 2001). Identities are "multiple and complex, and even changing" (Greishaber & Cannella, 2001, p. 13) and "are always historically produced through a range of discursive practices" (Weedon, 1997, p. 146). Further, as children come to understand and discuss gender, experiences along with culture and context contribute to their perceptions of gender (Iorio & Visweswariah, 2011; Wohlwend, 2007; Lind, 2005; Oschner, 2000; Dyson, 1993: Heath, 1983; Yelland, 1998).

The Emergence of the Disney Princesses

Although the various princesses of Disney movies existed individually, in the year 2000, the princesses were joined together under the collective The Disney Princess (Cinderella, Sleeping Beauty, Ariel, Belle, Snow White, Jasmine, Mulan, and Pocahontas, Tiana [added in 2009]). This marketing scheme, born from Andy Mooney, Chairman of Disney Consumer Products Worldwide, while attending a Disney on Ice performance in Phoenix, Arizona, was a response to the children in attendance donning their own homemade princess costumes (Orenstein, 2011). To Mooney, the creation of a princess line was a huge branding prospect constructed with an ambiguous conception of princess. "Princess," Mooney admitted, is that its meaning is so broadly constructed that it actually has no meaning" (Orenstein, 2011, p. 13). This princess frame allowed for those characters to become part of the princess line without actually being princesses as well as expanding the possibilities of product.

Disney released the first princess items without any market testing, profiting over $300 million within the first year of sales (Orenstein, 2011). Targeted at children two to six years old, The Disney Princesses offer over 25,000 pieces to choose. By 2009, the revenue reached $4 billion

(https://www.disneyconsumerproducts.com/Home/display.jsp?contentId=dcp_home_ourfranchises_disney_princess_us&forPrint=false&language=en&preview=false&imageShow=0&pressRoom=US&translationOf=null&region=0),; "We simply gave girls what they wanted," Mooney said of the line's success, "although I don't think any of us grasped how much they wanted this (Orenstein, 2011, p. 14).

Under the guise of presenting family-friendly entertainment, Disney markets their products to their consumers—children—and misses the chance to empower children by choosing first to make a profit, ". . .behind the vocabulary of family fun and wholesome entertainment is the opportunity for teaching children that critical thinking and civic action in society are far less important to them then the role of passive consumers" (Giroux, 1999, p. 158). Targeting the young girl through programming and products, young girls are sold on The Disney Princesses (Kilbourne, 1999), framing childhood so it is harmonious with consumerism (Smoodin, 1994). Mooney's statement about giving girls what they want creates a façade of Disney as benign in their marketing choices and as responsive to their customer. The all-powerful Disney situates young girls as falsely empowered to have these "choices" and without knowing, young girls take on the passive consumer role. Inspiring critical thought or active democratic citizens is not a goal because thinkers and activists might question the choices of the company and lessen the profits.

Searching for Princesses

My journey into The Disney Princess marketing scheme began by visiting The Disney Store in October 2010, focusing first on the Halloween costumes. The front windows were simply decorated with three headless mannequins each dressed in a princess costume—one Sleeping Beauty, one Belle (from Beauty and the Beast), and one Cinderella—and nothing else. The choices inside the store continued along the Princess line with other characters taking on princesses themes—for example, Tinkerbell had a crown even though she is not a princess. Not only were costumes available, but an entire line of clothes depicting princesses and their storylines were present. Skirts with rosebuds on the hem to pay homage to Belle, T-shirts with face pictures of princesses, and dresses with dropped waists and tulle skirts illustrating the princesses across the bodice.

Although not deemed Disney-related costumes, other stores illustrated the strong influence the Disney

Princess marketing scheme on their own merchandise. On the Gymboree (children's clothing chain) website, girls' costumes included a Peacock Princess and Pumpkin Princess, both also available in the store. Target (large big box chain store) featured a whole row of princess costumes and accessories (which are always present no matter what time of year) as well as The Disney Princess and other princess costumes in the Halloween section of the store. Further, in the regular clothes department, infant and toddler T-shirts included a princess T-shirt for costume wear and licensed wear depicting The Disney Princesses. Costume Express catalog included the whole line of Disney Princess costumes (including infant sizes), a butterfly princess, kimono princess, pink kimono princess, Princess Wildflower (Native American princess), tower princess, pumpkin princess, and candy corn princess.

Continuing through the months after Halloween, I continued to visit stores, websites, and peruse catalogs. Princess seemed to be an ever-present theme. Gymboree had an entire line of everyday clothes focused on princess entitled Castle Princess. The colors of the clothes included lavender, mint green, and white with the word princess written in script on several pieces including shoes, bibs, and onesies. One onesie claimed "kiss me" on the front with a frog wearing a crown, reminiscent of the frog prince story, while another onesie was flanked with a tutu and matching tulle sleeves.

Tutus seemed to be part of many stores lines of clothes. Gymboree has its own tutu shop with a plethora of choices including sparkle, striped, and ruffled hem tutus. Leggings are also trimmed in tulle for a tutu-like feel for those girls wanting to wear pants. Even lines of clothing with non-related princess themes included a tutu skirt. For example, the Greek Isle Style line included a two-tiered blue sparkle tutu while the Burst of Spring line included a tutu resembling a strawberry. Upon a visit to The Gap (family clothing chain), tulle skirts punctuated one wall in a rainbow of colors. Old Navy (family clothing chain) had its own tutu bathing suit for the days princesses wanted to hit the water.

Other stores continued a princess theme. For example, the store at the local zoo displayed a Jungle Princess shirt. Carters (children's clothing store) added princess shirts to their line, heralding from the wall when I walked into their store. In a Land of Nod (children's furniture, toy, gear, and clothing chain) catalog, categories are presented as ways to label children. The princess category is described as, "Hear ye! Hear ye! The Princess approaches.

In preparation, we, her loyal subjects, have polished her crown, dispatched all local dragons, and assembled a collection of the girliest gifts from lands near and far." The child dressed in this section is wearing a tutu advertising offerings including a petal pusher tutu. For further ideas beyond the paper catalog, an actual website is offered— www.landofnod.com/princess.

Interestingly enough, as my search for princesses ended, I experienced a little déjà vu. I walked back into The Disney Store in March 2011 to witness another window of just princesses. Three headless mannequins back again—Sleeping Beauty, Belle, and Cinderella. This time in princess nightgowns, fancy enough to wear at the ball. Complete with drapes of chiffon, sparkles, and ribbons. Inside the store, an organic shirt proclaiming, "Once a princess, always a princess," cotton princess dresses with mesh and ruffle tutu-like skirt, and princess swimsuits. The beginning and end of my short-term observation punctuated with a plethora of princess as imagined by corporate decision-makers.

Clothing and Identity: Looking through the Theory Lens

The Disney Princesses have created a discourse, which manifests itself throughout the retail market. This discourse is steeped in capitalism, consumerism, and materialism, offering "an artifact of culture" (Apple & Christian-Smith, 1991; Aronowitz & Giroux, 1991) reflective of both the historical and present perspective on the society (Foucault, 1972). The ease of success in the marketplace (Orenstein, 2011) and development of a discourse positions The Disney Princesses in a place of power over people and sculpting society (Foucault, 1972). As young girls choose to wear a princess product, they are perpetuating the discourse and continuing to give power to a corporate conception of princess. This is evident as the children engage in playing princess define princess as "What Disney says." Through this princess discourse, Disney has found a way to state what is normal and acceptable (Foucualt, 1995; Gallagher, 1999). Other retailers continue to perpetuate this as normal when they also place princess items in their stores. As young girls dress in princess-themed items, there is an acceptance of corporations as systems of power, making decisions about what someone should wear. Disney's perpetuation of children's innocence through The Disney Princesses is an imposition on young girls' identities of what is right. At the same time, this choice aligns with the societal ideas of children as innocent (Grieshaber & Cannella, 2001) and continues to set a societal dichotomy of right and wrong in terms of childhood identity. If society believes young girls as innocent is the right identity and Disney supports this belief, adults and peers engage in surveillance, judging those that do not follow the norm (Foucault, 1995) or, in this case, choose not to wear princess clothes.

Disney knows that its princess products sell. Consider the very simple window dressing schemes I observed on two occasions over a short period of time. Just three mannequins, headless, wearing princess products, placed all alone in the window. Essentially, the discourse speaks for itself. Here is how you speak princess, wear our products. The choice for these windows is like a public slap in the face reiterating Mooney's statement that the products are just giving girls what they want as well as implying to the consumer, why think, we have already given you the means to express being a princess. There is no need for imagination. Disney is kind enough to present the mannequins as headless so children can easily imagine themselves dressed in the presented garb. In considering other retailers' version of princesses, The Land of Nod offers an actual script for parents and children to consider when becoming a princess. If a young girl can be The Land of Nod princess, then The Land of Nod princess clothing is critical and ensures a sale for the company.

And how does all of this impact young girls' identities? Identities are formed through interactions with others (Grieshaber & Cannella (Eds.), 2001; MacNaughton, 2000, MacNaughton & Hughes, 2001). When young children interact with corporations' conceptions of princess, then the identity emerges as a mixture of the child and the corporation. Whether it is a Disney or Gymboree princess, a system based in profit is having some influence on how identity is shaped. What should be noted is that a variety of companies do carry princess-related products that may or may not emulate Disney definition of princess. Could the differential frames of princess be a resistance to Disney corporate definition of princess? Could Gymboree, The Gap, and The Land of Nod become sources of resistance for young girls? Or could their presence offer young girls a myriad of ways to consider princess? With several means of defining princess, young girls could be interacting with different perspectives as they shape their identities. But should princesses be the only way a young girl can consider her identity?

Even with possible resistance in mind, it should be noted that the presentations of princess is still through a capitalist and consumer lens. The choice for retailers to add princess to their clothing lines is probably not steeped in offering young girls different experiences to influence their identities. Rather, the purpose is to make money. The awareness of this purpose delineates a whole other question—Should retailers with the purpose of making money be an influence on young girls' identities? MacNaughton discusses how the interactions between children and other people can "protect or transform their identities" (2000, p. 28). Essentially, money-making corporations are providing the defining ideas of princess to young girls based in consumerism. Navigating the princess products alone, a young girl's interaction could delineate an identity based on consumption. For example, a girl chooses to purchase more princess products in order to ensure her own identity as a girl. Yet, it should be noted, that the very presence of the corporate princess could be a site of critique. The active interaction between a child and an adult discussing the limitations and purposes of marketing like The Disney Princesses could empower a young girl to consider other marketing strategies with a critical lens. These types of experiences influence identity development in a completely different manner.

Young girls can define self as princess but at the same time can be defining self through consumption (as previously suggested in their allegiance to corporate-defined princesses). Engaging in the "Princess" culture could function as a symbol of success and social class. For example, a child clothed in The Disney Princesses could be symbolic of a family with enough money to afford the clothes as well as imply the ability to purchase the related entertainment like going to the movies, owning the DVD, or vacationing at Disneyworld. In this facet, The Disney Princesses influence family identity and possible social transformation of the family able to afford fun and leisure activity (Tricarico, 2008).

Throughout this discussion, I consider my own observations in terms of theory, exploring a postmodern perspective on identity. Yet, it is important to note how my interpretations are based on how I assume young girls are influenced by the corporate idea of princess. Children's voices are definitely missing from the conversation. Research about young girls' developing identities in conjunction with princess clothing which includes interviews with children is imperative to further understanding the impact of princess. This discussion should be a first step in many exploring the influence of marketing practices on young girls' identities.

And Her Identity Lived Happily Ever After?

The presence of Princesses is part of the current young girl's environment. Walking into Nordstroms (department store), my daughter sees The Disney Princesses on a T-shirt. At sixteen-months-old, her reaction is to point and then move on to something else, but what happens when she wants to stay and look? Should a corporation's conception of princess be one of the experiences my daughter interacts with in order to form her own identity? She may not have a choice, as it seems princesses in some form seem to be everywhere, from the zoo store to the department store. The choice may begin with me. Much like Orenstein (2011) suggests, my part is not about restricting my daughter's access to the world, but to empower her so she "can thrive within it" (p. 191). As her mother, I am positioned to offer her many experiences to influence her identity development. So yes, she will see princess clothing but I will be available to listen to her viewpoint, share my perspective, and interact with her beyond her initial "princess" experience.

Consider the experience with the preschoolers I share at the beginning of this essay. How might have I responded to these two young girls upon their statement of how Disney defines princess? My response could have included questions about why Disney gets to decide what a princess is or if there are other ways to consider a princess besides Disney's suggestion. I might have asked about who benefits each time they buy another piece of The Disney Princess clothing or how they treat friends that do not follow the Disney Princess ideal in both clothing and defining princess. Maybe Disney has given us a way to help young girls begin to develop their critical thinking processes and civil action abilities as part of their identities or at least to begin to see all the possibilities a young girl may have—regardless of how she dresses.

Discussion Questions

1. How might a parent help his or her daughter to reject the role of a passive consumer and gravitate toward critical thinking and active democratic citizenship?
2. Explain the meaning of the phrase "Corporate princess could be a site of critique between parent and child."
3. How does Stone's (1965) ubiquitous mother and investiture through child's dress fit with Iorio's reading?
4. How can the "girlie-girl" look be contested while wearing a princess costume?

References

Apple, M. & Christian-Smith, L. K. (1991). *The politics of the textbook*. New York: Routledge.

Aronowitz, S. & Giroux, H. A. (1991). *Postmodern education: Politics, culture, and social criticism*. Minneapolis: University of Minnesota Press.

Dyson, A. (1993). *Social worlds of children learning to write in an urban primary school*. New York: Teachers College Press.

Enhrenreich, B. (2007). The bonfire of the Disney Princess. *The Nation*, December 24. Retrieved from http://www.thenation.com/article/bonfire-disney-princesses.

Foucault, M. (1972). *The archeology of knowledge*. New York: Pantheon.

Foucault, M. (1995). *Discipline and punish: The birth of the prison*. New York: Vintage.

Gallagher, S. (1999). An exchange of gazes. In J. Kincheloe, S. Steinberg, & L. Villaverde (Eds.), *Rethinking intelligence* (pp. 69–84). New York: Routledge.

Giroux, H. (1999). *The mouse that roared: Disney and the end of innocence*. New York: Rowman & Littlefield.

Grieshaber, S. & Cannella, G. (2001). *Embracing identities in early childhood education: Diversity and possibilities*. New York: Teachers College Press.

Heath, S. B. (1983). *Ways with words: Language, life, and work in communities and classrooms*. New York: Cambridge University Press.

Iorio, J. & Visweswariah, H. (2011). Do daddies wear lipstick? And other child-teacher conversations exploring constructions of gender. In T. Jacobson (Ed.), *Gender in early childhood*. St. Paul, MN: Red Leaf Press.

Kilbourne, J. (1999). *Deadly persuasion*. New York: Free Press.

Lind, U. (2005). Identity and power, "meaning," gender and age: Children's creative work as a signifying practice. *Contemporary Issues in Early Childhood* 6(3): 256–68.

MacNaughton, G. (2000). *Rethinking gender in early childhood education*. Thousand Oakes: Paul Chapman Publishing, Ltd.

MacNaugton, G. & Hughes, P. (2001). Fractured or manufactured: Gendered identities and culture in the early years. In S. Grieshaber & G. Cannella, (Eds.), *Embracing identities in early childhood education: Diversity and possibilities* (pp. 114–132). New York: Teachers College Press.

Ochsner, M. (2000). Gendered make-up. *Contemporary Issues in Early Childhood*, 6(2): 209–13.

Orenstein, P. (2006, July 24). What's Wrong with Cinderella? *New York Times*. Retrieved from www.NYTimes.com.

Orenstein, P. (2011). *Cinderella ate my daughter: Dispatches from the front lines of the new girlie-girl culture*. New York: Harper.

Reilly, A. & Cosbey, S. (Eds.) (2008). *Men's fashion reader*. New York: Fairchild Books.

Smoodin, E. (1994). *Disney discourse: Producing the magic kingdom*. New York: Routledge.

Strauss, G. (2004, March 2). Princesses Rule the Hearts of Little Girls. *USA Today*. Retrieved from www.USAToday.com.

Tricarico, D. (2008). Dressing up Italian Americans for the youth spectacle: What difference does a guido perform? In A. Reilly & S. Cosbey (Eds.), *Men's fashion reader* (pp. 265–278). New York: Fairchild.

Weedon, C. (1997). *Feminist practice and postructuralist theory*. Oxford: Basil Blackwell.

Wolhwend, K. (2007). Friendship meeting or blocking circle? Identities in the laminated spaced of playground conflict. *Contemporary Issues in Early Childhood* 8 (1): 73–88.

Yelland, N. (Ed.) (1998). *Gender in early childhood*. New York: Routledge.

11.2
Costuming the Imagination: Origins of Anime and Manga Cosplay

Theresa Winge

All over the world, cosplay fans gather at conventions and parties to share their appreciation of and affection for anime and manga (McCarthy 1993; Napier 2001; Poitras 2001). These fans, who also refer to themselves as *otaku*, wear detailed makeup and elaborate costumes modeled after their favorite anime, manga, and related video game characters (Poitras 2001; Richie 2003). Cosplayers spend immeasurable monies and hours constructing or purchasing costumes, learning signature poses and dialogue, and performing at conventions and parties, as they transform themselves from "real world" identities into chosen (fictional) characters. This is the essence of cosplay, or kosupure (Aayama and Cahill 2003; Richie 2003).

The term cosplay combines costume and play (or role-play). Cosplay also refers to the activities, such as masquerades, karaoke, and posing for pictures with other otaku, that are associated with dressing and acting like anime, manga, and video game characters (Macias and Machiyama 2004; Poitras 2001). While the term cosplay encompasses various types of costumed role-playing, such as science fiction, fantasy, horror, mythology, fetish, and so forth, this chapter focuses only on Japanese and North American cosplay related to anime, manga, and video games.

My objective here is to provide the reader with an understanding of anime and manga cosplay, cosplayers, and their social structures. First, I explore the origin stories of cosplay to establish contributions from both Japan and North America. Next, I discuss the distinguishing characteristics of Japanese and North American cosplay to determine the similarities and differences between the two cultural settings. I contextualize four cosplay elements: (1) anime and manga cosplayers, (2) social settings, (3) character and roleplaying, and (4) dress, which includes clothing or costumes, makeup, wigs or hairstyles, jewelry, and accessories. Last, I offer an introduction to the anime and manga cosplay social structures (i.e., interactions, environments, and experiences) in order to provide the reader with an awareness of the complexities and dynamics of the cosplay world.

Origin Stories of Cosplay

The few sources that discuss the origins of cosplay are primarily found on Web sites, online publications, and weblogs. Constructed and maintained by anime and mangafans, these sources communicate information about anime and manga (most with a personal bias). Therefore, it is not surprising that the specific origins of anime and manga cosplay are highly debated topics among anime and manga *otaku* (Hlozek 2004). One side speculates that cosplay began in North America, during the 1960s, when people dressed as and role-played their favorite science fiction and fantasy characters, such as Spock from *Star Trek* and Robin from *Batman* (Bruno 2002a). This type of costumed role-playing (not yet called cosplay) spanned a variety of genres and may have inspired Japanese anime and manga fans to dress as their favorite characters. On the other side of the debate are those who speculate that cosplay was imported from Japan, coming to North America with the formations of anime and manga fan clubs (Bruno 2002a; Ledoux and Ranney 1997).

The origin story that appears to have the most evidence to support it actually blends the Japanese and North American contributions. In 1984 Takahashi Nobuyuki (known in the United States as "Nov Takahashi"), founder of and writer for Studio Hard, an anime publishing company, attended World-Con, a science fiction convention, in Los Angeles (Bruno 2002a; Hlozek 2004). He was impressed with the costumed science fiction and fantasy fans whom he saw, especially those competing in the masquerade (Bruno 2002a). Consequently, when he returned to Japan and wrote about his experiences at the convention, he focused on the costumed fans and the masquerade. Moreover, Takahashi encouraged his Japanese readers to incorporate costumes into their anime and manga conventions (Bruno 2002a).

Takahashi was unable to use the word masquerade because this word translated into Japanese means "an aristocratic costume party," which is drastically different from the costume competitions seen at conventions (Bruno 2002a). Instead, he created the phrase costume play, which was eventually shortened to kosupure, or cosplay (Bruno 2002a). As a result, Takahashi added two new words to the subculture and pop culture lexicon: cosplay and cosplayer.

In 1980, at the San Diego, California, Comic-Con, several fans dressed as anime and manga characters in the masquerade (Ledoux and Ranney 1997). It was not long before anime and manga otaku were donning cosplay dress to Japanese conventions (Bruno 2002a). During the 1980s, there was a growing demand for Japanese anime (and manga) imports (Drazen 2003), and an increasing number of otaku attended North American science fiction and fantasy conventions (Hlozek 2004; Poitras 2001). As a result, these types of North American conventions began to include anime- and manga-focused activities, such as panels, guest speakers, anime video rooms, and masquerades (i.e., organized costumed performances). In time, otaku organized conventions expressly for fans of anime, manga, and related media. Overall, North American and Japanese cosplay have many commonalities, such as a dedicated fan base and the use of costumes. They also have distinguishing characteristics, such as variations within masquerade competitions, appropriate locations for wearing cosplay dress, and cosplay markets.

Context of Cosplay

The context of anime and manga cosplay is a combination of the presence of basic components and related interactions between those components. The four basic components are anime and manga cosplayer, social settings, (fictional) character and role-playing, and dress (e.g., hair, costume, makeup, and accessories, including weapons). Furthermore, these components facilitate complex interactions between people (e.g., cosplayers, spectators, masquerade judges , etc.), environments (e.g., personal, private, public, and virtual), and fantasy (e.g., imagination, fictional characters, etc.). The following four sections are an overview of the basic components and complex interactions that create the context of cosplay.

Anime and Mango Cosplayer

Anime and manga cosplayers may be any age, gender, and ethnicity. They have varied educational backgrounds, occupations, disposable incomes, and resources. Essentially, an anime or manga cosplayer can be almost anyone who expresses his or her fandom and passion for a character by dressing and acting similarly to that character. Since the exact cosplay demographics are currently unknown, this is an area in need of further research.

A cosplayer researches and studies an already existing anime or manga character with a keen eye for detail, in order to create a cosplay character. The interpretation usually takes shape by reading or watching the chosen character within its given medium (i.e., manga, anime, or video game). The level of research and study is ultimately guided by the cosplayer's objectives (e.g., masquerade participation, socializing, etc.).

Cosplayers exist at various places along a cosplay continuum, which is based on their level of commitment. At one end are cosplayers content with dressing (e.g., wig, makeup, and costume) as their chosen character and attending conventions and events for socializing and having fun. At the other end are those cosplayers obsessed with a given character, re-creating that character with meticulous attention to detail and performing as that character as often as time and money allow. Between these extremes, there are cosplayers who research, study, and practice their characters and participate in cosplay events, such as masquerade and karaoke. Regardless of his or her place on the cosplay continuum, each cosplayer has an extraordinary level of dedication and commitment to the depiction of a chosen character, based on individual objectives that may include, but are not limited to, the following criteria: humor, accurate depiction, and casual participation.

Social Settings

Cosplay is primarily a social activity associated with various activities and conventions, where cosplayers gather to share their passions for anime and manga characters (Aoyama and Cahill 2003). The cosplay social settings may include, but are not limited to, the following: masquerades (i.e., character based costume or performance competitions), photograph sessions, themed parties, karaoke, club meetings, and conventions. While the social settings for cosplay may vary greatly, conventions are often the primary space where large numbers of cosplayers gather, socialize, and perform.

Conventions are held at all times of the year, around the world, for fans of science fiction, fantasy, horror, anime, manga, and the like to share their interests and passions with like-minded individuals (Poitras 2001). The dedicated cosplayer may attend conventions on the average of one a month. As a result, many science fiction and fantasy conventions include a variety of activities, such as discussion panels, skits, film screenings, and masquerades specifically aimed at anime and manga *otaku*.

The convention activity that attracts the most interest from otaku, especially cosplayers, is the masquerade.

Cosplayers compete in masquerades by posing or acting in skits relevant to their characters. At science fiction and fantasy conventions, anime and manga cosplayers compete against various genres of cosplayers. Despite slight variations between each masquerade, participants are generally judged on three main criteria: accuracy of the costume's appearance to the actual character; construction and details of the cosplay dress; and entertainment value of the skit and/or accuracy to the character.

Spectators play an important role in the social settings of cosplay. In fact, it could be argued that cosplay events, especially the masquerade, would be pointless if it were not for the spectators, even if they are composed of friends and other cosplayers. Spectators use applause, verbal cues, and laughter to encourage cosplayers to perform and interact.

Furthermore, the cosplay social settings exist beyond the stage of a masquerade. Cosplayers interact with each other, often role-playing their chosen characters while participating in hallway conversations, karaoke parties, and online chat rooms. These social settings take any shape or form desired by cosplayers. Often the settings extend beyond tangible spaces, into virtual spaces, such as Web sites, weblogs, and online journals (Poitras 2001). Cosplayers utilize Web sites to register and plan activities for conventions, as well as to promote and communicate about their fandom for anime and manga cosplay. They also use weblogs and online journals to confide in others, express opinions, and argue about the finer details of cosplay. Additionally, traditional print media, such as the magazines *Animerica* and *Newtype,* feature several pages per issue of cosplay photographs from recent conventions.

Character and Role-playing

An otaku chooses an anime, manga, or video game character to cosplay based on personal criteria. A resourceful cosplayer has few limitations in character choice, beyond his or her imagination. The pool of characters to choose from is vast, including characters from anime feature movies and serials, manga single image and series, and related video games. Some cosplay characters are featured in all three media, such as Dragon Ball *Z* and Fist of the North Star. In fact, there are so many characters to choose from that they have been informally classified into subgenres.

Among these subgenres are mecha, cyborg, furry, and Lolita. Mechas (short for "mechanicals") are giant robot characters, often piloted or operated by humans (Napier 2001). Some examples of mecha characters are Gundam Wing Zero (Gundam Wing television series, 1995–96) and EVA units (Neon Genesis Evangelion television series, 1995–96). Cyborgs are part machine and part human, such as Major Kusanagi Motoko (Ghost in the Shell, 1995) and the Knight Sabers (Bubblegum Crisis, 1987–91). (Figure 11.8) Furries are characters that have "fur," and the cosplay costumes for them are usually created from faux fur. Some examples are Totoro, a giant, gray catlike creature (My Neighbor Totoro, 1988) and Ryo-ohki (an alternate romanization of Ryôôki), a cute, furry cabbit (cat-rabbit) (Tenchi muyô yôôki series, 2000, known by the alternate romanization Tenchi Muyô Ryo-ohki in the United States). A Lolita character attempts to convey a kawaii image, which is young, childlike, and cute (Aoyama and Cahill 2003; Schodt 1996). The character may don a baby-doll dress trimmed with layers of lace, kneesocks, and sometimes carry a stuffed animal or a parasol. A common anime reference for the Lolita character is the Wonder Kids' Lolita Anime I: Yuki no kurenai keshô and Shôjo bara kei (1984); however, this character has an earlier reference in Vladimir Nabokov's Lolita (1955). Both of these references for the Lolita character define and emphasize its sexualized imagery; however, not all Lolita cosplayers intend to communicate that image.

Certain anime and manga characters are more popular than others, which results in trends within cosplay. The popularity of anime and manga characters is most evident by the numerous observations of cosplayers dressed as the same character at a convention. For example, in the September 2003 issue of Newtype, there is a photograph of multiple depictions of Inuyasha (i.e., a half dog demon and half human male, with silver or black hair and dog ears, wearing a red kimono-style garment with a sword) at the Anime Expo convention in Anaheim, California. Another example is the frequent sightings of Lolita characters at anime and manga conventions. The Lolita genre is so popular that there are numerous Web sites, costume shops, and publications dedicated to it. An additional cosplay character type is known as "crossplay" (Hlozek 2004). Crossplay is where a cosplayer employs gender reversal (i.e., a female who dresses as a male character or vice versa). Depending on the cosplayer's objectives, the crossplay may portray the opposite gender with accuracy or it may have humorous intentions within its display (e.g., dress, role-playing, etc.). For example, at CONvergence 2004 (a science fiction and fantasy convention held in Bloomington, Minnesota) there were several males dressed as each of the Sailor Moon Scouts (teenage heroines who assist Sailor Moon in her endeavors to save the world from evil), and a young woman was dressed as Tuxedo Mask (the young hero who often assists Sailor Moon and the Scouts in their quest). In this example, crossplay was utilized for humorous effect and social levity. These Scouts had deep voices and visible chest and leg hair, along with five o'clock shadows, and this Tuxedo Mask had a high-pitched voice and curvaceous silhouette. Moreover, the group was continuously making gender-related puns and jokes aimed at further identifying and establishing their gender role reversals.

Crossplay among cosplayers is not unusual, considering the many gender reversals, confusions, and ambiguities within anime and manga. For example, Oscar Francois de Jarjayes, from the Rose of Versailles (1972–74). was raised as a male; however, she is actually a female. The story centers on Oscar's ambiguity and duality. Another example is the Three Lights from Sailor Moon. In the manga, the Three Lights females pose as human males in a rock band, but in the anime they transform from male pop stars into female sailor senshi-Sailor Starlights.

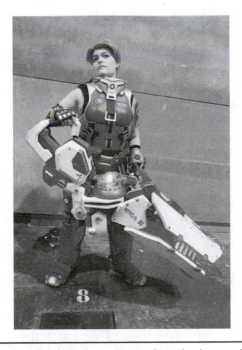

Figure 11.8 A cyborg is a person whose body contains mechanical or electrical devices and whose abilities are greater than the abilities of normal humans.

The cosplayer relies on dress and role-playing to display a given character. Cosplay role-playing is the ability to dress, walk, talk, and act similar to the chosen anime or manga character in order to portray a character in a desired fashion. Role-playing is an essential skill for a cosplayer, regardless if he or she is accurate to a character, creating a parody, or just having fun. Role-playing a character is greatly aided by cosplay dress.

Dress

Cosplay dress includes all body modifications and supplements, such as hair, makeup, costume, and accessories, including wands, staffs, and swords. This dress is often referred to as a "costume"; however, cosplay dress goes well beyond a simple costume. Cosplay dress may be the most important tool the cosplayer has to nonverbally communicate his or her chosen character and character traits. This dress functions as character identification and provides a basis for role-playing and interactions with other cosplayers. Cosplay dress also enables cosplayers to move from their actual identities to their chosen cosplay characters, and sometimes back again. For example, "Sailor Bubba," a bearded male cosplayer (and crossplayer) dressed as Sailor Moon (i.e., manga and anime teenage, female heroine with magical powers), speaks with a deep voice, walks with a gait natural to a 6-foot-tall, 250-pound man, and has dark black chest hair poking out of the top of his schoolgirl uniform. Still, anime and manga cosplayers recognize the dress and accept his change in personality (and gender) when a man in a tuxedo and top hat, the costume for Tuxedo Mask, enters the room. Suddenly it is a cosplay version of Sailor Moon and Tuxedo Mask having a conversation about saving the world (with not-so-subtle references to a room party as the scene for the next battle with a villain called "Mr. Jagermeister").

Each cosplayer determines the accuracy of his or her cosplay dress and character-portrayal. For some cosplayers the costume must be an exact replica of that worn by an anime character, which is no easy feat, given the unrealistic aspects of animated costumes. These cosplayers take extreme care to get every physical detail correct, such as adding padding for muscles, dyeing hair to bright, unnatural colors, and wearing platform shoes. They often spend significant amounts of money and time to create the perfect replica of their character's dress (Aoyama and Cahill 2003). Still other cosplayers are content with the bare minimum of dress that communicates their chosen character.

Typically, cosplay dress is either self-created or purchased, or a combination of the two. Wigs, cosmetics, and jewelry are often purchased because these items are difficult to make or may be less expensive than construction from raw materials. The constructed portions of cosplay dress usually include the clothing, but may also include foam swords and (faux) gem-encrusted wands. Some portions of cosplay dress that usually are a combination of purchased and constructed often need to be modified. such as shoes and accessories.

Japanese and North American Cosplay

A distinguishing characteristic between Japanese and North American cosplay is the way in which cosplayers perform in competition. In North America, during masquerades cosplayers wear their dress onstage and perform skits, often humorous but not necessarily an exact mime of their chosen character. In Japan, cosplayers also wear their dress on stage during competitions; however, they usually give only a static display, such as striking their character's signature pose or reciting the motto of their chosen character (Bruno 2002b).

Another distinguishing characteristic is where cosplay dress is worn. In North America, cosplayers wear their dress in nearly any setting (Bruno 2002b). For example, fully costumed/dressed cosplayers may leave a convention and eat at a nearby restaurant. In Japan, cosplayers are not welcome in certain areas beyond the convention, and some conventions request that cosplayers not wear their dress outside the convention (Bruno 2002b). Both Japanese and North American cosplayers gather with friends for cosplay at conventions and private events.

Since Japanese culture values community above the individual, cosplayers exist as a subculture, outside the acceptable norms of the dominant culture, where acts of discrimination have occurred by the dominant culture (Aoyama and Cahill 2003; Richie 2003). As a result, Japanese cosplayers have a negative reputation as individualists within some areas of Japanese culture (Bruno 2002b; Richie 2003). In Japan, unlike North America, there are areas, such as the Akihabara and Harajuku districts in Tokyo, strictly designated for cosplay costume shops, cafes, and restaurants (Prideaux 2001). Although Japanese cosplayers may venture into areas not designated for cosplayers, such activity is discouraged because of the negative reputation of cosplayers, and to protect young female cosplayers from unwanted attention (Richie 2003).

A final distinguishing characteristic between Japanese and North American cosplay is the available goods and markets for cosplayers. In Japan, there are districts where anime and manga cosplayers are the target market for consumable goods, such as cosplay costumes, accessories, and publications. North American anime and manga conventions feature dealers who sell a limited selection of cosplay items (e.g., magazines, DVDs, action figures, etc.). Within science fiction and fantasy conventions, anime and manga cosplayers compete with other fandoms, such as *Star Trek* and *Star Wars* fans, for a portion of the market. Outside the convention setting, anime and manga cosplayers must resort to catalogs and online shops for cosplay items, such as wigs, costumes, and makeup.

During the latter portions of the twentieth century, Japan and North America exchanged pop and subcultural ideas (Napier 2001; Poitras 2001). This is evident in Hollywood movies influenced by Japanese anime (e.g., *The Matrix* was influenced by *Ghost in the Shell*). An example of how Japanese anime and manga story lines have been influenced by North American subcultural activities is the *Record of Lodoss War* stories, which were influenced by *Dungeons and Dragons* role-playing games (Poitras 2001). This Japanese and North American exchange has extended to anime and manga and is apparent within the sources of inspiration for anime and manga cosplay.

Social Structures of Cosplay

Cosplay is a highly social activity that occurs in specific environments, such as anime and manga conventions, karaoke events, and dub meetings (Aoyama and Cahill 2003). Therefore it provides significant social benefits for cosplayers, who are often labeled "geeks" (i.e., socially and culturally inferior individuals) by the dominant culture. As a result, the anime and manga cosplay subculture provides cosplayers with "social structures" (Merton 1968). This social structure is composed of social interactions, environments, and experiences.

Most of the social interactions take place via the cosplay character(s). The character provides a (protective) identity for the cosplayer, which may allow for more confident and open interactions. Moreover, cosplay dress and environment(s) permit the cosplayer to role-play the character he or she is dressed as and engage in such social activities within a "safe" and "supportive" social structure. In this way the cosplay social structure is established, developed, and maintained.

The environments and spaces created for and by cosplay provide cosplayers with a variety of spaces for social interactions. Some of these environments include, but are not limited to, the following: an intimate space (dress), a private space (solitary rehearsals and research), a public space (interactions with other cosplayers, both in person and virtual), and a performance space (ranging from small parties to masquerades). Cosplay merges fantasy and reality into "carnivalesque" environments and spaces, where individuals have permission to be someone or something other than themselves (Bakhtin 1968; Napier 2001; Richie 2003). It is here that cosplay characters, distinctive from their anime and manga origins, emerge and interact with other cosplay characters. This further suggests the malleable identities of the cosplayers created in these environments where people are "not themselves" but instead are fictional anime and manga characters.

Cosplay social interactions and environments provide cosplayers with unique and significant experiences. These experiences include making new friends to claiming a moment in the limelight. Moreover, cosplay experiences appear to have real benefits for the cosplayers, because of the continued participation and growing interest in cosplay and related activities. The variety of cosplay experiences contributes to the social structure of cosplay.

In summary, cosplay inspired by anime, manga, and related video games expands not only the anime and manga art form but also the interactions of two global cultures—Japan and North America. The interactions begin with origin stories of cosplay and continue as cosplayers share fandom from both Japan and North America (via surfing the Internet and attending conventions). The impact of these interactions is visually evident at conventions where the context of cosplay, which includes social settings, cosplayers, characters and role-playing, and dress, is on display. Moreover, these interactions contribute to, build on, and develop into the social structures of cosplay, providing cosplayers with unique interactions, environments, and experiences.

Notes

1. In North America, *otaku* refers to an anime and manga (hardcare) fan or enthusiast. However, in Japan, *otaku* is an honorific and is used to address a good friend or the like (Shodt 1996).
2. In this chapter, I utilize J. B. Eicher's (2002) definition of dress—any body modification or supplement,

3. *Jagermeister* is an herbal (anise) liqueur that is popular in North America.

References

Aoyama, T., and J. Cahill. 2003. Cosplay Girls: Japani Live Animation Heroines. Tokyo: DH.

Bakhtin, M. 1968. Rabelais and His World. Trans. H. Iswolsky. Cambridge, MA: MIT.

Bruno, M. 2002a. "Cosplay: The Illegitimate Child of SF Masquerades." *Glitz and Glitter Newsletter*, Millennium Costume Guild. October. http://millenniumcg.tripod.com/glitzglitter/1002artirles.html (accessed March 20, 2005).

Bruno, M. 2002b. "Costuming a World Apart: Cosplay in America and Japan." *Glitz and Glitter Newsletter*, Millennium Costume Guild. October. http://millenniumcg.tripod.com/glitzgliaedl002articles.html (accessed March 20, 2005).

Drazen, P. 2003. *Anime Explosion! The What? Why?& Wow! Of Japanese Animation.* Berkeley, CA: Stone Bridge.

Eicher, J. B. 2000. "Dress," in Routledge *International Encyclopedia of Women*: Global Women's *Issues* and Knowledge, ed. C. Kramarae and D. Spender. London: Routledge.

Hlozek, R. 2004. Cosplay: The New Main Attraction. May. http://www.jivemgazine.com/article,php?pid=l953 (accessed March 20, 2005).

Ledoux, T., and D. Ranney. 1997. *The Complete Anime Guide*, 2nd ed. Issaquah, WA: Tiger Mountain.

Marias, P., and Marhiyama, T. 2004. *Cruising the Anime City: An Otaku Guide to Neo Tokyo.* Berkeley, CA: Stone Bridge.

McCarthy, H. 1993. *Anime!ABeginners Guide to Japanese Animation.* London: Titan Books.

Merton, R. K. 1968. *Social Theory and Social Structure.* New York: Free Press.

Napier, S. 2001. *Anime from Akira to PrincessMononoke: Experiencing Contemporary Japanese Animation.* New York: Palgrave.

Poitras, G. 2001. *Anime Essentials: Eveything a Fan Needs to Know.* Berkeley, CA: Stone Bridge.

Prideaux, E. 2001. "Japanese Trend Sees Teens Dress in Costume." CNews. Associated Press (Tokyo), February 7.

Richie, D. 2003. *Image Factory: Fads and Fashions in Japan.* London: Reaktion Books.

Schodt, F. L. 1996. *Dreamland Japan: Writings on Modern Manga.* Berkeley, CA: Stone Bridge.

Discussion Questions

1. How do the divisions of environments Winge offers compare to the public, private, and secret self model? Compare Winge's divisions to the PPSS model in Table 11.1.

2. What are the cultural similarities and differences in cosplay between Japan and North America?

3. Winge notes the benefits to geeks who costume at cosplay conventions. Can you think of other benefits?

11.3
Balancing Personal Needs and Authenticity When Designing Historic Styles of Dress
Dina C. Smith and Casey R. Stannard

Today there are roughly 4,500 members in the Jane Austen Society of North America. Groups like this frequently meet for reenactment events such as balls and teas to celebrate the Regency period, the time period in which Austen lived. "Regency" is typically used to refer to the time period from 1795 to 1820 by these hobbyists.

During reenactment events, female members are encouraged to wear "Regency" gowns that mimic the

---

Adapted from an article that originally appeared in *Clothing and Textiles Research Journal*.

styles fashionable in that time period (see Figure 11.9). Regency gowns had a long, straight skirt, an empire waistline, and typically had low necklines. The gowns were often made of soft and subtle fabrics with white being an especially fashionable color. Although Regency gowns appear to be loose in fit as a whole and simple to create, the bodices and sleeves are intended to be fitted to the individual wearer, which pose several challenges when constructing the gowns.

Regency dress as worn by the members of various historical reenactment groups can be thought of as a *historic style of dress*. A historic style of dress imitates historic dress but is not an exact copy and is distinguished from "historic costume," used to refer to actual historic garments (Marendy, 1993). Many reenactors are very concerned with making their Regency dress authentic to the actual historic garments worn in the past. In fact, there is such a strong desire to dress authentically that many individuals have created internet-based instructions (referred to as blogs for the remainder of this work) for properly creating and dressing in Regency attire.

These blogs were frequently visited by Dina, who was a member of a local reenactment group, to get ideas for making her own Regency attire. After investigating other research, we found that no researchers have dealt with Regency dress as a historic style of dress worn today.

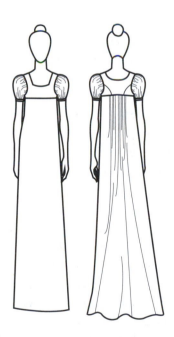

Figure 11.9 Line drawing of Regency gown (drawing by Casey Stannard).

Therefore, we decided to examine the design decisions related to the personal needs of the wearer and desire for authenticity of reenactors creating Regency gowns.

Conceptual Framework

The Functional, Expressive, Aesthetic Consumer Needs Model

To understand the design decisions made when creating Regency gowns as a historic style of dress, the needs of the reenactor had to be considered. Because Regency reenactors have to fulfill various needs when designing their gowns, we consulted the FEA [Functional, Expressive, Aesthetic] Consumer Needs Model, which was developed to describe consumer needs for contemporary clothing (functional, expressive, and aesthetic) that should be addressed when designing apparel (Lamb & Kallal, 1992, p. 42).

According to Lamb and Kallal (1992), functional needs relate to the utility of a garment and include fit, mobility, comfort, and [ease of] donning and doffing. Expressive needs "relate to the communicative aspects of dress" and convey the wearer's values, roles, status, and self-esteem (Lamb & Kallal, 1992, p. 43). Aesthetic needs relate to the beauty and attractiveness of a garment. Aesthetic needs include art elements, design principles, and the body/garment relationship. Design principles include "line, form, color, texture, and pattern" (Lamb & Kallal, 1992, p. 43). While design limitations were not part of the FEA Model, the authors explained, "Designers must deal with conflicts between competing FEA priorities as well as with production or price constraints" (Lamb & Kallal, 1992, p. 44). Therefore, designers of Regency gowns were anticipated to experience similar constraints or limitations.

Authenticity

Authenticity is "the attempt, to the best of an individual's ability, to use what they [sic] believe to be a method used in historical times to produce an artifact that reproduces something from an [sic] historical time" (Turner, 2010, p. 27). Wearers of historic styles of dress often value and strive to achieve authenticity in dress (Marendy, 1993; Strauss, 2001). According to Strauss (2001), reenactors' perceptions of authenticity in dress rely on three "elements of authenticity" (p. 152), which included: "accuracy of construction" (p. 153), "method of construction" (p. 154), and "material accuracy" (p. 154). Accuracy of construction referred to conforming dress items to the "historical specifications of original artifacts" (Strauss, 2001, p. 153). Method of construction referred to the sewing techniques used to make the garment such as hand or machine-sewing. Material accuracy refers to whether or not the materials used in the design are the same as an original artifact (Strauss, 2001). These three elements are standards by which reenactors evaluate dress authenticity. It can be difficult to create authentic historic styles of dress, as many historic materials are no longer available and the construction is not easy. Additionally, while historically accurate patterns can be found, they must be altered to fit the modern figure.

We decided to investigate blogs about the making of the Regency historic style of dress using netnography. Kozinets (2002) defined this research method as "ethnography of the Internet" that "adapts ethnographic research techniques to study the cultures and communities that are emerging through computer-mediated communications" (p. 62).

An extensive Google search using terms such as "Regency dress" and "Pride and Prejudice sewing" was conducted. Only blogs where designers described the making of Regency gowns were included. The blogs primarily contained essays and photographs of the garments within various stages of construction.

Results

We examined blogs that detailed the creation of 19 gowns. The authors were all female, designers, and wearers of the Regency gowns. Therefore, the authors are called designers for the remainder of the paper.

Nearly all the designers made gowns to attend Regency events such as a Jane Austen festival, a Jane Austen tea, or a Regency ball. Other designers made gowns for historical recreation challenges, such as the Historical Sew Fortnightly. The gowns discussed in these blogs were made to be both wearable and authentic.

Personal Needs

Personal needs of the designer were important design considerations and mirrored the needs (i.e., functional, expressive, and aesthetic) described in the FEA Consumer Needs Model (Lamb & Kallal, 1992). Instances of all three types of needs were considered by the designers; however, the expressive needs were the least frequently mentioned. The aesthetic needs were the most commonly explored.

Many of the designers created their gowns to fulfill specific functional needs. For example, to achieve

mobility one designer removed the train of her gown to make it more suitable for dancing. Donning and doffing the gowns were also important functional considerations. Many of the designers chose to use modern closures (e.g., zippers, hooks and eyes, etc.) to help with these processes.

Sometimes the designers described expressive needs or aspects they wanted their gowns to communicate. For example, Edelweiss Patterns (2013, November 17) stated, "I wanted the feel of the gown to be sumptuously elegant, yet with a sweetness to it to distinguish it from anything that Caroline Bingley would have worn" (para. 2), such as "garish colors and gaudy trims." By referencing an antagonist of Jane Austen's *Pride and Prejudice*, published in 1813, this designer communicated that she wanted to be finely dressed but not project a conceited demeanor.

The designers often followed their personal preferences for aesthetic details relating to the general line, shape, size, and so forth (Lamb & Kallal, 1992). The designers commonly made alterations based on aesthetics. One designer altered the aesthetics of her gown because she felt a puffier sleeve would make the gown more suitable for eveningwear.

Authenticity

An overarching desire for authenticity was evident. Designers looked to primary sources for inspiration to guide them in creating an authentic-looking gown. Fashion plates were a common source of inspiration. Two designers based their gowns on Regency portraits. Original historic garments from personal or museum collections were also studied for inspiration.

Other designers created their gowns based on general Regency attributes and secondary sources, which included images of gowns posted on pinterest.com and tumblr.com, as well as gowns made by other reenactors. Some of the designers used Regency films for inspiration, but this source of inspiration was less common. Clearly, the designers were highly concerned with authenticity in their garments.

Strauss (2001) discussed three aspects of authenticity (i.e., accuracy of construction, methods of construction, and material accuracy). We found that the designers were in opposition to Strauss's (2001) claim that historic styles of dress needed all three elements of authenticity to be considered authentic. While the designers perceived and evaluated the authenticity of their gowns using these three elements, they did not feel the garments needed all three of them. Instead, designers felt the presence of at least one historically accurate element compensated for the absence of the others.

Pattern. Strauss (2001) stated, "The garments worn by most serious reenactors were patterned after original museum artifacts, thus appearing authentic" (p. 153). The designers also viewed patterns based on historic garments as the most accurate. Several of the designers used published patterns based on historic garments like Janet Arnold's *Patterns of Fashion 1* (1964). Online Regency patterns such as Sense and Sensibility patterns were also popular.

Several designers stated that they combined multiple patterns (an act referred to as "frankensteining"). For example, one designer used two patterns based on historic garments and consulted an online pattern for instructions on the neckline closure. Many of the designers demonstrated a sophisticated understanding of patternmaking by picking and choosing desired characteristics of the final garment.

The designers "frankensteined" the patterns to resolve fit issues, which they frequently encountered when using historical reproduction patterns. These fit issues occurred because the patterns were made for the exact size and proportions of the original wearer, which vary significantly from contemporary bodies. Interestingly, after the designers "frankensteined" the patterns in order to fit the patterns to their figures (which changed the line, proportions, and overall design), they still viewed their gowns as authentic.

Construction. Strauss (2001) also found that "method of construction" contributed to authenticity (p. 154). The designers placed high value on accurate construction methods, but many found the use of modern construction techniques was unavoidable. Five designers used sewing machines, though only one designer explained her motivation for doing so was to save time. She, along with one other designer, stated that machine-sewing reduced the authenticity of their gowns.

Four designers reported sewing Regency gowns completely by hand. The Fashionable Past sewed her gown by hand because she was "striving for accuracy" and tried to copy an original 1820s gown "as closely as possible" (The Fashionable Past, n.d., para. 2). Among the designers, the use of patterns based on historic garments appeared to compensate for choosing machine-sewing, resulting in a gown the designers viewed as authentic.

Material. Material referred to the fabric and other components needed to create the design. Some designers mentioned buying materials from online vendors who carried more authentic materials to achieve material accuracy. However, the designers often chose less authentic materials.

There was a preference among the designers for using materials they had on hand, regardless of authenticity. This was a way to reduce the cost of a gown. The designers also frequently used modern materials because they considered them to be less expensive alternatives. In addition, modern materials were thought to perform better and were easier to sew.

Limitations

The designers of Regency gowns encountered limitations that impacted their designs. A desire to create authentic gowns led the designers to negotiate a balance between their personal needs, their desire for authenticity, and various limitations. As previously mentioned, the selection of materials, patterning, and construction techniques were influenced by limitations.

A limitation in skill barred some of the designers from achieving the desired authentic looking gowns. This limitation relates to the "inability to accurately replicate materials of the past" (Strauss, 2001, p. 155). Challenges faced while constructing Regency gowns further revealed how the designers' construction skills impacted their designs. Several designers noted the difficulty of properly setting in the sleeves. Two other designers noted difficulty in replicating historic gown details.

Financial limitations influenced materials selection. Strauss (2001) listed "financial limitations" (p. 155) as a barrier to authenticity as "authentic items were generally more expensive" (p. 155). Limitations in time and the perceived worth of effort were evidenced in the decisions the designers made while constructing their gowns. Some designers left off elements that would take too long to construct like piping along seamlines.

Historic Styles of Dress Design Considerations Model

The Regency gowns were designed with personal needs, desire for authenticity, and limitations of the designer in mind. This research led to the development of the *Historic Styles of Dress Design Considerations Model* (Figure 11.10), which incorporates categories from the FEA Consumer Needs Model (Lamb & Kallal, 1992, p. 42), as well as Strauss's (2001) "elements of authenticity" (p. 152). We have included these as Material, Construction, and Pattern.

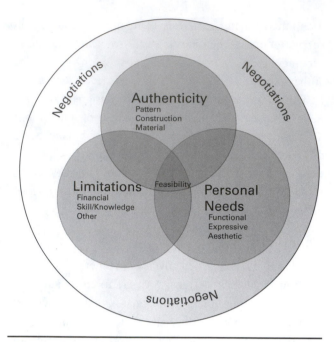

Figure 11.10 Historic Styles of Dress Design Considerations Model.

Limitations found among the designers included financial, knowledge/skill, and other. These are listed within the "Limitations" circle. Personal needs, authenticity, and limitations are depicted as overlapping circles encased within a larger circle labeled "Negotiations."

Limitations and authenticity. In most cases, this intersection was one in which concern for authenticity preceded the limitations that the designers faced. For example, some designers selected materials based on the historic garments they used for inspiration. However, the designers were sometimes unable to use historically-accurate materials due to the limited availability and the financial expense.

Likewise, designers proceeded with authenticity by basing the design of their gowns on historic garments or patterns but then were limited in their ability to replicate the construction of these garments or patterns (i.e., limitations in skill). For example, one designer omitted the lining in the sleeves of her gown after experiencing difficulty constructing the sleeves.

Personal needs and authenticity. Each of the three types of personal needs could impact the authenticity of a gown. Within the sample, the most frequent intersection was between the functional needs of the designer and her desire for authenticity. For example, American Duchess (2009, June 23) used an inauthentic closure. She explained,

"Why did I use buttons? In my sewing experience, I have found buttons to be the most secure of closures. . . Period? Not so much, but FUNCTIONAL!" (para. 12).

Another example of the intersection between aesthetic needs and authenticity was one in which designers drew from authentic sources of inspiration but made alterations to suit their aesthetic needs.

Limitations and personal needs. The intersection between limitations and personal needs also impacted the Regency gowns. While designing a ball gown, Cation Designs (2013, February, 1) was unable to find white cotton fabric for the price she "was willing to spend" and selected a "celadon-colored sheet" as a "unique and cheaper" alternative (para. 2). The designer explained that she then "had to figure out how to dress it up so that it would look appropriately fancy" (para. 2). In this case, both a limitation and a personal aesthetic need impacted authenticity.

Feasibility. The intersection between personal needs, limitations, and authenticity is depicted at the center of the model, resulting in a feasible project that is perceived as authentic. The Dreamstress (2009, October 17), illustrated this intersection when she faced a limitation in materials, the personal need for fit, all while desiring an authentic-looking design. When The Dreamstress (2009, October 14) documented her project, she asked, "So, how long do you think it will take me to turn a pile of muslin into a plausibly accurate Regency frock?" (para. 7). First, she had to deviate from the original historic pattern because her fabric was not wide enough for the pattern (limitation). Later, she changed the construction of the bodice to fit her bust (personal need): "I went for a gathered and slightly scooped apron front rather than the flatter bias cut rectangle of the original" (para. 10). Despite the fact that her gown was impacted by these limitations and personal needs, the The Dreamstress viewed her gown as fairly historically accurate. This designer's discussion is an example of how a project can be perceived as authentic even when it balances the three aspects of authenticity, personal needs, and limitations.

Conclusions

We examined the design decisions related to the personal needs and desire for authenticity of designers creating Regency gowns as a historic style of dress. Regency gown designers' desire for authenticity led them to seek out historical sources that enabled them to produce authentic designs. Personal needs relating to function, expression, and aesthetics, in addition to limitations, such as financial limitations and limitations in knowledge, influenced decisions in patterning and construction of the gowns. The designers often had to make compromises among these elements while designing historic styles of dress.

References

Arnold, J. (1964). *Patterns of fashion 1: Englishwomen's dress and their construction 1660–1860*. London, United Kingdom: MacMillan Publishers, LTD.

American Duchess: Historical Costuming. (2009, June 23). Guts: 1790s wrap-front gown details [Web log post]. Retrieved from http://americanduchess .blogspot.com/search/label/Regency%20Voile

Cation Designs. (2013, February 1). Channeling Caroline and Charlotte [web log post]. Retrieved from http:// cationdesigns.blogspot.com/2013/02/channeling-caroline-and-charlotte.html

The Dreamstress. (2009, October 17). Madame Recamier needs to recline on her recamier [weblog post]. Retrieved from http://thedreamstress.com/2009/10 /madame-recamier-needs-to recline-on-her-recamier/

Edelweiss Patterns. (2013, November 17). The hand sewn silk regency ball gown [web log post]. Retrieved from http://www.edelweisspatterns.com/blog/?p=4310

The Fashionable Past: Katherine's Dress Site. (n.d.). The background. Retrieved from http://www.koshka-the -cat.com/background.html

Kozinets, R. V. (2002). The field behind the screen: Using netnography for marketing research in online communities. *Journal of Marketing Research, 39*, 61–72.

Lamb, J. M., & Kallal, M. J. (1992). A conceptual framework for apparel design. *Clothing and Textiles Research Journal, 10*(2), 42–47. doi: 10.1177/0887302X 9201000207

Marendy, M. (1993).The development and the evaluation of costume reproduction pattern blocks for an 1880's woman's dress. *Clothing and Textiles Research Journal, 11*(4), 41–52. doi: 10.1177/0887302X9301100406

Strauss, M. D. (2001). A framework for assessing military dress authenticity in Civil War reenacting. *Clothing and Textiles Research Journal, 19*(4), 145–157. doi: 10.1177/0887302X0101900401

Turner, A. L. (2010). Honored values and valued objects: The Society for Creative Anachronism. (Unpublished doctoral dissertation). Oregon State University, Corvallis, OR.

Discussion Questions

1. What, do you think, enabled some designers to machine sew a Regency Style dress (when the originals were hand sewn) and to consider the gowns authentic?

2. What method did the authors use to collect and analyze data?

3. What is 'frankensteining'?

An extended version of this article appears in *Clothing and Textiles Research Journal, 34*(4), 287–302.

CHAPTER 12
DRESS AND TECHNOLOGY
Kimberly A. Miller-Spillman

After you have read this chapter, you will understand:

- **Where research on apparel technology is performed**
- **The variety of innovation within the apparel industry**
- **How technology, status, and time intersect**
- **Consumer preferences for apparel technology**
- **How tradition and technology are related to culture**

In this chapter we observe the many effects that technology has on dress and fashion. For example, prior to the 1850s the method of obtaining clothing was to visit a seamstress or tailor and to sew by hand at home to mend and keep clothes up-to-date. However, the invention of the sewing machine changed the social custom of visiting a seamstress or tailor to going to a store for readymade clothing. Later, women could purchase a home sewing machine and paper patterns (available in the 1860s) to create their own clothing at home. The invention of the sewing machine also made mass production of apparel possible and created a new social class of factory workers. At the conclusion of this chapter you will have the opportunity to reflect on the changes brought about by the Industrial Revolution in the late 1800s and early 1900s and compare those changes to the current state of the apparel industry.

Technology and fashion both change rapidly, replacing the old with the new. For instance, the invention of the cage crinoline in the 1850s offered women a lightweight alternative to expand skirt widths without layers of heavy, starched petticoats (Tortora & Eubank, 2010). The weight of the petticoats had become a health and safety concern for women as they moved through daily tasks. In this case, innovation in women's support garments allowed women healthier and safer lives (see Figure 12.1).

During any given era, there are consumers who will embrace new technology and those who reject it.

Figure 12.1 Early technology: the cage crinoline (1850s–1870s) provided women with the desired silhouette without weighing down the wearer.

Technophobes come in all ages, but, in general, older consumers tend to stick with familiar processes while younger consumers embrace new technology (see Figure 12.2). A consumer's adaptation of technology is influenced by their generational cohort. **Generation Z** refers to people born between the early to mid-1990s through 2010 (also known as the Internet Generation). They were born after the World Wide Web became increasingly available, and they are the first generation to be born completely in an era of postmodernism and globalism. College students today have grown up with mobile technology, thus creating a consumer who expects technology to continue making life easier, faster, and convenient.

Figure 12.2 Today's college students have always had technology as a part of their lives.

RESEARCH IN THE APPAREL INDUSTRY

Innovation is the development of something new, whether a thought or idea, a practice, or a tool or implement. Technological advances in apparel can be found in a variety of places. **University faculty** is one group that conducts research on apparel technology by obtaining funding from the government, corporations, and the military. **Entrepreneurs** who have a hot idea for the latest in wearable electronics merge nanotechnology with apparel. The **U.S. Military** is one of the largest producers and consumers of apparel and has a vested interest in researching wearable technology to assist soldiers in the field. For more information on technology and the fashion industry, see the reading "5 Technology Trends Transforming the Fashion Industry" at the end of this chapter.

VARIETY OF INNOVATIONS IN THE APPAREL INDUSTRY

Nanotechnology is the science of making electronics as tiny as possible. When nanotechnology companies partner with apparel companies, it results in the development of **wearable electronics**. Everything you can imagine—and probably a few things that you can't—has been tried or is in the process of being tested (Warren, 2001). From clothes that "talk" to washing machines, telling the washer how the garment should be cleaned, to a global positioning system woven into a jacket collar to track a wandering child or an Alzheimer's patient, wearable electronics can do amazing things. There's clothing that adjusts to your changes in size, clothes that change color to match another garment in your closet, children's sleepwear that sounds an alarm if a baby stops breathing, gym-suit fabrics that absorb odors and can be worn three or four times without offending other exercisers, and fiber-optic wedding dresses or disco trousers that sparkle.

Other innovations in the apparel industry can be found in **clothing for specific needs**, a segment of the apparel industry that accommodates consumers outside of the mainstream (Watkins, 1995a). Clothing for specific needs includes astronauts, firefighters, disabled individuals, and older adults. Any specialized occupation, such as football players, motocross riders, hockey players, people in the microchip manufacturing industry, and underwater divers, could fit under the broad umbrella of clothing for specific needs. For example, "smart" spacesuits can monitor an astronaut's physical condition. This once sophisticated and expensive technology is trickling down to consumers who are willing to pay $20 to $60 for a T-shirt (or running bra) that monitors heart rate, body temperature, respiration, and number of calories burned and can warn the wearer of a potential heart attack or heat stroke (accessed on November 17, 2017, at https://inhabitat.com/ecouterre/electronic-sports-bra-monitors-vital-signs-communicates-with-smartphones/).

A new technology that can make textiles germ-free was developed by a researcher at the University of Georgia. This inexpensive technology can be applied to medical linens and clothing, face masks, athletic socks, and diapers. Given that many "new" technologies are initially expensive and are not available at the price points the public can afford, it will be interesting to see how rapidly this technology will become available (UGA News Service).

New technologies target Generation Z consumers, which include having clothing that changes color from day to night, trousers that multitask by doubling as keyboards, and iPod or GPS systems built directly into their designs at the fiber level. Instead of having pockets sized for electronic devices in your clothing, your wardrobe will actually be your BlackBerry. Of course, the challenge is to manufacture these garments in quantities so that they are affordable. Companies can be encouraged to develop these designs if there is enough consumer demand.

Another innovation was developed by a former consumer economics student at the University of Georgia. Justin Niefer used his marketing skills to become an entrepreneur. Niefer is cofounder of the company **Evoshield**, which produces a lightweight, malleable substance that hardens to fit the wearer's body and disperses impact. The primary application for the product is in sports, namely baseball and football. A YouTube video features Niefer demonstrating the product's effectiveness (www.youtube.com/watch?v=KUjSylfDcgw).

Innovations in digital technology are revolutionizing the process of design by using digital methods rather than **screen printing** methods. Apparel designers are happy to no longer be limited by screen printing. **Digital printing** has given designers the ability to produce a fabric pattern that will follow the shape of the body, thus looking less "flat" and more natural. Screen prints restrict the complexity of prints as well as the number of colors that can be produced on a garment. (You may want to count the number of colors on your favorite T-shirt.) There is much more flexibility with digital printing, and designers are thrilled to have more choices (see Figure 12.3).

Other designers are excited by innovations in electronics added to dress. The Galaxy Dress (www.youtube.com /watch?v=rX9FOGFxN9A) was the commissioned centerpiece of the "Fast Forward: Inventing the Future" exhibit at the Museum of Science and Industry in Chicago in 2009. The Galaxy Dress is one example of the many developments in clothing technology. Turkish designer and two-time winner of the British Designer of the

Figure 12.3 This digital print follows body contours.

Year award Hussein Chalayan is a staunch supporter of technology in fashion and has created dresses that glow with built-in LEDs or emit spectacular red lasers. For Chalayan, the future of technology and dress is already here. For example, **STEM** programs in Kentucky with middle-school students are increasing interest in technology and fashion careers. (See reading "Middle-School Kids, Sewing, and STEM" at the end of this chapter.) (See Figure 12.4.)

Still other designers prefer to experiment with eco-friendly methods to create clothing. Designer Suzanne Lee discusses how a person can grow his or her own clothes at www.ted.com/talks/suzanne_lee_grow_your_ own_clothes.html. Still others show how clothes can be differently applied. See a demonstration at www. youtube.com/watch?v=ScvdFeh1aOw. The concept that clothing is nondiscursive (McCraken, 1988)—or fixed for several hours at a time—may be obsolete by 2020 if these technologies appeal to consumers.

TECHNOLOGY, STATUS, AND TIMING

Technology and fashion have a lot in common. Both thrive on the status of being the latest "it" item. Therefore, the friend with the latest technology for his or her iPhone holds

Figure 12.4 This 3-D printed shoe design is an example of technology and fashion.

a certain status among friends. The same phenomenon occurs in fashion when one member of a group shows up wearing the latest fashion. Technology as well as fashion depends on timing to achieve status. For example, timing was critical for Target customers to purchase a Missoni item in 2011. Customers employed the technology of the Internet to purchase a reasonably priced Missoni outfit that was fashionable. Target customers were so excited by the Missoni sale that they shut down the retailer's website from an overwhelming number of orders.

CONSUMER PREFERENCES FOR APPAREL TECHNOLOGY

Given enough consumer demand, more innovative technologies will reach the mass consumer. For example, one technology is already available—however, not widespread—computerized **body scanners** take 10 seconds to collect thousands of body measurements to produce a garment that fits an individual precisely (see Figure 12.5). The individual steps into a cylinder (much like the airport scanner), fully clothed, for 10 seconds and a computer prints out her exact measurements. With the measurements, a company can produce a perfect-fitting pair of jeans for between $160 and $180. If women complain that finding well-fitting jeans are hard to find, why are they not demanding this technology at an affordable price? Consumer acceptance is one reason and price is another. Perhaps the average-size woman is not

comfortable knowing that all of her body measurements can be seen by store employees, nor does she want to invest $160 on a pair of jeans.

The next step in this technology would allow the customer to select fabric, color, and style details such as pant leg fullness and pocket style from an array of options. Not only would the garment be customized to fit precisely, but also the consumer would take part in designing the style of garments she or he wants. This process is called **co-design** (Fiore, Lee, & Kunz, 2004; Lee et al., 2002; Lee et al., 2011). Apparel industry experts often refer to custom-fit garments ordered through a mass retailer or producer as **"made-to-measure"**(Gellers, 1998). Garments ordered through a mass retailer or producer for which the consumer has made personal style design choices are referred to as **mass customized** (Pine, 1993).

Made-to-measure and mass-customized apparel is already available (Coia, 2003; Lee & Chen, 1999), but advances in computerized imaging and production systems probably will make customized apparel more readily accessible and less expensive sometime around the year 2020.

Only a small minority of consumers (about 9 percent) had purchased apparel through the Internet by early 1999 (Yoh et al., 2003). But more than one-third of shoppers had purchased apparel via the Internet by 2001 (Pastore, 2001), and apparel is now one of the top five most purchased product categories ("Online Spending," 2003). Why shouldn't we believe that these modes of shopping will play a more substantial role in how consumers shop by 2020?

Mass customization of fit is beginning to attract more customers; Lands' End has found that four of its top-selling products are in the customized-fit category (Coia, 2003). And the chances are good that a variety of modes of shopping will continue to be used through the next 10 years. Made-to-measure apparel will require extensive development of computer systems and new retail systems. The eventual changes in the fashion system that could result from widespread use of made-to-measure and mass-customized ordering are almost too immense to comprehend, but certainly intriguing. Increased variety and diversity in appearances and more uniqueness in what can be purchased could certainly emerge. The fashion system will become increasingly complex during the 21st century and consumers will determine which technologies are implemented and which are not.

Figure 12.5 Computerized body scanners can take a customer's precise body measurements.

TECHNOLOGY, TRADITION, AND CULTURE

Tradition in all fields has a habit of slowing things down. The terms *Western* and *non-Western* are often used interchangeably with *industrial* and *non-industrial* and create boundaries between cultures that embrace technology and those that do not. Cultures are often described by their level of technology. Think of the Egyptian pyramids and the roads and bridges engineered by the ancient Romans. In the apparel industry, one can create a technology continuum with a back-strap loom on one end and computer-operated industrial looms on the opposite end (see Figure 1.2b in Chapter 1 to view these looms side-by-side). What one gains in speed and standardization with computer-operated looms, one loses in creativity and variation of handmade items.

Is tradition gender-specific? Women in most developing countries are considered more traditional than men. Women are often the last to give up their traditional dress and their cultural traditions because women are more likely than men to stay at home with children while men are more likely to seek employment away from the home. In fact, "women's work" often invokes images of slow, repetitive, low-tech labor that takes place in the home while women tend children. "Men's work" invokes images that are fast paced and include high production. Although not all developing countries divide labor between the private sphere (female) and the public sphere (male), many do (Barnes & Eicher, 1992).

Tradition is naturally resistant to innovation, and technological change is not always embraced with open arms. However, preserving traditions is valuable to cultural richness and to maintaining the history of a culture. In the reading "For Dignity and Development, East Africa Curbs Used Clothes "Imports"" (at the end of this chapter), author Kimiko de Freytas-Tamura describes how imports of secondhand clothes from the United States undermine efforts in East Africa to develop their own textile industry.

On the other end of the technology continuum is a computerized loom used in most industrialized countries. This loom requires human intervention only when there is a problem (i.e., a thread has broken). The computerized loom needs to be programmed and maintained by a human, but the actual work of producing the cloth is done by the machine.

The apparel industry itself is resistant to change. Susan Watkins provides two examples, heat sealing and molding, as possible alternatives for the American apparel industry (Watkins, 1995b). Some of these processes have been around since the 1950s and were perfected after initial endeavors. These processes, which are practiced in European apparel industries, are time-efficient and economical. However, adopting these processes would mean changing the way clothing is designed, produced, and marketed in the United States. The American apparel industry evidently is not ready for these changes.

More recently, clothing researchers Armstrong and LeHew have considered the impact of the apparel industry on the environment and recommend a new dominant social paradigm for the apparel industry (see the reading "Shifting the Dominant Social Paradigm in the Apparel Industry: Acknowledging the Pink Elephant"). A **paradigm** is defined as an assembly of practices and protocols characterizing a discipline or field (Kuhn, 1996). Beginning with the Industrial Revolution the apparel industry's paradigm has dictated the exploitation of the earth's resources, which is now taking its toll on the environment. This mind-set of the apparel industry, to produce new fashions quickly while ignoring the earth's limits, is now being called into question by eco-conscious consumers. How can the apparel industry re-create itself so that it will be profitable and eco-friendly? Tradition has prevented the industry from changing and consumers are just now realizing that the costs of their consumer goods include costs to the earth. Armstrong and LeHew admit that changing the apparel industry will be difficult—but it can be done.

Summary

Technology and dress is a wide-ranging topic with many avenues for innovation. Many groups and individuals are currently involved in the research and development of new technologies in dress. Many innovations are in the works that join nanotechnology and clothing to create wearable electronics. Time and status are important elements of both technology and fashion. Consumers may not be uniformly receptive of new technology and may reject technology or take time to adopt new technologies. However, new technology connected to dress will undoubtedly appeal to those who can afford it and eventually trickle down to the mass consumer. Both technology and traditions to create dress are uniquely tied to culture. Interventions into cultural groups with new technology should be considered carefully before moving forward.

Key Terms

Clothing for specific needs
Co-design
Body scanners
Digital printing
Entrepreneurs

Evoshield
Generation Z
Innovation
Made-to-measure
Mass customized

Nanotechnology
Paradigm
Screen printing
Spray-on clothes
STEM

Technophobe
University faculty
U.S. Military
Wearable electronics

Learning Activity 12.1

DRESS AND TECHNOLOGY

Objective

To find the most current information on wearable electronics.

Procedure

Given how quickly technology changes you would want to do this often: do an online search to find out what is currently available in technology and dress. Use the following terms or a combination of terms to search for current information. You should prepare a report on your findings to share with the class. This can also be done in groups.

CuteCircuit

DuPont and smart garments

Fiber-optics and dress

ICD+ Smart garments

Levi-Strauss

Luminex

M-Dress

Nanotechnology and clothing

Philips NV

Smart fabrics

Technology and clothing

Textronics

Wearable electronics

References

Barnes, R. and J. B. Eicher (eds.) (1992), *Dress and Gender: Making and Meaning*, Oxford: Berg Press.

Coia, A. (2003), Channeling E-Tail Resources," *Apparel*, 44(12): 18–20.

Fiore, A. M., S. Lee and G. Kunz (2004), "Individual Differences, Motivations, and Willingness to Use a Mass Customization Option for Fashion Products," *European Journal of Marketing*, 38(7): 835–49.

Gellers, S. (1998, July 8), "Made-to-Measure: Raising the Stakes for Better Clothing," *Daily News Record*, 9: 16.

Kuhn, Thomas S. (1996), *The Structure of Scientific Revolutions* (3rd ed.), Chicago: University of Chicago Press.

Lee, S. and J. C. Chen (1999, December), "Mass Customization Methodology for Apparel Manufacturing with a Future," *Journal of Industrial Technology*, 16(1). Available online: www.nait.org.

Lee, H. H., M. L. Damhorst, J. R. Campbell, S. Loker and J. L. Parsons (2011), "Consumer Satisfaction with a Mass Customized Internet Apparel Shopping Site," *International Journal of Consumer Studies*, 35(3): 316–29.

Lee, S., G. Kunz, A. M. Fiore, and J. R. Campbell (2002), "Acceptance of Mass Customization of Apparel: Merchandising Issues Associated with Preference for Product, Process, and Place," *Clothing and Textiles Research Journal*, 20(3): 138–46.

McCraken, G. (1988), *Culture and Consumption*, Bloomington: Indiana University Press.

Pastore, M. (2001, January 16), "Consumer Continues Online Purchases." Available online: www.clickz.com/stats/markets/retailing/article.php/560781.

Pine, B. J., II (1993), *Mass Customization: The New Frontier in Business Competition*, Boston: Harvard Business School Press.

Tortora, P. G. and K. Eubank (2010), *Survey of Historic Costume: A History of Western Dress* (5th ed.), New York: Fairchild Books.

Warren, S. (2001), "Ready-to-Wear Watch?Dogs: 'Smart' Garments Keep Track of Vital Signs, Hide Odor," *Wall Street Journal*, October 10, B1, B3.

Watkins, S. M. (1995a), *Clothing: The Portable Environment* (2nd ed.), Ames: Iowa State University Press.

Watkins, S. M. (1995b), "Stitchless Sewing for the Apparel of the Future," in M. E.

Yoh, E., M. L. Damhorst, S. Sapp and R. Laczniak (2003), "Consumer Adoption of the Internet: The Case of Apparel Shopping," *Psychology and Marketing*, 20(12): 1095–118.

5 Technology Trends Transforming the Fashion Industry
Launchmetrics

The innovations taking place at the intersection of fashion and technology are profoundly amazing and transformative. In many respects, the fashion industry today bears little resemblance to that of a decade ago—and will change even more in the decade ahead.

Legendary businessman Peter Drucker famously said, "Trying to predict the future is like trying to drive down a country road at night with no lights while looking out the back window." He's right, which is why I'm not going to try to predict the future here.

I am, however, going to energize your imagination with five trends that will help create that unpredictable future—trends that are taking shape right now, that Fashion GPS is tracking closely, and with which all of us in the fashion industry will need to grapple in the years ahead.

1. Wearable Technology Blurs the Line Between Tech and Fashion

What it's about: The most obvious examples of wearable technology today are Google Glass and a variety of smartwatches—but these are rudimentary first steps into the realm of wearable tech.

What happens, for example, when smart fabrics (you may already be aware of the San Francisco conference in April focusing on this trend) enable fashions to incorporate sensors that emit aromas or interact with the environment in different ways? Imagine fashions that alter their color or texture based on surrounding conditions of light, heat or sound.

Or, for another example, imagine fashions that seamlessly and invisibly incorporate biofeedback to support an individual's health and wellness. Would you like some smartclothes to go with your smartwatch and smartphone?

Why it matters: The days of fabric as a strictly static resource are coming to a close—the days of fabric as an active (and interactive) resource are just beginning.

2. Fashion Week Becomes 52 Fashion Weeks Each Year

What it's about: Digital Fashion Week is something of a curiosity now, but it's the beginning of what could be a sea change in the fashion world.

Just as the internet and the 24/7 news cycle have been laying waste to weekly news magazines and daily newspapers, the hyper-networked fashion world to come is likely to transform any given Fashion Week into worldwide industry event that lasts 365 days a year.

This transformation will probably occur in stages, the first of which is global participation in local events. Live streaming of runway shows is already commonplace, and the impact of the social media component of those streams is only beginning to be understood and leveraged in a way that can benefit fashion brands.

Why it matters: Consider 1,000 people in New York and 1,000 people in San Francisco viewing an Amsterdam Fashion Week event. A new product hits the runway and the buzz in San Francisco is off the meter, while the reaction in New York is ho-hum at best. The retail implications for the brand presenting that product—and understanding the buzz both quantitatively and qualitatively—could make or break the product launch. That's a single data point. Now imagine a flood of data points 365 days a year.

3. 3D Printing Means Everyone Becomes a One-Person Factory

What it's about: If you haven't heard much about 3D printing, brace yourself: Imagine having a printer in your home or office that, instead of putting ink to paper, actually creates three-dimensional solid objects. Print a pair of shoes? A handbag? A dress? Yep: All of the above . . . and more.

According to Forbes, 3D printing will be a $3.1 billion industry by 2016 and a $5.2 billion industry by 2020. I think those predictions are too conservative.

To understand how 3D printing will transform the fashion industry in the years ahead, compare and contrast life today with life before computers and smartphones and the internet. That's the kind of transformative change that will be brought about by easily affordable 3D printing.

Over the past 20 years, the near-ubiquity of computers has democratized information and media. Publishing and broadcasting, once available to just a privileged few, are now available to anyone with an idea and a laptop or tablet—and that idea can be made available to anyone on the planet with the click of a mouse.

Why it matters: Think about designers in offices, apartments and garages developing accessory prototypes—or engaging in full-on production without any middleman whatsoever. Or imagine designers creating scale models of—well, of models wearing the designs they've created; how might those scale models be used to popularize and sell fashion? The possibilities are endless. The impacts will be enormous.

4. Smart Use of Metadata Will Give Brands a Competitive Edge

What it's about: You've been hearing plenty in the news lately about metadata and the NSA, and you're probably familiar with metadata as it relates to web pages. But consider other kinds of metadata.

How customers and potential customers interact with online product databases (GPS Styles, for one example) can reveal patterns of interest and intent that can suggest which products have the greatest possibility for success.

Gathering metadata is the easy part: Every digital action leaves a footprint, and capturing those footprints is a relatively minor issue. However, as everything that everyone in the industry does takes on a digital component, the volume of data capable of being captured is incalculable. This begs the question of how to make sense of it all.

Why it matters: Knowing how to sift through the haystack of information to identify needles of insight that can help weave profitable new strategies—that's where the smart use of data-mining technologies coupled with strategic analysis will drive new avenues of success for fashion brands large and small worldwide.

5. Technology Will Make Everything You Know Today Obsolete in 10 Years

What it's about: Moore's Law states that the processing power of computers will double every two years. The term originated around 1970, and it's held fairly true since then (though some analyses of Moore's Law say the doubling occurs every 18 months).

In other words: A decade from now, the processing power of the average computer—or smartphone—will be 32 times stronger than it is today.

Imagine the seismic shifts that power will create: Those needles I referred to above might be easier for the entrepreneur to find. The digital capabilities of today's biggest fashion brands will be dwarfed by the startup brands of 2024. The technology trends starting to emerge today will accelerate exponentially over the coming decade.

Why it matters: The truly successful fashion brands of tomorrow will be those that can not only recognize and cope with the pace of change, but embrace it. They will be aware of both the megatrends and microtrends in our industry—and will be flexible enough to strategically act on them with bold conviction.

Discussion Questions

1. Which of the five trends did you find most interesting? Did any trend sound like a job possibility for you in the future?
2. Do a quick search on your computer to find out what the current value is of the 3D printing industry.
3. Do you see yourself 3D printing shoes, handbags or other fashion items at home in the future?

12.2
Middle School Kids, Sewing, and STEM

Marjorie Baker

What do science, technology, engineering, math (STEM), fashion, and sewing have in common? Ask that of anyone who sews and they will quickly say that sewing involves all of the above. That is exactly how teaching sewing to youth is being approached using recently introduced curricula from Cornell and the University of Minnesota (Style Engineers) and the University of Nebraska-Lincoln (STEAM Clothing). Marjorie Baker,

Original for this text.

University of Kentucky Extension Associate for Clothing and Textiles is actively involved with integrating both of these curricula to teach sewing and expose youth to STEM careers through their interest in fashion and design. The Kentucky 4-H Fashion Leadership Board, a selected group of fashion minded high school aged 4-H youth were used to kick start this before Baker realized how beneficial these programs would be for all youth. After all, sewing, especially clothing involves fibers and fabric (science), using a machine (technology), fitting pieces together that actually fit a 3-D form (engineering) and both body and fabric measurements (math). The Nebraska curriculum includes color and other principles of design (art) to complete the STEAM acronym. Sewing involves pre-engineering skills as well as being a valuable life skill that:

- Increases hand-eye coordination
- Improves critical thinking among youth
- Is sustainable
- Is fashionable
- Builds self esteem

Baker used the idea of integrating fashion and science to earn a grant from the National 4-H Council funded by HughesNet to implement STEM activities during summer camp. She recruited 4-H and FCS Cooperative Extension agents from across Kentucky to join her, reaching a total of 500 4-H youth. Using the Style Engineers curriculum was a perfect fit. Agents were free to select the activities they thought would benefit their youth. Some chose day camps that focused only on the sewing portions while others chose hands on science activities during traditional resident camp settings. At the end of the summer, the overall consensus was that the young designers had a lot of fun learning about sewing, textiles, and engineering, as well as related STEM careers.

The Style Engineers curriculum, funded by the National Science Foundation was first introduced in 2015. As more funding is secured, more activities will be added. The program currently includes five educational "Modules" – *Patternmaking Tools and Tech, Marvelous Materials, Smart Clothing, We are Engineers, and Movement Improvement.* Each module includes a video relating the unit to careers in the fashion and apparel industry. All materials are available at www.styleengineers.org.

Patternmaking Tools and Tech progressively teaches how to transform a two-dimensional material into a three-dimensional item. Whether it's for the body or a fashion accessory, visualizing the flat pattern requires thoughtful planning and fabric manipulation. Beginning hand sewing and machine sewing is introduced, as well. Let's take a closer look at the activities.

Gremlin Pin Hand Sewing teaches the beginner how to thread a needle, knot the thread, sew a running stitch and sew a button all the while creating a cute wearable pin in the matter of an hour's time.

Amazing Maze is designed to teach the beginner how to maneuver a sewing machine, stitching straight, turning corners, and stopping while "sewing" their way out of the paper maze. Once smooth movement and speed is acquired, the student is ready to sew on fabric, creating do-it-yourself (DIY) projects like tote bags and skirts.

DIY Bags and Totes vary in difficulty. There are six projects to choose from to explore 2-D to 3-D transformation and construction techniques like zippers and linings.

DIY Wrap Skirt is the curriculum's introduction to garment sewing and pattern making. Mathematical measurements and calculations are used to find the radius and circumference for creating the personalized skirt pattern.

Flatten your Clementine is a simple exercise in drawing a design on the 3-D object and envisioning what the design would look like flattened out. After several designs are examined, the students begin to think more creatively and can then transfer that thinking to the next activity.

Spectacular Skirts expands upon this spatial visualization by using miniature skirts on half-scale dress forms. Students are asked to examine how each skirt fits around the body and to make a tissue pattern or draw the shape of the flat pattern they think was used to create each skirt. The first skirt is a flared skirt. Looking at the skirt, one's first thought might be that the pattern is a trapezoid shape being smaller at the top with a wider lower edge. In reality the pattern is actually a full circle. The second skirt is a full skirt with gathers at the waist. Again the silhouette is smaller at the top and fuller at the lower edge, in some ways, similar to the first. However the actual pattern is a simple rectangle, wider than it is long. The third skirt is a straight skirt with darts at the waist line. By the third skirt, students begin to understand and can identify the actual pattern that was used, adding that a discussion of darts and gathers has now been introduced. The fourth skirt is a peg skirt with tucks around the waistline that create fullness in the hip area but is smaller at the hemline. At this point, the students have experienced the previous shapes and can more easily create a tissue pattern or identify the flat pattern shape, one that looks like an upside down flared skirt pattern.

Floral Pattern Puzzle is another exercise in spatial awareness. By adding pattern and color to the shapes, the young designer must cut paper pieces apart and fit them together to create a miniature paper blouse.

Free Draping with Fabric challenges the student to manipulate fabric on a half-scale dress form to create their 3-dimensional design. Fabric shape, weight, structure and texture can dictate garment patternmaking and construction techniques, influencing the finished look of the garment.

The **Marvelous Materials** module explores the physical and some chemical properties of fabric and materials used in adorning and protecting the body. From creating a polymer to testing the stretch limits of spandex, these hands-on activities are enough to get all participants excited about the world of fashion and textiles.

Fabric Structures: A Close Look lays the foundation for examining fabric structures. Knowing the characteristics and being able to distinguish between knit, woven, and non-woven fabrics greatly influences garment design and fabric choice.

Knit Bombing examines the structure of knit fabric and its advantage for smooth close fitting garments. Students are challenged to cover 3-D objects with fabrics creating a wrinkle-free surface. Knit fabric is the clear winner in this experiment.

Expand Band is a fun activity where a group of 4 to 8 students gather in the center of a giant elastic band made from multi directional stretch spandex fabric. How far will it stretch? Spandex is capable of stretching up to 7 times its original length and returning. Not only do the students test the stretch ability of the fabric, but they also test the strength and type of stitching that joins the fabric. *Expand Band* proved to be one of the most fun illustrations of performance based fabric during the summer camp experience.

Thermal Wrap, *Polar Walk*, and *Alien Incubation*, all explore the thermal insulative properties associated with different fabrics. Designing clothing to protect and maintain comfortable body temperature is important for everyday wear as well as for extreme sports and protective gear for fire fighters and astronauts. Thermometers and temperature guns are used to measure heat loss via conduction and convection.

Whacky Armor involves making a shear thickening viscoelastic polymer to test its protective properties against sudden force. This substance, in its relaxed state is soft and pliable but when forcefully hit, becomes solid, thus protecting against broken bones when used in protective gear like vests and knee pads for extreme and contact sports. During the 2006 Winter Olympics, the US and Canadian ski teams made history with their "soft armor." The *Knee Drop and Spin* activity illustrates how *Whacky Armor* protects the knees.

Movement Improvement explores how clothing is engineered to maximize movement, especially in athletic wear.

Bendable Action – Young designers learn how different pattern shapes can enable/inhibit movement. Further discussion introduces how pleats, gathers, and slits enable ease of movement.

Fabric Flex – Fiber content and fabric structure directly affect the way the fabric conforms and moves with the body. Different fabric types are tested for their percentage of stretch. Fabric terms used add to the vocabulary of the young designers.

Joint Jive illustrates how the body's skeletal structure moves and how different body positions affect the fit and movement of clothing. Clothing acts like a "second skin". Knowing that the body has different types of joints, the designer must understand that they require different amounts of ease or stretch in order to move comfortably.

Smart Clothing may well be the most intriguing module. Today's clothing goes beyond just covering the body. It can monitor heart rate and body temperature, change appearance with your emotions and even charge your battery for electronic devises. This module introduces using conductive sewing thread, soft circuitry, and light emitting diode (LED) lights to illuminate wearable items. Electronic-textiles (E-textiles) and soft circuitry have shown to be an engaging way to teach electronics, especially for girls who may not ever be exposed to it, with the added bonus of introducing them to the older craft of sewing.

Space Dough Introductory and *Space Dough Advanced* cover the basics of simple and parallel circuits using a salt based dough mixture as the conductive material. Students can mix up their own dough from household ingredients or use commercial Play-Doh®. Learning about polarity, conductive materials and LEDs opens the door to creating wearable technology.

Illuminating Fashion – Circuit Cards is an exercise in "sewing" and following a diagram to better understand polarity. Using a hole punched paper diagram and yarns, the student "sews" from hole to hole connecting all the "positive" holes with one piece of yarn and all the "negative" holes with a second piece of yarn. Positive and negative lines can never touch, if they do, the result is a short circuit.

Illuminating Fashion – Hand Sewing and *LED Bracelet – Felt or Foam* require understanding how soft circuits work and how to use a hand sewing needle and thread to sew with conductive thread to create a wearable accessory that lights up. Both involve creating parallel circuits.

Illuminating Fashion – Applique – Machine Sewing and *Illuminating Fashion – LED Bracelet* require understanding how soft circuits work and how to use a sewing machine and conductive thread in the bobbin to create a wearable accessory that lights up. Both involve creating parallel circuits.

Illuminating Fashion – Skirts takes the *DIY Skirts* activity from the **Patternmaking, Tools and Tech** module a step further by incorporating electronics into a wearable garment. Parallel circuits are sewn by machine with conductive thread in the bobbin and LEDs and battery pack added. Other decorative elements can also be added to increase the visual impact and creative design.

We are Engineers develops the thought process behind solving problems by encouraging team work in creating new designs and events. The Engineering Design Process (EDP) is as important to the fashion designer as it is to the engineer that builds bridges.

Sketchstorming reviews what the young designers have learned and how they can apply it to their fashion designs. This activity includes fashion croquis for the students to sketch their design or describe in words how they plan to implement their designs.

Confetti Rain is a group activity in problem solving. The goal is to construct an umbrella that protects from an imaginary and uncommon substance falling from the sky. The EDP comes into play as the groups discuss how they can build a product that solves the problem.

Operation Design Challenge – This group activity is the culmination of multiple activities and references concepts about the EDP, movement, adding LEDs to garments, insulation, impact protection, and patternmaking and construction of a garment. It is suggested that at least one or two activities from each module be done before completing this capstone activity. Design challenges are issued to each group for them to develop a prototype garment that meets the requirements of the challenge.

Engineering the Runway – It's time to show off all the designs that the young designers have created throughout the process of working through the modules. Planning and practice are required to write a script detailing each proto type garment from the design challenge to coordinating the choreography takes. This may end up being an activity that takes more than one day to complete. Parents and friends were invited to the final event and the young designers were recognized for their participation and completion of the program.

The recent "Maker's" movement has ignited interest in creating hand crafted items. 4-H has been doing this for over 100 years, teaching youth to learn by doing. While the Style Engineers curricula's main focus is exposing young designers to possible STEM related careers and thinking into the future, it lacked fundamental skill building for more advanced sewing. To fill this void, Baker chose another curriculum to integrate into Kentucky's 4-H Clothing program, one which was recently adopted by National 4-H and developed by University of Nebraska called STEAM Clothing. This curriculum focuses on teaching the integration of science, technology, engineering, art, and math as it relates to sewing and clothing construction/fashion design. A clothing portfolio including samples of sewing techniques and fashion ideas, as well as a textile scrapbook that includes identifying different fibers and fabrics are two examples of STEAM Clothing projects that the young designers find useful while building a solid foundation for future projects. (Figure 12.6)

Quote from a beginner teen sew-er:

I have very much enjoyed my experiences learning with STEAM. It allowed me, as a student to learn the "whys" and "hows" of sewing and fashion. I like STEAM because it teaches the basics of fashion in a way that is easy to understand, and to relay to others. I also liked the way that the STEAM Clothing book "Sewing FUNdamentals" used hands-on activities to make the lessons stick. I especially enjoyed the fact that all of the aspects of STEAM are easily connected to one another.

The STEAM Clothing curriculum consists of three levels of leader guides that each include sections solely devoted to doing science experiments that explore the physical and chemical properties of textiles. Learning how to identify fibers by burning them and looking at them under a magnifier to testing how different cleaning products and light exposure affect them are just a few examples.

In conclusion, after the initial year of introducing the STEM concepts as they relate to teaching sewing to

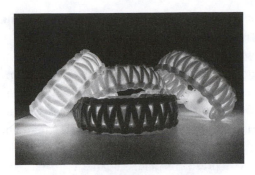

Figure 12.6 Middle school kids in Kentucky get a lesson in fashion engineering through 4-H.

4-H youth in Kentucky, Baker expects to see a change in how the clothing projects are viewed. She worked in collaboration with the state's 4-H SET specialists to train numerous Kentucky 4-H Youth Development agents and volunteers to understand and use these two curricula. 4-H'ers are highly motivated to exhibit what they learn at county and state fair. Updating the current fair classes is the next step to undertake in showing the world that using a needle and thread is an essential life skill, more than just sewing, it's engineering!

Discussion Questions

1. Think back to your Middle School days. Would the STEM and STEAM programs been of interest to you? Why or why not?
2. How, by integrating STEM and sewing, can girls learn about the sciences through their interest in fashion?
3. Can you think of other methods to teach sewing in STEM or STEAM based activities?

12.3
For Dignity and Development, East Africa Curbs Used Clothes Imports

Kimiko de Freytas-Tamura

KIGALI, Rwanda—In Kenya, they are called the "clothes of dead white people." In Mozambique, they are the "clothing of calamity."

They are nicknames for the unwanted, used clothing from the West that so often ends up in Africa.

Now, a handful of countries here in East Africa no longer want the foreign hand-me-downs dumped on them because they're trying to manufacture their own clothes.

But they say they're being punished for it—by the United States.

Here in East Africa, Rwanda, Kenya, Uganda, Tanzania, South Sudan and Burundi have been trying to phase out imports of secondhand clothing and shoes over the last year, saying the influx of old items undermines their efforts to build domestic textile industries. The countries want to impose an outright ban by 2019.

Across Africa, secondhand merchandise is the primary source of clothing—much as it is for cars, planes, hospital equipment, computers and sometimes even drugs that have passed their expiration date.

Buses with Japanese lettering are ubiquitous. Planes in Congo have signs in Italian. Aspirin from Europe past its sell-by-date floods markets in Cameroon. Old medical equipment from the Netherlands lies idle in hospitals in

Figure 12.7 An Akan Chief wears local clothing while some African countries claim that secondhand clothing from the U.S. and Europe are thwarting their efforts to build their own textile industry.

South Africa. Ghana has become a dumping ground for huge amounts of electronic waste.

Rwanda, in particular, is seeking to curb the import of secondhand clothes, not only on the grounds of protecting a nascent local industry, but also because it says wearing hand-me-downs compromises the dignity of its people. (Figure 12.7)

But when countries in East Africa raised their import tariffs on used garments last year—to such a high level that they constituted a de facto ban—the backlash was significant.

In March, the Office of the United States Trade Representative threatened to remove four of the six East African countries included in the Africa Growth and Opportunity Act, a preferential trade deal intended to lift trade and economic growth across sub-Saharan Africa. (Burundi and South Sudan, gripped by upheaval, had already been expelled from the trade deal because their governments were accused of perpetrating state violence.)

Under the deal, products like oil, coffee and tea are allowed access to American markets with low tariffs. But the White House has the right to terminate the agreement with a country if it feels that the relationship doesn't benefit the United States.

The dispute has thrown into relief the perennial debate among countries, especially developing ones, over how to balance protectionism with the risk of damaging their relationship with an interconnected world.

The American response reflects a desire to both protect jobs and have open access to small but promising markets. The East African nations are trying to replicate the success stories in Asia and even the United States, where infant manufacturing industries were initially protected and nurtured before they were able to compete on the global market.

Rwanda's president, Paul Kagame, who has been the most vocal leader about the used-clothing ban among the East African nations, said that the region should go ahead with the ban even if it meant sacrificing some economic growth.

"We have to grow and establish our industries," Mr. Kagame said in June. "This is the choice we find that we have to make. We might suffer consequences. Even when confronted with difficult choices, there is always a way."

East Africa imported $151 million worth of used clothes and shoes in 2015, mostly from Europe and the United States, where consumers regularly buy new clothes and dispose of old ones, often giving them away to charities. At least 70 percent of donated garments end up in Africa, according to Oxfam, a British charity that also sells used, donated clothes to the continent.

The American threat, officials in the region say, is an example of a Western nation bullying countries that are trying to move beyond what the continent is typically known for: exporting raw materials, not finished products.

For countries like Rwanda, a small landlocked state with few natural resources to extract and export, building local manufacturing is vital for development, officials contend.

"Politically and morally it is wrong," Mukhisa Kituyi, the secretary general of the United Nations Conference on Trade and Development and Kenya's former trade minister, said of the American threat to remove countries from the trade deal. "The leadership of Rwanda and East Africa is right and should not lose sight of the bigger picture they have in mind."

The trade relationship between the United States and East Africa should be founded on mutual respect, he added, "and should not go down the way of 19th century England when it started a war with China over opium," he said of Britain's determination to pry open Chinese markets to sell drugs.

East Africa could export garments worth up to $3 billion annually within a decade, according to McKinsey, the consultancy.

Behind the American response to the East African ban is a group of 40 used clothing exporters, known as the Secondary Materials and Recycled Textiles Association. It says that 40,000 American jobs, like sorting and packing clothes, are at risk. Clothing thrown away by Americans, the association says, will end up in landfills in the United States and damage the environment if not sold abroad.

The organization, which describes the East African tariffs as "taking advantage of U.S. generosity," lobbied for the American response. It did so on the grounds that the East African countries were contravening rules that require them to show they are "making progress" toward eliminating trade barriers to American goods and investment.

"It's hard to argue that the U.S. should continue to give preferential access to its market if the country is taking steps that harms U.S. companies," said Grant Harris, who served as the principal adviser to former President Barack Obama on issues related to Africa.

The United States often uses the trade deal as a negotiating tool. In 2015, South Africa nearly lost its eligibility over a ban on American chicken imports, which it said were killing the country's poultry industry. Last year, the United States warned the tiny nation of Lesotho that it could lose its eligibility if the government failed to enact political reforms.

As South Africa did on chicken imports, Kenya blinked and withdrew its support for the used-clothing ban because it risked losing its lucrative textiles exports to the United States; globally, Kenya exported about $380 million of clothing globally in 2015, much of it made for American companies. The United States Trade Representative now says it will not review Kenya's eligibility.

Despite the possible ejection from the trade deal, which American officials say will be decided at the end of the year, the remaining members appear determined to uphold the ban.

Underlying their protectionist move is the damage done in the 1980s and 1990s by economic liberalization. That, and a combination of debt crises, falling cotton prices and cheap Chinese imports, wiped out textile industries across the continent.

While African economies were being pushed by institutions like the International Monetary Fund to open up trade, the West protected its textile industries by restricting imports of yarns and fabrics from developing countries.

"Removing barriers to trade made it easier to import and export things but made African economies more vulnerable to imports, and manufacturing industries in particular became uncompetitive," said Andrew Brooks, author of "Clothing Poverty: The Hidden World of Fast Fashion and Second-hand Clothes."

The current dispute over the trade deal, he said, exposed "the underbelly of globalization."

Kenya, for example, had half a million workers in the garment industry a few decades ago. That number has shrunk to 20,000 today, and production is geared toward exporting clothes often too expensive for the local market. In Ghana, jobs in textiles plunged by 80 percent between 1975 and 2000. Many people in Zambia, which produced clothes locally 30 years ago, can now only afford to buy imported secondhand clothes.

Although many support government efforts to build national textile industries, they say that the ban on used clothing should be done incrementally.

In Rwanda, where the per capita gross domestic product is $700, many people oppose the ban, saying it has thrown thousands out of jobs distributing and selling secondhand clothes and has hurt the nation's youth in particular.

Since Rwandan import tariffs on used garments have been raised 12 times, clothes sellers in Kigali have watched their revenues plummet. The government decision was premature, they said, put in place before the country was able to produce clothes that are affordable. And though the ban excludes imports of secondhand clothing, it hasn't stopped the influx of more expensive new clothing from China.

Peter Singiranumwe, 26, relied on selling used clothing to help pay for his rent and studies in telecommunications and engineering. "Now I'll have to stop because I don't make enough money anymore," he said. "It's impossible."

And the question remains whether Rwanda, Tanzania and Uganda are ready to build a textile industry of their own.

Vital ingredients for that to happen are still missing, and cutting off imports of used clothing alone is unlikely to fix the problem, some in the industry say. Energy and transportation costs in Rwanda are among the highest in Africa, there is a dearth of skilled workers in tailoring and light manufacturing, and imports of high-quality materials like fabric and yarn are prohibitively expensive.

There's also the question of the size and purchasing power of the local consumer market. "Do we have a ready market here to which we can feed 'Made In Rwanda' clothes to the population?" asked Johannes Otieno, the manager of Utexrwa, which makes uniforms for the army, the police and hospitals.

Mr. Otieno said he opposes the East African ban on secondhand clothing, questioning what Rwanda would do if the United States ejected it from the trade deal.

"A country cannot survive alone," he said. "We depend on America for a lot of things. We're not stable enough to say, 'We don't need you anymore.'"

A version of this article appears in print on October 12, 2017, on Page A4 of the New York edition with the headline: East Africa Curbs Imports on America's Hand-Me-Downs.

Discussion Questions

1. How can the U.S. help East African countries without harming U.S. companies who sell second hand clothing?
2. How do you respond to this statement in the reading: ". . . is an example of Western nation bullying countries trying to move beyond exporting raw materials".
3. What, if anything, can you do as an individual to help East African countries in their wish to export clothing?

12.4
Shifting the Dominant Social Paradigm in the Apparel Industry: Acknowledging the Pink Elephant
Cosette M. Armstrong and Melody L. A. LeHew

Fashion . . . suggests a passing trend or fad—something transient, superficial and often rather wasteful. It represents the opposite of longevity and, as such, would appear to be an impediment to sustainability

Walker 2006:71

It is reasonable to conclude that the apparel industry is a guilty culprit in the current ecological crisis. Since the Industrial Revolution, the industry's impact has grown unceasingly, and there are now social, environmental, and economic consequences that must be addressed. Industrialization has been characterized by an endless hunger for growth and expansion that the ecosystem cannot accommodate. Central to this system is an accounting approach in which costs of environmental goods and services are never expressed in the economic bottom line; meanwhile, natural capital and assets continuously evaporate. No business could survive using this model. Thus, industrialization has ignored the natural scale and limits of our natural world in the name of progress (Schumacher 1973). A key component of this denial of limits is the problematic pink elephant of consumerism that is becoming increasingly difficult

to ignore when attempting to define a new mindset for the apparel industry: a sustainable one. In this paper, the authors explore what a new mindset for the industry might look like.

A fundamental driver of consumerism and this subsequent denial of limits are essential to the concept of fashion where newness becomes an end in itself, and resource limits are best ignored. Products that rely heavily on the concept of fashion, like apparel, are at odds with sustainability, which raises a unique set of challenges for designers and product developers. Their decisions are *the* chief instigators of environmental and social impacts because choices made early in the design process, such as materials selection and production method, significantly influence the impact of a product's life cycle. Products encoded for a specific purpose, result in a domino effect throughout the remainder of the product development process (see Armstrong and LeHew 2011 for more details).

But, fashion is an important aspect of modern culture and may, therefore, be a powerful conduit for the transition to environmentally friendly and socially responsible production and consumption (Walker 2006: 74–75). If designers are perceptive and open to the

Adapted from a previously published article.

principles of sustainability, the concept of fashion may be used to attract attention, energy, and imagination around sustainable solutions. Fields such as engineering and industrial design have recently demonstrated a shift in practice that may serve as a basis for a new paradigm for the apparel industry.

A paradigm is defined as an assembly of practices and protocols characterizing a discipline or field (Kuhn 1996). A paradigm shift occurs as knowledge evolves; old procedures and rules are replaced as a new paradigm makes them flawed. Such an event in a scientific community (where the concept originated) can be abrupt as new knowledge replaces old.

A shift within a *social* paradigm, on the other hand, may occur in stages over time as the diverse values and beliefs of members of the social system evolve. Here, dominant ways of thinking may remain even after a new paradigm has indicated a more enlightened way of going about things. Thus, a Dominant Social Paradigm (DSP) is a chief indicator of social behavior, and therefore, plays a primary role in maintaining or changing unsustainable practices (Dunlap and Van Liere 1984). A DSP is essentially a belief system that characterizes a community (Shafer 2006) and the practice and protocols in the current apparel industry community are shaped by the DSP of the twentieth century.

Characteristics of the DSP which currently perpetuates unsustainability in the Western world include (1) unlimited growth in free markets, (2) a liberal regulatory environment, (3) an emphasis on individualism and private ownership, and (4) an over-reliance on technology as a solution to environmental problems (Shafer 2006: 124–126). At present, the apparel industry over too heavily on technology to solve its environmental problems, focusing on efficiency and new technology, rather than addressing the pink elephant (consumerism). The authors argue in this paper that if the apparel industry is going to make a meaningful shift toward a more sustainable DSP, a more sustainable *pattern* of practice and acknowledgement and navigation of the pink elephant will be prerequisites. The authors explore a number of emerging sustainable approaches from other fields to propose a new DSP for the apparel industry.

Industrial Ecology

Industrial Ecology (IE) is a supply chain organization which supports sustainable design and product development, using the principles of sustainable development. Embodying the Golden Rule, sustainable development is defined as meeting the needs of the present without prohibiting future generations from meeting their own needs (World Commission on Environment and Development 1987). Sustainable development emphasizes the environmental health, social equity, and economic viability of industrial systems. This approach is based on the idea that industry, economy, and technology should work in concert with nature. Just as nature regenerates itself infinitely and uses solar energy as its only input, IE addresses how natural resources are consumed and given new life in a system where disposal of waste is not an option (Graedel and Allenby 1995).

Industrial ecology (IE) pays special attention to material and energy use, the preservation of local landscapes and biodiversity, and cooperation and communication throughout the supply chain. First, materials use is minimal; form matches function precisely. Any waste generated in production is given new life when used to create new products (e.g. Climatex carpet, Kenaf International paper, Lafarge cement). Thus, products are often designed with remanufacturing and reuse in mind, avoiding the extraction of new materials. To reduce contamination, toxic materials are used only when and where they are necessary and are not stored or transported long distances. Further, all energy used for production, preferably solar, results in some type of material transformation. Finally, the products which result from IE are more reflective of the real costs to the environment (Graedel and Allenby 1995). Table 12.1 compares IE to the apparel industry.

On the positive side, the apparel industry has integrated its supply chain, formed strategic partnerships, and advanced its technological sophistication (Keiser and Garner 2008), aligning itself in many ways to IE. But, challenges remain for the apparel industry. These are the key components required for a paradigm shift: the development of partnerships *outside* the apparel supply chain, a more cooperative than competitive approach in the market, and a more realistic costing strategy which acknowledges the real costs of products to the environment and people.

Sustainable Approaches

Sustainable design (SD) and sustainable product development (SPD) approaches fall along a continuum, from approaches that permit the consumer to maintain traditional consumption habits (the pink elephant) to approaches that require significant changes to the consumer culture. Four levels of intervention occupy the continuum between these two polar positions (Vezzoli and Manzini 2007).

TABLE 12.1

COMPARING THE APPAREL SUPPLY CHAIN TO INDUSTRIAL ECOLOGY

	Apparel Supply Chain	Industrial Ecology
Scope	Global	Local
Scale	Large	Large
Supply chain relationships	Integrated, cooperative, but not completely reliant	Integrated, cooperative, collaborative, reliant
Relationships outside specific industry	Limited	Strategic partnerships within & without
Environment	Highly competitive	Highly cooperative
Basis of competition	Speed of delivery; product innovation; manufacturing expertise; technology; resources	Efficiency, productivity, product innovation
Tools	Technology	Technology
Customer	Well-defined niches; specialized consumer preference	Narrow niches that complement current market assortment
Costing	Market price	Ecological value

The *first and lowest level* of intervention, called end-of-pipe strategies, addresses only the consequences of traditional consumption by adjusting the materials and energy levels used to create products. Common considerations at this level are things like ease of maintenance and repairs, upgrading, component recovery for remanufacturing or re-use, materials recycling, and ease of sorting and collection in the disposal stage. Considerations may also be made to ensure that packaging, instructions, and overall appearance of the product encourage efficient and environmentally friendly use.

The *second level* makes similar substitutions to increase efficiency in the production systems, but is encompassed by a life cycle assessment (LCA). LCA is an analysis of a product's life cycle and its environmental impact. Thus, impacts are reduced across the product's life cycle. This framework produces products that replace existing ones with environmentally conscious elements and are also considered socially acceptable by consumers.

The *third level* of intervention begins to address consumer culture (the pink elephant). Instead of producing traditional products, this system designs new ways for consumers to achieve satisfaction that may or may not include a tangible product.

Lastly, *the fourth level*, and by far the most challenging is one in which new qualitative criteria for sustainable lifestyles are created. At this level, *designers lead consumers* into a more sustainable pattern of consumption. Here, design is heavily reliant on the designer's ability to perceive human needs that are more social than material in nature. It is fair to assume that these latter two levels of intervention are distinct in the high degree to which the pink elephant is acknowledged and navigated. These intervention levels are noted in the following discussion of sustainable approaches.

Design for Environment and Design for X

Design for environment (DfE) is an approach that seeks sustainability while retaining competitiveness. Design for X (DfX) refers to specific design strategies such as design for disassembly. In this case, each design strategy has its own set of methods and measurements, but both rely on technology (Guidice, La Rosa, and Risitano 2006).

Cradle to Cradle

The most widely recognized set of principles for sustainable product design is McDonough and Braungart's

(2004) *Cradle to Cradle* (C2C) procedure, which aligns with the principles of DfE and IE. C2C is the antithesis to the current cradle-to-grave production model and has three primary tenets: celebrate diversity, use solar income, and waste equals food.

The waste equals food tenet has attracted attention in the industry, inspiring an increase of materials analyses to determine the biological (biodegradable) or technical (recyclable) food value of products at the end of their life cycle. The C2C protocol was recently used to create a production model for sustainable apparel in the industry. The model, called Cradle to Cradle Apparel Design (C2CAD), includes consideration for consumer preferences, materials analysis, collaboration in the supply chain, and an analysis of the environmental impacts of the production process. However, the model does not address the first or second principle of C2C with any confidence. When Gam (2007) attempted to implement the model in a manufacturer of children's knitwear in Korea, the manufacturer could not comply with the tenets outlined in the model. Collaboration in the supply chain, knowledge and expertise for analysis of materials selection, and considerations for energy use were absent.

Product Service Systems

Products and services have always been linked. But recently, product service systems (PSS) have received renewed attention as a possible channel to increase consumer satisfaction while dematerializing the traditional production-consumption system. In developed countries, an increase in consumption of material goods is equated with an increase in quality of life, though no relationship has ever been documented. PSS seeks to replace product ownership with utility. When material consumption is substituted by services, this increases the likelihood of using fewer material resources and energy, giving way to fewer products and less waste (Maxwell and Van der Vorst 2003). Businesses may compensate for lost revenue from material goods by selling unique services that support their products. PSS is a direct and long-term approach with customers, the creation of collaborative networks with various stakeholders, and low capital intensity. Admittedly, this approach requires a dramatic shift in traditional consumption habits.

Emotionally Durable Design, Slow Design, and Design Activism

Design strategies situated at the highest level on the intervention continuum most often emphasize the exceptional delivery of human needs; basics needs which transcend social and cultural norms. These approaches to design have the potential to yield the most sustainable products because they incorporate consumer behavior into the product strategy. Importantly, these strategies more successfully acknowledge and navigate around the pink elephant.

The *emotionally durable* product-consumer relationship can be created through designing for attachment, creating a symbiotic relationship of mutual need and caring through product attributes that stimulate things like memory development and pleasure. In this approach, lifelong partnerships (consumer-to-product, consumer-to-manufacturer) are subsequently formed that make it easy to nurture a product's life through repair, upgrades, and service.

Slow design implies that the design is no longer controlled by time, which eliminates the need for constant updates and production to compete in the marketplace. Slow design has been used interchangeably with design for well-being. Here, the designer focuses on well-being (social and environmental) early in the design process instead of only individual well-being (economic). Thus, the well-being of individuals is less dependent on acquisition and more reliant on sustainable development to create products which embody deeper meaning for the consumer.

Design activism is a powerful force for change in which designers are inspired by issues personal to them and the world. These products may be designed for humanitarian aid (natural disasters, postwar), services to the poor or excluded (homeless, disabled, elderly), or human rights (fair trade, ethical trade).

Tools for Sustainable Approaches

A variety of conceptual and scientific tools have evolved to support strategic decision-making during sustainable design and sustainable product development processes. However, the most common scientific tool used to support SD and SPD approaches is the previously mentioned Life Cycle Assessment. In a LCA, products and the production processes used to create them are systematically summed up in an environmental impact equation, typically categorized across the product life cycle stages. The five life cycle stages are material, design, distribution, use, and disposal. The LCA is an important decision-making tool, as it offers a precise way to compare the impact of different product life cycle stages to each other as well as to make product comparisons. There are generally three types of LCAs: inventory analyses (resource use, impacts), impact analyses (description and assessment impacts), and improvement analyses (discovery of opportunities to reduce environmental burdens) (Lowe, Warren, and Moran 1997: 52). Conducting a LCA requires ample time and money and only addresses the environmental impact of the product, but does not account for social and economic impacts on the environment.

To There from Here: A New Dominant Social Paradigm for the Apparel Industry

When we compare apparel design and product development processes to sustainable approaches we find some commonalities (Table 12.2): both originate from similar disciplines; both rely on multidisciplinary collaboration and concurrent and iterative activities; both rely on sophisticated technology; and both are beholden to basic

TABLE 12.2

COMPARISON OF APPAREL DESIGN AND PRODUCT DEVELOPMENT PROCESSES TO SUSTAINABLE APPROACHES

Method	Apparel Design & Product Development	Sustainable Design & Product Development
Origins	Industrial design, engineering, & architecture	Industrial design, engineering, architecture, environmental, agriculture
Authored by	Academicians; tested in industry	Collaboration of academic & industry; industry
Purpose	Education	Solve environmental issues in industry
Process	Collaborative, sequential & non-linear, concurrent, iterative	Collaborative, non-linear, concurrent, iterative
Team	Multidisciplinary; Design, product development, merchandising, marketing, production, manufacturing related to apparel	Multidisciplinary; Design, product development, marketing, production, manufacturing, pollution prevention, environmental risk, occupational health & safety, waste management, ecological conservation, & other stakeholders
Tools	Technology	Technology; scientific & conceptual tools
Common activities	Market & consumer research, design, costing, sample making, line development, line presentation, pre-production preparation & technical development, sourcing, production, quality assurance, marketing, packaging, distribution	Marketing & consumer research, defining the problem, evaluating solutions quantitatively & qualitatively, backcasting, risk analysis, prototype development, prototype modeling of product system, communication of environmental qualities to market
Guiding information	Trend, market, & consumer research	LCA & analysis; model nature's system; checklists; the Golden Rule
Costing	Market price	Ecological value
Product	New line/collection or products; Ever-changing, disposable, beholden to concept of fashion	Single product, revised product, product-service system; Reflective of art, science, culture, nature, place; form fits function

responsibilities such as market research, preproduction tasks, production, marketing, distribution, and retailing. But, there are considerable disagreements between the two approaches that merit exploration for a new Dominant Social Paradigm in the apparel industry.

First, the most important difference is that of costing. Apparel products are sold at market price rather than their ecological value, whereas sustainable product development products reflect the real costs of the impacts of resource use. This is why sustainable products typically cost more than traditionally made products. Developing a metric for ecological costing has been problematic and we may not be able to afford the resources we are using. Market mechanisms of the global economy such as quotas, tariffs, and subsidies further complicate this effort. These systems are implemented to protect developing countries from the rigors of the free market; however, these manipulations often drive down prices, ignoring the real cost of the ensuing impacts on people and the planet.

This picture gets muddier when structures designed to offer economic assistance to developing countries from firms like the International Monetary Fund and the World Bank are considered. In this case, loans are made to developing countries to stimulate struggling economies on a short-term basis and stabilize the economic system. But, these firms have a tendency to impose unrealistic terms, which can prompt countries to over produce to stay current on these loans (Weisbrot 2009). In sum, these market mechanisms complicate global trade because they impact how products are valued; inflating values for exportation from developing countries and deflating it for consumption in developed countries (Schor 2005). Economies around the globe, particularly those reliant on apparel and textile business, have collapsed under these conditions.

There are some cases of changing costing policies. A number of product developers are beginning to shift their costing policies to better reflect real costs of production, rather than the price retailers are willing to pay for goods. This suggests that these strategies may inspire changes for sustainability throughout the apparel supply chain (Interfaith Center on Corporate Responsibility 2010). Nevertheless, this predicament is not easily solved. But being aware of the standards, regulations, and monetary policies that drive the machine is a beginning. A new Dominant Social Paradigm for the industry would undoubtedly reflect the real costs of doing apparel business in social and environmental terms.

Second, the cooperative nature of product development expands in the context of sustainable product development and industrial ecology. Sustainable product development relies heavily on partnerships with many stakeholders *outside* the apparel field, such as environmental expertise on waste that could be used for raw materials. This cooperation would bring up issues of efficiency, risk reduction, and survival. Further, consultation with stakeholders is central to decision making. As the apparel industry is already increasingly integrated, it is well poised to begin reaching beyond the context of its own vacuum. A new Dominant Social Paradigm for the apparel industry would include an expansion of infrastructure designed to foster collaboration and cooperation. Partnerships may reflect greater inclusion of outside organizations that offer sustainability-related savvy, such as assisting firms with materials analyses or environmental impact assessments. Additionally, the diminishing availability of virgin materials will drive the need to form partnerships with unrelated industries to source waste that may be used for materials or with companies that may process or redesign second-hand apparel. To foster such symbiotic arrangements, the development of collaborative and cooperative skills among apparel industry professionals cannot be underestimated.

Third, it is clear that sustainable design and product development approaches utilize a variety of conceptual and scientific tools to better balance market demands with ecosystem health, a prospect virtually untouched by apparel firms. A new Dominant Social Paradigm for the industry would embrace continuous research and exploration related to the impact of its products. Though the apparel industry has begun to dabble with these tools, future industry professionals must also have the competence to utilize and administer such tools. Most recently, a pilot of the Eco Index was launched through a collaboration of two outdoor organizations and the Zero Waste Alliance that seems like a promising step toward the development of tools to analyze apparel and textile products. But, the use of these tools admittedly command greater knowledge of the natural sciences. In the new Dominant Social Paradigm, apparel industry professionals would understand the mechanics of sustainability science and be able to administer a variety of impact analyses.

Finally, the apparel industry must come to grips with its own belief system. A new Dominant Social Paradigm would scrutinize the following industry tendencies: the purpose and consequences of economies of scale, a relentless competitive environment, and, the use of the concept of fashion that may degrade rather than enhance quality of life. In a new Dominant Social Paradigm, the practice of creating products that are only responsive to the market, rather than to the ecosystem's limits would seem simplistic and wasteful. Recently, several common industry concepts were described as increasingly dysfunctional in light of sustainability, such as: Growth is good, progress equals material progress, and consumers as a profit-making resource. These components characterize the pink elephant which has contributed to a growing conflict of interest between producers and consumers. Some propose a needs, rather than wants, approach to marketing, such as well-being marketing (Varey 2010). Whatever the case, a new DSP for the industry would focus on creating apparel products that are more efficient in material use, production, and consumer utility, while also delivering the fundamental human needs of consumers; needs that are inherently more social than material. Apparel industry professionals would hold competences such as perceiving human needs and ecosystem limits, working cooperatively *with* the market rather than trying to dominate it, and understanding local culture and tradition. In the new Dominant Social Paradigm, practice in the industry would encompass the Golden Rule, better supporting sustainable development.

Conclusion

Though the apparel industry is a substantial source of livelihood for many people worldwide, it is also a principal culprit in the ecological crisis. Social, environmental, and economic consequences in the industry pose a threat to sustainability on an unimaginable scale, and some argue that the apparel industry has been tardy in its response. Nevertheless, it is fair to suggest that the future will require a new *pattern* of thinking and action, *a new dominant social paradigm*, far beyond the one that created the industrial world. Solutions or adaptations must work in step with the ecological realities of today, acknowledging the pink elephant of growth, consumption, and limitless accumulation.

References

Armstrong, Cosette M. and Melody L.A. LeHew. 2011. "Sustainable apparel product development: In search of a new dominant social paradigm for the field using sustainable approaches." *Fashion Practice*, 3(1): 29–62.

Dunlap, Riley E., and Kent D. Van Liere. 1984. Commitment to the Dominant Social Paradigm and Concern for Environmental Quality. *Social Science Quarterly*, 65:1013–1028.

Gam, Hae Jin. 2007. Development and Implementation of a Sustainable Apparel Design and Production Model. Ph.D. dissertation, Oklahoma State University, United States—Oklahoma. Accessed April 25, 2009, from Dissertations & Theses: Full Text database. (Publication No.AAT 3259611).

Graedel, Thomas E. and Braden Richard, Allenby. 1995. *Industrial Ecology*. Englewood, New Jersey: Prentice Hall.

Guidice, Fabio, Guido La Rosa, and Antonio Risitano. 2006. *Product Design for the Environment: A Life Cycle Approach*. Boca Raton, FL: Taylor & Francis Group.

Interfaith Center on Corporate Responsibility (ICCR). 2010. Best Current Practices in Purchasing: The Apparel Industry, http://www.asyousow.org/publications/Apparel_Report.pdf, accessed July 16, 2010.

Keiser, Sandra J. and Myrna B. Garner. 2008. *Beyond Design*. New York: Fairchild Publications, Inc.

Kuhn, Thomas S. (1996). *The Structure of Scientific Revolutions* (3rded.). Chicago, IL: University of Chicago Press.

Lowe, E. A., John L. Warren, and Stephen R. Moran. 1997. *Discovering Industrial Ecology*. Columbus, OH: Battelle Press.

Maxwell, Dorothy and Rita Van der Vorst. 2003. "Developing Sustainable Products and Services." *Journal of Cleaner Production*, 11: 883–895.

McDonough, William and Michael Braungart. 2004. *Cradle to Cradle*. New York: North Point Press.

Schor, Juliet B. 2005. "Prices and Quantities: Unsustainable Consumption and the Global Economy." *Ecological Economics*, 55: 309–320.

Schumacher, E.F. 1973. *Small is Beautiful*. New York: Harper & Row, Publishers, Inc.

Shafer, William Eugene. 2006. Social Paradigms and Attitudes Toward Environmental Accountability. *Journal of Business Ethics*, 65: 121–147.

Varey, Richard J. 2010. "Marketing Means and Ends for a Sustainable Society: A Welfare Agenda for Transformative Change." *Journal of Macromarketing*, 30(2): 112–126.

Vezzoli, Carlo A. and Ezio Manzini. 2007. *Design for Environmental Sustainability*. New York, NY: Springer.

Walker, Stuart. 2006. *Sustainable by Design: Explorations in Theory and Practice*. London, UK: Earthscan.

Weisbrot, Mark. 2009, October 13. "A New Role for the IMF?" *Tikkun Magazine*. http://www.tikkun.org /article.php/20091013105540620 , accessed June 19, 2010.

World Commission on Environment and Development (WCED). 1987. *Our Common Future*. Oxford: Oxford University Press.

Discussion Questions

1. Do you agree that the current dominant social paradigm (DSP) shaping apparel design, production, and consumption is at odds with a sustainable future? Discuss your view.

2. Several sustainable design and sustainable product development models were presented in the article. In your opinion, which model holds the greatest promise for firms in an apparel industry operating within a new ecologically minded dominant social paradigm? Discuss the reasons for your choice.

3. Describe the "pink elephant" presented in this article and its relevance to the fashion industry. Why might apparel designers, apparel marketers, and even apparel educators be reluctant to acknowledge the "pink elephant"?

4. Two readings in this chapter ("Excuse Me" and "Haute Technology") have mentioned aspects of a new industrial revolution in the apparel industry. Do you think that widespread use of these technologies could place enough pressure on the apparel industry to invest in a new Dominant Social Paradigm? Why or why not?

CHAPTER 13
ETHICS IN FASHION
Andrew Reilly

After you have read this chapter, you will understand:

- **The complex relationships between ethics and the fashion industry**
- **Some specific types of ethical dilemmas in the fashion industry**
- **How consumer demand for unique products can lead to unethical practices**

INTRODUCTION

Life is full of ethical dilemmas, and the fashion industry has its share of controversy around ethics. All one has to do is read or watch the news to find examples of ethical issues in the fashion field. For instance, John Galliano was fired from his job as head of the fashion house Dior and fined for anti-Semitic statements and behavior in a Paris bar in February 2011. Fashion designers often take on the status of celebrities and their behavior is watched carefully. Would you say that Galliano was a victim of freedom of speech? Do we hold celebrities to higher standards than regular people? Or did Galliano get what he deserved? Often ethical issues are not black and white; there is not always one "right" answer.

Ethics is the study of right and wrong. The origins of ethics date back to Greek philosophers Socrates (496–399 B.C.) and his student Aristotle (384–322 B.C.). Both argued that self-knowledge through questioning what was right and wrong was necessary to achieve enlightenment and fulfillment. There are no clear lines between what is right and wrong, and topics related to ethical issues are usually controversial and vary from culture to culture.

A civilization decides what is criminal based on its code of morality. As we have seen in prior chapters, morality varies from culture to culture. Examples from the fashion industry include co-opting ethnic costumes and using objectified images in advertising and promotions. In Westernized countries, it is acceptable for a woman to show her face, hair, and body shape in public; in some Islamic countries that might be illegal. The legal issue depends on who is in charge of the government. As recently as 2011 the government of Saudi Arabia has considered passing a law that would require women with "sexy eyes" to keep them covered in public. What is legal is not always considered ethical.

In the fashion industry many companies establish a code of ethics to guide decisions when morality and legality are in conflict with each other. Typical issues include knockoffs, human labor conditions, animal rights, environmental waste, and political agendas. In the reading "Eco-Fashion, Sustainability, and Ethics," Bonnie English wades through some of these issues. She discusses how the fashion industry—often associated with sketchy practices—can embrace sustainability in an industry predicated on change.

KNOCKOFFS, COPIES, AND COUNTERFEITS

In the fashion industry gray-market, knockoff, and counterfeit merchandise is a significant problem. **Gray-market** merchandise is a legitimate, genuine product but is not sold by an authorized representative. Rather, manufacturers that are hired to make the goods produce greater quantities than the contract specifies in order to sell them on the side, which is not only a violation of the contract but illegal as well. Sometimes this deceptive practice is known as third-shift manufacturing.

Unlike gray-market goods—which are authentic—**knockoffs** are variations of authentic goods. Knockoff merchandise use other items as inspiration and are considered imitations (such as Target creating an affordable version of a Dior couture gown). The creation of knockoffs is illegal in Europe, where fashion designs are protected for 25 years, but the practice is widely accepted in the United States and attempts to pass legislation have failed. However, unique marks, logos, prints, patterns, and inventions can apply for legal protection in the United States.

Counterfeit merchandise—copies of items, intended to defraud the consumer—is another problem (see Figure 13.1). Counterfeit goods are illegal because they violate trademarks and intellectual property laws. The Organization for Economic Cooperation and Development reported fake merchandise accounted for $461 billion in 2013. Other sources estimate this figure is as high as $1.8 trillion. The majority of merchandise is clothing, accessories, and handbags (Counterfeit.com, 2015), which French, Italian, and American brands hit hardest (OECD/EUPIO, 2016). Many consumers do not see purchasing counterfeit products as unethical (Ha & Lennon, 2006; Ang et al. 2001), perhaps due to the fact that the effects are not immediately visible. The counterfeit industry accounts for 7 percent of world trade and thousands of jobs lost (Yurchisin & Johnson, 2010). The counterfeit industry has also been linked to terrorist organizations and organized crime (Ha & Lennon, 2006; Geltner, 2004). Such organizations often use slave labor or sweatshops to manufacture the merchandise.

SWEATSHOPS

Sweatshops—work environments that endanger the physical and mental welfare of employees, underpay their employees, or use slave labor—are banned in many Westernized countries, but questionable practices that fall under the radar still exist. A 2006 report called "Conduct Unbecoming" (authored by the union Unite Here!) documents how the U.S. Department of Defense, the largest consumer of U.S.-made apparel, contracted with manufacturers whose businesses can be described as sweatshops. Workers earned less than the legal minimum wage and reported pay cuts and paycheck irregularities, little to no benefits, forced overtime, and unsafe work conditions that violated OSHA (Occupational Safety and Health Administration) standards. A situation like this is not uncommon in the fashion industry where many goods are produced in countries or areas with different labor laws. See Figure 13.2.

In many developing countries or territories, such as Saipan and Bangladesh, sweatshops are not illegal and are the means by which inexpensive products are manufactured. Workers earn literally pennies an hour; for example, in Bangladesh over 80 percent of people earn less than $2 per day (World Bank, 2004). According to one study, doubling the salary of people employed by sweatshops would increase the cost of the product by 1.8 percent, well under the 15 percent increase consumers say they are willing to pay to ensure their products are made ethically (Pollin, Burns, & Heintz, 2004). Additionally, workers must work long days in unsavory conditions, such as rooms with poor ventilation and abuse, and many women are forced to take birth control in order to avoid pregnancy and the resulting time off (Bernhardt et al., 2009).

While it is technically not illegal for U.S.-based companies to contract with sweatshops in foreign countries,

Figure 13.1 Counterfeit merchandise is a big problem in the fashion industry.

Figure 13.2 Sweatshop labor has long been a problem in the fashion industry, as workers are underpaid and receive no benefits from their employer.

it is not necessarily ethical. Nike, H&M, The Gap, Victoria's Secret, Walmart, Disney, and Sears were all "outed" for contracting with foreign sweatshops. Many consumers are demanding that companies take responsibility for their actions and contract only with manufacturers that pay their employees a fair wage and treat them with dignity. The result is that company representatives visit their contractors to verify that working conditions are safe and sound. However, as *BusinessWeek* reported in 2006, manufacturers are adept at hiding infractions and abuses, as discussed in the reading "Secrets, Lies, and Sweatshops."

Many U.S. consumers purchase apparel produced in the United States believing that it was made under ethically sound conditions. However, sometimes they can be misled. The "Made in . . ." label reports a country where the consumer believes the garment was manufactured, but the question of when a garment becomes a garment remains. A shirt can be made from cotton grown in one country that is made into yarns in another country, woven into fabric in another, designed in another, cut in another, sewn in another, and finished in another. At what point does the shirt become a "shirt"? Advocates for transparency in manufacturing are calling for labels that detail each step of the process. Until then, consumers who wish to purchase ethically traded products should purchase from fair-trade associations and companies that guarantee a fair wage and work condition to their employees. The country of origin label may be misleading in another way. For example, sweatshops are not uncommon on the island of Saipan but because the island is a commonwealth of the United States, garments manufactured there are labeled "Made in the U.S.A." Consumers trying to make ethical choices are frustrated by these types of issues.

BLOOD DIAMONDS

Blood diamonds are another ethically questionable area in fashion. Sometimes called conflict diamonds or war diamonds, blood diamonds come from war-torn areas (usually in developing nations) where the sale of such gems helps support an armed conflict. Typically, the diamonds are sold by insurgents or the party attempting to overthrow the current regime, and slaves are used to mine the diamonds. The sale of conflict diamonds from Angola was first banned by the United Nations in 1998; since then diamonds from Liberia, Sierra Leone, Côte d'Ivoire, and the Republic of Congo have been banned (the ban on diamonds from Liberia and the Republic of Congo has since been lifted).

Many consumers were unaware of the background of their diamond purchases. While efforts such as international bans are made to curtail the sale of blood diamonds, many are still on the market via smuggling through other countries or the black market. Consumers wanting to ensure that their diamond purchases are not from conflict areas should buy only those that come with a Kimberley Process Certification, which is a guarantee from the World Diamond Congress that the diamond is from a legitimate mine. The negative publicity surrounding blood diamonds—including a Hollywood blockbuster movie (*Blood Diamond*, 2006)—have helped to raise awareness of the controversy, but there are still many problems in the diamond industry, such as the wages of diamond miners, smuggling, and the underground diamond trade, that make it increasingly difficult for consumers to know if their diamonds are bloody or not.

ANIMAL PRODUCTS

The use of animals in fashion is an ethical issue due to the treatment of animals, which is frequently cruel and painful. Birds and other animals have a long history of use in fashion. In fact, The Metropolitan Museum of Art devoted an entire exhibition to the use of skins, furs, feathers, and animal prints in its 2004 exhibition "Wild: Fashion Untamed." Curator Andrew Bolton, in the book for this exhibition, states, "The history of fashion's appropriation of animal skins, prints, and symbolism is also a history of society's changing attitudes and ambivalences toward human-animal relations" (2004, p. 11).

In the late 19th and early 20th centuries, bird feathers and other parts (body and head) were extensively used in millinery to decorate women's hats. During this period hats were an essential accessory worn to complete a woman's daily outfit. Amy D. Scarborough (2009) found that at the end of the 19th century the Audubon Society and women's groups ignited efforts to stop the decline of birds related to millinery practices. They promoted their social-responsibility agenda through public lectures on the killing of birds for fashion, held fashion shows offering hat designs with no birds or feathers, and used other tactics to persuade fashionable women to stop accessorizing with birds. Scarborough found that although fashion magazines showed hats with birds and feathers in their pages, some also provided discourse on the fact that the use of birds and feathers in millinery was adversely affecting bird populations. In fact, one fashion magazine in particular,

Harper's Bazaar,[1] "changed the type of bird and plumage trimmings presented that reflected change in American bird protection legislation" (Scarborough, 2009, p. 107). This historic example shows us that combined efforts toward social responsibility can work to the betterment of the use of birds and animals in the fashion industry.

Animal fur and skins have always been used in clothing; the earliest examples of clothes are animal hides. The pelts and skins were necessary for warmth and protection from the elements. Throughout human history, animals have continued to be used for warmth and protection—but also for accessorizing and showing status and wealth. It is only in the last century that the use of animals has been questioned as being unethical.

The issue is not necessarily the product itself but how the animal is treated. The picture is not pretty. Animals are either hunted in the wilderness or raised specifically for their fur or skins in unsanitary and cramped cages. They are clubbed, suffocated, poisoned, skinned alive, and boiled alive or otherwise mutilated in efforts to retrieve their hides. Many consumers empathize with the animal and object to the treatment. However, there appears to be less empathy for the non-cuddly type of animal. Snakes, lizards, silkworms, and cows garner less outrage than baby mink, seals, and exotic animals like tigers and leopards. (See Figure 13.3.)

Animal activists argue that alternatives to animal products exist. Synthetic furs offer similar warmth, tactile, and visual qualities as the genuine article. Artificial silk is available, but for people who want the real deal there is wild silk—where the moth is allowed to break through before the cocoon is used for fabric production. However, others argue that the alternatives do not provide the same degree of aesthetics or exclusivity as the original.

The controversy has resulted in marketing campaigns and niche producers that promote "ethical fur" or "ethical leather" or "ethical skins." Hunters and farmers support the humane treatment of animals while in their care and provide good nutrition, housing, and veterinary care for the livestock. They also advocate the hunting of animals to help balance wilderness ecology rather than as a commercial response to the fashion industry. However, "ethical fur"

Figure 13.3 Products made from animal hides or skins are controversial due to the way animals are treated during harvesting.

is an oxymoron, as reported by Dannie Penman in, "Is 'Ethical Fur' the Fashion Industry's Most Cynical Con Yet?"

Consumers who want to avoid fur products or purchase products that have been made with animals raised and killed in humane conditions do not necessarily find it easy to make informed decisions. Often, fur is deliberately mislabeled. The Humane Society reports that fur from dogs is commonly labeled as other types of fur or not labeled at all. The Truth in Fur Labeling Act helps consumers make informed decisions when they are considering purchasing fur products. The law requires that fur items must be labeled with country of origin and type of fur, but an undercover investigation by the Humane Society reports some high-end retailers are ignoring this law.

Some counties and cities have addressed this issue by banning or outlawing the sale of fur or fur farms. In 2011, West Hollywood, California, became the first American city to ban the sale of fur clothing within city limits. In 2017, Berkley, California, did the same. Similarly, around the world, many nations have banned fur farming in its entirety or in part (Austria, Bosnia and Herzegovina, Croatia, Denmark, Germany, Japan, Macedonia, Slovenia, Switzerland, and the United Kingdom) or the importation of fur (India, New Zealand).

Summary

Discussed in this chapter are several ethical issues found in the fashion industry. The media has brought many of these issues to light, however, because within the fashion industry often these issues are not taken seriously. But given the breadth of fashion globally and the tremendous demand for unique and fashionable objects, ethical issues in fashion are not small considerations. Hopefully the reader is now aware of the many ways in which consumer demands can lead to unethical practices primarily because of the money involved. In the future, we hope that before buying a counterfeit item or an item made from an animal you will reflect on what you have read in this chapter.

Key Terms

Blood diamonds	Ethics	Knockoffs
Counterfeit	Gray-market	Sweatshops

Learning Activity 13.1

ANIMAL FASHION

In a small group, generate a list of all animals that have been used for clothing and/or fashion. Which animals get the most sympathy? Which animals aren't widely used anymore? Why?

Learning Activity 13.2

REAL OR FAKE?

The instructor will bring in an authentic product and a counterfeit. Students will analyze both products for differences and similarities. How easy or hard is it to distinguish the products? Would someone not trained in fashion be able to tell the difference? Discuss why people might prefer one to the other.

Learning Activity 13.3

CODE OF ETHICS

Look up your favorite brands and find their code of ethics. How do they compare to each other? What ethical situations are discussed or mentioned? Are any areas missing that you think should be addressed? Discuss your findings with classmates.

References

Ang, S. H., P. S. Cheng, E. A. C. Lim and S. K. Tambyah (2001), "Spot the Difference: Consumer Responses Towards Counterfeits," *Journal of Consumer Marketing*, 18(3): 219–35.

Bernhardt, A., R. Milkman, N. Theodore, et al. (2009), "Broken Laws, Unprotected Workers: Violations of Employment and Labor Laws in America's Cities," National Employment Law Project. Available online: http://www.academia.edu/9743602/Violations_of_Employment_and_Labor_Laws_in_Americas_Cities_Broken_Laws_Unprotected_Workers.

Bolton, A. (2004), *Wild Fashion Untamed*, New Haven: Yale University Press.

Conduct Unbecoming: Sweatshops and the U.S. Military Uniform Industry. (2006). New York: Unite Here!

"Counterfeit.com" (2015), *The Economist*. Available online: http://www.economist.com/news/business/21660111-makers-expensive-bags-clothes-and-watches-are-fighting-fakery-courts-battle.

"John Galliano Convicted for Anti-Semitic Rant. Aljazeera." Available online: www.aljazeera.com/news/europe/2011/09/201198124129538913.html.

Geltner, P. (2004), "Counterfeit Goods Fueling Terror Groups," *The Columbus Dispatch*, May 26, A11.

Ha, S. and S. J. Lennon (2006), "Purchase Intent for Fashion Counterfeit Products: Ethical Ideologies, Ethical Judgments, and Perceived Risks," *Clothing and Textiles Research Journal*, 24(4): 297–315. DOI: 10.1177/0887302X0623068.

The Humane Society (n.d.), "Fur in Fashion." Available online: www.humanesociety.org/issues/fur_fashion/.

OECD/EUIPO (2016), *Trade in Counterfeit and Pirated Goods: Mapping the Economic Impact*, Paris: OECD Publishing.

Pollin, R., J. Burns and J. Heintz (2004), "Global Apparel Production and Sweatshop Labour: Can Raising Retail Prices Finance Living Wages?" *Cambridge Journal of Economics*, 28(2), 153–71.

Scarborough, A. D. (2009), "Fashion Media's Role in the Debate on Millinery and Bird Protection in the United States in the Late Nineteenth and Early Twentieth Centuries." Unpublished doctoral dissertation, Oregon State University.

World Bank (2004), *World Development Indicators Online*. Available online: http://www.worldbank.org/data.

Yurchisin, J. and K. K. P. Johnson (2010), *Fashion and the Consumer*, New York: Berg.

Endnote

1. Prior to November 1929 the spelling of the magazine was *Harper's Bazaar*.

This introduction is based on a version originally written by Andrew Reilly, Kimberly A. Miller-Spillman, and Patricia Hunt-Hurst and appeared in *Meanings of Dress* edition 3.

13.1
Eco-Fashion, Sustainability and Ethics
Bonnie English

Our personal consumer choices have ecological, social, and spiritual consequences. It is time to re-examine some of our deeply held notions that underlie our lifestyles.

David Suzuki

Green as the New Black

While the 'Green Designer' exhibition was held as early as 1986 at the Design Centre in London and the label Esprit led the way with its inaugural Ecollection in November 1991, 'fashion as a design discipline has been late to investigate the theoretical greening of the design production loop, lagging behind industrial design and architecture' (Thomas, 2008: 526). Yet, interestingly, consumer activist group campaigns have tended to target fashion events more than other disciplines. Marketing strategists realize that, in the postmodernist age, when social and political commentary has become associated with both art and sartorial design, consumers now demand accurate and truthful labelling (provenance) and information relating to fair payment and healthy working conditions (fair trade) in order to make informed and conscientious decisions regarding their choice of clothing. For some, shopping has become an ethical minefield.[1] According to Thomas, 'potentially, there is an ideological connection between ethical trading and ethical fashion, thus conferring on both an altruistic intent and political stance' (2008: 532).

The dichotomy still remains that fashion, throughout history, has been driven by a desire to establish social class differentiation and status within a group through conspicuous consumption, but the desire to ally oneself voluntarily with an ideology has proved to be a stronger incentive in the twentieth and twenty-first centuries. In the 1970s, in particular, environmental concerns, including the energy crisis and the inhumane treatment of animals, led to major changes in the textile, fur and cosmetic industries. Subsequently, it became very fashionable to wear multilayered natural materials, such as wool, cotton

From *A Cultural History of Fashion in the 20th and 21st Centuries*, Bloomsbury Publishing, Plc.

and hemp, fake fur coats and to don natural complexions. Quentin Bell argued that one's degree of commitment to a cause became visibly evident in one's dress and that 'it is as though the fabric were indeed a natural extension of the body, or even of the soul' (1992: 19). Mixing art and politics, artist Kathleen Hamnett initially exhibited her 'environmental' T-shirts in the 1980s and has continued with garments donning activist slogans such as 'Make Trade Fair' and 'No More Fashion Victims'. She then turned to fashion design and today creates 'fashionable' clothing, adhering strictly to environmental and ethical guidelines. Quite rightly, Kate Fletcher (2007), in her essay 'Clothes That Connect', also argues that, in order for eco-fashion to be sustainable, its clothing must now be fashionably stylish as well as environmentally correct. American academic Theresa Winge postulates that eco-fashion has now become depoliticized (no longer associated with anti-war campaigns and anti-mainstream activities as it was in the 1960s and 1970s) and less stereotyped as a commodity fetish by celebrities, including actors George Clooney and Julia Roberts and photographer Annie Leibovitz, who promote sustainable fashion as an aesthetic life choice 'on the red carpets and in the pages of magazines' (2008: 513).

This chapter will deal mainly with environmental, design sustainability and ethical issues that relate to the choice and production of materials used for clothing, textiles and footwear. It will attempt to respond to a question posed by fashion writer David Lipke in Women's Wear Daily (31 March 2008), which asked, 'Is Green Fashion an Oxymoron?' How is it that 'an industry driven by disposable trends and aesthetic whims can reconcile itself to an era of conservation'? By briefly charting past and existing practices, this chapter will consider new strategies introduced and developed in the twenty-first century to foster sustainable textile production that could impact upon both developed and developing countries. By outlining the social, economic and environmental effects of current practices, including reference to fabric wastage, recycling and reusing materials, it will reinforce the need for a symbiotic liaison between the designer, the patternmaker and the manufacturer. It will consider new emphasis on the use of chemical-free organic fibers and textiles, the use of nontoxic dyes as well as methods of construction and deconstruction informed by environmental concerns. It will outline revived historical methodologies, including examples of fully fashioned and seamless knitwear, draped garments made from uncut, rectangular lengths of fabric and one-size-fits-all styling as well as current eco-fashion practices evident in the work of leading fashion, textile and footwear designers.

More Than Just a Marketing Strategy?

Since 2006, eco-fashion has attracted a much wider audience. It was a popular theme targeted by magazines, journals, Web sites, special events, educational institutions and corporate and commercial bodies. For example, at that time, Vanity Fair magazine brought out its 'Green Issue' outlining the designers[2] who had presented eco-fashion on the runway. Other niche magazine publications endorsing eco-fashion include the New Consumer, The Ethical Consumer and Ecology (United Kingdom), Organic Style (United States), Green and GreenPages (Australia) plus other mainstream magazines that contain photographs and articles featuring celebrity activists with environmental issues such as Elle, Glamour and Marie Claire. Numerous academic book publications and journal articles have proliferated, including the international journal Fashion Theory (Bloomsbury), which in 2008 dedicated a special issue to eco-fashion with writings from scholars around the world discussing the complexity of sustainability issues in fashion. More recently, a new ethical and sustainable magazine called SIX was launched in 2011 to celebrate the designers, individuals, independent brands and companies that are creating a more ethical and sustainable future for the fashion industry. Online sites have flourished, including the Ethical Fashion forum (www.ethicalfashionforum.com), which outlines how to combine sustainable practice with commercial success in fashion, and fashion-conscience. com, which operates vending portals that offer different 'interpretations' of ethical fashion. Exhibitions, trade fairs, global forums and eco-friendly design competitions and awards have attracted considerable local, national and international interest. Amongst many others,[3] more recent events include the Shanghai International Fashion Culture Festival in 2009, which included the 'Green Fashion' International Clothing and Textile Expo (covering a vast area of 50,000 square metres in its International Expo Centre), and exhibitions such as 'Eco-fashion: Going Green' at the Fashion Institute of Technology, New York, in 2010, which considered ecological practices, both good and bad, over the past 250 years. In terms of education, one UK MBA business degree, in conjunction with the conservation charity World Wildlife Fund, has incorporated sustainability at its core, entitled the 'One

Planet MBA' at the University of Exeter (Morgan, 2011).[4] Corporate social responsibility has influenced many fashion distributers and corporate retailers, including the Arcadia Group and Marks & Spencer, whose marketing campaign 'Look behind the label' highlighted its use of fair trade cotton and food products, becoming 'its most successful consumer campaign ever (Attwood, 2007, in Beard, 2008: 452), and the company aims to be carbon neutral by 2012. Walmart, the largest retailer in the world, became the biggest US producer of organic cotton in 2009. As well, in 2011, H&M launched its first eco-collection called Conscious made from recycled polyester, organic cotton and Tencel™, a natural manmade fiber; H&M caused a buzz when it partnered with the French fashion house Lanvin for its Waste collection, but seemingly, 'the line of dresses and bags were at too high a price point for many of its customers' (Kaye, 2011; Leon Kaye is the founder and editor of GreenGoPost.com); individual designer houses such as YSL adopted the strategy of upcycling preconsumer waste; and Issey Miyake opened his newest concept shop Elttob Tep (Pet Bottle spelled backwards) in Ginza selling innovative fabrics created from recycled plastics.

The Environmental Footprint

Sourcing Environmentally-Friendly Textiles

The fashion industry has relied on the production of textiles made from raw fibres that are cultivated in fields where considerable amounts of water are needed and chemicals used despite the fact that insecticides pollute both the air and water. The World Wildlife Fund has estimated that it takes 8,500 litres (2,245 gallons) of water to raise 1 kilogram (2.2 pounds) of cotton lint—enough to make one pair of blue jeans (Kaye, 2011)! Energy is expended in the spinning, weaving and knitting processes, and, along with the transportation and distribution of the raw and finished products, this increases greenhouse gas emissions. The production of synthetic fabrics depletes finite resources such as petroleum (that are nonrenewable and incapable of being fully biodegradable), and most textiles today are treated with various finishing chemicals, further polluting the environment and considered a health risk to humans. Whereas in the nineteenth century, dyes contained highly toxic chemicals and pesticides such as arsenic, in the twentieth century, one of the most polluting fibres to manufacture was viscose rayon. In Africa, mountains of plastic and polyester/synthetic throwaway apparel are being used for landfill, which will never break down. While there has been a resurgence in recent years of the rediscovered art of hand dyeing and fabric printing using natural vegetable dyes or azo-free dyeing, these craft-based techniques are too labour intensive and expensive to offer a solution to the global industry. According to Scaturro (2008: 469–88), textile conservator at the Cooper-Hewitt National Design Museum, Smithsonian Institution, New York, technology plays an ambivalent role in the environmental debate, as it acts as both a destructive and enabling force. Scaturro argues that it heralded the built-in system of redundancy through efficient 'fast fashion' products, which led to 'a profusion of detrimental textile manufacturing by-products and waste entering the ecosystem' as well as 'a vast amount of energy needed to make and take care of all the clothing produced'. As a more positive facilitator, she believes that, in the future, technology can serve to improve methods of clothing creation, consumption and disposal. 'This tension between technology, as a positive or negative factor in the sustainable reality of a culture's resources, is at the core of any discussion on technology and environmentalism' (Scaturro, 2008: 474). It seems that there are no easy solutions. For example, she points out that while the organic fiber advocate organisation Organic Exchange is committed to increasing the production of organic cotton by 50 per cent a year in the United States, the reality is that organic cotton does not produce the same yield or volume that conventional cotton can, making it more costly, and there is virtually no reduction in the harm that occurs during the subsequent dyeing and manufacturing process. It would seem that a national standard is required that oversees the entire production cycle not only of cotton yarns[5] but fabrics generated from renewable sources such as bamboo, seaweed, corn, soy, eucalyptus, milk and beechwood in the creation of polymers. For a successful outcome to occur, 'technology must be precisely applied to limit pollution and energy expenditures' (Scaturro, 2008: 480).

Experimental interdisciplinary research projects that investigate the possible interface between textiles, clothing, biological science and health are increasing. This collaborative work, based on nanotechnology, has created 'smart' fabrics, 'interactive textiles' and thermal shape memory fabrics, which can change colour through light and heat applications, control body temperature through microfibres, absorb odours and create scents that enhance well-being, protect skin tear and block out ultraviolet rays. Since the 1990s, wearable technology incorporating hybrid textiles and garments has been an expanding field requiring the expertise of scientists, computer analysts, electrochemistry and electronics specialists as well as textile and fibre engineers and, of course, fashion designers. Recent innovations have been developed by design professor Helen Storey of the London School of Fashion in collaboration with scientist Tony Ryan in dissolving fabrics, producing catalytic clothing that is both futuristic and life-changing. Their catalytic clothing (Dezeen, 2011) is a radical project in which photocatalysts, washed into the fabric, bind to the textile, creating an anti-pollutant surface that purifies the surrounding air. The photocatalyst gains its energy from light and breaks down pollutants in the air and turns them into non-harmful chemicals. This clothing technology has the power to change the way we live by making our lives greener and more sustainable.

Pattern Making—Fabric Wastage

Fabric in particular and fashion in general, by their very nature, are vehicles of built-in obsolescence—it's about waste. Pattern making is integral to the design process as technical and aesthetic considerations must be considered simultaneously. In today's fashion production, fabric (preconsumer) wastage equates to 15 to 20 per cent in traditional cut-and-sew methodologies. When methods are informed by environmental concerns, designers look back to historical precedents, including fully fashioned knitted garments that have no cutting, tube-knitted seamless garments informed by advanced technology (Miyake's APOC) or one-size-fits-all made from uncut rectangular lengths of fabric. When there are fabric off-cuts, this material must be able to be recycled, and this could include using it for quilts, as fibre, or as rags to make rugs, blankets, stuffing or other small craft items. This would allow all off-cuts to be made into new fabrics. Chemical companies like Wellman USA, an early leader in synthetic fiber recycling, and Japan's Teijin, which introduced Eco-Circle, have established successful polyester-recycling technology schemes.

In general terms, waste reduction is preferable to recycling or disposal, because 'recycling can impact negatively on the environment through transportation (fuel, emissions) and reprocessing (in particular, water, energy and chemical consumption)' (Gertsakis and Lewis in Rissanen, 2005: 3). Historical precedents established in fashion history present more sustainable constructive methods than are used today. These included ancient traditional and national costumes such as the Greek peplos made from two large rectangular pieces of fabric pinned at each shoulder, the Japanese kimono, which was made from eight rectangular pieces of fabric sewn together, and the Indian sari, which wraps around the body. Madeleine Vionnet and Madame Grès, renowned as masters of drape in the early decades of the twentieth century, were admired for their genius in manipulating cloth rather than cutting it; Zandra Rhodes's textile designs determined the shape and form of her garments in the 1970s and 1980s; Hishinuma's experimental use of triangles in the 1980s fitted together to form a modular unit as a means of preserving fabric; Miyake's APOC vision introduced in the 1990s used a tubular knitting system as a means of revolutionizing and simplifying garment construction; and the label MATERIALBYPRODUCT was created by Australian co-designers who developed a new system of pattern-making in the 2000s where the off-cuts are used as a decoration or extension of the main garment.[6]

Recycling and Vintage Clothing

Historically, recycling has been embedded in the fabric of society. Throughout the ages, garments were passed from mother to daughter, father to son or to other family members or friends. Worn parts were eliminated, clothing was resized and, in some cases, stylistically modified or redesigned. The 1970s back-to-nature era saw the mushrooming of secondhand clothing or charity stores opening in towns and cities across the Western world. Driven by a global energy crisis, these outlets allowed buyers, often of limited means, an opportunity to be seen as environmentally conscious. Many of these clothes that were recycled or 'upcycled' were originally made from 'good' materials as the integrity of the fabric prolonged the life of the garment, and their construction was based on quality craftsmanship. Garments originating in the 1920s and 1930s, for example, were valued for their uniqueness, their hand-beading and embroidery and for their ability to be easily transformed into contemporary pieces. It was a nostalgic decade, very much in keeping with postmodernist trends, which appropriated not only fashions from the past, but classic films and furniture also became popular modes of consumption as well. In humanistic terms, this heralded the reemergence of emotional connectivity—of acknowledging that clothing with links to the past can have an in-built memory. This tenet is now widely accepted and has proved to be an incentive for contemporary designers such as Yohji Yamamoto and Martin Margiela. Yamamoto's famous quote that he liked clothes that were old and worn and that throwing out an old coat was like throwing away an old friend is testament to this statement. Margiela experimented with the concept of degeneration and 'the effect of decay on the material structure of fabric', a theme 'that has been central to the work of many contemporary artists' (English, 2011: 138).

According to Kaye (2011), the stark reality of today's recycling dilemma is that in the United States alone, almost 11 million tonnes of textiles ends up in landfill. In Britain, 1 million tonnes of discarded apparel needs to be recycled annually. He points out that some of this post-consumer waste is used creatively: denim is making a comeback as a building insulator, and Walmart is working with vendors to increase the recycling of polyester and nylon for industrial use. Some clothing manufacturers are moving toward a closed-loop system: Patagonia, for example, allows consumers to drop off unwanted clothing bearing its label at company stores and allows consumers to post unwanted clothes back to its Nevada (US) service centre. In a recycling centre, 70 per cent is sent to be used as fibre, and 'items of higher quality end up in Eastern Europe or China where there is a market for used clothes that will not sell in "vintage" shops'.

According to Alexandra Palmer in Old Clothes: New Looks, second-hand clothing can adopt a form of exchange value, especially if the unwanted garments are high-end designer labels. Websites such as vintagecouture.com, established by Linda Lattner in 1999, have become lucrative businesses as the old garments are seen as a unique sign of individuality and connoisseurship. As in the art world, when the original designer becomes deceased, the clothing becomes more valuable. Vintage shopping can be viewed as a continuation of discount culture, while simultaneously achieving an individual identity and exclusivity that the brand names have lost (Palmer and Clark, 2005: 199). Designers such as John Galliano often draw inspiration from vintage clothing.

As the repurposing of textiles and the recycling of clothing has become the most responsible practice in eco-fashion in the twenty-first century, it is not surprising that the Internet now plays an important part in disseminating and sharing information, through commercial sites, online editorial magazines and blogs and social networks about ideas associated with reconstructive sewing methods and distribution outlets or Web sites such as eBay for preowned merchandise. Some vendors will operate smaller stores within these sites, reselling items sourced from local outlets. These online vending options, facilitating the global distribution of old clothing, are the antithesis of today's

'fast fashion' where newness and expendability have been canonized and ideals of novelty and profit firmly embedded in the industry's agenda. Fashion's inherent consumerism has increased exponentially since the Second World War, fuelled by the media, but is now being questioned following tragic world events and the global economic downturn experienced since 2000. Have these events forced some sectors in society to reevaluate their ethical standards, value systems and environmental concerns? Is the world developing a growing social consciousness?

According to Alexandra Palmer, the revival of second-hand clothing, in most cases, has little to do with environmental concerns. She argues that few 'vintage whores' (Palmer and Clark, 2005: 197) are motivated solely by altruistic motives, such as a concern for sustainable fashion, and are drawn, in part, to the aura of the clothing in its past life, its history concealed beneath the surface of the garment. Vintage wear also appeals to the younger generation for financial or economic reasons because it allows for a fast turnover of clothes in one's wardrobe. Historically, clothing was often used as barter, exchanged for cooking utensils for example, and this practice has been reinstated in modern society. This act of bartering, where one item is exchanged for another, has long been an inherent part of everyday life in the markets of Zambia and other parts of Africa, amongst other cultures, where nothing is wasted and the concept of reusing and modifying is indicative of the cultural ethos.

Eco-Designers

In today's society, individual designers have responded to this global issue by adopting a more responsible design methodology that can be formulated within existing technology. By using more holistic approaches, their work reflects sustainable practice in terms of textile development, minimizing fabric waste, manufacturing methods, and aftercare and disposal with an emphasis on innovative research to develop new products. Large footwear corporations, amongst others, in order to build a successful brand identity, have embraced eco-design as an effective marketing strategy. Nike, for example, recycles used rubber trainers for playground surfaces (Delong, 2009: 109).

While some designers recycle old products or use only organic materials, others are concerned more with design integrity, insisting on the evolution of an idea rather than responding to consumerist demands. Eco-consciousness is fundamental in the work and philosophy of both established and emerging international designers in their quest to reduce the fashion industry's environmental footprint. They include, amongst others, British designer Jessica Ogden and her use of secondhand fabrics; Russell Sage, who revamped trademark fabrics like Burberry; Katherine Hamnett's use of organic cotton and eco-awareness statements printed on her T-shirts; Americans Susan Cianciola, who used vintage fabrics for one-off garments, and Miguel Adrover, who presented a 'garbage collection' using unusual recycled products; and Yeohlee Teng, who produces one-size-fits-all garments and fights to preserve local rather than overseas production by producing nearly every garment she sells right in the Garment District in New York City. Luxury eco-brands are limited, with the exception of Stella McCartney and Ciel in the United Kingdom, Noir in Denmark, Fin in Norway and Linda Loudermilk in the United States.

Sustainability of craft, or the incorporation of hand-worked techniques, now referred to as 'slow design' has become central to the philosophy of eco-conscious designers. Brown's Eco Fashion (2010: 13) states that 'these traditional craft skills have become more valued and used, and eventually incorporated into the fashion industry through partnership with high-end designers'. Brown cites examples of fair trade, community based liaisons that have produced 'Indian embroidered sundresses, African beaded jewellery and Peruvian knitted sweaters'. With the eradication of traditional craft talent in the developed nations of North America and Western Europe, she argues, a greater appreciation has developed for the indigenous and inherited craft expertise in communities around the world. She provides specific examples of this practice:

Noir in Denmark is in partnership with Ugandan farmers and supports their development and production of organic long-staple cotton. Carla Fernandez of Taller Flora works with Mexican artisans, reinterpreting their techniques into highly sophisticated designs while learning from their knowledge: a truly collaborative process. With every design and every stitch, Alabama Chanin honours the women of the south of the USA, their history, their struggles and their everyday skills sets. Her work is a labour of love. (Brown, 2010: 13)

African designer Lamine Kouyate, with his label XULY. Bët, deconstructs and reconstructs recycled clothing 'by applying stitches on the outside of his garments to focus attention on the (frayed) edges where threads hold garments together' (Rovine, 2005: 215). According to Rovine, 'The garments incorporate visible seams, like healed wounds that have left their mark (by using red thread), the past lives of clothes that have been re-shaped into new forms' (2005: 219). Kouyate incorporates torn pockets and discoloured collars along with the old collar labels of used shirts and pant waistbands to visibly exaggerate the links with the garments' past lives and as a way to 'document the changing identities of these garments . . . and their attraction lies in the imaginative potential of their former life' (Rovine, 2005: 221).

Rebecca Earley from the Chelsea College of Art, London, transforms and reinvents discarded blouses from charity shops. She employs upcycling techniques, using heat photograms and overprinting the surface of the reshaped garments. Stains are covered with the reactive overlaid dyes, and when it completes its second life, the garment can be transformed a third time into a quilted waistcoat. A Textile Environmental Design student, Kate Goldsworthy, who works with Earley, has developed a method of bonding a lining made of recycled polyester fleece to the original textile without the use of adhesives or bonding agents to produce the textile for the waistcoat. Laser etching creates a delicate lacelike effect, with melted transparent materials digitally controlled to facilitate the process of fusing (Brown, 2010: 164).

Ethical Concerns

Exploitation and Reflective Practice

Fashion, in the second decade of the twenty-first century, has finally found its consciousness, and its designers, models and business entrepreneurs alike have joined global musicians to attempt to make the world a better place (Plate 29). It began in the 1970s and 1980s—a time when unethical practices were publicly highlighted in the fashion and associated industries with attention on the wearing of fur, feathers and animal skins and the inhumane and barbarous treatment of animals as well as their use in the research and development units of cosmetic companies.

Ethical practice relates to the culture of advertising and, in particular, the exploitation of child models to promote a prepubescent sexuality in fashion advertising, which fulfils a cosmetic function, distorting social values and attitudes. Over the past few decades, socially responsible practices drew attention to the rise of racial discrimination in modelling and the very limited number of African and Asian models used. While projecting an image of multiculturalism, American Vogue included only a handful of black celebrity faces on its covers between

2002 and 2009.[7] Fashion photographer Nick Knight made particular reference to this commercially driven racial favouritism in his film Untitled (2008) featuring Naomi Campbell. As well, the promotion of a poor body image—a trend impacting greatly upon young men and women worldwide—has led to a disturbing increase in anorexia and bulimia in today's society. A number of designers have attempted to counteract stereotypical and idealized gender and body images through their styling. In Italy in 2006, fashion agents signed agreements not to use underage or underweight models for runway shows.

Greenwashing is a term (like whitewashing) that has been adopted recently to describe a cover-up marketing ploy often used by individuals, companies and organizations to downplay the unethical practices that proliferate in the fashion industry, including the use of child labour. Labelling inconsistencies and misleading classifications confuse the buyer and often compromise provenance. Sandy Black, in Eco-Chic: The Fashion Paradox (2007), reports that those buying fair trade cotton may not necessarily have an organic product, and some companies blur the component content of blended fabrics. Workers' wages in Third World countries are difficult to contextualize, and Western designers are often misled into believing that workers are being paid a reasonable sum for their production practices. Australian journalist Elisabeth Wynhausen (2008: 28) tried to map the supply chain or trail of a designer garment. She found that manufacture took place in China if more than 300 garments in one style were required (otherwise a surcharge was imposed), as US orders of one style were often in the tens of thousands. The garment designs (often samples made from photographs of garments seen in New York shop windows) were handed to the trading houses in Hong Kong (or existing product was purchased there), which acted as the intermediaries between foreign buyers and Chinese factories. A shirt could be made and delivered to any major city worldwide for approximately one-half of the cost of making it on-shore. For smaller orders, local factories with in-house machinists were used, but a certain amount of outsourcing or subcontracting to sweatshops was also used, where migrant workers were unlawfully paid below minimum wage, contrary to restrictions imposed by the Australian government. A number of unscrupulous employers get work done outside their factories without registering with the Australian Industrial Registry, a requirement under the federal clothing trade's award. While unsustainable levels of clothing production and consumption may exist in the developed world, a more farreaching problem is 'the negative economic, social and environmental effects (that) tend to fall upon developing countries where an ever-increasing proportion of clothing is produced' (Rissanen, 2005: 7). With an estimated 30 to 50 per cent of British, European and American fashion manufactured goods now being produced off-shore, the subsequent exploitation of local and national factory and industry workers in terms of health and working conditions has led to concerns about the treatment of garment factory workers in locations such as the Pearl River Delta in China and the ghettos in India. This exploitation includes the use of very poorly paid sweatshop labour, using dangerous chemicals to produce textiles and clothing and the use of limited fossil fuels (already exhausted) to sustain the supply chains, leading to the gradual degradation of the environment.

It seems that there is 'no single organization or government body to regulate any specific "code of conduct" for the fashion industry although there are several trade associations with schemes set up to monitor and encourage ethical practices amongst commercial firms such as Ethical Trading Initiative in the UK, Solidaridad and the Clean Clothes Campaign in the Netherlands, Fair West in Australia or the Fair Labour Association in the USA' (Beard, 2008: 450). Regarding other problems such as 'counterfeit chic' (see Chapter 10) and the theft of creative intellectual property, some fashion industries are attempting to establish both formal and informal ethical codes. For example, in New York, Diane Von Furstenberg, as president of the Council of Fashion Designers of America, has been seeking greater government regulation of intellectual property design and fair trade policies. Despite highly globalized consumer markets, individual designers have fought to retain financial independence, allowing them to maintain a moral responsibility towards worker exploitation and providing protection for their own intellectual property. However, due to the limited supply of eco-friendly material, products often display an inflated exchange rate. For the limited, yet expanding, eco-conscious consumer base to become part of the mainstream or dominant culture will take time and money. Luxury sustainable goods offered by leading style labels help to reinforce the notion that eco-fashion of the twenty-first century represents a commodity that has an appeal to a much broader consumer market than its counterpart of the past. It also underlines the fact that guilt doesn't sell fashion, desire does.

References

Beard, N. D. (2008), 'The Branding of Ethical Fashion and the Consumer: A Luxury Niche Market or Mass-Market Reality?' *Fashion Theory*, Vol. 12, No. 4, pp. 447–68.

Bell, Q. (1992), *On Human Finery*, London: Allison & Busby.

Black, S. (2007), *Eco-Chic: The Fashion Paradox*, London: Black Dog Publishing.

Brown, S. (2010), *Eco Fashion*, London: Laurence King.

DeLong, M. (2009), 'Innovations and Sustainability at Nike', *Fashion Practice: The Journal of Design, Creative Process & the Fashion Industry*, Vol. 1, No. 1, pp. 109–14.

English, B. (2011), *Japanese Fashion Designers: The Work and Influence of Issey Miyake, Yohji Yamamoto and Rei Kawakubo*, Oxford: Berg.

Fletcher, K. (2007), 'Clothes That Connect', in J. Chapman and N. Gant (eds), *Designers, Visionaries and Other Stories*, London: Earthscan.

Kaye, L. (2011), 'Textile Recycling Innovation Challenges Clothing Industry', *The Guardian*, 23 June.

Lipke, D. (2008), 'Is Green Fashion an Oxymoron?' *Women's Wear Daily*, 31 March.

Morgan, A. (2011), 'New Business Degree Makes Sustainability Its Starting Point', *The Guardian*, 14 April, www.guardian.co.uk/sustainable-business/blog/one-planetmba-university-exeter.com.

Palmer, A., and Clark, H. (eds) (2005), *Old Clothes, New Looks: Second Hand Fashion*, London: Berg.

Rissanen, T. (2005), 'From 15%–0: Investigating the Creation of Fashion without the Creation of Fabric Waste', presented at the conference Creativity: Designer Meets Technology , Europe 27–29 September, Copenhagen, Denmark, KrIDT, and Philadelphia University (US), www.kridt.dk/conference/speakers/Timo_Rissanen.pdf.

Rovine, V. L. (2005), 'Working the Edge: XULY.Bët's Recycled Clothing', in A. Palmer and H. Clark (eds), *Old Clothes, New Looks: Second Hand Fashion*, London: Berg.

Scaturro, S. (2008), 'Eco-tech Fashion: Rationalizing Technology in Sustainable Fashion', *Fashion Theory*, Vol. 12, No. 4, pp. 469–89.

Thomas, D. (2005), 'If You Buy One of These Fake Bags ...', *Harper's Bazaar*, April, pp. 75–76.

Thomas, S. (2008), 'From "Green Blur" to Ecofashion: Fashioning an Eco-lexicon', *Fashion Theory*, Vol. 12, No. 4, pp. 525–40.

Winge, T. M. (2008), 'Green Is the New Black: Celebrity Chic and the "Green" Commodity Fetish', *Fashion Theory*, Vol. 12, No. 4, pp. 511–24.

Notes

1. 'I'd rather go naked than wear fur' (PETA, or People for the Ethical Treatment of Animals, anti-fur campaign, 1994).

2. Nielsen 2008 Global Online Survey on Internet shopping habits. Eco-aware designers who were referenced included Armani, de la Renta, McCartney, Betsey Johnson and Tom Oldman.

3. The Ethical Fashion Show in Paris (2004–2006) and the Anti-apathy re: Fashion event held during London Fashion Week (February 2005); Sao Paulo, Brazil's Fashion Week in 2007, which introduced recycled e-fabrics for elegant evening gowns.

4. Only one of thirty-seven UK institutions since 2007 to have signed up to the United Nations' principles for responsible management education.

5. While sustainability advocates focus on water and fossil fuel scarcity, cotton, which requires large amounts of both resources, has faced a global shortage in the past year (Kaye, 2011).

6. Liliana Pomazan (English and Pomazan, 2010) describes this process: through this innovative technique, at least two garments are simultaneously cut from one length of cloth, one from the positive pieces and one from the negative. Depending on the design, the negative (anti) may be patched with other fabrics to complete the garment, or they may be left open and worn over the classic (positive) garment, almost as an accessory, or used as a diffusion line called 'waste collation' (2010: 220).

7. Halle Berry, December 2002; Liya Kebede, May 2005; Jennifer Hudson, March 2007; and Michelle Obama, March 2009.

Discussion Questions

1. Do you believe that eco-fashion can remain a strong movement in the fashion industry or do you think it is a "fashion" itself that will fade away? Justify your response.

2. How would you convince consumers that sustainable clothes are a better choice even if they are more expensive than other clothing options?

3. How can consumers be sure that their clothes are truly eco-friendly and sustainable if greenwashing is prevalent in the industry?

13.2
Secrets, Lies, and Sweatshops

Dexter Roberts and Pete Engard

American importers have long answered criticism of conditions at their Chinese suppliers with labor rules and inspections. But many factories have just gotten better at concealing abuses.

Tang Yinghong was caught in an impossible squeeze. For years, his employer, Ningbo Beifa Group, had prospered as a top supplier of pens, mechanical pencils, and highlighters to Wal-Mart Stores (WMT) and other major retailers. But late last year, Tang learned that auditors from Wal-Mart, Beifa's biggest customer, were about to inspect labor conditions at the factory in the Chinese coastal city of Ningbo where he worked as an administrator. Wal-Mart had already on three occasions caught Beifa paying its 3,000 workers less than China's minimum wage and violating overtime rules, Tang says. Under the U.S. chain's labor rules, a fourth offense would end the relationship.

Help arrived suddenly in the form of an unexpected phone call from a man calling himself Lai Mingwei. The caller said he was with Shanghai Corporate Responsibility Management & Consulting Co., and for a $5,000 fee, he'd take care of Tang's Wal-Mart problem. "He promised us he could definitely get us a pass for the audit," Tang says.

Lai provided advice on how to create fake but authentic-looking records and suggested that Beifa hustle any workers with grievances out of the factory on the day of the audit, Tang recounts. The consultant also coached Beifa managers on what questions they could expect from Wal-Mart's inspectors, says Tang. After following much of Lai's advice, the Beifa factory in Ningbo passed the audit earlier this year, Tang says, even though the company didn't change any of its practices.

For more than a decade, major American retailers and name brands have answered accusations that they exploit "sweatshop" labor with elaborate codes of conduct and on-site monitoring. But in China many factories have just gotten better at concealing abuses. Internal industry documents reviewed by *Business Week* reveal that numerous Chinese factories keep double sets of books

to fool auditors and distribute scripts for employees to recite if they are questioned. And a new breed of Chinese consultant has sprung up to assist companies like Beifa in evading audits. "Tutoring and helping factories deal with audits has become an industry in China," says Tang, 34, who recently left Beifa of his own volition to start a Web site for workers.

A lawyer for Beifa, Zhou Jie, confirms that the company employed the Shanghai consulting firm but denies any dishonesty related to wages, hours, or outside monitoring. Past audits had "disclosed some problems, and we took necessary measures correspondingly," he explains in a letter responding to questions. The lawyer adds that Beifa has "become the target of accusations" by former employees "whose unreasonable demands have not been satisfied." Reached by cell phone, a man identifying himself as Lai says that the Shanghai consulting firm helps suppliers pass audits, but he declines to comment on his work for Beifa.

Wal-Mart spokeswoman Amy Wyatt says the giant retailer will investigate the allegations about Beifa brought to its attention by *Business Week*. Wal-Mart has stepped up factory inspections, she adds, but it acknowledges that some suppliers are trying to undermine monitoring: "We recognize there is a problem. There are always improvements that need to be made, but we are confident that new procedures are improving conditions."

Chinese Export manufacturing is rife with tales of deception. The largest single source of American imports, China's factories this year are expected to ship goods to the U.S. worth $280 billion. American companies continually demand lower prices from their Chinese suppliers, allowing American consumers to enjoy inexpensive clothes, sneakers, and electronics. But factory managers in China complain in interviews that U.S. price pressure creates a powerful incentive to cheat on labor standards that American companies promote as a badge of responsible capitalism. These standards generally incorporate the official minimum wage, which is set by local or provincial governments and ranges from $45 to $101 a month. American companies also typically say they hew to the government-mandated workweek of 40 to 44 hours, beyond which higher overtime pay is required. These figures can be misleading, however, as the Beijing government has had only limited success in pushing local authorities to enforce Chinese labor laws. That's another reason abuses persist and factory oversight frequently fails.

Some American companies now concede that the cheating is far more pervasive than they had imagined. "We've come to realize that, while monitoring is crucial to measuring the performance of our suppliers, it doesn't per se lead to sustainable improvements," says Hannah Jones, Nike Inc.'s (NKE) vice-president for corporate responsibility. "We still have the same core problems."

This raises disturbing questions. Guarantees by multi-nationals that offshore suppliers are meeting widely accepted codes of conduct have been important to maintaining political support in the U.S. for growing trade ties with China, especially in the wake of protests by unions and antiglobalization activists. "For many retailers, audits are a way of covering themselves," says Auret van Heerden, chief executive of the Fair Labor Assn., a coalition of 20 apparel and sporting goods makers and retailers, including Nike, Adidas Group, Eddie Bauer, and Nordstrom (JWN). But can corporation successfully impose Western labor standards on a nation that lacks real unions and a meaningful rule of law?

Historically associated with sweatshop abuses but now trying to reform its suppliers, Nike says that one factory it caught falsifying records several years ago is the Zhi Qiao Garments Co. The dingy concrete-walled facility set near mango groves and rice paddies in the steamy southern city of Panyu employs 600 workers, most in their early 20s. They wear blue smocks and lean over stitching machines and large steam-blasting irons. Today the factory complies with labor-law requirements, Nike says, but Zhi Qiao's general manager, Peter Wang, says it's not easy. "Before, we all played the cat-and-mouse game," but that has ended, he claims. "Any improvement you make costs more money." Providing for overtime wages is his biggest challenge, he says. By law, he is supposed to provide time-and-a-half pay after eight hours on weekdays and between double and triple pay for Saturdays, Sundays, and holidays. "The price [Nike pays] never increases one penny," Wang complains, "but compliance with labor codes definitely raises costs."

A Nike spokesman says in a written statement that the company, based in Beaverton, Ore., "believes wages are best set by the local marketplace in which a contract factory competes for its workforce." One way Nike and several other companies are seeking to improve labor conditions is teaching their suppliers more efficient production methods that reduce the need for overtime.

The problems in China aren't limited to garment factories, where labor activists have documented sweatshop conditions since the early 1990s. Widespread violations of Chinese labor laws are also surfacing in factories supplying everything from furniture and household appliances to electronics and computers. Hewlett-Packard (HPQ), Dell (DELL), and other companies that rely heavily on contractors in China to supply notebook PCs, digital cameras, and handheld devices have formed an industry alliance to combat the abuses.

A compliance manager for a major multinational company who has overseen many factory audits says that the percentage of Chinese suppliers caught submitting false payroll records has risen from 46% to 75% in the past four years. This manager, who requested anonymity, estimates that only 20% of Chinese suppliers comply with wage rules, while just 5% obey hour limitations.

A recent visit by the compliance manager to a toy manufacturer in Shenzhen illustrated the crude ways that some suppliers conceal mistreatment. The manager recalls smelling strong paint fumes in the poorly ventilated and aging factory building. Young women employees were hunched over die-injection molds, using spray guns to paint storybook figurines. The compliance manager discovered a second workshop behind a locked door that a factory official initially refused to open but eventually did. In the back room, a young woman, who appeared to be under the legal working age of 16, tried to hide behind her co-workers on the production line, the visiting compliance manager says. The Chinese factory official admitted he was violating various work rules.

The situation in China is hard to keep in perspective. For all the shortcomings in factory conditions and oversight, even some critics say that workers' circumstances are improving overall. However compromised, pressure from multinationals has curbed some of the most egregious abuses by outside suppliers. Factories owned directly by such corporations as Motorola Inc. (**MOT**) and General Electric Co. (**GE**) generally haven't been accused of mistreating their employees. And a booming economy and tightening labor supply in China have emboldened workers in some areas to demand better wages, frequently with success. Even so, many Chinese laborers, especially migrants from poor rural regions, still seek to work as many hours as possible, regardless of whether they are properly paid.

In this shifting, often murky environment, labor auditing has mushroomed into a multimillion-dollar industry. Internal corporate investigators and such global auditing agencies as Cal Safety Compliance, SGS of Switzerland, and Bureau Veritas of France operate a convoluted and uncoordinated oversight system. They follow varying corporate codes of conduct, resulting in some big Chinese factories having to post seven or eight different sets of rules. Some factories receive almost daily visits from inspection teams demanding payroll and production records, facility tours, and interviews with managers and workers. "McDonald's (MCD), Walt Disney (DIS), and Wal-Mart are doing thousands of audits a year that are not harmonized," says van Heerden of Fair Labor. Among factory managers, "audit fatigue sets in," he says.

Some companies that thought they were making dramatic progress are discovering otherwise. A study commissioned by Nike last year covered 569 factories it uses in China and around the world that employ more than 300,000 workers. It found labor-code violations in every single one. Some factories "hide their work practices by maintaining two or even three sets of books," by coaching workers to "mislead auditors about their work hours, and by sending portions of production to unauthorized contractors where we have no oversight," the Nike study found.

The Fair Labor Assn. released its own study last November based on unannounced audits of 88 of its members' supplier factories in 18 countries. It found an average of 18 violations per factory, including excessive hours, underpayment of wages, health and safety problems, and worker harassment. The actual violation rate is probably higher, the FLA said, because "factory personnel have become sophisticated in concealing noncompliance related to wages. They often hide original documents and show monitors falsified books."

While recently auditing an apparel manufacturer in Dongguan that supplies American importers, the corporate compliance manager says he discussed wage levels with the factory's Hong Kong-based owner. The 2,000 employees who operate sewing and stitching machines in the multi-story complex often put in overtime but earn an average of only $125 a month, an amount the owner grudgingly acknowledged to the compliance manager doesn't meet Chinese overtime-pay requirements or corporate labor codes. "These goals are a fantasy," the owner said. "Maybe in two or three decades we can meet them."

Pinning down what Chinese production workers are paid can be tricky. Based on Chinese government figures, the average manufacturing wage in China is 64 cents an hour, according to the U.S. Bureau of Labor Statistics and demographer Judith Banister of Javelin Investments, a consulting firm in Beijing. That rate assumes a 40-hour week. In fact, 60- to 100-hour weeks are common in China, meaning that the real manufacturing wage is far less. Based on his own calculations from plant inspections, the veteran compliance manager estimates that employees at garment, electronics, and other export factories typically work more than 80 hours a week and make only 42 cents an hour.

BusinessWeek reviewed summaries of 28 recent industry audits of Chinese factories serving U.S. customers. A few factories supplying Black & Decker (BDK), Williams-Sonoma, and other well-known brands turned up clean, the summaries show. But these facilities were the exceptions.

At most of the factories, auditors discovered records apparently meant to falsify payrolls and time sheets. One typical report concerns Zhongshan Tat Shing Toys Factory, which employs 650 people in the southern city of Zhongshan. The factory's main customers are Wal-Mart and Target (TGT). When an American-sponsored inspection team showed up this spring, factory managers produced time sheets showing each worker put in eight hours a day, Monday through Friday, and was paid double the local minimum wage of 43 cents per hour for eight hours on Saturday, according to an audit report.

But when auditors interviewed workers in one section, some said that they were paid less than the minimum wage and that most of them were obliged to work an extra three to five hours a day, without overtime pay, the report shows. Most toiled an entire month without a day off. Workers told auditors that the factory had a different set of records showing actual overtime hours, the report says. Factory officials claimed that some of the papers had been destroyed by fire.

Wal-Mart's Wyatt doesn't dispute the discrepancies but stresses that the company is getting more aggressive overall in its monitoring. Wal-Mart says it does more audits than any other company—13,600 reviews of 7,200 factories last year alone—and permanently banned 141 factories in 2005 as a result of serious infractions, such as using child labor (Figure 13.4). In a written statement, Target doesn't respond to the allegations but says that it "takes very seriously" the fair treatment of factory workers. It adds that it "is committed to taking corrective action—up to and including termination of the relationship for vendors" that violate local labor law or Target's code of conduct. The Zhongshan factory didn't respond to repeated requests for comment.

An audit late last year of Young Sun Lighting Co., a maker of lamps for Home Depot (HD), Sears (SHLD), and other retailers, highlighted similar inconsistencies. Every employee was on the job five days a week from 8 a.m. to 5:30 p.m., with a lunch break and no overtime hours, according to interviews with managers, as well as time sheets and payroll records provided by the 300-worker factory in Dongguan, an industrial city in Guangdong Province. But other records auditors found at the site and elsewhere—backed up by auditor interviews with workers—revealed that laborers worked an extra three to five hours a day with only one or two days a month off during peak production periods. Workers said they received overtime pay, but the "auditor strongly felt that these workers were coached," the audit report states.

Young Sun denies ever violating the rules set by its Western customers. In written answers to questions, the lighting manufacturer says that it doesn't coach employees on how to respond to auditors and that "at present, there are no" workers who are putting in three to five extra hours a day and getting only one or two days off each month. Young Sun says that it follows all local Chinese overtime rules.

Home Depot doesn't contest the inconsistencies in the audit reports about Young Sun and three other factories in China. "There is no perfect factory, I can guarantee you," a company spokeswoman says. Instead of cutting off wayward suppliers, Home Depot says that it works with factories on corrective actions. If the retailer becomes aware of severe offenses, such as the use of child labor, it terminates the supplier. A Sears spokesman declined to comment.

Coaching of workers and midlevel managers to mislead auditors is widespread, the auditing reports and *Business Week* interviews show. A document obtained last year during an inspection at one Chinese fabric export factory in the southern city of Guangzhou instructed administrators to take these actions when faced with a

Figure 13.4 A factory in Delhi, India with young factory workers.

surprise audit: "First notify underage trainees, underage full-time workers, and workers without identification to leave the manufacturing workshop through the back door. Order them not to loiter near the dormitory area.

Secondly, immediately order the receptionist to gather all relevant documents and papers." Other pointers include instructing all workers to put on necessary protective equipment such as earplugs and face masks.

Some U.S. retailers say this evidence isn't representative and that their auditing efforts are working. *Business Week* asked J.C. Penney Co. (JCP) about audit reports included among those the magazine reviewed that appear to show falsification of records to hide overtime and pay violations at two factories serving the large retailer. Penney spokeswoman Darcie M. Brossart says the company immediately investigated the factories, and its "auditors observed no evidence of any legal compliance issues." In any case, the two factories are too small to be seen as typical, Penney executives argue. The chain has been consolidating its China supply base and says that 80% of its imports now come from factories with several thousand workers apiece, which are managed by large Hong Kong trading companies that employ their own auditors. Quality inspectors for Penney and other buyers are at their supplier sites constantly, so overtime violations are hard to hide, Brossart says.

Chinese factory officials say, however, that just because infractions are difficult to discern doesn't mean they're not occurring. "It's a challenge for us to meet these codes of conduct," says Ron Chang, the Taiwanese general manager of Nike supplier Shoetown Footwear Co., which employs 15,000 workers in Qingyuan, Guangdong. Given the fierce competition in China for foreign production work, "we can't ask Nike to increase our price," he says, so "how can we afford to pay the higher salary?" By reducing profit margins from 30% to 5% over the past 18 years, Shoetown has managed to stay in business and obey Nike's rules, he says.

But squeezing margins doesn't solve the larger social issue. Chang says he regularly loses skilled employees to rival factories that break the rules because many workers are eager to put in longer hours than he offers, regardless of whether they get paid overtime rates.

Ultimately, the economics of global outsourcing may trump any system of oversight that Western companies attempt. And these harsh economic realities could make it exceedingly difficult to achieve both the low prices and the humane working conditions that U.S. consumers have been promised.

Discussion Questions

1. How can the average consumer be sure that he or she is purchasing goods manufactured ethically?

2. Many times working in sweatshop conditions is preferable to living on the street, engaging in prostitution, or going hungry. What would you do if you had the authority to close down a sweatshop but the consequences would be that 100 people were out of work?

13.3
Is 'Ethical Fur' the Fashion Industry's Most Cynical Con Yet?

Danny Penman

A deeply disturbing investigation into a trend sweeping the catwalks.

Fur crazy: London, New York and Milan were buzzing with new takes on furs during their shows, like this one by British designer Giles Deacon for Emanuel Ungaro.

As models strode down the Paris catwalks last week draped in ready-to-wear collections, it was clear that fur is once again the height of fashion.

London, New York and Milan were also buzzing with new takes on mink, fox, and raccoon furs during their shows.

'This year's autumn and winter collections are completely orientated around fur,' says Shelly Vella, Fashion Director at Cosmopolitan magazine. 'Fur is not just back—it's everywhere.

'The fur industry has re-branded itself as the ethical alternative to "fast fashion". I think this is complete nonsense. People are losing their morality.'

But fashion is a fickle business and the fur trade knows how to manage changes in taste better than most. Over the past decade it has spent tens of millions of pounds re-branding itself as a purveyor of 'ethical fashion'.

Although many in the fashion industry have embraced such claims, an undercover film shot by an animal welfare group—and seen exclusively by the Mail—will surely give them pause for thought.

Filmed last month in Maryland and Pennsylvania, the footage shows animals being crushed, strangled and drowned as trappers struggle to keep up with booming demand from the fashion industry.

The investigator from Respect For Animals spent two years infiltrating two groups of American trappers, who catch animals in the wild as an alternative to raising and killing them on fur farms.

The groups were chosen not because they were regarded as being the most cruel, but because they were believed to be among the most humane. In fact, their pelts are eligible to be sold under the fur industry's Origin Assured scheme, the trade's equivalent to the organic label.

The footage shows foxes, raccoons, otters and mink being caught in leg-hold traps. These steel-jawed traps clamp on to an animal's leg with sharp teeth and hold it until the trapper returns.

They were banned in the UK in 1958 and across Europe in 1995 because of their 'intolerable cruelty'.

In the undercover film, a young raccoon is caught in such a trap when it tries to cross a stream. The creature quakes with terror as the trapper approaches and then repeatedly hits it on the head with a metal-tipped pole, breaking its nose and jaw.

Cruel: The undercover footage shows a fox flailing in a leg-hold trap. When the trapper arrives, he crushes the fox by kneeling on its chest. The animal's ribs can be heard popping as the trapper discusses what its pelt is worth

Mark Glover, director of Respect For Animals says: 'We'd love to believe that such blatant cruelty is unusual. But it is entirely normal—and perfectly legal. In fact, such methods are enshrined in U.S. and Canadian governments guidelines on the "humane killing" of trapped animals.'

The film shows countless disturbing deaths. In one scene, a fox can be seen flailing in a leg-hold trap. When the trapper arrives, he crushes the fox by kneeling on its chest. The animal's ribs can be heard popping as the trapper discusses what its pelt is worth.

Although the fur trade will not be keen for its customers to know it, crushing is one of the standard methods of killing because it doesn't damage an animal's fur.

Who Knew?

More than two million cats and dogs are killed for their fur in China each year

'Our industry upholds the highest standards of animal welfare,' says Rebecca Phillips, of the International Fur Trade Federation (IFTF). 'We condemn cruelty. Such behaviour is not normal.'

I would love to believe what the IFTF is telling me—but I have doubts. Earlier this month I was given footage and photographs shot by trappers.

These paint a portrait of an industry rife with cruelty. George, whose name has been changed, is a typical U.S. trapper who earns a few thousand dollars a year trapping to supplement his income as a construction site labourer.

One of his videos shows an elegant bobcat being strangled with a wire noose. Another shows George stabbing wolves in the throat with a blade that's been cleverly designed to minimise damage to the animal's fur. Such behaviour was meant to have ceased 16 years ago when leg-hold traps were banned across Europe. As part of the same law, the EU also banned fur from countries still using 'cruel' traps.

'Responsible choice': Fashion types now like to portray furs and skins as 'natural, and bio-degradable' materials.

At the time it was hailed as a victory for welfare because it would have had the knock-on effect of forcing U.S., Russian and Canadian trappers to use alternatives.

But it didn't work out like that. Instead, the proposals sparked ferocious lobbying and talk of a 'trade war'.

To defuse the row, just months before the import ban was due to come into force, the European Commission over-rode the new regulations.

Although the fur trade won this crucial battle, they also realised that in order to prosper in the long run they would need to polish their public image. And they did so with remarkable aplomb. Fur was re-branded as ethical, green and animal friendly. And, with an eye to the future, it was to become the antithesis of High Street 'fast fashion'.

Fashion types now like to portray furs and skins as 'natural, and bio-degradable' materials that are the 'responsible choice'.

But just how true are such claims? It might seem reasonable to think that, ethics aside, fur is indeed eco-friendly. Appearances, however, can be deceptive.

According to a study at the University of Michigan, the energy needed to produce a fur coat from farmed animals is 15 times greater than that required for a fake one.

Fur from wild animals fares little better. It still has to be dried and tanned—and these processes consume significant amounts of energy and release toxic chemicals into the environment. In fact, the World Bank ranks fur processing as the world's fifth biggest toxic metal polluter.

And ironically, given fur's allure as a sexy material, tanning relies on chemicals such as toluene and lead. Both reduce human fertility.

Perhaps the most curious claim made by the industry is that fur is the ethical choice for those who care about animal welfare.

'Ironically, given fur's allure as a sexy material, tanning relies on chemicals such as toluene and lead - which both reduce human fertility'

Several years ago the IFTF, now headed by the disgraced former Lib Dem MP Mark Oaten, developed the scheme known as Origin Assured. This offers 'assurances on the humane treatment of animals'. So how does this claim stand up? Under this scheme, fur trappers are still allowed to use leg-hold traps and to crush and drown animals.

Despite all of this, the rehabilitation of fur has been astonishing. More than 400 designers now use it. It has also become a lucrative industry that's doubled in size over the past decade and is now worth around £11?billion.

British designers have been at the forefront of this renaissance with Pringle, Belstaff, Alexander McQueen and Jasper Conran leading the fray.

So what do you do if you love the look of fur, but can't stomach the suffering? The obvious solution is to buy fake, or vintage fur, made out of discarded pieces of old fur.

Sadly, neither is a guaranteed cruelty-free option. In Britain there are currently no requirements to label real or vintage fur.

Chinese manufacturers capitalise on this by using cheap off-cuts of real fur or the pelts of rabbits that may have been skinned alive and passing them off as fake.

This means cheap fur can find its way into High Street shops—even if the retailer has an anti-fur policy. How often is real fur passed off as faux? It's impossible to say.

'Consumers are buying real fur, thinking it is fake,' says Mr Glover, of Respect for Animals. 'They would be horrified to know their actions are causing such suffering.'

Discussion Questions

1. Is "ethical fur" a con?
2. How can consumers be educated on the realities of fur harvesting?

GLOSSARY

Abductive inference A natural, instinctive mode of reasoning that is hardwired into human cognition and expressed though "spontaneous conjectures" that provisionally explain unusual observations (Ch. 1)

Achieved roles Roles that we work to earn, for example, college graduate (Ch. 9)

Agency A concept used by feminists to describe the resistance women use to combat patriarchy (Ch. 8)

Agonic power Power attributed to doing something of a physical nature (Ch. 5)

Airbrushed image To alter (an image, especially a photograph) by means of an airbrush or other technique in order to increase its attractiveness or conceal an unwanted part (Ch. 10)

Androgyny Combination of masculinity and femininity (Ch. 5)

Anticipatory socialization Dress up among children and adults that anticipate actual roles later in life (Ch. 11)

Appearance management behaviors (AMBs) Activities that create a desired aesthetic and generally relate to one or more of the five senses. They are divided into routine and non-routine behaviors (Ch. 4)

Ascribed role A position people acquire through no fault or virtue of their own, for example, age, gender, skin color, and birth order (Ch. 9)

Blood diamonds Diamonds mined in areas where proceeds are used to support slavery or war; also known as conflict diamonds or war diamonds (Ch. 13)

Blue-collar dress Historically worn by male laborers in the United States (Ch. 9)

Body dissatisfaction A person's negative thoughts about his or her own body, including judgments about size and shape and muscle tone; generally involves a discrepancy between one's own body type and an ideal body type (Ch. 10)

Body image The mental construct people have about their bodies and includes "a person's perceptions, thoughts, and feelings about his or her body" (Grogan, 2008, p. 3) (Ch. 4) (Ch. 10)

Buddhism Indian religion founded by Buddha that stresses mindfulness, the concept of karma, and the idea that happiness can come only from within, not from possessions (Ch. 8)

Carnivalesque Any merrymaking, revelry, or festival as a program of sports or entertainment; where people are no longer themselves but become the characters they dress as (Ch. 11)

Channels of communication As through the five physiological senses (Berlo, 1960) (Ch. 3)

Christianity Monotheistic religious sect that includes Catholicism, Protestantism, and the Anabaptists (including the Amish and Mormons) (Ch. 8)

Classic A style that changes little from season to season but is generally popular across seasons (Ch. 2)

Clothing for specific needs A segment of the apparel industry that accommodates consumers outside of the mainstream, for example, astronauts, firefighters, disabled individuals, older adults, football players, motocross riders, and hockey players (Ch. 12)

Co-design A garment that has been customized to fit precisely and the consumer takes part in designing the style of garments she or he wants (Ch. 12)

Collective selection Fashions originate in specific social or subcultural groups (Blumer 1969). Also known as subcultural leadership (Ch. 2)

Collective selection theory The process of choosing from competing styles that match the current zeitgeist or spirit of the times (Ch. 1). Fantasy dress can help individuals relax, escape the responsibilities for everyday life, and prepare for future societal changes (Ch. 11)

Colorism The privileging of lighter skin tones (Ch. 4)

Communication The production and exchange of meanings (Fiske, 1990, p. 2) through dress (Ch. 3)

Computerized body scanners Take 10 seconds to collect thousands of body measurements to produce a garment that fits an individual precisely (Ch. 12)

Conk A hairstyle popular among African American men in the early and middle 20th century that used caustic lye to straighten hair (Ch. 7)

Consumer consumption fantasy Purchasing items to fulfill a fantasy as a cosplayer, for example, a storm trooper in *Star Wars*, a Civil War Confederate (or Union) solider, or any type of costumed character you want to be (Ch. 11)

Cosplay A combination of costume + play (Ch. 11)

Costume Body supplements and modifications that indicate the "out-of-everyday" social role or activity. The word costume is reserved for use in discussions of dress for the theater, folk and other festivals, ceremonies, and rituals (Roach-Higgins and Eicher, 1992, p. 10) (Ch. 11)

Context Combinations of elements and surrounding situations (Ch. 3)

Counterfeit Exact copies of branded merchandise that are intended to defraud the consumer (Ch. 13)

Cross-cultural research Comparing two cultures on a set of issues such as men's and women's appearance in fashion magazines (Ch. 10); example: Sino-Japanism dress compared to U.S. dress between 1890 and 1927 (Ch. 11)

Culture A set of human-made objective and subjective elements that in the past increased the probability of survival and resulted in satisfaction of the participants in an ecological niche, and shared among those who could communicate with each other because they had a common language and lived in the same time and place (Triandis, 1994, p. 22) (Ch. 1)

Cultural authentication A process of assimilation through which a garment or an accessory external to a culture is adopted and changed (Ch. 1)

Cultural appropriation When one person or culture uses the unique creations of another culture for their benefit (Ch. 7)

Cultural ideal A person who personifies the ideal for her time (Ch. 10)

Digital print methods Use a computer to print out a fabric; the print can come from a cell phone (Ch. 12)

Drag Gender performance, usually lampooned (Ch. 5)

Dramaturgical approach A way to express everyday dress using the theater as a model of front stage and back stage dress and behavior (Ch. 1)

Dress The total arrangement of all outwardly detectable modifications of the body and all material objects added to it (Ch. 1)

Dress code A list of what clothing styles are acceptable and which ones are not (Ch. 9)

Early adopters Majority of consumers who adopt a style early in its life cycle (Ch. 2)

Eclectic Mixing and matching a diverse array of styles and influences in any one appearance or throughout a wardrobe (Ch. 3)

Euro-American idealized images Human bodies and faces that are digitally retouched to appear flawless (Ch. 10)

Entrepreneurs Businesspeople who have ideas for the next hottest wearable electronics (Ch. 12)

Ethnicity Learned cultural heritage that is shared by a group of people (Ch. 7)

Ethnocentrism Judging people from other cultures and backgrounds by one's own cultural standards and beliefs (Ch.1); the belief that one's own culture has the "right" way to do things (Ch. 4)

Escapist fantasy A fantasy that helps a person to forget their troubles while pretending to be someone else from another time period or another planet (Ch. 11)

Ethics The study of right and wrong (Ch. 13)

Evoshield A lightweight, malleable substance that hardens to fit the wearer's body and disperses impact. The primary application for the product is in sports (Ch. 12)

Fad A style that has a short, quick popularity (Ch. 2)

Fantastic socialization Dress up among children and adults that are not roles that can be played later in life but involve imagination and creativity (Ch. 11)

Fantasy The free play of creative imagination and to indulge in reverie, create or develop imaginative and often fantastic views or ideas (Ch. 11)

Fantasy proneness A psychological medical test to determine an individual's propensity toward childhood memories, hypnosis, excessive daydreaming, and creative experiences (Ch. 11)

Fashion followers Consumers who adopt a style at the tail end of its life cycle (Ch. 2)

Fashion innovators The people who create a new style (Ch. 2)

Fashion leaders Authorities on appearance matters who are valued for their opinions; they help disseminate a trend to wider audiences (Ch. 2)

Fashion life cycle A continuum of stages that illustrates the acceptance or popularity of a trend (Ch. 2)

First impression The first step in person perception; interviewers say it takes five seconds to develop a first impression of a job candidate (Ch. 9)

Five factor model of personality A personality test that includes the factors: neuroticism, openness to experience, agreeableness, and conscientiousness (Ch. 11)

Flapper Epitome of the flat-chested, straight figure of the 1924 to 1928 period (Ch. 10)

Fundamentalism A conservative religious doctrine that opposes intellectualism and worldly accommodation in favor of restoring traditional, otherworldly religion (Ch. 8)

Gender Social construction of one's male or female identity (Ch. 5)

Generation Z Refers to people born between the early to mid-1990s through 2010 (also known as the Internet Generation) (Ch. 12)

Gibson Girl Female cultural ideal of the early 1900s (Ch. 10)

Global citizenship Someone who identifies with being part of an emerging world community and whose actions contribute to building this community's values and practices (Ch. 1)

Grammar rule Rules on how to arrange dress learned as a child from parents and significant others, for example, American women cannot be seen in public topless (Ch. 3)

Gray-market Legitimate merchandise sold through illegal channels; also known as third shift manufacturing (Ch. 13)

Haptics A type of nonverbal communication that includes touch (Ch. 3)

Hedonic power Power attributed to passivity, or being looked at (Ch. 5)

Hinduism Indian religion that combines South Asian and Western beliefs; themes include dharma (morals/ethics/duties), samsara (the continuing cycle of birth, life, death, and rebirth), and karma (action and subsequent reaction) (Ch. 8)

"I" Mead (1934) defines the "I" as the impulsive and unpredictable part of the self (Ch. 11)

Idealized image Any image in which attempts are made to make the subject appear "better," perfect, flawless according to a standard (usually a Western standard) of thin, white, blonde, muscular, etc. (Ch. 10)

Identity An organized set of characteristics that expresses the various aspects of who you are; who one is as an individual and where one fits in as a member of society (Ch. 1)

Ideology A set of ideas that do not hold up under the rigors of scientific investigation and that support the interest of dominant groups (Ferrante, 1995) (Ch. 8)

Influencer A person who has *the power to influence* many people, as through social media or traditional media; for example, a female fashion blogger (Ch. 10)

Innovation The development of something new, whether a thought or idea, a practice, or a tool or implement (Ch. 12)

Islam Religion based on the principle of submission to Allah, or God; its holy texts are the Koran and the Hadith (or sayings of the Prophet) (Ch. 8)

Judaism Religion originating in prophesies about the God Yahweh; its religious knowledge is founded in the Torah, the first five books of the Hebrew Bible (Ch. 8)

Kinetics A type of nonverbal communication that includes facial expressions, physical movement and actions (such as hand gestures) (Ch. 3)

Knockoffs Variations of authentic goods; products "inspired by" better-known branded products (Ch. 13)

Late adopters Majority of consumers who adopt a style late in its life cycle (Ch. 2)

Looking glass self Imagining how important others may think of you, or what characteristics others may assign to you based on appearance (Ch. 1)

Made-to-measure Apparel industry experts often refer to custom-fit garments ordered through a mass retailer or producer as "made-to-measure" (Ch. 12)

Magic moments When a Civil War reenactor believes that he or she has crossed over into the actual historic moment through mental time travel (Ch. 11)

Market-infrastructure theory (Sproles, 1985) Only items sold in business retail environments can become fashions (Ch. 2)

Mass customized Garments ordered through a mass retailer or producer for which the consumer has made personal style design choices (Ch. 12)

Material culture analysis Physically describes the design and construction of the garments and interprets the functions and meanings of the garments (Severa & Horswill, 1989) (Ch. 1)

"Me" Mead (1934) defines the "Me" as the social conscious part of the self that considers what is socially acceptable (Ch. 11)

Modesty Covering part of the body that otherwise exposed would be considered sexual (Ch. 6); the quality of not being too proud or confident about yourself or your abilities; covering the body so as not to show it off (Ch. 8)

Model of clothing in context A theory that emphasizes the combinations of elements and surrounding situations that make up context (Ch. 3)

Monotheism A belief in a single God, that is, Christianity, Islam, and Judaism (Ch. 8)

Morality Conformity to ideals of right human conduct (Ch. 8)

Nanotechnology The science of making electronics as tiny as possible (Ch. 12)

Nonverbal communication Communicating that does not necessarily involve verbal expression through speaking or writing (Ch. 3)

Nondiscursive Because dress often tends to be stable or unchanging for many hours of the day dress is usually nondiscursive—or fixed—behavior (McCracken, 1988) (Ch. 3)

Nostalgia Yearning for another time that is viewed with reverence and longing (Ch. 3)

Objectification The action of degrading someone to the status of a mere object (Ch. 10)

Openness to experience A factor in the five factor model of personality that includes fantasy, aesthetics, feelings, actions, ideas, and values. Persons who score high on this factor are curious; have broad interests; and are creative, original, imaginative, untraditional, artistic, perceptive, and insightful (Ch. 11)

Paradigm An assembly of practices and protocols characterizing a discipline or field (Ch. 12)

Paralinguistics A type of nonverbal communication that includes the sound of the voice while delivering verbal communications (Ch. 3)

Participant observation A type of ethnography research in which the researcher participates in the event while observing what other members say and do. In many instances this is a better way to obtain information than surveys or interviews (Ch. 11)

Patriarchy Refers to cultural beliefs and values that give higher prestige to men than to women; likely to be the ideology that undergirds all world religions (Ch. 8)

Perceptual elements The integral units of fabric and apparel that can be perceived by humans, these elements are the basic elements of design, for example, color, fiber, and condition of dress items (Ch. 3)

Person perception Refers to the way we learn and think about others and their characteristics, intentions, and inner states (Ch. 9)

Photoshopped image An image that has been analyzed with a graphics-editing program to create and manipulate images (Ch. 10)

Pluralism The acceptance of differences in others while not necessarily wanting to adopt those differences for the self (Ch. 1)

Polysemic The ability to send a great amount of messages all at one time (as through dress) (Ch. 3)

Polytheism A belief in many gods, for example, Buddhism, Hinduism, Confucianism, Taoism, and Shintoism (Ch. 8)

Porn chic "Fashion and related trend-based behaviors linked to the porn industry that have become mainstreamed in the dress of women and girls" (Lynch, 2012, p. 3) (Ch. 6)

Postmodern A term useful in summarizing trends in consumer life at the end of the 20th century and the beginning of the 21st century in which consumer choices are characterized by eclectic, nostalgic, simulation, and questioning of rules (Ch. 3)

Private self The part of the self that we only let family members and friends see; broadly, the dress after 5:00 pm and on weekends (Ch. 11)

Profane Mundane; that which is considered an ordinary element of everyday life (Ch. 8)

Program One's response to one's own appearance (Ch. 1)

Proxemics A type of nonverbal communication that includes the amount of physical distance between people (Ch. 3)

Public, private, and secret self model Model created by Joanne Eicher about dress and parts of the self that was later expanded and revised by Eicher and Miller, 1994 (Ch. 11)

Public self The part of the self that we let everyone see; broadly, the dress worn for everyday wear between 9:00 a.m. and 5:00 p.m. (Ch. 11)

Questioning traditions Interesting mixes of fabrics that challenge old rules about not mixing patterns in one look (Ch. 3)

Race Visible and distinctive characteristics that are determined by biology (Ch. 7)

Religion A set of beliefs, symbols, and practices that is based on the idea of the sacred and unites believers in a socioreligious community (Ch. 8)

Retouched digital image Transforming or altering a photograph using various methods and techniques to achieve desired results (Ch. 10)

Reviews Other's reactions to an individual's appearance (Ch. 1)

Roles Positions that people occupy in a group or society (Ch. 1)

Role theory The idea that within a society a certain position or status has norms and expectations, including expectations on how to dress (Ch. 1)

Role-related dress Dress that has become inextricably tied to a particular occupation (Ch. 9)

Runway showpiece item A statement piece made by a designer to show at the end of a runway show. This piece is not for sale and is typically fantastic for the purpose of earning the respect of the consumer and inspiring the consumer to purchase other items from their line (Ch. 11)

Sacred Refers to that which people define as extraordinary, inspiring a sense of awe and reverence (Ch. 8)

Screen print methods Limited colors and options than the digital method (Ch. 12)

Secret Self The part of the self that is kept secret or shared with an intimate (Ch. 11)

Self-esteem Confidence in one's own worth or abilities; self-respect (Ch. 10)

Self-indication process A process of learning who we are through continued reflection and action with others. Constant experimentation and exploration is the process of self-indication (Blumer, 1969) (Ch. 3)

Semiotics The study of signs and sign systems (Ch. 1) (Ch. 3)

Sex Biological designation based on sex organs (Ch. 5)

"Show royal blue, sell navy blue" A retail slogan that recommended bright colors to attract customers to their store, then the customer would buy the more practical navy blue (Ch. 11)

Simulations A postmodernist concept in which simulations are becoming as valuable as what is real and rare (Baudrillard, 1983) (Ch. 3)

Slut Walks organized marches of women in miniskirts from several countries (i.e., South Africa, Canada, and the United States) who wish to send the message that how they dress does not give men permission to rape them (Ch. 3)

Social comparison theory A theoretical framework of human behavior of the tendency to compare ourselves to others in regard to appearance for purposes of self-evaluation (Ch. 10)

Social identity theory Theory developed by Tajfel and Turner (1986) for understanding how people create social groups. Includes the following steps: categorizing people into groups, identifying into one of the groups, groups comparing themselves to other groups and developing group distinctiveness (Ch. 7) (Ch. 2)

Social responsibility Social responsibility is the idea that businesses should balance profit-making activities with activities that benefit society; it involves developing businesses with a positive relationship to the society in which they operate. For example, it is the media's social responsibility to notify its readers of retouched photos. (Ch. 10)

Spornosexual "The modern day man who's often at the gym working on fitness. He's chiseled, tanned and hot. He prefers to spend his time, and his money, on his physical upkeep. And he doesn't shy away from showing off his results" (Engle, 2014, n.p.). (Ch. 6)

Spray-on clothes Fibers in a spray can that fit the body very closely and once dry you can take the clothing off and wash and dry it. (Ch. 12)

Status or prestige The social stratification with which groups and individuals are ranked and organized by legal, political, and cultural criteria (Ch. 9)

STEM Acronym for programs that introduce science and technology to students: S = science, T = technology, E = engineering, M = math (Ch. 12)

Sweatshops Work environments that endanger the physical and mental welfare of employees, underpay their employees, or use slave labor (Ch. 13)

Symbolic interaction theory (Kaiser, Nagasawa, & Hutton, 1995): Styles are given meaning by negotiations between the individual and society, where individuals strive to illicit a certain reaction via appearance from society and alter appearance until it is achieved (Ch. 1) (Ch. 2)

Taking on the role of the other Taking on other people's perspectives to understand their responses (Ch. 1)

Technophobe A person who is afraid to try new technology (Ch. 12)

Theory A set of ideas that describe, explain, and predict outcomes and relationships and guide the development of hypotheses (Ch. 1)

Theory of shifting erogenous zones Theory conceived by Laver (1969) to explain changes in fashions; that styles change in order to expose certain parts of the body until overexposure yields boredom and a new body part is exposed to create interest (Ch. 6)

Transgender or transpeople A person whose gender identity does not align with their sex assigned at birth (Ch. 5)

Transnational style A quickly shifting style of dress worn simultaneously in many world locations (Eicher, Evenson & Lutz, 2008, p. 54) (Ch. 1)

Trickle-across theory (King, 1963) A style can simultaneously appear across all levels of society as a function of different retail stores offering it to different consumers (Ch. 2)

Trickle-down theory (Simmel, 1904; Veblen, 1912) Social theory that fashion develops as a function of a class emulation; a style originates in the uppermost level of society and is copied by successively lower levels of society (Ch. 2)

Trickle-up theory (Hedbidge, 1979) Fashions begin in the lower class and are adopted by successively higher levels of society (Ch. 2)

Twiggy Thin, frail, female cultural ideal of the 1960s (Ch. 10)

Undercoding Meanings tend to be vague and hard to verbalize (Umberto Eco, 1976) as through dress (Ch. 3)

Uniqueness theory Concept that fashion begins from original or new styles (Ch. 2)

Unisex Lacking gender designation, masculinity, or femininity (Ch. 5)

University faculty Those who conduct research in their area of expertise with grants from the government, corporations, and the military (Ch. 12)

U.S. Military One of the largest producers and consumers of apparel and has a vested interest in researching wearable technology to assist soldiers in the field (Ch. 12)

Wearable electronics When nanotechnology companies partner with apparel companies it results in the development of wearable electronics. Examples include global positioning system in the clothing of toddlers and Alzheimer's patients; alarms in baby's sleepwear that alert if the child has stopped breathing; fiber optic wedding dresses and disco trousers (Ch. 12)

Western cultural ideal The ideal man or woman from a European American culture that includes a thin body, a muscular body, and light-colored skin (Ch. 10)

Western idealized images Human bodies and faces that are digitally retouched to appear flawless (Ch. 10)

White-collar dress Historically worn by male executives in the United States (Ch. 9)

Wish fulfillment psychology Marketing psychology that helps a consumer fulfill a wish or fantasy (Ch. 11)

World dress Describes similar types of body modifications and supplements worn by many people in various parts of the world no matter where the types of dress or the people themselves originated (Eicher & Evenson, 2015, p. 46) (Ch. 1)

Zeitgeist German word meaning "spirit of the times"; the essence or feeling of an era (Ch. 2)

CREDITS

Chapter 1

1.1 monkeybusinessimages/iStock.com
1.2a In Pictures Ltd./Corbis via Getty Images
1.2b SEBASTIEN BOZON/AFP/Getty Images
1.3 © The Winters Group
1.4 Andrey Arkusha/Shutterstock.com
1.5 drbimages/iStock.com
1.6a, b Courtesy of Cassidy Herrington
1.7 Joe Raedle/Getty Images
1.8a © Joseph Hancock, All Rights Reserved.
1.8b © Joseph Hancock, All Rights Reserved.
1.9 Photo Courtesy of Dan McQuade.

Chapter 2

2.1 Fairchild Books
2.2 Lisa Berg
2.3 MartinaP/Shutterstock.com
2.4 WWD / © Conde Nast
2.5 Everett Historical/Shutterstock.com
2.6, 2.7 Jay McCauley Bowstead
2.8–14 Pamala Gomes

Chapter 3

3.1 Alex Wong/Getty Images
3.2 English Heritage/Heritage Images/Getty Images
3.3 Damhorst, 2005
3.4 KMazur/WireImage/Getty Images
3.5 Steve Granitz/WireImage/Getty Images
3.6 H. Armstrong Roberts/ClassicStock/Getty Images
3.7 Chris Moore/Catwalking/Getty Images
3.8–10 Fairchild Books

Chapter 4

4.1 Courtesy of Susan Kaiser
4.2 Bartosz Hadyniak/iStock.com
4.3 Bettmann/Getty Images
4.4 Universal History Archive/UIG via Getty Images
4.5 katalinamas/IStock.com
4.6 Kypros/Getty Images
4.7 Featureflash Photo Agency/Shutterstock.com
Table 4.1 Courtesy of Barnes and Eicher
4.8 Yann Layma/The Image Bank/Getty Images

Chapter 5

5.1 jsp/Shutterstock.com
5.2 chippix/Shutterstock.com
5.3 Everett Historical/Shutterstock.com
5.4 CREATISTA/iStock.com
5.5 CREATISTA/Shutterstock.com
5.6 Jack Burlot/Apis/Sygma/Sygma via Getty Images
5.7 Carl-Johan De Geer
5.8 Bettman/Getty Images
5.9–11 Courtesy of Katalin Medvedev and Lioba Moshi

Chapter 6

6.1 Silver Screen Collection/Getty Images
6.2 felixmizioznikov/iStock.com
6.3 Everett Historical/Shutterstock.com
6.4 WhiteHaven/Shutterstock.com

Chapter 7

7.1 Charles 'Teenie' Harris/Carnegie Museum of Art/Getty Images
7.2 encrier/iStock.com
7.3 KateONeill/iStock.com
7.4 Guy Marineau/Condé Nast via Getty Images
7.5, 7.6 Photograph by Edwin Rosskam for the Farm Security Administration-Office of War Information photograph Collection, Library of Congress.
7.7 Christine Beaule
7.8 Andrés Herbas

Chapter 8

8.1 Neilson Barnard/Getty Images for FASHION NEX
8.2 zaihan/iStock.com
8.3 snik2016/iStock
8.4 David Turnley/Corbis/VCG via Getty Images
8.5 Godruma/iStock.com
8.6 Mary Lou Carter
8.7 Creative Commons
8.8 Richard Harris Photography
8.9 Laurence Koltys, photographer
8.10 NARINDER NANU/AFP/Getty Images

Chapter 9

9.1 Steve Debenport/iStock.com
9.2 PeopleImages/iStock.com
9.3 michaeljung/iStock.com
9.4 Werner Forman/Universal Images Group/Getty Images
9.5 Stefan Zaklin/Getty Images
9.6a,b Laura Cavanaugh/Getty Images for AWXII
9.7 Brendon Thorne/Getty Images for AIF
9.8 Brooke Erin Duffy and Emily Hund

Chapter 10

10.1 Levan Verdzeuli/Getty Images

10.2   The Delineator/Library of Congress
10.3   Axelle/Bauer-Griffin/FilmMagic/Getty Images
10.4   Education Images/UIG via Getty Images
10.5   Massimo Merlini/iStock.com
10.6a   Mike Marsland/WireImage/Getty Images
10.6b   Image courtesy of The Advertising Archives
10.7   Giannoni / WWD / © Conde Nast

Chapter 11

11.1   Image Courtesy of The Advertising Archives
11.2   WWD / © Condé Nast
11.3   Visions of America/UIG via Getty Images
11.4   Image Courtesy of The Advertising Archives
11.5   Victor Boyko/Getty Images
11.6   DeAgostini/Getty Images
11.7   Jeffrey Greenburg/UIG via Getty Images
11.8   Oscar Gonzalez/NurPhoto via Getty Images
11.9, 11.10   Courtesy of Casey Stannard

Chapter 12

12.1   Library of Congress
12.2   pixelfit/iStock.com
12.3   Victor VIRGILE/Gamma-Rapho via Getty Images
12.4   Estrop/Getty Images
12.5   Courtesy of Unique Solutions Design Ltd.
12.6a   K A Vallis
12.6b   Marjorie Baker
12.7   Education Images/UIG via Getty Images

Chapter 13

13.1   Aquino / WWD / © Conde Nast
13.2   Liuser/iStock.com
13.3   ChiccoDodiFC/iStock.com
13.4   Michael Gottschalk/Photothek via Getty Images

INDEX